A Reading/Language Arts Program

## Program Authors

Dr. Diane August
Educational Researcher - Center for Applied Linguistics
Washington D.C.

Dr. Donald R. Bear
University of Nevada, Reno
Reno, Nevada

Dr. Janice A. Dole
University of Utah
Salt Lake City, Utah

Dr. Jana Echevarria
California State University, Long Beach
Long Beach, California

Dr. Douglas Fisher
San Diego State University
San Diego, California

Dr. David J. Francis
University of Houston
Houston, Texas

Dr. Vicki L. Gibson
Longmire Learning Center, Inc.
College Station, Texas

Dr. Jan E. Hasbrouck
Educational Consultant - J.H. Consulting
Seattle, Washington

Dr. Scott G. Paris
University of Michigan
Ann Arbor, Michigan

Dr. Timothy Shanahan
University of Illinois at Chicago
Chicago, Illinois

Dr. Josefina V. Tinajero
University of Texas at El Paso
El Paso, Texas

**Contributors**

Time Magazine, The Writers' Express, Accelerated Reader

Students with print disabilities may be eligible to obtain an accessible, audio version of the pupil edition of this textbook. Please call Recording for the Blind & Dyslexic at 1-800-221-4792 for complete information.

B

The McGraw·Hill Companies

**Macmillan/McGraw-Hill**

Published by Macmillan/McGraw-Hill, of McGraw-Hill Education, a division of The McGraw-Hill Companies, Inc., Two Penn Plaza, New York, New York 10121.



Printed in the United States of America

6 7 8 9 RMN 14 13 12 11

# Program Authors

**Dr. Donald R. Bear**

University of Nevada, Reno

- Author of *Words Their Way* and *Words Their Way with English Learners*
- Director, E.L. Cord Foundation Center for Learning and Literacy

**Dr. Jan E. Hasbrouck**

Educational Consultant

- Developed Oral Reading Fluency Norms for Grades 1–8
- Author of *The Reading Coach: A How-to Manual for Success*

**Dr. Timothy Shanahan**

University of Illinois at Chicago

- Member, National Reading Panel
- President, International Reading Association, 2006
- Chair, National Literacy Panel and National Early Literacy Panel

**Dr. Diane August**

Educational Researcher

- Principal Investigator, Developing Literacy in Second-Language Learners: Report of the National Literacy Panel on Language-Minority Children and Youth
- Member of the New Standards Literacy Project, Grades 4–5

**Dr. Douglas Fisher**

San Diego State University

- Co-Director, Center for the Advancement of Reading, California State University
- Author of *Language Arts Workshop: Purposeful Reading and Writing Instruction* and *Reading for Information in Elementary School*

**Dr. Vicki Gibson**

Longmire Learning Center, Inc.
College Station, Texas

- Owner and Director
- Author of *Differentiated Instruction: Grouping for Success*

**Dr. Scott G. Paris**

University of Michigan, Ann Arbor

- Chair, Graduate Program in Psychology, University of Michigan
- Principal Investigator, CIERA, 1997–2004

**Dr. Janice A. Dole**

University of Utah

- Investigator, IES Study on Reading Interventions
- National Academy of Sciences, Committee Member: Teacher Preparation Programs, 2005–2007

**Dr. Jana Echevarria**

California State University, Long Beach

- Author of *Making Content Comprehensible for English Learners: The SIOP Model*
- Principal Researcher, Center for Research on the Educational Achievement and Teaching of English Language Learners

**Dr. David J. Francis**

University of Houston

- Director of the Center for Research on Educational Achievement and Teaching of English Language Learners (CREATE)
- Director, Texas Institute for Measurement, Evaluation, and Statistics

**Dr. Josefina V. Tinajero**

University of Texas at El Paso

- Past President, NABE and TABE
- Co-Editor of *Teaching All the Children: Strategies for Developing Literacy in an Urban Setting* and *Literacy Assessment of Second Language Learners*

# Contributing Authors

**Dr. Adria F. Klein**
Professor Emeritus,
California State University,
San Bernardino

- **President, California Reading Association, 1995**
- **Co-Author of *Interactive Writing* and *Interactive Editing***

**Dr. Doris Walker-Dalhouse**
Minnesota State University,
Moorhead

- **Author of articles on multicultural literature and reading instruction in urban schools**
- **Co-Chair of the Ethnicity, Race, and Multilingualism Committee, NRC**

**Dolores B. Malcolm**
St. Louis Public Schools
St. Louis, MO

- **Past President, International Reading Association**
- **Member, IRA Urban Diversity Initiatives Commission**
- **Member, RIF Advisory Board**

**In memory of our esteemed colleague and friend, Dr. Steven A. Stahl**

# Program Consultants

**Kathy R. Bumgardner**
Language Arts Instructional Specialist
Gaston County Schools, NC

**Dr. Cheryl Dressler**
Literacy Consultant
English Learners

**Linda Diamond**
CEO, Consortium on Reading Excellence
Author of *Teaching Reading Sourcebook*
Berkeley, CA

**Norma Hashimoto**
Teacher on Special Assignment/
Reading Content Expert
Fresno Unified School District
Fresno, CA

**Elizabeth Jimenez**
CEO, GEMAS Consulting
Pomona, CA

**Dr. Sharon F. O'Neal**
Associate Professor
College of Education
Texas State University
San Marcos, TX

**Dinah Zike**
Dinah-Might Adventures, L.P.
San Antonio, TX

# California Program Reviewers

**Meagan Baedeker**
Teacher, Grades K–1
Canyon Vista School
Aliso Viejo, CA

**Christina Lee Ballantyne**
Teacher, Grade 4
Cherry Chase School
Sunnyvale, CA

**Virginia Bateman**
Lead Teacher, Grades K–6
Department of Education
Folsom, CA

**Donna Bengle**
Teacher, Grade 2
Vencil Brown Elementary School
Roseville, CA

**Kathleen Best**
Teacher, Grade 1
Longfellow Elementary School
Riverside, CA

**Carol Cleland**
Teacher, Grade 3
Isador Cohen Elementary
Sacramento, CA

**Irene Constantine**
Teacher, Grade 2
Del Lago Elementary School
Mission Viejo, CA

**Jenika Cracchiolo**
Teacher, Grade 1
Canyon Vista School
Aliso Viejo, CA

**Vicki Crow**
Teacher, Grade K
Wegeforth School
San Diego, CA

**Malaura Easton**
Teacher, Grade K
La Pluma Elementary
La Mirada, CA

**Lillian Gamble**
Teacher, Grade 1
Isador Cohen Elementary
Sacramento, CA

**Leticia Gonzalez**
Vice Principal
Cohasset Street Elementary
Van Nuys, CA

**Patricia Hernandez**
Teacher, Grade K
Temperance-Kutner Elementary
Fresno, CA

**Veronica Izzard**
Teacher, Grades 4–5
Ramona School
Oxnard, CA

**Merry Jones**
Teacher, Grade 3
Fallon Elementary and Middle School
Dublin, CA

**Celia Kuehm**
Coordinator, Dual Immersion
Meyler St. School
Torrance, CA

**Carol Lazar**
Reading Specialist, Retired
Brekke Elementary
Santa Barbara, CA

**Allison Lott**
Teacher, Grade 6
Easterby Elementary School
Fresno, CA

**Delia Nuño**
Vice Principal
Balderas Elementary
Fresno, CA

**Soung Pae-Wegenka**
Research Teacher
Chula Vista Elementary
Chula Vista, CA

**Linda Perry**
Coordinator
Sacramento County Office of Education
Forest Ranch, CA

**Dianne M. Priest**
Reading Council President, Retired
Saratoga, CA

**Nona Reimer**
Teacher, Grade 5
John Malcom School
Laguna Niguel, CA

**Lupe Robles**
Teacher, Grade 2
Pearson Elementary
Modesto, CA

**Azar Sadrian**
ELL Coordinator
Gold Trail School
Placerville, CA

**Karen Sarafian-Hames**
Teacher, Grade 1
Foulks Ranch Elementary School
Elk Grove, CA

**Elestine Smittick**
Literacy Expert
Local District 3
Inglewood, CA

**Raenna Summers**
Teacher, Grade 4
Citrus Heights School
Citrus Heights, CA

**Soma Varma**
Teacher, Grade 1
Greenville Fundamental School
Santa Ana, CA

**Ruth Williams**
Principal
Kelly Elementary School
Compton, CA

# California Treasures Matrix

The literature in *California Treasures* is organized around six themes common to all grades. These themes address the intellectual and social demands students will face in school and in the workplace.

- The Science and History/Social Science units cover important content-area information at each grade level. The Personal Experiences and Creative Expression units help students explore their interests and creativity. The Teamwork unit deals with the critical skill of working together and solving problems.
- This organization enables schools to focus on and build deep understanding of common ideas and concepts as students progress through the grades.

**Theme Overview Chart**

| | Personal Experiences | History/Social Science | Creative Expression | Teamwork | Science | Spotlight on Grade ___ |
|---|---|---|---|---|---|---|
| GRADE 1 | All About Us | Our Families, Our Neighbors | Have Fun! | Let's Team Up | Nature Watch | Adventures |
| GRADE 2 | Friends and Family | Community Heroes | Let's Create | Better Together | Growing and Changing | The World Around Us |
| GRADE 3 | Let's Learn | Neighborhoods and Communities | Express Yourself | Our Teams | Those Amazing Animals | Storytellers |
| GRADE 4 | Growing Up | Making a Difference | The Power of Words | Working Together | Habitats | Problem Solving |
| GRADE 5 | Taking a Stand | The American West | Using Your Wits | Team Up to Survive | Investigations | Changes |
| GRADE 6 | Our Stories | Ancient Civilizations | A Question of Values | Achieving Dreams | Our Incredible Earth | Rescue 9-1-1 |

| KINDERGARTEN | | | | | |
|---|---|---|---|---|---|
| | Unit 1 Families | Unit 2 Friends | Unit 3 Transportation | Unit 4 Food | Unit 5 Animals |
| | Unit 6 Neighborhood | Unit 7 Weather | Unit 8 Plants | Unit 9 Amazing Creatures | Unit 10 I Know a Lot! |

# Theme: Let's Learn

## Planning the Unit



## Using the Student Book



## Wrapping Up the Unit



## Additional Resources



**Theme Opener**

**Main Selections**

**Progress Monitoring**

# Theme: Let's Learn

Theme Opener, pp. xvi–2/3

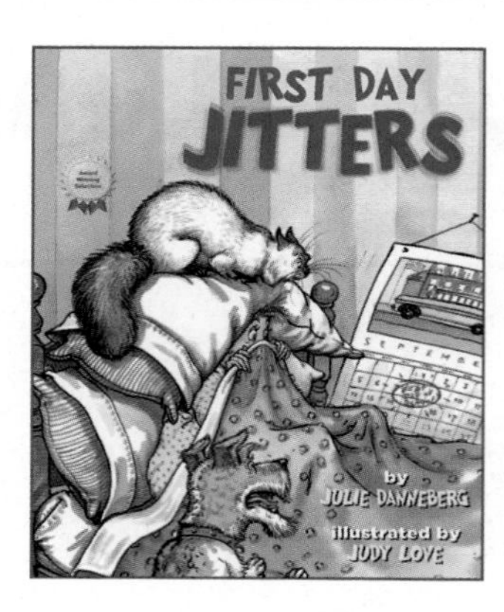

pp. 6A–33KK

pp. 34A–65II

| | WEEK 1 | WEEK 2 |
|---|---|---|
| **ORAL LANGUAGE** | | |
| • Listening Comprehension<br>• Speaking/Viewing | **Theme**<br>Teachers<br>**Build Background** | **Theme**<br>The Power of Books<br>**Build Background** |
| **WORD STUDY** | | |
| • Vocabulary | **Vocabulary**<br>*chuckled, nervous, nonsense, fumbled, trudged*<br>Word Parts/Prefixes *un-, non-* | **Vocabulary**<br>*auditions, adventure, exploring, sparkling, fantastic, success*<br>Word Families |
| • Phonics/Word Study | **Phonics**<br>Short Vowels | **Phonics**<br>Final *e* |
| • Spelling | **Spelling**<br>Words with Short Vowels | **Spelling**<br>Words with Final *e* |
| **READING** | | |
| • Comprehension | **Comprehension**<br>**Strategy:** Analyze Story Structure<br>**Skill:** Character, Setting, Plot | **Comprehension**<br>**Strategy:** Make Inferences and Analyze<br>**Skill:** Cause and Effect |
| • Fluency | **Fluency**<br>Repeated Reading: Phrasing | **Fluency**<br>Repeated Reading: Intonation |
| • Skill-Based Practice Readers | **Approaching**<br>*The New House*<br>**On Level**<br>*The New Kid*<br>**Beyond**<br>*The New Hometown*<br>**English Learners**<br>*The First Day* | **Approaching**<br>*Puss in Boots*<br>**On Level**<br>*Anansi Wins Back the World's Stories*<br>**Beyond**<br>*Aladdin and His Lamp*<br>**English Learners**<br>*Anansi and the Three Tasks* |
| **LANGUAGE ARTS** | | |
| • Writing | **Writing**<br>Topic Development: Moment | **Writing**<br>Topic Development: Moment |
| • Grammar | **Grammar**<br>Statements and Questions | **Grammar**<br>Commands and Exclamations |

pp. 66A–77QQ

pp. 78A–111KK

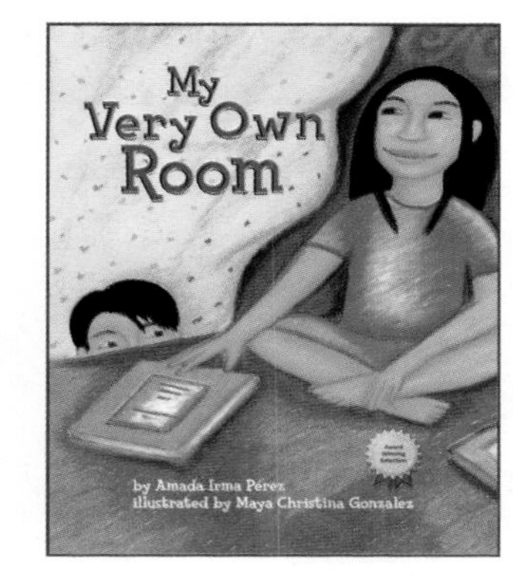


pp. 112A–145II

**Review and Assess**

## WEEK 3

**Theme**
Building Schools

**Build Background**

**Vocabulary**
*donate, unaware, members, contribute*

Thesaurus/Synonyms

**Phonics**
Long *a*

**Spelling**
Words with Long *a*

**Comprehension**
**Strategy:** Summarize
**Skill:** Main Idea and Details

**Fluency**
Repeated Reading: Pacing

**Approaching**
*Jay Beckwith and Julia Morgan: Two Builders*

**On Level**
*Jay Beckwith and Julia Morgan: Two Builders*

**Beyond**
*Jay Beckwith and Julia Morgan: Two Builders*

**English Learners**
*Two Builders*

**Writing**
Personal Narrative: Description

**Grammar**
Subjects

## WEEK 4

**Theme**
Learning to Read

**Build Background**

**Vocabulary**
*passion, bothering, admire, concentrate, ached, splendid*

Dictionary/Multiple-Meaning Words

**Phonics**
Long *o*

**Spelling**
Words with Long *o*

**Comprehension**
**Strategy:** Generate Questions
**Skill:** Compare and Contrast

**Fluency**
Repeated Reading: Expression

**Approaching**
*Running with Wolves*

**On Level**
*Katie and the Wolf*

**Beyond**
*A Dog's Life*

**English Learners**
*The Wolf*

**Writing**
Topic Development: Object, Setting

**Grammar**
Predicates

## WEEK 5

**Theme**
Those Special Books

**Build Background**

**Vocabulary**
*separate, determination, storage, exact, ruined, luckiest*

Word Parts/Suffixes, *-er, -est*

**Phonics**
Long *i*

**Spelling**
Words with Long *i*

**Comprehension**
**Strategy:** Monitor Comprehension
**Skill:** Make and Confirm Predictions

**Fluency**
Repeated Reading: Phrasing

**Approaching**
*The Slightly Tipping Tree House*

**On Level**
*A Winter Adventure*

**Beyond**
*The Science Fair*

**English Learners**
*Safe in the Storm*

**Writing**
Topic Development: Object, Setting

**Grammar**
Compound Sentences

## WEEK 6

**Writing**
Writing Workshop

**Unit 1 Assessment, 151M–151N**

**Comprehension**
Character, Setting, Plot; Cause and Effect; Main Idea and Details; Compare and Contrast; Make and Confirm Predictions

**Vocabulary Strategies**
Word Parts/Prefixes; Word Families; Thesaurus/Synonyms; Dictionary/Multiple-Meaning Words; Word Parts/Suffixes

**Text Features/Literary Elements/Study Skills**
Bar Graphs; Personification; Italics, pronunciations, bold or colored type; Guide words, Headings, Captions

**Grammar**
Statements and Questions; Commands and Exclamations; Subjects; Predicates; Compound Sentences

**Writing**
Topic Development: Moment; Personal Narrative: Description; Topic Development: Object, Setting

**Fluency Assessment**

**Diagnose and Prescribe**
Interpret Assessment

# Unit 1 Resources

## Literature

Literature Big Books (6)

Student Book (2)

StudentWorks Plus eBook

Read-Aloud Anthology Includes Plays for Readers Theater

Content Reader

Approaching Level

On Level

Beyond Level

Skill-Based Practice Readers

English Learners

EL Readers

Classroom Library Books (18)

Oral Vocabulary Cards (30 sets)

## Teaching Support

Teacher's Edition

Teacher's Resource Book

Available on Jump Drive

symbol rare

Vocabulary Cards

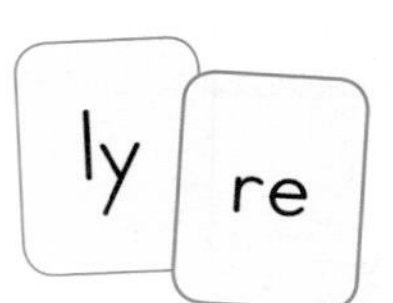
Word-Building Cards

should does

High-Frequency Word Cards Cards

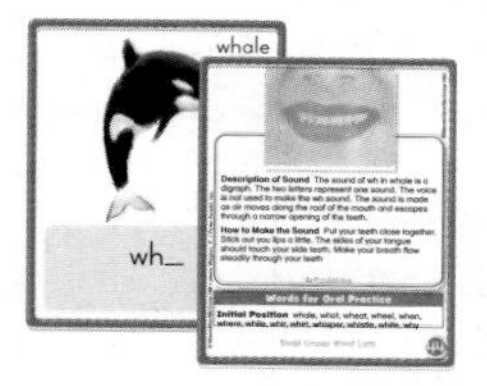
Sound-Spelling Cards

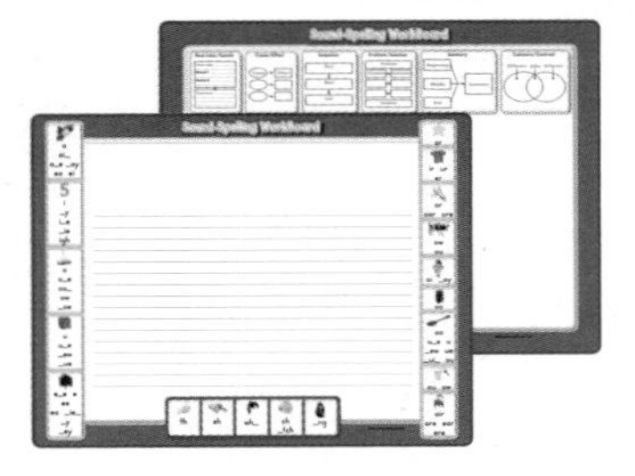


Transparencies

Sound-Spelling WorkBoards

## Class Management Tools

How-to Guide

Weekly Contracts

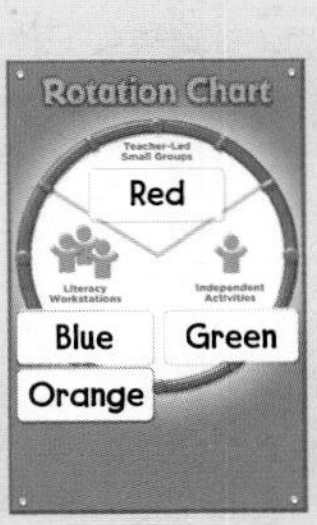


Rotation Chart

## Student Practice

**Practice Book**

Additional Reproducibles:

Approaching Beyond

**Handwriting**

- Cursive

**Home-School Connection**

- Take-Home Stories
- Homework Activities

Available on Jump Drive

Literacy Workstation Flip Charts

## Differentiated Resources

Visual Vocabulary Resources

EL Resource Book

Newcomer Resources

**English Learners**

Intervention Anthology

Teacher's Guide

**Intervention**

## Assessment

Progress Monitoring

Diagnostic

Summative

# Digital Resources

## Digital Learning

### PREPARE
- Professional Development Videos
- Parent Connection

### PLAN/ORGANIZE

Go to **www.macmillanmh.com** for Online Lesson Planner

### TEACH
- Theme Launcher Video
- Classroom Presentation Toolkit
- Vocabulary PuzzleMaker
- Sound Pronunciation CD

Theme Launcher Video

### STUDENT RESOURCES

- 

- Listening Library
- Fluency Solutions Audio CD
- Online Games and Activities

### ONLINE

**www.macmillanmh.com**
- Meet the Author/Illustrator
- Computer Literacy Lessons
- Theme Research Toolkit
- Oral Language Activities
- Vocabulary and Spelling Activities
- Leveled Reader Database

### CD-ROM
- Vocabulary PuzzleMaker
- Handwriting
- TeacherWorks Plus Interactive Lesson Planner
- StudentWorks Plus
- Accelerated Reader Quizzes

## Digital Assessment

**Assessment Online**
- Administer the **Unit Assessment** electronically.
- Score all tests electronically.
- Prescriptions for Reteaching.
- Student Profile System.

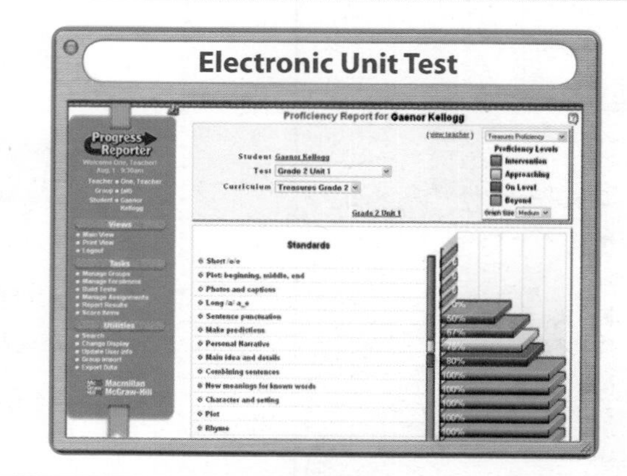

# Professional Development

## Classroom Videos

- Hear from leading reading researchers and watch expert teachers as they discuss and model key instructional routines and classroom management techniques.
- These videos cover areas such as phonics, writing, comprehension, English learners, and assessment. Clips from many of these videos can be accessed through links in the **online Teacher's Edition**.

**Professional Development Video:** Classroom Routines

## Online Courses and Support

- Deepen your understanding of key instructional strands through online course offerings.
- Courses include Teaching English Learners, Classroom Management, Building Comprehension, and others.
- Work with colleagues to practice and refine new instructional techniques and strategies.

## Leadership Handbook

- Ideal for principals and coaches, this resource enables you to quickly and easily evaluate *California Treasures* implementation.
- Sections include Implementing Your New Curriculum, Intervention, Differentiated Instruction, Mentors/Coaches, Effective Professional Development, Date-Driven Instruction, and Observation Checklists.

## Instructional Routine Cards

- Detailed routines and QuickStudy Sheets are available for all the instructional routines in the program.
- Great for program training and ongoing professional development.

# Diagnostic Assessments

### Screening and Diagnosis

Use your state or district screener to identify students at risk. In addition, see tests in our **Diagnostic Assessment** book for information on determining the proficiency of students according to a specific standard or prerequisite skill.

Diagnostics should be given during the first unit after you have had time to observe students and they become familiar with classroom routines. Use the diagnostics to determine students in need of intervention or to identify specific prerequisite skill deficiencies that you need to teach during Small Group differentiated instruction time.

# Progress Monitoring Assessments

California Progress Monitoring Assessment

### Meeting Grade-Level Expectations

Use these tests at the end of each unit (every 6–8 weeks). Weekly tests are also available. These tests cover all domains and strands in the content standards. Multiple questions and next-steps information are provided.

### Ongoing Informal Assessments

- Daily Quick Check Observations
- Weekly Tests/Selection Tests; Critical Thinking (Student Book)
- Weekly Fluency Practice Passages

### Formal Assessment

- Unit Assessments
- Fluency Assessments
- Write on Demand Prompts

**Unit Assessment Student Book**

# Summative Assessments

### Links to California State Test (CST)

Use the STAR California Standards Tests (grades 2–11) and the tests provided in **Summative Assessment**. Give every tri-semester, mid-year, or end-of year to determine whether students have mastered the grade-level content standards and to document long-term academic growth.

## Digital Assessment

**Assessment Online**

- Administer the **Unit Assessment** electronically.
- Score all tests electronically.
- Prescriptions for Reteaching.
- Student Profile System.

## CA Test Alignment

| GRADE 3 UNIT 1 ASSESSED SKILLS | California State Test |
| --- | --- |
| **COMPREHENSION STRATEGIES AND SKILLS** | |
| • Strategies: Analyze story structure; Make Inferences; Summarize; Generate Questions; Monitor Comprehension | ◆ |
| • Skills: Character, Setting, Plot; Cause and Effect; Main Idea/Details; Compare and Contrast; Make and Confirm Predictions | ◆ |
| **VOCABULARY STRATEGIES** | |
| • Word Parts: Prefixes *un-, non-*; Suffixes *-er, -est* | ◆ |
| • Word Families | ◆ |
| • Thesaurus: Synonyms | ◆ |
| • Dictionary: Multiple-Meaning Words | ◆ |
| **PHONICS** | |
| • Short Vowels | ◆ |
| • Final *e* | ◆ |
| • Long *a* | ◆ |
| • Long *o* | ◆ |
| • Long *i* | ◆ |
| **TEXT FEATURES AND STUDY SKILLS** | |
| • Bar Graphs | |
| • Italics, Pronunciations, bold or colored type | |
| • Encyclopedia Article: Guide Words, Headings, Captions, Index | ◆ |
| • Dictionary | ◆ |
| • Personification | |
| **GRAMMAR, MECHANICS, USAGE** | |
| • Statements and Questions | ◆ |
| • Commands and Exclamations | ◆ |
| • Subjects and Predicates | ◆ |
| • Compound Sentences | ◆ |
| • Subjects; Correct Sentences | ◆ |
| • Predicates; Complete Sentences | ◆ |
| • Compound Sentences; Punctuate Compound Sentences | ◆ |

# Theme Project

CA CONTENT STANDARD W 3.1.3 Understand the structure and organization of various reference materials.

CA CONTENT STANDARD R 3.2.1 Use titles, tables of contents, chapter headings, glossaries, and indexes to locate information in text.

**Introduce the Theme** Write this theme statement on the board: *Learning helps you find out about the world around you.* Ask: *If you could choose any place or time in history to learn about in depth, what would you choose and why?*

Help students get ready for their theme project by brainstorming some subjects they find interesting. The subjects can range from a place to a person to science to basketball. Have students pick a subject and pick a method to research it (Internet, library). Then have them research that subject using that method.

LOG ON **Theme Launcher Video**
**www.macmillanmh.com**

## Research and Inquiry

### Self-Selected Theme Project

**State the Problem and Identify Needed Information** Tell students that they will research subjects they think are interesting and want to know more about. Students exploring subjects such as science or history/social science can read books at their local library. Students interested in subjects such as baseball or swimming can use reputable Web sites on the Internet. Other sources students can use for research include encyclopedias, atlases, magazines, newspapers, and textbooks.

**Identify Resources for Finding Information** Have students make a list of all the places they can look to find information, such as library and media centers, bookstores, and the Internet.

**Research Strategies**

**Cite and Record Sources**

- Give credit for others' ideas, images, and information.
- Use bibliographic information to cite sources and understand the importance of doing so.
- Do not pass off others' ideas and words as your own.

**Find the Information** Have students locate informational resources and use titles, tables of content, chapter headings, glossaries, and indexes to locate information about their chosen subject.

**Organize the Information** After students collect their research information, have them list it by topic and subtopic.

See the Unit Closer on pages 151K–151L for **Step 5: Create the Presentation** and **Step 6: Review and Evaluate.**

# Introduce Theme Project

**LET'S LEARN**

Review with students what they have found out so far about the importance of learning and how people learn.

- Help students point out places in their community where people go to learn things. (museums, schools, libraries, media centers, Internet, etc.) Explain what kinds of things people can learn when they visit each place.
- Read and discuss the Research Activity on page 4 of the **Student Book**. Help students begin thinking about the subject they would like to choose as the focus for their theme project.

## CA Connect to Standards

**Speaking and Listening**

Share with students that often when they give a presentation, the audience is allowed to ask them questions afterwards. When asked a question, students must be aware that they should respond with appropriate elaboration. Have them practice answering questions with a partner.
LAS 3.1.3

# Unit 1 Opener



## The Big Question

**Why is Learning Important?**

What do schools, books, and museums have in common? They all help you learn. Learning helps you find out about the world around you.

In school you learn subjects, such as science and history. Outside of school you learn, too. You read street signs, recipes, and Web sites, and go to museums. Everywhere you go, you also learn how to make friends and get along with others.

Learning can help you become who you want to be. You may study science and become a doctor. You may study writing, and become an author. So keep learning about new things!

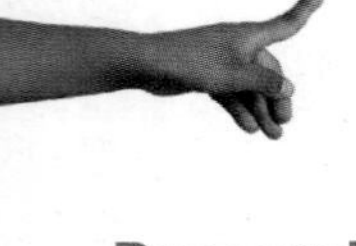

### Research Activities

In this unit you will read about ways to learn and why learning is important. Choose something that you would like to learn more about. Research and write as much as you can about this topic. Write about what makes topic interesting to you.

### Keep Track of Ideas

As you read, look for ideas about learning. Some selections are about learning in school. Others are about learning at home or outdoors. Use the Layered Book. On the top section, write "Let's Learn." On each layer write connections from the weekly selections that tell about how the characters learn.

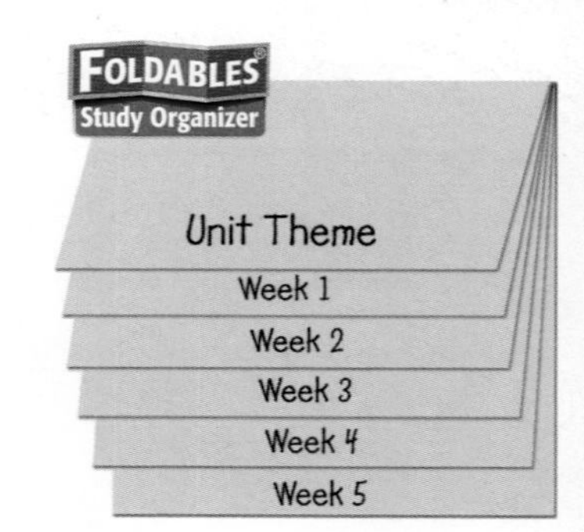


## Research Toolkit

**Conduct Your Unit 1 Research Online with:**

**Research Roadmap**
Follow step-by-step guide to complete your research project.

**Online Resources**
- Topic Finder and other Research Tools
- Videos and Virtual Fieldtrips
- Photos and Drawings for Presentations
- Related Articles and Web Resources

**California Web Site Links**

Go to **www.macmillanmh.com** for more information.

**California People**

**Maria Azucena Vigil**
**Teacher**
Ms. Vigil has been a California teacher for many years. She was the 1992 Teacher of the Year.

### KEEP TRACK OF IDEAS

Go to page 303 of the **Teacher's Resource Book** for instructions on how to create a Layered Book study organizer for this unit. Give students time to create the Foldables.

Read Keep Track of Ideas on page 5 of the **Student Book**. Model how students will be using their Foldables to keep track of ideas as they read through the stories in the unit. Explain that keeping track of ideas they read about will help them with ideas for their own unit project.

### RESEARCH TOOLS

Tell students that as they read the stories in this unit, they will learn about important people and events in California, both past and present. Students will be able to use the Research Tools to help them learn more about California people and places and how different things contributed to California history and culture.

### Character Building: Patience

Use the dolls to show that everyone learns things at a different pace. Explain that *different* does not mean *bad* and that we have to be patient with others.

# Start Smart At a Glance

## WHOLE GROUP

### Phonics/Word Study
Multisyllabic Word Strategy
6 Syllable Types
Spelling Link

### Vocabulary
Vocabulary Routine
Vocabulary Strategies
Morphology
Dictionary/Thesaurus

### Comprehension
Reading Narrative Text
Reading Informational Text
Key Strategies
Monitoring Comprehension

### Fluency
Establish Yearly Goals

### Writing
Set Up Writer's Notebook
Establish Writing Habits
Use Rubrics
On-Demand Writing
Conferences and Revision Assignments

### Assessment
Diagnostic Assessments

## Teacher Tools

**Technology to help plan and implement instruction**

**PREPARE**
- Professional Development Videos
- Parent Connection

**PLAN/ORGANIZE**

Go to **www.macmillanmh.com** for Online Lesson Planner

All-In-One Planner and Resource Center

**TEACH**
- Theme Launcher Video
- Classroom Presentation Toolkit
- Vocabulary PuzzleMaker
- Sound Pronunciation CD

**ASSESS**

Assessment Online

ExamView® CD-ROM

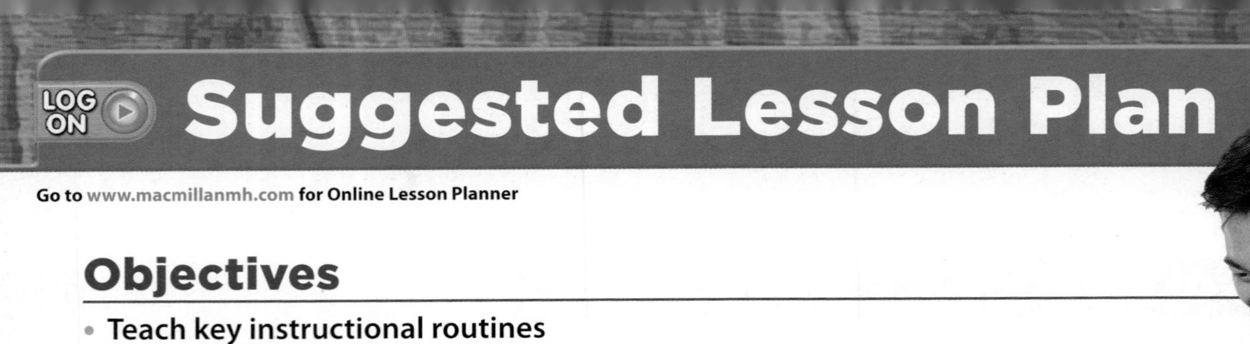

# Suggested Lesson Plan

Go to www.macmillanmh.com for Online Lesson Planner

## Objectives

- Teach key instructional routines
- Review previous-grade skills
- Establish classroom procedures
- Assess skills

## Whole Group

TeacherWorks Plus — All-In-One Planner and Resource Center (CD-ROM)

| PACING | DAYS 1 - 2 | DAYS 3 - 4 |
|---|---|---|
| Phonics/Word Study | Decoding Strategy, S4–S5 | Reading Real and Nonsense Words, S7 |
| Vocabulary | Define/Example/Ask Routine, S8 | Building Robust Vocabulary, S9<br>Morphology, S11 |
| Comprehension/ Fluency | Reading Narrative Text, S14–S15 | Reading Informational Text, S16–S17 |
| Writing | Set Up Writer's Notebook, S22 | Establish Writing Habits, S22 |
| Independent Work | Distribute Materials<br>Student Contract | Reading Inventory<br>Self-Selected Reading |

## Resources

**Read-Aloud Anthology**

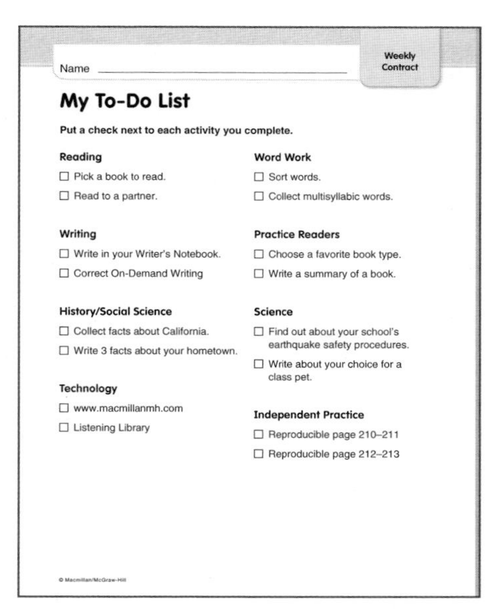

Name ______________________ Weekly Contract

### My To-Do List

Put a check next to each activity you complete.

**Reading**
- ☐ Pick a book to read.
- ☐ Read to a partner.

**Writing**
- ☐ Write in your Writer's Notebook.
- ☐ Correct On-Demand Writing

**History/Social Science**
- ☐ Collect facts about California.
- ☐ Write 3 facts about your hometown.

**Technology**
- ☐ www.macmillanmh.com
- ☐ Listening Library

**Word Work**
- ☐ Sort words.
- ☐ Collect multisyllabic words.

**Practice Readers**
- ☐ Choose a favorite book type.
- ☐ Write a summary of a book.

**Science**
- ☐ Find out about your school's earthquake safety procedures.
- ☐ Write about your choice for a class pet.

**Independent Practice**
- ☐ Reproducible page 210–211
- ☐ Reproducible page 212–213

© Macmillan/McGraw-Hill

**Student Contract**

**Content Reader**

| DAYS 5-6 | DAYS 7-8 | DAYS 9-10 |
|---|---|---|
| Reading Real and Nonsense Words, S7 | Reading Real and Nonsense Words, S7 | Link to Spelling, S7 |
| Vocabulary Strategies (Context Clues) Prefixes and Suffixes, S10–S11 | Using a Dictionary, S12 | Using a Thesaurus, S13 |
| Key Comprehension Strategies, S18–S19 | Key Comprehension Strategies, S18–S19 | Monitor Comprehension, S20 |
| Using Rubrics, S23 | On-Demand Writing, S24 | Writing Conferences and Revision Assignments, S25 |
| Online Activities<br>Small-Group Rotation Practice | Online Activities<br>Small-Group Rotation Practice | Check Contract<br>Assess Classroom Management Routines |

## Prepare

**WHOLE GROUP**

**PHONICS/WORD STUDY**
- Multisyllabic Word Strategy
- 6 Syllable Types
- Decoding Words
- Link to Spelling

**VOCABULARY**
- Vocabulary Routine
- Build Robust Vocabulary
- Vocabulary Strategy: Context Clues
- Morphology (Prefixes/Suffixes)
- Dictionary/Thesaurus

**CONTENT STANDARDS**
R 3.1.2, R 3.1.4, R 3.1.6, R 3.1.7, R 3.1.8; W 3.1.3; LC 3.1.8

# Phonics/Word Study

## Multisyllabic Word Strategy

**EXPLAIN/MODEL**

CA CONTENT STANDARD **R 3.1.2** Decode regular multisyllabic words.

Explain to students that they will be reading many unfamiliar words this year. You will be helping them decode these words and use word parts to determine each word's meaning. To help them, you will use a consistent Decoding Strategy that will make reading these unfamiliar multisyllabic words easier.

Distribute copies of the **Decoding Strategy Chart** on page S28. Then do the following:

- Write the word *rebuilding* on the board. Do not pronounce the word.
- Have students read aloud Step 1 of the Decoding Strategy: *Look for word parts (prefixes) at the beginning of the word.*

**Think Aloud** Let's look at this word. It is spelled *r-e-b-u-i-l-d-i-n-g*. This is a long word. To help me read it, I will look for parts of the word that I know. I start by looking at the beginning. In this word I see the prefix *re-*. A **prefix** is a word part that always appears at the beginning of a word. It changes the meaning of the word. The prefix *re-* means "again." Let's underline the prefix *re-*. I have seen this prefix in many words, such as *remake* and *reheat*.

- Have students read aloud Step 2 of the Decoding Strategy: *Look for word parts (suffixes) at the end of the word.*

**Think Aloud** Then I look at the end of the word. There are many common word parts that appear at the end of a word. These are called suffixes. A **suffix** can change the meaning of a word and often its part of speech. For example, it can change a noun, such as *boat*, into a verb, such as *boating*. I see the common suffix *-ing* at the end of this word.

- Have students read aloud Step 3 of the Decoding Strategy: *In the base word, look for familiar spelling patterns. Think about the six-syllable spelling patterns you have learned.*

**Think Aloud** All that's left in this word are the letters *b-u-i-l-d*. These letters form the word *build*. That's a word I already know how to read.

- Have students read aloud Step 4 of the Decoding Strategy: *Sound out and blend together the word parts.*

**Think Aloud** Let's put the word parts together: *re-build-ing.*

- Have students read aloud Step 5 of the Decoding Strategy: *Say the word parts fast. Adjust your pronunciation as needed. Ask yourself: "Is it a word I've heard before? Does it make sense in this sentence?"*

**Think Aloud** Now let's say the word parts quickly: *rebuilding.* That's a word I have heard before. I know they were rebuilding the homes destroyed by the earthquake. Using the word parts, I can also figure out what the word means. Since *re-* means "again," I can figure out that *rebuilding* means "building again."

**PRACTICE**

Guide students in using the **Decoding Strategy Chart** to read these and other words: *uncooked, rewinding, disappeared, preordered, undercooked.*

## Word Building

Tell students that they will have an opportunity to work with word parts to see how many words they can form. Display the following **Word-Building Cards**: *un, re, ed, ing, ful, chain, block, fill, call, color.*

Ask students to do the following:

- Read each syllable.
- Ask yourself: *Does this syllable normally appear at the beginning of a word, at the end, or somewhere in the middle?*
- Then use the word parts to form words. Once you make a real word—a word you have heard before—record it on your paper. See how many words you can make.

### Objective

- Read multisyllabic words

### Materials

- Decoding Strategy Chart: TE Reproducible, p. S28

### Quick Phonics Survey

Throughout the first few weeks of school, notice students who struggle decoding words. Following the Start Smart weeks, assess those students' decoding abilities using the Quick Phonics Survey in **Diagnostic Assessment**. Use the results to provide additional phonics instruction.

ON YOUR OWN **TE Reproducible,** page S28

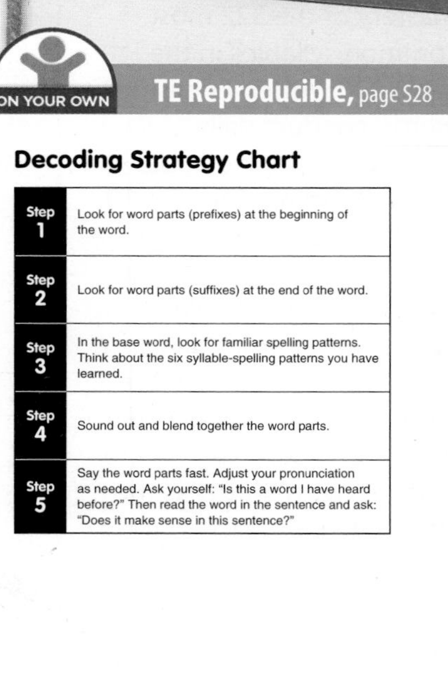

**Decoding Strategy Chart**

| | |
|---|---|
| Step 1 | Look for word parts (prefixes) at the beginning of the word. |
| Step 2 | Look for word parts (suffixes) at the end of the word. |
| Step 3 | In the base word, look for familiar spelling patterns. Think about the six syllable-spelling patterns you have learned. |
| Step 4 | Sound out and blend together the word parts. |
| Step 5 | Say the word parts fast. Adjust your pronunciation as needed. Ask yourself: "Is this a word I have heard before?" Then read the word in the sentence and ask: "Does it make sense in this sentence?" |

### Objectives

- Learn 6 syllable types
- Decode real and nonsense words
- Spell multisyllabic words

#### Materials

- None

### Syllable Fluency

To help students gain mastery of the 322 most common syllables in the top 5,000 written English words, conduct daily syllable fluency work. Use **Word-Building Cards 1–10**. Display one card at a time. Have students chorally read each common syllable. Repeat at varying speeds and in random order. Have students work with partners during independent time to write as many words as they can containing each syllable.

# Phonics/Word Study

## 6 Syllable Types

Tell students that they will be working with the six most common syllable types in English words this year. Knowing these syllable types will help them read long, unfamiliar words.

Discuss the following **syllable types**. Write the name of each on the board and several examples for students to record in their Writer's Notebooks.

1. **CLOSED** These syllables end in a consonant. The vowel sound is generally short. The vowel is enclosed (or closed in) by the consonants. (Examples: rab/bit, nap/kin)
2. **OPEN** These syllables end in a vowel. The vowel sound is generally long. The vowel is open and free to say its name. (Examples: ti/ger, pi/lot)
3. **CONSONANT + *le*** Usually when *le* appears at the end of a word and a consonant comes before it, the consonant + *le* form the final syllable. (Examples: ta/ble, lit/tle)
4. **VOWEL TEAM** Many vowel sounds are spelled with vowel digraphs, or teams, such as *ai, ay, ee, ea, oa, ow, oo, oy, oi, ie,* and *ei.* The vowel teams must stay together and appear in the same syllable. (Examples: ex/plain/ing, team/mate)
5. ***r*-CONTROLLED** When a vowel is followed by the letter *r*, the vowel and the *r* must appear in the same syllable. Therefore, they act as a team that cannot be broken up. (Example: tur/tle, mar/ket)
6. **FINAL (SILENT) *e*** (VCe) When a word has a vowel-consonant-*e* spelling pattern, the vowel and the final silent *e* must stay in the same syllable. (Examples: com/pete, de/cide)

**PRACTICE**

Write the following syllables on the board: *pub, ble, ver, mar, ount, tle, cade, vise, pro, aim, cab, ite, co, ate, ple, ma, eed, irt, ran, mid, cle, ta, ide, den, gle, ore, oach, par, ba, oon*. Have students sort the syllables according to type. Draw a Syllable Sort Chart on the board. Have students write each syllable under the correct heading.

| Closed | Open | Consonant + *le* | Vowel Team | *r*-Controlled | Final (Silent) *e* |
|---|---|---|---|---|---|
| | | | | | |

## Decoding Words

Write the following word lists on the board. These lists contain both real and nonsense words. Use one word list per day to assess students' general decoding abilities.

### Word Lists

**List 1:** (real) ***tab, peg, give, gob, hub, fuss, cell, puff, fizz, hog***
(nonsense) ***gat, ved, hib, mog, lun, quat, lem, fid, mog, sug***

**List 2:** (real) ***clamp, wreck, chick, brisk, stomp, help, shrub, think, when, grand***
(nonsense) ***shuzz, chend, stiss, threg, phum, whep, flod, belp, slamp, crint***

**List 3:** (real) ***space, preach, dries, boast, train, spray, knight, squeeze, ply, whole, huge***
(nonsense) ***sote, feam, boap, glay, cright, deest, sny, flain, shabe, pabe***

**List 4:** (real) ***flair, shook, scorch, term, vault, quirk, churn, barge, halt, broil***
(nonsense) ***boit, stoud, plar, loy, mern, noof, gurst, torth, blirch, stook***

**List 5:** (real) ***absent, bonus, reptile, exclaim, poodle, pumpkin, mutate, compete, appoint, scribble***
(nonsense) ***rigfap, churnit, bapnate, deatloid, foutnay, moku, wolide, lobam, nagbo, flizzle***

## Link to Spelling

**CA CONTENT STANDARD LC 3.1.8** Spell correctly one-syllable words that have blends, contractions, compounds, orthographic patterns (e.g., qu, consonant doubling, changing the ending of a word from -y to -ies when forming the plural), and common homophones (e.g., hair-hare).

**DICTATION** Dictate the following words for students to spell: *smell, queen, running, babies, pair, pear, trick, shrub, blaze, grain, cheat, flight, throat, germ, fault, pork, point, mouth, bloom, problem, frozen, crisis, deleted, stampede, complaining, unclear, formal, border, gentle, bridle.* Provide context sentences for the homophones *pear* and *pair.*

- Pronounce one word at a time. Have students clearly state the word. Then repeat the word for students and use it in a sentence. Prompt students to write one syllable at a time for multisyllabic words.
- After dictation is completed, write the words on the board. Ask students to proofread their spellings and correct any errors by writing the correct spelling beside the incorrect spelling. Collect the pages to analyze each student's spelling errors.

### Spelling Inventory

Throughout the first few weeks of school, notice students who frequently misspell words. Following the Start Smart weeks, assess these students' spelling abilities using the Spelling Inventory in **Diagnostic Assessment**. Use the results to differentiate weekly spelling lists.

## Objective

- Build vocabulary

### Materials

- None

### Academic Language

Academic words include those harder Tier 2 words that appear in much of students' reading materials as well as the language of instruction. The words chosen for instruction were selected from the **Living Word Vocabulary** list, Avril Coxhead's list of **High-Incidence Academic Words**, and Andrew Biemiller's **Words Worth Teaching** list.

### Three Tiers of Words

**Tier 1** words are those commonly used in speech, such as *mom*, *table*, and *book*.

**Tier 2** words are those words found in many sources that have wide applicability, such as *compare, enormous,* and *vital*. A lack of knowledge of these words can severely hinder comprehension of text.

**Tier 3** words are those content-specific words that do not appear in many sources and can be taught at point of use, such as *lava, bipartisan,* and *Louisiana Purchase*.

# Vocabulary

## Vocabulary Routine

CA CONTENT STANDARD **R 3.1.4** Use knowledge of antonyms, synonyms, homophones, and homographs to determine the meanings of words.

Tell students that throughout the year you will be introducing them to new words that will appear in many texts they read. Knowing these words will help them become better readers. When introducing these words, you will use the same **Define/Example/Ask** routine. Describe the routine to students.

**DEFINE** You will tell them the meaning of the word using student-friendly language—words they already know. (Example: *The word* enormous *means "very big."*)

**EXAMPLE** You will give them an example of how the word is used, using their own common experiences. (Example: *Our school has an enormous gym. It is bigger than any other room in the school.*)

**ASK** You will ask them a question that helps them connect the word to known words and use the word in speaking. (Example: *What have you seen that is enormous? What words mean the same, or nearly the same, as* enormous*? What words mean the opposite of* enormous*?*)

Always have students pronounce the words multiple times throughout the instruction. In addition, compare words that sound almost the same to help students avoid confusion. For example, when teaching the word *carnivore*, write the words *carnivore* and *carnival* on the board, one on top of the other. Pronounce each word slowly and carefully, and have students repeat. Then help students compare the spellings of the two words. Ask: *What's the same in both words? What's different?*

### Vocabulary Routine

Use the routine below to model the **Define/Example/Ask** routine.

**Define:** To **adapt** means to change.
**Example:** We had to adapt to our new class schedule when reading class was moved to the afternoon.
**Ask:** What have you had to adapt to? What words mean the same as *adapt*? SYNONYM

---

**Define:** A **mentor** is a person, usually older, whom you admire and from whom you can learn a lot.
**Example:** Mrs. Rodriguez, a local police officer, is a mentor to our class. She teaches us what it takes to be a good citizen. EXAMPLE
**Ask:** Who is a mentor to you? Why? Who could you mentor?

---

**Define:** To **succeed** means to achieve a goal.
**Example:** We all succeeded at passing this week's spelling test.
**Ask:** What is the opposite of succeeding? ANTONYM

## Build Robust Vocabulary

Tell students that in order to learn words well, they need many opportunities to read, write, and speak these words. You will provide daily opportunities for them to do this. Use the following extension activities to illustrate the types of exercises students will be doing throughout the year.

**CONNECT TO WORDS** Read aloud the following sentence prompts, one at a time. Engage students in a discussion. Use the discussion to evaluate each student's depth of word meaning.

1. Which would be harder to **adapt** to—a new way of getting to school or a new teacher? Why?
2. What are the qualities of a good **mentor**?
3. What does it take to **succeed** at a sport?
4. I will **succeed** in school this year because ______.
5. A **mentor** can help me by ______.
6. When you **adapt** to a new place, you must ______.

**WORD SQUARES** Ask students to create Word Squares for each word in their Writer's Notebooks.

- In the first square, students write the word.
- In the second square, students write their own definitions of the word and any related words, such as synonyms. Remind students that **synonyms** are words that have the same or nearly the same meaning. **Related words** include words with the same base, such as *succeed, success, successful; adapt, adaptation.*
- In the third square, students draw a simple illustration that will help them remember the word. They might also want to write a mnemonic that will help them remember the word. (Example: *My pa rates high* for *separate.*)
- In the fourth square, students write nonexamples, including antonyms for the word. Remind students that **antonyms** are words that have the opposite meaning. (Example: succeed/fail)

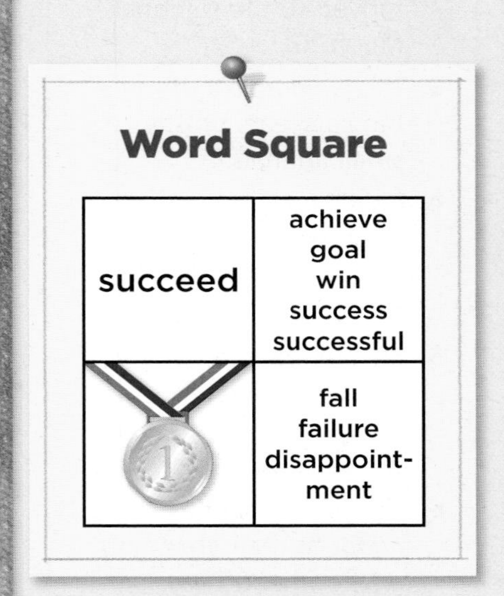

### Objectives

- Use context clues
- Identify prefixes and suffixes

### Materials

- None

### Example Sentences

1. A *predator* is an animal that hunts other animals for food.
2. The *enormous*, or very large, dinosaur is being moved to the National Museum.
3. The *cougar*, like other big cats, eats mostly small animals.
4. Unlike most animals that hunt during the day, *nocturnal* animals hunt only at night.
5. We are reading about *mammals*, such as apes, cows, horses, and whales.
6. The parrots had to *adapt* to their changing environment. They moved to a deeper part of the forest where trees were not being cut down. They also began eating different plants and insects.

# Vocabulary

## Vocabulary Strategy: Context Clues

CA CONTENT STANDARD
**R 3.1.6** Use sentence and word context to find the meaning of unknown words.

**EXPLAIN/MODEL**

Tell students that they can sometimes use the words surrounding a new, unfamiliar word to figure out its meaning. This is a good strategy to use when reading alone, especially when a dictionary or glossary is not readily available. Explain the following types of context clues:

- **Definition** The author provides a direct definition of an unfamiliar word, right in the sentence. The signal words *is, are, means,* and *refers to* are used. (Example: A *predator* is an animal that hunts other animals for food.)
- **Appositive Definition** An appositive is a word or phrase that defines or explains an unfamiliar word that comes before it. It is set off by commas and begins with the signal word *or*. (Example: The *enormous*, or very large, dinosaur is being moved to the National Museum.)
- **Synonym** The author uses another word or phrase that is similar in meaning or can be compared to the unfamiliar word. The signal words *also, as, identical, like, likewise, resembling, same, similarly,* and *too* are used. (Example: The *cougar*, like other big cats, eats mostly small animals.)
- **Antonym** The author uses another word or phrase that means about the opposite of, or is in contrast to, an unfamiliar word. The signal words *but, however, in contrast, instead of, on the other hand, though,* and *unlike* are used. (Example: Unlike most animals that hunt during the day, *nocturnal* animals hunt only at night.)
- **Example** The author gives several words or ideas that are examples of the unfamiliar word. The signal words *for example, for instance, including, like,* and *such as* are used. (Example: We are reading about *mammals*, such as apes, cows, horses, and whales.)
- **General** The author provides clues to the word's meaning in the surrounding words and sentences. (Example: The parrots had to *adapt* to their changing environment. They moved to a deeper part of the forest, where trees were not being cut down. They also began eating different plants and insects.)

**PRACTICE**

Provide the sentences in the Example Sentences box. Model using the different types of context clues.

# Morphology

CA CONTENT STANDARD
R 3.1.8 Use knowledge of prefixes (e.g., un-, re-, pre-, bi-, mis-, dis-) and suffixes (e.g., -er, -est, -ful) to determine the meaning of words.

## PREFIX

- Tell students that a **prefix** is a word part that is added to the beginning of a word. The word to which a prefix is added is called the **root word** or base word.
- Common prefixes include *un, re, dis, in, non, over, mis*, and *sub*.
- You can use the meaning of the prefix to determine the meaning of the whole word. This is called the word-part clue strategy.
- However, there are limitations. For example, not all words that begin with *un* begin with a prefix. For example, the letters *u-n* at the beginning of *unhappy* is a prefix; the letters *u-n* at the beginning of the word *uncle* are not a prefix. To determine whether or not a group of letters is a prefix, remove the letters from the word. What remains must be a known word.
- Write the following words on the board: *unwrap, under, uncle, unbelievable, united.* Guide students to determine which words begin with prefixes and which are "pretenders."
- Point out to students that most prefixes have more than one meaning. For example, the prefix *un* can mean "not," as in *unhappy*, or "do the opposite of," as in *untie*.

## SUFFIX

- Tell students that a **suffix** is a word part that is added to the end of a word, changing its meaning, and often its part of speech. The word to which a suffix is added is called the **root word** or base word.
- Common suffixes include *s, es, ed, ing, ly*, and *ful*.
- Point out to students that a suffix sometimes changes the spelling of the base word. For example, when the suffix *-ing* is added to a CVC word, the final consonant is doubled (run/running); when a suffix is added to a word ending in a consonant and *y,* you change the *y* to *i* before adding the suffix (fly/flies); and when a suffix is added to a word ending in *e,* you drop the *e* before adding the suffix (make/making).
- Write the following words on the board: *unafraid, happily, joyful, clapping, remake, mislead, appointed*. Guide students to identify the prefix and/or suffix in each word, then use the meaning of the prefix or suffix to define the whole word.

# Start Smart

## Objective

- Use a dictionary and thesaurus

## Materials

- TE Reproducible, p. S29
- Grammar and Writing Handbook, pp. 46–47

ON YOUR OWN **TE Reproducible,** page S29

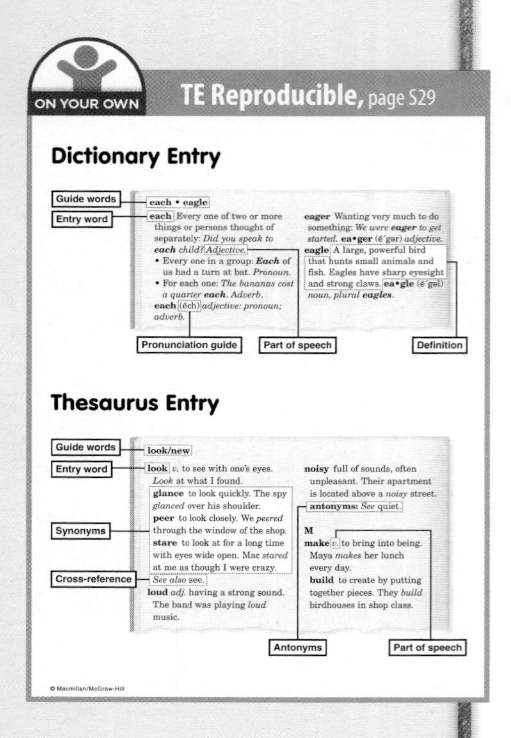

### Dictionary Entry

each • eagle

**each** Every one of two or more things or persons thought of separately: *Did you speak to **each** child? Adjective.*
• Every one in a group: ***Each** of us had a turn at bat. Pronoun.*
• For each one: *The bananas cost a quarter **each**. Adverb.*
**each** (ēch) *adjective: pronoun; adverb.*

**eager** Wanting very much to do something: *We were **eager** to get started.* **ea•ger** (ē´gər) *adjective.*
**eagle** A large, powerful bird that hunts small animals and fish. Eagles have sharp eyesight and strong claws. **ea•gle** (ē´gəl) *noun, plural **eagles**.*



### Thesaurus Entry

look/new

**look** *v.* to see with one's eyes. *Look* at what I found.
**glance** to look quickly. The spy *glanced* over his shoulder.
**peer** to look closely. We *peered* through the window of the shop.
**stare** to look at for a long time with eyes wide open. Mac *stared* at me as though I were crazy.
*See also* see.
**loud** *adj.* having a strong sound. The band was playing *loud* music.

**noisy** full of sounds, often unpleasant. Their apartment is located above a *noisy* street.
**antonyms:** *See* quiet.

**M**
**make** *v.* to bring into being. Maya *makes* her lunch every day.
**build** to create by putting together pieces. They *build* birdhouses in shop class.





# Vocabulary

## Using a Dictionary

**CA CONTENT STANDARD R 3.1.7** Use a dictionary to learn the meaning and other features of unknown words.

Tell students the following:

- A **dictionary** lists words in alphabetical order.
- The **entry words** show the spelling and syllables.
- The **guide words** show the first and last words on the page. Words on the page come between the guide words alphabetically.
- The **pronunciation** of each word is shown in parentheses.
- The **part of speech** is shown after the pronunciation.
- Often the **origin** of the word, such as the language from which the word comes, is shown in the dictionary entry.
- You use a dictionary to look up a word you've never seen or heard before. You can also use a dictionary to confirm a word's meaning to make sure you are using it correctly.

Use TE Reproducible page S29, **Grammar and Writing Handbook** page 46, or a classroom dictionary to model the above for students, including how to use the dictionary's **pronunciation key**. Focus on how to use what you find in a dictionary, such as how to look up the meaning of a word and choose the appropriate definition to make sure it fits the context of the sentence. Tell students that the first entry for a word may not be the one they are looking for. They should read all the entries. Likewise they need to read all the definitions for the word to see which one matches the context in which the word is used.

Write the following sentence on the board. *She will pitch the tent at the campsite before it gets dark.*

**Think Aloud** I know that *pitch* can mean "to throw a ball," such as a baseball. That doesn't make sense in this sentence. The word *pitch* must have more than one meaning. I will look in a dictionary to see what other meanings it might have. As I look in the dictionary, I see that *pitch* can mean "to set up firmly in the ground." Now that makes sense in this sentence. You have to set up a tent by putting the tent poles firmly in the ground. I can replace these words to see if it makes sense in the sentence: She will "set up" the tent at the campsite before it gets dark.

In addition, point out how the dictionary can be used to expand one's understanding of word meanings and learn about **multiple-meaning words**.

## Using a Thesaurus

CA CONTENT STANDARD
**W 3.1.3** Understand the structure and organization of various reference materials (e.g., dictionary, thesaurus, atlas, encyclopedia).

Tell students the following:

- A **thesaurus** is a reference book that lists words and their **synonyms**, or words of similar meaning. A thesaurus also includes **antonyms**, or words with opposite meanings.
- The word that you look up in a thesaurus is called the **entry word**. Entry words are usually listed in alphabetical order. Some thesauruses are organized by concept or category.
- **Guide words** show the first and last entries on each page.
- Some entries include a **cross-reference** that will guide you to other words with similar or opposite meanings.

Use TE Reproducible page S29, **Grammar and Writing Handbook** page 47, or a classroom thesaurus to model the above for students. Focus on how to use what you find in a thesaurus, such as how to look up the synonym for a word and use it to revise your writing. In addition, point out how the thesaurus can be used to expand one's understanding of related words.

Focus students' attention on how a thesaurus lists words with similar meanings. However, the words in one entry represent **shades of meaning** of one concept. List the words *depressed, sad, happy,* and *ecstatic* on the board in that order. Point out that *depressed* is an extreme form of *sad* and *ecstatic* is an extreme form of *happy*. When using a thesaurus, remind students to choose the word that best represents the shade of meaning of the word they want to use in their writing.

### English Learners

UNIVERSAL ACCESS

**Survival Skills** If you have any newcomers in your class, use the Start Smart weeks to teach these students how to introduce themselves (*Hello. My name is* ___.) as well as the names of important classroom items. Spend some individual time teaching basic commands such as *Sit down* and *Take out your book* by modeling each. In addition, teach basic requests, such as *May I use the restroom?* Enlist the help of any students who speak the newcomer's primary language.

# Read

## WHOLE GROUP

**COMPREHENSION**
- Reading Narrative Text
- Reading Informational Text
- Reading Strategies

**FLUENCY**
- Establish Yearly Goals

**CONTENT STANDARDS**
R 3.1.3, R 3.2.0, R 3.3.0, R 3.3.1

ON YOUR OWN **TE Reproducible,** page S30

**Genres**

| Type | Key Characteristics | Examples |
|---|---|---|
| Drama (Play) | | |
| Fable | | |
| Fairy Tale | | |
| Fantasy | | |
| Fiction | | |
| Folklore (Folktale, Trickster Tale) | | |
| Historical Fiction | | |
| Humor | | |
| Legend | | |
| Mystery | | |
| Poetry | | |
| Realistic Fiction | | |
| Science Fiction | | |
| Short Story | | |
| Autobiography | | |
| Biography | | |
| Essay (Persuasive) | | |
| Narrative Nonfiction | | |
| Nonfiction | | |
| Speech | | |



# Comprehension

TESTED SKILL

## Reading Narrative Text

**CA CONTENT STANDARD R 3.3.0** Students read and respond to a wide variety of significant works of children's literature. They distinguish between the structural features of the text and literary terms or elements (e.g., theme, plot, setting, characters).

**Read Aloud**

Tell students that **story structure** refers to the way the author has organized the events of the plot using story elements such as character, setting, and theme. When analyzing story structure, readers focus on the following story elements:

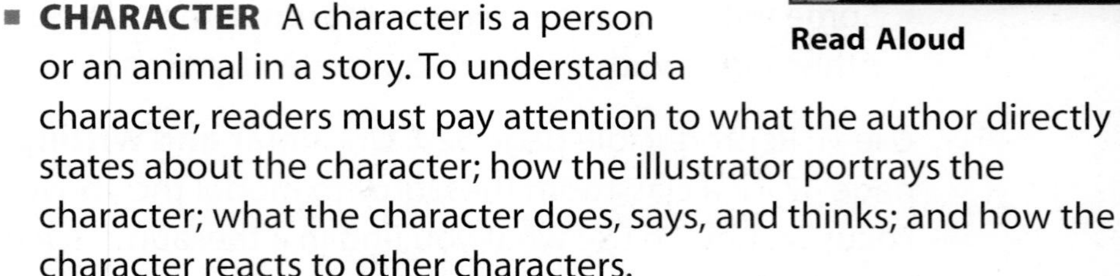

- **CHARACTER** A character is a person or an animal in a story. To understand a character, readers must pay attention to what the author directly states about the character; how the illustrator portrays the character; what the character does, says, and thinks; and how the character reacts to other characters.

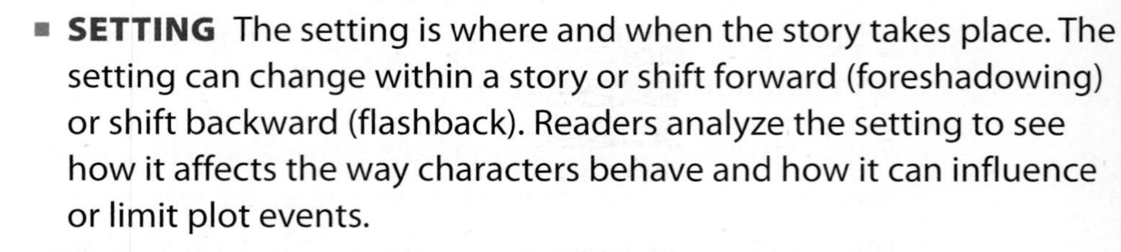

- **SETTING** The setting is where and when the story takes place. The setting can change within a story or shift forward (foreshadowing) or shift backward (flashback). Readers analyze the setting to see how it affects the way characters behave and how it can influence or limit plot events.

**CA CONTENT STANDARD R 3.2.0** Students read and understand grade-level-appropriate material. They draw upon a variety of comprehension strategies as needed.

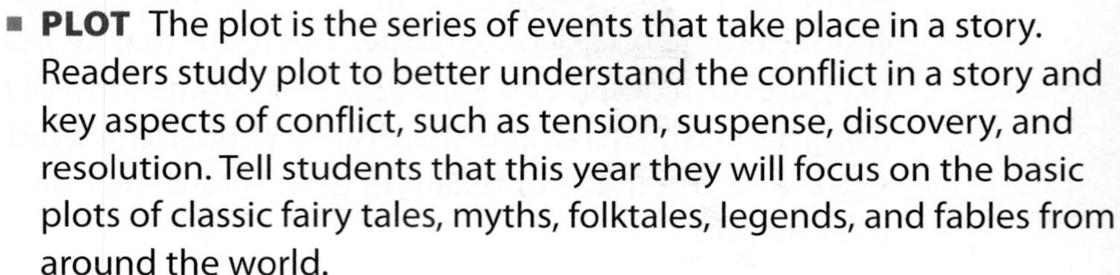

- **PLOT** The plot is the series of events that take place in a story. Readers study plot to better understand the conflict in a story and key aspects of conflict, such as tension, suspense, discovery, and resolution. Tell students that this year they will focus on the basic plots of classic fairy tales, myths, folktales, legends, and fables from around the world.
- **THEME** The theme is the overall idea, or message about life, that the author wants to convey to readers in a story. By discovering the theme of a story, a reader will understand what the author thinks is both important and meaningful.

Use "Arachne the Spinner" on **Read-Aloud Anthology** pages 75–78 to model each of the above. Read the story once without stopping. Then revisit the story and discuss each aspect of narrative text.

## Genres

CA CONTENT STANDARD
**R 3.3.1** Distinguish common forms of literature (e.g., poetry, drama, fiction, nonfiction).

Tell students that throughout the year they will be learning more about different story **genres**. Knowing the characteristics of a genre will help them predict the kinds of information the author will provide as they read. This year they will focus on learning the structural differences of fables, myths, legends, and fairy tales.

Distribute TE Reproducible page S30. Review the name of each genre and help students list key characteristics they know for each. Tell students that as they read new stories, they will be recording examples of each genre type and adding to the list of characteristics.

## QAR

Tell students that asking and answering questions is one way to improve their reading comprehension. To help students answer questions provided in the **Student Book** and on tests, you will be teaching them a strategy called **QAR: Question Answer Relationships**.

Explain to students that there are two types of question answer relationships. One type is "In the Book" answers. These answers fall into two categories: answers that are "Right There" and answers that you have to "Think and Search" to find. Define each.

- **RIGHT THERE** The answer is in one specific place in the text. Words from the question and words that answer the question are often "right there" in the same sentence.
- **THINK AND SEARCH** The answer is in the text. Readers need to "think and search," or put together different parts of the text, to find the answer. The answer can be within a paragraph, across paragraphs, or even across chapters and books.

Another type is "In My Head" answers. Define each.

- **AUTHOR AND ME** The answer is not in the text. To answer the question, readers need to think about how the text and what they already know fit together.
- **ON MY OWN** The answer is not in the text. Readers need to use their own ideas and experiences to answer the question.

Write each type on a Classroom Chart. Tell students that they will practice using QAR every week as they answer the **Critical Thinking** questions in their Student Book.

### Objectives

- Read narrative text
- Identify genres

### Materials

- Read-Aloud Anthology, pp. 75–78
- TE Reproducible, p. S30

### Differentiated Instruction

Use the *Managing Small Groups How-To Guide,* Rotation Chart, and Weekly Contracts to set up your small group classroom routine. Remember that small groups should be flexible and dynamic. Base the groupings on student needs as assessed through daily Quick Checks and weekly or unit **Progress Monitoring Assessments**. Students should NOT be placed in one group and remain there for an extended period of time. Some students may need additional support on one skill, while meeting grade-level expectations on another. The goal of all small group instruction is ensuring students access to core content and grade-level standards. Set high expectations and use the preteach and reteach lessons to help students achieve this.

### Objective

- Comprehend informational text

### Materials

- TE Reproducibles, pp. S35–S41

# Comprehension

## Reading Informational Text

Content Reader

Tell students that **nonfiction** surrounds us—in textbooks, magazines, posters, and online articles. Nonfiction looks quite different from fiction. Nonfiction contains special **text features** such as maps, charts, diagrams, time lines, boldface words, and other graphic aids. These features sometimes graphically show a difficult concept to make it easier to learn and remember; at other times these features add information to the main text.

Tell students that when reading nonfiction, they will learn how to:

- Preview the text by reading the title and section or chapter headings to determine the main ideas presented in the text.
- Use the graphic aids to take additional meaning from the text and integrate this information with that provided by the text.
- Identify the text structure, or the way the author organized the text, to increase their understanding and retention of the text information.

Use a selection from the **Content Reader** or a nonfiction textbook in your classroom. Have students read the chapter title and all the main headings. Model how you use the title and headings to determine what you will read about and figure out the main ideas of the selection. Then have students preview the photographs, illustrations, and other graphics.

Tell students that they will read the main text on each page first. Then they will stop, look at the other graphic features on the page, and figure out if they illustrate a concept in the main text or add information. Once completed, they will continue reading. At the end of the selection, have students explain how previewing and reading the text in this way helped them better understand what they read.

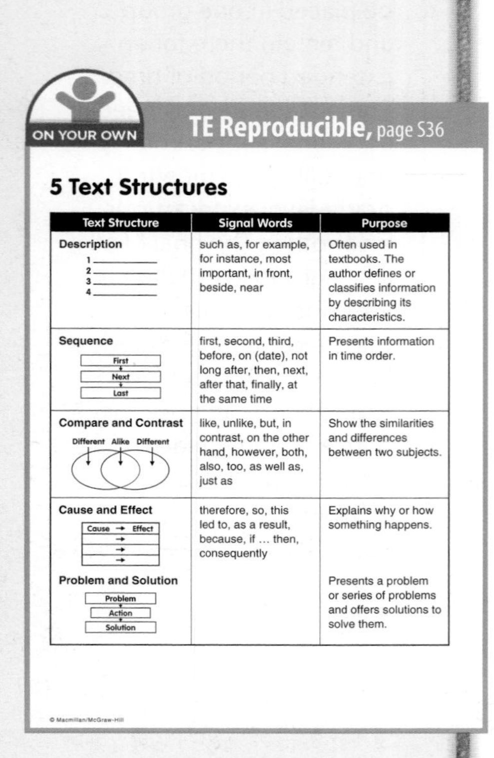
ON YOUR OWN

**TE Reproducible,** page S36

### 5 Text Structures

| Text Structure | Signal Words | Purpose |
|---|---|---|
| Description (1, 2, 3, 4) | such as, for example, for instance, most important, in front, beside, near | Often used in textbooks. The author defines or classifies information by describing its characteristics. |
| Sequence (First → Next → Last) | first, second, third, before, on (date), not long after, then, next, after that, finally, at the same time | Presents information in time order. |
| Compare and Contrast (Different, Alike, Different) | like, unlike, but, in contrast, on the other hand, however, both, also, too, as well as, just as | Show the similarities and differences between two subjects. |
| Cause and Effect (Cause → Effect) | therefore, so, this led to, as a result, because, if … then, consequently | Explains why or how something happens. |
| Problem and Solution (Problem → Action → Solution) | | Presents a problem or series of problems and offers solutions to solve them. |

## Nonfiction Text Structures

Tell students that **text structure** refers to the organizational pattern a writer uses to present information in a nonfiction text. Distribute copies of TE Reproducible page S36 and do the following:

- Define each type of text structure: description, sequence, compare/contrast, cause/effect, and problem/solution.
- Explain that each text structure contains signal words that alert the reader that the text is structured in a specific way.
- Point out the graphic organizer associated with each text structure. Tell students that when they encounter a key signal word in the text, they will use the appropriate graphic organizer to record information from the text. This will help them organize their learning and better understand it.

Tell students that they will use **nonfiction writing frames** to help them summarize what they read in writing and remember more quickly these main nonfiction text structures. Distribute copies of TE Reproducibles pages S37–S41. Review the writing frame for each text structure, one per day. Have students store or copy these in their Writer's Notebooks. Use selections in the **Content Reader** to demonstrate how to fill out each frame and use it to summarize.

## Note Taking

Tell students that when they read nonfiction text, they will periodically take notes to help them better remember that information. Note taking will also help them determine the main ideas, or most important information, in the text.

- Distribute copies of TE Reproducible page S35.
- Use a selection from the Content Reader or a chapter from your social studies or science textbook.
- Model how to fill out the note-taking form for one chapter in the book. Students will list the main idea of each paragraph or section of text, make drawings to help them remember difficult concepts, then use the main ideas to write a brief summary of the chapter.
- Model taking notes at least once a week for the first 6–8 weeks of school, or until students feel comfortable taking notes on their own. Use this note-taking procedure while reading any content-area textbook or when students are conducting independent research.

ON YOUR OWN **TE Reproducible,** pages S37–S41

**Description Writing Frame**

**Use the Writing Frame below to summarize the selection.**

People are trying to help by ______

First, they are ______

This is important because ______

They are also ______

This is important because ______

**Rewrite the completed summary on another sheet of paper. Keep it as a model for writing a summary of an article or selection using this Text Structure.**



ON YOUR OWN **TE Reproducible,** page S35

**Notetaking (Cornell Notes)**

| Main Ideas | Key Words/Drawings |
|---|---|
| | |

| Summary |
|---|
| |

## Objective

- Use reading strategies

### Materials

- TE Reproducible, pp. S42–S47

Use TE Reproducibles pages S42–S47 to model each strategy and provide guided practice. Use one page every 1-2 days.

ON YOUR OWN **TE Reproducible,** pages S42–S47

**Comprehension Passage: Summarize**

**Read the passage. Then complete the questions.**

**Ben Franklin**

Ben Franklin invented many handy objects. We can say that Ben invented swim fins. We can also say that Ben invented mail routes. In the old days, mail came in many different ways. Ben's routes were fast, and mail always came the same way. We still use many of Ben's mail routes today.

Ben Franklin also remade many old objects, so that they worked better. Flames in lamps make smoke. Smoke would get trapped inside and make glass lamps gray. Ben made a lamp that let the smoke escape. In Ben's lamp the glass stayed clean. We can say that Ben reinvented the old lamp in a better way.

Ben had strong work habits. Ben did not sleep late and he went to bed early. His habits made him feel good and allowed him to accomplish a lot. Ben was a good and smart man.

1. Underline the first sentence in each paragraph. This sentence is the topic sentence of each paragraph.
2. Circle two important details in each paragraph.
3. Now write a summary of Ben Franklin's contributions.



# Comprehension

## Key Reading Strategies

**CA CONTENT STANDARD R 3.2.0** Students read and understand grade-level-appropriate material. They draw upon a variety of comprehension strategies as needed.

Tell students that a **reading strategy** is a technique or process consciously used by a reader to understand a text. Point out the following:

- Skilled readers use strategies every time they read. The strategies a reader uses depend on the text demands.
- Strategies can be used before, during, and after reading.
- Students will learn a small set of strategies throughout the year that they can use as they read in class and independently.

### SUMMARIZE

Tell students that a summary is a short statement of the most important ideas in a passage or a text.

- When summarizing, a reader must identify what a passage or selection is about—the most important ideas—and restate them in his or her own words.
- If you can summarize a part of a text, then you understand what it's mostly about and can then continue reading.

### VISUALIZE

Tell students that when you visualize, you form a mental picture as you read or listen.

- When visualizing, you combine what you already know with descriptive text details to picture events, characters, and settings.
- If you don't feel like you are understanding what you read, or are having a hard time understanding a concept in the text, you can stop and try to picture it to help you make sense of the text.

### GENERATE QUESTIONS

Tell students that good readers ask questions about a text before, during, and after reading. Then they look for answers.

- Good readers ask questions as they read, such as *Do I understand what is taking place in this part of the text? What does this word or phrase mean? Why has the author included this information?*
- Good questions to ask include *Who? What? Why? Where?* and *What if?*
- Asking good questions helps a reader focus on the most important information in a text.

### MAKE, REVISE, AND CONFIRM PREDICTIONS

Tell students that when they predict, they use text clues, along with prior knowledge, to infer what might happen next in a story.

- Text clues may include a character's behavior, a series of cause-and-effect relationships, or a series of events.
- Readers also use story structure or pattern of predictability to make logical guesses about upcoming story events or character actions.
- Readers evaluate earlier predictions to either confirm their accuracy or to recognize that the original prediction must be revised. This is one way to check understanding while reading.

### MAKE INFERENCES

Tell students that making inferences asks readers to call upon their understanding of the text, examine their own experiences, and then conclude certain information based on these factors.

- Authors don't always tell readers directly everything that takes place in a story or text, so a good reader must take what details the author does offer and infer, or reasonably assume, certain conclusions.
- Making inferences helps a reader better understand the text and make logical predictions.

### EVALUATE

Tell students that when they evaluate as a strategy, they call upon their own critical judgment to understand a text.

- Good readers need to be suspicious of biases, opinions presented as fact, and techniques of persuasion.
- Readers also evaluate literary devices, such as personification or foreshadowing, to see how they might slant or prejudice their interpretation.
- Any judgment the reader makes must be supported by the text.
- Judgments must also apply to the sources a writer uses. Are they sound and reliable? What is the author's purpose—to entertain, persuade, or instruct?

### Comprehension

Observe students during the first few weeks of school. Notice students who struggle reading grade-level text. Assess those students' reading comprehension abilities using the Leveled Passages in **Diagnostic Assessment**. Use the results to provide appropriate small group instruction.

# Start Smart

## Objective

- Monitor comprehension

## Materials

- TE Reproducible, p. S31

# Comprehension

## Monitor Comprehension/Clarify

In addition to the six key reading strategies, students will be using two strategies with every story they read: **monitoring comprehension** and **making connections**.

Tell students that as they read, they need to monitor their comprehension and stop and check if they understand what they are reading. If they do not understand something, they need to use self-correction techniques, called **Fix-Up Strategies**, to help them make sense of their reading. Explain the following:

- When we read, we need to stop at regular intervals and ask ourselves what we just read. We also need to stop when we have a problem or get confused by the text.
- Clarifying our understanding can involve one or more of the following Fix-Up Strategies: rereading, summarizing, adjusting reading rate, answering questions about the text, reading ahead for helpful information, note taking, and outlining.

Create a classroom Fix-Up Strategies Chart with students. List the different ways a reader stops and monitors his or her reading. Model each of these strategies as you begin reading the selections in the **Student Book** during Whole Group time or the **Skill-Based Practice Readers** during Small Group time.

## Make Connections

Tell students that good readers connect what they read to their personal experiences, other books they have read, and other things they know about the world around them.

- **TEXT-TO-SELF** You connect the text to experiences you have had in your own life. For example, if you read a story about a family going on vacation to Yosemite, you can connect their experiences to family vacations you have taken.
- **TEXT-TO-TEXT** You connect the text to other texts you have read. For example, after reading several selections on one theme in the Student Book, you will tell how each new selection adds to your growing knowledge of that theme.
- **TEXT-TO-WORLD** You connect the text to the outside world and other things you have learned. For example, if you read a selection about how the government is organized, you can connect it to your town's government and any related news stories.

ON YOUR OWN **TE Reproducible,** page S31

**Reading Interest Survey**

**Circle YES or NO to answer each question.**

1. Reading is fun. YES NO
2. Reading is a good way to spend spare time. YES NO
3. I like having someone read aloud to me. YES NO
4. I learn from reading. YES NO
5. I read for fun every day. YES NO
6. Most books are long and boring. YES NO
7. I have several favorite books at home. YES NO
8. There should be more time in school for free reading. YES NO
9. I would rather watch TV than read. YES NO
10. I am a good reader. YES NO

**Put a checkmark √ next to your answer.**

| Check what you like to do. | Very Much | Sometimes | Very Little |
|---|---|---|---|
| Read about animals. | | | |
| Read adventure stories. | | | |
| Read funny books. | | | |
| Read magazines. | | | |
| Read about real places. | | | |
| Read about real people. | | | |
| Read newspapers. | | | |
| Read online articles. | | | |
| Read mysteries. | | | |
| Read fantasies. | | | |

# Fluency

## Establish Yearly Goals

**CA CONTENT STANDARD**
**R 3.1.3** Read aloud narrative and expository text fluently and accurately and with appropriate pacing, intonation, and expression.

Tell students that fluency involves three key aspects of our reading: speed, accuracy, and expression. Explain the following:

- **SPEED/PACE** The rate at which we read is important. We need to read at a pace appropriate for the level of text difficulty. In Grade 3 the goal by the end of the year is to read 107 words correct per minute (WCPM). Explain to students that you will be testing them on their rate throughout the year to meet this goal. Rereading previously read books is one way they will increase their rate.
- **ACCURACY** Correctly identifying words is key to skilled, fluent reading. Explain to students that the work they do in phonics and word study will help them read longer and harder words. They will also use **Speed Drills** to help them become automatic at reading those words with more complex spelling patterns. TE Reproducible page S34 provides a sample.
- **EXPRESSION/INTONATION** Good readers read with proper phrasing and intonation. They read dialogue the way the character would have said it. They speed up when the action in a story gets exciting, and they slow down on difficult parts of a text. This means that the reader is decoding and comprehending the text at the same time—the hallmark of a skilled, fluent reader. Explain to students that they will be performing **Readers Theater** plays throughout the year to work on their oral expression of text.

### Objective

- Build fluency

### Materials

- TE Reproducible, p. S34

### Fluency

At the end of the Start Smart weeks, assess each student's oral reading fluency to establish each child's baseline. The goal for the beginning of Grade 3 is 71 words correct per minute (WCPM). See **Diagnostic Assessment** for tests and scoring guidelines. Use the results to provide appropriate small group instruction.

**TE Reproducible,** page S34

**Syllable Speed Drill**

| | | | | |
|---|---|---|---|---|
| ing | un | ture | dis | com |
| im | ter | ment | er | der |
| ver | ble | tion | num | re |
| est | ple | de | ex | en |
| bout | per | tle | pro | dif |
| fore | fa | el | ful | pic |
| por | tween | hap | nev | ness |
| non | mis | ly | ic | less |
| lect | heav | sub | rep | semi |
| ma | mid | tend | pre | cial |

# Write

**WHOLE GROUP**

**WRITING**
- Writer's Notebook
- Rubrics
- On-Demand Writing
- Writing Conferences
- Revision Assignments

**CA CONTENT STANDARDS**
W 3.1.0, W 3.1.4

**Daily Journal Prompts**

Use the following writing prompts throughout the Start Smart unit.

- Write about your dream vacation.
- Write about your favorite book.
- Write about your favorite thing to do outside of school.
- Write about a job you would like to have someday.
- Write about your favorite place in California.

# Writing

## Set Up Writer's Notebooks

Tell students that they will be writing every day. You want them to record their writings in Writer's Notebooks. These notebooks will be used to:

- Record on-demand writings. Students will write as much as they can as well as they can for a predetermined amount of time. Once completed, students will check their writing during Independent Time and correct any errors. Then, during conferences, you will analyze their writing to see if any additional errors were made that they didn't correct or notice. This is one way you will help them become better writers and individualize writing instruction.
- Make word lists associated with word study skills, such as words with prefixes, suffixes, synonyms, and antonyms.
- Write drafts of any major writing pieces.
- Complete revision assignments based on writing needs.
- Write their responses to readings to develop a deeper understanding of the text.

Have students write their name on the front of their Writer's Notebook. Then have them turn to the first page and write the date. Remind them that they will write the date at the beginning of each new piece they write.

Ask students to write for five minutes as much as they can as well as they can. Tell them that you want them to write a description of themselves, including what they like to do in and out of school.

Then have students turn to the back of their Writer's Notebooks. Have them record the following headings on separate pages: *synonyms, antonyms, idioms, prefixes, suffixes, multiple-meaning words, related words*. Students will use these pages to record words they learn associated with each word type.

## Establish Writing Habits

Tell students that one writing habit they will be using all year is carefully rereading and revising their work. This will help them check for grammar, usage, and mechanics errors. It will also give them an opportunity to strengthen their writing based on feedback they receive from you or their classmates.

CA CONTENT STANDARD
**W 3.1.4** Revise drafts to improve the coherence and logical progression of ideas by using an established rubric.

Teach students the proofreading marks shown. Use these marks when you proofread pieces with students. Tell students that these marks will be used in every grade; they are common to all students in the school. Therefore, it is good to learn and use them. Write the marks on a chart and post it in the classroom for all to see and use.

## Use Rubrics

Tell students that they will also be using rubrics as they write and revise this year. Tell them that you will give them rubrics before they begin writing to help them understand the expectations for each piece and what they need to do to create a piece that meets the highest standards.

Distribute copies of the Writing Rubric on TE Reproducible page S33. Discuss with students the following:

- **IDEAS AND CONTENT/GENRE** include the information you put in a piece of writing, including the characteristics of the genre.
- **ORGANIZATION AND FOCUS** is how you organize, or order, that information. Will clear organization help the reader understand what you are writing?
- **SENTENCE STRUCTURE/FLUENCY** involves using a variety of sentence types to add interest to the writing. It also involves using complete sentences with coherent thoughts and ideas.
- **VOICE** is how you tell the story. What do you add to the writing to make it your own?
- **WORD CHOICE** includes the specific, descriptive words you choose to paint a vivid picture in the reader's mind.
- **CONVENTIONS** refers to writing sentences with correct grammar, spelling, and word usage.
- **PRESENTATION** is how the writing looks. Did you use your best handwriting? Is it typed in an easy-to-read format and font?

Have students use the Writing Rubric to write about an adventure that happened to them in the past. Help them use the rubric to plan their writing, then evaluate it during the revision phase. Finally, use the rubric to score the piece and explain to students how it could be revised to receive a higher score.

### Objectives

- Set up Writer's Notebook
- Learn proofreading marks and use rubrics

### Materials

- TE Reproducible, p. S33

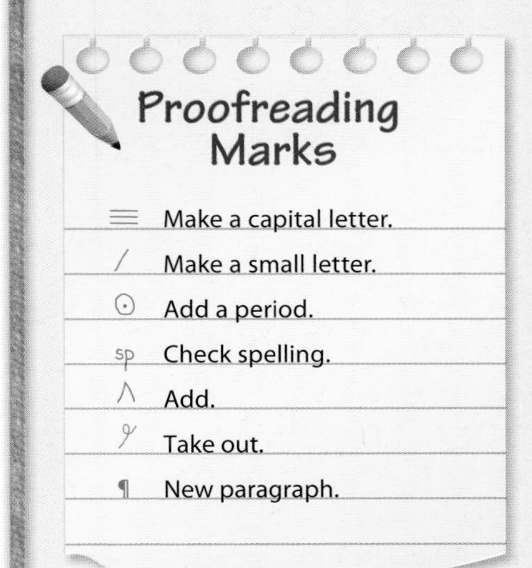

**TE Reproducible,** page S33

### Writing Rubric

| ④ Excellent | ③ Good | ② Fair | ① Poor |
|---|---|---|---|
| **Ideas and Content/Genre** | | | |
| The writer creates a cohesive story with carefully chosen details. | The writer relates a personal experience with adequate detail. | The writer relates a personal experience but may lose focus. | The writer does not share a personal experience. |
| **Organization and Focus** | | | |
| The writer grabs the reader's attention with a strong beginning and end. | The text has a recognizable beginning and ending. It presents ideas in order. | The writer presents the events in order but does not use time-order words. | The text has no clear beginning or endings. The sequence is hard to follow or confusing. |
| **Voice** | | | |
| The writer shows originality and a strong personal message. | The writer makes an effort to share a message. Some attempts are more effective than others. | The writer tells a story in a predictable way. The writer shows a lack of personal involvement. | The writer appears detached from the experience and the reader. |
| **Word Choice** | | | |
| The text uses both challenging and everyday language in a natural way. | The text uses appropriate words and some colorful language. | The text uses words that are not precise or lack description. | The text uses words that are inappropriate for the purpose or audience. |
| **Sentence Structure/Fluency** | | | |
| The text contains creative, effective sentences that flow smoothly and vary in structure. | The text contains complete sentences that vary in structure. | The text contains mostly simple sentences and few sentences with complex structures. | The sentences contain fragments and run-ons and are difficult to understand. |
| **Conventions** | | | |
| The text needs little editing. Most conventions are used correctly. | The spelling, capitalization, punctuation, and usage are mostly correct. | The text has frequent errors that make it hard to read. | The text repeats a lot of errors in spelling, word choice, punctuation, and usage. |
| **Presentation** | | | |
| The text is easy to read. The formatting improves the message. | The text is readable. The formatting supports the message. | The text is somewhat difficult to read. The format or spacing is not uniform. | The text is very difficult to read. The formatting hurts understanding. |

## Objective

- Write on demand

### Materials

- None

# Writing

## On-Demand Writing

**CA CONTENT STANDARD**
**W 3.1.0** Students write clear and coherent sentences and paragraphs that develop a central idea. Their writing shows they consider the audience and purpose. Students progress through the stages of the writing process.

Tell students that every week they will be writing on demand. That means they will be given a writing prompt and told how many minutes they must write without stopping. Explain the following:

- *In Write-on-Demand assignments, you will write as much as you can as well as you can.*
- *The amount of time you write without stopping will slowly increase throughout the year.*
- These Write-on-Demand assignments mirror those that will appear on their key assessments, such as Unit Tests. Therefore these assignments will help students develop the writing stamina needed to do well on these tests.
- You will work with them to revise their Write-on-Demand pieces to tailor your writing instruction to their specific needs. This will help each of them become better writers.

Explain the following Write-on-Demand steps.

**STEP 1 Read and analyze the prompt.**
Write the following prompt on the board: *Your neighborhood is littered with trash. What can you do to help?*

Ask students to chorally read the prompt. Discuss what the writing expectation is: You will create a Problem and Solution piece that explains the problem (a littered neighborhood) and what you can do to clean it up (the solution to the problem).

**STEP 2 Plan your writing.**
Tell students that they will write an interesting introduction to their writing that grabs the reader's attention and establishes the problem (a littered neighborhood). They will then write about how to solve the problem. Suggest that they write a possible solution in each subsequent paragraph, or write each step to solve the problem, one step in each paragraph. They will end the piece with a strong conclusion that sums up their thinking on the problem and solution.

**STEP 3 Write for the allotted time, staying focused.**
Tell students that they will write for five minutes without stopping. They will write as much as they can as well as they can. They should not stop and revise after each sentence or paragraph. Rather, they can use time at the end if they have it. Remind students that both the amount they write and the quality of their writing are important.

**STEP 4 Evaluate your writing.**
Once completed, ask students their impressions of the writing experience. *What was difficult? How did the time restriction affect your writing? What could you do differently next time?* Then ask students to proofread their writing during Independent Time. Tell them that you will review their writing during conferences, review their proofreading marks, and give them a specific revision assignment that will help them improve their writing.

## Conferences

Tell students that each week you will be meeting with several of them during Small Group time to review their Writer's Notebook pieces. The purpose of these conferences is to determine the specific writing skills they need to work on to become better writers. These may include writing more precise details, working on a specific grammar or mechanics skill, or reorganizing their writing so it flows better and is easier for the reader to understand.

## Revision Assignments

Tell students that revision assignments are a regular part of their writing work in their Writer's Notebooks. These assignments help you work with each of them on one skill at a time until each has mastered it. Explain the following:

- Revision assignments involve marking up a specific section of their writing, such as underlining a sentence, and then asking them to revise it in a specific way.
- Revision assignments require them to use your feedback to make their writing better. They show how much you value their writing and step by step how to develop into skilled writers.

Write the following on the board: *This summer I went to the beach with my family. We swam for hours. We played beach volleyball. <u>We also took a boat to watch the whales.</u> We had fun at the beach.*

Revise

Then write the following revision assignment beneath it: *This sentence made me curious. Pretend that this event happened in slow motion. Write three or four more sentences that describe exactly what happened.*

With students, revise the passage above, using the revision assignment as a guide. Model using proofreading marks as appropriate.

### Anchor Papers

Student models for each writing mode (Scores 1–4) are provided in the **Teacher's Resource Book**.

Revise

### Revision Assignments

Use the Revision Assignment to focus each student's rewrites. These can be printed from the Jump Drive for ease of use.

# Diagnostic Assessments

## Skill Assessment and Placement

Observe students throughout the Start Smart unit as they complete assignments, respond orally in class, and read aloud. Take note of individual students' skill needs.

**Fluency Benchmark** Following the Start Smart weeks, assess each student's fluency level. This test will show which students are below grade-level, on level, and above level based on national fluency norms.

For students below level, use the *Diagnostic Assessment Decision Tree* in **Diagnostic Assessment** to determine which tests need to be administered to figure out each student's specific skill needs. The results of these tests will assist you in determining which students need intervention and help you provide appropriate small group lessons to fill in skill gaps and get all struggling readers on level.

**DIAGNOSTIC ASSESSMENTS INCLUDE . . .**

- **Fluency Passages** (determine fluency rates; WCPM scores correlated to national norms developed by program author Jan Hasbrouck)
- **Leveled Passages** (determine reading level and comprehension abilities)
- **Quick Phonics Survey** (determine decoding abilities and skill deficiencies; developed by program author Jan Hasbrouck)
- **Vocabulary** (determine speaking and reading vocabulary proficiency; tests for English learners based on CELDT word lists)
- **Spelling Inventory** (determine encoding abilities; developed by program author Donald Bear)
- **Basic Assessments** (determine lower-level skill deficiencies, when applicable; includes high-frequency words, phonemic awareness, and alphabet recognition)

**Diagnostic Assessment**

| Diagnose | | Prescribe |
|---|---|---|
| **Use the results of the Diagnostic Assessments to provide appropriate small group instruction. Focus on rebuilding lower-level skills needed to accelerate student progress. Use the Intervention Kit (K–3) and/or the Intervention Anthology for additional support.** | | |
| | **IF...** | **THEN...** |
| **FLUENCY**<br>Fluency Passages (WCPM) | Students are below grade level . . . | See the Assessment Decision Tree. Assess decoding skills using Quick Phonics Survey and comprehension abilities using the Leveled Passages.<br>**Evaluate for intervention.** |
| **COMPREHENSION**<br>Leveled Passages | Students are below grade level . . . | Consider students' reading level when providing preteach and reteach lessons to support students while reading the Core selections. |
| **PHONICS/WORD STUDY**<br>Quick Phonics Survey<br>Spelling Inventory | Students are below grade level . . . | Assess basic skills, such as phonemic awareness and high-frequency words. |
| **VOCABULARY**<br>Reading Vocabulary | Students are below grade level . . . | Assess English learners' vocabulary. The assessment is correlated to the CELDT. |
| **WRITING**<br>Writing Inventory<br>(Use the Write-on-Demand Prompt to get a writing sample from each student.) | Students are below grade level . . . | Provide additional practice during the building strong sentences and building strong paragraph lessons in Weeks 1, 2, 4, 5. |

## WRITE-ON-DEMAND SCORING RUBRIC

**PROMPT** **What was the most interesting thing you did this summer? Tell me about it in detail. Write for five minutes.**

| 4 Excellent | 3 Good | 2 Fair | 1 Unsatisfactory |
|---|---|---|---|
| • More than 7 sentences<br>• Almost no spelling or grammar errors<br>• Cohesive ideas, focused and organized | • 5–7 sentences<br>• A few spelling and grammar errors<br>• Well-developed ideas and facts provided | • 4–5 sentences<br>• Several spelling and grammar errors<br>• Some good information; some vague | • Fewer than 4 sentences<br>• Many spelling and grammar errors<br>• Few developed ideas or accurate information |

Name ____________________________

# Decoding Strategy Chart

| Step | |
|---|---|
| Step 1 | Look for word parts (prefixes) at the beginning of the word. |
| Step 2 | Look for word parts (suffixes) at the end of the word. |
| Step 3 | In the base word, look for familiar spelling patterns. Think about the six syllable-spelling patterns you have learned. |
| Step 4 | Sound out and blend together the word parts. |
| Step 5 | Say the word parts fast. Adjust your pronunciation as needed. Ask yourself: "Is this a word I have heard before?" Then read the word in the sentence and ask: "Does it make sense in this sentence?" |

Name ______________________________

# Dictionary Entry

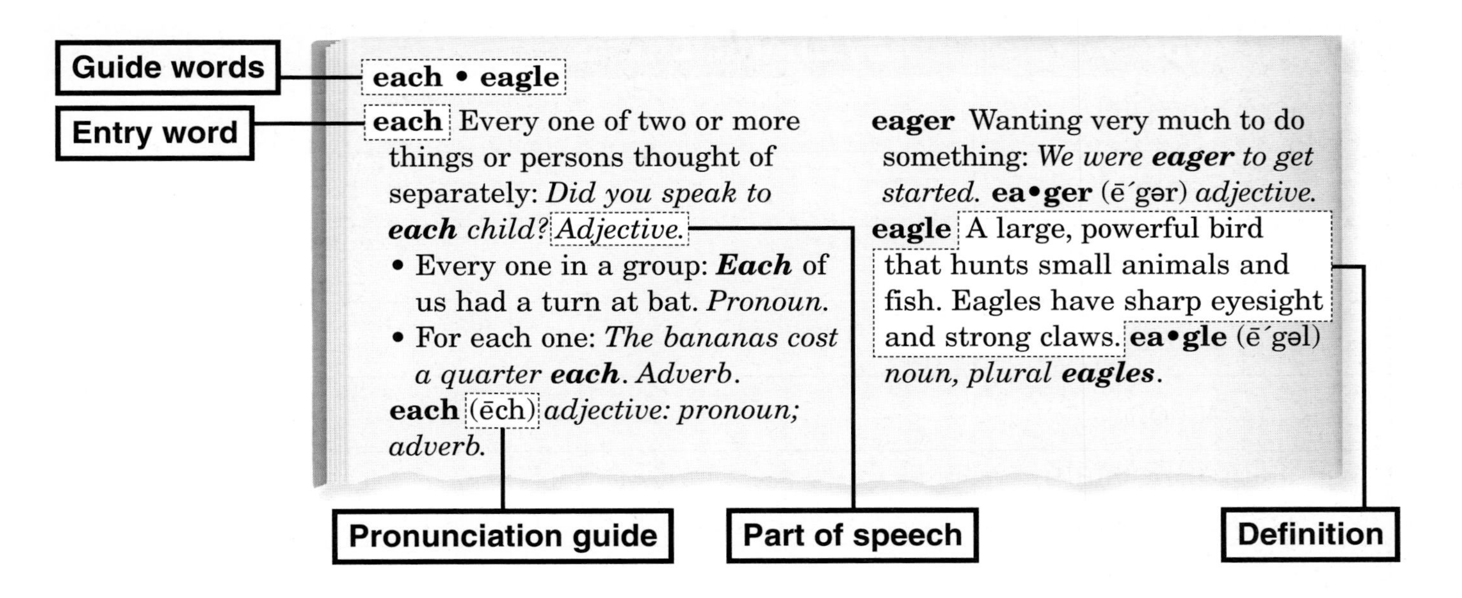


# Thesaurus Entry

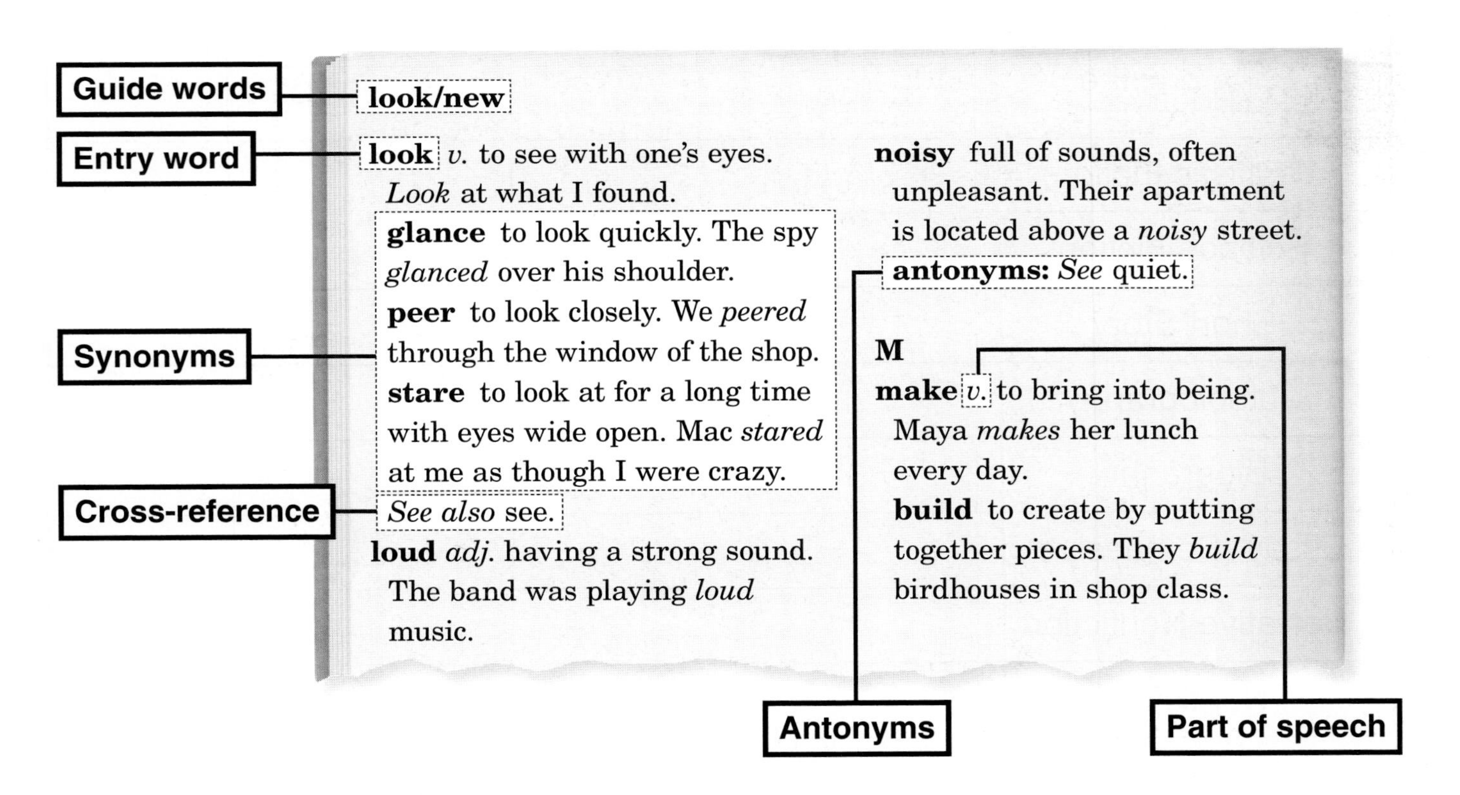

Name ______________________________



# Genres

| Type | Key Characteristics | Examples |
|---|---|---|
| Drama (Play) | | |
| Fable | | |
| Fairy Tale | | |
| Fantasy | | |
| Fiction | | |
| Folklore (Folktale, Trickster Tale) | | |
| Historical Fiction | | |
| Humor | | |
| Legend | | |
| Mystery | | |
| Poetry | | |
| Realistic Fiction | | |
| Science Fiction | | |
| Short Story | | |
| Autobiography | | |
| Biography | | |
| Essay (Persuasive) | | |
| Narrative Nonfiction | | |
| Nonfiction | | |
| Speech | | |

Name ______________________________



# Reading Interest Survey

**Circle YES or NO to answer each question.**

1. Reading is fun. YES NO
2. Reading is a good way to spend spare time. YES NO
3. I like having someone read aloud to me. YES NO
4. I learn from reading. YES NO
5. I read for fun every day. YES NO
6. Most books are long and boring. YES NO
7. I have several favorite books at home. YES NO
8. There should be more time in school for free reading. YES NO
9. I would rather watch TV than read. YES NO
10. I am a good reader. YES NO

**Put a checkmark √ next to your answer.**

| Check what you like to do. | Very Much | Sometimes | Very Little |
|---|---|---|---|
| Read about animals. | | | |
| Read adventure stories. | | | |
| Read funny books. | | | |
| Read magazines. | | | |
| Read about real places. | | | |
| Read about real people. | | | |
| Read newspapers. | | | |
| Read online articles. | | | |
| Read mysteries. | | | |
| Read fantasies. | | | |

Name ______________________________

Weekly Contract

# My To-Do List

**Put a check next to each activity you complete.**

### Reading

- ☐ Pick a book to read.
- ☐ Read to a partner.

### Word Work

- ☐ Sort words.
- ☐ Collect multisyllabic words.

### Writing

- ☐ Write in your Writer's Notebook.
- ☐ Correct On-Demand Writing

### Practice Readers

- ☐ Choose a favorite book type.
- ☐ Write a summary of a book.

### History/Social Science

- ☐ Collect facts about California.
- ☐ Write 3 facts about your hometown.

### Science

- ☐ Find out about your school's earthquake safety procedures.
- ☐ Write about your choice for a class pet.

### Technology

- ☐ www.macmillanmh.com
- ☐ Listening Library

### Independent Practice

- ☐ Reproducible page 210–211
- ☐ Reproducible page 212–213

Name ______________________



# Writing Rubric

| ④ Excellent | ③ Good | ② Fair | ① Poor |
|---|---|---|---|
| **Ideas and Content/Genre** | | | |
| The writer creates a cohesive story with carefully chosen details. | The writer relates a personal experience with adequate detail. | The writer relates a personal experience but may lose focus. | The writer does not share a personal experience. |
| **Organization and Focus** | | | |
| The writer grabs the reader's attention with a strong beginning and end. | The text has a recognizable beginning and ending. It presents ideas in order. | The writer presents the events in order but does not use time-order words. | The text has no clear beginning or endings. The sequence is hard to follow or confusing. |
| **Voice** | | | |
| The writer shows originality and a strong personal message. | The writer makes an effort to share a message. Some attempts are more effective than others. | The writer tells a story in a predictable way. The writer shows a lack of personal involvement. | The writer appears detached from the experience and the reader. |
| **Word Choice** | | | |
| The text uses both challenging and everyday language in a natural way. | The text uses appropriate words and some colorful language. | The text uses words that are not precise or lack description. | The text uses words that are inappropriate for the purpose or audience. |
| **Sentence Structure/Fluency** | | | |
| The text contains creative, effective sentences that flow smoothly and vary in structure. | The text contains complete sentences that vary in structure. | The text contains mostly simple sentences and few sentences with complex structures. | The sentences contain fragments and run-ons and are difficult to understand. |
| **Conventions** | | | |
| The text needs little editing. Most conventions are used correctly. | The spelling, capitalization, punctuation, and usage are mostly correct. | The text has frequent errors that make it hard to read. | The text repeats a lot of errors in spelling, word choice, punctuation, and usage. |
| **Presentation** | | | |
| The text is easy to read. The formatting improves the message. | The text is readable. The formatting supports the message. | The text is somewhat difficult to read. The format or spacing is not uniform. | The text is very difficult to read. The formatting hurts understanding. |

Name ______________________________

# Syllable Speed Drill

| | | | | |
|---|---|---|---|---|
| ing | un | ture | dis | com |
| im | ter | ment | er | der |
| ver | ble | tion | num | re |
| est | ple | de | ex | en |
| bout | per | tle | pro | dif |
| fore | fa | el | ful | pic |
| por | tween | hap | nev | ness |
| non | mis | ly | ic | less |
| lect | heav | sub | rep | semi |
| ma | mid | tend | pre | cial |

Name ______________________________

Comprehension

# Notetaking (Cornell Notes)

| Main Ideas | Key Words/Drawings |
| --- | --- |
| | |

| Summary |
| --- |
| |

Name ______________________________



# 5 Text Structures

| Text Structure | Signal Words | Purpose |
|---|---|---|
| **Description**<br>1 ____<br>2 ____<br>3 ____<br>4 ____ | such as, for example, for instance, most important, in front, beside, near | Often used in textbooks. The author defines or classifies information by describing its characteristics. |
| **Sequence**<br>First → Next → Last | first, second, third, before, on (date), not long after, then, next, after that, finally, at the same time | Presents information in time order. |
| **Compare and Contrast**<br>Different Alike Different | like, unlike, but, in contrast, on the other hand, however, both, also, too, as well as, just as | Show the similarities and differences between two subjects. |
| **Cause and Effect**<br>Cause → Effect<br>→<br>→<br>→ | therefore, so, this led to, as a result, because, if… then, consequently | Explains why or how something happens. |
| **Problem and Solution**<br>Problem → Action → Solution | therefore, so, this led to, as a result, because, if… then, consequently | Presents a problem or series of problems and offers solutions to solve them. |

Name ______________________________

# Description Writing Frame

**Use the Writing Frame below to summarize the selection.**

People are trying to help by ______________________________

______________________________.

First, they are ______________________________

______________________________

______________________________.

This is important because ______________________________

______________________________

______________________________.

They are also ______________________________

______________________________

______________________________.

This is important because ______________________________

______________________________

______________________________.

**Rewrite the completed summary on another sheet of paper. Keep it as a model for writing a summary of an article or selection using this Text Structure.**

Name ______________________________



# Compare and Contrast Writing Frame

**Use the Writing Frame below to summarize the selection.**

Both ______________ and ______________ are similar in many ways.

They are similar because ________________________________________

________________________________________________________________.

They are also similar because ____________________________________

________________________________________________________________.

In some ways, though, ______________ and ______________
are different.

They are different because _______________________________________

is ______________________________________________________________.

So, ______________ and ______________ have both similarities
and differences.

**Rewrite the completed summary on another sheet of paper. Keep it as a model for writing a summary of an article or selection using this Text Structure.**

Name ______________________________

# Cause and Effect Writing Frame

**Use the Writing Frame below to summarize the selection.**

Many of our Earth's animals are in danger. There are several things we can do to help them.

We can ______________________________

______________________________.

The effect of this is ______________________________

______________________________.

We can also ______________________________

______________________________.

The effect of this is ______________________________

______________________________.

In addition, we can ______________________________

______________________________.

The effect of this is ______________________________

______________________________.

Therefore, it's important to help Earth's animals so that they ______________

______________________________.

Name ______________________________

# Problem and Solution Writing Frame

**Use the Writing Frame below to summarize the selection.**

Most inventions solve problems. Here are some examples.

One problem was that ______________________________

______________________________.

This problem was solved when ______________________________

______________________________.

Another problem was that ______________________________

______________________________.

This problem was solved when ______________________________

______________________________.

Another problem was that ______________________________

______________________________.

This problem was solved when ______________________________

______________________________.

**Rewrite the completed summary on another sheet of paper. Keep it as a model for writing a summary of an article or selection using this Text Structure.**

Name ________________________________



# Sequence Writing Frame

**Use the Writing Frame below to summarize the selection.**

The first step in making a ______________ is to ______________________

_____________________________________________________________.

After that, you must ___________________________________________

_____________________________________________________________

_____________________________________________________________.

Thirdly, you need to ___________________________________________

_____________________________________________________________

_____________________________________________________________.

Finally, you _______________________________________________

_____________________________________________________________

_____________________________________________________________.

**Rewrite the completed summary on another sheet of paper. Keep it as a model for writing a summary of an article or selection using this Text Structure.**

Name ______________________________

# Comprehension Passage: Summarize

**Read the passage. Then complete the questions.**

## Ben Franklin

Ben Franklin invented many handy objects. We can say that Ben invented swim fins. We can also say that Ben invented mail routes. In the old days, mail came in many different ways. Ben's routes were fast, and mail always came the same way. We still use many of Ben's mail routes today.

Ben Franklin also remade many old objects, so that they worked better. Flames in lamps make smoke. Smoke would get trapped inside and make glass lamps gray. Ben made a lamp that let the smoke escape. In Ben's lamp the glass stayed clean. We can say that Ben reinvented the old lamp in a better way.

Ben had strong work habits. Ben did not sleep late and he went to bed early. His habits made him feel good and allowed him to accomplish a lot. Ben was a good and smart man.

1. Underline the first sentence in each paragraph. This sentence is the topic sentence of each paragraph.
2. Circle two important details in each paragraph.
3. Now write a summary of Ben Franklin's contributions.

______________________________

______________________________

______________________________

Name ______________________________

# Comprehension Passage: Visualize

**Read the passage. Then complete the questions.**

## The Toad

I went to my little yellow rowboat. An old toad saw me. "It is midday. I need to eat!" he croaked. "Let's go!" I told him. I began to row.

Suddenly, we saw a glow on a small hilltop. Large golden bowls sat on the land. We rowed over. We saw a bowl of hot roasted nuts. We saw a bowl of green beans. We saw a bowl of ripe blackberries. We saw a loaf of warm bread. We ate and ate! We did not stop. We had cold juice to complete the feast. When we finished, we were full.

"Mmm!" I said.

"Mmm!" croaked the toad.

What a daydream! Will the toad be in my dreams when I go to bed? I hope so!

1. Underline the descriptive words and phrases in the first two paragraphs, such as *little*, *yellow*, and *old*.
2. Circle the words that describe the place in the second paragraph.
3. Now write what you pictured in your mind when you read the first two paragraphs.

______________________________________________

Name ______________________________

# Comprehension Passage: Generate Questions

**Read the passage. Then complete the questions.**

## Cubby's New Pals

It was sunset. The sun was dropping in the sky, like a big red ball. Cubby was eating his supper. The silky wolf cub was sad. He wanted the kids to return to the woods.

"They seem so sweet," he said, "and it is very neat that they can speak to us."

"Yes," said Mom. "If kids trust us, we help them."

"Will we see them soon?" asked Cubby. His eyes gleamed.

"They usually come on the weekends," said Mom. "Now eat your dinner. It is time to sleep."

1. Underline the words or phrases that tell who or what the selection is about.
2. Write what you know about wolf cubs.

______________________________

______________________________

3. Now write the questions you asked as you read the story.

______________________________

______________________________

______________________________

# Comprehension Passage: Make, Confirm, Revise Predictions

**Read the passage. Then complete the questions.**

## A Box of My Own

Herb was the third of five kids. They lived in the smallest house on the block with their mom and dad. They had a dog, cat, and bird. Herb was never bored.

"I wonder what it would be like to have a room of my own?" Herb sighed.

"Herb!" called Mom from the kitchen. "We had to get a new fridge today. It is taller than the old one. Will you put the box out on the curb?"

Herb perked up. "May I have it?" he blurted. "I can set it up under the shadiest tree. I'll hang my drawings on the wall. I'll put a *Do Not Disturb* sign on the door. I'll read books in peace and quiet."

"Superb!" said Mom. "A box of your own is a perfect hideaway!"

1. Read the first paragraph. Write why you think Herb is never bored. ______________________________
2. Read the third paragraph. Write what Herb might do with the big box? ______________________________
3. Underline the words or phrases that explain what Herb did with the box.

Name ________________________________

# Comprehension Passage: Make Inferences

**Read the passage. Then complete the questions.**

## Cicily's Pictures

Cicily looked around the park. A mist hung low touching the trees. "What a change," said Cicily. "This looks like the warmest day we have had so far."

In front of Cicily was a tree with a bird making a giant nest. "This looks like the pigeon nest on our ledge at home in the city. Birds are smart," she said.

"Some birds are smarter than others. Some make their own nests while some don't know how," said Dad. "You should take pictures of some of the amazing nests you see in the park and in the city."

"I did!" Cicily pulled some pictures out of her bag. "Which one do you think is nicest, the pictures of the park or the city?"

Dad looked at all of the pictures. "I think the park pictures are nicer than the pictures of the city because of the ancient trees."

I think so too," said Cicily. "This picture won me a prize in school."

1. Read the first paragraph. Write where you think Cicily lives. Underline the words that give you clues.
2. Which picture won Cicily a prize? How do you know?

Name ____________________

# Comprehension Passage: Evaluate

**Read the passage. Then complete the questions.**

## Look! A Flying Bag!

"Look!" said Joseph. "I will hold this paper bag over the fire. When I let it go, it will fly!"

"I think you are crazy!" said a man in a black hat. "A bag cannot fly!"

Joseph held the open bag over the fire. When he let it go, it flew into the air. Every man in the room gasped. They were all amazed.

"It is a trick," said the man in the black hat.

"No," said Joseph. "It is a fact that a bag of hot air can fly. One day, men and women will fly in balloons."

**1.** How does the man in the black hat feel about the experiment?

______________________________

**2.** How does Joseph feel about the man's reaction?

______________________________

**3.** How do you think the man in the black hat will respond to Joseph's last comment?

______________________________

______________________________

The Big Question

## Big Question Board

Tell students that the units in their **Student Book** are organized around themes. That is, in each unit they will be exploring an important topic. For example, one unit will be related to an important Grade 3 science concept; another unit will be related to an important Grade 3 history/social science concept. Each selection in the unit will build on students' growing knowledge of the topic. Then explain the following:

- Together you will create a Big Question Board, like a large bulletin board, in the classroom.
- This board will contain the unit theme, sentence strips listing how each selection adds information to the theme, research collected throughout the unit, unit vocabulary, strategy charts, phonics charts, and other important pieces of information from the unit.
- Establish a wall, or a portion of a wall, in the classroom for the Big Question Board. Create a banner reading: "Big Question Board." Add to the board as you begin reading the selections in Unit 1.

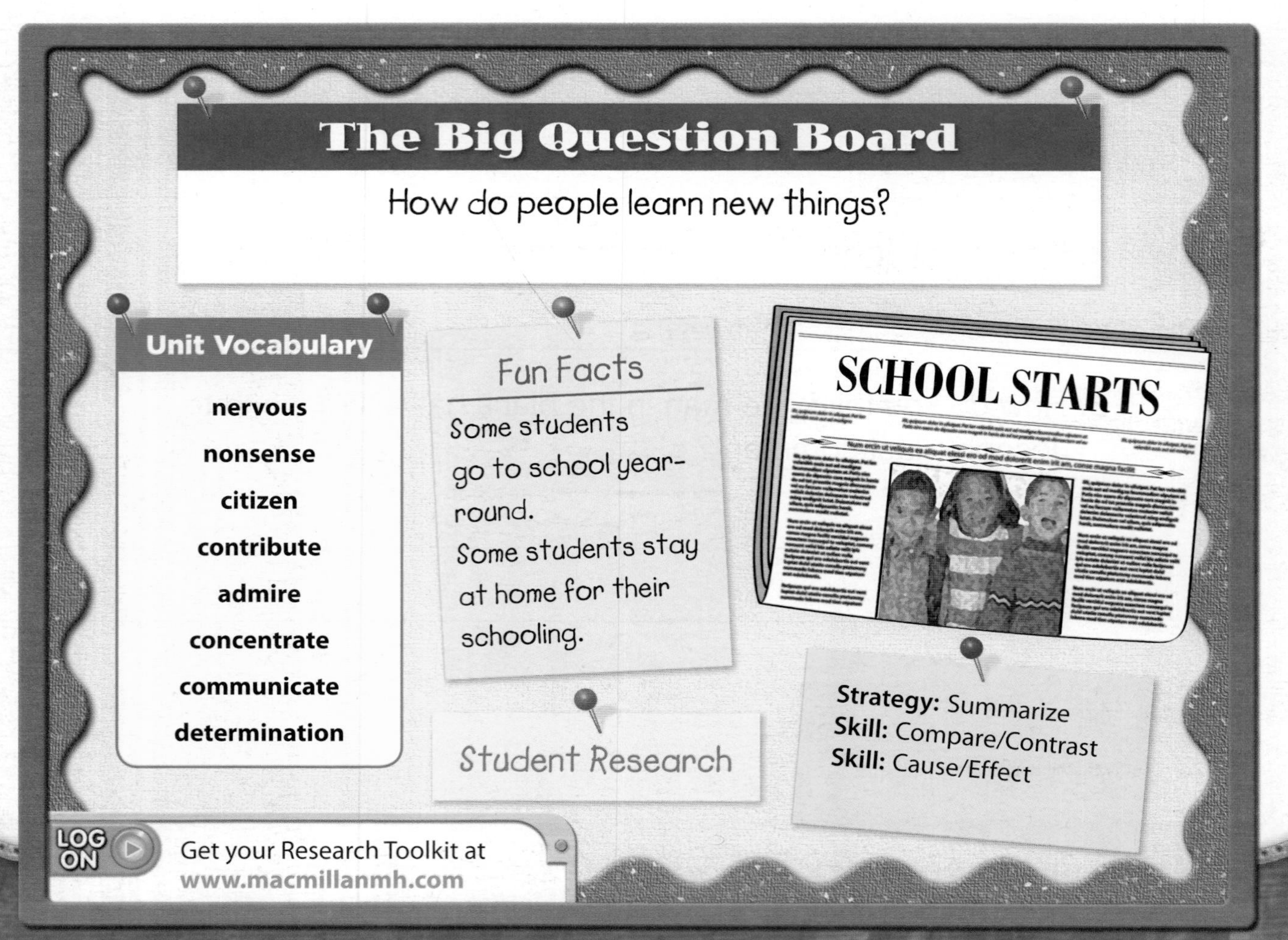

# Week 1 At a Glance

## WHOLE GROUP

### Phonics/Word Study
Short Vowels, Multisyllabic Words

### Vocabulary
Robust Words: *chuckled, nervous, nonsense, fumbled, trudged*

Word Parts: Prefixes *un-, non-*

### Comprehension
Strategy: Analyze Story Structure
Skill: Character, Setting, Plot

### Fluency
Phrasing

### Spelling
Short Vowels: *clap, step, sick, rock, luck, crop, snack, mess, head, shut, miss, stamp, jump, click, pond*

### Grammar/Mechanics
Statements and Questions

Capitalization and Punctuation in Statements and Questions

### Writing
Topic Development: Moment

### Read Aloud
Genre: Poetry

## SMALL GROUP

### Differentiated Instruction for Tested Skills

Approaching Level | On Level | Beyond Level | English Learners

## Teacher Tools

Technology to help plan and implement instruction

### PREPARE
- Professional Development Videos
- Parent Connection

### PLAN/ORGANIZE

### TEACH
- Theme Launcher Video
- Classroom Presentation Toolkit
- Vocabulary PuzzleMaker
- Sound Pronunciation CD

### ASSESS

# Weekly Literature

## Student Book

**A mix of fiction and nonfiction connected to:**

- Unit Theme
- California Content Standards

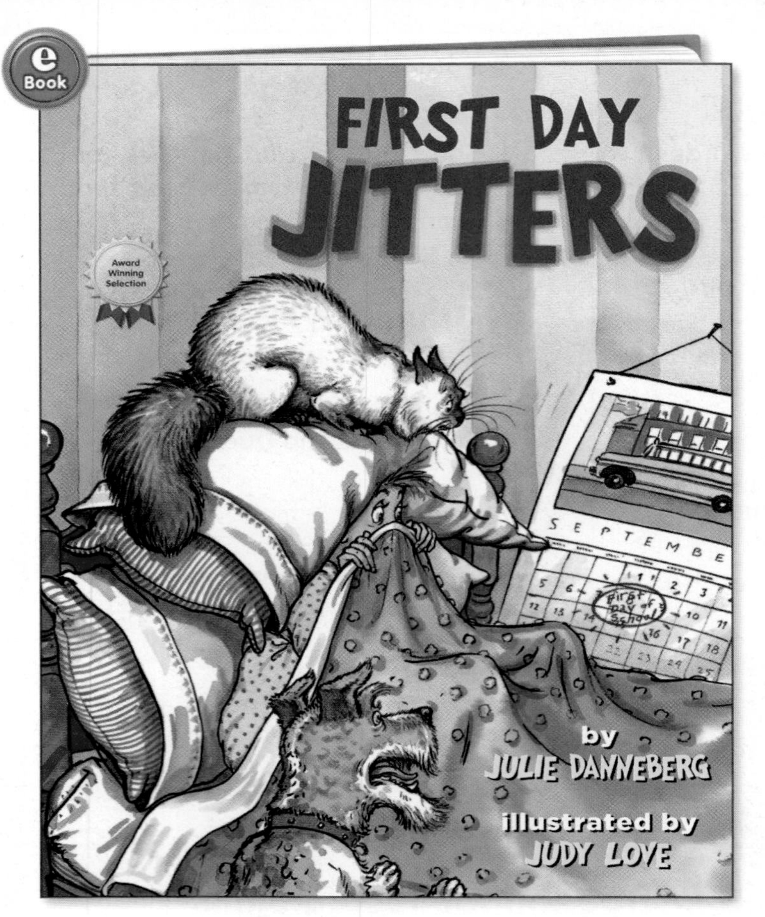


**Main Selection**

Genre Realistic Fiction

**Preteach Vocabulary and Comprehension**

Genre Realistic Fiction

**Paired Selection**

Genre Nonfiction

## Support Literature

**Resources to build robust vocabulary, fluency, and content knowledge**

**Interactive Read-Aloud Anthology**

- Listening Comprehension
- Readers Theater Plays

**Content Reader**

- Meets all California Science and History/Social Science Standards

# Resources for Differentiated Instruction

## Skill-Based Practice Readers

- Same Theme
- Same Vocabulary/Phonics
- Same Comprehension Skills

Approaching Level

On Level

Beyond Level

English Learner

On Level Practice Reader sheltered for English Learners

## StudentWorks Plus

- eBook
- Use for preteaching
- Summaries in multiple languages
- Word-by-Word Reading
- Assessment

## Practice Book and Reproducibles

Also available:

Approaching Reproducible

Beyond Reproducible

## Home-School Connection

- Family letters in English, Spanish, Hmong, Vietnamese, Cantonese, Khmer
- Take-Home Stories

## Intensive Vocabulary

Build robust vocabulary with fiction and nonfiction

**Oral Vocabulary Cards**

## Intervention Kit

- Intervention Anthology
- Phonemic Awareness Teacher's Edition
- Phonics/Word Study Teacher's Edition
- Comprehension Teacher's Edition
- Vocabulary Teacher's Edition
- Fluency Teacher's Edition
- Writing and Grammar Teacher's Edition

## Visual Vocabulary Resources

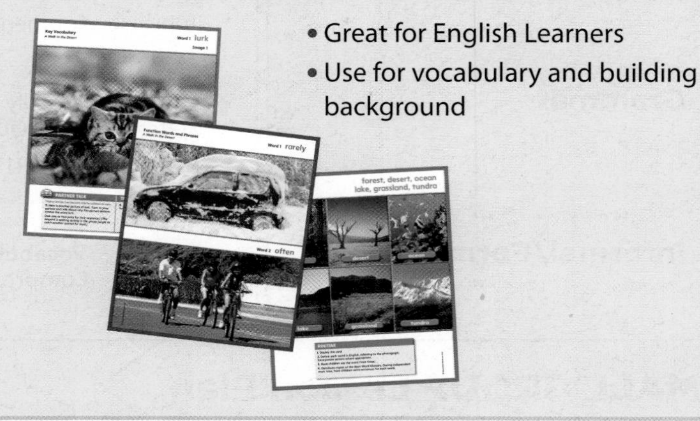


- Great for English Learners
- Use for vocabulary and building background

# Suggested Lesson Plan

LOG ON Go to www.macmillanmh.com for Online Lesson Planner

First Day Jitters, pp. 10–27

| WHOLE GROUP | DAY 1 | DAY 2 |
|---|---|---|
|  15–20 min **ORAL LANGUAGE**<br>• Listening Comprehension<br>• Speaking/Viewing | **Listening/Speaking/Viewing**<br>**Focus Question** How do you feel about new people, places, and things?<br>Read Aloud: "Give Me Normal," 6L–6M<br>Build Background, 6 | **Listening/Speaking**<br>**Focus Question** Why does Sarah try to avoid going to school? |
| 30–40 min **WORD STUDY**<br>• Vocabulary |  **Vocabulary** R 3.1.1<br>*chuckled, nervous, nonsense, fumbled, trudged,* 9, 31A<br>Practice Book, 10 | **Vocabulary** R 3.1.1, R 3.1.8<br>Review Words, Word Parts/Prefixes, 31A<br>Practice Book, 15 |
| • Phonics/Word Study | **Strategy:** Word Parts/Prefixes *un-, non-*, 8 | **Phonics**<br>Read Short Vowel Words, 6N<br>Practice Book, 9 R 3.1.1 |
| • Spelling |  **Spelling** Pretest, 31C<br>Practice Book, 16 LC 3.1.8 | **Spelling** Word Sorts, 31C<br>Reproducible, SP1 LC 3.1.8 |
|  30–40 min **READING**<br>• Comprehension | **Read** "Tina's Try-Out Day," 8–9<br> Student Book<br> **Comprehension**, 9A–9B<br>**Strategy:** Story Structure<br>**Skill:** Character, Setting, Plot R 3.3.3<br>Practice Book, 11 | **Read** *First Day Jitters,* 10–27<br>Student Book<br>**Comprehension**, 10–27<br>**Strategy:** Analyze Story Structure<br>**Skill:** Character, Setting, Plot R 3.3.3<br>Practice Book, 12 |
| • Fluency | **Fluency** Model Fluency, 6M R 3.1.9 | **Fluency** Repeated Reading: Phrasing, 29A R 3.1.9 |
|  30–40 min **LANGUAGE ARTS**<br>• Writing | **Writing**<br>**Daily Writing Prompt** Describe how you felt the first time you tried a new activity, such as bike riding or cooking.<br>Topic Development: Moment, 32–33B W 3.1.1 |  **Writing**<br>**Daily Writing Prompt** Write about a new activity that you'd like to try. Explain why you'd like to try this activity.<br>Topic Development: Moment, 33C<br>Practice Book, 20 W 3.1.1 |
| • Grammar | **Grammar** Daily Language Activities, 31E<br>Statements and Questions, 31E<br>Reproducible, GR1 LC 3.1.1 | **Grammar** Daily Language Activities, 31E<br>Statements and Questions, 31E<br>Practice Book, 18 LC 3.1.1 |
| **ASSESSMENT**<br>• Informal/Formal | **Quick Check** **Vocabulary**, 8<br>**Comprehension**, 9B | **Quick Check** **Comprehension**, 23 |

 45–60 min **SMALL GROUP Lesson Plan** — **Differentiated Instruction 33K–33JJ**

## California Standards

| Vocabulary | Comprehension | Writing | Social Studies |
|---|---|---|---|
| Vocabulary Words<br>Word Parts/ Prefixes<br>R 3.1.8 | Strategy: Story Structure<br>Skill: Character, Setting, Plot<br>R 3.3.3 | Topic Development: Moment<br>W 3.1.1, W 3.1.4 | Government and the citizen<br>HSS 3.4.2, HSS 3.4.1 |

## DAY 3

**Listening/Speaking**

**Focus Question** Read "Tina's Try-Out Day." How is Tina's situation similar to Sarah's? How do Tina and Sarah react differently to their situations?

Summarize, 29

**Vocabulary** R 3.1.1, R 3.1.8, R 3.1.8
Review Words, Related Words, 31B

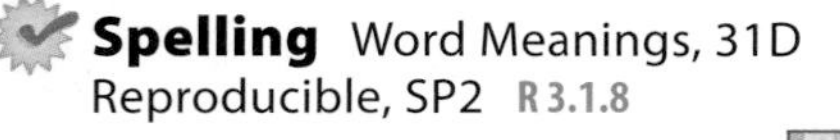

**Spelling** Word Meanings, 31D
Reproducible, SP2 R 3.1.8

**Read** *First Day Jitters,* 10–27

**Comprehension**
Critical Thinking, 29

**Review Skill:** Self-Selected Strategy, 29B

Student Book

**Fluency** Repeated Reading: Phrasing, 29A
Practice Book, 13 R 3.1.9

**Writing**

**Daily Writing Prompt** Paint a picture of your classroom in words. For example, describe its size, shape, and furniture.

**Topic Development: Moment,** 33D W 3.1.1

**Grammar** Daily Language Activities, 31E
Mechanics and Usage, 31F

Reproducible, GR2 LC 3.1.1

**Quick Check** **Fluency**, 29A

## DAY 4

**Listening/Speaking/Viewing**

**Focus Question** Why are teachers, such as Sarah Jane Hartwell in *First Day Jitters,* good citizens?

**Vocabulary** R 3.1.1, R 3.1.8, R 3.1.8

**Content Vocabulary:** *citizen, community, laws, nations,* 30

Review Words, Morphology, 31B

**Spelling** Proofread, 31D
Practice Book, 17 R 3.1.8

**Read** "How to Be a Good Citizen," 30–31

Student Book

**Comprehension**
**Nonfiction:** Informational Essay, 3

**Text Feature:** Bar Graph, 30

Practice Book, 14 R 3.2.1

Content Reader

**Fluency** Repeated Reading: Phrasing, 29A R 3.1.9

**Writing**

**Daily Writing Prompt** Imagine that you are Mr. Hartwell. Write what you would say to persuade Sarah to go to school.

**Reading/Writing Connection,** 33E–33F W 3.1.1

**Grammar** Daily Language Activities, 31E
Statements and Questions, 31F
Practice Book, 19 LC 3.1.1

**Quick Check** **Vocabulary**, 31A–31B

## DAY 5 Review and Assess

**Listening/Speaking/Viewing**

**Focus Question** Who are the main characters in *First Day Jitters* and "How to Be a Good Citizen"? Does "How to Be a Good Citizen" have characters, a setting, and a plot? Why or why not?

**Vocabulary** R 3.1.1, R 3.1.8, R 3.1.8
Assess Words, Connect to Writing, 31B

**Spelling** Posttest, 31D
Reproducible, SP3 R 3.1.8

**Read** Self-Selected Reading R 3.3.2

Student Book

**Comprehension**

Critical Thinking, 31

**Fluency** Practice, 29A R 3.1.3

**Writing**

**Daily Writing Prompt** Pretend that you're a reporter for the school newspaper. Write a short article about Mrs. Sarah Jane Hartwell.

**Conferences/Revision (Assignments),** 33G–33H W 3.1.1, W 3.1.4

**Grammar** Daily Language Activities, 31E
Statements and Questions, 31F
Reproducible, GR3 LC 3.1.1

**Weekly Assessment, 33I–33J**

# Differentiated Instruction

## What do I do in small groups?

## Focus on Skills

**IF...** **students need additional instruction and practice based on your Quick Check observations of the following skills:**

- **Phonics/Word Study**
  Short vowels
- **Vocabulary Words**
  *chuckled, nervous, nonsense, fumbled, trudged*
  **Strategy:** Word Parts
- **Comprehension**
  **Strategy:** Analyze Story Structure
  **Skill:** Character, Setting, Plot
- **Fluency**

**THEN...**

| | |
|---|---|
| Approaching<br>English Learners | Preteach and Reteach Skills |
| On Level | Consolidate Learning |
| Beyond | Enrich and Accelerate Learning |

## Suggested Small Group Lesson Plan

| Focus on Skills | DAY 1 | DAY 2 |
|---|---|---|
| **Phonics/Word Study**<br>• **Short vowels** | English Learners Preteach Short vowels, 33DD | On Level Reteach Short vowels, 33U |
| **Vocabulary**<br>• **Week 1 Words**  | Approaching Preteach; Academic Language, 33K, 33M<br>On Level Review, 33U<br>Beyond Practice Reader Lesson 1, 33AA<br>English Learners Preteach; Academic Language, 33CC–33DD | Approaching Practice Reader Lesson 1, 33P<br>Beyond Practice Reader Lesson 2, 33BB<br>English Learners Preteach Vocabulary; Access to Core Content, 33DD–33EE |
| **Comprehension**<br>• **Strategy:** Analyze Story Structure<br>• **Skill:** Character, Setting, Plot | Approaching Prepare to Read, 33K<br>Beyond Practice Reader Lesson 1, 33AA<br>English Learners Prepare to Read, 33CC | Approaching Reteach; Practice Reader Lesson 1, 33O–33P<br>Beyond Practice Reader Lesson 2, 33BB<br>English Learners Practice Reader, 33II |
| **Fluency**<br>• **Repeated Reading** | | |

## Skill-Based Practice Readers

Apply skills and strategies while reading appropriate leveled books.

**Leveled Practice Database**
Go to **www.macmillanmh.com**.

## Manipulatives

Use for Hands-on Learning

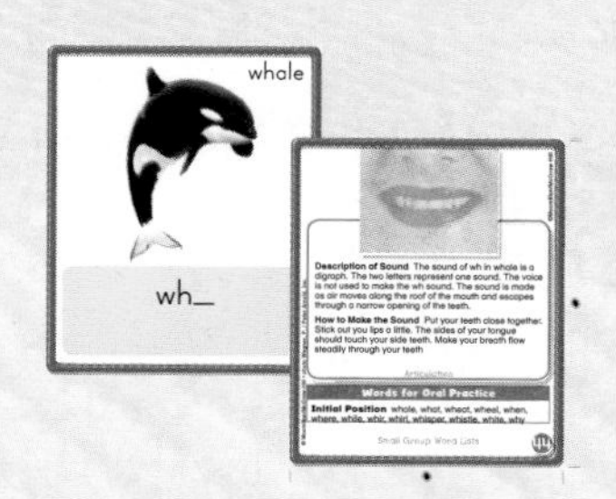


**Sound-Spelling Cards**

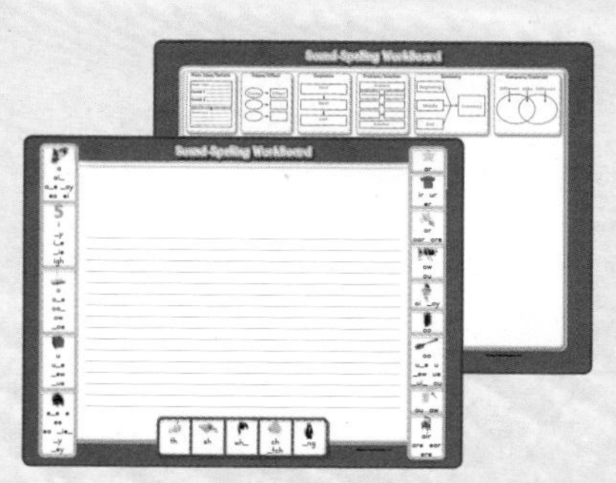

**Sound-Spelling WorkBoards**

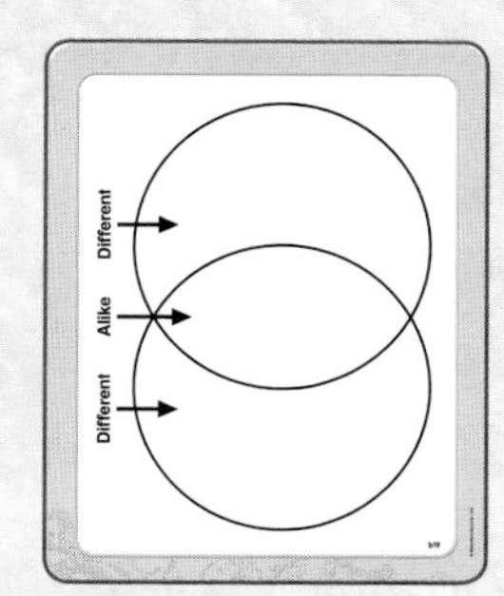


**Vocabulary/Comprehension Write-on/Wipe-off Board**

**FOLDABLES®** Hands-on activities for reinforcing weekly skills

| DAY 3 | DAY 4 | DAY 5 |
|---|---|---|
| **Approaching** Short vowels, 33L<br>**Beyond** Extend and Accelerate, 33Y | **English Learners** Grammar, 33GG | **Approaching** Short Vowels, 33L |
| **Approaching** Practice Reader Lesson 2, 33Q<br>**On Level** Practice Reader Lesson 1, 33W<br>**English Learners** Preteach Vocabulary; Access to Core Content, Grammar, 33DD–33EE, 37GG | **Approaching** Review Vocabulary, 33N<br>**On Level** Practice Reader Lesson 2, 33X<br>**Beyond** Enrich, 33Y<br>**English Learners** Vocabulary, 33II–33JJ | **English Learners** Vocabulary, Practice Reader, 33II |
| **Approaching** Practice Reader Lesson 2, 33Q<br>**On Level** Practice Reader Lesson 1, 33W<br>**English Learners** Practice Reader, 33II | **Approaching** Practice Reader Lesson 3, 33R<br>**On Level** Practice Reader Lesson 2, 33X<br>**English Learners** Practice Reader, 33II | **Approaching** Book Talk, 33JJ<br>**On Level** Book Talk, 33JJ<br>**Beyond** Book Talk, 33JJ<br>**English Learners** Book Talk, 33JJ |
| | **Approaching** Reread, Model, 33S<br>**On Level** Reread, Model, 33V<br>**Beyond** Reread, Model, 33Z<br>**English Learners** Reread, Model, 33FF | **Approaching** Self-Selected Reading, 33T<br>**On Level** Self-Selected Reading, 33V<br>**Beyond** Self-Selected Reading, 33Z |

# Managing the Class

## What do I do with the rest of my class?

- Literacy Workstations
- Practice Book
- Online Activities
- Classroom Library

## Classroom Management Tools

**Weekly Contract**

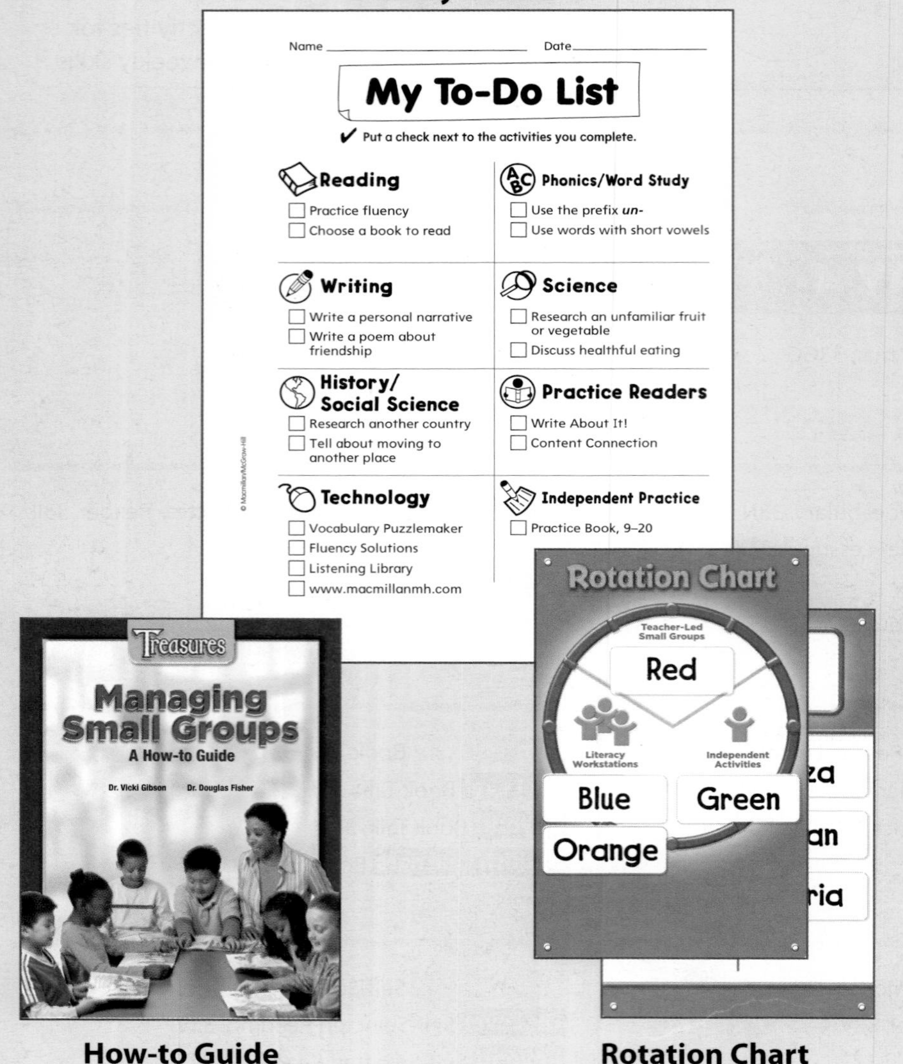
Name ____ Date ____

My To-Do List

✔ Put a check next to the activities you complete.

**Reading**
- ☐ Practice fluency
- ☐ Choose a book to read

**Phonics/Word Study**
- ☐ Use the prefix *un-*
- ☐ Use words with short vowels

**Writing**
- ☐ Write a personal narrative
- ☐ Write a poem about friendship

**Science**
- ☐ Research an unfamiliar fruit or vegetable
- ☐ Discuss healthful eating

**History/ Social Science**
- ☐ Research another country
- ☐ Tell about moving to another place

**Practice Readers**
- ☐ Write About It!
- ☐ Content Connection

**Technology**
- ☐ Vocabulary Puzzlemaker
- ☐ Fluency Solutions
- ☐ Listening Library
- ☐ www.macmillanmh.com

**Independent Practice**
- ☐ Practice Book, 9–20



**How-to Guide**

**Rotation Chart**

## Digital Learning

**StudentWorks Plus**
- Summaries in Multiple Languages
- Word-by-Word Reading
- Assessment

**Meet the Author/Illustrator**

**Mary Hoffman**
- Mary grew up in Manchester, England.
- Mary never wears anything blue.
- When Mary was a girl, she wanted to be a garage mechanic.

Other books written and by Mary Hoffman
- Hoffman, Mary. *Boundless Grace.* New York: Puffin, 2000.
- Hoffman, Mary. *The Color of Home.* New York: Dial, 2002.
- Hoffman, Mary. *Starring Grace.* Frances Lincoln Childrens Books, 2003.

- Read Other Books by Author or Illustrator

## Classroom Library

Use the trade books to apply skills. See lessons on pages T2–T7. See also **Theme Bibliography**, pages T8–T9, to select books for 30 minutes of daily independent reading.

Approaching

On Level

Beyond

# Independent Activities

**ONLINE INSTRUCTION** www.macmillanmh.com

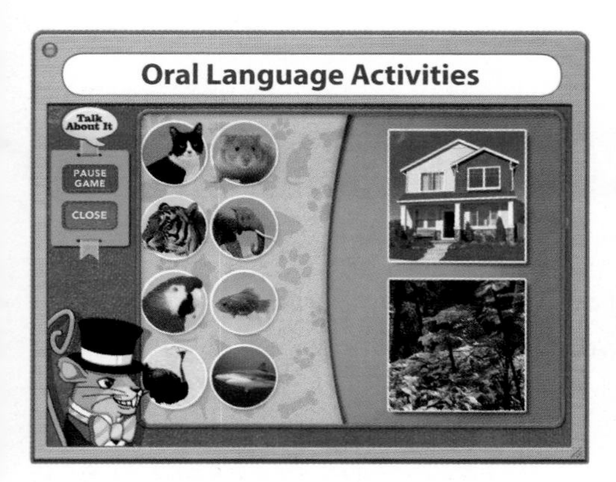


- Focus on Unit Vocabulary and Concepts
- English Learner Support

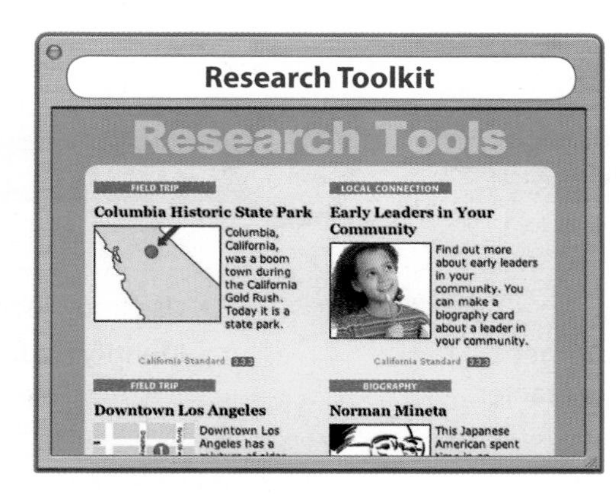


- Research Roadmap
- Research and Presentation Tools
- Theme Launcher Video
- Links to CA Science and History/Social Science Programs

- Focus on Keyboard and Internet Skills
- Media Literacy

- Differentiated Lists and Activities

## Available on CD

**LISTENING LIBRARY**
Recordings of selections

- Main Selections
- Paired Selections
- Practice Readers
- EL Readers

**FLUENCY SOLUTIONS**
Recorded passages at two speeds for modeling and practicing fluency

## Practice Book

Also Available:

Approaching Reproducible

Beyond Reproducible

## Literacy Workstation Flip Charts

Daily independent and partner activities connected to the weekly skills. See pages 6J–6K.

# Managing the Class

## What do I do with the rest of my class?

## Reading

### Objectives

- Read aloud text to a partner fluently and accurately
- Read and determine what a character is like using the author's portrayal to write a message from that character

## Phonics/Word Study

### Objectives

- Use knowledge of prefixes to determine word meanings
- Identify and sort words by vowel sounds

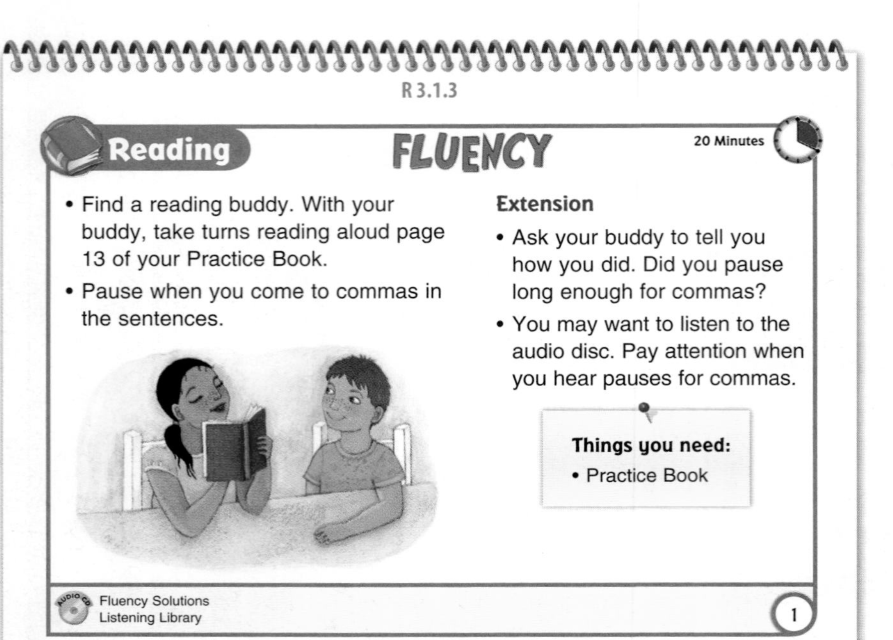

R 3.1.3

**Reading** FLUENCY — 20 Minutes

- Find a reading buddy. With your buddy, take turns reading aloud page 13 of your Practice Book.
- Pause when you come to commas in the sentences.

**Extension**

- Ask your buddy to tell you how you did. Did you pause long enough for commas?
- You may want to listen to the audio disc. Pay attention when you hear pauses for commas.

**Things you need:**
- Practice Book

Fluency Solutions Listening Library

1

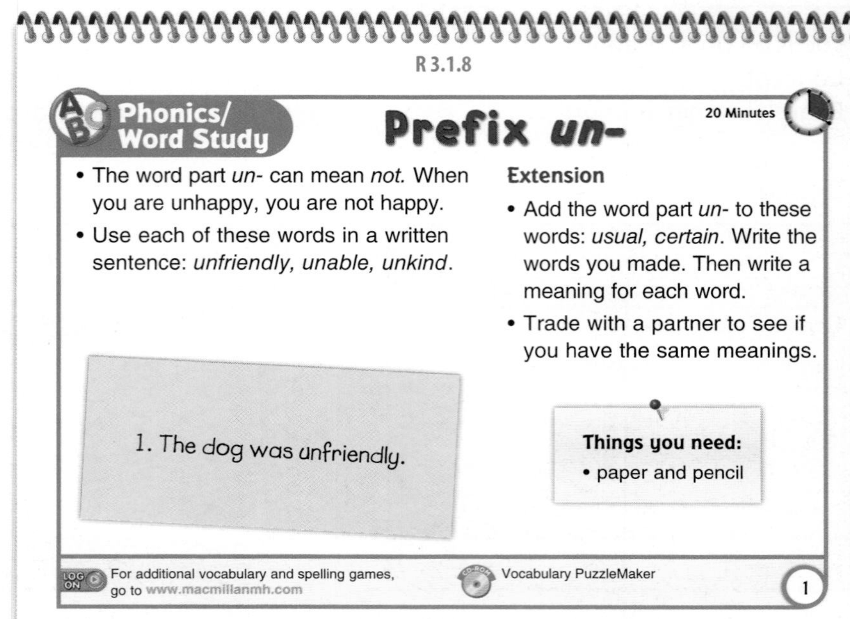

R 3.1.8

**Phonics/Word Study** Prefix *un-* — 20 Minutes

- The word part *un-* can mean *not.* When you are unhappy, you are not happy.
- Use each of these words in a written sentence: *unfriendly, unable, unkind*.

1. The dog was unfriendly.

**Extension**

- Add the word part *un-* to these words: *usual, certain*. Write the words you made. Then write a meaning for each word.
- Trade with a partner to see if you have the same meanings.

**Things you need:**
- paper and pencil

For additional vocabulary and spelling games, go to www.macmillanmh.com

Vocabulary PuzzleMaker

1

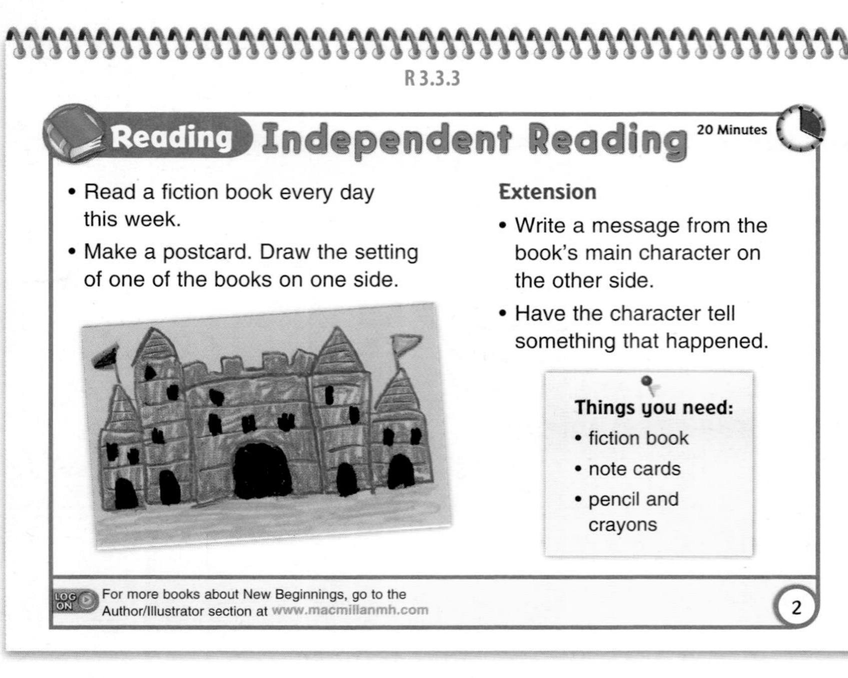

R 3.3.3

**Reading** Independent Reading — 20 Minutes

- Read a fiction book every day this week.
- Make a postcard. Draw the setting of one of the books on one side.

**Extension**

- Write a message from the book's main character on the other side.
- Have the character tell something that happened.

**Things you need:**
- fiction book
- note cards
- pencil and crayons

For more books about New Beginnings, go to the Author/Illustrator section at www.macmillanmh.com

2

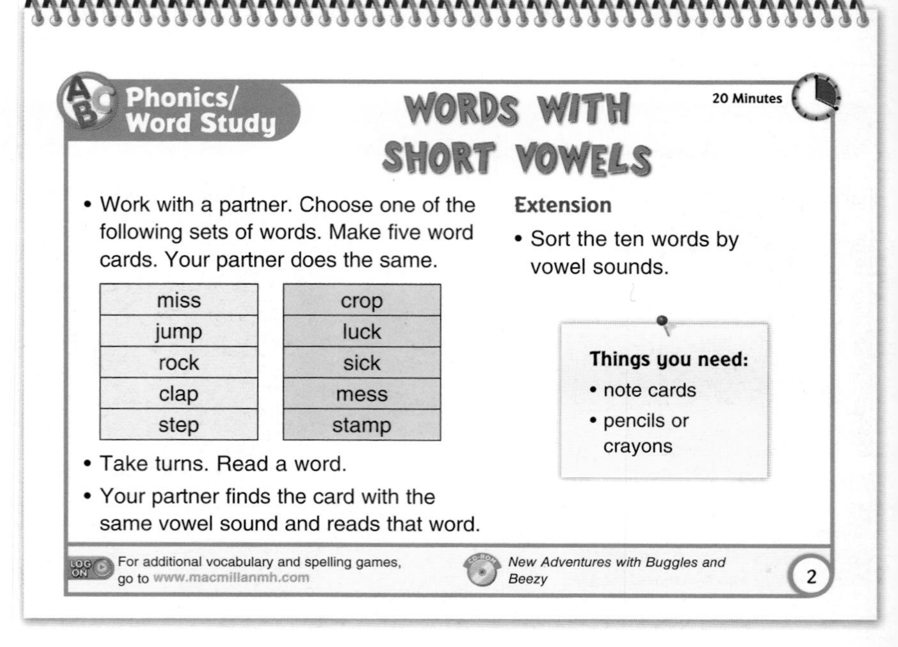

**Phonics/Word Study** WORDS WITH SHORT VOWELS — 20 Minutes

- Work with a partner. Choose one of the following sets of words. Make five word cards. Your partner does the same.

| miss | crop |
|---|---|
| jump | luck |
| rock | sick |
| clap | mess |
| step | stamp |

- Take turns. Read a word.
- Your partner finds the card with the same vowel sound and reads that word.

**Extension**

- Sort the ten words by vowel sounds.

**Things you need:**
- note cards
- pencils or crayons

For additional vocabulary and spelling games, go to www.macmillanmh.com

*New Adventures with Buggles and Beezy*

2

# Literacy Workstations

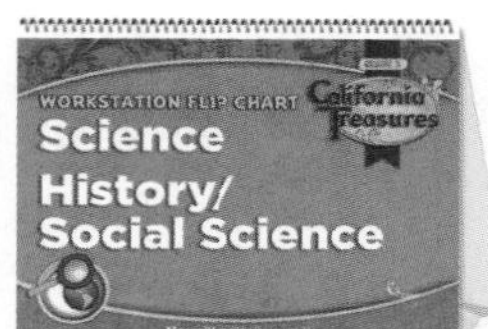


**Literacy Workstation Flip Charts**

## Writing

### Objectives

- Write a personal narrative with well-chosen details to develop the plot about meeting one of your friends
- Write a poem about friends

## Content Literacy

### Objectives

- Research a fruit or vegetable to learn about its different functions including growth and survival
- Research immigrants and their cultural and religious traditions and contributions

W 3.2.1

**Writing**  PERSONAL NARRATIVE — 20 Minutes

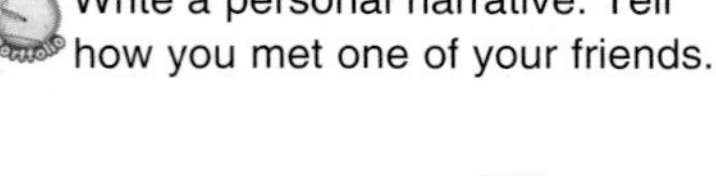

- Write a personal narrative. Tell how you met one of your friends.

**Extension**

- Draw a picture. Show an activity you and your friend do together.
- In your response journal, write a list of your favorite books. Then tell your list to a friend.

**Things you need:**
- paper and pencil
- crayons
- journal

1

LS 3.3.a

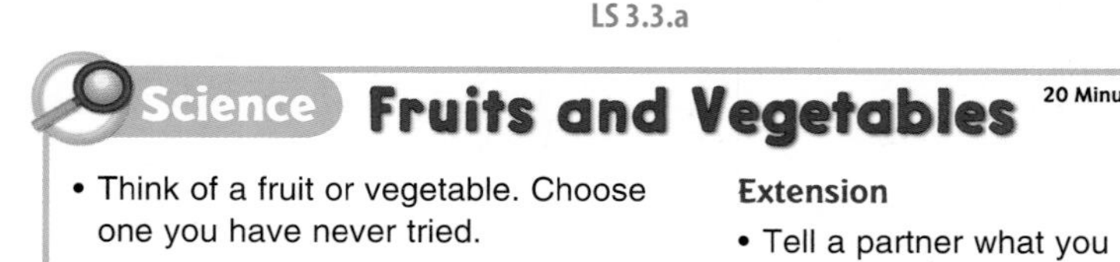

**Science** Fruits and Vegetables — 20 Minutes

- Think of a fruit or vegetable. Choose one you have never tried.
- Use a cookbook, an encyclopedia, or the Internet. Learn about the food. Where does it grow? What vitamins does it have?

**Extension**

- Tell a partner what you learned.
- If your food is healthful, you might want to try it.

**Things you need:**
- cookbook, encyclopedia, or computer

Internet Research and Inquiry Activity
Students can find more facts at www.macmillanmh.

1

W 3.2.2

**Writing** 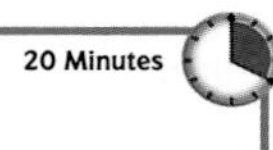 Poem — 20 Minutes

- Think about your friends. Why do you like them?
- Write a poem about friends. Use what you know. Your poem does not have to rhyme.

**Extension**

- Write another poem using the letters in your name.

**Things you need:**
- paper
- pencil

2

HSS 3.3.1

 **History/Social Science** New Beginnings — 20 Minutes 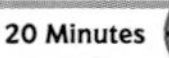

- Immigrants are people who move to another country. Do you know any immigrants?
- Think about moving to another country. What will you bring? Name three things.
- Write a few sentences. Tell about these things. Tell why they are important.

**Extension**

- Find a partner. Take turns. Tell what you will pack. Tell why.

**Things you need:**
- paper
- pencil

2

# Prepare

## WHOLE GROUP

**ORAL LANGUAGE**
- Read Aloud
- Build Background
- Connect to Theme

**PHONICS/WORD STUDY**
- Short Vowels

**VOCABULARY**
- Teach Words in Context
- Word Parts: Prefixes *un-*, *non-*

**COMPREHENSION**
- Strategy: Analyze Story Structure
- Skill: Character, Setting, Plot

**CA STANDARDS**
R 3.1.1, R 3.1.2, R 3.1.3, R 3.1.8, R 3.3.1, R 3.3.3, LAS 3.1.9

## SMALL GROUP

- Differentiated Instruction, pp. 33K–33JJ

### Intensive Vocabulary

To provide 15–20 minutes of additional vocabulary instruction, see **Oral Vocabulary Cards** 5-Day Plan. The pre- and post-tests are on **Teacher Resource Book** pages 269–272.

# Read Aloud

## Read "Give Me Normal"

**Read Aloud**

**GENRE: POEM**

Share with students the following key characteristics of a **poem**:

CA CONTENT STANDARD **R 3.3.1** Distinguish common forms of literature.

- A poem is a piece of writing that usually tells about a strong feeling or experience.
- Poems may paint a picture of a person or an event using colorful, descriptive language.
- Some poems do not rhyme. Poems that do not rhyme are called free-verse poems.

**FOCUS ON VOCABULARY**

Introduce the following words, using the **Define/Example/Ask** routine. Tell students that knowing these words will help them visualize the scenes in the poem in their minds.

### Vocabulary Routine

Use the routines below to discuss the meaning of each word.

**Define:** Something **normal** is usual or expected.
**Example:** It is normal for my baby brother to cry when he is upset.
**Ask:** Is it normal to have a snowstorm in the summer?

**Define:** Something that is **inflated** is filled up with air or gas.
**Example:** I inflated my new bike tire with air after the old one popped on a pebble.
**Ask:** What decorations might need to be inflated for a party?

**Define:** **In my book** means in my opinion.
**Example:** Roller coasters are not a lot of fun in my book.
**Ask:** When would you use the phrase "in my book"?

**LISTENING FOR A PURPOSE**

Ask students to listen carefully as you read "Give Me Normal" on **Read-Aloud Anthology** pages 9–11. Use the Think Aloud and Genre Study prompts provided.

EL **Interactive Reading** Build students' oral language by engaging them in talk about the poem's basic meaning.

- After the third stanza say, *Turn to your partner and discuss what the narrator thinks is strange about Ms. Roys.*

- After the last stanza, say, *Tell your partner what the narrator does when she is worried. Explain how you know.*

**Think/Pair/Share** Use Copying Master 7, "This was mostly about . . . ," to help students summarize what they learned about the narrator of the poem and her first day of school. When completed, have students turn to a partner and orally summarize the poem. Then have a few students share their summaries with the class.

**RESPOND TO THE POEM**

Ask students the **Think and Respond** questions on page 11. Point out the color imagery *yellow stovepipe hat, black patent leather shoes, a bright red table*. Ask students how the words help them picture the teacher and classroom.

## Model Fluency

Reread the poem. Tell students that this time you want them to focus on phrasing, one important aspect of fluent reading.

CA CONTENT STANDARD **LAS 3.1.9** Read prose and poetry aloud with fluency, rhythm, and pace, using appropriate intonation and vocal patterns to emphasize important passages of the text being read.

Point out to students that you pause in your reading when you see a comma and stop at a period. Make sure that you do not pause or stop at the end of a line unless you see punctuation. Model an example.

**Think Aloud** Listen as I read the first stanza. The poet is describing what Ms. Roys is wearing. I will pause at commas and stop at the end of the sentence:

Ms. Roys met us
On the first day of school,
With a yellow stovepipe hat
On her head,
A skirt that stuck out
As if there were wires
Underneath it,
And black patent leather shoes
Like I wore in kindergarten.

Did you notice where I paused in my reading? Now you try. Repeat the stanza after me, using the same phrasing that I do.

**Establish Fluency Focus** Remind students that you will be listening for these same qualities in their reading throughout the week. You will help them improve their reading by adjusting their phrasing and paying attention to punctuation.

Point out that good readers show their understanding of a story by reading it in these expressive ways. It shows that the reader is decoding and comprehending at the same time. That's the hallmark of a skilled, fluent reader.

### Readers Theater

**BUILDING LISTENING AND SPEAKING SKILLS**
Distribute copies of "Take Me to Your Litter" **Read-Aloud Anthology**, pages 132–145. Have students practice reading the play throughout the unit. Assign parts and have the students present the play or perform it as a dramatic reading at the end of the unit.

CA CONTENT STANDARD **R 3.1.3** Read aloud narrative and expository text fluently and accurately with appropriate pacing, intonation, and expression.

## Objective

- Decode multisyllabic words with short vowel spellings

## Materials

- Sound-Spelling Cards
- Practice Book, p. 9
- Transparency 1
- Word-Building Cards
- Teacher's Resource Book, p. 178

### English Learners
UNIVERSAL ACCESS

**Transfer Sounds** In Spanish, the letters *a, e, i, o,* and *u* stand for different sounds. For example, the letter *e* stands for the long *a* sound and the letter *i* stands for the long *e* sound. Spanish-speaking students may pronounce English short vowel words using the sounds common in Spanish. Use the Approaching Level phonics lessons to provide additional decoding and pronunciation practice.

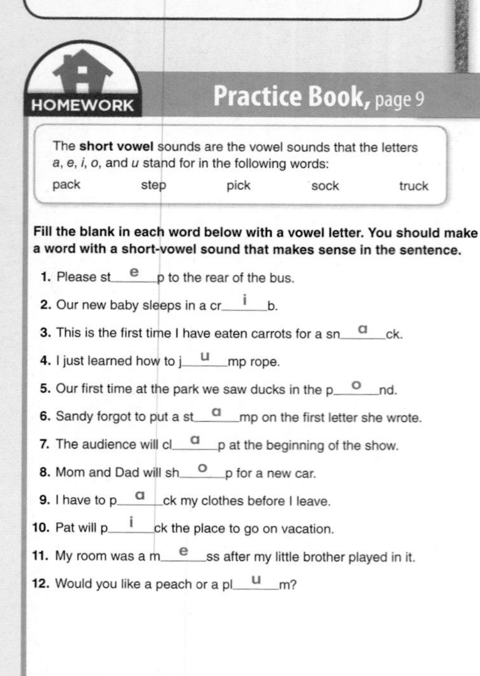

HOMEWORK **Practice Book,** page 9

The **short vowel** sounds are the vowel sounds that the letters *a, e, i, o,* and *u* stand for in the following words:
pack step pick sock truck

**Fill the blank in each word below with a vowel letter. You should make a word with a short-vowel sound that makes sense in the sentence.**

1. Please st__e__p to the rear of the bus.
2. Our new baby sleeps in a cr__i__b.
3. This is the first time I have eaten carrots for a sn__a__ck.
4. I just learned how to j__u__mp rope.
5. Our first time at the park we saw ducks in the p__o__nd.
6. Sandy forgot to put a st__a__mp on the first letter she wrote.
7. The audience will cl__a__p at the beginning of the show.
8. Mom and Dad will sh__o__p for a new car.
9. I have to p__a__ck my clothes before I leave.
10. Pat will p__i__ck the place to go on vacation.
11. My room was a m__e__ss after my little brother played in it.
12. Would you like a peach or a pl__u__m?

**Approaching Reproducible,** page 9
**Beyond Reproducible,** page 9

# Phonics

## Short Vowels

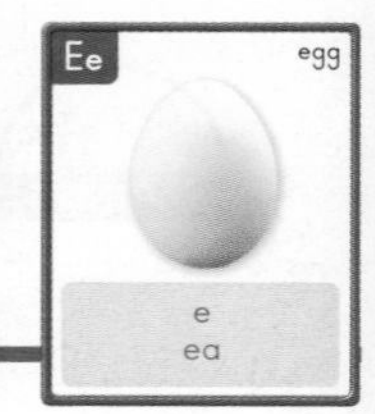


### EXPLAIN/MODEL

Display the *Apple*, *Egg*, *Insect*, *Octopus*, and *Umbrella* **Sound-Spelling Cards** for the short vowels. Point to each card and say the sound. Have students repeat. Then provide a sample word for each spelling. For example, the /a/ sound can be spelled *a* as in *apple*.

- **/a/** as in *apple*
- **/e/** as in *egg* and *head*
- **/i/** as in *insect*
- **/o/** as in *octopus*
- **/u/** as in *umbrella*

Write other words containing each short vowel sound on the board, underline the short vowel spelling, and blend each one. Model blending the word *flat*.

**Think Aloud** Look at this word. It is spelled f-l-a-t. I see the letter a, which is the spelling for the /a/ sound. Listen and watch as I sound out the word: /fffIllaaat/, flat. (Run your finger under the word as you sound it out.)

### PRACTICE/APPLY

**CA CONTENT STANDARD R 3.1.1** Know and use complex word families when reading to decode unfamiliar words.

**Read Word List** Display **Transparency 1**. The first line includes short vowel words students will encounter in the upcoming selections. Have students underline the short vowel sound in each word. Then have them chorally read the words.

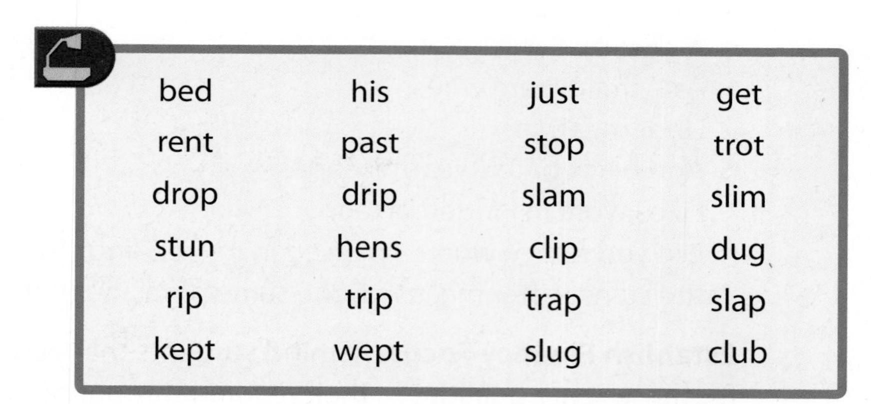

| | | | |
|---|---|---|---|
| bed | his | just | get |
| rent | past | stop | trot |
| drop | drip | slam | slim |
| stun | hens | clip | dug |
| rip | trip | trap | slap |
| kept | wept | slug | club |

**Phonics Transparency 1**

**Sort Words** Ask students to sort the words by spelling pattern. Then have them write the word sort in their Writer's Notebooks.

| a | e | ea | i | o | u |
|---|---|---|---|---|---|
| | | | | | |

## Read Multisyllabic Words

CA CONTENT STANDARD
**R 3.1.2** Decode regular multisyllabic words.

**TRANSITION TO LONGER WORDS** Help students transition from reading one-syllable to multisyllabic words with short vowel sounds. Have students read a word in the first column, then model how to read the longer word in the second column. Point out the added syllable(s), such as a prefix or suffix, to help students gain awareness of these common word parts.

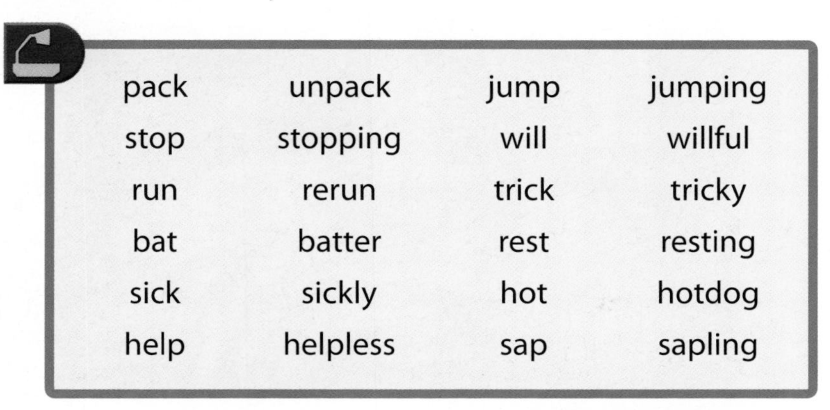

| | | | |
|---|---|---|---|
| pack | unpack | jump | jumping |
| stop | stopping | will | willful |
| run | rerun | trick | tricky |
| bat | batter | rest | resting |
| sick | sickly | hot | hotdog |
| help | helpless | sap | sapling |

**Phonics Transparency 1**

**BUILD WORDS** Use **Word-Building Cards** *con, test, text, tent, tact, pub, lic, lish*. Display the cards. Have students use the word parts to build as many short-vowel multisyllabic words as possible. These and other words can be formed: *contest, context, content, contact, public, publish*.

**CONNECT TO 6 SYLLABLE TYPES** To further help students break apart longer words to decode them, explain the following:

- **Closed Syllables** When a syllable ends in a consonant, it is called a closed syllable. The vowel is "closed in" by the consonants. Most closed syllables have short vowel sounds. (fab/ric)

**APPLY DECODING STRATEGY** Guide students to use the **Decoding Strategy** to decode the following words comprised of short-vowel closed syllables: *backpack, basket, cactus, princess, napkin, plastic, muffin, puppet, dentist, zigzag*. Write each word on the board. Remind students to look for short-vowel spellings in step 3 of the Decoding Strategy procedure.

## Build Fluency

**SPEED DRILL** Distribute copies of the **Short Vowels Speed Drill** in the **Teacher's Resource Book**. Use the Speed Drill routine to help students become fluent reading words with short-vowel spelling patterns.

### Syllable Fluency

Use **Word Building Cards 1-10**. Display one card at a time. Have students chorally read each common syllable. Repeat at varying speeds and in random order. Have students work with partners during independent time to write as many words as they can containing each syllable. Add these lists to the **Unit 1 Big Question Board.**

### Decoding Strategy

**Decoding Strategy Chart**

| | |
|---|---|
| Step 1 | Look for word parts (prefixes) at the beginning of the word. |
| Step 2 | Look for word parts (suffixes) at the end of the word. |
| Step 3 | In the base word, look for familiar spelling patterns. Think about the six syllable-spelling patterns you have learned. |
| Step 4 | Sound out and blend together the word parts. |
| Step 5 | Say the word parts fast. Adjust your pronunciation as needed. Ask yourself: "Is this a word I have heard before?" Then read the word in the sentence and ask: "Does it make sense in this sentence?" |

# Oral Language

## Build Background

**ACCESS PRIOR KNOWLEDGE**

Share the following information:

The first day of school is a big day for everyone. Look at the photo of the students and teacher. What expression do you see on the students' faces? What is the teacher's expression? What do these expressions tell you about how they feel?

Write the following words on the board and briefly define each one using the **Define/Example/Ask** routine: **excited** (happy and interested), **assist** (help).

**FOCUS QUESTION** Ask students to read "Talk About It" on **Student Book** page 7. Then have students turn to a partner and describe the photo. Ask:

- Do you think the teacher in the photo is excited? Why or why not?
- How do you think the teacher in the photo is assisting the student? How do you think the student feels?

**BUILD WRITING FLUENCY**

Ask students to write in their Writer's Notebook what they know about teachers. Tell students to write as much as they can as well as they can. Students should write for five minutes without stopping. Meet with individuals during Writing Conference time to provide feedback and revision assignments. Students should self-correct any errors they notice prior to the conference.

**English Learners**

UNIVERSAL ACCESS

During the discussion, build on students' responses to help them move to the next level of language acquisition. For example, if a student answers *yes* to the first question, say: *That's correct. The teacher looks excited. Say it with me.* (Students repeat sentence.) *I see the smile on her face. Therefore, the teacher is happy and excited to be teaching on the first day of school. Now turn to your partner and tell about this picture.*
Provide the following frames orally or in writing to help students respond in complete sentences.

**Beginning/Early Intermediate** The teacher is _____.

**Intermediate** The teacher feels excited because ____.

**Early Advanced** On the first day of school, the teacher and students feel ____ because _____.

# Unit Theme

## Big Idea

Teachers, like students, are often nervous on the first day of school as they meet their new classes.

### CONNECT TO THEME

Ask students what they know about teachers and the first day of school.

- What kinds of things do teachers and students have to learn on the first day of school?
- How does it feel to meet new people?

### USE THEME FOLDABLES

Write the **Big Idea** statement on the board. Ask students to copy it on their Unit Theme Foldables. Remind them to add details as they complete this week's readings.

## Digital Learning

**PRETEACH** Have Approaching Level students and English Learners listen to the selection on **StudentWorks Plus**, the interactive eBook, before reading with the class. The recording contains summaries in multiple languages, word-by-word reading support, a bilingual glossary, and comprehension questions with corrective feedback.

For Web site activities for oral language development, go to www.macmillanmh.com.

FOLDABLES® Study Organizer

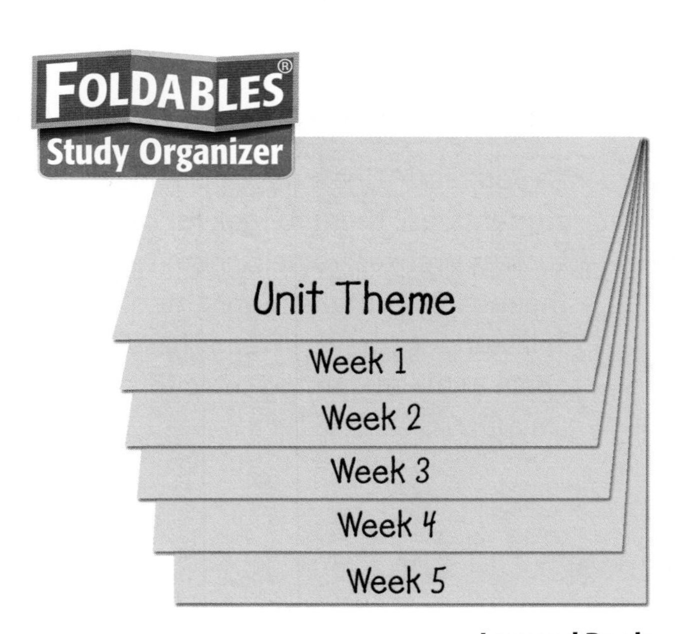


**Layered Book**

# Vocabulary

STRATEGY
**WORD PARTS**

CA CONTENT STANDARD R 3.1.8 Use knowledge of **prefixes** and suffixes to determine the meaning of words.

**Prefixes** Explain to students that a prefix is a word part that is added to the beginning of a base word. The prefix changes the base word's meaning. Point out that the prefixes *un-* and *non-* often mean "not."

Ask students to read "Word Parts: Prefixes" in the bookmark on **Student Book** page 8. Then model for students how to use the meaning of a prefix and a base word to figure out the meaning of an unfamiliar word.

**Think Aloud** I read that Tina felt unhappy when she saw the other girls at the field. In the word *unhappy*, I see the prefix *un-* at the beginning of the word. I know that the prefix *un-* usually means "not." I also see the base word *happy*. I can figure out the meaning of the word *unhappy* by putting together the meaning of the prefix *un-* and the base word *happy*. The word *unhappy* means "not happy" or "not feeling glad."

## Read "Tina's Tryout Day"

As you read "Tina's Tryout Day" with students, ask them to look for clues, such as prefixes, to help them reveal the meanings of the highlighted words. Tell students they will read these words again in the upcoming selection *First Day Jitters.*

**Vocabulary**

**nervous** **nonsense**
**fumbled** **trudged**
**chuckled**

**Word Parts**
Prefixes are word parts added to the beginning of words. The prefixes *non-* and *un-* usually mean "not."
*nonsense* = the opposite of sense

# TINA'S TRYOUT DAY

by Amy Helfer

Tina woke up to her buzzing alarm clock. She rubbed her eyes and wondered why she was up so early. Then she remembered: it was tryout day!

### THE BIG DAY

A few weeks ago, Tina decided she would try out for the Comets, her school's softball team. Tina ran downstairs to the kitchen. "Mom!" she shouted. "It's tryout day!"

"I know," answered Mom. "I made you breakfast."

"I'm too **nervous** to eat."

"You'll have more energy if you do," said Mom.

Tina still felt a bit sick, but she ate some breakfast anyway. Then she ran up to her room and **fumbled** into her clothes.

"Slow down!" Mom **chuckled**. "You'll use up all your energy before you get there."

### ON THE FIELD

Tina got to the field and saw many girls already there. She suddenly felt unhappy.

8

**Quick Check**

**Can students identify word meanings?**

During **Small Group Instruction**

**If No** → **Approaching Level** Reteach the words using the Vocabulary lesson, pp. 33M–33N.

**If Yes** → **On Level** Consolidate the learning using p. 33U.

**Beyond Level** Extend the learning using p. 33Y.

"What am I doing?" Tina asked herself. "I'll never make the team."

Her mom gave her a hug. "That's **nonsense**," she said. "Get out there and do your best. You will be great!"

### PLAY BALL!

The girls had to run, field, bat, catch, and throw balls. Even though Tina stumbled while fielding, she thought she did well.

Afterward, Tina was really tired and **trudged** off the field. One of the coaches called her name. "What do you think, Tina?" she asked. "Would you like to join the Comets?"

Tina forgot how tired she was and jumped high into the air. "Oh, boy!" she shouted. "Would I ever!"

### Reread for Comprehension

**Analyze Story Structure**

**Character, Setting, Plot** Every story has characters, a setting, and a plot. They make up the story's structure. **Characters** are people in the story. The **setting** is when and where the story takes place. The **plot** tells all the events in the story. It has a beginning, middle, and end.

A Story Map helps you analyze the story structure. Reread the selection to find the characters, setting, and plot.

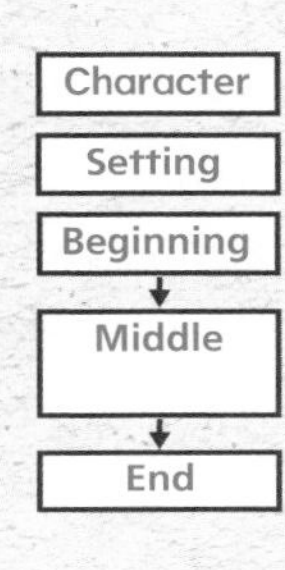


9



# Vocabulary

### TEACH WORDS

Introduce each word using the **Define/Example/Ask** routine. Model reading each word using the syllable-scoop technique.

### Vocabulary Routine

**Define:** The word **nervous** means "a little afraid or worried."
**Example:** I feel nervous when I ride on an airplane.
**Ask:** What makes you feel nervous? EXAMPLE

- You may have **chuckled**, or laughed quietly, when you saw something funny. *I chuckled when I heard the joke.* How is *chuckled* different from *laughed out loud*? COMPARE AND CONTRAST
- **Nonsense** is a silly or untrue idea or thought. *I was afraid to go to the library. My friend said my fears were nonsense.* What is something that you think is nonsense? EXAMPLE
- If something is **fumbled**, it is done in a clumsy or awkward way. *He was tired and fumbled into his pajamas.* When have you fumbled into something? EXAMPLE
- **Trudged** describes a way of walking slowly or dragging one's feet. *The tired student trudged up the hill to his house.* Can you think of a reason why you might have trudged somewhere? EXPLANATION

### English Learners

UNIVERSAL ACCESS

**Preteach Vocabulary**
See pages 33DD and 33M to preteach the vocabulary words to **English Learners** and **Approaching Level** students. Use the **Visual Vocabulary Resources** to demonstrate and discuss each word. Use the Interactive Question-Response Guide to preteach the content in "Tina's Tryout Day" and develop meaning.

HOMEWORK **Practice Book,** page 10

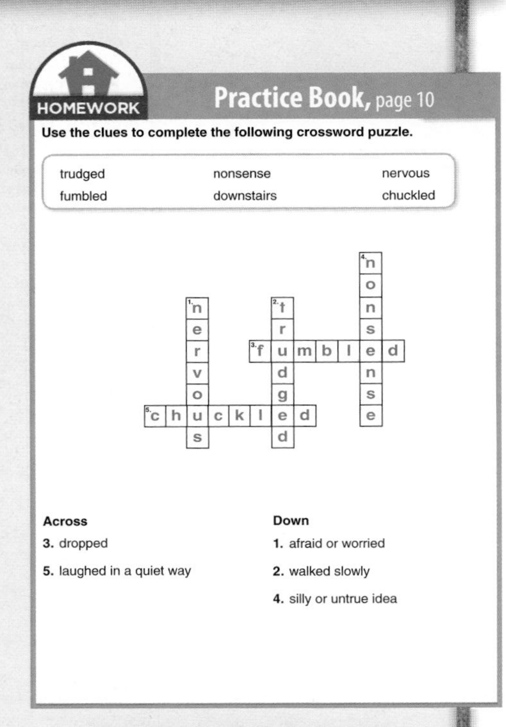
Use the clues to complete the following crossword puzzle.

trudged, nonsense, nervous, fumbled, downstairs, chuckled

Across
3. dropped
5. laughed in a quiet way

Down
1. afraid or worried
2. walked slowly
4. silly or untrue idea

**Approaching Reproducible,** page 10
**Beyond Reproducible,** page 10

### Objectives

- Analyze story structure
- Understand character, setting, and plot
- Use academic language: *story structure, character, setting, plot*

#### Materials

- Transparencies 1a, 1b, 11
- Practice Book, p. 11

### Skills Trace

| Character, Setting, Plot | |
|---|---|
| Introduce | U1: 9A–B |
| Practice/ Apply | U1: 10–29; Practice Book, 11–12 |
| Reteach/ Review | U1: 330–33JJ; U2: 313A–B, 314–339, 345M–HH; Practice Book 145–146 |
| Assess | Weekly Tests; Unit 1, 3, 6 Tests |
| Maintain | U1: 59B; U4: 33B; U6: 387A–B |

### English Learners

UNIVERSAL ACCESS

**Academic Language** Preteach the following academic language words to **English Learners** and **Approaching Level** students during Small Group time: *character, setting, plot, dialogue.* See page 33K.

# Reread for Comprehension

## STRATEGY
### ANALYZE STORY STRUCTURE

**What Is It?** Explain that the main parts of a story are the characters, setting, and a plot. This is called **story structure**.
**Why Is It Important?** Point out that by identifying the parts of a story and seeing how they fit together, a reader can understand what happens and why it happens.

## SKILL
### CHARACTER, SETTING, PLOT

**CA CONTENT STANDARD R 3.3.3** Determine what characters are like by what they say or do and by how the author or illustrator portrays them.

#### EXPLAIN

**What Is It?** The **setting** is when and where the story takes place. The **characters** are the people in the story. Their actions move along with the plot. A **plot** is made up of events in a story and has a beginning, middle, and end.
**Why Is It Important?** Authors develop the plots in made-up stories through the characters, settings, and events. To understand a story, readers must be able to identify these story elements.

Transparency 1a

**Vocabulary**
nervous, nonsense, fumbled, trudged, chuckled

**Word Parts**
Prefixes are word parts added to the beginning of words. The prefixes *non-* and *un-* usually mean "not."
*nonsense* = the opposite of sense

**TINA'S TRYOUT DAY**
*by Amy Helfer*

Tina woke up to her buzzing alarm clock. She rubbed her eyes and wondered why she was up so early. Then she remembered: it was tryout day!

**THE BIG DAY**

A few weeks ago, Tina decided she would try out for the Comets, her school's softball team. Tina ran downstairs to the kitchen. "Mom!" she shouted. "It's tryout day!"

"I know," answered Mom. "I made you breakfast."

"I'm too **nervous** to eat."

"You'll have more energy if you do," said Mom.

Tina still felt a bit sick, but she ate some breakfast anyway. Then she ran up to her room and **fumbled** into her clothes.

"Slow down!" Mom **chuckled**. "You'll use up all your energy before you get there."

**ON THE FIELD**

Tina got to the field and saw many girls already there. She suddenly felt unhappy.

8

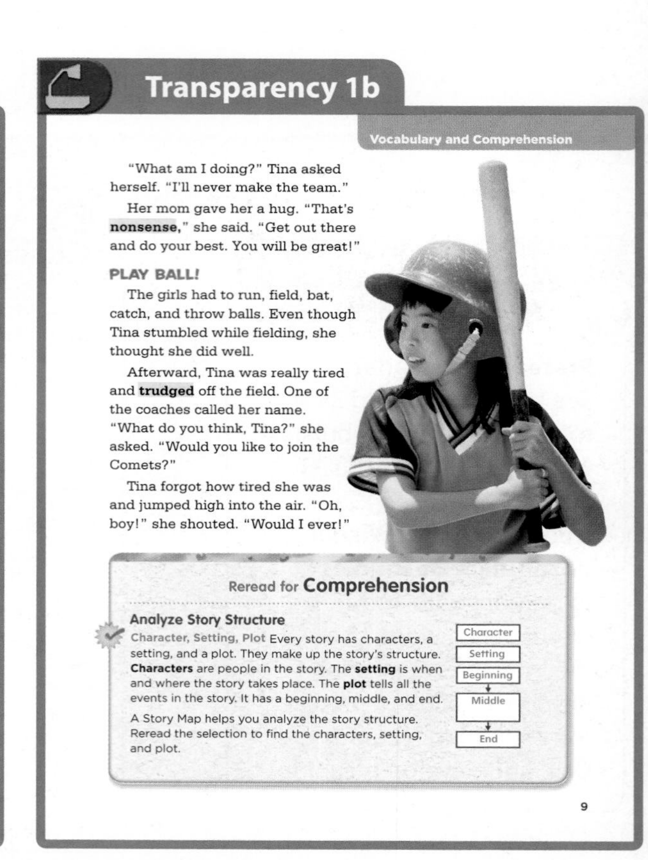

Transparency 1b

Vocabulary and Comprehension

"What am I doing?" Tina asked herself. "I'll never make the team."

Her mom gave her a hug. "That's **nonsense**," she said. "Get out there and do your best. You will be great!"

**PLAY BALL!**

The girls had to run, field, bat, catch, and throw balls. Even though Tina stumbled while fielding, she thought she did well.

Afterward, Tina was really tired and **trudged** off the field. One of the coaches called her name. "What do you think, Tina?" she asked. "Would you like to join the Comets?"

Tina forgot how tired she was and jumped high into the air. "Oh, boy!" she shouted. "Would I ever!"

Reread for **Comprehension**

**Analyze Story Structure**
Character, Setting, Plot Every story has characters, a setting, and a plot. They make up the story's structure. **Characters** are people in the story. The **setting** is when and where the story takes place. The **plot** tells all the events in the story. It has a beginning, middle, and end.
A Story Map helps you analyze the story structure. Reread the selection to find the characters, setting, and plot.

Character
Setting
Beginning
Middle
End

9

Student Book pages 8–9 available on Comprehension Transparencies 1a and 1b

- Readers can learn about characters by paying attention to what they say or do. Understanding a character's personality can help readers understand what happens in the story. Illustrations also give the reader information about the character.

### MODEL

**How Do I Use It?** Read aloud the first few paragraphs of "Tina's Tryout Day" from **Student Book** page 8. Use **Transparency 11** to record the characters, settings, and plot.

**Think Aloud** I see that Tina is the main character of the story. In the beginning of the story, she seems to be at home. This is the setting. As I read I'll look for the events in the beginning, the middle, and the end of the story. In the beginning, Tina wakes up and feels nervous because she is going to try out for the school's softball team. Tina tells her mother that she is nervous, but I can also tell by her actions, because she rubs her stomach and feels sick. I'll keep reading to find out what happens next in the plot.

### GUIDED PRACTICE

Continue by helping students identify what happens after Tina runs downstairs in the section of the story titled "The Big Day." (See the second sentence in the Beginning box on the story map.)

### APPLY

Have students reread the remainder of "Tina's Tryout Day" and complete the Story Map. Have them add information to the Character and Setting boxes as necessary. Help them see that in the middle of the story the setting has changed. Tina is now on the ball field, and she is trying out for a place on the team.

Continue filling in the Story Map with students. Help them complete the End box on the Story Map. Help them understand that at the story's end, Tina is asked to join the team. Ask students to retell the story to a partner using their completed Story Maps.

### Quick Check

**Can students identify the characters, settings, and plot in a story?**

During **Small Group Instruction**

**If No →** Approaching Level Reteach the skill using the Comprehension lesson, pp. 33O–33R.

**If Yes →** On Level Consolidate the learning using pp. 33W–33X.

Beyond Level Extend the learning using pp. 33AA–33BB.

### Transparency 11

**Story Map**

**Characters**
Tina and her mother; the coach

**Setting**
Tina's home; the softball field

**Beginning**
Tina is nervous.
She talks to her mom at home about softball tryouts.

↓

**Middle**
Tina is on the field at school.
She is nervous, but she is trying hard.

↓

**End**
Tina thought she played well.
She gets chosen for the team.

**Graphic Organizer Transparency**

HOMEWORK **Practice Book,** page 11

The **plot** includes the important events that happen in the beginning, middle, and end of a story. The **characters** are the people or animals in the story. The **setting** is when and where the story happens.

**Read the story, then answer the questions below.**

At 9:00 A.M. on his first day of work at the supermarket, Josh was given shopping cart duty. It was cold out, and Josh did not want this task, but he was a good worker.

Josh started his search for carts by walking up and down the supermarket parking lot. He started a train of shopping carts and after an hour Josh had twenty-five carts. He pushed them all into the front of the store.

Josh was about to go out for more carts when his boss called out to him, "Hold on there, Josh. You're such a good worker that we are making you a cashier. Come on in and start your training."

1. When does this story take place?
on Josh's first day of work, on a cold day
2. Where does this story take place?
at the supermarket where Josh works
3. Who is the main character in this story? How can you tell?
Josh. The story tells about what happens to him.
4. What is the first important event in this story?
Josh gets shopping cart duty.
5. What is the last important event in this story?
Josh moves up to cashier.

Approaching Reproducible, page 11
Beyond Reproducible, page 11

# Read

## WHOLE GROUP

**MAIN SELECTION**

- *First Day Jitters*
- Skill: Character, Setting, Plot

**PAIRED SELECTION**

- "How to Be a Good Citizen"
- Text Feature: Bar Graph

**CA STANDARDS**

R 3.1.6, R 3.2.1, R 3.2.2, R 3.2.3, R 3.2.4 R 3.3.1, R 3.3.3, R 3.3.5 , HSS 3.4.1, HSS3.4.2

## SMALL GROUP

- Differentiated Instruction, pp. 33K–33JJ

# Main Selection

**GENRE: REALISTIC FICTION**

CA CONTENT STANDARD R 3.3.1 Distinguish common forms of literature.

Have a student read the definition of Realistic Fiction on **Student Book** page 10. Some realistic fiction stories may be humorous. Students should look for clever language, unexpected events, and humorous illustrations.

**STRATEGY**
**ANALYZE STORY STRUCTURE**

Remind students that when they **analyze story structure**, they will identify the setting and characters. They will also identify plot events in the beginning, middle, and end of the story.

**SKILL**
**CHARACTER, SETTING, PLOT**

CA CONTENT STANDARD R 3.3.3 Determine what characters are like by what they say or do and by how the author or illustrator portrays them.

**Characters** are the people in the story. **Setting** is where the story takes place. The **plot** is made up of the events and characters' actions in the story.

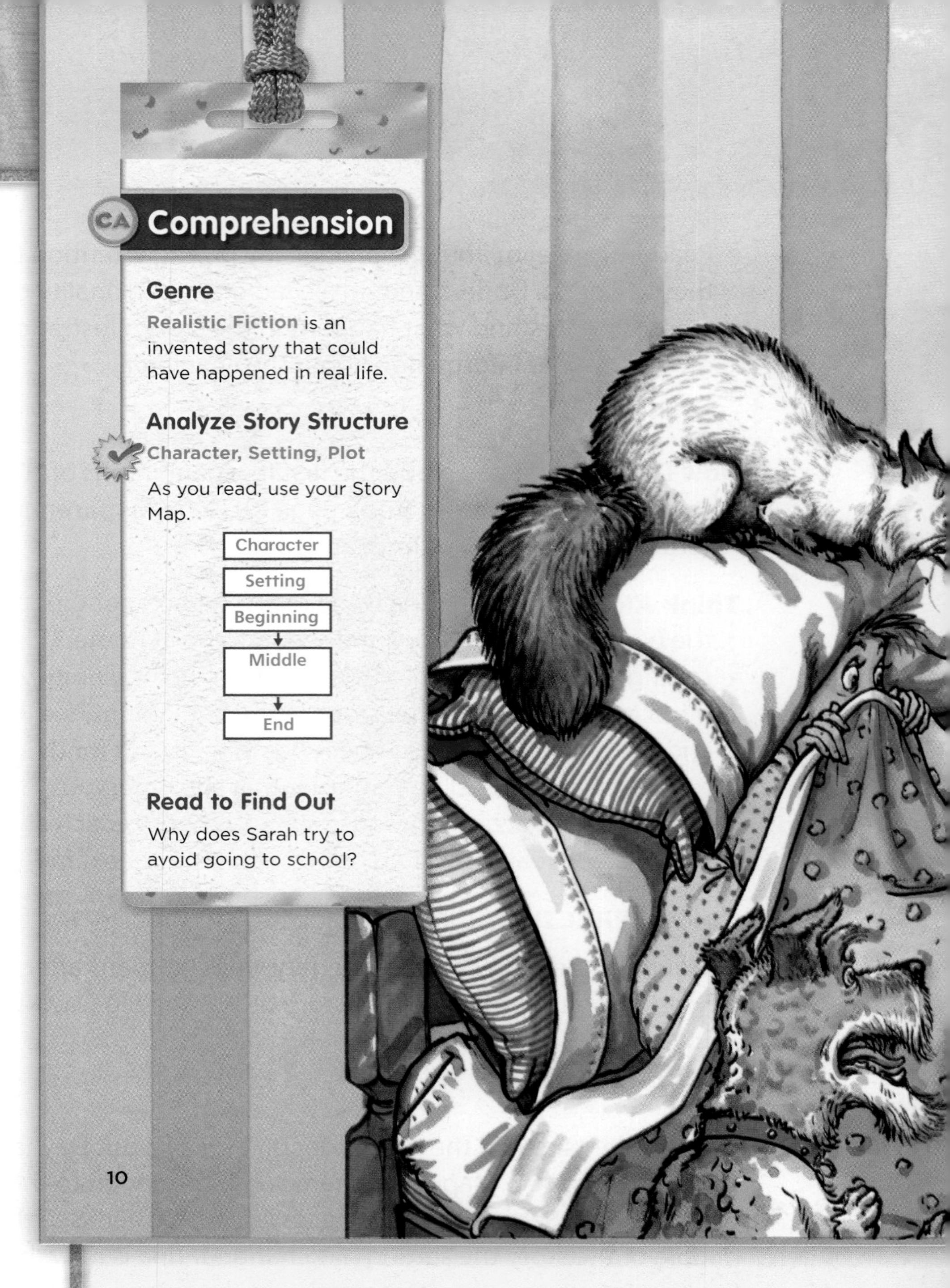

## Comprehension

**Genre**

**Realistic Fiction** is an invented story that could have happened in real life.

**Analyze Story Structure**

**Character, Setting, Plot**

As you read, use your Story Map.



**Read to Find Out**

Why does Sarah try to avoid going to school?

10

## Vocabulary

**Vocabulary Words** Review the tested words while reading: **nervous, fumbled, chuckled, nonsense,** and **trudged**.

**Additional Selection Words** Students may be unfamiliar with these words. Pronounce the words and give student-friendly explanations as needed.

**tunneled** (p. 14): dug farther, as if to make a deep hole

**clammy** (p. 23): cool, damp, and sticky

**weakly** (p. 23): without strength

**slumped** (p. 23): fell against something because of a weak feeling

**gushed** (p. 24): talked with so much feeling that it seemed silly

## Preview and Predict

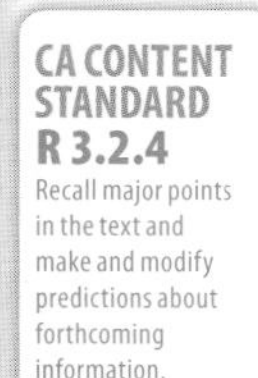


**QUICK WRITE** Ask students to read the title, preview the illustrations, think about the genre, and write their predictions about the plot and how the story will be organized.

## Set Purpose

**FOCUS QUESTION** Discuss the "Read to Find Out" question on **Student Book** page 10. Remind students to look for the answer as they read.

Point out the Story Map in the Student Book and on **Practice Book** page 12. Explain that students will fill it in as they read.

## Read *First Day Jitters*

Use the questions and Think Alouds to support instruction about the comprehension strategy and skill.

### PARTNERS — Read Together

If your students need support to read the Main Selection, use the prompts to guide comprehension and model how to complete the graphic organizer. Allow students time to fill in their organizers before you provide the answers.

Use **Think/Pair/Share**. When asking a question, have students *think* about their answer, then discuss it with a *partner*. Finally, have selected students *share* their answers with the group. Provide sentence frames for discussion, such as *The first characters I learn about in the story are* ______ *and* ______, to help students use academic language. Students should support their answers with evidence from the text.

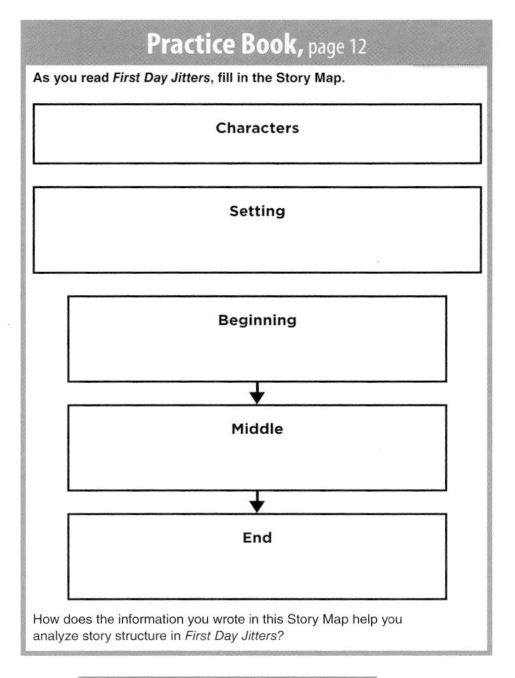

**Practice Book,** page 12

As you read *First Day Jitters*, fill in the Story Map.

Characters

Setting

Beginning

Middle

End

How does the information you wrote in this Story Map help you analyze story structure in *First Day Jitters?*

**Approaching Reproducible,** page 12

**Beyond Reproducible,** page 12

# Develop Comprehension

## 1 STRATEGY
### ANALYZE STORY STRUCTURE

**Teacher Think Aloud** I know that the story I'm about to read is fiction, or a made-up story about characters. I know that as I read a made-up story, I can look for the way the story is organized. This is called the **story structure.** I will look for who the characters are and will pay attention to what they are like, what they do or say, and how the illustrator draws them. I will look for the setting, or where and when the story takes place. I will also keep track of the characters' actions and the events in the story. They make up the story's plot. By understanding a story's structure, I can understand what is happening in it and why.

## Monitor Comprehension

### Monitor and Clarify: *Read Ahead*

**Explain** Sometimes it is hard to figure out what is happening in a story. When students do not understand a character's actions, or what is happening, they can use the read-ahead strategy to get more information and clear up their confusion.

**Model** It is not clear on page 13 why Sarah doesn't want to get out of bed. By reading ahead, it becomes clear from the dialogue that Sarah doesn't want to get up because she doesn't want to start over at a new school.

**Apply** Have students use the read-ahead strategy to help them understand confusing parts of the story. After they have finished the story, have them tell how reading ahead helped them understand these confusing parts.

"Sarah, dear, time to get out of bed," Mr. Hartwell said, poking his head through the bedroom doorway. "You don't want to miss the first day at your new school do you?"

"I'm not going," said Sarah, and pulled the covers over her head.

2

13

# Develop Comprehension

**2 SKILL**
**CHARACTER, SETTING**

Which **characters** appear at the beginning of the story? (Sarah and Mr. Hartwell) What is the **setting**? When and where does the story take place? (The story begins in Sarah's bedroom on the morning of the first day of school.) Fill in the Characters and Setting boxes in the Story Map with this information.

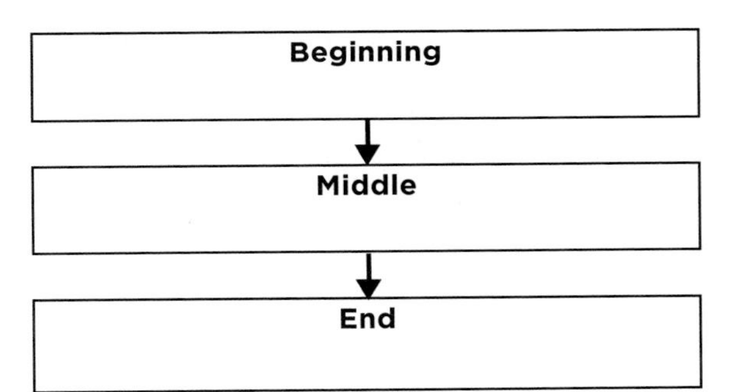


**Beginning**

**Middle**

**End**

## English Learners

**UNIVERSAL ACCESS**

Prepare students to read the story *prior* to the whole class reading. Use the Interactive Question-Response Guide on page 33EE to preteach the story content, build language, and develop meaning. This will enable students to participate successfully in the whole class reading and discussion.

**Beginning/Early Intermediate** Emphasize those questions and responses marked Beginning/Early Intermediate. In addition, focus on Key Words, Basic Words, and Function Words/Phrases.

**Intermediate** Use all the questions and prompts in the Interactive Question-Response Guide.

**Early Advanced** Extend language by using more complex sentence frames in the Interactive Question-Response Guide.

## Phonics/Word Study

**APPLY DECODING SKILLS** While reading, point out words with the sound/spelling patterns, syllable types, and word parts students have learned. Help students blend these words. You may wish to focus on selection words with short vowel spellings, such as *bed, miss, just, wish, sick, rushed,* and *class.*

# Develop Comprehension

### 3 GENRE: REALISTIC FICTION

Now that you know the elements of **realistic fiction**, what do you expect to find in the rest of the story? (I think that Sarah and Mr. Hartwell will continue to argue, but that Sarah will eventually go to school. I also think that the events in the story will continue to be funny. These are things that could happen in real life.)

"Of course you're going, honey," said Mr. Hartwell, as he walked over to the window and snapped up the shade.

"No, I'm not. I don't want to start over again. I hate my new school," Sarah said.

3 She tunneled down to the end of her bed.
4

**Character, Setting, Plot**
What plot events have taken place so far?

## Comprehension

CA CONTENT STANDARD R 3.3.5
Recognize the similarities of sounds in words and rhythmic patterns in a selection.

### Literary Devices: Onomatopoeia

**Explain** Onomatopoeia is when words sound like the sound they name. In the phrase *the buzz of a bee,* the word *buzz* is an example of onomatopoeia. It sounds like the noise a bee makes. Authors use onomatopoeia to help readers "hear" what happens in a story.

**Discuss** Read the first sentence on page 14. Help students see that *snapped* has a sharp sound like a window shade quickly rolling up. This word helps readers understand that Mr. Hartwell opened the shade loudly to get Sarah out of bed.

**Apply** Have students read the first sentence in the third paragraph on page 18. Ask: *What word is an example of onomatopoeia in this sentence?* (*sighed*) *How does it help you understand how Mr. Hartwell is feeling?* (A sigh shows that someone is tired of something.)

15



# Develop Comprehension

4 SKILL
PLOT

What do we know about the **plot** so far? What events have taken place? Let's add this information to the Beginning box on our Story Map. (Sarah does not want to get out of bed on the first day of school. She wants to hide under the covers. She says she hates her new school. Mr. Hartwell tells her that she is going to school.)

| Characters |
| --- |
| Sarah and Mr. Hartwell |

| Setting |
| --- |
| home on the morning of the first day of school |

| Beginning |
| --- |
| Sarah won't get out of bed. She wants to hide under the covers. |

| Middle |
| --- |
| |

| End |
| --- |
| |

# Develop Comprehension

**5 SKILL**
**CHARACTER**

What kind of person is Mr. Hartwell? What has the author done to help you learn about this **character**? (Mr. Hartwell is the kind of person who knows that rules must be followed. He uses kindness in dealing with others. He talks calmly to Sarah about going to school and he calls her "sweetheart.")

**6 MONITOR AND CLARIFY: READ AHEAD**

Where is Sarah on pages 16 and 17? How can **reading ahead** help you to find out? (Sarah is still at home in bed. I can find out where she is by reading ahead. On page 18 the illustration shows Sarah still in bed with the pillow over her head. She is still talking about staying in bed and not going to school. The strategy helped me figure out what was happening in this part of the story.)

"How can you hate your new school, sweetheart?" Mr. Hartwell **chuckled**. "You've never been there before! Don't worry. You liked your other school, you'll like this one. Besides, just think of all the new friends you'll meet."

5
6

16

"That's just it. I don't know anybody, and it will be hard, and ... I just hate it, that's all." **7** 

17



# Develop Comprehension

**7** **SKILL**
**PLOT**

What does the illustration on pages 16 and 17 show you about how Sara feels about her new school? How does it help you understand the story's **plot** so far? (The illustrations show what Sara imagines about her new class on the first day of school. On page 16, she imagines the students looking friendly and polite, but on page 17 she imagines the students teasing one another and misbehaving in other ways. The illustration shows that Sara is not sure what to expect at school. It helps the reader understand why she doesn't want to get out of bed and go to school.)

**8** **SKILL**
**CHARACTER**

Think about Sarah's **character**. What do her actions so far tell you about her? (Sarah gets nervous and is scared to try new things. She tries to hide from new situations that she thinks will make her uncomfortable.)

**English Learners**
UNIVERSAL ACCESS

**STRATEGIES FOR EXTRA SUPPORT**

**Question 8 CHARACTER**
Help students understand that the characters are the people in the story. Ask: *Who have you met in the story so far? Let's look at the pictures to help us. What do you know about these people? What have they done so far? What do you think they will do next?*

# Develop Comprehension

**9 GENRE: REALISTIC FICTION**

Mr. Hartwell asks Sarah what everyone will think if she doesn't show up at school. Why is her answer funny? Is it something a real person would say? Use what you know about **realistic fiction** to help you answer the question. (Sarah says everyone will think she is lucky and will wish they were home, too. Her answer is funny because it's a surprise. A reader expects her to say that she doesn't care what people will think. Real people might say this because they could feel the same way that Sarah does about going to school.)

9 "What will everyone think if you aren't there? We told them you were coming!"

"They will think that I am lucky and they will wish that they were at home in bed like me."

Mr. Hartwell sighed. "Sarah Jane Hartwell, I'm not playing this silly game one second longer. I'll see you 10 downstairs in five minutes."

18

## Vocabulary

CA CONTENT STANDARD R 3.1.6 Use sentence and word context to find the meaning of unknown words.

### Context Clues

**Explain/Model** Good readers look at how a word is used in a sentence. Context clues can help them understand a difficult word. Read the word *sighed* in the third paragraph on page 18 in context.

**Think Aloud** I see the word *sighed*. I think that this word is probably a verb because it has an *-ed* ending. In this part of the story, Mr. Hartwell and Sarah are arguing about Sarah going to school. I read that Mr. Hartwell is irritated with Sarah. Using context clues, I think the word *sighed* tells how Mr. Hartwell said the words.

**Apply** Tell students to use context clues to help them figure out other difficult words, such as *moaned* on page 21.

# Develop Comprehension

**10 SKILL**
**CHARACTER**

Mr. Hartwell says, "I'm not playing this silly game one second longer." What does this dialogue and the illustration tell you about his **character**? (Mr. Hartwell wants Sarah to stop wasting time and get ready for school. He has lost his patience with her and is getting frustrated.)

# Develop Comprehension

11 **SKILL**
**CHARACTER**

How does Sarah get out of bed? What do her actions when she gets out of bed tell you about her **character**? (She gets out of bed in a very clumsy way. It shows that she still does not want to get up and go to school.)

12 **SKILL**
**PLOT**

Think about the story's **plot**? What does Sarah do from the time she gets out of bed until she goes downstairs? What is the last thing she does on page 21? Fill in the Middle box on the Story Map. (Sarah gets out of bed and gets dressed for school. She goes downstairs and takes her lunchbox.)

| Characters |
| --- |
| Sarah and Mr. Hartwell |

| Setting |
| --- |
| home on the morning of the first day of school |

| Beginning |
| --- |
| Sarah won't get out of bed. She wants to hide under the covers. |

↓

| Middle |
| --- |
| Sarah gets out of bed, gets dressed for school, and takes her lunchbox. |

↓

| End |
| --- |
| |

Sarah
tumbled
out of bed.
She stumbled into the bathroom.
11 She **fumbled** into her clothes.

20

"My head hurts," she moaned as she **trudged** into the kitchen.

Mr. Hartwell handed Sarah a piece of toast and her lunchbox.

12
13

21

# Develop Comprehension

**13 SELF-SELECTED STRATEGY USE**

What strategies have you used so far to help you understand the selection? Where did you use them? Why? How did they help?

**RETURN TO PREDICTIONS AND PURPOSES**

Have students respond to the selection by confirming or revising their predictions and purposes for reading. Encourage them to revise or write additional questions to help focus their attention as they continue to read the selection.

## Extra Support

### Plot

If students have trouble answering question 12, ask them: *Where was Sarah at the beginning of the story?* (in her bedroom in bed) *What did she do? Why?* (She pulled the covers over her head. She did this because she wanted to stay home and not go to school.) *What did Mr. Hartwell do?* (He tried to persuade her to go to school.) *Why does she finally get up?* (Mr. Hartwell told her to get dressed and go downstairs.) *What does she do after she gets up?* (She gets dressed, goes downstairs, and takes her lunchbox.)

If students still have trouble, go back to pages 18–21 and have them use the illustrations and text to help them understand the events in the plot.

Stop here if you wish to read this selection over two days.

# Develop Comprehension

**14 SUMMARIZE**

What has happened so far in the story? Let's **summarize** to check our understanding. (Sarah wakes up on the first day of school, does not want to go, and says she is sick. Mr. Hartwell tells her to get up and get ready for school. Sarah says she hates her new school because she does not want to start over. Finally, she gets out of bed and gets dressed and takes her lunch box.)

**15 SKILL**
**CHARACTER**

Think about what you know about Sarah. How does the illustration on pages 22–23 help readers understand how this **character** feels? (The building looks very big and scary so it shows that Sarah is nervous. She does not want to go to school.)

**16 STRATEGY**
**WORD PARTS: PREFIXES**

What **prefix** and root word, or base word, do you see in the word *nonsense*? How can you use the prefix to help you figure out the meaning of *nonsense*? (The prefix is *non-* and the base word, or root word, is *sense*. *Non-* means "not," so *nonsense* means "something that does not make sense.")

They walked to the car. Sarah's hands were cold and clammy.

They drove down the street.

She couldn't breathe.

And then they were there.

"I feel sick," said Sarah weakly.

"**Nonsense**," said Mr. Hartwell. "You'll love your new school once you get started. Oh, look. There's your principal, Mrs. Burton." 16 17 18

Sarah slumped down in her seat.

**Character, Setting, Plot**
How does Mr. Hartwell feel about Sarah's attitude?

23



# Develop Comprehension

**17 STRATEGY**
**ANALYZE STORY STRUCTURE**

**Teacher Think Aloud** Paying attention to a **story's structure**—what a character does at the beginning, the middle, and the end—can help me understand it. At the beginning of the story, Sarah didn't want to go to school. Now that we are in the middle of the story, explain how Sarah's actions have changed.

*(Have students apply the strategy in a Think Aloud.)*

**Student Think Aloud** Sarah got out of bed and got dressed. Now she is driving to school with Mr. Hartwell. I can see she has changed since the beginning of the story, even though she still says she feels sick. The setting has changed from home to school. I'm not sure what will happen at the end, but I think everything will turn out okay.

**18 SKILL**
**CHARACTER**

How does Mr. Hartwell feel about Sarah's actions on the way to school? What does he think of her attitude? What does this show about Mr. Hartwell's **character**? (Mr. Hartwell thinks Sarah is being silly. He doesn't believe that she is sick and he is losing patience with her. He thinks that she will like school once she gets started.)

**English Learners**
**UNIVERSAL ACCESS**

**STRATEGIES FOR EXTRA SUPPORT**

**Question 18 CHARACTER**
Help students understand that *attitude* means how you feel about something. Discuss students' attitudes toward school. Ask: *How does Sarah feel about going to school? What is her attitude toward school? What does Mr. Hartwell think about what Sarah is doing? How do we know? What does he say?*

# Develop Comprehension

19 **SKILL**
**SETTING**

How has the **setting** changed since the beginning of the story? Why is it important? (It's later in the morning and school has started. The place has changed from Sarah's house to Sarah's new school.)

"Oh, Sarah," Mrs. Burton gushed, peeking into the car. "There you are. Come on. I'll show you where to go."

19

24

She led Sarah into the building and walked quickly through the crowded hallways. "Don't worry. Everyone is **nervous** the first day," she said over her shoulder as Sarah rushed to keep up. 20 21





# Develop Comprehension

## 20 SKILL
### CHARACTER

What kind of person is Mrs. Burton? How can you tell? What clues does the author give about this **character**? (She is kind, helpful, and understanding. She takes Sarah into the school and shows her where to go. She sees that Sarah is nervous, and she tries to make her feel better.)

## 21 STRATEGY
### ANALYZE STORY STRUCTURE

This is almost the end of the story. Think about the **setting** now. Think about the **events** in the beginning and middle of the story. Think about what kind of **character** Sarah is. Use this information to **analyze the story structure** and tell what you think will happen to Sarah.

**Student Think Aloud** Now Sarah is at school. At the beginning of the story, Sarah didn't want to go to school and she hid in bed. In the middle of the story, she got dressed and rode to school with Mr. Hartwell. Now she is on her way to her class with Mrs. Burton. Even though Sarah is nervous, I think that in the end she will like her new school and her new class.

# Develop Comprehension

**22 SKILL**
**PLOT**

What happens at the end of the story? What makes this event in the **plot** such a surprise? Let's add this to the End box to complete the Story Map. (Sarah is a teacher who meets her new class. It is surprising because I thought that Sarah was a new student, not a teacher. It is also surprising that a teacher would be so nervous on the first day of school.)

| Characters |
|---|
| Sarah and Mr. Hartwell |

| Setting |
|---|
| home on the morning of the first day of school |

| Beginning |
|---|
| Sarah won't get out of bed. She wants to hide under the covers. |

↓

| Middle |
|---|
| Sarah gets dressed for school and takes her lunchbox. |

↓

| End |
|---|
| Sarah is a teacher who meets her new class. |

When they got to the classroom, most of the children were already in their seats.

The class looked up as Mrs. Burton cleared her throat.

"Class. Class. Attention, please," said Mrs. Burton.

When the class was quiet she led Sarah to the front of the room and said, "Class, I would like you to meet ...

26

... your new teacher, Mrs. Sarah Jane Hartwell."

22

27

## Quick Check

**Can students identify the characters, setting, and plot?**

During **Small Group Instruction**

**If No →** Approaching Level Reteach the skill and have students apply it to a simpler text. Use Practice Reader lesson, pp. 33P–33R.

**If Yes →** On Level Have students apply the skill to a new text to consolidate learning. Use Practice Reader lesson pp. 33W–33X.

Beyond Level Have students apply the skill to a more complex text to extend learning. Use Practice Reader lesson, pp. 33AA–33BB.



# Develop Comprehension

CA CONTENT STANDARD R 3.2.4 Recall major points in the text and make and modify predictions about forthcoming information.

### RETURN TO PREDICTIONS AND PURPOSES

Review students' **predictions** and **purposes** for reading. Did students figure out why Sarah didn't want to go to school? (She was nervous.)

### REVIEW READING STRATEGIES

- **Analyze Story Structure** How did identifying the characters and settings, and keeping track of the story events help you understand and enjoy the story?
- **Monitor and Clarify: Read Ahead** Do you understand the strategy of reading ahead to get more information and figure out confusing parts of a story? When might you use it again?
- **Decoding** What difficult words did you encounter? How did the Reading Multisyllabic Words strategy help you sound out these words?
- **Self-Selected Strategy Use** What strategies did you use to make sense of what you read? Where? How were these strategies helpful?

### RESPONSE TO LITERATURE

Provide the following prompt: *Write about why it's important to be ready for your first day of school. Use details from the story to support your answer.*
As students write, remind them to:

- Show their understanding of the story.
- Give examples of the story.
- Use correct grammar, spelling, punctuation, and capitalization.

## Author and Illustrator

**OFF TO SCHOOL WITH JULIE AND JUDY**

Have students read the biographies of the author and illustrator. Ask:

- How do you think Julie Danneberg feels about being a teacher like Sarah? How do you think she feels about the first day of school?
- Why do Judy Love's illustrations help to make the ending a surprise?

**WRITE ABOUT IT**

**Author's Craft: Humor**

Discuss with students what feelings they experienced while reading *First Day Jitters*. Ask them to write how they feel about the events that took place in the story. What parts of the story did they find humorous? Why were these parts funny? Have students include whether or not they liked the story and why.

### Author's Purpose

Guide students to use the genre (realistic fiction) and content to figure out the author's purpose. Help them see that the author wrote a funny story about realistic events. It does not give information about a topic. Help them conclude that the purpose of this story is to entertain.

## OFF TO SCHOOL WITH JULIE AND JUDY

**AUTHOR**

**JULIE DANNEBERG** knows all about teaching. She has been a teacher for many years and really enjoys it. Julie says that being around kids all day gives her lots of ideas for stories. She starts every day by working on her writing for an hour.

**Another book** by Julie Danneberg: *First Year Letters*

**ILLUSTRATOR**

**JUDY LOVE** decided that she wanted to illustrate books when she was seven or eight years old. Judy gets ideas for her illustrations from her favorite hobbies: gardening, visiting museums, and making costumes for children's plays.

Find out more about Julie Danneberg and Judy Love at **www.macmillanmh.com**.

**Author's Purpose**

Did Julie Danneberg write to inform or entertain readers in *First Day Jitters*? What details help you figure out the author's purpose?

28

### Author's Craft

**Humor**

Julie Danneberg uses humor to make *First Day Jitters* fun to read.

- **Humor** is what makes a story funny. Humorous characters often act in surprising ways or say funny things. For example: *When the class was quiet she led Sarah to the front of the room and said, "Class, I would like you to meet . . . your new teacher, Mrs. Sarah Jane Hartwell."* (pp. 26–27)
- Discuss why the ending is funny. Help students see that the surprise at the end of the story makes readers laugh. Mrs. Burton's introduction is humorous.

To help students see the humor in the ending, ask them how they pictured Sarah. Then discuss why other parts of the story are funny.

## Critical Thinking

### Retell the Story

Use your Story Map to help you retell *First Day Jitters.* Tell about what happened in the beginning, middle, and end of the story.

Character
Setting
Beginning
Middle
End

### Think and Compare

1. Why was Sarah so **nervous** about going to school? Use details from the story's **plot** to support your answer. **Analyze Story Structure: Character, Setting, Plot**
2. At first, why might most readers think Sarah is a student? Use story details to support your answer. **Analyze**
3. How would you feel if you were a teacher on the first day at a new school? Explain. **Apply**
4. Why are many people nervous when they are in new situations? **Evaluate**
5. Read "Tina's Tryout Day" on pages 8–9. How is Tina's situation similar to Sarah's? How are Tina's and Sarah's reactions different? Use details from both selections in your answer. **Reading/Writing Across Texts**

29

## Answering Questions

CA CONTENT STANDARD R 3.2.3 Demonstrate comprehension by identifying answers in the text.

### Think and Search

Model the Think and Search strategy with question 2. Students will need to find information in several places in the story to answer the question.

**Question 2 Think Aloud** To answer this question, I will look in several places in the story. In the beginning Sara acts like a child when she won't get out of bed. She says she hates like, which sounds like a child, not an adult. She keeps saying she feels sick as Mr. Hartwell drives her to school. All her words and actions until the end of the story. By using the Think and Search strategy—looking for answers in several places—I was able to find details about Sara that helped me answer the question.

## Critical Thinking

### SUMMARIZE

Have partners summarize *First Day Jitters* in their own words. Remind students to use their Story Maps to help them organize their summaries about characters, setting, and plot.

### THINK AND COMPARE

Sample answers are given.

1. **Character, Setting, Plot** Sarah was nervous and worried because it was her first day at a new school and she was afraid she might not like it.
2. **Analyze** Answers should include details about Sarah's childish words and actions throughout the story until she walks into the classroom.
3. **Text-to-Self** I would be nervous because it is not easy meeting a lot of new people at one time and showing them what to do. USE ON MY OWN
4. **Text-to-World** Many people feel nervous in new situations because it takes time to become comfortable around new people and new surroundings.

### FOCUS QUESTION

5. **Text-to-Text** Both Sarah and Tina are nervous about a new situation. They are different because Tina is excited even though she is nervous. She wants to try out for the team. Sarah is nervous and afraid and doesn't want to go to school.

# Fluency

## Repeated Reading: Phrasing

CA CONTENT STANDARD
**R 3.1.3** Read aloud narrative and expository text fluently and accurately and with appropriate pacing, intonation, and expression.

**EXPLAIN/MODEL** Tell students they will be doing a choral reading. Model reading **Transparency 1**, pausing at commas and the ellipsis (three dots) and stopping at periods. Explain that on the transparency one slash shows a pause and two slashes show a full stop.

**Transparency 1**

When they got to the classroom,/ most of the children were already in their seats.//

The class looked up as Mrs. Burton cleared her throat.//

"Class.// Class.// Attention,/ please,"/ said Mrs. Burton.//

When the class was quiet she led Sarah to the front of the room and said,/ "Class,/ I would like you to meet . . . / your new teacher,/ Mrs. Sarah Jane Hartwell."//

from *First Day Jitters*, pages 26–27

**PRACTICE** Reread the first two sentences. Have students chorally repeat. Divide them into two groups. Have groups alternate reading sentences. Remind students to pay attention to the pauses and stops shown by the slash marks. Provide corrective feedback as needed.

**DAILY FLUENCY** Students will practice fluency using **Practice Book** page 13 or the **Fluency Solutions Audio CD**. The passage is recorded at a slow practice speed and a faster fluent speed.

### Quick Check

**Can students read fluently?**

During **Small Group Instruction**

**If No** → **Approaching Level** Use the Fluency lesson and model, p. 33S.

**If Yes** → **On Level** See Fluency p. 33V.

**Beyond Level** See Fluency p. 33Z.

### Objectives

- Read accurately with proper phrasing
- 61–81 WCPM

### Materials

- Transparency 1
- Practice Book, p. 13
- Fluency Solutions Audio CD

### English Learners

UNIVERSAL ACCESS

**Echo-Read for Fluency**
First, discuss the meaning of the passage to ensure that students understand it. Explain this is the part where the principal of the school introduces Sarah to the class and readers find out she's the new teacher. Have students echo-read after you. Students can also read along with the recording on **Fluency Solutions Audio CD**.

AUDIO CD

**Practice Book,** page 13

**As I read, I will pay attention to phrasing.**

One Monday in November, Jay and his mother drove
9 to a yellow brick building with a sign in front that said:
21 "Rosewood Middle School." It was a big building—much
30 taller than Jay's old school.
35 Jay's mother filled out lots of forms. Before they left,
45 the school principal, Ms. Tucker, came out of her office
55 and shook Jay's hand. "Welcome to Rosewood," she said.
64 "We'll see you tomorrow."
68 On Tuesday morning, Jay's older sister, Eva, gave him
77 a ride to school. "Are you nervous?" she asked.
86 Jay shrugged and then nodded. "I hate being the new kid,"
97 he admitted. 99

**Comprehension Check**

1. Who is the main character and what is the story about? **Plot Development** Jay; going to a new school for the first time
2. Why is Jay nervous? **Plot Development** Jay is nervous because he does not like being the new kid at school.

| | Words Read | – | Number of Errors | = | Words Correct Score |
|---|---|---|---|---|---|
| First Read | | – | | = | |
| Second Read | | – | | = | |

**Approaching Reproducible,** page 13

**Beyond Reproducible,** page 13

# Comprehension

**REVIEW SKILL**
**SELF-SELECTED STRATEGY USE**

### EXPLAIN/MODEL

- Tell students that good readers **select** and use many **strategies** as they read. These strategies are conscious techniques readers use to understand a text. The strategies vary depending on the demands of the text and the reader's purpose. For example, if the text contains a lot of hard words, the reader might stop and summarize after every page to check understanding.
- Explain that this year students will learn a few basic strategies that they can use while reading in class or independently. These include summarize; visualize; generate questions; make inferences; and make, confirm, and revise predictions.
- Tell students that good readers always begin by previewing a text. This involves reading the title, looking at the illustrations, and determining the selection's genre. For example, if the selection is a fantasy, the reader knows what kinds of story events might happen—things that could not happen in real life. The reader also knows that this story is fiction and, therefore, will have a clear beginning, middle, and end.
- If the selection is nonfiction, the reader will read the title and headings to learn the selection's main ideas. Then the reader will read and look for signal words that tell how the author organized the text.
- Then the reader will begin reading, selecting, and using strategies as needed to check understanding.

### PRACTICE/APPLY

Tell students that with every selection they read this year, they will have an opportunity to tell what strategies they are selecting and using. They will also explain why these strategies are helpful. This will help them verbalize their strategy use, understand that there is more than one way to monitor comprehension of a text, and assist the teacher as appropriate strategies are modeled in the text. Ask:

- What strategies did you use while reading *First Day Jitters*?
- How did these strategies help you understand the text?

## Objectives

- Self-select strategies to aid comprehension
- Use academic language: *strategy, summarize, visualize, generate questions, inferences*

**Content Reader**

For content correlated to California Science and History/Social Science standards, see pages 144–149 in the **Content Reader**.
**HSS 3.4.1, HSS 3.4.2**

# Paired Selection

CA CONTENT STANDARD R 3.2.1 Use **titles**, tables of contents, chapter headings, glossaries, and indexes to locate information in text.

**GENRE: NONFICTION**

Have students read the bookmark on **Student Book** page 30. Explain that a nonfiction informational essay often contains

- factual information about a topic
- a title that tells the topic of the article and subheadings that tell the topic of each section.
- text features, such as graphs, that give more information about the topic

## Text Feature: Bar Graphs

**EXPLAIN** Point out the **bar graph** on page 31. Explain that this graph shows information about the number of students who answered a survey question. Point out the features of this bar graph.

- The bar graph has a title that tells the reader what the graph is about.
- The labels on the left side show what is being compared.
- The numbers at the bottom show the number of students.
- Thick lines called bars show how many students chose each quality.

**APPLY** Ask students what qualities are shown at the left of the graph. (the four qualities of a good citizen: respect, responsibility, honesty and fairness, courage) Ask what the numbers at the bottom of the graph show. (the number of students who chose each quality as the best)

# How to Be a Good Citizen

1

by Jan Smith

A **citizen** is a person who lives in a **community**. Each citizen has certain rights and duties. Here is how you can be a good citizen.

**Be Respectful** Be kind and fair to everyone. Always tell the truth.

**Be Responsible** Follow the **laws**, or rules, of your **nation**, your state, and your town. Obeying the laws keeps you and the community safe.

**Be Active** Take part in school and community activities. Help your neighbors.

**Be Informed** Learn about your state and nation. Knowing your history can bring your community closer together.

**Be Courageous** Always try to help others, even when it is difficult. Dr. Martin Luther King, Jr., is an example of a good citizen. He fought for equal rights for all citizens. Follow these tips and you'll be on your way to becoming a great citizen!

### Content Vocabulary

**History/Social Science Words** Explain the words using the **Define/Example/Ask** routine. Definitions are provided below.

**citizen** (p. 30): a person who lives in a community and has rights and responsibilities

**community** (p. 30): a place where people live, work, and play

**laws** (p. 30): rules made by the government of a nation, town, or community

**nation** (p. 30): a group that shares one government, history, culture, and language

## Qualities of Good Citizens

### Reading a Bar Graph

This bar graph shows the answers to a survey.
A survey asks what people think about something.

**Survey Question:**
**What is the most important quality of a good citizen?**

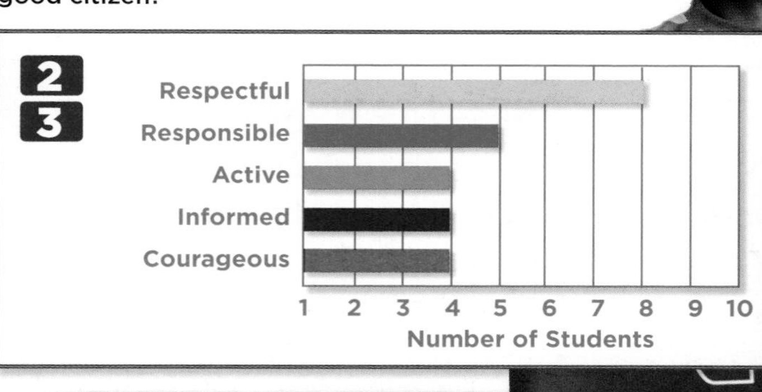

### Critical Thinking

1. Look at the bar graph. How many people answered the survey question? Which quality received the most votes? **Reading a Bar Graph**
2. What are some things you can do to be a good citizen? **Apply**
3. How is Sarah Jane Hartwell in *First Day Jitters* a good citizen? **Reading/Writing Across Texts**

#### History/Social Science Activity

Work with a partner. Survey your classmates about what it takes to be a good citizen. Make a bar graph that shows your findings.

Find out more about good citizens at **www.macmillanmh.com.**

31

# Read

## Paired Selection

### 1 TEXT FEATURES: HEADINGS

CA CONTENT STANDARD HSS 3.4.2 Understand the importance of public virtue and the role of citizens.

Look at the title and section headings on page 30. What what information do they give about how a person can be a good citizen? (The title tells what the whole article is about—how to be a good citizen and each section head tells one way to be a good citizen: be respectful, be responsible, be honest and fair, and be courageous.)

### 2 TEXT FEATURE: BAR GRAPHS

What does each bar on the **bar graph** show? (Each bar shows the number of people who chose that quality.)

### 3 TEXT FEATURE: BAR GRAPHS

Look at the **bar graph**. Do more people think that responsibility or courage is the most important quality of a good citizen? (More people think that responsibility is the most important quality.)

## Critical Thinking

1. Twenty-five people answered. "Respect" received the most votes. READING A BAR GRAPH
2. Answers may include helping with chores, respecting property, and keeping promises. APPLY

3. **FOCUS QUESTION** As a teacher she will probably help others in her community, follow her school's rules, and be fair to her students. READING/ WRITING ACROSS TEXTS

### History/Social Science

Have students display their bar graphs and explain what information the graphs show.

## English Learners

### UNIVERSAL ACCESS

**Content Vocabulary** Draw pictures to illustrate the meaning of the content vocabulary words. For example, to illustrate laws, draw a police officer saying "no" to kids who want to cross the street at a green light. Have students repeat the words a few times.

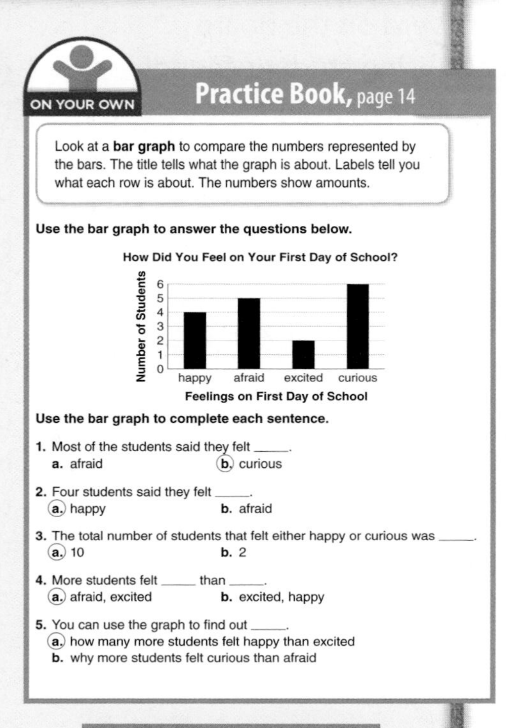

ON YOUR OWN **Practice Book,** page 14

Look at a **bar graph** to compare the numbers represented by the bars. The title tells what the graph is about. Labels tell you what each row is about. The numbers show amounts.

**Use the bar graph to answer the questions below.**

**How Did You Feel on Your First Day of School?**



**Use the bar graph to complete each sentence.**

1. Most of the students said they felt _____.
   a. afraid (b.) curious
2. Four students said they felt _____.
   (a.) happy b. afraid
3. The total number of students that felt either happy or curious was _____.
   (a.) 10 b. 2
4. More students felt _____ than _____.
   (a.) afraid, excited b. excited, happy
5. You can use the graph to find out _____.
   (a.) how many more students felt happy than excited
   b. why more students felt curious than afraid

Approaching Reproducible, page 14
Beyond Reproducible, page 14

# Connect Language Arts

## WHOLE GROUP

**VOCABULARY**
- Tested Words

**SPELLING**
- Short Vowels

**GRAMMAR**
- Statements and Questions

**CONTENT STANDARDS**
R 3.1.4, R 3.1.8, LC 3.1.1, LC 3.1.8

## SMALL GROUP

- Differentiated Instruction, pp. 33K–33JJ

ON YOUR OWN **Practice Book**, page 15

The **prefixes** *un-* and *non-* are word parts that can be added to the beginning of base words. They form new words with new meanings. *Un-* means "not" or "the opposite of." *Non-* means "not" or "without."

*un + kind = unkind* *non + stop = nonstop*

**Add the prefix *un-* or *non-* to the words in the box. Then complete the sentences below with the new words.**

| | | |
|---|---|---|
| un usual | un happy | un safe |
| non stick | un wrap | non skid |

1. We learn to make unusual foods in cooking class.
2. First the teacher may unwrap the ingredients.
3. We usually cook in nonstick pans.
4. The kitchen floor is covered with nonskid mats.
5. Without the mats, the kitchen could be unsafe.
6. I would be unhappy to miss cooking class.

**Approaching Reproducible**, page 15
**Beyond Reproducible**, page 15

# Build Robust Vocabulary

## Day 1 Teach/Practice

### CONNECT TO WORDS

- Practice this week's vocabulary words using the following prompts:

1. Would you be more likely to *chuckle* at a scary movie or a funny one?
2. When do you get *nervous*? How do you act?
3. What idea or fear do you think is *nonsense*?
4. Is a man who *fumbles* into his coat being careful with his clothing?
5. If you *trudged* through something rather than walked, how did you look? Show me.

### ACADEMIC VOCABULARY

- Review the important academic vocabulary words for the week. These words include: *story structure, character, setting, plot, prefix, bar graph, phrasing, punctuation, poem*.
- Write each word on the board. Define each using student-friendly language and ask students to select the word you are defining. Then point to words in random order for students to define.

## Day 2 Review

### CONNECT TO WORDS

- Review the definitions of this week's vocabulary words using **Student Book** pages 8–9. Discuss each word using the following prompts:

1. What is something that makes you *chuckle*?
2. Do you think a person who gets *nervous* around deep water would want to travel in a boat? Explain.
3. What does it mean to call something *nonsense*? Explain.
4. What might cause someone to *fumble* into something?
5. Would you be more likely to *trudge* when you are tired or full of energy?

### WORD PARTS: PREFIXES

- Remind students that knowing the meaning of a prefix and a base word can help them figure out the meaning of an unfamiliar word.
- Display **Transparency 1**. Read the first sentence and model using the prefix to figure out the meaning of the underlined word.
- Have students identify the word parts that help them define the remaining underlined words.
- Have students write the following words and their meanings in their writer's notebooks using their knowledge of the meanings of the prefixes *un-* and *non-* : *nondrip, unpaid, unwise, nonslip*.

CA CONTENT STANDARD
R 3.1.8 Use knowledge of prefixes and suffixes to determine the meaning of words.

CA CONTENT STANDARD
R 3.1.4 Use knowledge of **antonyms**, **synonyms**, homophones, and homographs to determine the meanings of words.

## Day 3 Reinforce

### CONNECT TO WORDS

- Ask students to create Word Squares for each word in their Writer's Notebooks.
- In the first square, students write the word. (Example: *chuckled*)
- In the second square, students write their own definition of the word and any related words, such as synonyms. (Example: *laugh, giggle, snicker, smile*)
- In the third square, students draw a simple illustration that will help them remember the word. (Example: *drawing of person smiling and a speech bubble that says, "Ha ha!"*)
- In the fourth square, students write nonexamples, including antonyms for the word. (Example: *cry, weep, shed tears, sob*)

### RELATED WORDS

- Help students generate words related to *trudged*.
- Draw a T-chart on the board. One column is headed "Moving Slowly"; the other column is headed "Moving Quickly."
- Have students list words they know to add to each column. Students can use a student-level thesaurus to find more synonyms and antonyms for *trudged*, such as (slowly) *crawl, stumble, plod, shuffle*; (quickly) *run, skip, scamper, sprint, dash, gallop*.

## Day 4 Extend

### CONNECT TO WORDS

- Review this week's vocabulary using the following sentence stems. Have students orally complete each one.

**1.** I chuckled when I saw the _____ .

**2.** The boy trudged because _____.

**3.** The girl felt nervous because _____.

**4.** I might fumble into something when _____.

**5.** It is nonsense to be _____.

### MORPHOLOGY

- Use the additional selection vocabulary word *weakly* as a springboard to learn other words.
- Write the word *weakly* on the board. Underline *-ly*. Explain that the suffix *-ly* usually means "in a certain way or manner." The word *weakly* means "done in a weak way."
- Write the words *harshly* and *swiftly* on the board. Have students underline *-ly* in each word and identify the base word.
- Use the word parts to define each word. Explain that *-ly* means "in a certain way" and *harsh* means "rough or unpleasant." Therefore, *harshly* means "in an unpleasant way." *Swiftly* means "in a quick way" because *swift* means "quick or fast."

## Day 5 Assess and Reteach

### POSTTEST

- Display **Transparency 2.** Have students complete the cloze sentences using one of this week's vocabulary words.
- Note how quickly and accurately students can complete this task. Work with students who make errors or require too much time to complete this task during Small Group time.

### CONNECT TO WRITING

- Have students write sentences in their Writer's Notebooks using this week's vocabulary. Tell students to write sentences that tell about meeting their teacher on the first day of school.
- EL Provide the Day 4 sentence stems for students needing extra support.

# 5-Day Spelling

Go to page T17 for **Differentiated Spelling Lists**. Pretests and Posttest are available in Teacher's Resource Book.

## Spelling Words

| | | |
|---|---|---|
| clap | crop | miss |
| step | snack | stamp |
| sick | mess | jump |
| rock | head | click |
| luck | shut | pond |

**Review** cat, can, man
**Challenge** bathtub, anthill

## Dictation Sentences

1. The children clap with their hands.
2. Pat took a small step.
3. She felt **sick** last night.
4. That rock is heavy.
5. Good **luck** in the game!
6. The farmer had a good crop.
7. A carrot is a healthy snack.
8. My dog made a huge mess!
9. Try not to hit your **head**.
10. Please shut the door.
11. I **miss** my old school.
12. I need a stamp for the letter.
13. How high can you jump?
14. I heard a faint click.
15. This pond is not deep.

## Review/Challenge Words

1. Jill's cat is gray.
2. That man is our new teacher.
3. Tom can teach his dog tricks.
4. I filled the bathtub with water.
5. Ants live in an anthill.

Words in **bold** type are from the main selection.

# Short Vowels

CA CONTENT STANDARD
**LC 3.1.8** Spell correctly one-syllable words that have blends, contractions, compounds, orthographic patterns (e.g., qu, consonant doubling, changing the ending of a word from -y to -ies when forming the plural), and common homophones (e.g., hair-hare).

## Day 1 Pretest

### ASSESS PRIOR KNOWLEDGE

- Model for students how to spell the word *step*. Segment the word sound-by-sound, then attach a spelling to each sound. Point out that *step* follows a spelling pattern for short vowel sounds.
- Use the Dictation Sentences. Say the underlined word, read the sentence, and repeat the word. Have students write the words.
- Have students self-correct their tests. Remind them that the letters *a*, *e*, *i*, *o*, and *u* followed by a consonant usually indicates a short vowel sound.
- Have students cut apart the **Spelling Word Cards BLM** on **Teacher's Resource Book** page 102 and figure out a way to sort them. Have them save the cards for use throughout the week.

## Day 2 Word Sorts and Review

### WORD SORTS

- Have students take turns sorting words and explaining how they sorted them. When students have finished the sort, discuss any words that have unexpected vowel spellings. (*head*)
- Review the spelling words pointing out the short vowel spellings. Use the cards on the Spelling Word Cards BLM. Write the key words *mat, hen, sit, top,* and *bug on* the board. Model how to sort words by short vowel sounds. Place one or two cards under the correct key words.

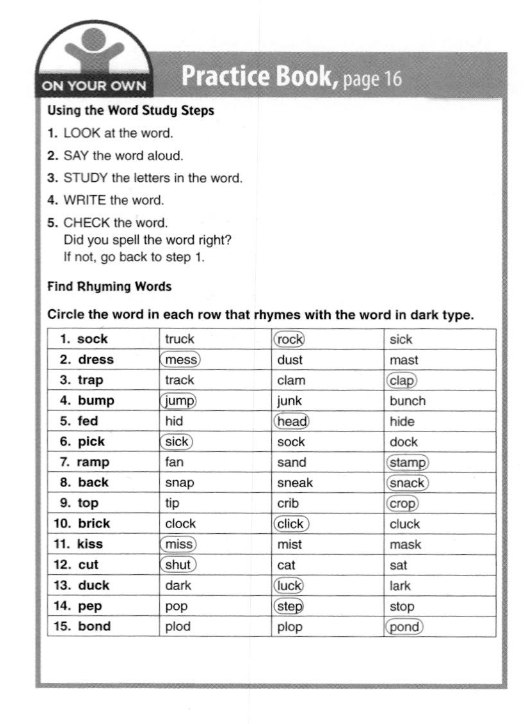

ON YOUR OWN **Practice Book,** page 16

**Using the Word Study Steps**

1. LOOK at the word.
2. SAY the word aloud.
3. STUDY the letters in the word.
4. WRITE the word.
5. CHECK the word.
   Did you spell the word right?
   If not, go back to step 1.

**Find Rhyming Words**

**Circle the word in each row that rhymes with the word in dark type.**

| | | | |
|---|---|---|---|
| 1. **sock** | truck | (rock) | sick |
| 2. **dress** | (mess) | dust | mast |
| 3. **trap** | track | clam | (clap) |
| 4. **bump** | (jump) | junk | bunch |
| 5. **fed** | hid | (head) | hide |
| 6. **pick** | (sick) | sock | dock |
| 7. **ramp** | fan | sand | (stamp) |
| 8. **back** | snap | sneak | (snack) |
| 9. **top** | tip | crib | (crop) |
| 10. **brick** | clock | (click) | cluck |
| 11. **kiss** | (miss) | mist | mask |
| 12. **cut** | (shut) | cat | sat |
| 13. **duck** | dark | (luck) | lark |
| 14. **pep** | pop | (step) | stop |
| 15. **bond** | plod | plop | (pond) |

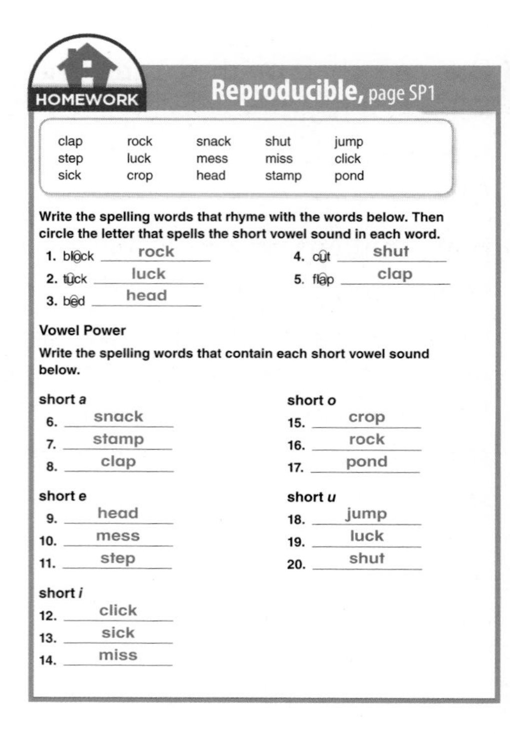

HOMEWORK **Reproducible,** page SP1

| | | | | |
|---|---|---|---|---|
| clap | rock | snack | shut | jump |
| step | luck | mess | miss | click |
| sick | crop | head | stamp | pond |

**Write the spelling words that rhyme with the words below. Then circle the letter that spells the short vowel sound in each word.**

1. block rock
2. tuck luck
3. bed head
4. cut shut
5. flap clap

**Vowel Power**

**Write the spelling words that contain each short vowel sound below.**

**short *a***
6. snack
7. stamp
8. clap

**short e**
9. head
10. mess
11. step

**short *i***
12. click
13. sick
14. miss

**short *o***
15. crop
16. rock
17. pond

**short *u***
18. jump
19. luck
20. shut

## Day 3 Word Meanings

### DEFINITIONS

Display the definitions below. Have students write the clues and the spelling words that go with them in their Writer's Notebooks.

1. a stone (rock)
2. not open (shut)
3. not well (sick)
4. a small meal (snack)
5. a body of water (pond)

Challenge students to come up with other clues for spelling words, review words, or challenge Words.

Have partners write a context rich sentence for each spelling word, leaving a blank where the word should go. Then have them trade papers and fill in the missing words.

## Day 4 Proofread

### PROOFREAD AND WRITE

Write the sentences below. Have students circle each misspelled word and write the word correctly.

1. You can stap on the rock. (step)
2. The pig likes to jumpe in the mud. (jump)
3. The farmer has a nice croop of corn. (crop)
4. The girl was seck with a fever. (sick)

**Error Correction** Some students will leave off the first letter of a final blend, such as the letter *m* in *jump*. Help these students segment the word sound by sound by orally stretching the sounds, /juuummmp/. Each sound should be held for two to three seconds. Then have students attach a spelling to each sound they hear.

## Day 5 Assess and Reteach

### POSTTEST

Use the Dictation Sentences on page 31C for the Posttest.

If students have difficulty with any of the words in the lesson, have them place them on a list called *Spelling Words I Want to Remember* in their Writer's Notebooks. Look for students' use of these words in their writings.

Challenge students to search for other words with short vowel spelling patterns and add them to the Unit 1 Big Question Board.

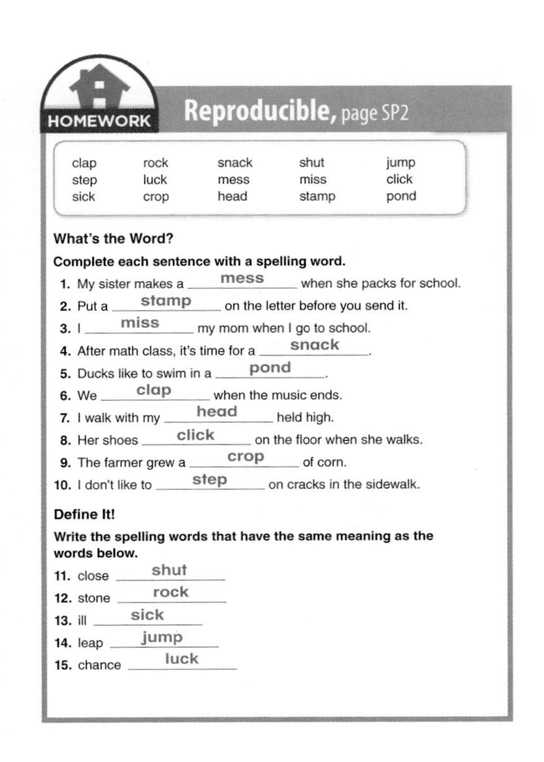

HOMEWORK **Reproducible,** page SP2

| clap | rock | snack | shut | jump |
|---|---|---|---|---|
| step | luck | mess | miss | click |
| sick | crop | head | stamp | pond |

**What's the Word?**

**Complete each sentence with a spelling word.**

1. My sister makes a ___mess___ when she packs for school.
2. Put a ___stamp___ on the letter before you send it.
3. I ___miss___ my mom when I go to school.
4. After math class, it's time for a ___snack___.
5. Ducks like to swim in a ___pond___.
6. We ___clap___ when the music ends.
7. I walk with my ___head___ held high.
8. Her shoes ___click___ on the floor when she walks.
9. The farmer grew a ___crop___ of corn.
10. I don't like to ___step___ on cracks in the sidewalk.

**Define It!**

**Write the spelling words that have the same meaning as the words below.**

11. close ___shut___
12. stone ___rock___
13. ill ___sick___
14. leap ___jump___
15. chance ___luck___

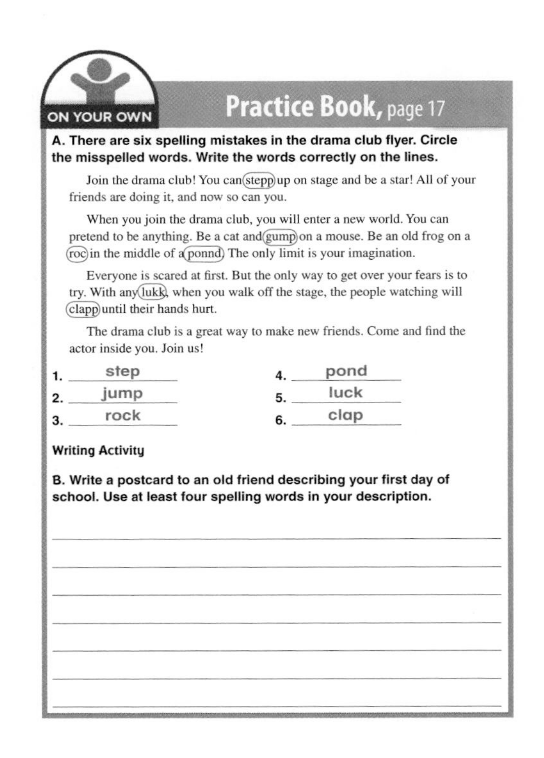

ON YOUR OWN **Practice Book,** page 17

**A. There are six spelling mistakes in the drama club flyer. Circle the misspelled words. Write the words correctly on the lines.**

Join the drama club! You can stepp up on stage and be a star! All of your friends are doing it, and now so can you.

When you join the drama club, you will enter a new world. You can pretend to be anything. Be a cat and gump on a mouse. Be an old frog on a roc in the middle of a ponnd. The only limit is your imagination.

Everyone is scared at first. But the only way to get over your fears is to try. With any lukk, when you walk off the stage, the people watching will clapp until their hands hurt.

The drama club is a great way to make new friends. Come and find the actor inside you. Join us!

1. ___step___
2. ___jump___
3. ___rock___
4. ___pond___
5. ___luck___
6. ___clap___

**Writing Activity**

**B. Write a postcard to an old friend describing your first day of school. Use at least four spelling words in your description.**

HOMEWORK **Reproducible,** page SP3

**Look at the words in each set below. One word in each set is spelled correctly. Look at Sample A. The letter next to the correctly spelled word in Sample A has been shaded in. Do Sample B yourself. Shade the letter of the word that is spelled correctly. When you are sure you know what to do, go on with the rest of the page.**

**Sample A:** Ⓐ lump Ⓑ lumpe Ⓒ lumpp Ⓓ luump

**Sample B:** Ⓔ tacke Ⓕ taak Ⓖ tack Ⓗ takk

1. Ⓐ klap Ⓑ claap Ⓒ clap Ⓓ clapp
2. Ⓔ stepp Ⓕ step Ⓖ steap Ⓗ stap
3. Ⓐ sick Ⓑ siick Ⓒ sik Ⓓ syck
4. Ⓔ rawk Ⓕ roock Ⓖ rocke Ⓗ rock
5. Ⓐ lucke Ⓑ luck Ⓒ lucc Ⓓ luk
6. Ⓔ krop Ⓕ cropp Ⓖ crop Ⓗ crope
7. Ⓐ snaak Ⓑ snacc Ⓒ snack Ⓓ snac
8. Ⓔ messe Ⓕ mess Ⓖ meass Ⓗ mas
9. Ⓐ head Ⓑ haed Ⓒ hed Ⓓ heade
10. Ⓔ shut Ⓕ shutt Ⓖ schut Ⓗ schutt
11. Ⓐ miss Ⓑ mis Ⓒ myss Ⓓ mys
12. Ⓔ stemp Ⓕ stampe Ⓖ Stampp Ⓗ stamp
13. Ⓐ jump Ⓑ jumpe Ⓒ juump Ⓓ juumpe
14. Ⓔ cliek Ⓕ click Ⓖ clyck Ⓗ cliik
15. Ⓐ ponde Ⓑ pawnd Ⓒ paund Ⓓ pond

# Connect
## Grammar

# 5-Day Grammar

# Statements and Questions

## Daily Language Activities

Use these activities to introduce each day's lesson. Write the day's activities on the board.

**DAY 1**
**1.** I goe to school. **2.** I like mi teacher. **3.** Her name iz Miss Jones. (1: go; 2: my; 3: is)

**DAY 2**
**1.** jim eats a snck. **2.** When iz the game? **3.** this is my first day (1: Jim; snack; 2: is; 3: This; day.)

**DAY 3**
**1.** who is your teacher. **2.** my teacher is Mr. Chen **3.** he is a nice maan. (1: Who; teacher?; 2: My; Chen.; 3: He; man.)

**DAY 4**
**1.** we have a teacher **2.** how many students ate a snack **3.** i want to jomp rope. (1: We; teacher.; 2: How; snack?; 3: I; jump)

**DAY 5**
**1.** Our class went to the ponde **2.** We watched the ducks **3.** How many ducks were there. (1: pond.; 2: ducks.; 3: there?)

## English Learners
UNIVERSAL ACCESS

**Transfer Skills** Speakers of many Asian languages often form questions by adding words to statements, such as *The hat is pretty, no?* or *You see or not see the cat?* Provide additional sample sentences for students to repeat and use to ask about classroom objects.

## Day 1 Introduce the Concept

### INTRODUCE SENTENCES AND SENTENCE FRAGMENTS

- A **sentence** is a group of words that expresses a complete thought.
- A **sentence fragment** is a group of words that does not express a complete thought.
- Every sentence begins with a capital letter.

**Examples:**
Sentence: Sue walked to school.
Sentence Fragment: My teacher.

- Use the Teach/Practice/Apply routine and the English Learner supports on the transparency to provide additional instruction and practice.

See Grammar Transparency 1 for modeling and guided practice.

HOMEWORK **Reproducible,** page GR1

- A **sentence** is a group of words that tells a complete thought.
- Every sentence begins with a capital letter.
  Sentence: Peter looked at the building.
  Not a sentence: At the building.

**Write *yes* if the words make a sentence. Write *no* if they do not.**

1. Peter's family is moving to a new town. yes
2. Went to a new school. no
3. Peter worries about his first day. yes
4. Drove him to school. no
5. He sits quietly in the car. yes
6. Unlike his other school. no
7. Bigger and newer. no
8. Felt lost. no
9. Then he saw his classroom. yes
10. Bright and sunny. no
11. Made friends. no
12. Peter had a lot of fun. yes
13. Peter's new teacher. no
14. Not nervous. no
15. He can't wait to go back. yes

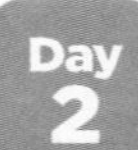

## Day 2 Teach the Concept

### REVIEW SENTENCES

Review how to identify complete sentences and sentence fragments. Remind students that sentences begin with capital letters.

### INTRODUCE STATEMENTS AND QUESTIONS

Present the following:

- A **statement**, or declarative sentence, is a sentence that tells something. It ends in a period.
- A **question**, or interrogative sentence, is a sentence that asks something. It ends in a question mark.

**Examples:**
I like my new friends.
When is the first day of school?

See Grammar Transparency 2 for modeling and guided practice.

ON YOUR OWN **Practice Book,** page 18

- A **statement** is a sentence that tells something. It ends with a period.
- A **question** is a sentence that asks something. It ends with a question mark.
  Statement: There are many ways to make new friends.
  Question: What do you do to make friends?

**Write *statement* if the sentence tells something. Write *question* if the sentence asks something. Put the correct end mark at the end of the sentence.**

1. Meg liked to make new friends statement, .
2. She said hello to the new student statement, .
3. How would you greet a new student question, ?
4. She told him about their school statement, .
5. She told him how they had fun statement, .
6. What would you say about your school question, ?
7. She showed him around the school statement, .
8. Where would you take a new student question, ?
9. What would you ask someone new question, ?
10. Do you like to hear about new places question, ?
11. We like our school statement, .
12. What was your school like question, ?
13. We have a lot of fun reading statement, .
14. Have fun at your new school statement, .

CA CONTENT STANDARD
**LC 3.1.1** Understand and be able to use complete and correct declarative, interrogative, imperative, and exclamatory sentences in writing and speaking.

## Day 3 Review and Practice

### REVIEW SENTENCES

Review statements and questions. Provide examples for each.

### MECHANICS AND USAGE: CAPITALIZATION AND PUNCTUATION

- Begin every sentence with a capital letter.
- Use a period at the end of a statement.
- Use a question mark at the end of a question.

As students write during the week, remind them to check for capitalization in the first word of a sentence and to edit for correct use of end punctuation for statements and questions (declarative and interrogative sentences).

See Grammar Transparency 3 for modeling and guided practice.

HOMEWORK **Reproducible,** page GR2

- Every sentence begins with a capital letter.
- A **statement** is sentence that tells something. It ends with a period.
- A **question** is a sentence that asks something. It ends with a question mark.
  Statement: It takes time to learn about a new place.
  Question: Do you like going to new places?

**After each sentence, write *statement* or *question* for the kind of sentence it is. Then write the sentence correctly. Use capital letters and end marks.**

1. maps can help you find your way statement; Maps can help you find your way.
2. do you know how to use a map question; Do you know how to use a map?
3. you can ask others for help statement; You can ask others for help.
4. can you give me directions question; Can you give me directions?
5. do you know where I can find Room 3A question; Do you know where I can find Room 3A?
6. soon you will know your way around statement; Soon you will know your way around.
7. you will feel right at home statement; You will feel right at home.
8. will you show others how to find places question; Will you show others how to find places?

## Day 4 Review and Proofread

### REVIEW STATEMENTS AND QUESTIONS

Ask students to tell what a statement is and what a question is. Ask what punctuation mark goes at the end of each.

### PROOFREAD

Have students proofread/edit the following sentences. Have them identify whether each sentence is a statement or a question.

1. who is in third grade? (Who; question)
2. My teacher is very nice (nice.; statement)
3. carol and Sue jump rope. (Carol; statement)
4. What time is lunch. (lunch?; question)

See Grammar Transparency 4 for modeling and guided practice.

ON YOUR OWN **Practice Book,** page 19

- A sentence is a group of words that tells a complete thought.
- A **statement** is sentence that tells something.
- A **question** is a sentence that asks something.

**Read the description of Carly's first day at camp. Circle the mistakes and rewrite the paragraph.**

I woke up early. it was the first day of camp. I didn't know what to expect. Would I know anyone in my group Would we do things I like to do? Would we swim in the lake or the pool? I've never gone swimming outside before

The bus was already filled with campers. I looked nervously down the aisle? Then I saw Lisa. she had been on my soccer team. I sat down next to her. Now I didn't even mind the rain. It would be fine because I had a friend with me.

I woke up early. It was the first day of camp. I didn't know what to expect. Would I know anyone in my group? Would we do things I like to do? Would we swim in the lake or the pool? I've never gone swimming outside before.

The bus was already filled with campers. I looked nervously down the aisle. Then I saw Lisa. She had been on my soccer team. I sat down next to her. Now I didn't even mind the rain. It would be fine because I had a friend with me.

## Day 5 Assess and Reteach

### ASSESS

Use the Daily Language Activity or **Reproducible** page GR3 for assessment.

### RETEACH

Use Reproducible page GR3 and selected pages from the **Grammar and Writing Handbook** for additional reteaching.

Check students' writing for use of the skill. Assign Grammar Revision Assignments in their Writer's Notebooks, as needed.

See Grammar Transparency 5 for modeling and guided practice.

HOMEWORK **Reproducible,** page GR3

**A. Read each group of words. Write *yes* if the group of words forms a sentence. Write *no* if it does not form a sentence.**

1. I remember my first day of school. yes
2. Looked strange. no
3. Was lost. no
4. I know my way around. yes
5. Have friends. no

**B. Decide if the sentence is a statement or a question. Write your answer on the line. Rewrite the sentence using the correct punctuation and capitalization.**

6. do you remember your first day of school question; Do you remember your first day of school?
7. Maybe you were excited statement; Maybe you were excited.
8. maybe you were scared statement; Maybe you were scared.
9. Do you know anyone in your class question; Do you know anyone in your class?
10. did you make new friends question; Did you make new friends?
11. It seems long ago now statement; It seems long ago now.
12. Do you like your new school question; Do you like your new school?

Write

WHOLE GROUP

WRITING
- Focus on Moment

CONTENT STANDARDS
W 3.1.2, W 3.1.4, LAS 3.1.3

SMALL GROUP

- Differentiated Instruction, pp. 33K–33JJ

5-Day Writing

| | |
|---|---|
| DAY 1 | Skill Introduction |
| DAY 2 | Minilesson 1<br>Revision Assignments |
| DAY 3 | Minilesson 2<br>Revision Assignments |
| DAY 4 | Reading/Writing Connection<br>Focus on Moment |
| DAY 5 | Writing Conferences |

The Writers' Express
Immediate Impact. Lasting Transformation. wex.org

**Research Proven Writing Approach**

# Topic Development: Focus on a Moment

## Professional Development

### WHAT IS FOCUS?

**Focus is a writer's ability to stick with and develop one central moment, place, or object.**

### WHY TEACH FOCUS?

Focus is the first skill in the writing scope and sequence because research has shown it drives students to develop a set of abilities that are fundamental to powerful writing.

Below are a few of the common problems that students overcome as they learn to focus.

- listing without including any detail or development
- touching on a subject without really developing it
- including some detail without developing a theme or message

### WHAT HAPPENS WHEN STUDENTS FOCUS ON A MOMENT?

Often students begin their writing by listing every aspect of the day's activity. It is important to encourage them to focus on one part of the experience. When students write about one moment rather than jumping from event to event, they develop descriptive details and an emotional response to this moment in time.

### ASSESSMENT: WHAT WILL I SEE IN MY STUDENTS' WRITING?

When writers focus on the most vital moments in their own experience, they can include detailed descriptions of thoughts and events. By showing their unique perspective on the world, they invite the reader to connect with their experience.

*One day my mom was cooking. I asked if I could help her and she said yes. I helped with the onions and peppers. I put them into a pan and fried them in a pan. I was stirring them and stirring them. I was very tired from stirring them all that time.*

This student focused on a moment when she helped her mother. Her specific details and sustained focus allow the reader to picture what this experience was like for her.

**TARGETING FOCUS: USING OVER-THE-SHOULDER CONFERENCES**

You can use an Over-the-Shoulder Conference to let a student know that he has done a great job with focus or to remind him why focus is so important. For example,

- You might recognize how well the student has focused.
  *This is great! You've already written three quarters of a page just about swinging the jump rope.*
- You might remind the student to focus.
  *I can see you're going to write about the kickball game in PE class. Which moment are you going to choose?*

**POST STUDENT EXCERPTS**

While students are working on focus, you should post strong student examples of focus, and make sure to discuss briefly how these excerpts demonstrate the skill particularly well. In discussing the new set of excerpts posted around the room, you might say:

**Think Aloud** We've spent lots of time this week talking about why focusing on a moment is an important writing skill. Take a look at the writing I hung up today. Does anyone see a great example of how focused writing helps you picture what was happening in one moment? How does it let you imagine how the writer felt?

**SHARING CIRCLE**

Sharing plays a vital role in the writing process because of what it teaches students about community, as well as writing. In Sharing Circle, students repeat a protocol that lets them appreciate each other's work, pinpoint the impact their writing is making on their readers, and gain confidence in their skills.

When you and your students target the skill of Focusing on a Moment, you might begin Sharing Circle by saying:

**Think Aloud** During sharing today, I want everyone to listen carefully for details that really help you picture a specific moment. When you make your comments to the reader, make sure to tell him or her why those details stood out to you.

Throughout the unit, students will use the skill of focus to write strong sentences and paragraphs. This skill will be used as you guide them through the writing of a Personal Narrative in the middle of the unit and they create a Personal Narrative independently at the end of the unit.

## Objective

- Introduce Skill: Focus

### Materials

- none

## Notes from Research

**Why teach focus?**

- When a writer skips from subject to subject, he starts over and over again and doesn't give himself a chance to develop the depth of his ideas.
- When a writer sticks with one subject and examines it closely, he often discovers something only he thinks, feels, or sees.
- Focus gives students a tool for digging down to an observation that's all their own, to get below the typical ways of talking about the world.
- Students who learn to communicate their "distinctive take" on the world find out that people want to listen to what they say. Listeners respond excitedly, which helps students to discover the power to make people pay attention and gives them a reason to keep writing.

### Objective

- Focus on a moment and write to a prompt

#### Materials

- Writer's Notebook
- Transparency 1

**Writing Professional Development Guide**

See **Writing Professional Development Guide** for student examples and additional research information.

# Writer's Craft

## Strong Sentences: Focus on a Moment

**TEACH/MODEL**

**Set Purpose** Tell students that today you are going to learn a new writing skill. It is called focus. Ask: *How many of you have ever looked through a camera? What can you see?*

> **Students:** *Just what the camera is looking at. Like a picture of my mom.*
> **Teacher:** *That's right. Even though there might be a lot going on around you and your mom, when you take a picture with a camera you are focusing on one special thing—in this case, your mom. It's very similar when we focus in our writing.*

**Focus Drawings** Post the following definition of Focus.

> **Focus is picking one thing or action and writing a lot about it.**

Explain to students that they are going to do a drawing exercise and then write about it. Hand out paper and colored pencils to students. Tell students to draw a picture of themselves. They MUST include these three things in their picture. Post these on the board:

- Show what you look like.
- Show you wearing your favorite clothes.
- Show one thing you like to do.

## Teacher Write Aloud

**PRACTICE/APPLY**

Model for students how to focus on the small details of an object or a setting. Record your observations on the board or chart paper.

**Teacher:** *What are some of your favorite things to do?*
**Student:** *I like to play hockey!*
**Teacher:** *I want you to draw yourself participating in your favorite activity. What might you draw if you're playing hockey?*
**Student:** *Me in my hockey pads and uniform, with my stick shooting a puck.*
**Teacher:** *Great. Now I know what you will be focused on today—you playing hockey. It's like I'm taking a picture of you doing your favorite activity with my camera. There might be a lot happening around you, but I'm just focusing on you playing hockey.*

Tell students to pay attention to the small details of what they are doing, what they are wearing, and what they look like. Ask students to work quickly. Give them approximately 15 minutes to draw. Make sure they include all three things in their drawings.

**Summarize Learning** Explain the following:

**Think Aloud** Today you really focused on three things in your drawings: what you look like, your favorite clothes, and your favorite thing to do. Now you are going to pick one thing and write as much as you can about it. That is what focus is all about.

Ask students to take out their Writer's Notebooks and remind them that they will be writing for a full 10 minutes. Ask the questions below to spark writing ideas. Then post the Writing Prompt on **Transparency 1**.

- Raise your hand if you had fun drawing your favorite clothes.
- Raise your hand if you had fun drawing your favorite activity.
- Raise your hand if you drew yourself sitting; —standing.

**Transparency 1**

Pick ONE of the THREE parts of your picture. Write only about that one part of the picture.

**Writing Transparency**

### Daily Journal Prompts

**Focus on Moment**

Use these and other prompts for independent daily journal writing.

- Write about a moment when you were surprised.
- Write about a moment when you helped someone.
- Write about a moment when you got hurt. Describe what happened and how you felt.
- Write about a moment when you were angry or upset.

## Objective

- Select a single idea and write two sentences to expand it

### Materials

- Writer's Notebooks
- Practice Book, p. 20

### Teacher-to-Teacher

**Two Is Enough**

Two sentences may not seem like much, but we've found that it can be very difficult for student writers to add even one more sentence to a piece that they think they have already finished. Adding two sentences challenges students to stick with something even when they think they have nothing more to say.

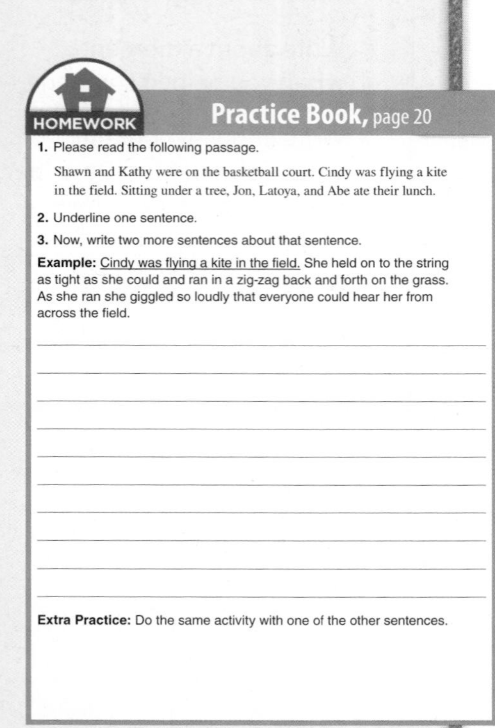

HOMEWORK **Practice Book,** page 20

**1.** Please read the following passage.

Shawn and Kathy were on the basketball court. Cindy was flying a kite in the field. Sitting under a tree, Jon, Latoya, and Abe ate their lunch.

**2.** Underline one sentence.

**3.** Now, write two more sentences about that sentence.

**Example:** Cindy was flying a kite in the field. She held on to the string as tight as she could and ran in a zig-zag back and forth on the grass. As she ran she giggled so loudly that everyone could hear her from across the field.

**Extra Practice:** Do the same activity with one of the other sentences.

**Approaching Reproducible,** page 20

**Beyond Reproducible,** page 20

# Minilesson 1

**Strong Sentences** | Developing a Single Moment in Time

### TEACH/MODEL

**Write Strong Sentences** Ask students to copy the following passage into their Writer's Notebooks, or use **Practice Book** page 20. They then underline one sentence and write two more sentences about that sentence.

**Shawn and Latoya were on the basketball court. Cindy was flying a kite in the field. Sitting under a tree, Juan, Kathy, and Abe ate their lunch.**

Explain that the writer could tell an entire story about each one of these moments. For example, what might have happened on the basketball court? (Latoya got a basket, Shawn double-dribbled, etc.) Tell students to rewrite the sentence and write two more sentences focusing on that moment.

### PRACTICE/APPLY

- Students work independently to write about one of the sentences. Circulate and provide Over-the-Shoulder Conferences.
- Ask for students to share their work. If possible, try to find one student for each of the three sentences.

**Summarize Learning** Discuss the following:

**Think Aloud** So, what do you think? Was today's writing interesting? Unique? Everyone came up with their own way to focus on one moment. For the next few weeks, we will work on developing one moment in our writing. The goal is to give our readers a clear picture of one moment that is happening in our writing.

# Minilesson 2

**Strong Sentences** Developing a Single Moment in Time

### TEACH/MODEL

**Write Strong Sentences** Ask students to copy the following passage into their Writer's Notebook. They then choose one sentence and write two more sentences about that sentence.

**Dave made a sandwich. He went back to the kitchen to get something to drink. Debbie ate half of Dave's sandwich.**

Explain that the writer could tell an entire story about each one of these moments. For example, how might Dave have made his sandwich? (He took two slices of bread and slathered them with mayonnaise. He put cheese, meat, and pickles in the middle.)

### PRACTICE/APPLY

- Students work independently to write about one of the sentences. Circulate and provide Over-the-Shoulder Conferences.
- Ask for students to share their work. If possible, try to find one student for each of the three sentences.

**Summarize Learning** Explain the following:

**Think Aloud** What examples of focused writing can you remember from today? Is it getting easier to find moments of focus in writing? Remember, focus is picking one moment and writing a lot about it. How do you think focus makes writing better? (writer is staying on topic, writing is more detailed, etc.)

## Objective

- Select a single idea and write two sentences to expand it

### Materials

- Writer's Notebooks

## Teacher-to-Teacher

Students are motivated to write when writing is about communicating and developing their ideas. This curriculum is designed to emphasize this aspect of writing, and uses the motivation that comes from this urge to communicate to develop specific writing skills. Keep this in mind as you encourage students to focus on one moment in their writing.

## English Learners

UNIVERSAL ACCESS

**Sentence Frames**
Provide sentence frames to help students develop the moment. *Dave made a sandwich. First, he got the ____. Then he ____. When he was done, he ____.*

Provide language as needed. Also, have available a bilingual picture dictionary for students to reference.

# Reading and Writing Connection

## Writer's Craft

**STRONG SENTENCES: FOCUS ON MOMENT**

Use the example from *First Day Jitters* to show the author's skilled use of focus.

- Ask: *When was a time you didn't want to get out of bed?*
- Have students read aloud the excerpt from *First Day Jitters*. Ask: *What part of the passage could you "see" happening as you read it? What small actions could the author show because she focused on a moment?*

**USE FOCUS TO WRITE ABOUT TEXT**

Remind students to use the skill of focusing on a moment when they write about *First Day Jitters* so that they are able to include lots of details.

CA CONTENT STANDARD LAS 3.1.3 Respond to questions with appropriate elaboration.

**Engagement Prompt** These prompts have been designed to help students deepen their connection to the text and to discover their own perspective on it.

- *Focus on a moment when you didn't want to go to school.*

**Response Prompt** These prompts have been designed to help students explore more deeply their reactions to particular passages in the reading.

- *Focus on a moment in the story when you hoped Sarah would get her way.*

CA **Writing**

**Focus on Moment**
When you **focus on moment**, your reader will see a strong image of what you are writing about.

# Reading and Writing Connection

Read the passage below. Notice how author Julie Danneberg focuses on a moment of time.

An excerpt from *First Day Jitters*

"Sarah, dear, time to get out of bed," Mr. Hartwell said, poking his head through the bedroom door. "You don't want to miss the first day at your new school do you?"

"I'm not going," said Sarah, and pulled the covers over her head.

The author focuses on the moment when Mr. Hartwell first tries to get Sarah up. She uses details about what the two characters did and said to help us feel as though we're watching the moment.

**Unit 1 Writing: Personal Narrative (Description)**

| | |
|---|---|
| Week 1 | • Strong Sentences: Focus on Moment |
| Week 2 | • Strong Paragraphs: Focus on Moment |
| Week 3 | • Personal Narrative (Guided Writing) |
| Week 4 | • Strong Sentences: Focus on Setting/Object |
| Week 5 | • Strong Paragraphs: Focus on Setting/Object |
| Week 6 | Personal Narrative (Independent Writing) |

## Read and Find

Read Kendall's writing below. What did she do to focus on a moment? Use the tips below to help you.

### Fresh Baked Cookies!

by Kendall W.

I watched my mom carefully reach into the oven with the oven mitt. She slid out the tray of cookies. The heat from the cookies made the air above the cookie sheet shimmer. I closed my eyes and breathed in deeply to smell their yummy scent.

Read about the freshly baked cookies.

### Writer's Checklist

- [x] Does the writer pick a short amount of time and write a lot about it?
- [x] Does the writer include specific details about her experience?

- [ ] Can you picture the **moment** the way Kendall experienced it?

33

# Write

**Literary Analysis Prompt** These prompts have been designed to help students deepen their connection to the text and discover their own perspective on it.

- *Focus on a place in the story where you thought the author made Sarah seem like a real person.*

## Use Student Model

Have students chorally read the student sample at the top of **Student Book** page 33. Discuss what this student writer did to focus on a moment in time. Use the Writer's Checklist.

Write the following journal prompt on the board:

**Think about your first day of school. Select one moment that was memorable. Write three to five sentences about that moment.**

Tell students that you will be reading and commenting on their writing during Writing Conference time.

Model how to use the Writer's Checklist to write and revise their work.

- What is the moment you chose?
- What sentences did you add to tell about that moment? Will readers be able to clearly picture that moment? If not, what details could you add?

# Conferences

## Writing Journals

### Objective

- Students will meet with the teacher to discuss writing and receive revision assignments

### Materials

- Writer's Notebooks
- Revision Assignments

### Teacher-to-Teacher

**Over-the-Shoulder Conferences**

Use these quick, focused opportunities to comment while students are writing.

- **Step 1** Quietly move close enough to a student that you can read the journal entry he or she is writing.
- **Step 2** Read part of what you see. You don't need to start from the beginning or read the entire piece.
- **Step 3** Show the student a spot in the writing where he or she is using a particular skill or describing something that piques your interest.
- **Step 4** Whisper a sentence or two about why you noticed that spot in the writing and ask a question that will nudge the student to add a detail or clarify.
- **Step 5** Move on to the next student. Select students strategically. You should see 12–15 students in a 15-minute period.

### DYNAMIC FEEDBACK SYSTEM

**Purpose** One of the best ways for students to develop skills is by understanding how their writing affects their readers. Your targeted comments direct students to notice the impact they've made by using a specific skill. Your comments should aim to:

- Engage and encourage students by showing them your appreciation for what they've written.
- Focus students' attention on developing one particular skill.

**Steps in the Dynamic Feedback System**

1. Read and appreciate the writing.
2. Notice how the student uses the targeted skill. (e.g. focus: Ask: *For how many sentences does the student stay on a topic?)*
3. Write comments in which you show how the writing has an impact on you. Direct your comments to those places in the piece where the student has used the targeted skill.
4. Meet with and give the student a revision assignment.

### WRITE EFFECTIVE COMMENTS ON FOCUS

**Sample Comments for Focus** At least one of your comments should highlight the way the student uses the skill of focus. Here are some sample comments. Use these comments to get you started.

- *I like the way you really focused on the moment when [your sister took the remote control from you].*
- *Will you tell me more about this moment? You made me curious!*
- *This is a great description of when you [ate something sour]. Can you tell me more about this moment?*
- *Which of these moments do you think you could write the most about?*

# Revision Assignments

CA CONTENT STANDARD
**W 3.1.4** Revise drafts to improve the coherence and logical progression of ideas by using an established rubric.

## IMPROVE WRITING

**What Is It?** Revision assignments play a crucial role in the dynamic feedback system. They enable you to work with each student on one skill at a time until the student has mastered it.

Revision assignments involve marking a specific section of a student's journal entry and then asking the student to revise it in a specific way. By requiring students to put to use your feedback to revise their own writing, revision assignments show clearly how that feedback has affected what students are able to do next.

**Sample Revision Assignments for Focus** Here are some examples of effective revision assignments for focus. Use them to get started. You may also use the preprinted Revision Assignment Notes or create your own revision assignments based on these.

*In your Writer's Notebook, I have underlined a fantastic moment that needs more focus. Find the sentence. Rewrite the sentence. Write two more sentences focusing on that moment.*

*Pick a single moment in your entry and pretend that you can freeze time. Now think about your frozen moment and describe every detail you can think of how that scene looks. Underline the moment. Rewrite the sentence. Write two more sentences focusing on that moment.*

[Write, underline, or bracket the sentence.] *There are so many interesting moments in this entry that I'm having a hard time imagining any of them in detail. Write two sentences just about* [insert specific moment from journal entry].

### Revision Assignment Notes

Use the Revision Assignment Notes to focus students' rewrites.

**Available on Jump Drive**

### Daily Handwriting

Have students review the manuscript alphabet, and letter and word spacing. See Handwriting pages 4–6 for daily practice. W 3.1.2

Mark students' Journal Checklists to indicate mastered skills.

**Reproducible,** page 222

| STAGE 1 Establishing Habits | | |
|---|---|---|
| ☐ Write Journal Entries | ☐ Practice Skill Drills | ☐ Engage in Experience |
| ☐ Respond to Feedback | ☐ Develop Vocabulary | ☐ Share Writing |

| STAGE 2 Strengthening Voice | | |
|---|---|---|
| Expressive Skills | Topic Development | ☐ Moment ☐ Object ☐ Setting |
| | Showing | ☐ Include unique observations<br>☐ Recognize showing and telling |
| | Strong Verbs | ☐ Recognize and use strong verbs |
| | Sensory Detail | ☐ Use multiple senses<br>☐ Choose sensory detail effectively |
| | Dialogue and Evidence I | ☐ Include dialogue |
| | Character Development | ☐ Believable<br>☐ Change and growth |
| | Logical Structure I: Distinguishing Moments | ☐ Use chronological order<br>☐ Distinguish moments |
| Technical Skills | Sentence Mechanics & Usage I: The Complete Sentence | ☐ Capitals and end punctuation<br>☐ Parts of speech<br>☐ Possessives<br>☐ Commas in a series |
| | Subject/Verb Agreement I | ☐ With present tense<br>☐ With simple past tense |
| | Punctuating and Formatting Dialogue & Quotations | ☐ Quotation marks |

**Writing Journal Checklist**

# Administer the Test

## Weekly Reading Quick Check,

**Passage and questions, Unit 1 Week 1**

**ASSESSED SKILLS**

- Vocabulary Words; Word Parts/Prefixes *un-, non-*
- Character, Setting, Plot
- Statements and Questions; Focus on Moment
- Short Vowels

*Selection Test Also Available.*

**Progress Monitoring, Unit 1 Week 1**

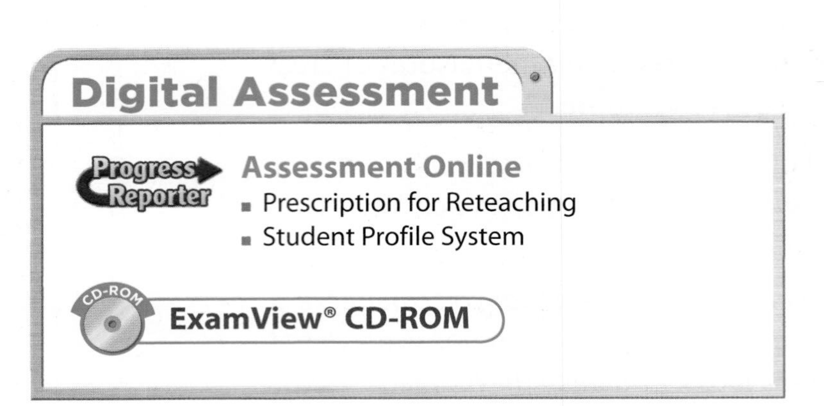

## Unit Fluency Assessment

Assess fluency for one group of students per week. Use the Oral Fluency Record Sheet to track the number of words read correctly. Fluency goal for all students: **61–81 words correct per minute (WCPM).**

| | |
|---|---|
| Approaching Level | Weeks 1, 3, 5 |
| On Level | Weeks 2, 4 |
| Beyond Level | Week 6 |

**Diagnostic, Unit 1 Fluency**

| Diagnose | | Prescribe |
|---|---|---|
| **Review the assessment answers with students. Have them correct their errors. Then provide additional instruction as needed.** | | |
| | **IF...** | **THEN...** |
| **VOCABULARY WORDS**<br>**VOCABULARY STRATEGY**<br>Word Parts/Prefixes *un-, non-* | 0–2 items correct . . . | LOG ON Online Practice: Go to **www.macmillanmh.com.**<br>CD-ROM Vocabulary PuzzleMaker |
| **COMPREHENSION**<br>Skill: Character, Setting, Plot | 0–2 items correct . . . | SPIRAL REVIEW See Character, Setting, Plot lessons Unit 1, Week 2, page 59B. |
| **WRITING AND GRAMMAR**<br>Statements and Questions<br>Focus on Moment | 0–1 items correct . . . | See Focus lessons in Unit 1, Week 2. |
| **PHONICS AND SPELLING**<br>Words with Short Vowels | 0–2 items correct . . . | LOG ON Online Practice: Go to **www.macmillanmh.com**<br>Intervention Kit: Phonics/Word Study |
| **FLUENCY** | 55–60 WCPM | AUDIO CD Fluency Solutions Audio CD |
| | 0–54 WCPM | Intervention Kit: Phonics/Word Study |

## WRITE-ON-DEMAND SCORING RUBRIC

**PROMPT** **What happens on the first day of school? Write as much as you can as well as you can. Write for 5 minutes.**

| 4 Excellent | 3 Good | 2 Fair | 1 Unsatisfactory |
|---|---|---|---|
| • More than 7 sentences<br>• Almost no spelling or grammar errors<br>• Cohesive ideas, focused and organized | • 5–7 sentences<br>• A few spelling and grammar errors<br>• Well-developed ideas and facts provided | • 4–5 sentences<br>• Several spelling and grammar errors<br>• Some good information; some vague | • Fewer than 4 sentences<br>• Many spelling and grammar errors<br>• Few developed ideas; little accurate information |

**Daily Planner**

| | |
|---|---|
| DAY 1 | • Prepare to Read<br>• Academic Language<br>• Vocabulary (Preteach) |
| DAY 2 | • Comprehension<br>• Practice Reader Lesson 1 |
| DAY 3 | • Phonics/Decoding<br>• Practice Reader Lesson 2 |
| DAY 4 | • Phonics/Decoding<br>• Vocabulary (Review)<br>• Practice Reader Lesson 3 |
| DAY 5 | •Self-Selected Reading |

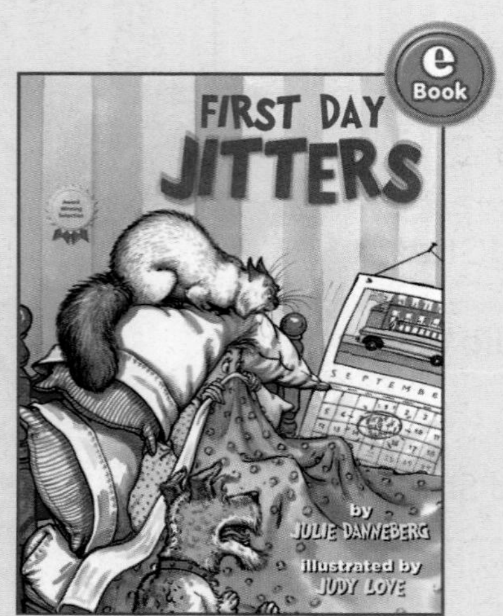


**StudentWorks Plus**

**Academic Language**

Academic words include those harder Tier 2 words that appear in much of students' reading materials as well as the language of instruction. The words chosen for instruction were selected from the **Living Word Vocabulary** list and Avril Coxhead's list of **High-Incidence Academic Words**.

Strategic

# Approaching Level

## Prepare to Read

**Objective** Preview *First Day Jitters*
**Materials** • **StudentWorks Plus** • self-stick notes

### PREVIEW TEXT

- Have students preview *First Day Jitters* using the **StudentWorks Plus**. This version of the Student Book contains oral summaries in multiple languages, online multilingual glossaries, word-by-word highlighting, and questions that assess and build comprehension.
- Remind students that listening carefully to and following along with the word-by-word reading will help them prepare for the reading of the selection with the class. Ask students to place self-stick notes on any challenging words or places that confuse them. Discuss these with students prior to the reading of the selection with the rest of the class.
- Ask students to write three or four sentences in their Writer's Notebooks telling what they learned about doing something for the first time.

## Academic Language

**Objective** Teach academic language
**Materials** • none

### PRETEACH LANGUAGE OF INSTRUCTION

Tell students that there are many important lesson words you will be using this week. You want them to become familiar with these words *before* the lessons. These words also appear in the directions of the tests they will be taking this year.

Preteach the following academic words: *realistic fiction, setting, plot, characters, story structure, prefixes, nonfiction, bar graph.*

- Define each word using student-friendly language. Tell students that *prefixes* are word parts added to the beginning of a base word that change the meaning of the base word. For example, when you play in a *fair* way, you follow the rules. The prefix *un-* means "not." When you play in an *unfair* way, you do not follow the rules. Underline the prefix *un-* in *unfair* to help students remember this.
- In addition, relate each word to known words. For example, connect *characters* to *people* and *setting* to *place* or *location*.
- Highlight these words when used throughout the week and reinforce their meanings.

Strategic

# Approaching Level

## Phonics/Decoding

**Objective** Decode words with short vowels

**Materials**
- **Approaching Reproducible,** p. 9
- **Sound-Spelling WorkBoards**

TESTED SKILL

### PHONICS MAINTENANCE

- Distribute a **WorkBoard** to each student. Say a short vowel sound taught this week. Have students find the **Sound-Spelling Card** on the board for each sound.
- Review the spelling(s) for each sound by providing a sample word containing that spelling. Guide students to write the word on the board. Model how to segment the word and write the spelling for each sound, as needed. In addition, point out spelling hints, such as words with short vowel sounds often having a CVC (consonant-vowel-consonant) pattern.
- Dictate the following words for students to spell: *bed, miss, clasp, risk, flop, must, help*. Write each word on the board and have students self-correct their work.

### RETEACH SKILL

CA CONTENT STANDARD R 3.1.2 Decode regular multisyllabic words.

**Short Vowels** Point to the short vowel Sound-Spelling Cards on the WorkBoard and review the spellings for each sound. State each spelling and provide a sample word.

- Write the words below on the board. Model how to decode the first word in each row, then guide students as they decode the remaining words. For the multisyllabic words, divide the words into syllables using the syllable-scoop procedure to help students read one syllable at a time.
- When completed, point to the words in random order for students to chorally read. Repeat several times.

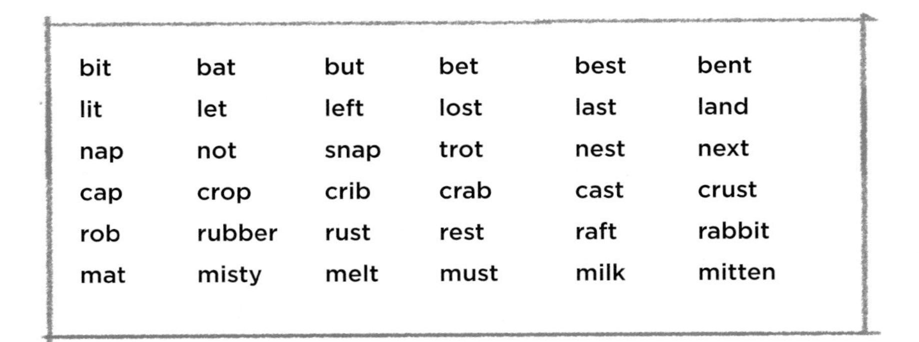

| | | | | | |
|---|---|---|---|---|---|
| bit | bat | but | bet | best | bent |
| lit | let | left | lost | last | land |
| nap | not | snap | trot | nest | next |
| cap | crop | crib | crab | cast | crust |
| rob | rubber | rust | rest | raft | rabbit |
| mat | misty | melt | must | milk | mitten |

Sound-Spelling WorkBoard

### English Learners
UNIVERSAL ACCESS

**Minimal Contrasts** Focus on articulation. Make the /a/ and /e/ sounds and point out your mouth position. Have students repeat. Use the articulation photos on the small **Sound-Spelling Cards**. Repeat for short vowel sounds /i/, /o/, and /u/. Then have students say each sound together, noticing the slight difference in mouth position. Continue by having students read minimal contrast pairs, such as bat/bet, cot/cut, pet/pit.

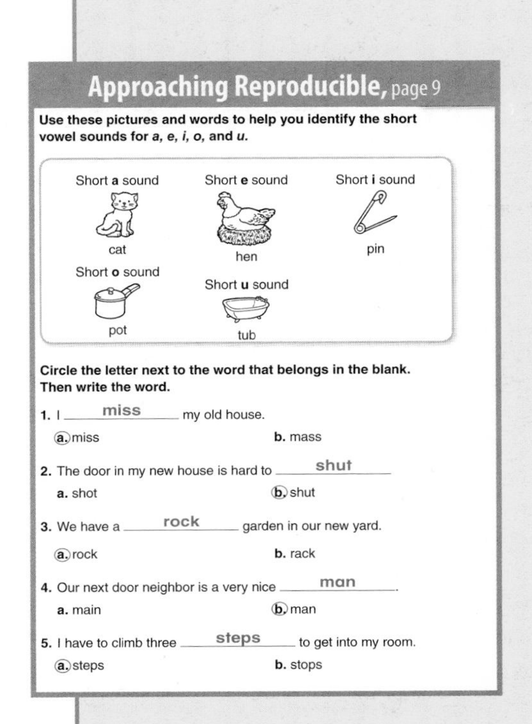

Approaching Reproducible, page 9

Use these pictures and words to help you identify the short vowel sounds for *a*, *e*, *i*, *o*, and *u*.

Short **a** sound — cat
Short **e** sound — hen
Short **i** sound — pin
Short **o** sound — pot
Short **u** sound — tub

Circle the letter next to the word that belongs in the blank. Then write the word.

1. I ___miss___ my old house.
   a. miss b. mass
2. The door in my new house is hard to ___shut___.
   a. shot b. shut
3. We have a ___rock___ garden in our new yard.
   a. rock b. rack
4. Our next door neighbor is a very nice ___man___.
   a. main b. man
5. I have to climb three ___steps___ to get into my room.
   a. steps b. stops

Strategic

# Approaching Level

## Vocabulary

**Objective** Preteach selection vocabulary

**Materials** • **Visual Vocabulary Resources** • **Approaching Reproducible,** p. 10

TESTED SKILL

### PRETEACH VOCABULARY

Use the **Visual Vocabulary Resources** to preteach the key selection words *chuckled, nervous, nonsense, fumbled, trudged*. Focus on two words per day. Use the following routine that appears in detail on the cards.

- Define the word in English and provide the example given.
- Define the word in Spanish, if appropriate, and indicate if the word is a cognate.
- Display the picture and explain how it illustrates or demonstrates the word.
- Then engage students in structured partner talk about the image, using the key word.
- Ask students to chorally say the word three times.
- Point out any known sound-spellings or focus on a key aspect of phonemic awareness related to the word.
- Distribute copies of the Vocabulary Glossary in the **English Learners Resource Book**.

### Corrective Feedback

Throughout the lessons, provide feedback based on students' responses. If the answer is correct, ask another question. If the answer is tentative, restate key information to assist the student. If the answer is wrong, provide corrective feedback such as hints or clues, refer to a visual such as a Sound-Spelling Card or story illustration, or probe with questions to help the student clarify any misunderstanding.

### Approaching Reproducible, page 10

**Read the vocabulary words. Then read the sentence at the left of each picture. Write the correct vocabulary word in the sentence at the right of the picture.**

nervous trudged nonsense chuckled fumbled

|  |  |  |
|---|---|---|
| 1. Annie walked with heavy steps. | | Annie trudged down the street. |
| 2. Some hairstyles are silly. | | Mom said that my new hairstyle is nonsense. |
| 3. Jen worried about singing. | | Jen was nervous when she began to sing. |
| 4. Fred dropped the ball. | | Fred fumbled the ball in his first game. |
| 5. Jay laughed at the joke. | | Jay chuckled at the joke. |

Strategic

# Approaching Level

## Vocabulary

**Objective** Review vocabulary and high-frequency words

**Materials** • **Vocabulary Cards** • **High-Frequency Word Cards**

### REVIEW VOCABULARY

**Review Words** Display the Vocabulary Cards for *chuckled, nervous, nonsense, fumbled,* and *trudged*. Point to each word, read it aloud, and have students chorally repeat.

Then provide the following word sets. Ask students to name the word in each set that is not related to the other words.

- chuckled, cried, laughed, giggled
- nervous, uneasy, relaxed, scared
- nonsense, foolish, silly, serious
- fumbled, graceful, tripped, clumsy
- trudged, slow, ran, walked

### HIGH-FREQUENCY WORDS

**Top 250 Words** The ability to read accurately and effortlessly the most frequently used words in written English will help students develop reading fluency. Display **High-Frequency Word Cards 1–10**. Then do the following:

- Display one card at a time and ask students to chorally state each word.
- Have students spell each word aloud.
- Ask students to write each word in their Writer's Notebooks as they state aloud each letter. Then have them read the word again.
- When completed, quickly flip through the word card set as students chorally read the words.
- Provide opportunities for students to use the words in speaking and writing. For example, provide sentence starters such as *I always* ________ for oral and written practice. Or point to a word card and ask a questions such as *What word means the opposite of this word?* (when pointing to the *after* word card).
- Continue the routine throughout the week.

### Word Webs

Have students create word webs in their Writer's Notebooks for each vocabulary word. Write the related words provided and ask students to add other words, phrases, and illustrations.

Student Book

Strategic

# Approaching Level

## Comprehension

**Objective** Reteach analyze story structure and character, setting, plot

**Materials** • **Student Book:** "Tina's Tryout Day"

### RETEACH STRATEGY: ANALYZE STORY STRUCTURE

- **Define** Tell students that a story's structure is made up of the characters, setting, and events in the story. It also includes a beginning, middle, and end. Knowing how these parts of the story fit together helps the reader understand what happens and why.

  Relate the word *structure* to the word *building*. A building is put together using many different parts and pieces. Likewise, the structure of a story is put together using elements like characters, setting, and events.
- **Relate to Real Life** Ask students to imagine that they are working on a school play. A new students comes to join the crew but knows nothing about the play. They have to tell the student about the characters, settings, and events that occur so that the new student can help design sets and costumes. These elements make up the structure of the play.
- **Set Purpose** Remind students that good readers think about a story's structure as they read. They try to figure out how the characters, setting, and main events fit together. This helps them understand what happens and why it happens.

### RETEACH SKILL: CHARACTER, SETTING, PLOT

**CA CONTENT STANDARD R 3.3.3** Determine what characters are like by what they say or do and by how the author or illustrator portrays them.

- **Define** Tell students that a character is a person or animal in a story. The setting is where and when the story takes place, and the plot is made up of the events in the story. A plot has a beginning, middle, and end.
- **Relate to Real Life** Ask students to think about their favorite movie. Ask them to name one person or animal in the movie. Tell them that this is one of the characters. Ask: *Where does the movie take place?* Tell them this is the setting. Then have students explain what happens in the movie. Explain that this is the movie's plot.
- **Set Purpose** Remind students that good readers identify the characters, setting, and plot as they read. This helps them better understand what is happening in a story and helps them make predictions about what might happen next.
- **Apply** Work with students to identify the characters, setting, and plot in "Tina's Tryout Day." Then have them use these parts of the story structure to retell the story. Students will apply this strategy and skill to a simpler text as they read *The New House*.

#### Corrective Feedback

Read the story with students. Ask: *Who did you meet? Where does the story take place? What happens?* Circle the names of characters and places in the story. Underline clues that tell about the events of the plot. Explain that the items circled and underlined are parts of the story structure.

Strategic

# Approaching Level

## Practice Reader Lesson 1

**Objective** Read to apply skills and strategies

**Materials**
- **Practice Reader:** *The New House*
- **Approaching Reproducible,** p. 12

### BEFORE READING

**Preview and Predict** Have students read the title and preview the first chapter. Ask students to make predictions about who the characters are, where they are, and what will happen to them in this section. Students should note any questions they have before they read.

**Review Vocabulary Words** Have students read the vocabulary words on the inside front cover. Briefly define each and ask students to state related words they have learned.

**Set a Purpose for Reading** *Let's read to find out how Skye feels about her new house.*

### DURING READING

**STRATEGY**
**ANALYZE STORY STRUCTURE**

Remind students that the characters, setting, and plot make up the structure of a story.

**SKILL**
**CHARACTER, SETTING, PLOT**

Remind students to think about the characters, setting, and plot as they read. Read Chapter 1 with students. Help students complete the Story Map.

As you read, help students decode unknown words. In addition, ask open-ended questions to facilitate rich discussion, such as *Why does the author want us to know about Skye's old house?* Build on students' responses to develop deeper understanding of the text.

Stop after each two pages and ask students to summarize the information they read to check their understanding before reading on. If they struggle, help students reread the difficult pages or passage. Then model how to figure out the characters, setting, and important events of the story.

### AFTER READING

Ask students to compare Skye's new home to their home. *How are the two places the same? How are they different?* Have students comment on which part of Skye's story they liked the best.

Practice Reader

**Digital Learning**

Use the **Practice Reader Audio CD** for fluency building *after* students read the book with your support during Small Group time.

Practice Reader

Strategic

# Approaching Level

## Practice Reader Lesson 2

**Objective** Reread to apply skills and strategies and develop fluency

**Materials**
- **Practice Reader:** *The New House*
- **Approaching Reproducible,** p. 13

### BEFORE READING

**Review Strategy and Skill** Review students' completed Story Maps from the first read. Remind students that the characters are the people or animals in the story, the setting is where and when the story takes place, and the plot is make up of the important events in the story. The story structure is made up of all of these elements.

**Review Vocabulary Words** Have students search the book for each vocabulary word. Ask students to read aloud the sentence containing the word and state the word's definition or provide related words. Point out any context clues provided, such as surrounding words.

**Set a Purpose for Reading** *Let's reread to check our understanding of the information in the book and to work on our reading fluency.*

### DURING READING

Reread *The New House* with students. Have them read silently two pages at a time, or read aloud to a partner. Stop and have students summarize before reading the next two pages. Model oral summaries as needed.

### AFTER READING

**Check Comprehension** Have partners complete the Comprehension Check on page 16. Review students' answers. Help students find evidence for their answers in the text.

**Model Fluency** Model reading the Practice Reader fluency passage on **Approaching Reproducible** page 13. Tell students to pay close attention to your phrasing, or how you group certain words together, as you read. Then read one sentence at a time and have students echo-read the sentences, copying your phrasing.

During independent reading time, have students work with a partner using the fluency passage. One student reads aloud, while the other repeats each sentence back. If students need additional support, have them listen to the "practice speed" version of the passage on the **Fluency Solutions Audio CD**.

**Approaching Reproducible,** page 13

**As I read, I will pay attention to phrasing.**

Dad took Skye's hand as they went down the steps to
11 the street. "Forty steps!" he said. "And I never have to
22 shovel them again." Skye just sighed.
28 At the hardware store, Skye trudged slowly behind
36 Dad. When he asked her to pick a color for her new room,
49 she just shrugged.
52 Dad looked upset. "I know you're sad about moving,"
61 he said. "But we want Grandma to come and live with
72 us." 73

**Comprehension Check**

1. Why is Skye sad? **Plot Development** Skye is sad because she is moving to a new house.
2. Where did Dad and Skye go? **Plot Development** They went to the hardware store.

| | Words Read | – | Number of Errors | = | Words Correct Score |
|---|---|---|---|---|---|
| First Read | | – | | = | |
| Second Read | | – | | = | |

Strategic

# Approaching Level

## Practice Reader Lesson 3

**Objective** Build fluency

**Materials** • **Practice Reader:** *The New House*

### FOCUS ON FLUENCY

**Timed Reading** Tell students that they will be doing a final timed reading of the fluency passage from *The New House* that they have been practicing. With each student, follow these directions:

- Place the passage facedown.
- When you say "Go," the student begins reading the passage aloud.
- When you say "Stop," the student stops reading the passage.

As they read, note words students mispronounce and their overall phrasing. Stop after one minute. Help students record and graph the number of words they read correctly.

### REREAD PREVIOUSLY READ BOOKS

- Distribute copies of this week's **Practice Readers** or sample books from the classroom library. Have students select two to reread. Tell students that rereading these books will help them develop their skills. The more times they read the same words, the quicker they will learn these words. This will make the reading of other books easier.
- Circulate and listen in as students read. Stop students periodically and ask them how they are figuring out difficult words and how they are monitoring their comprehension. Note students who need additional work with specific decoding or comprehension skills.
- Have students read other previously read Practice Readers during independent reading time or for homework.

### Meet Grade-Level Expectations

As an alternative to this day's lesson, guide students through a reading of the On Level Practice Reader. See page 33W. Since both books contain the same vocabulary, phonics, and comprehension skills, the scaffolding you provided will help most students gain access to this more challenging text.

### Book Talk

See page 33JJ. Students will work with peers of varying language abilities to discuss this week's Practice Readers.

Student Book

Student Book

### Decodable Text

Use the Reading *Triumphs* Anthology and the decodable stories in the **Teacher's Resource Book** to help students build fluency with basic decoding

Strategic

# Approaching Level

## Fluency

**Objectives** Reread selections to develop fluency; develop speaking skills

**Materials** • **Student Book:** *First Day Jitters,* "How to Be a Good Citizen"

### REREAD FOR FLUENCY

CA CONTENT STANDARD **R 3.1.3** Read aloud narrative and expository text fluently and accurately and with appropriate pacing, intonation, and expression.

- Have students reread a portion of *First Day Jitters*. Suggest that they focus on two to four of their favorite pages from the selection. Work with students to read the pages with appropriate phrasing.
- Provide time for students to read their sections of text to you. Comment on their phrasing and provide corrective feedback by modeling proper fluency.

### DEVELOP SPEAKING/LISTENING SKILLS

- Have students practice reading "How to Be a Good Citizen."
- Work with students to read with appropriate phrasing. Model reading a few lines at a time. Emphasize how you group words into phrases by paying attention to punctuation like commas and periods. Have students repeat.
- Provide time for students to read aloud the selection to partners. Ask students to give examples of when their partner used proper phrasing.

CA CONTENT STANDARD **LAS 3.1.7** Use clear and specific vocabulary to communicate ideas and establish the tone.

- Have students discuss other ways that they can be good citizens. Have them use clear and specific vocabulary to communicate their ideas and establish the tone.

Strategic

# Approaching Level

## Self-Selected Reading

**Objective** Read independently to identify character, setting, and plot

**Materials** • **Classroom Library** • other fiction books

### APPLY SKILLS TO INDEPENDENT READING

- Have students choose a fiction book for independent reading. (See the **Theme Bibliography** on pages T8–T9 for book suggestions.) Remind them that the characters are the people or animals in the story, the setting is where and when the story takes place, and the plot is made up of the events in the beginning, middle, and end of the story. Have students read their books and record the characters, setting, and story events on a Story Map.
- After reading, ask students to use their Story Maps to write or orally state a summary of the book. Provide time for students to share their summaries and comment on their reactions to the book. Ask: *Would you recommend this book to a classmate? Why or why not?*

Classroom Library

## Daily Planner

| | |
|---|---|
| DAY 1 | • Vocabulary |
| DAY 2 | • Phonics |
| DAY 3 | • Practice Reader Lesson 1 |
| DAY 4 | • Practice Reader Lesson 2<br>• Fluency |
| DAY 5 | • Self-Selected Reading |

Benchmark

# On Level

## Vocabulary

**Objective** Review vocabulary

**Materials** • **Vocabulary Cards**

TESTED SKILL

### REVIEW PREVIOUSLY TAUGHT WORDS

**Review Words** Display the **Vocabulary Cards** *chuckled, nervous, nonsense, fumbled,* and *trudged*. Point to each word, read it aloud, and have students chorally repeat.

Then provide the following Yes/No questions. Ask students to answer each question, justifying their answer. Allow other students to respond. Use the discussions to determine each student's depth of word knowledge.

- Do you feel *nervous* before taking a test?
- Do people usually *chuckle* during a funny movie?
- Is it *nonsense* to want to get good grades?
- Do you think graceful people usually *fumble* into things?
- Are people who *trudge* full of energy?

## Phonics/Word Study

**Objective** Decode multisyllabic words with short vowels

**Materials** • **Sound-Spelling WorkBoards**

TESTED SKILL

### RETEACH SKILL

CA CONTENT STANDARD R 3.1.2 Decode regular multisyllabic words.

- **Short Vowel Words** Point to the five short vowel **Sound-Spelling Cards** on the **WorkBoard** and review the spellings for these sounds. State each spelling and provide a sample word.
- Write the words below on the board. If necessary, divide the words into syllables using the syllable-scoop procedure to help students read one syllable at a time. When completed, point to the words in random order for students to chorally read.

| | | | | |
|---|---|---|---|---|
| content | cotton | nonstop | fossil | rotten |
| tidbit | zigzag | finish | upset | kickstand |
| topic | fabric | velvet | button | ribbon |

- **Spelling** Dictate the following words for students to spell on their WorkBoards: *problem, petted, sunset, scatter, cliff*. Guide students to use the Sound-Spelling Cards and model how to segment words, such as spelling a word syllable by syllable.

Sound-Spelling WorkBoard

Benchmark

# On Level

## Fluency

**Objectives** Reread selections to develop fluency; develop speaking skills

**Materials** • **Student Book:** *First Day Jitters,* "How to Be a Good Citizen"

### REREAD FOR FLUENCY

CA CONTENT STANDARD R 3.1.3 Read aloud narrative and expository text fluently and accurately and with appropriate pacing, intonation, and expression.

- Have students reread *First Day Jitters*. Work with students to read with appropriate phrasing. Model as needed.
- Provide time for students to read a section of text to you. Comment on their phrasing and provide corrective feedback.

### DEVELOP SPEAKING/LISTENING SKILLS

- Have students practice reading "How to Be a Good Citizen."
- Work with students to read with appropriate phrasing. Model reading a few lines at a time. Emphasize how you group words together into phrases by following the punctuation. Have students repeat.
- Provide time for students to read aloud the selection to the class. Ask students to identify times when the reader paused for a comma or stopped for a period.
- Have students ask each other questions about being a good citizen and answer the questions with details and elaboration.

CA CONTENT STANDARD LAS 3.1.3 Respond to questions with appropriate elaboration.

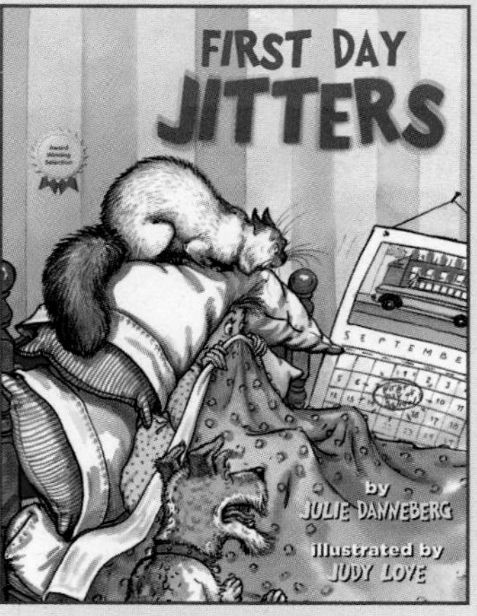

Student Book

Student Book

## Self-Selected Reading

**Objective** Read independently to identify character, setting, and plot

**Materials** • **Classroom Library** • other fiction books

### APPLY SKILLS TO INDEPENDENT READING

- Have students choose a fiction book for independent reading. (See the **Theme Bibliography** on pages T8–T9 for book suggestions.) Have students read their books and write down the characters, setting, and plot.
- After reading, ask students to use their Story Map to write a summary of the book. Provide time for students to share their summaries and comment on their reactions to the book. Ask: *Would you recommend this book to a classmate? Why or why not?*

Classroom Library

Practice Reader

Benchmark

# On Level

## Practice Reader Lesson 1

**Objective** Read to apply strategies and skills

**Materials**
- **Practice Reader:** *The New Kid*
- **Practice Book,** p. 12

### BEFORE READING

**Preview and Predict** Have students read the title and preview the book by reading the chapter titles and looking at the illustrations. Ask students to predict who the main characters are, where the story takes place, and what they think will happen at the beginning, middle, and end of the story.

**Review Vocabulary Words** Have students read the vocabulary words on the inside front cover. Ask students to state related words they have learned. Review definitions, as needed.

**Set a Purpose for Reading** *Let's read to find out what happens to Jay on his first day at a new school.*

### DURING READING

**STRATEGY**
**ANALYZE STORY STRUCTURE**

Remind students that the characters, setting, and story events make up the story's structure.

**SKILL**
**CHARACTER, SETTING, PLOT**

**CA CONTENT STANDARD R 3.3.3** Determine what characters are like by what they say or do and by how the author or illustrator portrays them.

Remind students that characters are people or animals in a story. The setting is where and when the story takes place, and the plot is made up of important events in the beginning, middle, and end of the story.

Read Chapter 1 with students. Ask open-ended questions to facilitate rich discussion, such as *What does the author want us to know about Jay's character?* Build on students' responses to develop deeper understanding of the text. Have students fill in the first section of the Story Map, then continue reading.

**Context Clues** As they read, have students point out this week's new vocabulary words and any context clues the author provides, such as nearby words with similar meanings.

### AFTER READING

Ask students to compare Jay's experience with their own or a friend's experience of starting at a new school or moving to a new place. *How were the experiences the same? Different?*

Benchmark

# On Level

## Practice Reader Lesson 2

**Objective** Reread to apply skills and strategies and develop fluency

**Materials**
- **Practice Reader:** *The New Kid*
- **Practice Book,** p. 13

### BEFORE READING

**Review Strategy and Skill** Review students' completed Story Maps from the first read. Remind students that the characters are the people in the story, the setting is where and when the story takes place, and the plot is made up of the important story events.

A story's structure is made up of the characters, the setting, and the plot. Have students use their Story Maps to summarize the story. If students' summaries are incomplete, provide a model summary or use a student summary and revise it as a group. Have students copy the revised summary in their Writer's Notebooks.

**Set a Purpose for Reading** *Let's reread to check our understanding of the information in the story and to work on our reading fluency.*

### DURING READING

Reread *The New Kid* with students. Have them read silently two pages at a time, or read aloud to a partner. Stop and have students summarize before reading the next two pages. Model oral summaries as needed.

### AFTER READING

**Check Comprehension** Have partners complete the Comprehension Check on page 16. Review students' answers. Help students find evidence for their answers in the text.

**CA CONTENT STANDARD R 3.1.3** Read aloud narrative and expository text fluently and accurately and with appropriate pacing, intonation, and expression.

**Model Fluency** Model reading the Practice Reader fluency passage on **Practice Book** page 13. Tell students to pay close attention to your phrasing as you read. Then read one sentence at a time and have students echo-read the sentences, copying your phrasing.

During independent reading time, have students work with a partner using the fluency passage. One student reads aloud, while the other repeats each sentence back. If students need additional support, have them listen to the "practice speed" version of the passage on the **Fluency Solutions Audio CD**.

Practice Reader

### Book Talk

See page 33JJ. Students will work with peers of varying language abilities to discuss this week's Practice Readers.

### Practice Book, page 13

**As I read, I will pay attention to phrasing.**

One Monday in November, Jay and his mother drove
9 to a yellow brick building with a sign in front that said:
21 "Rosewood Middle School." It was a big building—much
30 taller than Jay's old school.
35 Jay's mother filled out lots of forms. Before they left,
45 the school principal, Ms. Tucker, came out of her office
55 and shook Jay's hand. "Welcome to Rosewood," she said.
64 "We'll see you tomorrow."
68 On Tuesday morning, Jay's older sister, Eva, gave him
77 a ride to school. "Are you nervous?" she asked.
86 Jay shrugged and then nodded. "I hate being the new kid,"
97 he admitted. 99

**Comprehension Check**

1. Who is the main character and what is the story about? **Plot Development** Jay; going to a new school for the first time
2. Why is Jay nervous? **Plot Development** Jay is nervous because he does not like being the new kid at school.

| | Words Read | – | Number of Errors | = | Words Correct Score |
|---|---|---|---|---|---|
| First Read | | – | | = | |
| Second Read | | – | | = | |

**Daily Planner**

| | |
|---|---|
| DAY 1 | • Practice Reader Lesson 1 |
| DAY 2 | • Practice Reader Lesson 2 |
| DAY 3 | • Phonics |
| DAY 4 | • Vocabulary<br>• Fluency |
| DAY 5 | • Self-Selected Reading |

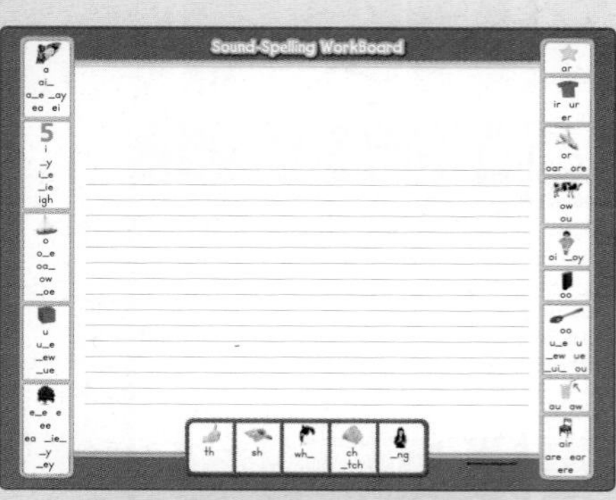
Sound-Spelling WorkBoard

Advanced

# Beyond Level

## Phonics/Word Study

**Objective** Decode multisyllabic words with short vowels

**Materials** • **Sound-Spelling WorkBoards**

TESTED SKILL

### EXTEND/ACCELERATE

CA CONTENT STANDARD R 3.1.2 Decode regular multisyllabic words.

- **Read Multisyllabic Words with Short Vowels** Write the words below on the board. Challenge students to read the words, using known word parts. When completed, point to the words in random order for students to chorally read.

| | | | | |
|---|---|---|---|---|
| chapter | freshest | undressed | invented | investment |
| frantic | drumstick | citizen | unpacked | fantastic |
| magnetic | unlatched | backpacking | vanishing | resident |

- **Define Words** Ask students to use their knowledge of word parts to figure out the meanings of the above words. Then have partners find the words in a dictionary and confirm or revise the meanings. Challenge students to use these words in this week's writing assignments.
- **Spell Short Vowel Words** Dictate the following words for students to spell on their **WorkBoards:** *inspecting, fastest, instrument, artistic, reckless.* Write the words for students to self-correct.

## Vocabulary

**Objectives** Review prefixes; write a poem

**Materials** • none

TESTED SKILL

### ENRICH VOCABULARY

CA CONTENT STANDARD R 3.1.8 Use knowledge of prefixes and suffixes to determine the meaning of words.

- **Review Prefixes** Remind students that prefixes are added to the beginning of a word to change its meaning. Review common prefixes like *un-* and *non-*. Have students brainstorm a list of prefixes and them write a short story, using as many prefixes as they can.
- **Write a Poem** Ask students to think about spending a day in the desert. Challenge them to write a poem about their day, using the vocabulary words they have learned in this week's selections and adding personification.

Advanced

# Beyond Level

## Fluency

**Objectives** Reread selections to develop fluency; develop speaking skills

**Materials** • **Student Book:** *First Day Jitters,* "How to Be a Good Citizen"

### REREAD FOR FLUENCY

**CA CONTENT STANDARD R 3.1.3** Read aloud narrative and expository text fluently and accurately and with appropriate pacing, intonation, and expression.

- Have students reread *First Day Jitters.* Work with students to read the book with the appropriate phrasing.
- Provide time for students to read a section of text to you. Comment on their phrasing and provide corrective feedback.

### DEVELOP SPEAKING/LISTENING SKILLS

**CA CONTENT STANDARD R 3.1.3** Read aloud narrative and expository text fluently and accurately and with appropriate pacing, intonation, and expression.

- Have students practice reading "How to Be a Good Citizen."
- Work with students to read with appropriate phrasing. Model reading a few lines at a time. Emphasize how you group words together according to the punctuation to make the sentences sound like normal speech. Have students repeat.

**CA CONTENT STANDARD LAS 3.1.9** Read prose and poetry aloud with fluency, rhythm, and pace, using appropriate intonation and vocal patterns to emphasize important passages of the text being read.

- Provide time for students to read aloud the selection to the class. Ask students to identify when the reader paused or stopped for punctuation.
- Challenge students to present an oral summary of "How to Be a Good Citizen."

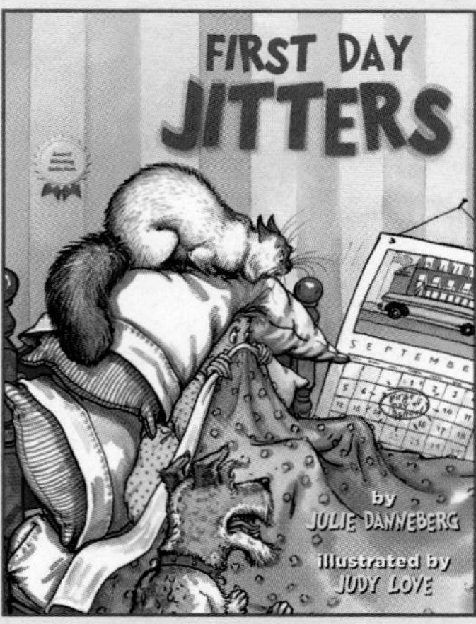

Student Book

Student Book

## Self-Selected Reading

**Objective** Read independently to identify the characters, setting, and plot of a story

**Materials** • **Classroom Library** • other fiction books

### APPLY SKILLS TO INDEPENDENT READING

- Have students choose a fiction book for independent reading. (See the **Theme Bibliography** on pages T8–T9 for book suggestions.) Have students read their books and write down the characters, setting, and plot.
- After reading, ask students to use their story maps to write a summary of the book. Provide time for students to share their summaries and comment on their reactions to the book. Ask: *Would you recommend this book to a classmate? Why or why not?*

Classroom Library

Practice Reader

Advanced

# Beyond Level

## Practice Reader Lesson 1

**Objective** Read to apply strategies and skills

**Materials**
- **Practice Reader:** *The New Hometown*
- **Beyond Reproducible,** p. 12

### BEFORE READING

**Preview and Predict** Have students preview the book by reading the title and chapter titles and looking at the illustrations. Ask students to predict what they think this book is about and where and when it takes place.

**Review Vocabulary Words** Have students read the vocabulary words on the inside front cover. Ask students to state each definition and any related words they have learned.

**Set a Purpose for Reading** *Let's read to find out how Nicky feels about her new hometown.*

### DURING READING

**STRATEGY**
**ANALYZE STORY STRUCTURE**

Ask students to define *story structure*. If necessary, remind students that the story structure is made up of the characters, setting, and story events.

**SKILL**
**CHARACTER, SETTING, PLOT**

**CA CONTENT STANDARD R 3.3.3** Determine what characters are like by what they say or do and by how the author or illustrator portrays them.

Ask students to define the terms *character, setting,* and *plot*. Remind students that the characters are the people or animals in the story, the setting is where and when the story takes place, and the plot is made up of the main story events.

Read the book with students. Ask open-ended questions to facilitate rich discussion, such as *What is the author's message about moving to a new place? How does the author show that Nicky's attitude has changed by the end of the story?* Build on students' responses to develop deeper understanding of the text. Have students fill in the Story Map independently as they read.

### AFTER READING

Ask students to compare themselves to Nicky. *How would they act if they were in Nicky's situation? Would they act the same as Nicky, or would they behave differently?* Prompt them to write tips for newcomers about how to adjust to life in a new town.

Advanced

# Beyond Level

## Practice Reader Lesson 2

**Objective** Reread to apply skills and strategies and develop fluency

**Materials**
- **Practice Reader:** *The New Hometown*
- **Beyond Reproducible,** p. 13

### BEFORE READING

**Review Strategy and Skill** Review students' completed Story Maps from the first read. Have students use it to summarize the story.

Remind students that a summary includes the characters, setting, and main events from the book. If students' summaries are incomplete, provide a model summary or use a student summary and revise it as a group. Have students copy the revised summary in their Writer's Notebooks.

**Set a Purpose for Reading** *Let's reread to check our understanding of the information in the book and work on our reading fluency.*

### DURING READING

Have students reread *The New Hometown* silently or with a partner. If reading in pairs, prompt students to stop every two pages and summarize or ask their partner probing questions.

### AFTER READING

**Check Comprehension** Have students independently complete the Comprehension Check on page 16. Review students' answers. Help students find evidence for their answers in the text.

**CA CONTENT STANDARD R 3.1.3** Read aloud narrative and expository text fluently and accurately and with appropriate pacing, intonation, and expression.

**Model Fluency** Model reading the Practice Reader fluency passage on **Beyond Reproducible** page 13. Tell students to pay close attention to your phrasing as you read. Then read one sentence at a time and have students echo-read the sentences, copying your phrasing.

During independent reading time, have students work with a partner using the fluency passage. One student reads aloud, while the other repeats each sentence back. Students can check their fluency by reading along with the "expert speed" version of the passage on the **Fluency Solutions Audio CD**.

Practice Reader

**Book Talk**

See page 33JJ. Students will work with peers of varying language abilities to discuss this week's Practice Readers.

**Beyond Reproducible,** page 13

**As I read, I will pay attention to phrasing.**

"Come on, lazy bones! What are you doing inside on this
11 beautiful day?" Mom said, as she walked into Nicky's room.
21 Nicky was lying on her bed, turning the pages of a
32 magazine. She looked up at her mother and sighed.
41 "What's there to do?" she asked.
47 "Let's hop in the car and go explore our new town," said
59 Mom. She watched as Nicky rolled slowly off the bed.
69 Then they both headed downstairs.
74 "I can't believe we have to drive every time we want to
86 buy something!" Nicky said. "I used to be able to walk to
98 all the stores by myself!"
103 Mom nodded her head a little sadly. "I know this is very
115 different from living in the city. It will take awhile for us to
128 get used to being in a new place, but maybe this little town
141 will surprise us." 144

**Comprehension Check**

1. How does Nicky feel about living in a new town? **Plot Development** Nicky seems sad and misses the city.
2. What advice does Nicky's mom give her? **Plot Development** Nicky's mom says that it will take time to get used to living in a new place.

| | Words Read | – | Number of Errors | = | Words Correct Score |
|---|---|---|---|---|---|
| First Read | | – | | = | |
| Second Read | | – | | = | |

30 MINUTES DAILY

## Daily Planner

| | |
|---|---|
| DAY 1 | • Build Background Knowledge<br>• Vocabulary |
| DAY 2 | • Vocabulary<br>• Access to Core Content *First Day Jitters* |
| DAY 3 | • Vocabulary<br>• Grammar<br>• Access to Core Content *First Day Jitters* |
| DAY 4 | • Vocabulary<br>• Writing/Spelling<br>• Access to Core Content "How to Be a Good Citizen" |
| DAY 5 | • Vocabulary<br>• Practice Reader *The First Day*<br>• Self-Selected Reading |

StudentWorks Plus

# English Learners

## Prepare to Read

**Content Objective** Describe the first day at a new school
**Language Objective** Use key words to describe the first day at a new school
**Materials** **StudentWorks Plus** (interactive eBook)

### BUILD BACKGROUND KNOWLEDGE

CA CONTENT STANDARD R 3.1.3 Read aloud narrative and expository text fluently and accurately and with appropriate pacing, intonation, and expression.

- Have students preview *First Day Jitters* using **StudentWorks Plus,** the interactive eBook. This version of the Student Book contains oral summaries in multiple languages, online multilingual glossaries, word-by-word highlighting, and questions that assess and build comprehension.
- Students can build their word reading fluency by reading along as the text is read or by listening during the first reading and, at the end of each paragraph, returning to the beginning of the paragraph and reading along.
- Students can build their comprehension by reviewing the definitions of key words in the online glossary and by answering the comprehension questions. When appropriate, the text required to answer the question is highlighted to provide students with additional support and scaffolding.
- Following the reading, ask students to respond in writing to a question that links the story to their personal experiences, such as: *Have you ever moved to a new neighborhood or gone to a new school? If so, describe what it was like and how you felt on your first day there.*

## Academic Language

**Language Objective** Use academic language in classroom conversations

- This week's academic words are **boldfaced** throughout the lesson. Define the word in context and provide a clear example from the selection. Then ask students to generate an example or a word with a similar meaning.

### Academic Language Used in Whole Group Instruction

| Theme Words | Key Selection Words | Strategy and Skill Words |
|---|---|---|
| **excited**<br>**assist** | **chuckled**<br>**nervous**<br>**nonsense**<br>**fumbled**<br>**trudged** | **analyze**<br>**structure**<br>**character**<br>**setting**<br>**plot**<br>**prefixes**<br>**statements**<br>**questions**<br>**capitalize** |

# English Learners

## Vocabulary

**Language Objective** Demonstrate understanding and use of key words by describing the first day at a new school

**Materials** • **Visual Vocabulary Resources** • **English Learner Resource Book**

TESTED SKILL

### PRETEACH KEY VOCABULARY

**All Language Levels** Use the **Visual Vocabulary Resources** to preteach the key selection words *chuckled, nervous, nonsense, fumbled,* and *trudged*. Focus on 1–2 words per day. Use the following routine that appears in detail on the cards.

- Define the word in English and provide the example given.
- Define the word in Spanish, if appropriate, and indicate if the word is a cognate.
- Display the picture and explain how it illustrates or demonstrates the word. Engage students in structured partner-talk about the image, using the key word.
- Ask students to chorally say the word three times.
- Point out any known sound-spellings or focus on a key aspect of phonemic awareness related to the word.
- Distribute copies of the Vocabulary Glossary in the **English Learner Resource Book** page 14.

### PRETEACH FUNCTION WORDS AND PHRASES

**All Language Levels** Use the Visual Vocabulary Resources to preteach the function words and phrases *tumbled out of, drive down the street, slump down,* and *tunnel down*. Focus on one word per day. Use the detailed routine on the cards.

- Define the word in English and, if appropriate, in Spanish. Point out if the word is a cognate.
- Refer to the picture and engage students in talk about the word; for example, students will Partner Talk using sentence frames or they will listen to sentences and replace a word or phrase with the new function word.
- Ask students to chorally repeat the word three times.

### TEACH BASIC WORDS

For **Beginning** and **Early Intermediate** students, use the Visual Vocabulary Resources to teach the basic words *bedroom, doorway, window, shade, kitchen,* and *bathroom*. Teach these "household" words using the routine provided on the card.

**Visual Vocabulary Resources**

**EL Resource Book,** page 14

Use the word chart to study this week's vocabulary words.
Write a sentence using each word in your writer's notebook.

| Word | Context Sentence | Illustration |
| --- | --- | --- |
| nervous | She was nervous when she went up to bat. | When do you feel nervous? |
| fumbled | I fumbled the ball. | |
| chuckled | Dad chuckled at my joke. | |
| nonsense | The class was silly. Ms. Norris asked for no more nonsense. | |
| trudged | The kids trudged up the steep hill. | When you trudge, do you feel tired or strong? |

Student Book

English Learner Resource Book

# English Learners

## Access to Core Content

**Content Objective** Read grade-level text
**Language Objective** Discuss text using key words and sentence frames
**Materials** • **English Learner Resource Book,** pp. 2–13

TESTED SKILL

### PRETEACH MAIN SELECTION (PAGES 10–27)

Use the Interactive Question-Response Guide on **English Learner Resource Book pages 2–11** to introduce students to *First Day Jitters*. Preteach half of the selection on **Day 2** and half on **Day 3**.

- Use the prompts provided in the guide to develop meaning and vocabulary. Use the Partner Talk and whole-class responses to engage students and increase student talk.
- When completed, have partners reread the story.

### PRETEACH PAIRED SELECTION (PAGES 30–31)

Use the Interactive Question-Response Guide in the English Learner Resource Book pages 12–13 to preview the paired selection "How to Be a Good Citizen." Preteach the selection on **Day 4**.

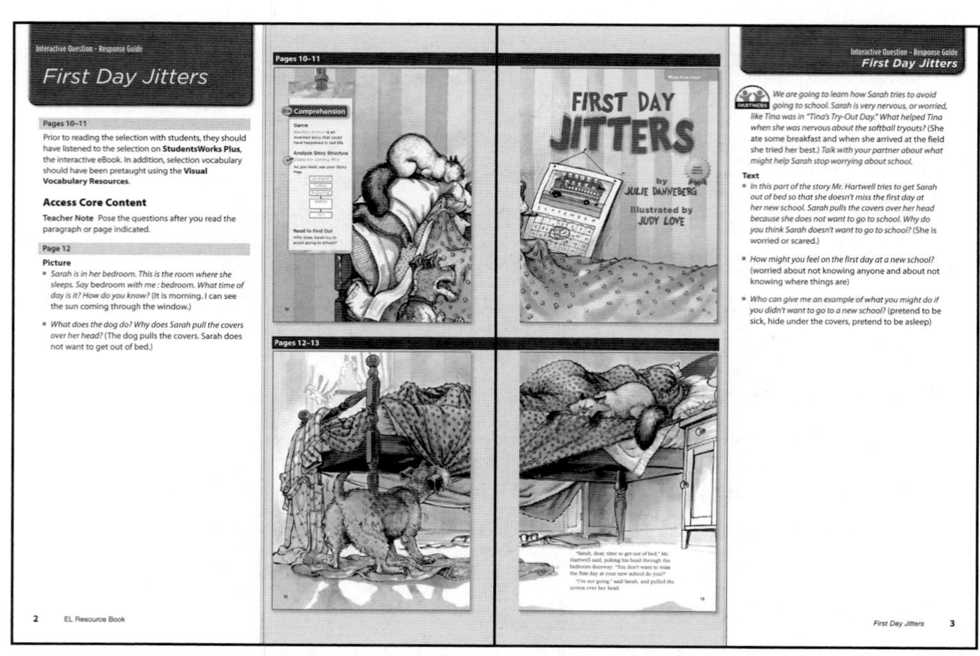
Interactive Question - Response Guide

*First Day Jitters*

Pages 10–11

Prior to reading the selection with students, they should have listened to the selection on **StudentsWorks Plus**, the interactive eBook. In addition, selection vocabulary should have been pretaught using the **Visual Vocabulary Resources**.

**Access Core Content**

**Teacher Note** Pose the questions after you read the paragraph or page indicated.

Page 12

**Picture**

- *Sarah is in her bedroom. This is the room where she sleeps. Say* bedroom *with me : bedroom. What time of day is it? How do you know?* (It is morning. I can see the sun coming through the window.)
- *What does the dog do? Why does Sarah pull the covers over her head?* (The dog pulls the covers. Sarah does not want to get out of bed.)

Interactive Question - Response Guide

*First Day Jitters*

PARTNERS *We are going to learn how Sarah tries to avoid going to school. Sarah is very nervous, or worried, like Tina was in "Tina's Try-Out Day." What helped Tina when she was nervous about the softball tryouts?* (She ate some breakfast and when she arrived at the field she tried her best.) *Talk with your partner about what might help Sarah stop worrying about school.*

**Text**

- *In this part of the story Mr. Hartwell tries to get Sarah out of bed so that she doesn't miss the first day at her new school. Sarah pulls the covers over her head because she does not want to go to school. Why do you think Sarah doesn't want to go to school?* (She is worried or scared.)
- *How might you feel on the first day at a new school?* (worried about not knowing anyone and about not knowing where things are)
- *Who can give me an example of what you might do if you didn't want to go to a new school?* (pretend to be sick, hide under the covers, pretend to be asleep)

Interactive Question-Response Guide Sample

# English Learners

## Fluency

**Content Objective** Reread selections to develop fluency; develop speaking skills
**Language Objective** Tell a partner what a selection is about
**Materials** • **Student Book:** *First Day Jitters,* "How to Be a Good Citizen"

### REREAD FOR FLUENCY

CA CONTENT STANDARD R 3.1.3 Read aloud narrative and expository text fluently and accurately and with appropriate pacing, intonation, and expression.

- Have students reread a portion of *First Day Jitters*. Suggest that they focus on two to four of their favorite pages from the selection. Work with students to read the pages with appropriate phrasing; for example, read one sentence at a time, pointing out how you follow punctuation such as commas to group certain words together as you read. Have students echo-read the sentences, copying your phrasing.
- Provide time for students to read their sections of text to you. Comment on their phrasing and provide corrective feedback by modeling proper fluency.

### DEVELOP SPEAKING/LISTENING SKILLS

- Have students practice reading "How to Be a Good Citizen." Work with students to read with accuracy and appropriate phrasing.
- Provide time for students to read to a partner. Ask students to discuss the characteristics of a good citizen. Provide the sentence frame: *A good citizen is* _____.

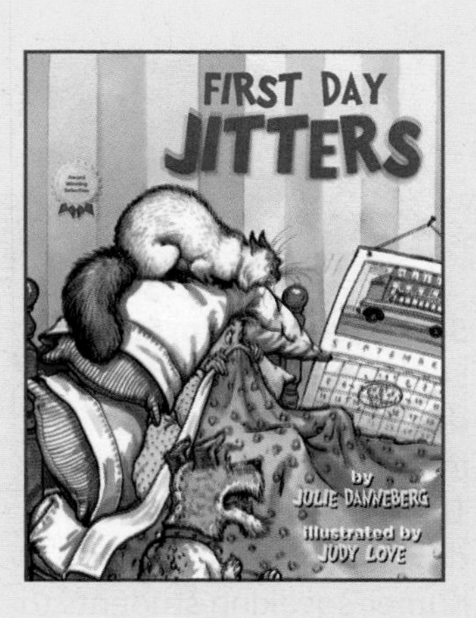

Student Book

## Self-Selected Reading

**Content Objective** Read independently
**Language Objective** Orally retell information learned
**Materials** • **Classroom Library** • other fiction books

### APPLY SKILLS TO INDEPENDENT READING

- Have students choose a fiction book for independent reading. (See the **Theme Bibliography** on pages T8–T9 for book suggestions.)
- After reading, ask students to orally summarize the book. Provide time for students to comment on their reactions to the book and share them with classmates. Ask: *Would you recommend this book to a classmate? Why or why not?*

Classroom Library

## Transfer Skills

**Sentence Structure** Unlike English, Hmong and Khmer do not use subject-verb inversion in questions. This may make it more difficult for Hmong- and Khmer-speaking students to identify questions and form them correctly. Have these students practice expressing statements (The teacher is Mr. Green.) as questions (Is the teacher Mr. Green?) as you point out the correct placement of subject and verb in each.

## Corrective Feedback

During whole group grammar lessons, follow the routine on the **Grammar Transparencies** to provide students with extra support. This routine includes completing the items with English Learners while other students work independently, having students reread the sentences with partners to build fluency, and providing a generative task such as writing a new sentence using the skill.

# English Learners

## Grammar

**Content Objective** Identify statements and questions
**Language Objective** Speak in complete sentences, using sentence frames

TESTED SKILL

### STATEMENTS AND QUESTIONS

- Remind students that a statement tells something and ends in a period, and that a question asks something and ends in a question mark. Write examples of each on the board, such as: *My friend has brown hair. What color hair do you have?*
- Write sentences on the board, such as those provided below. Have students provide the correct end punctuation, either a period or a question mark.

  *Who is your new teacher* ____

  *I am looking for Room 108* ____

  *Today is the first day of school* ____

  *What time is lunch* ____

### PEER DISCUSSION STARTERS

- Write the following sentences on the board.

  Many students are ____ on their first day of school.

  It is hard to be new at something because ____.
- Pair students and have them complete each sentence frame. Ask them to expand on their sentences by providing as many details as they can from this week's readings. Circulate, listen in, and take note of each student's language use and proficiency.

## English Learners

UNIVERSAL ACCESS

Build on students' responses to help move them to the next level of language acquisition; for example, if students say "Many students are nervous on their first day of school," say "That's correct. Many students are nervous. They have to meet new teachers and learn new routines. They might be afraid of getting lost. However, some students are excited or happy on their first day of school. Now turn to your partner and ask why some students might be excited or happy on their first day of school."

Provide the following sentence frames orally or in writing for support.

**Beginning/Early Intermediate** A new student feels ____.

**Intermediate** A new teacher might be nervous because ____.

**Early Advanced** It is easier to start out at a new school when ____.

# English Learners

## Writing/Spelling

**Content Objective** Spell words correctly
**Language Objective** Write in complete sentences, using sentence frames

**VOCABULARY**

- Write the key vocabulary words on the board: *chuckled, nervous, nonsense, fumbled, trudged*. Have students copy each word on their **WorkBoards**. Then help them say each word and write sentences for each word. Provide sentence starters such as:

  *_____ chuckled at the teacher's joke.*

  *Some _____ get nervous on the first day of school.*

  *School is for _____, not for nonsense.*

  *He fumbled in his _____ for his new pencil case.*

  *The students trudged _____ down the hallway.*

- Help students spell words using their growing knowledge of English sound-spelling relationships. Model how to segment the word students are trying to spell and attach a spelling to each sound (or spellings to each syllable if a multisyllabic word). Use the **Sound-Spelling Cards** to reinforce the spellings for each English sound.
- Dictate the following words for students to spell: *bit, bat, sit, not, cut, net, lot, get, but,* and *cat*. Guide students using the Sound-Spelling Cards as they spell each word.
- When completed, review the meanings of words that can be easily demonstrated or explained. Use actions, gestures, and available pictures.

Sound-Spelling WorkBoard

### Phonics/Word Study

For English Learners who need more practice with this week's phonics/spelling skill, see the Approaching Level lesson on page 33L. Focus on minimal contrasts, articulation, and those sounds that do not transfer from the student's first language to English. For a complete listing of transfer sounds, see pages T18–T33.

Practice Reader

# English Learners

## Practice Reader

**Content Objective** Read to apply skills and strategies
**Language Objective** Retell information using complete sentences
**Materials** • **Practice Reader:** *The First Day* • **English Learner Resource Book,** p. 15

TESTED SKILL

### BEFORE READING

CA CONTENT STANDARD R 3.2.4 Recall major points in the text and make and modify predictions about forthcoming information.

- **Preview** Read the title *The First Day*. Ask: *What's the title? Say it again.* Repeat with the author's name. Then page through the book. Use simple language to tell about each page. Immediately follow up with questions, such as: *They are in a car. Where do you think they are going? The teacher does not look happy. Why might that be? It must be time for lunch. Does this look like our cafeteria?*
- **Review Skills** Use the inside front cover to review the phonics skill and vocabulary words.
- **Set a Purpose** Say: *Let's read to find out about Jay's first day in a new school.*

### DURING READING

- Have students whisper-read each page, or use the differentiated suggestions below. Circulate, listen in, and provide corrective feedback, such as modeling how to blend a decodable word or clarifying meaning by using techniques from the Interactive Question-Response Guides.
- **Retell** Stop after every two pages and ask students to state the main ideas they have learned so far. Reinforce language by restating students' comments when they have difficulty using story-specific words. Provide differentiated sentence frames to support students' responses and engage students in partner talk where appropriate.

### English Learners

UNIVERSAL ACCESS

#### Beginning/Early Intermediate

**Echo-Read** Have children echo-read after you.

**Check Comprehension** Point to pictures and ask questions such as: *Where is Jay going today?*

#### Intermediate

**Choral-Read** Have children choral-read with you.

**Check Comprehension** Ask questions/prompts such as: *Is Jay happy to be at a new school? What does the author tell you about Jay's feelings?*

#### Early Advanced

**Choral-Read** Have children choral-read.

**Check Comprehension** *Ask: What makes Jay feel better? Find sentences that show how Jay's feelings begin to change.*

# English Learners

## AFTER READING

CA CONTENT STANDARD **LAS 3.1.3** Respond to questions with appropriate elaboration.

**Book Talk** Write the **Book Talk Prompts** below on the board or distribute copies of **English Learner Resource Book** page 15. Students will work with peers of varying language abilities to discuss them. Form groups so that students who read the Beyond Level, On level, Approaching Level, and English Learner versions of *The First Day* are in the same group.

Help students determine who will be the Leader for the discussion. Then have students discuss the following:

- **Describe how difficult it can be to move to a new home or neighborhood.**
- **Tell some ways to explore these new places.**
- **Explain why being in a new place can make you feel nervous.**
- **Give examples of how to become more comfortable in your new home or new school.**
- **Retell how making new friends or meeting new people is important to do when you are in a new school or neighborhood.**
- **Write one question about the book to ask your group.**
- **Write one question about the book to ask your group.**

**English Learner Resource Book**

**Develop Listening and Speaking Skills** Tell students to remember the following:

- Use clear and specific vocabulary to communicate ideas. Suggest they use the weekly vocabulary words in their discussions.
- Take turns speaking and listening. Give everyone a chance to speak.
- Retell, paraphrase, and explain information shared by others.
- Clarify and enhance the discussion through the use of pictures and props. Ask, *how does this picture help you better understand the story?*
- Connect and relate prior knowledge and experiences to ideas brought up in the discussion. Ask, *have you ever felt the same way as the character feels on this page?*

CA CONTENT STANDARD **LAS 3.1.2** Connect and relate prior experiences, insights, and ideas to those of a speaker.

### Newcomer

**Survival Skills: Introduce Self** Teach children how to introduce themselves, ask for other classmates' names, and say *Hello/Goodbye.* Use the sentence frames *My name is ______* and *What is your name?* Model dialogues, such as *Hello. My name is <insert name>. What is your name?* Have children repeat and practice with a partner.

## Big Question Board LAS 3.1.2, LAS 3.1.6

**WRAP UP** Tell students to add information learned this week related to the unit theme *Personal Experiences: Let's Learn*. Students should record how *First Day Jitters* adds to their growing knowledge of the theme. Students should also record any research facts they have uncovered throughout the week or questions they want to explore as they continue reading the selections in the unit. Have students present the information they learned. Remind them of the following speaking and listening skills:

- **Speaking** Tell students that when presenting information, they should have a clear beginning, middle, and end. They should also provide concrete details related to their topic to help the listeners understand the information. Suggest that they write what they want to say on three note cards: a beginning card, middle card, and ending card. Have them practice prior to giving the presentation.
- **Listening** Tell students to listen carefully and try to connect what they hear to their prior experiences. Provide time for them to share any thoughts or insights that can add to the information shared.

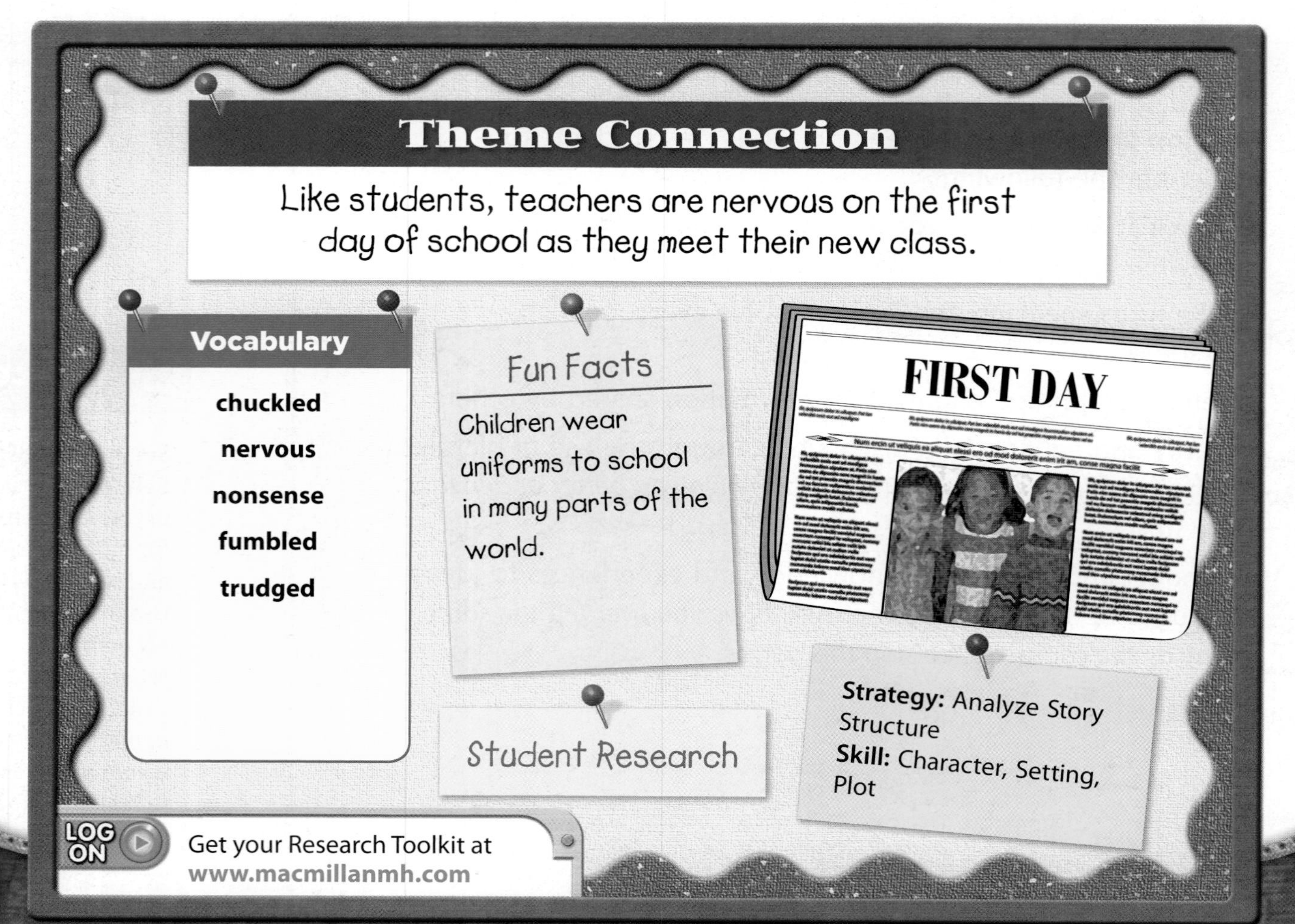

# Week 2 At a Glance

## WHOLE GROUP

### Phonics/Word Study
Final *e*, Multisyllabic Words

### Vocabulary
Robust Words: *auditions, adventure, exploring, sparkling, fantastic, success*

Word Families

### Comprehension
Strategy: Make Inferences and Analyze
Skill: Cause and Effect

Skill: Character, Setting, Plot

### Fluency
Intonation

### Spelling
Final *e*: *date, fine, rose, lake, life, home, safe, rice, globe, plane, wise, smoke, grade, smile, come*

### Grammar/Mechanics
Commands and Exclamations

Punctuation in Commands and Exclamations

### Writing
Topic Development: Moment

### Read Aloud
Genre: Poetry

## SMALL GROUP

### Differentiated Instruction for Tested Skills

Approaching Level | On Level | Beyond Level | English Learners

## Teacher Tools

### Technology to help plan and implement instruction

**PREPARE**
- Professional Development Videos
- Parent Connection

**TEACH**
- Theme Launcher Video
- Classroom Presentation Toolkit
- Vocabulary PuzzleMaker
- Sound Pronunciation CD

**PLAN/ORGANIZE**

Go to **www.macmillanmh.com** for Online Lesson Planner

TeacherWorks Plus™ All-In-One Planner and Resource Center

**ASSESS**

Assessment Online

ExamView® CD-ROM

# Weekly Literature

## Student Book

**A mix of fiction and nonfiction connected to:**

- Unit Theme
- California Content Standards

### Main Selection

**Genre** Realistic Fiction

### Preteach Vocabulary and Comprehension

**Genre** Fiction

### Paired Selection

**Genre** Legend

## Support Literature

**Resources to build robust vocabulary, fluency, and content knowledge**

### Interactive Read-Aloud Anthology

- Listening Comprehension
- Readers Theater Plays

### Content Reader

- Meets all California Science and History/Social Science Standards

# Resources for Differentiated Instruction

## Skill-Based Practice Readers

AUDIO CD

- Same Theme
- Same Vocabulary/Phonics
- Same Comprehension Skills

Approaching Level

On Level

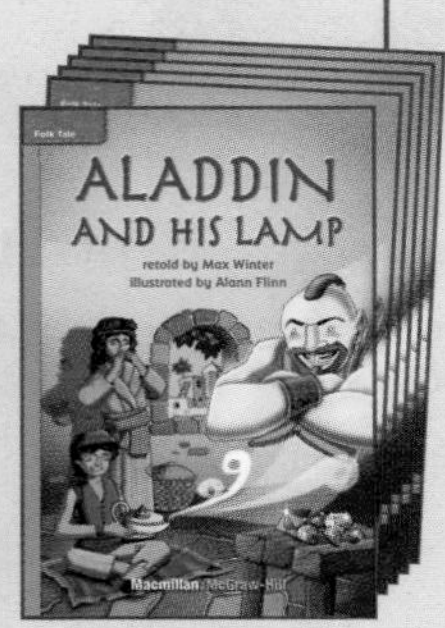


Beyond Level

English Learner

On Level Practice Reader sheltered for English Learners

## Intensive Vocabulary

Build robust vocabulary with fiction and nonfiction

Oral Vocabulary Cards

## Intervention Kit

- Intervention Anthology
- Phonemic Awareness Teacher's Edition
- Phonics/Word Study Teacher's Edition
- Comprehension Teacher's Edition
- Vocabulary Teacher's Edition
- Fluency Teacher's Edition
- Writing and Grammar Teacher's Edition

## StudentWorks Plus

- eBook
- Use for preteaching
- Summaries in multiple languages
- Word-by-Word Reading
- Assessment

## Practice Book and Reproducibles

Also available:

**Approaching Reproducible**

**Beyond Reproducible**

## Home-School Connection

- Family letters in English, Spanish, Hmong, Vietnamese, Cantonese, Khmer
- Take-Home Stories

## Visual Vocabulary Resources

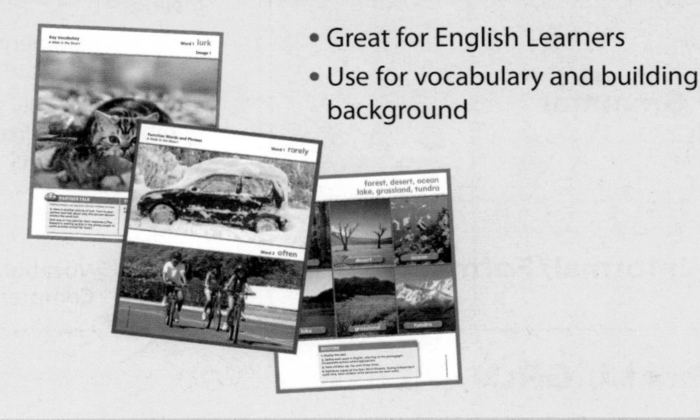

- Great for English Learners
- Use for vocabulary and building background

# Suggested Lesson Plan

LOG ON

Go to www.macmillanmh.com for Online Lesson Planner

**Amazing Grace, pp. 38–57**

| WHOLE GROUP | DAY 1 | DAY 2 |
| --- | --- | --- |
| **ORAL LANGUAGE**  15–20 min<br>• Listening Comprehension<br>• Speaking/Viewing | **Listening/Speaking/Viewing**<br>**Focus Question** What are some ways in which we can enjoy the power of books?<br>Read Aloud: "The Sure-Footed Shoe Finder," 34L–34M<br>Build Background, 34 | **Listening/Speaking**<br>**Focus Question** How do books help Grace achieve her dreams? |
| **WORD STUDY**  30–40 min<br>• Vocabulary<br>• Phonics/Word Study<br>• Spelling |  **Vocabulary** R 3.2.2<br>*auditions, adventure, exploring, sparkling, fantastic, success* 37, 63A<br>Practice Book, 22<br>**Strategy:** Word Families, 36<br> **Spelling** Pretest words with Final e, 63C<br>Practice Book, 28 LC 3.1.8 | **Vocabulary** R 3.1.4, R 3.2.2 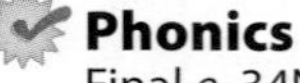<br>Review Words, Word Families, 38, 63A<br>Practice Book, 27<br> **Phonics**<br>Final *e*, 34N–34O<br>Practice Book, 21 R 3.1.1, R 3.1.2<br>**Spelling** Word Sorts, 63C LC 3.1.8<br>Reproducible, SP4 |
| **READING** 30–40 min<br>• Comprehension<br>• Fluency | **Read** "The Big Show," 36–37<br> Student Book<br>**Comprehension**, 37A–37B<br>**Strategy:** Make Inferences and Analyze R 3.2.2<br>**Skill:** Cause and Effect<br>Practice Book, 23<br>**Fluency** Model Fluency, 34M R 3.1.3 | **Read** *Amazing Grace*, 38–57<br>Student Book<br>**Comprehension**, 38–57<br>**Strategy:** Make Inferences and Analyze R 3.2.2 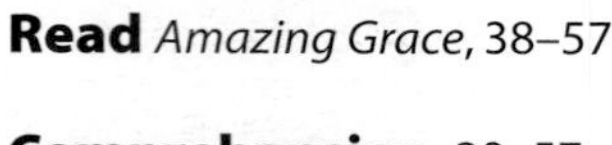<br>**Skill:** Cause and Effect<br>Practice Book, 24<br>**Fluency** Repeated Reading: Intonation, 59A R 3.1.3 |
| **LANGUAGE ARTS**  30–40 min<br>• Writing<br>• Grammar |  **Writing**<br>**Daily Writing Prompt** Write about a time you felt bored. What did you do to overcome the feeling?<br>Topic Development: Moment, 64–65 W 3.1.1, W 3.2.1b<br>**Grammar** Daily Language Activities, 63E<br>Commands and Exclamations, 63E<br>Reproducible, GR4 LC 3.1.1 |  **Writing**<br>**Daily Writing Prompt** Describe a fictional character you would like to be.<br>Focus on a Moment, 65A W 3.1.1, W 3.2.1b<br>Practice Book, 32<br> **Grammar** Daily Language Activities, 63E<br>Commands and Exclamations, 63E<br>Practice Book, 30 LC 3.1.1 |
| **ASSESSMENT**<br>• Informal/Formal | **Quick Check** **Vocabulary**, 36<br>**Comprehension**, 37B | **Quick Check** **Comprehension**, 57 |

 45–60 min

**SMALL GROUP Lesson Plan** | **Differentiated Instruction 65I–65HH**

## California Standards

**Vocabulary**
Vocabulary Words
Word Families
R 3.1.4

**Comprehension**
**Strategy:** Make Inferences and Analyze
**Skill:** Cause and Effect
R 3.2.2

**Writing**
Focus on a Moment
W 3.1.1, W 3.2.1b, W 3.1.4

**Physical Science**
PS 3.2.a

## DAY 3

### Listening/Speaking

**Focus Question** Read "The Big Show" on pages 36–37. Compare the play that the children made with the class play in *Amazing Grace*. How are they alike? How are they different?

Summarize, 59

### Vocabulary R 3.1.4, R 3.2.2

Review Words, Related Words, 63B

### Spelling Word Meanings, 63D

Reproducible, SP5 LC 3.1.8

**Read** *Amazing Grace*, 38–57

Student Book

### Comprehension

Critical Thinking, 59

**Review Skill:** Character, Setting, Plot, 59B R 3.3.3

### Fluency Repeated Reading: Intonation, 59A

Practice Book, 25 R 3.1.3

### Writing

**Daily Writing Prompt** Write about a time you were determined to do something.

**Focus on a Moment**, 65B W 3.1.1, W 3.2.1b

### Grammar Daily Language Activities, 63E

Mechanics and Usage, 63F
Reproducible, GR5 LC 3.1.1

**Quick Check** **Fluency**, 59A

## DAY 4

### Listening/Speaking/Viewing

**Focus Question** How are stories important to the people in the legend and Grace in *Amazing Grace*?

### Vocabulary R 3.1.4, R 3.2.2

Review Words, Morphology, 63B

### Spelling Proofread, 63D LC 3.1.8

Practice Book, 29

**Read** "The Storytelling Stone," 60–63

Student Book

### Comprehension

Language Arts: Legend

**Literary Element:** Personification, 60 R 3.3.2

Practice Book, 26

### Fluency Repeated Reading: Intonation, 59A R 3.1.3

Content Reader

### Writing

**Daily Writing Prompt** What makes someone a good storyteller?

**Reading/Writing Connection**, 65C–65D W 3.1.1

### Grammar Daily Language Activities, 63E

Commands and Exclamations, 63F
Practice Book, 31 LC 3.1.1

**Quick Check** **Vocabulary**, 63B

## DAY 5 Review and Assess

### Listening/Speaking/Viewing

**Focus Question** What are some of the main causes and effects in *Amazing Grace* and "The Storytelling Stone"? How does knowing these things help you understand the stories?

### Vocabulary R 3.1.4, R 3.2.2

Assess Words, Connect to Writing, 63B

### Spelling Posttest, 63D LC 3.1.8

Reproducible, SP6

**Read** Self-Selected Reading, 34J R 3.3.2

Student Book

### Comprehension

Critical Thinking, 63 HSS 3.2.1

### Fluency Practice, 34J R 3.1.3

### Writing

**Daily Writing Prompt** Compare and contrast a story you liked when you were younger to a story you love now.

**Conferences/Revision (Assignments)**, 65E–65F W 3.1.4

### Grammar Daily Language Activities, 63E

Commands and Exclamations, 63F
Reproducible, GR6 LC 3.1.1

**Weekly Assessment, 65G–65H**

# Differentiated Instruction

## What do I do in small groups?

## Focus on Skills

**IF...** **students need additional instruction and practice based on your Quick Check observations of the following skills:**

**Phonics/Word Study**
Final *e*

**Vocabulary Words**
*auditions, adventure, exploring, sparkling, fantastic, success*
**Strategy:** Word Families

**Comprehension**
**Strategy:** Make Inferences and Analyze
**Skill:** Cause and Effect

**Fluency**

**THEN...**

| | |
|---|---|
| Approaching / English Learners | Preteach and Reteach Skills |
| On Level | Consolidate Learning |
| Beyond | Enrich and Accelerate Learning |

## Suggested Small Group Lesson Plan

| Focus on Skills | DAY 1 | DAY 2 |
|---|---|---|
| **Phonics/Word Study** • **Final *e*** | **English Learners** Preteach Final *e*, 65J | **On Level** Reteach Final *e*, 65S |
| **Vocabulary** • **Week 2 Words**  | **Approaching** Preteach; Academic Language, 65I, 65K<br>**On Level** Review, 65S<br>**Beyond** Practice Reader Lesson 1, 65Y<br>**English Learners** Preteach; Academic Language 65AA–65BB | **Approaching** Practice Reader Lesson 1, 65N<br>**Beyond** Practice Reader Lesson 2, 65Z<br>**English Learners** Preteach Vocabulary; Access to Core Content, 65BB–65CC |
| **Comprehension** • **Strategy:** Make Inferences/Analyze • **Skill:** Cause and Effect | **Approaching** Prepare to Read, 65I<br>**Beyond** Practice Reader Lesson 1, 65Y<br>**English Learners** Prepare to Read, 65AA | **Approaching** Reteach; Practice Reader Lesson 1, 65M–65N<br>**Beyond** Practice Reader Lesson 2, 65Z<br>**English Learners** Practice Reader, 65GG |
| **Fluency** • **Repeated Reading** | | **Beyond** Practice Reader Lesson 2, 65Z |

## Skill-Based Practice Readers

Apply skills and strategies while reading appropriate leveled books.

**Leveled Practice Database**
Go to **www.macmillanmh.com**.

## Manipulatives

Use for Hands-on Learning

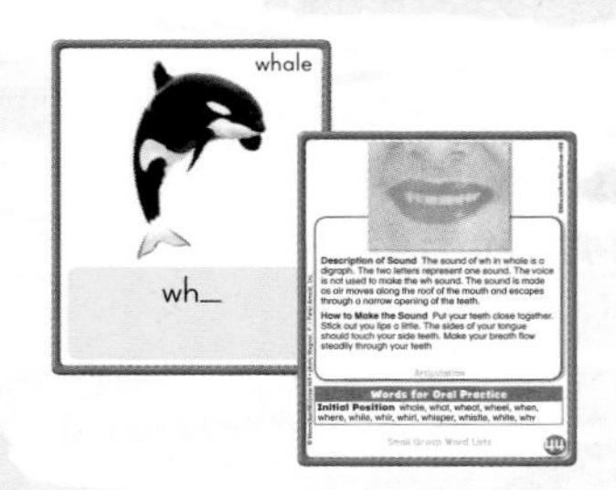


**Sound-Spelling Cards**

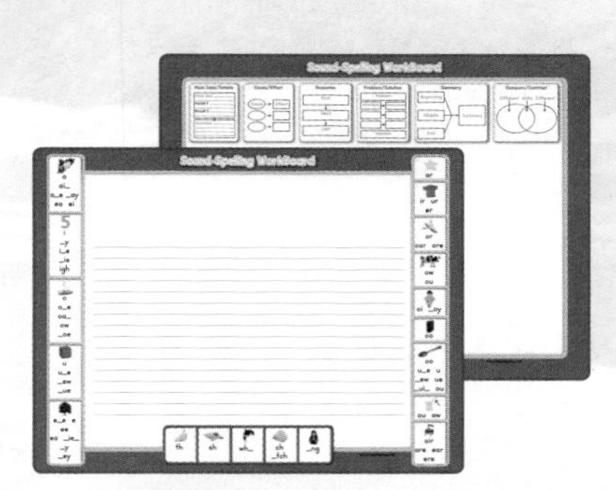

**Sound-Spelling WorkBoards**

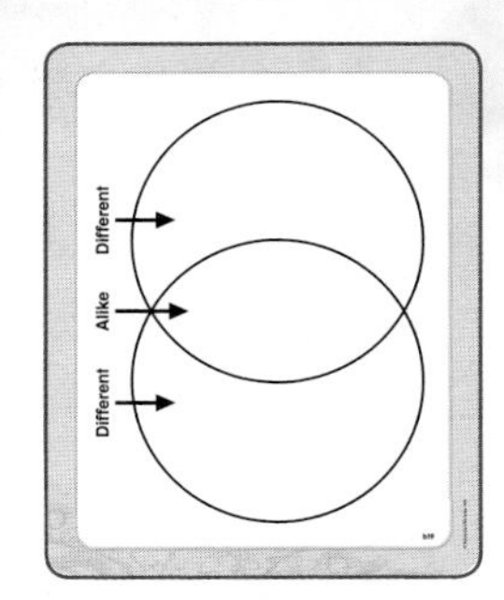


**Vocabulary/Comprehension Write-on/Wipe-off Boards**

Hands-on activities for reinforcing weekly skills

| DAY 3 | DAY 4 | DAY 5 |
|---|---|---|
| **Approaching** Final *e*, 65J<br>**Beyond** Extend and Accelerate, 65W | **Approaching** Final *e*, 65J<br>**English Learners** Writing/Spelling, 65FF | **English Learners** Review Final *e*, 65J |
| **Approaching** Practice Reader Lesson 2, 65O<br>**On Level** Practice Reader Lesson 1, 65U<br>**English Learners** Preteach Vocabulary; Access to Core Content, Grammar, 65BB–65CC, 65EE | **Approaching** Review Vocabulary, 65L<br>**On Level** Practice Reader Lesson 2, 65V<br>**Beyond** Enrich, 65W<br>**English Learners** Vocabulary, 65GG–65HH | **English Learners** Vocabulary, Practice Reader 65GG |
| **Approaching** Practice Reader Lesson 2, 65O<br>**On Level** Practice Reader Lesson 1, 65U<br>**English Learners** Practice Reader, 65GG | **Approaching** Practice Reader Lesson 3, 65P<br>**On Level** Practice Reader Lesson 2, 65V<br>**English Learners** Practice Reader, 65GG | **Approaching** Book Talk, 65HH<br>**On Level** Book Talk, 65HH<br>**Beyond** Book Talk, 65HH<br>**English Learners** Book Talk, 65HH |
| **Approaching** Practice Reader Lesson 2, 65O | **Approaching** Reread, Model, 65Q<br>**On Level** Reread, Model, 65T<br>**Beyond** Reread, Model, 65X<br>**English Learners** Reread, Model, 65DD | **Approaching** Self-Selected Reading, 65R<br>**On Level** Self-Selected Reading, 65T<br>**Beyond** Self-Selected Reading, 65X<br>**English Learners** Self-Selected Reading, 65DD |

## What do I do with the rest of my class?

- Literacy Workstations
- Practice Book
- Online Activities
- Classroom Library

## Classroom Management Tools

**Weekly Contract**

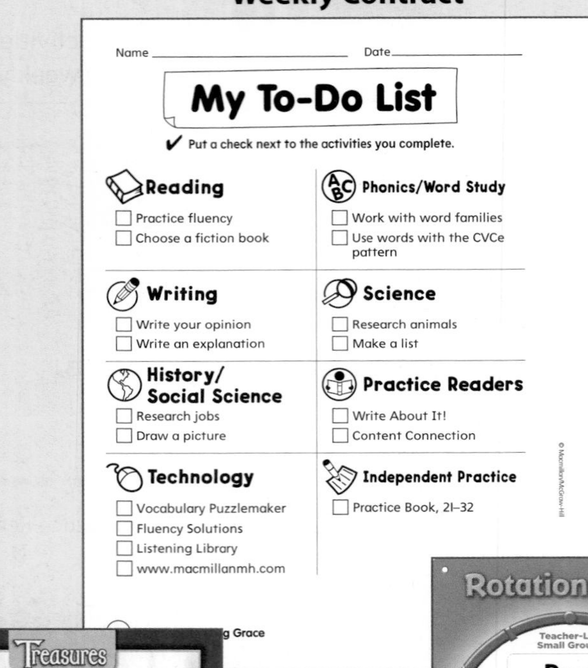

Name ________ Date ________

**My To-Do List**

✔ Put a check next to the activities you complete.

| | |
|---|---|
| **Reading**<br>☐ Practice fluency<br>☐ Choose a fiction book | **Phonics/Word Study**<br>☐ Work with word families<br>☐ Use words with the CVCe pattern |
| **Writing**<br>☐ Write your opinion<br>☐ Write an explanation | **Science**<br>☐ Research animals<br>☐ Make a list |
| **History/ Social Science**<br>☐ Research jobs<br>☐ Draw a picture | **Practice Readers**<br>☐ Write About It!<br>☐ Content Connection |
| **Technology**<br>☐ Vocabulary Puzzlemaker<br>☐ Fluency Solutions<br>☐ Listening Library<br>☐ www.macmillanmh.com | **Independent Practice**<br>☐ Practice Book, 21–32 |

How-to Guide

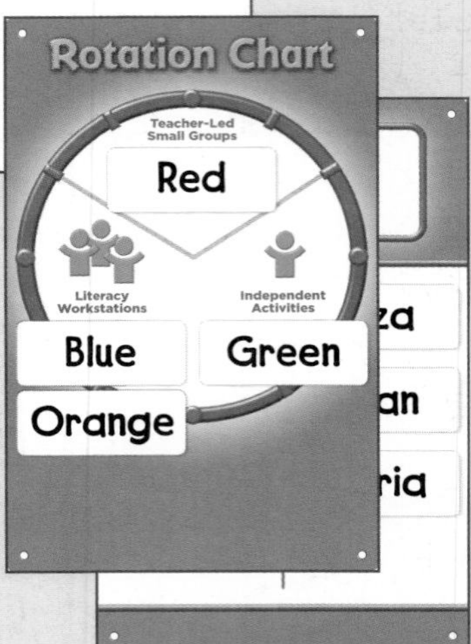


Rotation Chart

## Digital Learning

**StudentWorks Plus**

- Summaries in Multiple Languages
- Word-by-Word Reading
- Assessment

**Meet the Author/Illustrator**

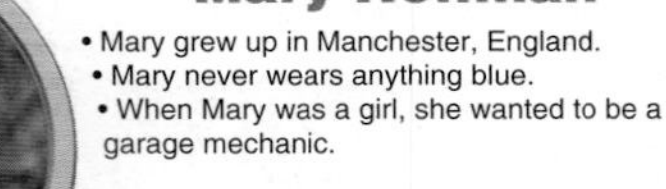

**Mary Hoffman**

- Mary grew up in Manchester, England.
- Mary never wears anything blue.
- When Mary was a girl, she wanted to be a garage mechanic.

Other books written and by Mary Hoffman

- Hoffman, Mary. *Boundless Grace.* New York: Puffin, 2000.
- Hoffman, Mary. *The Color of Home.* New York: Dial, 2002.
- Hoffman, Mary. *Starring Grace.* Frances Lincoln Childrens Books, 2003.

- Read Other Books by Author or Illustrator

## Classroom Library

Use the trade books to apply skills. See lessons on pages T2–T7. See also **Theme Bibliography**, pages T8–T9, to select books for 30 minutes of daily independent reading.

Approaching

On Level

Beyond

# Independent Activities

**ONLINE INSTRUCTION** www.macmillanmh.com

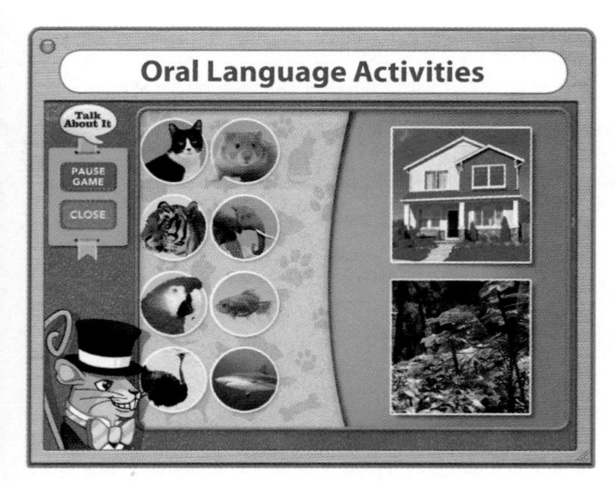


- Focus on Unit Vocabulary and Concepts
- English Learner Support

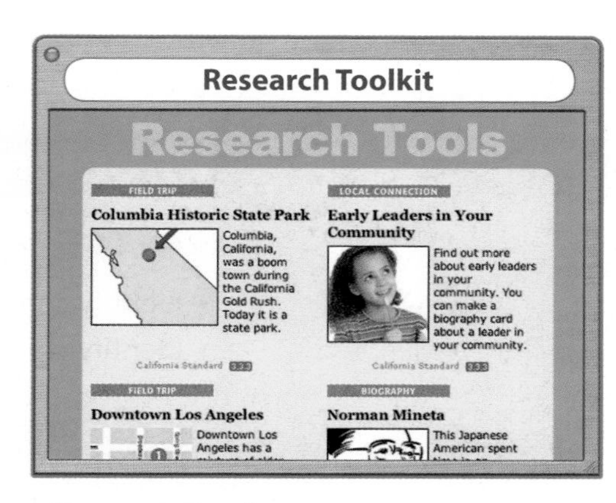


- Research Roadmap
- Research and Presentation Tools
- Theme Launcher Video
- Links to CA Science and History/Social Science Programs

- Focus on Keyboard and Internet Skills
- Media Literacy

- Differentiated Lists and Activities

## Available on CD

**LISTENING LIBRARY**
Recordings of selections
- Main Selections
- Paired Selections
- Practice Readers
- EL Readers

**FLUENCY SOLUTIONS**
Recorded passages at two speeds for modeling and practicing fluency

## Practice Book

Also Available:

**Approaching Reproducible**

**Beyond Reproducible**

## Literacy Workstation Flip Charts

Daily independent and partner activities connected to the weekly skills. See pages 34J–34K.

# Managing the Class

## What do I do with the rest of my class?

## Reading

### Objectives

- Read for fluency with partner reading
- Practice reading questions with an asking voice
- Practice reading ahead to help understanding

## Phonics/Word Study

### Objectives

- Identify common word parts
- Identify words with final e

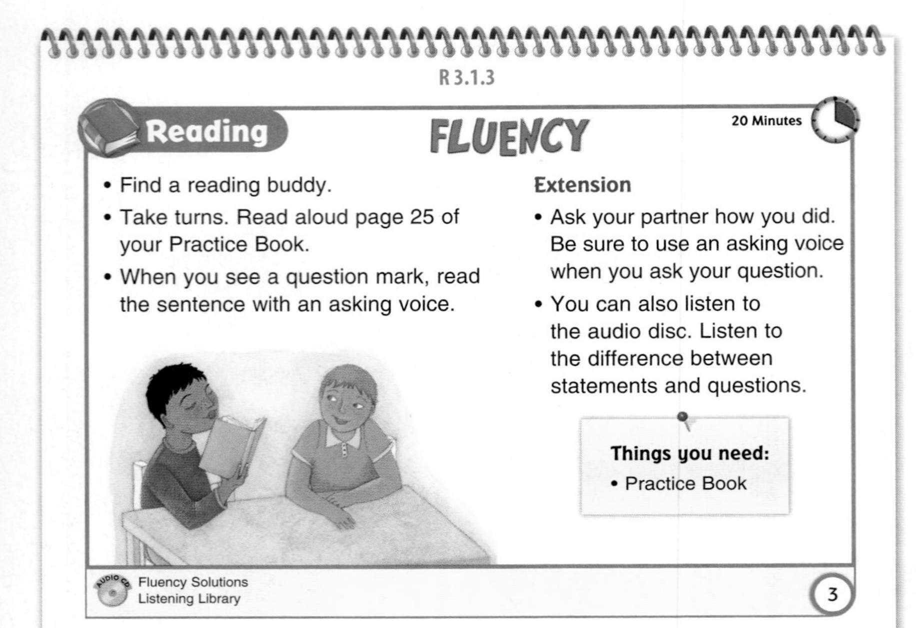

R 3.1.3

**Reading** — **FLUENCY** — 20 Minutes

- Find a reading buddy.
- Take turns. Read aloud page 25 of your Practice Book.
- When you see a question mark, read the sentence with an asking voice.

**Extension**

- Ask your partner how you did. Be sure to use an asking voice when you ask your question.
- You can also listen to the audio disc. Listen to the difference between statements and questions.

**Things you need:**
- Practice Book

Fluency Solutions
Listening Library

3

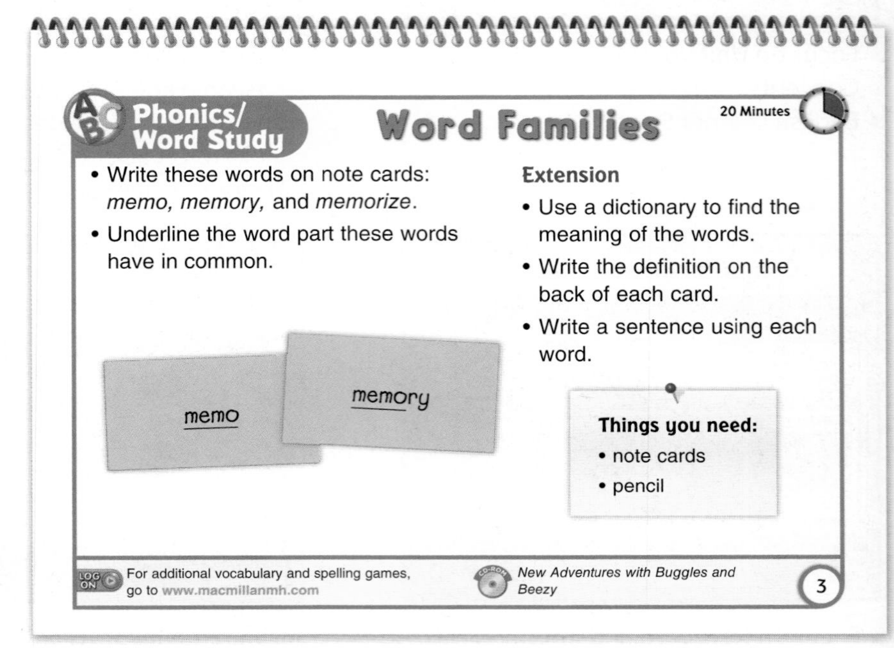

**Phonics/Word Study** — **Word Families** — 20 Minutes

- Write these words on note cards: *memo, memory,* and *memorize*.
- Underline the word part these words have in common.



**Extension**

- Use a dictionary to find the meaning of the words.
- Write the definition on the back of each card.
- Write a sentence using each word.

**Things you need:**
- note cards
- pencil

For additional vocabulary and spelling games, go to www.macmillanmh.com

*New Adventures with Buggles and Beezy*

3

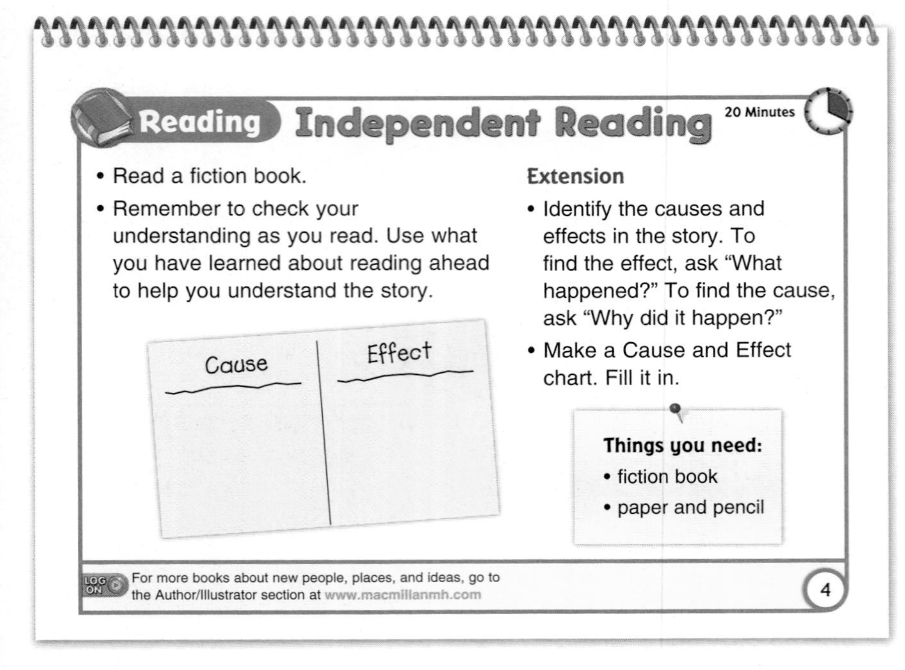

**Reading** — **Independent Reading** — 20 Minutes

- Read a fiction book.
- Remember to check your understanding as you read. Use what you have learned about reading ahead to help you understand the story.



**Extension**

- Identify the causes and effects in the story. To find the effect, ask "What happened?" To find the cause, ask "Why did it happen?"
- Make a Cause and Effect chart. Fill it in.

**Things you need:**
- fiction book
- paper and pencil

For more books about new people, places, and ideas, go to the Author/Illustrator section at www.macmillanmh.com

4

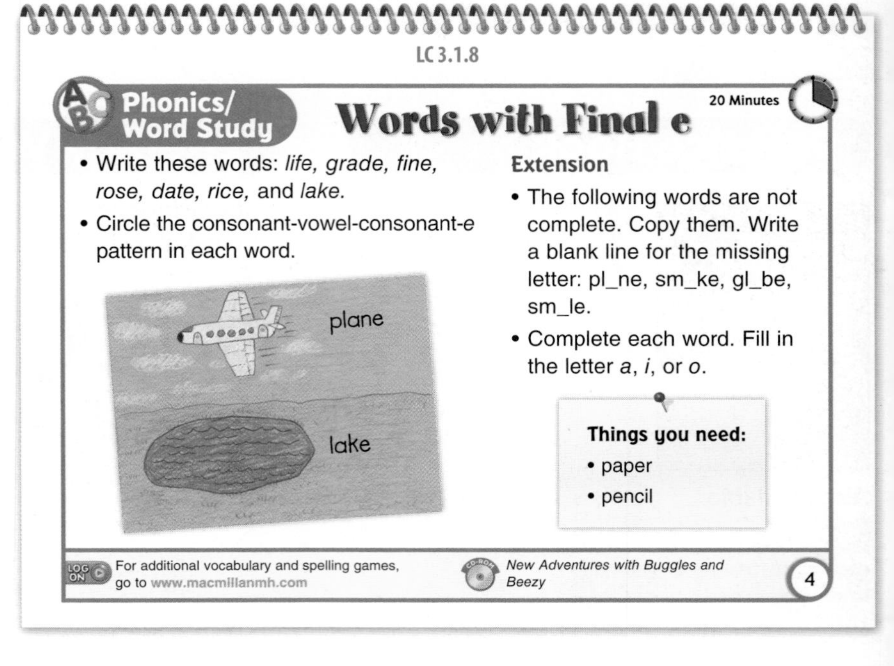

LC 3.1.8

**Phonics/Word Study** — **Words with Final e** — 20 Minutes

- Write these words: *life, grade, fine, rose, date, rice,* and *lake*.
- Circle the consonant-vowel-consonant-*e* pattern in each word.



**Extension**

- The following words are not complete. Copy them. Write a blank line for the missing letter: pl_ne, sm_ke, gl_be, sm_le.
- Complete each word. Fill in the letter *a*, *i*, or *o*.

**Things you need:**
- paper
- pencil

For additional vocabulary and spelling games, go to www.macmillanmh.com

*New Adventures with Buggles and Beezy*

4

# Literacy Workstations

**Literacy Workstation Flip Charts**

## Writing

### Objectives

- Write a paragraph giving your opinion about a fiction book
- Write a paragraph with step-by-step instructions on how to do an activity

## Content Literacy

### Objectives

- Research different kinds of jobs that people have
- Write a paragraph about a job you would like to have
- Research sensory details about different animals

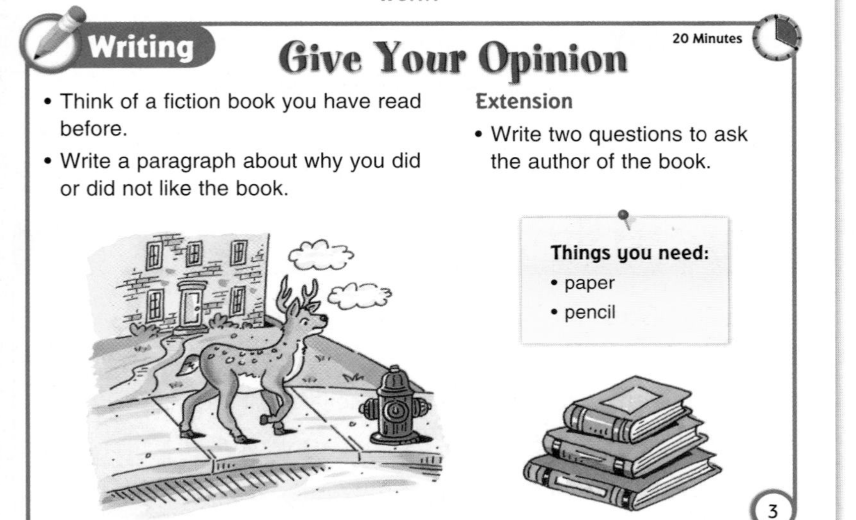
W 3.1.1

Writing — **Give Your Opinion** — 20 Minutes

- Think of a fiction book you have read before.
- Write a paragraph about why you did or did not like the book.

**Extension**

- Write two questions to ask the author of the book.

**Things you need:**
- paper
- pencil

3

W 3.1.3

History/Social Science — **Jobs** — 20 Minutes

- Use the Internet, encyclopedia or other sources. Look up different jobs people have.
- What kind of job would you like to have? Write a paragraph about why you would like to have that job.

**Extension**

- Draw a picture of a person that has that job.

**Things you need:**
- encyclopedia or reference books
- paper
- pencil

3

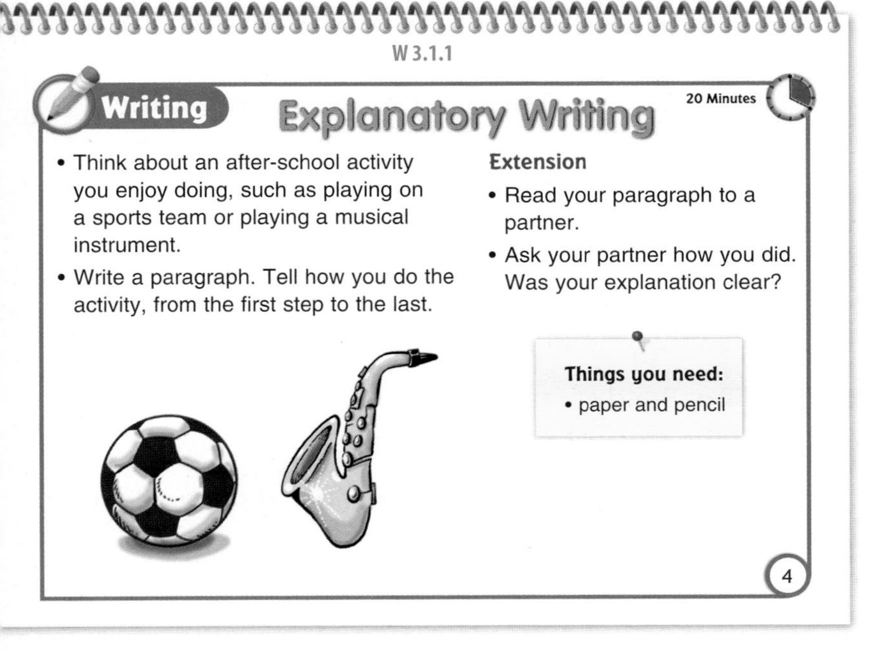
W 3.1.1

Writing — **Explanatory Writing** — 20 Minutes

- Think about an after-school activity you enjoy doing, such as playing on a sports team or playing a musical instrument.
- Write a paragraph. Tell how you do the activity, from the first step to the last.

**Extension**

- Read your paragraph to a partner.
- Ask your partner how you did. Was your explanation clear?

**Things you need:**
- paper and pencil

4

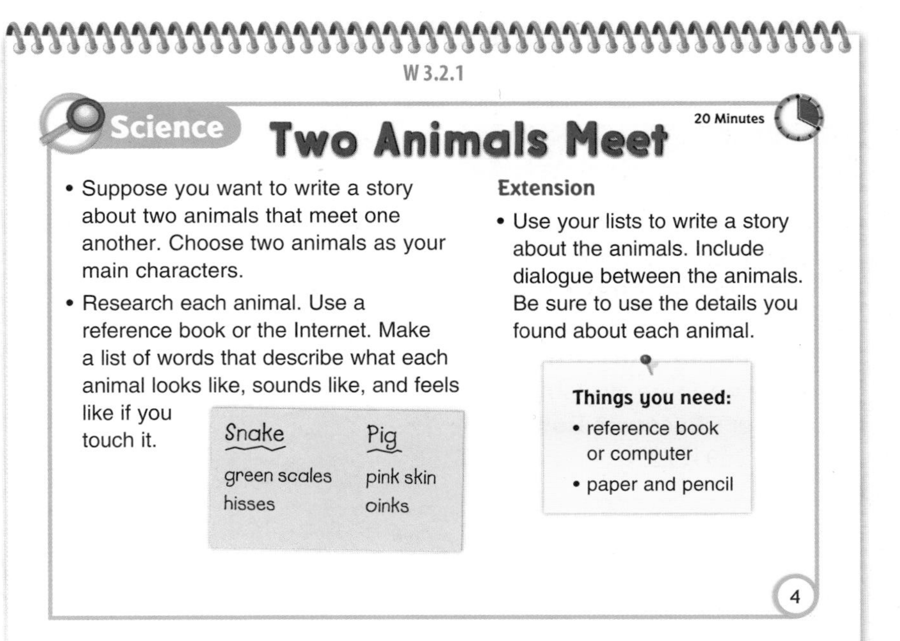
W 3.2.1

Science — **Two Animals Meet** — 20 Minutes

- Suppose you want to write a story about two animals that meet one another. Choose two animals as your main characters.
- Research each animal. Use a reference book or the Internet. Make a list of words that describe what each animal looks like, sounds like, and feels like if you touch it.

| Snake | Pig |
|---|---|
| green scales | pink skin |
| hisses | oinks |

**Extension**

- Use your lists to write a story about the animals. Include dialogue between the animals. Be sure to use the details you found about each animal.

**Things you need:**
- reference book or computer
- paper and pencil

4

# Prepare

## WHOLE GROUP

**ORAL LANGUAGE**
- Read Aloud
- Build Background
- Connect to Theme

**PHONICS/WORD STUDY**
- Final *e* Words

**VOCABULARY**
- Teach Words in Context
- Word Families

**COMPREHENSION**
- Strategy: Make Inferences and Analyze
- Skill: Cause and Effect

**CA CONTENT STANDARDS**
R 3.1.2, R 3.1.3, R 3.3.1, R 3.3.3
LAS 3.1.4, LAS 3.1.9, LAS 3.2.2

## SMALL GROUP

- Differentiated Instruction, pp. 65I–65HH

### Intensive Vocabulary

To provide 15–20 minutes of additional vocabulary instruction, see **Oral Vocabulary Cards** 5-Day Plan. The pre- and posttests for the week are available on **Teacher's Resource Book** pages 269–272.

# Read Aloud

## Read "The Sure-Footed Shoe Finder"

**Read Aloud**

**GENRE: POEM**

Share with students the following characteristics of **poetry**:

CA CONTENT STANDARD **R 3.3.1** Distinguish common forms of literature.

- A rhyming poem describes objects or actions using colorful words that form a picture in the reader's mind.
- A rhyming poem often has a rhythm created by a regular pattern of stressed and unstressed syllables and a pattern of rhyming words at the end of lines.

**FOCUS ON VOCABULARY**

Introduce the following words, using the **Define/Example/Ask** routine. Tell students that knowing these words will help them picture in their minds what the poem is describing.

### Vocabulary Routine

Use the routine below to discuss the meaning of each word.

Define: A **mate** is one of a pair of things that match each other.
Example: I often end up with only one glove because I've lost its mate.
Ask: What do you wear that has a mate?

Define: When something moves with a **lurch**, it moves forward quickly with a jerking motion.
Example: If you press on the gas pedal suddenly, a car will lurch ahead.
Ask: How is lurching different from sliding?

Define: **Mere** means "only" or "just."
Example: Since I am a mere beginner, I don't ice skate very well.
Ask: Can you easily hear someone who speaks in a mere whisper? Explain.

**LISTENING FOR A PURPOSE**

Ask students to listen carefully as you read "The Sure-Footed Shoe Finder" in the **Read-Aloud Anthology**, pages 38–40. Use the Think Alouds and genre study prompt provided.

**EL** **Interactive Reading** Build students' oral language by engaging them in talk about the story's basic meaning.

- After the first stanza, say, *Turn to your partner and discuss what you think this poem will be about.*

CA CONTENT STANDARD
LAS 3.1.4
Identify the musical elements of literary language.

- After the first third stanza, say, *Turn to your partner and discuss which words rhyme.*
- After the fourth stanza, say, *The fourth stanza talks about customers. Do you think this poem is a story or an advertisement? Discuss your opinion with a partner.*

**Think/Pair/Share** Use **Copying Master 3**, "I was able to picture in my mind. . .," to help students visualize what the poem is describing. When completed, have students turn to a partner and orally summarize the poem. Then have a few students share their summaries with the class.

### RESPOND TO THE POEM

Ask students the **Think and Respond** questions on page 40. Then have students think of a common problem people have and describe an imaginary machine that would help to solve the problem. Have them include words that describe how the machine looks and sounds.

## Model Fluency

Reread the poem. Tell students that this time you want them to focus on your **intonation** as you read.

Point out that you pay attention to raising your voice at question marks and and lowering it at periods as well as emphasizing the poem's regular rhythm. Model an example.

CA CONTENT STANDARD
LAS 3.2.2
Plan and present dramatic interpretations of experiences, stories, poems, or plays with clear diction, pitch, tempo, and tone.

**Think Aloud** Listen as I read the first two lines of the poem. Pay attention to how my voice sounds at the end of each sentence:

How many times has this happened to you?
You're late for the school bus and can't find a shoe.
It might take two hours unless you have got
the Sure-Footed Shoe Finder there on the spot!

Did you hear how my voice went up when I came to the end of the first sentence, "How many times has this happened to you?" My voice went up because this sentence is a question. At the end of the next sentence, "You're late for the school bus and can't find a shoe," my voice dropped because this sentence is a statement and ends in a period. The last sentence is an exclamation, so I speed up a little and emphasize the last few words, "there on the spot!" Now you try. Repeat each sentence after me, using the same intonation that I do.

**Establish Fluency Focus** Remind students that you will be listening for these same qualities in their reading throughout the week. You will help them improve their reading by using proper intonation at periods, question marks, and exclamation marks.

### Readers Theater

**BUILDING LISTENING AND SPEAKING SKILLS**
Distribute copies of "Take Me to Your Litter," **Read-Aloud Anthology** pages 132–145. Have students practice reading the play throughout the unit. Assign parts and have students present the play or perform it as a dramatic reading at the end of the unit.

CA CONTENT STANDARD
LAS 3.1.9
Read prose and poetry aloud with fluency, rhythm, and pace, using appropriate intonation and vocal patterns to emphasize important passages of the text being read.

## Objectives

- Decode multisyllabic words with final *e* spellings

### Materials

- Sound-Spelling Cards
- Practice Book, p.21
- Transparency 2
- Word-Building Cards
- Teacher's Resource Book 179

### English Learners

UNIVERSAL ACCESS

**Transfer Sounds** Students speaking Cantonese may have difficulty pronouncing and perceiving the long vowel sounds. Speakers of Hmong may have difficulty specifically with long *a* and long *o*. Use the Approaching Level phonics lessons to provide additional pronunciation/decoding practice.

HOMEWORK

**Practice Book,** page 21

A final silent **e** often makes the vowel in that syllable have the long vowel sound. For example:
conf**u**s**e** ref**i**n**e** disl**i**k**e** panc**a**k**e** al**o**n**e** qu**o**t**e**

**Circle the word that has a long vowel sound and a final silent e. Then write it on the line to complete the sentence.**

1. We read a book about a storm called a hurricane.
   rainstorm blizzard (hurricane)
2. We looked at a globe to see where one can form.
   map (globe) book
3. We learned when a hurricane might arrive.
   begin appear (arrive)
4. We found out the storm can bring huge winds.
   high brisk (huge)
5. The amount of rain can surprise you.
   (surprise) surround frighten
6. Scientists can compute how strong the storm will be.
   complain (compute) tell
7. No two storms are exactly alike.
   always similar (alike)
8. Our class wrote a report about hurricanes.
   read printed (wrote)

Approaching Reproducible, page 21

Beyond Reproducible, page 21

# Phonics

## Final *e*

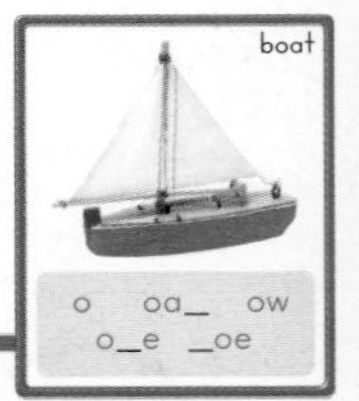


### EXPLAIN/MODEL

Display the *Train, Five, Boat, Cube,* and *Tree* **Sound-Spelling Cards** for the long vowel sounds. Tell students that when a word is spelled with a vowel, a consonant, and a final *e* at the end, the vowel sound is usually long. The final *e* and the vowel before it act as a team. Point to the final *e* spelling on each card and provide a sample word. For example:

- **a_e** as in *cane*
- **e_e** as in *Steve*
- **i_e** as in *bite*
- **o_e** as in *robe*
- **u_e** as in *cute*

Write the sample words on the board, underline the final *e* spelling, and model blending each one.

**Think Aloud** Look at the first words I wrote: c-a-n-e. I see the final *e* spelling *a_e* in *cane*. Listen and watch as I sound out the word: /kān/*cane*. (Run your finger under the word as you sound it out.)

### PRACTICE/APPLY

**Read Word List** Display **Transparency 2**. The first two lines include final *e* words students will encounter in the upcoming selections. Have students underline the final *e* spelling in each word. Then have them chorally read the words.

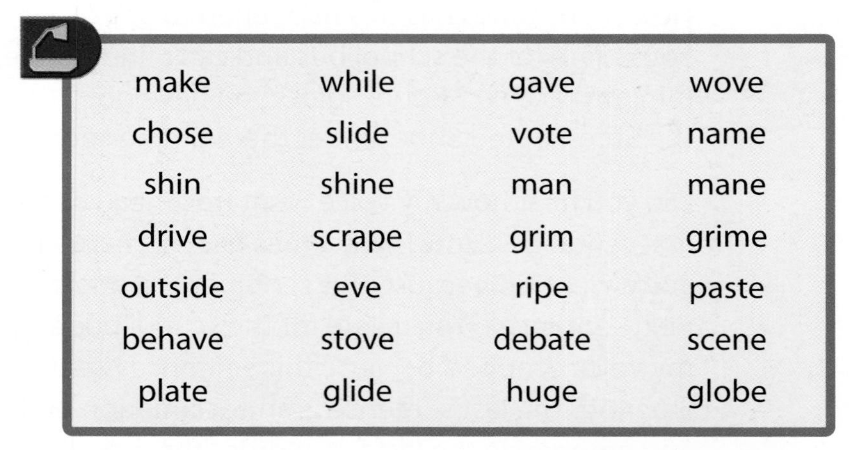

| | | | |
|---|---|---|---|
| make | while | gave | wove |
| chose | slide | vote | name |
| shin | shine | man | mane |
| drive | scrape | grim | grime |
| outside | eve | ripe | paste |
| behave | stove | debate | scene |
| plate | glide | huge | globe |

**Phonics Transparency 2**

**Sort Words** Ask students to sort the words by spelling pattern. Then have them write the sort in their Writer's Notebooks.

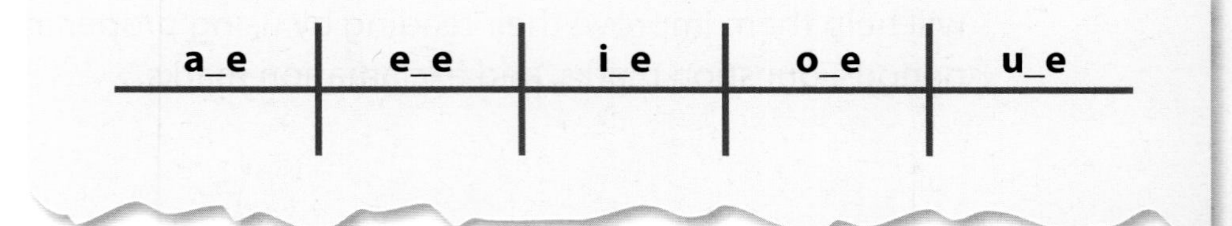

## Read Multisyllabic Words

CA CONTENT STANDARD
R 3.1.2 Decode regular multisyllabic words.

**TRANSITION TO LONGER WORDS** Help students transition from reading one-syllable to multisyllabic final *e* words. Have students read the word in the first column, then model how to read the longer word in the second column. Point out the added syllable(s), such as prefix or suffix, to help students gain awareness of these common word parts.

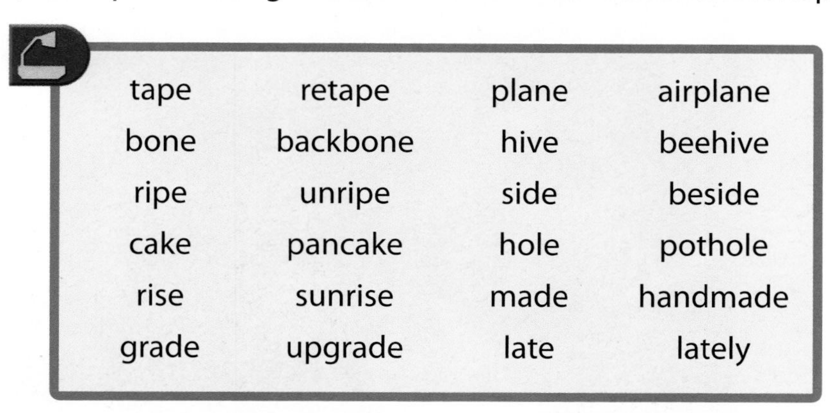

| | | | |
|---|---|---|---|
| tape | retape | plane | airplane |
| bone | backbone | hive | beehive |
| ripe | unripe | side | beside |
| cake | pancake | hole | pothole |
| rise | sunrise | made | handmade |
| grade | upgrade | late | lately |

**Phonics Transparency 2**

**BUILD WORDS** Use **Word-Building Cards** *dis, re, grace, pute, like, place, use, vise, make***.** Display the cards. Have students use the word parts to build as many final *e* multisyllabic words as possible. These and other words can be formed: *disgrace, dispute, dislike, displace, replace, reuse, revise, remake.*

**CONNECT TO 6 SYLLABLE TYPES** To further help students break apart longer words to decode them, explain the following:

- **Final *e* Syllables** When a word a vowel-consonant-*e spelling* pattern, the vowel and the final silent *e* must stay in the same syllable. (es/cape, rep/tile)

**APPLY DECODING STRATEGY** Guide students to use the **Decoding Strategy** to decode the following words: *mistake, provide, combine, suppose, awoke, describe, stampede, hopeless, concrete, boneless, promote, forgave.* Write each word on the board. Remind students to look for syllables with final *e* spellings in step 3 of the Decoding Strategy procedure.

## Build Fluency

**SPEED DRILL** Distribute copies of the **Final *e* Speed Drill** in the **Teacher's Resource Book**. Use the Speed Drill routine to help students become fluent reading words with final *e* spelling patterns.

### Syllable Fluency

Use **Word-Building Cards 11–20**. Display one card at a time. Have students chorally read each common syllable. Repeat at varying speeds and in random order. Have students work with partners during independent time to write as many words as they can containing each syllable. Add these lists to the **Unit 1 Big Question Board**.

### Decoding Strategy

**Decoding Strategy Chart**

| | |
|---|---|
| Step 1 | Look for word parts (prefixes) at the beginning of the word. |
| Step 2 | Look for word parts (suffixes) at the end of the word. |
| Step 3 | In the base word, look for familiar spelling patterns. Think about the six syllable-spelling patterns you have learned. |
| Step 4 | Sound out and blend together the word parts. |
| Step 5 | Say the word parts fast. Adjust your pronunciation as needed. Ask yourself: "Is this a word I have heard before?" Then read the word in the sentence and ask: "Does it make sense in this sentence?" |

# Oral Language

## Build Background

**ACCESS PRIOR KNOWLEDGE**

Share the following information:

To perform in a play, actors have to prepare. They memorize what their characters say and then they rehearse together until their performances are perfect. Many plays for children are created from books that tell funny or exciting stories.

Write the following words on the board and briefly define each one using the **Define/Example/Ask** routine: **performance** (when an actor, dancer, or musician entertains people) **rehearse** (to practice), **costume** (what an actor or dancer wears during a performance).

**FOCUS QUESTION** Ask students to read "Talk About It" on **Student Book** page 35. Then have them turn to a partner and describe the photo. Ask:

- Do you think the children are in a performance? Why?
- What costumes are the performers wearing?

WRITE ON DEMAND

**BUILD WRITING FLUENCY**

Ask students to write in their **Writer's Notebook** what they know about performing in a play. Tell students to write as much as they can as well as they can. Students should write for five minutes without stopping. Meet with individuals during Writing Conference time to provide feedback and revision assignments. Students should self-correct any errors they notice prior to the conference.

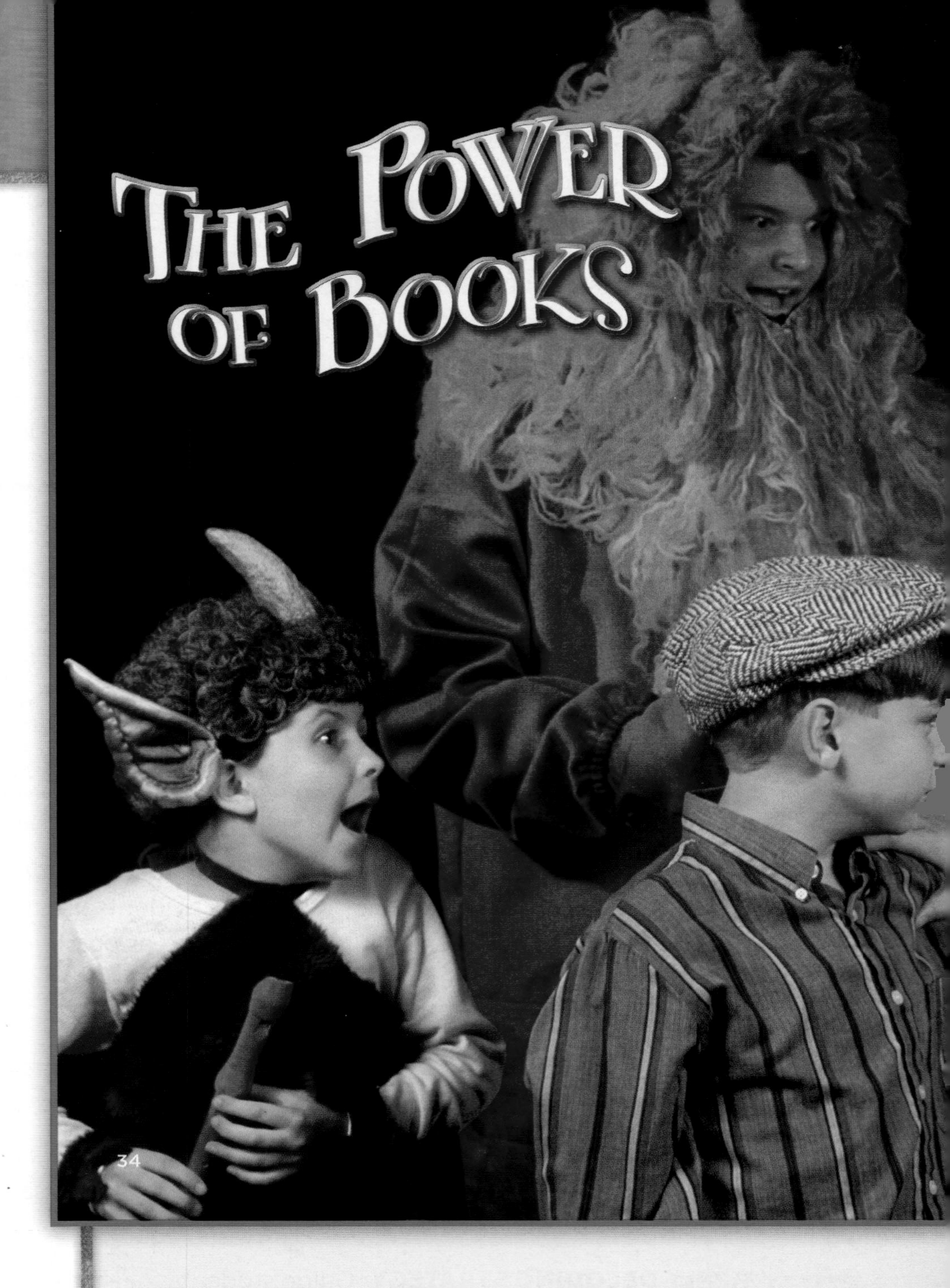


**English Learners**

UNIVERSAL ACCESS

During the discussion, build on students' responses to help them move to the next level of language acquisition. For example, if a student answers *yes* to the first question, say:

*That's correct. The children are in a performance. They are performing in a play. Say it with me.* (Students repeat sentence.) *They will entertain people who are watching the play.*
*Now turn to your partner and tell about this picture.*
Provide the following frames orally or in writing to help students respond in complete sentences.

**Beginning/Early Intermediate** These children are ____.

**Intermediate** These actors are pretending to____.

**Early Advanced** The actors will rehearse ____ and ______.

# Unit Theme

## Big Idea

Books can introduce us to new people, places, and ideas. In school we read a wide range of books.

### CONNECT TO THEME

Ask students what they have learned so far in this unit about how to share different ways that people learn and experience new things.

- What characters have we read about so far? What new experiences did these characters have? What did they learn from these experiences?
- How can books help people learn and experience new things?

### USE THEME FOLDABLES

Write the **Big Idea** statement on the board. Ask students to copy it on their Unit Theme Foldables. Remind them to add details as they complete this week's readings.

## Digital Learning

**PRETEACH** Have **Approaching Level** students and **English Learners** listen to the selection on **StudentWorks Plus**, the interactive eBook, before reading with the class. The recording contains summaries in multiple languages, word-by-word reading support, a bilingual glossary, and comprehension questions with corrective feedback.

For Web site activities for oral language development, go to **www.macmillanmh.com**.

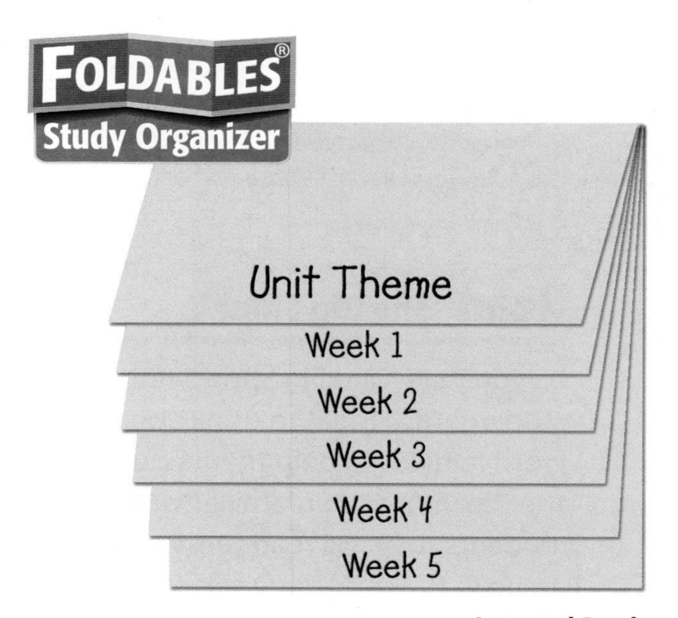


**Layered Book**

# Vocabulary

**STRATEGY**
**WORD FAMILIES**

Explain to students that when several words have the same word part or base word, they belong to the same **word family**. For example, the words *weekend, weekly,* and *weekday* all belong to the same family because they all contain the same base word *week*. If readers know the meaning of *week,* they can probably figure the meaning of other words in this word family.

Ask students to read "Word Families" in the bookmark on **Student Book** page 36. Then model for students how to use word families to determine the meaning of the word *adventurers.*

**Think Aloud** I see the word *adventurers* in the sentence, "The rest of the friends played the parts of the other adventurers." I think that *adventurers* is related to the word *adventure,* which means "something that a person does that is exciting or dangerous." Since the friends are called "adventurers," I think that adventurers are people who do something exciting or dangerous. By knowing the meaning of *adventure*, I was able to figure out the meaning of *adventurers*.

## Read "The Big Show"

As you read "The Big Show" with students, ask them to think about word families to help them figure out the meanings of unfamiliar words. Tell students they will read these words again in the upcoming selection *Amazing Grace*.

**Vocabulary**

| | |
|---|---|
| adventure | sparkling |
| exploring | fantastic |
| auditions | success |

**Word Parts**

**Word Families** are groups of words that have the same base word or word part.

*Adventure* and *adventurer* belong to the same word family.

by Amelia Thomas

Sue and Jake watched the pouring rain make puddles in Sue's backyard. They tried to think of a way to keep busy indoors. Suddenly, Jake had an idea. "Let's do a play."

"That's a great idea!" said Sue. "We can write a play about a book we like."

Jake and Sue found a favorite **adventure** book about **exploring** a lost kingdom. It was an exciting story with a brave girl and her strong dog.

Sue and Jake wrote all afternoon. Then they phoned their friends Tomás, Nita, Jill, and Kate. "We are having **auditions** for our play," said Jake. "Come and read for a part."

The play sounded like fun, so all the friends came. Nita was chosen to play the explorer because she was a good actor. Of course, her dog Fred played the dog. The rest of the friends played the parts of the other adventurers.

Tomás and Jill made colorful posters covered with **sparkling** glitter to tell others about their wonderful show. Jake and Sue made a stage in Sue's backyard. Nita and Kate made costumes.

36

**Quick Check**

**Can students identify word meanings?**

During **Small Group Instruction**

**If No** → **Approaching Level** Reteach the words using the Vocabulary lesson, p. 65K.

**If Yes** → **On Level** Consolidate the learning using p. 65S.

**Beyond Level** Extend the learning using p. 65W.

The next weekend, family and friends came to see the show. It was going well until the end. That's when Sue's cat leaped into the middle of the stage. Fred barked and chased the cat. Nita tripped over Fred. Sue started to cry. *The show is ruined*, she thought.

But then everyone stood up and clapped. "You were **fantastic**!" they yelled. "We want to see another show next week!"

Sue stopped crying and smiled. "We were a **success**! They liked us!" she said.

Reread for **Comprehension**

**Make Inferences and Analyze**

Cause and Effect

A **cause** is why something happens. The **effect** is what happens. Sometimes you need to analyze what happens in a story and make inferences about why these events happen. Reread the story. Use your Cause and Effect Chart to record causes and their effects.

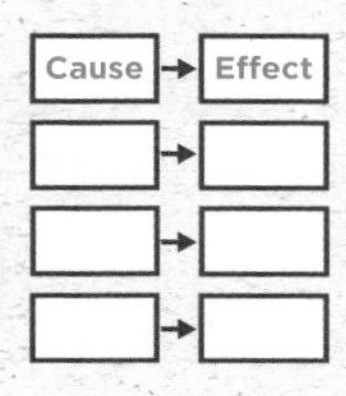






# Vocabulary

## TEACH WORDS

Introduce each word using the **Define/Example/Ask** routine. Model reading each word using the syllable-scoop technique.

### Vocabulary Routine

**Define:** An **adventure** is an exciting experience that may be dangerous, too.
**Example:** The journey to the moon was a great adventure.
**Ask:** Why do people like to have adventures? EXPLANATION

- **Exploring** means traveling around a place to find out what it is like. *My friends were exploring the town's new library.* Why do you think scientists are exploring outer space? EXPLANATION
- At **auditions**, performers try out for a part in a show and judges choose the best performer for each part. *My sister is going to auditions to try to get the lead acting role in the play.* How would you prepare if you were going to a singing audition? EXAMPLE
- Things that are **sparkling** are shiny and very bright. *The city lights were sparkling against the night sky.* What do you sometimes see sparkling up high in the night sky? COMPARE AND CONTRAST
- When something is **fantastic**, it is really wonderful or really good. *The fantastic ballplayer made three home runs in a row.* What is a synonym for *fantastic*? SYNONYM
- When something you do is a **success**, it means that it has a good result. *Our school fair was a success. Everyone had a great time.* What is an antonym for *success*? ANTONYM

## English Learners

UNIVERSAL ACCESS

**Preteach Vocabulary**
See pages 65K and 65BB to preteach the vocabulary words to **English Learners** and **Approaching Level** students. Use the **Visual Vocabulary Resources** to demonstrate and discuss each word. Use the Interactive Question-Response Guide to preteach the content in "The Big Show" and develop meaning.

**Practice Book, page 22**

Read the story. Choose words from the box to complete the sentences. Then write the answers on the lines.

auditions adventure exploring sparkling fantastic success

My friends and I love adventure stories. We wish we could go exploring with the story characters. We can't do that. But we do learn all sorts of things from these exciting tales.

Sometimes we put on a play about a story we're reading. We hold auditions to see who will play each part. From the book, we learn where and when the story takes place. Then we take old clothes and add decorations like sparkling jewels to make costumes. We make the costumes look like clothes the story characters wore. People who see our plays often say the costumes are fantastic. The right costumes help make a play a success.

**Approaching Reproducible, page 22**
**Beyond Reproducible, page 22**

## Objectives

- Make inferences and analyze
- Identify cause and effect
- Use academic language: *make inferences, cause, effect*

### Materials

- Transparencies 2a, 2b, and 8
- Graphic Organizer
- Practice Book, p. 23

## Skills Trace

**Cause and Effect**

| | |
|---|---|
| **Introduce** | U1: 37A–37B |
| **Practice/ Apply** | U1: 38–59; Practice Book 23–24 |
| **Reteach/ Review** | U1: 65M–HH; U5: 203A–B, 204–207, 211U–PP; Practice Book 279–280 |
| **Assess** | Weekly Tests; Unit 1, 3 Tests |
| **Maintain** | U1: 73B; U5: 229B |

## English Learners

UNIVERSAL ACCESS

**Academic Language**
Preteach the following academic language words to **English Learners** and **Approaching Level** students during Small Group time: *make inferences, cause, effect.* See page 65AA.

# Reread for Comprehension

## STRATEGY
### MAKE INFERENCES AND ANALYZE

CA CONTENT STANDARD
**R 3.2.2** Ask questions and support answers by connecting prior knowledge with literal information found in, and inferred from, the text.

**What Is It?** Explain that readers use information in the text, including pictures, as well as their own experiences to figure out a fact or information that the author has not included in a story. This is called **making inferences.**

**Why Is It Important?** Point out that making inferences and analyzing helps readers better understand what causes characters to act in a certain way and why certain events happen in a story.

## SKILL
### CAUSE AND EFFECT

**EXPLAIN**

**What Is It?** A **cause** is an event that makes something else happen. An **effect** is what happens as a result.

**Why Is It Important?** Point out that thinking about cause and effect relationships helps readers understand why something happened in the plot. It also helps readers understand why characters act in a certain way.

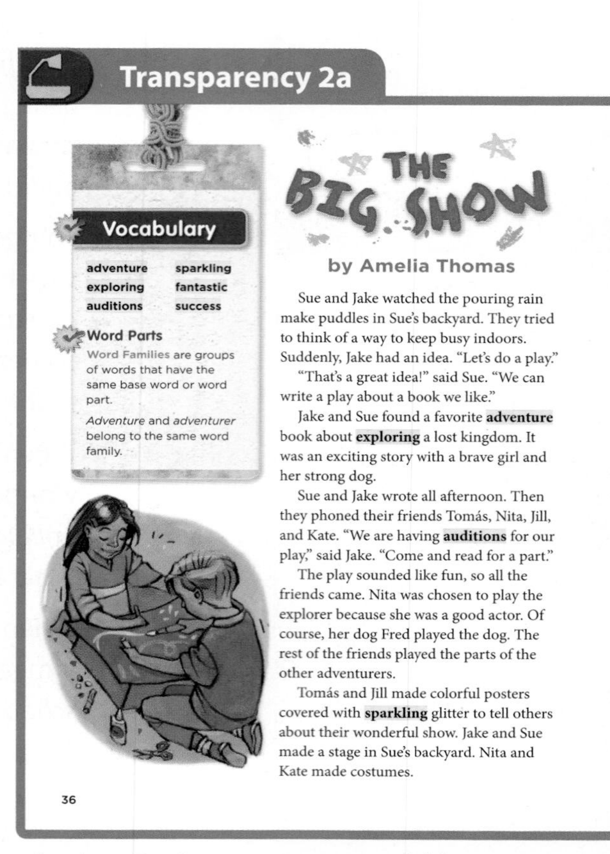

Transparency 2a

**Vocabulary**
adventure, sparkling, exploring, fantastic, auditions, success

**Word Parts**
Word Families are groups of words that have the same base word or word part.
*Adventure* and *adventurer* belong to the same word family.

THE BIG SHOW
by Amelia Thomas

Sue and Jake watched the pouring rain make puddles in Sue's backyard. They tried to think of a way to keep busy indoors. Suddenly, Jake had an idea. "Let's do a play."

"That's a great idea!" said Sue. "We can write a play about a book we like."

Jake and Sue found a favorite **adventure** book about **exploring** a lost kingdom. It was an exciting story with a brave girl and her strong dog.

Sue and Jake wrote all afternoon. Then they phoned their friends Tomás, Nita, Jill, and Kate. "We are having **auditions** for our play," said Jake. "Come and read for a part."

The play sounded like fun, so all the friends came. Nita was chosen to play the explorer because she was a good actor. Of course, her dog Fred played the dog. The rest of the friends played the parts of the other adventurers.

Tomás and Jill made colorful posters covered with **sparkling** glitter to tell others about their wonderful show. Jake and Sue made a stage in Sue's backyard. Nita and Kate made costumes.

36

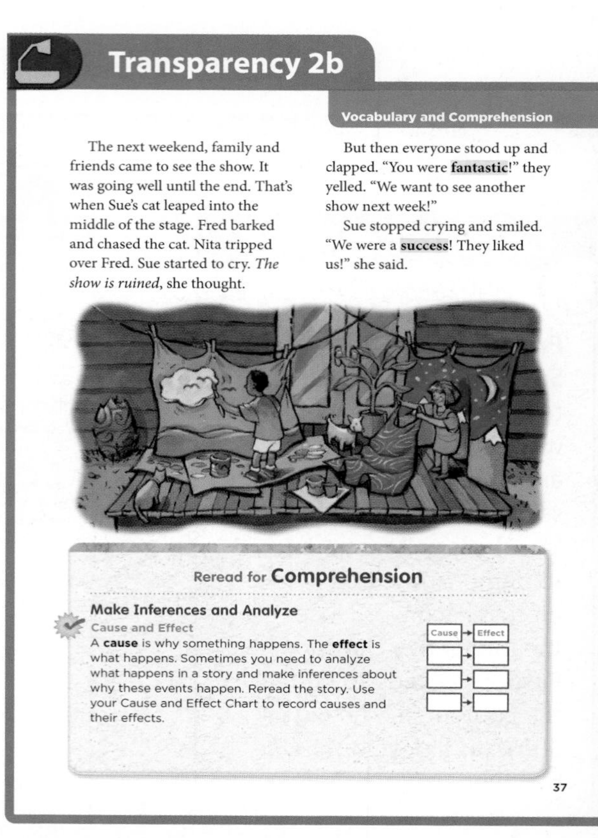

Transparency 2b

Vocabulary and Comprehension

The next weekend, family and friends came to see the show. It was going well until the end. That's when Sue's cat leaped into the middle of the stage. Fred barked and chased the cat. Nita tripped over Fred. Sue started to cry. *The show is ruined*, she thought.

But then everyone stood up and clapped. "You were **fantastic**!" they yelled. "We want to see another show next week!"

Sue stopped crying and smiled. "We were a **success**! They liked us!" she said.

Reread for **Comprehension**

**Make Inferences and Analyze**
Cause and Effect
A **cause** is why something happens. The **effect** is what happens. Sometimes you need to analyze what happens in a story and make inferences about why these events happen. Reread the story. Use your Cause and Effect Chart to record causes and their effects.

| Cause | Effect |
|---|---|
| | |
| | |
| | |

37

Student Book pages 36–37 available on Comprehension Transparencies 2a and 2b

- To find causes and effects, readers can ask these questions: *What happened?* (This is the effect.) *Why did it happen?* (This is the cause.)
- Sometimes readers find signal words or phrases such as *so, because, as a result, since,* and *due to to help them find causes and effects. If there are no signal words, then readers may use story clues and their own experiences to figure out a cause and effect.*

### MODEL

**How Do I Use It?** Read aloud the first two paragraphs of "The Big Show" on **Student Book** page 36. Use **Transparency 8** to record the causes and effects in the story.

**Think Aloud** After I read the first two paragraphs of the story, I can ask myself, *What did Sue and Jake do?* They wrote a play. Then I can ask myself, *Why did they write a play?* Because they had nothing to do. By asking myself these questions, I can figure out an effect—they wrote a play—and its cause—they had nothing to do. Since there were no signal words in this part of the story, I had to make an inference to figure out the cause and effect. Figuring out the cause and effect relationship helps me understand what the characters are doing in this part of the story.

### GUIDED PRACTICE

Continue by helping students identify another cause and effect in the first sentence in the fifth paragraph on page 36. Have them look for signal words. Help them see that the word *so* signals the effect, or what happens: All the friends came. Ask students, *What is the cause, or why they came?* (The play sounded like fun.)

### APPLY

Have students identify other causes and effects in the story and identify any signal words that help them. Ask them to complete the Cause and Effect Chart. Then discuss with them how finding causes and effects in a story can help them understand characters' actions and why certain events take place.

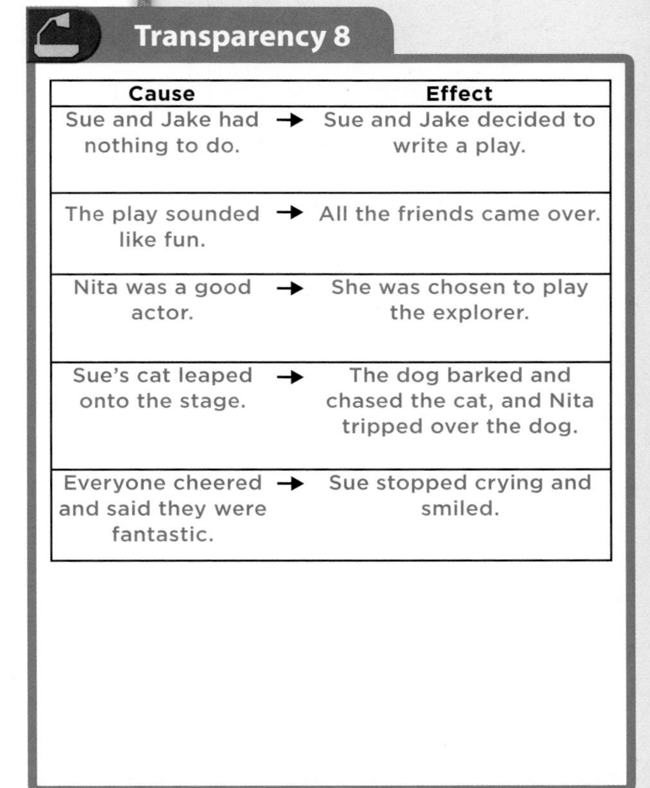

Transparency 8

| Cause | | Effect |
|---|---|---|
| Sue and Jake had nothing to do. | → | Sue and Jake decided to write a play. |
| The play sounded like fun. | → | All the friends came over. |
| Nita was a good actor. | → | She was chosen to play the explorer. |
| Sue's cat leaped onto the stage. | → | The dog barked and chased the cat, and Nita tripped over the dog. |
| Everyone cheered and said they were fantastic. | → | Sue stopped crying and smiled. |

**Graphic Organizer Transparency**

#### Quick Check

**Can students identify causes and effects?**

During **Small Group Instruction**

**If No →** **Approaching Level** Reteach the skill using the Comprehension lessons, pp. 65M–65P.

**If Yes →** **On Level** Consolidate the learning using pp. 65U–65V.

**Beyond Level** Extend the learning using pp. 65Y–65Z.

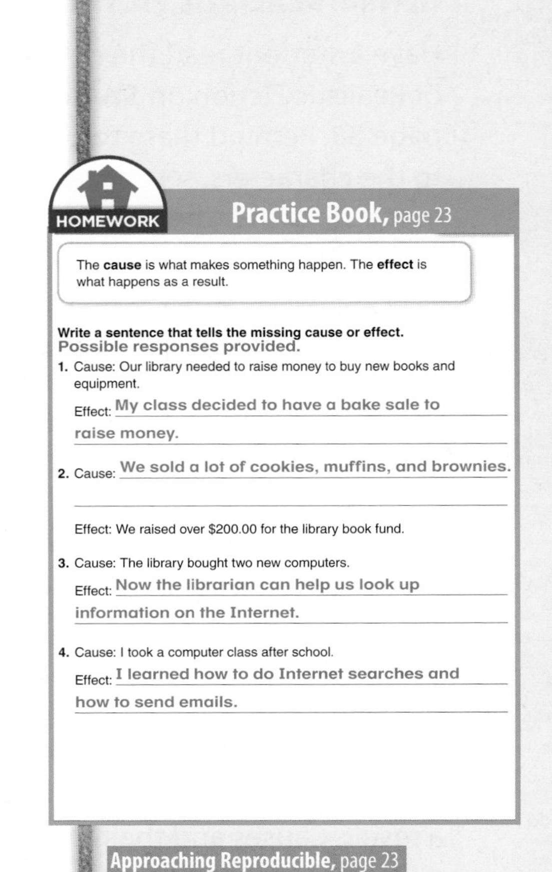

HOMEWORK **Practice Book,** page 23

The **cause** is what makes something happen. The **effect** is what happens as a result.

**Write a sentence that tells the missing cause or effect.**
Possible responses provided.

1. Cause: Our library needed to raise money to buy new books and equipment.
   Effect: My class decided to have a bake sale to raise money.
2. Cause: We sold a lot of cookies, muffins, and brownies.
   Effect: We raised over $200.00 for the library book fund.
3. Cause: The library bought two new computers.
   Effect: Now the librarian can help us look up information on the Internet.
4. Cause: I took a computer class after school.
   Effect: I learned how to do Internet searches and how to send emails.

**Approaching Reproducible,** page 23

**Beyond Reproducible,** page 23

# Main Selection

CA CONTENT STANDARD R 3.3.1 Distinguish common forms of literature.

**GENRE: REALISTIC FICTION**

Have a student read the definition of Realistic Fiction on **Student Book** page 38. Remind them to pay attention to the characters, setting, and dialogue in the story that they might recognize from real life.

**STRATEGY**

**MAKE INFERENCES AND ANALYZE**

CA CONTENT STANDARD R 3.2.2 Ask questions and support answers by connecting prior knowledge with literal information found in, and inferred from, the text.

Remind students that readers use what they learn from the text, including pictures, as well as their own experiences to **make inferences** and reach conclusions about a story.

**SKILL**

**CAUSE AND EFFECT**

CA CONTENT STANDARD R 3.2.3 Demonstrate comprehension by identifying answers in the text.

Explain that a **cause** is why something happens. An **effect** is what happens as a result. Causes and their effects make up the events in a story.

## Vocabulary

**Vocabulary Words** Review the tested words while reading: **auditions, adventure, exploring, sparkling, fantastic,** and **success**.

**Additional Selection Words** Students may be unfamiliar with these words. Pronounce the words, give student-friendly explanations as needed, and help students use any previously taught vocabulary strategies, such as word parts.

**memory** (p. 41): all the things stored in a person's mind

**companion** (p. 44): a person who goes along with another

**ballet** (p. 51): a dance that uses formal steps in which dancers balance on their toes

**stunning** (p. 51): very beautiful or impressive

## Preview and Predict

**CA CONTENT STANDARD R 3.2.4** Recall major points in the text and make and modify predictions about forthcoming information.

**QUICK WRITE** Ask students to read the title, preview the illustrations, think about the genre, and think about what will happen in this story. Then have them write their predictions about what will happen in the story.

## Set Purpose

**FOCUS QUESTION** Discuss the "Read to Find Out" question on **Student Book** page 38. Remind students to look for the answer as they read.

Point out the Cause and Effect chart in the Student Book and on **Practice Book** page 24. Explain that students will fill it in as they read.

## Read *Amazing Grace*

Use the questions and Think Alouds to support instruction about the comprehension strategy and skill.

### Read Together

PARTNERS

If your students need support to read the Main Selection, use the prompts to guide comprehension and model how to complete the graphic organizer. Allow students time to fill in their organizers before you provide the answers.

Use **Think/Pair/Share**. When asking a question, have students *think* about their answer, then discuss it with a *partner*. Finally, have selected students *share* their answers with the group. Provide sentence frames for discussion, such as *Grace's visit to the ballet caused her to* _____ and *The effect was*_____, to help students use academic language. Students should support their answers with evidence from the text.

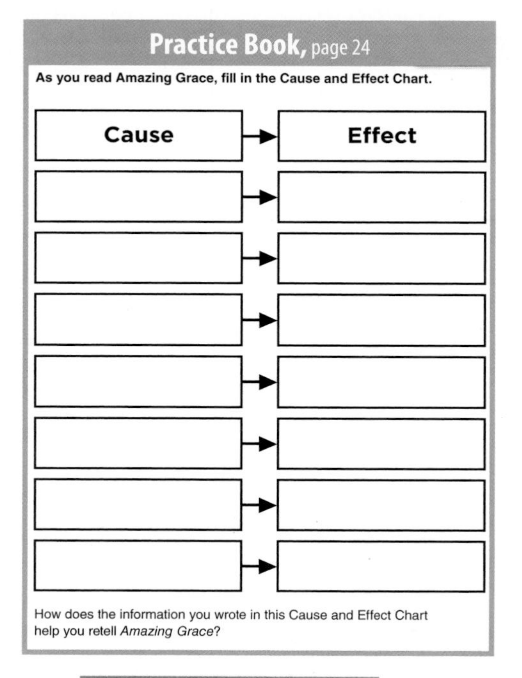

**Practice Book,** page 24

As you read Amazing Grace, fill in the Cause and Effect Chart.

| Cause | → | Effect |
|---|---|---|
| | → | |
| | → | |
| | → | |
| | → | |
| | → | |
| | → | |
| | → | |

How does the information you wrote in this Cause and Effect Chart help you retell *Amazing Grace*?

**Approaching Reproducible,** page 24

**Beyond Reproducible,** page 24

# Develop Comprehension

**1 STRATEGY**
**MAKE INFERENCES AND ANALYZE**

**Teacher Think Aloud** I know that in a fiction story, the author doesn't always tell everything that happens. To figure out the information that is left out, I will **make inferences**. To make inferences, I will think about what happens in the story and about similar experiences I've had. Then I can use these clues to figure out, or **analyze**, what is happening. Making inferences helps me understand the characters' actions and story events and helps me identify causes and effects. On page 41, I find out that Grace loves stories and enjoys acting them out. From my own experiences and information from the text, I can make an inference about the kind of person Grace is. I think she's a curious girl who enjoys stories because they help her experience new, exciting things by pretending that she is someone else.

40

## Monitor Comprehension

### Monitor and Clarify: *Reread*

**Explain** Tell students when they are confused by something in a story, such as a character's actions or the meaning of a word, they can reread that part of the story to figure out what is happening.

**Discuss** Tell students: *On page 42, I read that "Grace went into battle as Joan of Arc. . . and wove a wicked web as Anansi the Spider." I don't understand how Grace could do these things, so I will reread this page and the page before it. When I reread I learn that Grace likes acting out parts in stories, so this part is describing Grace as she pretends to be characters from different stories.*

**Apply** As students continue reading the story, have them use the reread strategy. After they have finished, have them share how rereading helped them understand confusing parts of the story.

Grace was a girl who loved stories.

She didn't mind if they were read to her or told to her or made up in her own head. She didn't care if they were in books or movies or out of Nana's long memory. Grace just loved stories.

After she had heard them, and sometimes while they were still going on, Grace would act them out. And she always gave herself the most exciting part.  

**Cause and Effect**
What happens when Grace reads a book?

41

# Develop Comprehension

## 2 SKILL
### CAUSE AND EFFECT

Think what happens when Grace hears a story. What is the **effect** on Grace? (Grace acts out the story and gives herself the best part. This is the effect of hearing the story.) Write the **cause and the effect** on your Cause and Effect Chart.

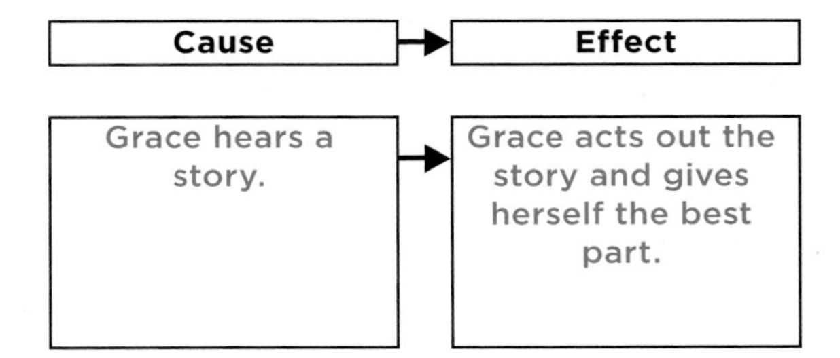

| Cause | Effect |
|---|---|
| Grace hears a story. | Grace acts out the story and gives herself the best part. |

## Phonics/Word Study

**APPLY DECODING SKILLS** While reading, point out words with the sound/spelling patterns, syllable types, and word parts students have recently learned. Help students blend these words. You may wish to focus on selection words with final *e* spelling patterns such as *wave, inside, gates, paved, lives, gave,* and *vote.*

## English Learners

**UNIVERSAL ACCESS**

Prepare students to read the story *prior* to the whole class reading. Use the Interactive Question-Response Guide on page 65CC to preteach the story content, build language, and develop meaning. This will enable students to participate successfully in the whole class reading and discussion.

**Beginning/Early Intermediate** Emphasize those questions and responses marked Beginning/Early Intermediate. In addition, focus on Key Words, Basic Words, and Function Words/Phrases.

**Intermediate** Use all the questions and prompts in the Interactive Question-Response Guide.

**Early Advanced** Extend language by using more complex sentence frames in the Interactive Question-Response Guide.

# Develop Comprehension

**3 CHARACTER**

What do the illustrations on this page tell you about Grace's **character**? (Grace makes costumes and pretends that she is in different places. She is very creative and has a big imagination.)

CA CONTENT STANDARD
R 3.3.3
Determine what characters are like by what they say or do and by how the author or illustrator portrays them.

Grace went into battle as Joan of Arc …
and wove a wicked web as Anansi the Spider.

She hid inside the wooden horse at the gates of Troy....

She went **exploring** for lost kingdoms....

She sailed the seven seas with a peg leg and a parrot.

3

4

43

# Develop Comprehension

## 4 WORD FAMILIES

CA CONTENT STANDARD R 3.1.1 Know and use complex word families when reading to decode unfamiliar words.

Knowing one word in a **word family** can help you figure out other words. How can knowing the meaning of *exploring* help you figure out the meaning of *explorer* or *exploration*? (I know that *exploring* means "traveling in unknown places and discovering what it is like." Since *exploration*, *explorer*, and *explored* belong to the same family, I can figure out that they all have to do with traveling to an unknown place.)

# Develop Comprehension

5 SKILL
CAUSE AND EFFECT

What **causes** Grace to play all the parts in adventure stories and fairy tales herself? (She had to play the parts herself because no one else was around.) Add this information to your Cause and Effect Chart.

| Cause | Effect |
|---|---|
| Grace is alone after reading adventure stories and fairy tales. | Grace acts out all the parts herself. |

She was Hiawatha, sitting by the shining Big-Sea-Water … and Mowgli in the backyard jungle.

Most of all Grace loved to act out **adventure** stories and fairy tales. When there was no one else around, Grace played all the parts herself. 5

She set out to seek her fortune, with no companion but her trusty cat—and found a city with streets paved in gold.

Or she was Aladdin, rubbing his magic lamp to make the genie appear.

44

Sometimes she could get Ma and Nana to join in, when they weren't too busy.

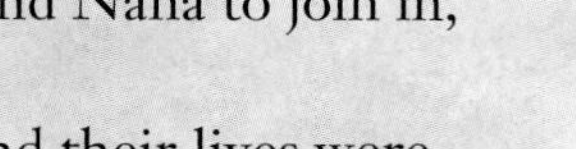

Then she was Doctor Grace and their lives were in her hands.

45



# Develop Comprehension

## 6 CHARACTER AND SETTING

What is the **setting** of the story? Who is the main **character**? (The main character in the story is a little girl named Grace. So far the story takes place in the present day, in Grace's home.)

# Develop Comprehension

## 7 STRATEGY
### MAKE INFERENCES AND ANALYZE

**Teacher Think Aloud** I know that **making inferences** can help me better understand a characters's actions in a story. In this part of the story, Raj tells Grace that Peter is a boy's name. Use your knowledge of Grace so far, her actions in this part of the story, and your own experiences to make an inference about what effect this comment has on her.

Prompt students to apply the strategy in a Think Aloud.

**Student Think Aloud** If I were Grace, I would feel very discouraged when Raj says that only boys can play Peter Pan. I know that Grace loves to play all the parts. I see that after Raj says she can't play Peter Pan, she keeps her hand up. I think that Grace really wants to play the part, so she keeps her hand up. I am sure that she feels mad because someone has said that she can't do something she wants to.

One day Grace's teacher said they would do the play *Peter Pan*. Grace knew who she wanted to be.

When she raised her hand, Raj said, "You can't be Peter—that's a boy's name."

But Grace kept her hand up.

46

"You can't be Peter Pan," whispered Natalie. "He isn't black." But Grace kept her hand up.

"All right," said the teacher. "Lots of you want to be Peter Pan, so we'll have **auditions** next week to choose parts." She gave them words to learn. **7** **8**

# Develop Comprehension

**8** **SKILL**
**CAUSE AND EFFECT**

Think about **cause and effect**. Why does the teacher decide to have auditions to choose parts for the play? What is the cause? What is the effect? (Lots of students wanted to be Peter Pan, so the teacher decides to have auditions to decide who will play each part.) Add this information to your Cause and Effect Chart.

| Cause | → | Effect |
| --- | --- | --- |
| Lots of students want to be Peter Pan. | → | The teacher decides to hold auditions. |

## English Learners

UNIVERSAL ACCESS

**STRATEGIES FOR EXTRA SUPPORT**

**Question 8 CAUSE AND EFFECT**
Help students identify causes and effects. Read the following sentence aloud: "Lots of you want to be Peter Pan, so we'll have auditions next week to choose parts." Ask: *Does this sentence contain a cause and effect signal word?* (Yes, it contains the signal word *so*.) What is the cause in this sentence? (Lots of the students want to be Peter Pan.) What is the effect? (They will have auditions.) Point out to students that they should look for signal words to help them find causes and effects. However, sometimes there are no signal words. Students should then ask themselves questions such as *What happened?* and *Why did it happen?* to find causes and effects.

# Develop Comprehension

## 9 STRATEGY
### MAKE INFERENCES AND ANALYZE

Read the last sentence on page 48. What lesson do you think Ma is trying to teach Grace? Use what you know and information from the text to **make an inference**. (Ma tells Grace that Raj is wrong and that a girl can be Peter Pan if she wants to. I think that Ma is trying to teach Grace that she can do and be anything she wants to, and can do the same things that boys can.)

## 10 CHARACTER

Read what Nana tells Grace on page 49. What do you learn about Nana's **character** from what she says? (Nana is a strong, positive person who believes that people can do anything they want to if they try hard and believe in themselves.)

## 11 GENRE: REALISTIC FICTION

What features of **realistic fiction** have you found so far in this story? (Answers should include that the events in the story could really happen, the story characters speak and act like people they know, and the story takes place in settings like ones that they know in real life—a home and a classroom.)

When Grace got home, she seemed sad.

"What's the matter?" asked Ma.

"Raj said I can't be Peter Pan because I'm a girl."

"That just shows what Raj knows," said Ma. "A girl can **9** be Peter Pan if she wants to."

48

Grace cheered up, then later she remembered something else. "Natalie says I can't be Peter Pan because I'm black," she said. 11

Ma looked angry. But before she could speak, Nana said, "It seems that Natalie is another one who don't know nothing. You can be anything you want, Grace, if you put your mind to it." 12 13

49

# Develop Comprehension

**12 SKILL**
**CAUSE AND EFFECT**

What **causes** Nana to say, "You can be anything you want, Grace, if you put your mind to it?" (Natalie told Grace that she couldn't be Peter Pan because she was black. This causes Nana to tell Grace that she can be Peter Pan if she really wants to.)

**13 SELF-SELECTED STRATEGY USE**

What strategies have you used so far to help you understand the selection? Where did you use them? Why? How did they help?

**RETURN TO PREDICTIONS AND PURPOSES**

Have students respond to the selection by confirming or revising their predictions and purposes for reading. Have them revise or write additional questions to help focus their attention as they continue to read the selection.

## Extra Support

**Cause and Effect**

Guide students who need help identifying causes and effects. Review questions to ask to figure out causes and effects. To find an effect, ask, *What happened?* To find a cause, ask, *Why did it happen?* Have them reread page 49. Ask: *What did Natalie say to Grace?* (Natalie said Grace could not be Peter Pan because she was black.) *What happened? How did this cause Ma to look?* (Ma looked angry.) *Why did this happen? What did Natalie do?* (Natalie said Grace couldn't play Peter Pan because she was black.) Then help students identify why Nana says that Grace can do anything she wants, if she puts her mind to it. (She says this because Natalie said that Grace couldn't be Peter Pan.)

Stop here if you wish to read this selection over two days.

# Develop Comprehension

**14 SUMMARIZE**

**Summarize** the events that have taken place so far in the story. (I have learned that Grace is a girl who loves stories and has a great imagination. She loves acting out stories and always gives herself the best parts. One day at school, the teacher says that the class will present the play *Peter Pan*. Grace wants to play Peter, but people say she can't because she is a girl and because she is black. At home she tells Ma and Nana. Ma looks angry, and Nana says that Grace can do anything she puts her mind to.)

**15 SKILL**
**CAUSE AND EFFECT**

What **causes** Nana and Grace to go into town? (They go into town because Nana wants to take Grace to the ballet.) Add this information to your Cause and Effect chart.

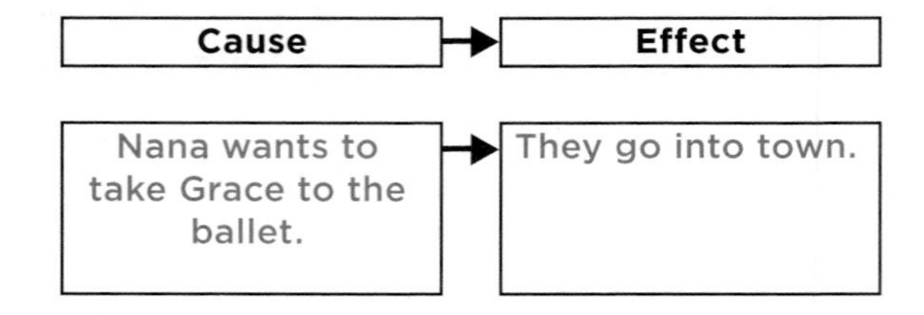

| Cause | Effect |
|---|---|
| Nana wants to take Grace to the ballet. | They go into town. |

**14**

On Saturday Nana told Grace they were going out. In the afternoon they caught a bus and train going into town. Nana took Grace to a grand theater. The sign outside read *Romeo and Juliet* in **sparkling** lights.

50

## Vocabulary

### Context Clues

**Explain/Model** Tell students they can use context clues to help find the meanings of difficult words. Context clues are words or information in the same sentence or in nearby sentences. Point to *ballerina* on page 51 and model using context clues to find the meaning.

**Think Aloud** I don't know the word *ballerina*, but clues tell me it has to do with dance. Nana took Grace to the ballet and had her look at a picture outside the theater: "Grace looked up and saw a beautiful young ballerina in a tutu." The next line says, "Above the dancer it said STUNNING NEW JULIET." Since this line comes after the one with *ballerina* in it, I think that *dancer* refers to the ballerina. A ballerina must be a type of dancer who performs in a ballet.

**Apply** Have students use context clues to help them with other difficult words or phrases.

"Are we going to the ballet, Nana?" asked Grace.

"We are, honey, but first I want you to look at this picture." **15**

Grace looked up and saw a beautiful young ballerina in a tutu. Above the dancer it said STUNNING NEW JULIET. **16**



# Develop Comprehension

**16 SETTING**

How do the illustrations on pages 50 and 51 help you to know that the **setting** has changed? (The illustrations show Nana and Grace on a busy street and standing outside a theater. Earlier in the story, the story took place in Grace's home and then at her school, so I know that the setting has changed.)

# Develop Comprehension

**17 STRATEGY**
**MAKE INFERENCES AND ANALYZE**

What lesson does Nana want to teach Grace? Use story clues about the characters' actions and feelings, what you know, and your own experiences to **make an inference**.

**Student Think Aloud** I know that grandmothers, like Nana, often want to help their grandchildren. From the story I know that Nana is taking Grace to see Rosalie, the ballerina, for a reason. Earlier, Raj and Natalie told Grace that she couldn't be Peter Pan. By taking Grace to the ballet, Nana shows her that Rosalie, who was from Trinidad, became a famous ballerina. Even though the author doesn't tell me this, I think that Nana wants to show Grace that if she works hard and believes in herself, she can do anything she wants, even play Peter Pan.

"That one is little Rosalie from back home in Trinidad," said Nana. "Her granny and me, we grew up together on the island. She's always asking me do I want tickets to see her Rosalie dance—so this time I said yes."

17

52

After the ballet Grace played the part of Juliet, dancing around her room in her imaginary tutu. I can be anything I want, she thought. 

53

# Develop Comprehension

18 **SKILL**
**CAUSE AND EFFECT**

What **causes** Grace to believe that she can be anything she wants? (Grace goes to see Rosalie dance as Juliet in the ballet. If Rosalie can do something as difficult as becoming a famous ballerina, then Grace can do those things, too.)

# Develop Comprehension

**19 SKILL**
**CAUSE AND EFFECT**

Why was Grace the best choice to play the part of Peter Pan? (She had been practicing being Peter all weekend and did well at the auditions.) Complete your Cause and Effect Chart.

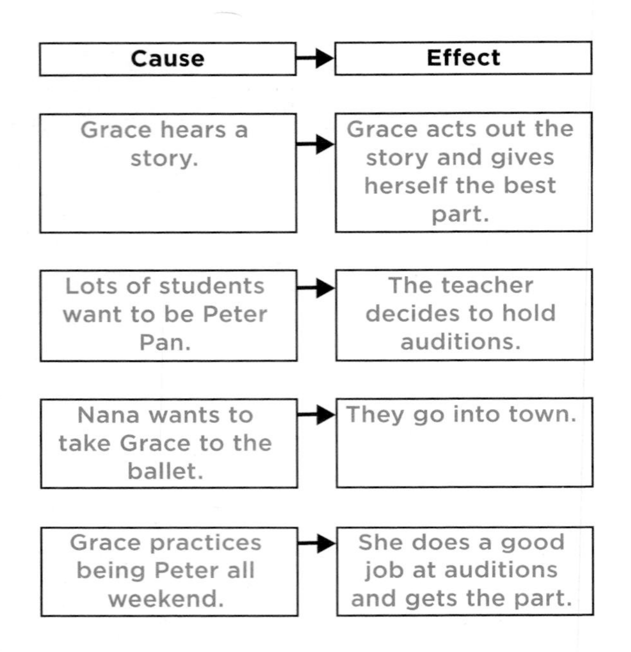

| Cause | Effect |
| --- | --- |
| Grace hears a story. | Grace acts out the story and gives herself the best part. |
| Lots of students want to be Peter Pan. | The teacher decides to hold auditions. |
| Nana wants to take Grace to the ballet. | They go into town. |
| Grace practices being Peter all weekend. | She does a good job at auditions and gets the part. |

On Monday the class met for auditions to choose who was best for each part.

When it was Grace's turn to be Peter, she knew exactly what to do and all the words to say—she had been Peter Pan all weekend. She took a deep breath and imagined herself flying.

When it was time to vote, the class chose Raj to be Captain Hook and Natalie to be Wendy. There was no doubt who would be Peter Pan. *Everyone* voted for Grace.

**19** **20** "You were **fantastic**!" whispered Natalie.

# Develop Comprehension

**20 GENRE: REALISTIC FICTION**

Do the events that occur on page 54 seem like things that would happen in real life? Does it make sense to have them in a **realistic fiction** story? (Yes, the events seem like they would happen in real life. People often have to audition to get a part in a play and they practice so that they do well. If they do well, they usually get the part. It makes sense to have these events in a realistic fiction story.)

# Develop Comprehension

**21 CHARACTER**

Grace says that she feels as if she could fly all the way home. What does this dialogue tell you about her **character**? (Grace means that she is happy and feels like she can do anything. It shows that she believes in herself and is proud of what she accomplished.)

## Listening/Speaking

CA CONTENT STANDARD LAS 3.1.3 Respond to questions with appropriate elaboration.

Have students share their Personal Response paragraphs. After speakers have finished, classmates can ask questions about the speaker's opinions and ideas. Then guide the speaker to respond to the questions with details and elaboration. Before the speaker answers questions, say: *Let's make sure we answer any questions using complete sentences. Let's make sure that we give details when we answer questions.* If students can successfully ask and answer questions, it shows that they listened carefully.

The play was a big **success** and Grace was an amazing Peter Pan.

After it was all over, she said, "I feel as if I could fly all the way home!" **21**

"You probably could," said Ma.

"Yes," said Nana. "If Grace puts her mind to it, she can do anything she wants."

57

# Develop Comprehension

### RETURN TO PREDICTIONS AND PURPOSES

Review students' **predictions** and **purposes**. Did they discover how books help Grace achieve her dreams? (Books allow Grace to use her imagination and practice playing different parts in stories. This practice helped her get the role of Peter.)

### REVIEW READING STRATEGIES

- **Make Inferences and Analyze** In what ways did making inferences about story characters and events help you to understand the selection?
- **Monitor and Clarify: Reread** Do you understand how the strategy of rereading can help you understand confusing parts of a story? When might you use it again?
- **Decoding** What difficult words did you encounter? How did the Reading Multisyllabic Words strategy help you sound out these words?
- **Self-Selected Strategy Use** What strategies did you use to make sense of what you read? Where? How were these strategies helpful?

### RESPONSE TO LITERATURE

Ask students to think about how books have affected their lives. Have them use their Writer's Notebooks to write about what they liked best about the character Grace and why. Have them use descriptive words to talk about the character.

**Quick Check**

**Can students identify causes and effects in the story?**

During **Small Group Instruction**

**If No →** **Approaching Level** Reteach the skill and have students apply it to a simpler text. Use Practice Reader lessons, pp. 65N–65P.

**If Yes →** **On Level** Have students apply the skill to a new text to consolidate learning. Use Practice Reader lesson, pp. 65U–65V.

**Beyond Level** Have students apply the skill to a more complex text to extend learning. Use Practice Reader lesson, pp. 65Y–65Z.

## Author and Illustrator

**AMAZING MARY AND CAROLINE**

Have students read the biographies of the author and illustrator. Ask:

- How do you think Mary Hoffman's experiences writing plays for her friends in primary school helped her write *Amazing Grace*?
- How do Caroline Binch's illustrations help you picture, or visualize, what what kind of person Grace is?

**WRITE ABOUT IT**

**Author's Craft: Alliteration**

Remind students how the author used alliteration in the story to create a rhythm with words and make phrases more interesting and memorable. Ask students to write a description of Grace or one of the other characters in the story. Have them use alliteration in their descriptions.

### Author's Purpose

Remind students that authors who write realistic fiction often write to inform or entertain. Ask them to use their Cause and Effect Charts and other clues from the story to show that the author's purpose was to write an entertaining story about a girl who learns she can be anything she wants, including Peter Pan.

# Amazing Mary and Caroline!

Mary Hoffman was interested in stories at a young age. When she was in primary school, she wrote plays for her friends to perform. As an adult, she has written over eighty children's books. She has also written other stories about Grace, including Boundless Grace.

Caroline Binch does more than draw pictures for children's books. She is a painter, a photographer, and a published author, too. She lives in England with her two dogs and cat.

Find out more about Mary Hoffman and Caroline Binch at **www.macmillanmh.com**.

**Another book** by Mary Hoffman and Caroline Binch: *Boundless Grace*

**Author's Purpose**

Fiction writers often tell stories that entertain or inform readers. What was Mary Hoffman's purpose for writing *Amazing Grace*? What clues in the story help you to understand the author's purpose?

58

CA CONTENT STANDARD R 3.3.5 Recognize the similarities of sounds in words and rhythmic patterns in a selection.

### Author's Craft

**Alliteration**

Alliteration is a literary device in which the same sound appears at the beginning of two or more words in a row. Authors often include alliteration in their stories to create a rhythm and make certain phrases more memorable and interesting.

- Example: "Grace went into battle as Joan of Arc...and wove a wicked web as Anansi the Spider." (page 42) The /w/ sound is repeated in the words *wove*, *wicked*, and *web*.
- Have students find other examples of alliteration in the story, such as, "She sailed the seven seas with a peg leg and a parrot." (page 43) Have students identify the sounds that repeat (*s* and *p*) and discuss how the rhythm and repeated sounds contribute to their enjoyment of the story.

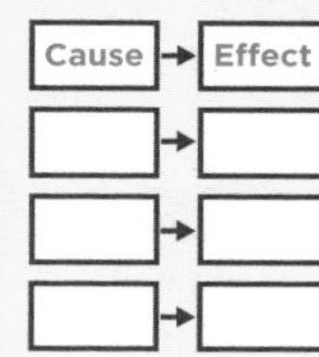

## Critical Thinking

### Retell the Story

Summarize the events in *Amazing Grace*. Then use your Cause and Effect Chart to help you understand why the events happened.

| Cause | Effect |
| --- | --- |
| | |
| | |
| | |

### Think and Compare

1. What **causes** Grace to be upset when she comes home from school in the middle of the story? What was the **effect** on Nana? **Make Inferences and Analyze: Cause and Effect**
2. Reread pages 50–53 of *Amazing Grace*. Why do you think Grace's Nana took her to see the ballet? **Analyze**
3. Grace helped her class play become a **success**. What activity or show have you helped make successful? **Apply**
4. What do Grace and her classmates learn about themselves after the play? **Evaluate**
5. Read "The Big Show" on pages 36–37. Compare the play that the children made with the class play in *Amazing Grace*. How are they alike? How are they different? Use details from both stories in your answer. **Reading/Writing Across Texts**

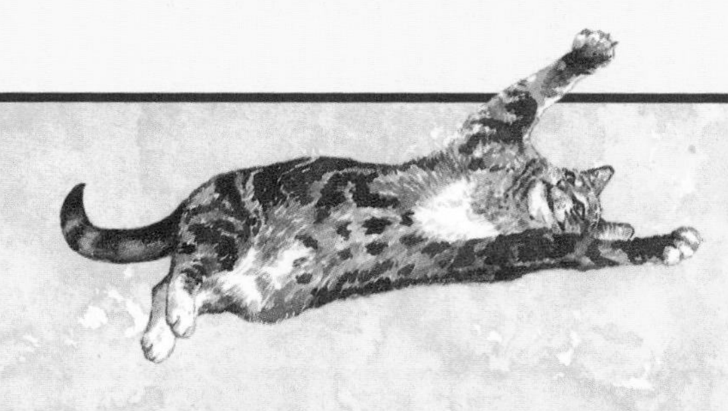

59

## Answering Questions

CA CONTENT STANDARD
R 3.2.2 Ask questions and support answers by connecting prior knowledge with literal information found in, and inferred from, the text.

### Author and Me

Model the Author and Me technique with question 4.

The answer is not in the selection. Link what you have learned in the text with what you already know.

**Question 4 Think Aloud** I know that people usually learn a lesson or find out something about themselves by finishing a task. I know that Grace and her classmates worked hard to put on a good show. Some of the students in Grace's class didn't think that she could be Peter, but she got the part and she was great. I think that Grace and her classmates learned that they can succeed and do anything they want if they work hard—even when someone tells them they can't.

## Critical Thinking

### SUMMARIZE

Have partners summarize *Amazing Grace* in their own words. Remind students to use their Cause and Effect Chart to help them organize their summaries.

### THINK AND COMPARE

1. **Cause and Effect** Grace is upset because Raj told her she could not be Peter Pan because she is a girl. Nana tells Grace that she can be anything she wants if she puts her mind to it.
2. **Analyze** Nana took her to see the ballet so she could see how successful Rosalie was as a ballerina playing Juliet. This helped Grace understand that she could be anything she wanted to be.
3. **Text-to-Self** Answers may vary. Students may say that they played a part in a school play, performed in a dance recital, or helped a sports team win a game.
4. **Text-to-World** Answers may vary. Students may say that Grace and her classmates learned how to put on a successful play. They also learned that you can play any role in a play if you believe in yourself and work hard. USE AUTHOR AND ME

### FOCUS QUESTION

5. **Text-to-Text** Answers may vary. Students may say that the shows were alike because children in both stories had to audition for parts, and the plays were successful. They were different because there were mistakes in "The Big Show," but everything went well in *Amazing Grace*.

### Objectives

- Read fluently with intonation
- 61–81 WCPM

### Materials

- Transparency 2
- Practice Book, p. 25
- Fluency Solutions Audio CD

### English Learners

UNIVERSAL ACCESS

**Develop Comprehension** Review the meaning of the passage sentence by sentence to ensure that students understand what they are reading. Have students retell what they have read. Model reading the passage phrase by phrase and the dialogue line by line. Then echo-read the passage with students.

### Practice Book, page 25

**As I read, I will pay attention to my intonation.**

| | |
|---|---|
| | Rainforests are home to over half the world's plants |
| 9 | and animals. When the rainforest is lost, the circle of life |
| 20 | breaks down. The climate changes. The plants and animals |
| 29 | die off. |
| 31 | People have come up with many ways to address this |
| 41 | problem. One way to save the forests is to learn all about |
| 53 | them. |
| 54 | Another way is to get wood from somewhere else. Now |
| 64 | there are tree farms where wood is grown. If you can get |
| 76 | trees from a farm, then you don't need to cut down a forest. |
| 89 | Cutting a rainforest tree should only be done as a last |
| 100 | **resort.** 101 |

**Comprehension Check**

1. What happens when the rainforest is lost? **Main Idea and Details**
   The circle of life breaks down, climate changes, and plants and animals die.
2. What are ways to help save the forests? **Main Idea and Details**
   learn about them, get wood from a tree farm

| | Words Read | – | Number of Errors | = | Words Correct Score |
|---|---|---|---|---|---|
| First Read | | – | | = | |
| Second Read | | – | | = | |

Approaching Reproducible, page 25

Beyond Reproducible, page 25

# Fluency

## Repeated Reading: Intonation

**CA CONTENT STANDARD R 3.1.3** Read aloud narrative and expository text fluently and accurately and with appropriate pacing, intonation, and expression.

**EXPLAIN/MODEL** Tell students that they will be echo-reading. Model reading **Transparency 2**. Emphasize intonation when reading the question and explain that your voice goes up at a question mark and goes down at a period. Using proper intonation when reading dialogue helps readers understand how characters sound.

### Transparency 2

On Saturday Nana told Grace they were going out. In the afternoon they caught a bus and train going into town. Nana took Grace to a grand theater. The sign outside read *Romeo and Juliet* in sparkling lights.

"Are we going to the ballet, Nana?" asked Grace.

"We are, honey, but first I want you to look at this picture."

Grace looked up and saw a beautiful young ballerina in a tutu. Above the dancer it said STUNNING NEW JULIET.

Fluency (from *Amazing Grace,* pages 50–51)

**PRACTICE** After you have read the entire passage, read one line at a time and have students echo-read the sentence. Point out how you raise your voice at the end of the question. Then have students work with partners and take turns reading and echo-reading the passage.

**DAILY FLUENCY** Students will practice fluency using **Practice Book** page 25 or the **Fluency Solutions Audio CD**. The passage is recorded at a slow practice speed and a faster fluent speed.

### Quick Check

**Can students read fluently?**

During **Small Group Instruction**

**If No** → **Approaching Level** Use the Fluency lesson and model, p. 65Q.

**If Yes** → **On Level** See Fluency, p. 65T.

**Beyond Level** See Fluency, p. 65X.

# Comprehension

**REVIEW SKILL**
**CHARACTER, SETTING, PLOT**

**EXPLAIN/MODEL**

CA CONTENT STANDARD
**R 3.3.3** Determine what characters are like by what they say or do and by how the author or illustrator portrays them.

Explain to students that fiction stories have characters, a setting, and a plot.

- **Characters** are the people and animals in a story. Readers learn about story characters from what they say, think, and do. They can also get information about characters from the illustrations.
- The **setting** is when and where a story takes place. The story may have one setting or the setting may change as the story goes on.
- The **plot** is made up of the events in a story. Most stories have a beginning, a middle, and an ending. In most plots the story begins with a character who has a problem. The plot follows the character as he or she tries to solve the problem.

Model how to identify characters, setting, and plot. Have students look at "The Big Show" on pages 36–37. Help them see that the story takes place on a rainy afternoon at Sue's house. The main characters are Sue and Jake. They are bored because it is raining, and they decide to write a play. The events in the story show how Sue and Jake write and perform a play with their friends. Point out that identifying the setting, characters, and plot in a story can help readers understand what happens in the story.

**PRACTICE/APPLY**

Ask the questions below to help students identify the characters, setting, and plot in *Amazing Grace*.

- What is the setting at the beginning of the story? (The story takes place in Grace's home in modern times.)
- Who is the main character in the story? What kind of person is she? How do you know? (The main character is Grace, who is a little girl with a big imagination. I know because she likes to act out the parts of her favorite characters from fairy tales and adventures. I can also tell this from the illustrations of her.)
- What important events happen at school on pages 46 and 47? (Grace wants to play Peter Pan in the school play, but several people tell her she can't because she is a girl and she is black.)
- What steps does Grace take to make sure she gets the role of Peter Pan in the class play? (She practiced all weekend before the audition and imagined she was flying during her audition.)

## Objectives

- Understand character, setting, and plot in a selection
- Use academic language: *character, setting, plot*

TESTED SKILL

**Skills Trace**

| Character, Setting, Plot | |
|---|---|
| **Introduce** | U1: 9A–B |
| **Practice/ Apply** | U1: 10–29; Practice Book 11-12 |
| **Reteach/ Review** | U1: 330–33JJ; U2: 313A–B, 314–339, 345M–HH; Practice Book 145–146 |
| **Assess** | Weekly Tests; Unit 1, 3, 6 Tests |
| **Maintain** | U1: 59B; U4: 33B; U6: 387A-B |

**Content Reader**

For content correlated to California Science and History/Social Science standards, see pages 24–29 in the **Content Reader**.
PS 3.2.a

# Paired Selection

**GENRE: LEGEND**

Have students read the bookmark on **Student Book** page 60. Explain that a legend

- is a story that is passed down from parents to children
- is based on the traditions of a people or region
- may use literary elements, such as personification
- may explain why something happens in nature

## Literary Elements: Personification

CA CONTENT STANDARD R 3.3.2 Comprehend basic plots of classic fairy tales, myths, folktales, **legends**, and fables from around the world.

**EXPLAIN** Some characters in legends are not human, but they have human characteristics. This is a special kind of literary element called personification.

- **Personification** is a literary element used when a storyteller gives an object, an animal, or a place human traits or a human personality. When an object or an animal in a story, such as a mirror, a tree, or a cloud, speaks or feels an emotion like a real person, it is personification.

**APPLY** Have students read the first two pages of the legend on pages 60–61. Discuss the callout that identifies personification. Then have students finish reading the legend and identify other examples of personification.

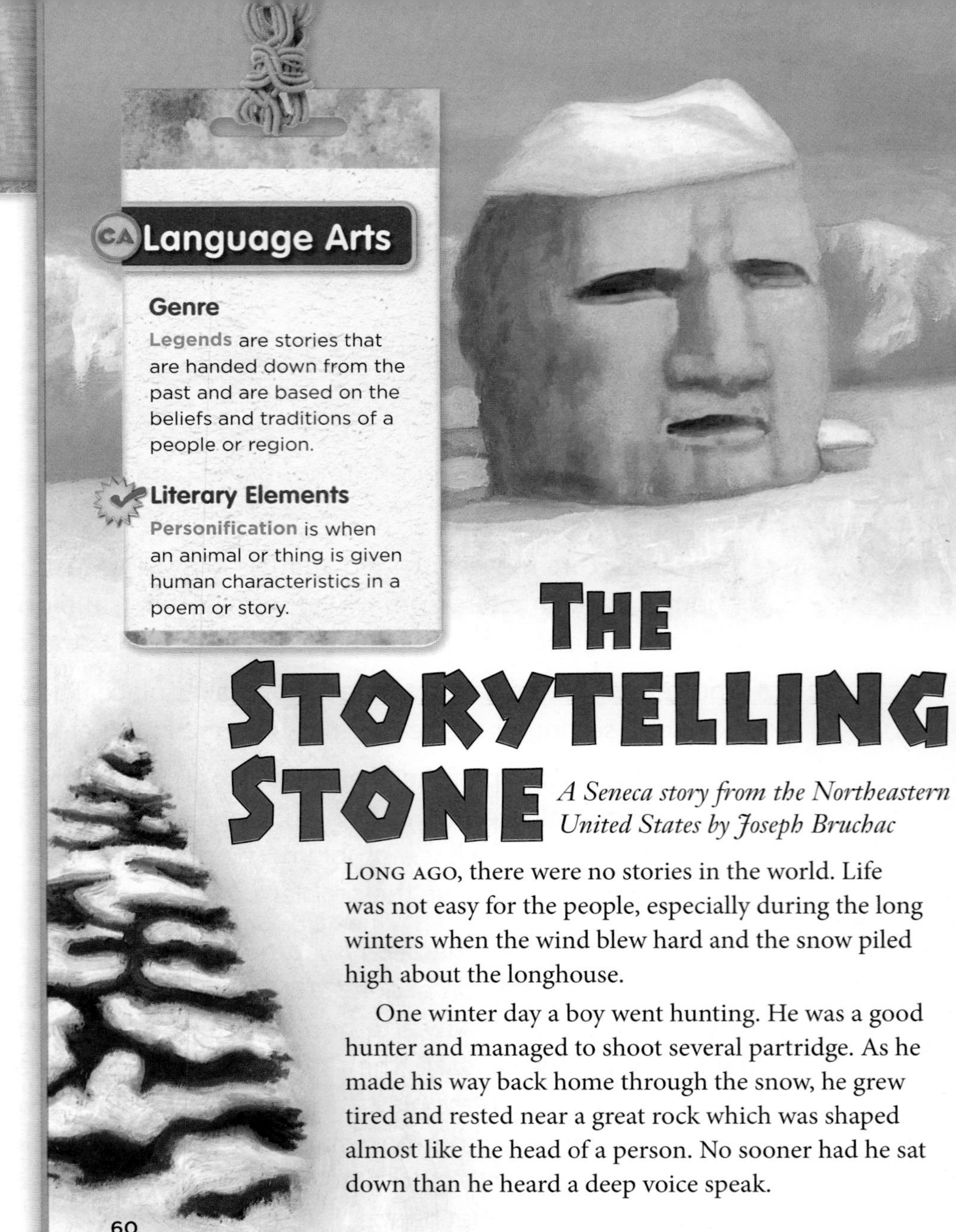


### Digital Learning

**Internet Research and Inquiry** Students can continue their unit research using the Research ToolKit on **www.macmillanmh.com**.

"I shall now tell a story," said the voice.

The boy jumped up and looked around. No one was to be seen.

"Who are you?" said the boy.

"I am Great Stone," said the rumbling voice which seemed to come from within the Earth. Then the boy realized it was the big standing rock which spoke. "I shall now tell a story."

**1**

The rock tells a story. This is an example of personification.

"Then tell it," said the boy.

"First you must give me something," said the stone. So the boy took one of the partridge and placed it on the rock.

**2**

"Now tell your story, Grandfather," said the boy.

Then the great stone began to speak. It told a wonderful story of how the Earth was created. As the boy listened he did not feel the cold wind and the snow seemed to go away. When the stone had finished the boy stood up.

"Thank you, Grandfather," said the boy. "I shall go now and share this story with my family. I will come back tomorrow."





## 1 LITERARY ELEMENT: PERSONIFICATION

How is Great Stone like a real person? What is it able to do? Why is this **personification**? (The stone can speak like a real person. It talks and tells stories to the human boy. When an object like a stone does something that only people can do, such as talking, it is personification.)

## 2 CAUSE AND EFFECT

What **causes** the boy to place a partridge on the rock? (Great Stone tells the boy he must give it something before it tells the story. This request causes the boy to give Great Stone one of the partridges.)

### Practice Book, page 26

**Personification** means giving human characteristics to an animal or thing. Examples:
The star raced across the sky. My old car coughed.

A **legend** is a story that is passed down orally from older people to younger ones. It may teach a lesson or explain why something happens. A legend often includes personification.

**Read the legend below. Then answer the questions.** Possible responses provided.

Father Sun and Mother Moon lived inside the rocks at Rock House. They didn't give any light to the sky, so the people and the animals lived in darkness. Coyote loved to play tricks. He thought it would be fun to dump fleas on Father Sun and Mother Moon. He gathered fleas in a bag and set out. On the way, he met Rabbit and Gopher. When he told them his plan, Rabbit and Gopher joined him on the path to Rock House. When they got to Rock House, they dumped the fleas down a hole in the rocks and ran away.

The fleas landed on Father Sun and Mother Moon. Mother Moon flew out of Rock House and began to fly around the Earth. Father Sun followed, racing around the Earth trying to get rid of those fleas. That is why, to this day, the Sun follows the Moon across the sky.

1. How does the author use personification in this legend? Coyote plays tricks and gathers fleas in a bag, Mother Moon and Father Sun live in a house.
2. What is this legend trying to explain? how the Earth gets light; how the sun and the moon move across the sky, providing light for Earth.

Approaching Reproducible, page 26

Beyond Reproducible, page 26

# Develop Comprehension

**3 CAUSE AND EFFECT**

What **effect** do the stories have on the people who live in the longhouse? (The stories cause the people to forget the cold and to be happy and sleep peacefully.)

**4 CAUSE AND EFFECT**

What **causes** Great Stone to speak for the last time? (Great Stone spoke for the last time because it had told the boy all its stories.)

**5 GENRE: LEGEND**

What elements of a **legend** can you find in this story? (This story has been passed down from parents to children for many generations. The story is based on the traditions of the Seneca who lived in the northeastern United States, and it explains how stories came to be part of Seneca culture.)

The boy hurried home to the longhouse. When he got there he told everyone something wonderful had happened. Everyone gathered around the fire and he told them the story he heard from the great stone. The story seemed to drive away the cold and the people were happy as they listened and they slept peacefully that night, dreaming good dreams. The next day, the boy went back again to the stone and gave it another bird which he had shot. **3**

"I shall now tell a story," said the big stone and the boy listened.

It went on this way for a long time. Throughout the winter the boy came each day with a present of game. Then Great Stone told him a story of the old times. The boy heard the stories of talking animals and monsters, tales of what things were like when the Earth was new. They were good stories and they taught important lessons. The boy remembered each tale and retold it to the people who gathered at night around the fire to listen. One day, though, when the winter was ending and the spring about to come, the great stone did not speak when the boy placed his gift of wild game.

62

**English Learners**
UNIVERSAL ACCESS

**Academic Language**
Guide students to see that the term *personification* is related to the word *person*. Have them complete the sentences: Great Stone is like a person because ____. This is personification because ____.

"Grandfather," said the boy, "Tell me a story."

Then the great stone spoke for the last time. "I have told you all of my stories," said Great Stone. "Now the stories are yours to keep for the people. You will pass these stories on to your children and other stories will be added to them as years pass. Where there are stories, there will be more stories. I have spoken. Naho."

4

Thus it was that stories came into this world. To this day, they are told by the people of the longhouse during the winter season to warm the people. Whenever a storyteller finishes a tale, the people always give thanks, just as the boy thanked the storytelling stone long ago.

5

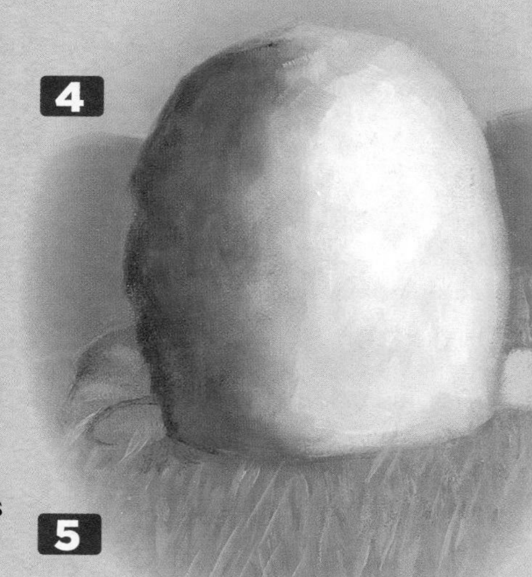

### Critical Thinking

1. How are Great Stone's actions like those of a real person's? Use details from the story in your answer. **Personification**
2. How do the stories help the boy and the people in the longhouse? **Analyze**
3. How are stories important to the people in the legend and Grace in *Amazing Grace*? Use details from the stories to support your answer. **Reading/Writing Across Texts.**

Find out more about personification at **www.macmillanmh.com**.

63



## Critical Thinking

### SUGGESTED ANSWERS

1. Great Stone knows the history of the earth and tells the boy important stories and lessons, just as an older person might teach a younger person. He also asks for something in return for his stories. People sometimes ask for something in return when they are giving something valuable, as Great Stone believes his stories are. PERSONIFICATION
2. The stories help the people live through the long, cold winter peacefully and teach them important lessons. ANALYZE

3. **FOCUS QUESTION** Stories are important to the people in the legend because they made them happy and taught them important lessons. Stories also made Grace happy because she enjoyed listening to them and acting them out. Stories also helped Grace learn important lessons about herself. She learned that she could act out any part and get any role in a play if she worked hard and put her mind to it. READING/WRITING ACROSS TEXTS

## CA Connect to Standards

CA CONTENT STANDARD HSS 3.2.1
Describe national identities, religious beliefs, customs, and various folklore traditions.

### Describe various folklore traditions of American Indian nations

Explain that American Indian nations in California have special stories and legends that are passed down from generation to generation. These stories help preserve their customs and cultures.

Have pairs of students choose an American Indian nation in California and do research to find legends and folklore belonging to that group. Have students collect their legends and folklore into an illustrated book and then present the stories orally to the class, as a storyteller might. Have them tell about the nation each story belongs to and explain the lesson the legend teaches.

# Build Robust Vocabulary

## Connect Language Arts

### WHOLE GROUP

**VOCABULARY**
- Tested words

**SPELLING**
- Final *e*

**GRAMMAR**
- Commands and Exclamations

**CA CONTENT STANDARDS**
R 3.1.1, R 3.1.4, LC 3.1.1, LC 3.1.3, LC 3.1.8

### SMALL GROUP

- Differentiated Instruction, pp. 65I–65HH

## Day 1 Teach/Practice

### CONNECT TO WORDS

- Practice this week's vocabulary words using the following prompts:
  1. What type of person might go to *auditions*?
  2. Would you rather read an *adventure* story or a biography? Why?
  3. Why is *exploring* a new place fun?
  4. What things have you seen that are *sparkling*?
  5. If a ballplayer missed a catch, would you say the player was *fantastic*? Why or why not?
  6. Would you rather that your class play be a *success* or a failure? Why?

### ACADEMIC VOCABULARY

- Review the important academic vocabulary words for the week. These words include: *make inferences, cause, effect, character, setting, plot, personification.*
- Write each word on the board. Define each using student-friendly language and ask students to select the word you are defining. Then point to words in random order for students to define.

## Day 2 Review

### CONNECT TO WORDS

- Review the definitions of this week's vocabulary words using **Student Book** pages 36–37. Discuss each word using the following prompts:
  1. Why does the director of a movie or play have *auditions*?
  2. What *adventure* story have you read recently?
  3. Where would you be *exploring* if you were in a submarine?
  4. Would you say that a star is *sparkling* or dull? Why?
  5. Would you smile or frown about something that is *fantastic*? Why?
  6. How can a business owner make sure that his business is a *success*?

### WORD FAMILIES

- Tell students that words that share a common word or word part often have similar meanings. Looking for common words can help them figure out unfamiliar words.
- Display **Transparency 3**. Read the first sentence and model how to find the meaning of the underlined word.
- Have students use their knowledge of word families to define the remaining underlined words.
- Have students write their own context-rich sentences for this week's vocabulary words in their Writer's Notebooks. Direct students to the sentences in the book or model an example first.

---

ON YOUR OWN

**Practice Book,** page 27

A **word family** is a group of words that have the same word part. This word part is called the base word. Knowing the meaning of the base word can help you figure out the meaning of other words in the word family.

**A. Read each sentence below. Circle the word that belongs to the same word family as the underlined word.**

1. My favorite books are about people who discover places no one has ever been before.
   a. extra  b. like  (c.) recover
2. When you read, you can imagine you're in a faraway place.
   a. interest  b. imaginary  (c.) think

**B. Read each poem below. Write two words that belong to the same word family as the underlined word.** Possible responses provided.

3. I would love to take a trip on a houseboat. household, playhouse, outhouse, firehouse, clubhouse
4. I read a story about a man in a lighthouse who saved hundreds of ships. lightning, flashlight, daylight, nightlight, highlight
5. Have you ever seen a waterfall? waterway, watermelon, underwater, watery, whitewater
6. It's fun to recite silly poems from memory. remember, memorize, memorial, memo

Approaching Reproducible, page 27
Beyond Reproducible, page 27

CA CONTENT STANDARD
**R 3.1.4** Use knowledge of antonyms, synonyms, homophones, and homographs to determine the meanings of words.

## Day 3 Reinforce

### CONNECT TO WORDS

- Ask students to create Word Squares for each word in their Writer's Notebooks.
- In the first square, students write the word. (Example: *fantastic*)
- In the second square, students write their own definition of the word and related words, such as synonyms. (Example: *fabulous, superb, extraordinary, marvelous, great*)
- In the third square, students draw a simple illustration that will help them remember the word. (Example: *drawing of person clapping with a big smile on his face)*
- In the fourth square, students write nonexamples, including antonyms for the word. (Example: *awful, poor, terrible)*

### RELATED WORDS

- Use the Additional Selection Vocabulary word *memory* as a springboard to learn other words.
- Write *memory* on the board; explain that it means "things stored in one's mind," or "the ability to recall things." Write *memorize, memorial,* and *remember* on the board. Point out that these words are in the same word family as *memory*.
- Have students use their knowledge of *memory* and a dictionary, if necessary, to figure out each word. Help them see that *memorize* means "to learn by heart." A *memorial* is a reminder of a person or an event.

CA CONTENT STANDARD
**R 3.1.1** Know and use complex word families when reading to decode unfamiliar words.

## Day 4 Extend

### CONNECT TO WORDS

- Review this week's vocabulary using the following sentence stems. Have students orally complete each one.

1. The drama teacher held auditions because ______.
2. I saw an exciting adventure movie about ______.
3. Scientists might go exploring in the ______ to find ______.
4. The ______ was sparkling in the light.
5. The food was fantastic because ______.
6. We knew the show was a success because ______.

### MORPHOLOGY

- Use the vocabulary word *audition* as a springboard to learn other words.
- Write the root *aud-* and the word *auditions* on the board. Underline the word part *aud-*. Point out that *aud-* means "hear"; an audition is a short performance in which a person's ability is seen and heard.
- Write the words *audio, audience, audible,* and *auditorium* on the board. Have students underline *aud* in each word. Then have them use the meaning of *aud-* and a dictionary, if necessary, to figure out the meanings—*audio* is recorded sound; an *audience* is the people who see and hear a performance; *audible* means "can be heard"; and an *auditorium* is a place where a performance is seen and heard.

## Day 5 Assess and Reteach

### POSTTEST

- Display **Transparency 4**. Have students complete the cloze sentences using one of this week's vocabulary words.
- Note how quickly and accurately students can complete this task. Work with students who make errors or require too much time to complete this task during Small Group time.

### CONNECT TO WRITING

- Have students write sentences in their Writer's Notebooks using this week's vocabulary. Tell students to write sentences that provide information they learned from this week's readings.
- **EL** Provide the Day 4 sentence stems for students needing extra support.

# 5-Day Spelling

Go to page T17 for **Differentiated Spelling Lists**. Pretests and Posttests are available in the Teacher's Resource Book.

## Spelling Words

| | | |
|---|---|---|
| date | **home** | wise |
| fine | safe | smoke |
| rose | rice | grade |
| lake | globe | smile |
| life | plane | come |

**Review** clap, crop, sick
**Challenge** sneeze, escape

## Dictation Sentences

1. What is today's date?
2. It is a fine day for a walk.
3. That is a pretty red rose.
4. May we swim in the lake?
5. I read about life in the sea.
6. I ran all the way **home**.
7. The park is a safe place to play.
8. We had rice with our dinner.
9. A globe is round.
10. We flew on a plane.
11. My grandma is very wise.
12. We smelled smoke from a fire.
13. We are in the third grade.
14. Grace had a big smile on her face.
15. Where did your family come from?

## Review/Challenge Words

1. Clap when the music ends.
2. It is not fun to be sick.
3. They pick their crop in the fall.
4. The dust made me sneeze.
5. I hope the tiger does not escape.

Words in **bold** type are from this week's selections.

# Final *e*

CA CONTENT STANDARD
**LC 3.1.8** Spell correctly one-syllable words that have blends, contractions, compounds, orthographic patterns, and common homophones.

## Day 1 Pretest

### ASSESS PRIOR KNOWLEDGE

- Model for students how to spell the word *lake*. Segment the word sound by sound, and then attach a spelling to each sound. Point out that the final *e* is silent.
- For students needing practice segmenting words or manipulating phonemes, see **Intervention Kit**.
- Use the Dictation Sentences. Say the underlined word, read the sentence, and repeat the word. Have students write the words.
- Have students correct their own tests. Remind students that words with the final *e* spelling usually have a long vowel sound.
- Have students cut apart the Spelling Word Cards BLM on **Teacher's Resource Book** page 103 and figure out a way to sort them. Have them save the cards for use throughout the week.

## Day 2 Word Sorts and Review

### SPIRAL REVIEW

Review short vowel sounds in the words *clap, crop,* and *sick*. Have students find words in this week's readings with the same sounds.

### WORD SORTS

- Have students take turns sorting words and explaining how they sorted them. When students have finished the sort, discuss any words that have unexpected vowel spellings. (*come*)
- Review the Spelling Words, pointing out the final *e* spellings. Use the cards on the Spelling Words BLM. Write the key words *date, fine,* and *rose* on the board. Model how to sort words by vowel sound and final *e*. Place one or two cards beneath the correct key words.

ON YOUR OWN **Practice Book,** page 28

**Using the Word Study Steps**
1. LOOK at the word.
2. SAY the word aloud.
3. STUDY the letters in the word.
4. WRITE the word.
5. CHECK the word. Did you spell the word right? If not, go back to step 1.

**Choose the spelling word that best completes the sentence.**
1. My favorite flower is a rose.
2. We have to fly in a plane to visit my grandparents.
3. I make sure to put the date on the top of my letters.
4. Dave swims in the lake every summer.
5. I looked at a globe to see the country where my pen pal was from.
6. Jill saw smoke at the top of the house and knew there was a fire.
7. My favorite meal for dinner is rice and chicken.
8. My younger sister is in the first grade.
9. I asked my uncle to come over to help me with my homework.
10. To live a long life you should exercise and eat healthy food.
11. I wrote my brother a letter to ask him when he was coming home.
12. My grandfather tells me to always do my homework so I can be wise when I grow up.
13. I smile every time I see my new puppy.
14. To be safe I look both ways when I cross the street.
15. I felt fine after a lot of rest.

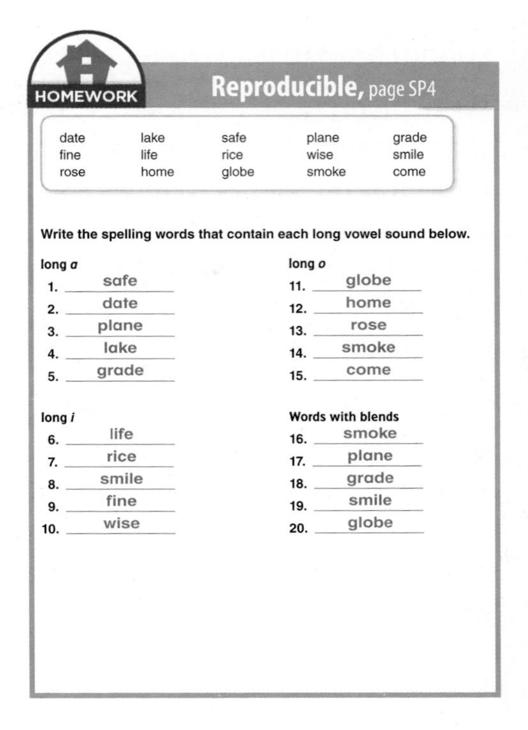
HOMEWORK **Reproducible,** page SP4

| | | | | |
|---|---|---|---|---|
| date | lake | safe | plane | grade |
| fine | life | rice | wise | smile |
| rose | home | globe | smoke | come |

**Write the spelling words that contain each long vowel sound below.**

long *a*
1. safe
2. date
3. plane
4. lake
5. grade

long *o*
11. globe
12. home
13. rose
14. smoke
15. come

long *i*
6. life
7. rice
8. smile
9. fine
10. wise

Words with blends
16. smoke
17. plane
18. grade
19. smile
20. globe

## Day 3 Word Meanings

### CATEGORIES

Display the group of words below. Have students copy the words into their Writer's Notebooks. Say the words aloud and ask students to complete each category with a spelling word.

1. bread, potato, ____ (rice)
2. tulip, daisy, ____ (rose)
3. clever, smart, ____ (wise)
4. sea, pond, ____ (lake)
5. house, hut, ____ (home)

Challenge students to come up with other category word groups for spelling words, review words, or challenge words.

Have partners write a sentence for each spelling word, leaving a blank where the word should go. Then have them trade papers and fill in the missing words.

## Day 4 Proofread

### PROOFREAD AND WRITE

Write the sentences below on the board. Have students circle and correct each misspelled word.

1. Did you pick a dayt to visit Tom's hoem? (date, home)
2. I picked a roas from the bush. (rose)
3. I smiyl when I get a good graid. (smile, grade)
4. The playn flew over a very large laik. (plane, lake)

**Error Correction** Some students may leave off the final e spelling, not realizing that the final e and the vowel before it act as a team. Other students may replace the final e spelling with another long vowel spelling, such as writing *smoak* for *smoke*. These students will need more work sorting and reading words containing final e spelling patterns.

## Day 5 Assess and Reteach

### POSTTEST

Use the Dictation Sentences on page 63C for the Posttest.

If students have difficulty with any words in the lesson, have students place them on a list called *Spelling Words I Want to Remember* in their Writer's Notebooks. Look for students' use of these words in their writings.

**Extra Support** Some students having spelling difficulties may need additional phonemic awareness instruction and practice. See the **Intervention Kit** for phoneme reversal, substitution, addition, deletion, and segmentation exercises.

Challenge students to find other words with final *e* and add them to the **Unit 1 Big Question Board**.

---

**HOMEWORK — Reproducible, page SP5**

| date | lake | safe | plane | grade |
|---|---|---|---|---|
| fine | life | rice | wise | smile |
| rose | home | globe | smoke | come |

**A. It Takes Three**

**Write a spelling word that goes with the other two words.**

1. pond, sea, lake
2. world, Earth, globe
3. smart, clever, wise
4. tulip, daisy, rose

**B. What Does It Mean?**

**Write a spelling word that matches each clue below.**

5. The place where you live home
6. The day of the year date
7. Not a frown smile
8. Flying machine plane
9. Rises from a fire smoke
10. Out of harm's way safe
11. A side dish rice
12. A class or year in school grade
13. Arrive come
14. Feeling well fine
15. A person's time on Earth life

**ON YOUR OWN — Practice Book, page 29**

**There are five spelling mistakes in this letter. Circle the misspelled words. Write the words correctly on the lines below.**

Dear Aunt Mary,

I am back in Boston! Our plain ride was fun. It was cool to look out the window and see the mountains and clouds. I even saw the layk when we were taking off! The people in those little cars had no idea I was watching them. It was great!

It was great to visit you, but I'm glad to be hoom saif and sound. We must make sure to talk often. I will try to write you as many letters as I can. Please com and see us soon.

Love,
Margaret

1. plane
2. lake
3. home
4. safe
5. come

**Writing Activity**

**Write a letter to your friend describing a trip you would like to take. Use at least three spelling words in your description.**

**HOMEWORK — Reproducible, page SP6**

**Look at the words in each set below. One word in each set is spelled correctly. Look at Sample A. The letter next to the correctly spelled word in Sample A has been shaded in. Do Sample B yourself. Shade the letter of the word that is spelled correctly. When you are sure you know what to do, go on with the rest of the page.**

**Sample A:** Ⓐ gayt Ⓑ gate Ⓒ gaat Ⓓ gat

**Sample B:** Ⓔ niec Ⓕ nice Ⓖ nyce Ⓗ naice

1. Ⓐ date Ⓑ dayt Ⓒ dait Ⓓ dayte
2. Ⓔ fin Ⓕ fyn Ⓖ fine Ⓗ faine
3. Ⓐ rose Ⓑ roze Ⓒ roase Ⓓ roaze
4. Ⓔ lake Ⓕ lacke Ⓖ layk Ⓗ laike
5. Ⓐ leyf Ⓑ lyfe Ⓒ life Ⓓ lyf
6. Ⓔ hoam Ⓕ home Ⓖ howme Ⓗ haum
7. Ⓐ saife Ⓑ saif Ⓒ seyfe Ⓓ safe
8. Ⓔ ric Ⓕ riis Ⓖ rice Ⓗ ryce
9. Ⓐ gloob Ⓑ gloab Ⓒ globe Ⓓ gloabe
10. Ⓔ playn Ⓕ plaen Ⓖ plaine Ⓗ plane
11. Ⓐ wyse Ⓑ wise Ⓒ waise Ⓓ wize
12. Ⓔ smoak Ⓕ smok Ⓖ smoake Ⓗ smoke
13. Ⓐ grayd Ⓑ grade Ⓒ graid Ⓓ graed
14. Ⓔ smyle Ⓕ smiyel Ⓖ smayle Ⓗ smile
15. Ⓐ come Ⓑ kome Ⓒ coome Ⓓ coam

# 5-Day Grammar

## Daily Language Activities

Write the sentences on the board.

**DAY 1**
who wrote the letter May wrote to her father he lives far away (1: Who; 2: letter?; 3: father.; 4: He; 5: away.)

**DAY 2**
Are you busy later Come to miy house after school what a great time we will have! (1: later?; 2: my; 3: school.; 4: What)

**DAY 3**
What a long letter this is? mail this letter today Put a stamp on the envelope (1: is!; 2: Mail; 3: today.; 4: envelope.)

**DAY 4**
What fun I had at your hom? call me soon. Let's play together another day (1: home!; 2: Call; 3: day.)

**DAY 5**
dave likes to write letters. His letters are funny Sometimes he tells jokes in them? (1: Dave; 2: funny.; 3: them.)

## English Learners

UNIVERSAL ACCESS

**Contrastive Analysis** Write on the board an example of a command and a question without punctuation. Punctuate the sentences with students. Discuss the difference between a command and a question. Note: Spanish punctuation uses an exclamation point or question mark at the beginning of a sentence.

# Commands and Exclamations

## Day 1 Introduce the Concept

**INTRODUCE COMMANDS AND EXCLAMATIONS**

Present the following:

- A **sentence** is a group of words that expresses a complete thought.
- A **command** is a sentence that tells someone to do something. It ends with a period.
- The word *you* is understood at the beginning of a command, but it is not usually written.
- An **exclamation**, or exclamatory sentence, is a sentence that shows excitement or strong feeling. It ends with an exclamation mark.

**Examples:**
Look at the package.
What a nice gift mom gave me!

See Transparency 6 for modeling and guided practice.

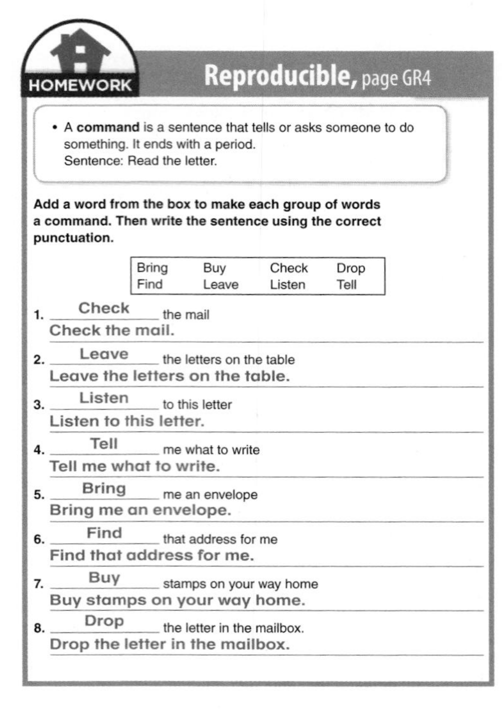

HOMEWORK **Reproducible,** page GR4

- A **command** is a sentence that tells or asks someone to do something. It ends with a period.
Sentence: Read the letter.

**Add a word from the box to make each group of words a command. Then write the sentence using the correct punctuation.**

| Bring | Buy | Check | Drop |
|---|---|---|---|
| Find | Leave | Listen | Tell |

1. Check the mail
Check the mail.
2. Leave the letters on the table
Leave the letters on the table.
3. Listen to this letter
Listen to this letter.
4. Tell me what to write
Tell me what to write.
5. Bring me an envelope
Bring me an envelope.
6. Find that address for me
Find that address for me.
7. Buy stamps on your way home
Buy stamps on your way home.
8. Drop the letter in the mailbox.
Drop the letter in the mailbox.

## Day 2 Teach the Concept

**REVIEW COMMANDS AND EXCLAMATIONS**

Review commands and exclamations with students.

Present the following:

- **Command:** A sentence that gives an order. It ends with a period.
- **Exclamation:** A sentence that shows excitement. It ends with an exclamation mark.

Have students give an example of each type of sentence.

See Transparency 7 for modeling and guided practice.

ON YOUR OWN **Practice Book,** page 30

- An **exclamation** shows strong feeling. It ends with an exclamation mark.
Sentence: What great news!

**Add a word from the box to make each group of words an exclamation. Then write the sentence correctly.**

| great | Hey | Look | Quick |
|---|---|---|---|
| see | too | What | Wow |

1. Look, there's a letter for you
Look, there's a letter for you!
2. What a surprise
What a surprise!
3. Quick, open the envelope
Quick, open the envelope!
4. Hey, it's from Aunt Cara
Hey, it's from Aunt Cara!
5. Wow, she has a new puppy
Wow, she has a new puppy!
6. That's great
That's great!
7. There's a picture, too
There's a picture, too!
8. Let me see
Let me see!

CA CONTENT STANDARD
**LC 3.1.3** Understand and be able to use complete and correct declarative, interrogative, imperative, and exclamatory sentences in writing and speaking.

## Day 3 Review and Practice

### REVIEW COMMANDS AND EXCLAMATIONS

Review punctuation in commands and exclamations. Remind students that the *you* at the beginning of a command is understood. An exclamation shows excitement.

### MECHANICS AND USAGE: PUNCTUATION IN COMMANDS AND EXCLAMATIONS

- Use a period at the end of a command.
- Use an exclamation mark at the end of an exclamation, or exclamatory sentence.

**Examples:**

What a pretty flower Sue sent! That flower is really beautiful!

Draw a picture.

See Transparency 8 for modeling and guided practice.

HOMEWORK **Reproducible,** page GR5

- A **command** tells or asks someone to do something. It ends with a period.
- An **exclamation** shows strong feeling. It ends with an exclamation mark.

**After each sentence, write *command* or *exclamation* for the kind of sentence it is. Then write the sentence correctly. Use capital letters and end marks.**

1. remember to write to grandfather command
   Remember to write to grandfather.
2. wow, I nearly forgot about that exclamation
   Wow, I nearly forgot about that!
3. whew, I'm glad you reminded me exclamation
   Whew, I'm glad you reminded me!
4. thank him for the gift command
   Thank him for the gift.
5. hand me that address book command
   Hand me that address book.
6. hey, I'll send him my new school picture exclamation
   Hey, I'll send him my new school picture!
7. that's a great idea exclamation
   That's a great idea!
8. write a note on the picture command
   Write a note on the picture.

## Day 4 Review and Proofread

### REVIEW TYPES OF SENTENCES

Ask students to explain the differences between statements, questions, commands, and exclamations. Ask what punctuation mark goes at the end of each type of sentence.

### PROOFREAD

Have students correct the errors in the following sentences and identify whether each sentence is a command or an exclamation.

1. what a great gift this is! (What; exclamation)
2. Write down your hobbies (hobbies.; command)
3. Tell me how to help? (help.; command)
4. What happy smiles the students have. (have!; exclamation)

See Transparency 9 for modeling and guided practice.

ON YOUR OWN **Practice Book,** page 31

- A **command** is a sentence that tells someone to do something.
- An **exclamation** shows strong feeling.

**Rewrite the letter from Steve fixing any mistakes you might find.**

Dear Chris,
What great news. I'm so happy to hear that you are coming to visit next month. wow, I can't believe it's been a year since you were last here I already have plans for things to do. I'll give you some hints. Bring your sleeping bag Pack a flashlight. Don't forget the bug spray. yes, we're going camping
I hope you'll do me another favor. Ask your dad for his chocolate chip cookie recipe His cookies are the best! Then I'll practice making them while you are here.
Sincerely yours,
Your favorite cousin,
Steve

Dear Chris,
What great news! I'm so happy to hear that you are coming to visit next month. Wow, I can't believe it's been a year since you were last here! I already have plans for things to do. I'll give you some hints. Bring your sleeping bag. Pack a flashlight. Don't forget the bug spray. Yes, we're going camping!
I hope you'll do me another favor. Ask your dad for his chocolate chip cookie recipe. His cookies are the best! Then I'll practice making them while you are here.
Sincerely yours,
Your favorite cousin,
Steve

## Day 5 Assess and Reteach

### ASSESS

Use the Daily Language Activity and **Reproducible GR6** for assessment.

### RETEACH

Use Reproducible GR6 and selected pages from the **Grammar and Writing Handbook** for additional reteaching.

Check students' writing for use of the skill. Assign Grammar Revision Assignments in their Writer's Notebooks, as needed.

See Transparency 10 for modeling and guided practice.

HOMEWORK **Reproducible,** page GR6

**A. Decide if the sentence is a *command* or an *exclamation*. Write your answer.**

1. Get ready to go. command
2. That's a great answer! exclamation
3. Oh no, I didn't get her address! exclamation
4. Find out where she lives. command
5. I cannot wait! exclamation
6. Mail that letter tomorrow. command
7. Put a stamp on the letter. command
8. She is going to be so happy! exclamation

**B. Rewrite the sentence using the correct punctuation.**

9. pack your bags tonight
   Pack your bags tonight.
10. we leave in two days
    We leave in two days!
11. don't forget your pillow
    Don't forget your pillow.

**Write a command sentence and an exclamation sentence about visiting a family member or a friend.** Possible answers are given.

I can't wait to see my uncle's new puppy!
Bring the leash.

# Write

## WHOLE GROUP

**WRITING**
- Focus on Moment

**CONTENT STANDARDS**
W 3.1.1, W 3.1.2, W 3.1.4, LAS 3.1.3

## SMALL GROUP

- Differentiated Instruction, pp. 65I–65HH

### 5-Day Writing

| | |
|---|---|
| DAY 1 | Skill Introduction |
| DAY 2 | Minilesson 1<br>Revision Assignments |
| DAY 3 | Minilesson 2<br>Revision Assignments |
| DAY 4 | Reading/Writing Connection<br>Focus on Moment |
| DAY 5 | Writing Conferences |

The Writers' Express
Immediate Impact. Lasting Transformation. wex.org

**Research Proven Writing Approach**

# Writer's Craft

## Strong Paragraphs: Developing a Single Moment of Action

**TEACH/MODEL**

**Set Purpose** Tell students that they are going to continue working on focus today. Remind them of the discussions and class work from the previous lesson (the introductory focus lesson). Remind students of the definition of *focus* (*picking one thing and writing a lot about it*).

Remind students how "focusing on a moment" means you are asking them to slow down and tell more about one moment rather than telling about every moment or occurrence in a given time frame (day, weekend, etc.) with little or no detail.

Display the prompt and read it to students.

**Write about one moment that happened over the weekend. Show what happened in that moment.**

**Make List** Ask students to name "moments" from their weekend that could be their starting point to answer the prompt. Basically you are generating a list of moments when students were "doing something."

**Share Lists** In the beginning many students will need help distinguishing individual moments from their experiences to add to the list. You will need to encourage and guide students to be specific. For example, if someone says, "I played," ask questions to elicit more detail such as "I played checkers with Mom." *What did you play? Who did you play with?*

**Teacher:** *What are some things you did that we could write on our list?*
**Students:** *went roller skating, ate at my grandmother's house, went to basketball practice*
**Teacher:** *Those all sounded like great ideas.*

Once you have a good-size brainstorm list (4–5 minutes at most should be enough time), stop and review the list with students. Check to see if it is clear that each of the items on the list is a separate moment that could be developed further.

## Teacher Write Aloud

**PRACTICE/APPLY**

Choose (or have any student choose) one moment from the list to develop further with the class and write it on another piece of chart paper. Explain to students that they are going to help you add details that show this moment (even if they weren't there).

As students offer details, write them on the new chart. Stop when you have four to five details to add to the originally chosen moment. The important thing to keep in mind here is that the details be relevant to the moment selected.

Guide students to give realistic details that are consistent with what could have actually happened had they been there (or when they had experienced a similar moment themselves). The idea is to add more details to the moment chosen so as to extend the focus on this moment. For example:

**Teacher:** *What moment did you choose?*
**Students:** *I played checkers with my Mom.*
**Teacher:** *What are some details to describe that?*
**Students:** *I was excited because I kept capturing her game pieces. My heart was racing and my hands were sweaty. I screamed when I won!*

**Summarize Learning** Say: *It sounds like most of us had fun over the weekend. Be sure to be specific in choosing one moment that happened over the weekend. Describe that moment in lots of detail.*

Ask students to take out their Writer's Notebooks. Ask the questions below to spark writing ideas. Then display the Writing Prompt on **Transparency 2**.

- Give me a thumbs up if you had a fun weekend.
- Give me a thumbs up if your weekend was awful.
- Give me a thumbs up if you did something silly over the weekend.
- Give me a thumbs up if you did chores over the weekend.

**Transparency 2**

Write about one moment that happened over the weekend. Show what happened in that moment.

**Writing Transparency**

### Objective

- Focus on a moment and write to a prompt

**Materials**

- Writer's Notebook
- Transparency 2

### Daily Journal Prompts

**Focus on Moment**

Use these and other prompts for independent daily journal writing.

- Write about something funny that happened in school. Describe what happened and what made it funny.
- Write about a moment that happened in the cafeteria. Show what happened in that moment.
- Write about a moment when you helped a family member.
- Write about a moment when you gave someone a gift. Describe what happened and how you felt.

## Objective

- Develop one moment of action in writing

### Materials

- Writer's Notebooks
- coat
- Practice Book, p. 32

### Teacher-to-Teacher

Focus is the first skill in the curriculum because it drives students to develop a set of abilities that are fundamental to powerful writing. In Grade 3, students will focus on developing particular moments or particular descriptions that are crucial to plot development, character development, or the overall mood of a piece. As students move through the curriculum, they will learn how to use this skill across genres.

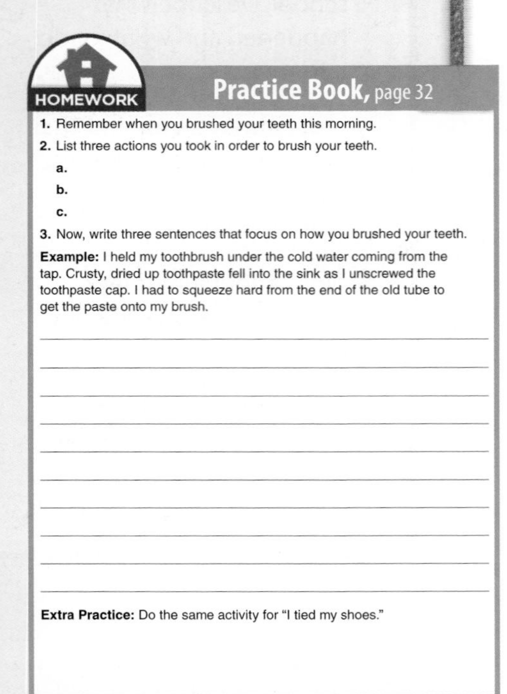
HOMEWORK **Practice Book,** page 32

1. Remember when you brushed your teeth this morning.
2. List three actions you took in order to brush your teeth.
   a.
   b.
   c.
3. Now, write three sentences that focus on how you brushed your teeth.

**Example:** I held my toothbrush under the cold water coming from the tap. Crusty, dried up toothpaste fell into the sink as I unscrewed the toothpaste cap. I had to squeeze hard from the end of the old tube to get the paste onto my brush.

**Extra Practice:** Do the same activity for "I tied my shoes."

**Approaching Reproducible,** page 32

**Beyond Reproducible,** page 32

# Minilesson 1

**Strong Paragraphs** Developing a Single Moment of Action

### TEACH/MODEL

**Write Strong Paragraphs** Tell students that focus can be tricky because sometimes we don't think about all the little steps that go into an action. For example, it's easy just to write, "I took a shot in basketball," and forget that aiming at the hoop, pushing out the ball, taking a little jump, and many other steps are part of that one action.

Ask students to give you directions on how to put on a coat. Remember, your job is to force them to think about the steps that go into it that they don't usually think about. Students will most likely skip steps as they tell you what to do, which will make the activity fun as you do exactly what they tell you.

### PRACTICE/APPLY

**Write Paragraphs** Write the following on the board. Have students copy the sentence in their Writer's Notebooks.

**I brushed my teeth.**

Have students write three more sentences that focus on how they brush their teeth to create a paragraph. Explain that "I brush my teeth" is the topic sentence; it tells the main idea of the paragraph. The sentences that follow, the ones they are adding, will provide the supporting details.

**Summarize Learning** Explain the following:

**Think Aloud** Can you see how focusing on the little details keeps your writing focused? I really liked the way [James] wrote about how [he rinsed with water his toothbrush before putting the toothpaste on the bristles]. This was a specific step in brushing teeth that helped the writing really focus on one moment of action and gave the reader a picture of what was happening. What other focused sentences did you hear in our writing today? I like the way you stayed on topic the whole time. Keep practicing this in your writing.

# Minilesson 2

**Strong Paragraphs** Developing a Single Moment of Action

### TEACH/MODEL

**Write Strong Paragraphs** Explain to students the goal of this lesson.

**Think Aloud** Recently, I performed a short action for you. Today, several students will act. Everyone will be responsible for writing down as much as you can remember about what our student actors do. Watch very carefully because when each student is done, you're going to write down as much as you can remember about what he/she did.

Have a student act like a monkey, waltz around the room, juggle, build a tower of books and knock it over, or some other activity that will make an action-packed moment. (You should choose the activity they'll be doing or at least approve their idea before they begin.) The action should only last for about 15–30 seconds.

### PRACTICE/APPLY

Have students write three to five sentences about what the student actor just did. They should use as much detail as possible to describe (his/her) actions.

**Summarize Learning** Students work independently. Circulate and provide Over-the-Shoulder Conferences. Ask for a few students to share their work. Point out that different writers described the event in different ways even though they were watching the same thing. Discuss the following:

**Think Aloud** From what I saw today, I think we may have some future actors in the room. Our actors were able to focus on a single moment in their performance. Because the acting was well done, writers had an easy time describing that moment because we were given an outstanding picture of exactly what we needed to write! What moments in our writing and acting were the most focused? How will you use this skill in your writing?

### Objective

- Describe an action they observe in the classroom

### Materials

- Writer's Notebooks

### Teacher-to-Teacher

**Model What You Mean**

By providing specific examples of the targeted skill through teacher write alouds, you provide clear models for students to follow.

### English Learners

UNIVERSAL ACCESS

**Sharing** Have English Learners share their writing with a peer first. Circulate and provide additional language. Re-cast students' sentences to make them complete and grammatically correct. Have students repeat. Then have them share with the larger group.

# Reading and Writing Connection

## Writer's Craft

**STRONG PARAGRAPHS: FOCUS ON MOMENT**

Use the example from *Amazing Grace* to show the author's skilled use of focusing on a moment.

- Ask: *What's one time that you felt left out?*
- Have students read aloud the excerpt from *Amazing Grace*. Ask: *What details did the author use to describe this moment in Grace's life? How did the author focus on Grace?*

**USE FOCUS TO WRITE ABOUT TEXT**

Remind students to use the skill of focusing on a moment when they write about *Amazing Grace* so that they are able to include lots of specific details.

CA CONTENT STANDARD LAS 3.1.3 Respond to questions with appropriate elaboration.

**Engagement Prompt** These prompts have been designed to help students deepen their connection to the text and discover their own particular perspective on it.

- *Focus on a moment when you felt discouraged like Grace did.*

**Response Prompt** These prompts have been designed to help students explore more deeply their reactions to particular passages in the reading.

- *Focus on a moment in the text that made you angry.*

CA Writing

**Focus on Moment**

Good writers **slow down a moment** in time and describe the action using strong details.

# Reading and Writing Connection

Read the passage below. Notice how author Mary Hoffman focuses on a moment in time.

An excerpt from *Amazing Grace*

The author focuses on the moment Grace learns an important lesson from her mother. We are able to picture this through the use of strong details.

Grace cheered up, then later she remembered something else. "Natlie says I can't be Peter Pan because I'm black," she said.

Ma looked angry. But before she could speak, Nana said, "It seems that Natalie is another one who don't know nothing. You can be anything you want, Grace, if you put your mind to it."

| Unit 1 Writing: Personal Narrative (Description) | |
|---|---|
| Week 1 | • Strong Sentences: Focus on Moment |
| Week 2 | • Strong Paragraphs: Focus on Moment |
| Week 3 | • Personal Narrative (Guided Writing) |
| Week 4 | • Strong Sentences: Focus on Setting/Object |
| Week 5 | • Strong Paragraphs: Focus on Setting/Object |
| Week 6 | Personal Narrative (Independent Writing) |

## Read and Find

Read Brian's writing below. What did he do to focus on a moment? Use the tips below to help you.

### A Special Day

by Brian J.

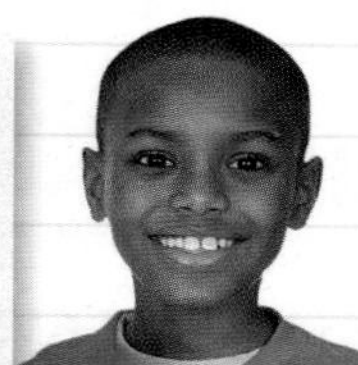

Read about a time I celebrated.

The candles were lit and my family started singing. My mind started to race as my mom walked over with the cake. What should I wish for? I puffed my cheeks and got ready to blow out my candles.

### Writer's Checklist

- ☑ Does the writer write about one object?
- ☑ Does the writer include specific details about that moment?
- ☐ Can you picture the **moment** the way Brian experienced it?

### Writing Strategies

CA CONTENT STANDARD W 3.1.1 Create a single paragraph: a. Develop a topic sentence. b. Include simple supporting facts and details.

**Paragraphs and Topic Sentences**

**Teach/Model** Tell students that a paragraph is a group of sentences that tell about one central, or main, idea. The main idea of the paragraph is the **topic sentence**, such as *I was courageous when I went mountain climbing.* The remaining sentences in the paragraph provide supporting facts and details, such as *I went to the highest mountain in our area. I put on my special equipment and climbed with a guide. It took me over an hour to reach the top.*

**Practice/Apply** Reinforce the characteristics of a strong paragraph as students write their responses to the Engagement Prompt, Response Prompt, Literary Analysis Prompt, or journal prompt.

# Write

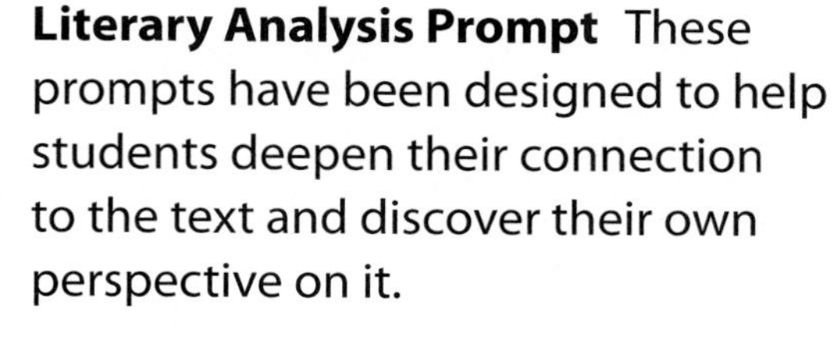

**Literary Analysis Prompt** These prompts have been designed to help students deepen their connection to the text and discover their own perspective on it.

- *Focus on a place in the text where the author used details to show that Grace was courageous.*

## Use Student Model

Have students chorally read the student sample at the top of **Student Book** page 65. Discuss what this student writer did to focus on a moment in time. Use the Writer's Checklist.

Write the following journal prompt on the board:

> **Think about a time you did something courageous. Select one specific moment, such as when you made the decision to act. Write a brief paragraph about that moment.**

Tell students that you will be reading and commenting on their writing during Writing Conference time.

Model how to use the Writer's Checklist to write and revise their work.

- What is the moment you chose?
- What sentences did you add to tell about that moment? Will readers be able to clearly picture that moment? If not, what details could you add?

## Objective

- Meet with the teacher to discuss writing and receive revision assignments

### Materials

- Writer's Notebooks
- Revision Assignments

### Teacher-to-Teacher

**Over-the-Shoulder Conferences**

Use these quick, focused opportunities to comment while students are writing.

- **Step 1** Quietly move close enough to a student that you can read the journal entry he or she is writing.
- **Step 2** Read part of what you see. You don't need to start from the beginning or read the entire piece.
- **Step 3** Show the student a spot in the writing where he or she is using a particular skill or describing something that piques your interest.
- **Step 4** Whisper a sentence or two about why you noticed that spot in the writing and ask a question that will nudge the student to add a detail or clarify.
- **Step 5** Move on to the next student. Select students strategically. You should see 12–15 students in a 15-minute period.

# Conferences

## Writing Journals

### DYNAMIC FEEDBACK SYSTEM

**Purpose** One of the best ways for students to develop skills is by understanding how their writing affects their readers. Your targeted comments direct students to notice the impact they've made by using a specific skill. Your comments should aim to:

- Engage and encourage students by showing them your appreciation for what they've written.
- Focus students' attention on developing one particular skill.

**Steps in the Dynamic Feedback System**

1. Read and appreciate the writing.
2. Notice how the student uses the targeted skill. (e.g. focus: Ask: *For how many sentences does the student stay on a topic?)*
3. Write comments in which you show how the writing has an impact on you. Direct your comments to those places in the piece where the student has used the targeted skill.
4. Meet with and give the student a revision assignment.

### WRITE EFFECTIVE COMMENTS ON FOCUS

**Sample Comments for Focus** At least one of your comments should highlight the way the student uses the skill of focus. Here are some sample comments. Use these comments to get you started.

- *You've focused on the moment when you [swallowed the bug] really well!*
- *I feel like I'm there watching you [score the winning basket].*
- *I enjoyed this moment and I want to know what else happened [when you ran down the hallway].*
- *You got me hooked! What happened next?*

# Revision Assignments

CA CONTENT STANDARD
**W 3.1.4** Revise drafts to improve the coherence and logical progression of ideas by using an established rubric.

## IMPROVE WRITING

**What Is It?** Revision assignments play a crucial role in the dynamic feedback system. They enable you to work with each student on one skill at a time until the student has mastered it.

Revision assignments involve marking a specific section of a student's journal entry and then asking the student to revise it in a specific way. By requiring students to put to use your feedback to revise their own writing, revision assignments show clearly how that feedback has affected what students are able to do next.

**Sample Revision Assignments for Focus** Here are some examples of effective revision assignments for focus. Use them to get started. You may also use the preprinted Revision Assignment Notes or create your own revision assignments based on these.

Revise

[Write, underline, or bracket the sentence.] *I underlined a place where I think you could write more about [planting the roses]. Write two more sentences about it.*

[Write, underline, or bracket the sentence.] *There are so many interesting action-packed moments in this entry that I'm having a hard time imagining any of them in detail. Write two sentences just about [insert specific moment from journal entry: your three-point shot, the victory lap you ran, etc].*

[Write, underline, or bracket the sentence.] *I put brackets around a section of your entry that is full of exciting moments. Underline one of those moments and write two more sentences about it.*

Revise

### Revision Assignment Notes

Use the Revision Assignment Notes to focus student's rewrites.

jump drive **Available on Jump Drive**

Daily Handwriting

Have students review writing numerals, punctuation marks, and writing sentences with proper word spacing. See Handwriting pages 7–9 for daily practice. **W 3.1.2**

Mark students' Journal Checklists to indicate mastered skills.

**Reproducible,** page 222

| | | |
|---|---|---|
| **STAGE 1** Establishing Habits | | |
| ☐ Write Journal Entries<br>☐ Respond to Feedback | ☐ Practice Skill Drills<br>☐ Develop Vocabulary | ☐ Engage in Experience<br>☐ Share Writing |
| **STAGE 2** Strengthening Voice | | |
| Expressive Skills | Topic Development | ☐ Moment ☐ Object ☐ Setting |
| | Showing | ☐ Include unique observations<br>☐ Recognize showing and telling |
| | Strong Verbs | ☐ Recognize and use strong verbs |
| | Sensory Detail | ☐ Use multiple senses<br>☐ Choose sensory detail effectively |
| | Dialogue and Evidence I | ☐ Include dialogue |
| | Character Development | ☐ Believable<br>☐ Change and growth |
| | Logical Structure I: Distinguishing Moments | ☐ Use chronological order<br>☐ Distinguish moments |
| Technical Skills | Sentence Mechanics & Usage I: The Complete Sentence | ☐ Capitals and end punctuation<br>☐ Parts of speech<br>☐ Possessives<br>☐ Commas in a series |
| | Subject/Verb Agreement I | ☐ With present tense<br>☐ With simple past tense |
| | Punctuating and Formatting Dialogue & Quotations | ☐ Quotation marks |

**Writing Journal Checklist**

# Administer the Test

## Weekly Reading Quick Check,

### Passage and questions, Unit 1 Week 2

**ASSESSED SKILLS**

- Vocabulary Words; Word Families
- Cause and Effect
- Commands and Exclamations; Topic Development: Moment
- Final *e*

*Selection Test Also Available.*

**Progress Monitoring, Unit 1, Week 2**

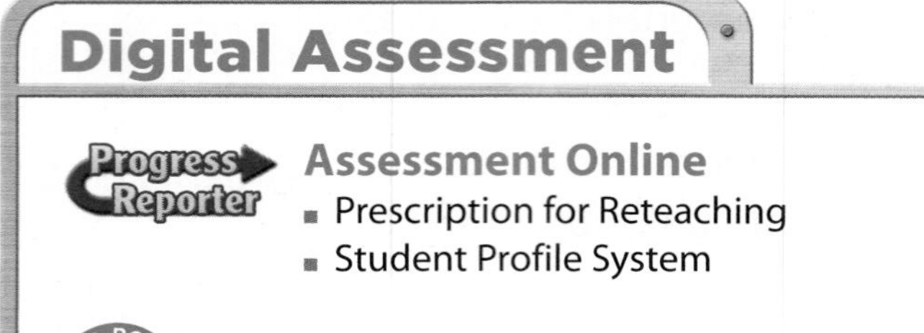

## Unit Fluency Assessment

Assess fluency for one group of students per week. Use the Oral Fluency Record Sheet to track the number of words read correctly. Fluency goal for all students: **61–81 words correct per minute (WCPM)**.

| | |
|---|---|
| Approaching Level | Weeks 1, 3, 5 |
| On Level | Weeks 2, 4 |
| Beyond Level | Week 6 |

**Diagnostic, Unit 1 Fluency**

## Diagnose | Prescribe

**Review the assessment answers with students. Have them correct their errors. Then provide additional instruction as needed.**

| | IF... | THEN... |
|---|---|---|
| **VOCABULARY WORDS**<br>**VOCABULARY STRATEGY**<br>Word Families | 0–2 items correct . . . | Reteach Skills: Intervention Kit<br>LOG ON Online Practice: Go to **www.macmillanmh.com**.<br>CD-ROM Vocabulary PuzzleMaker |
| **COMPREHENSION**<br>Skill: Cause and Effect | 0–2 items correct . . . | SPIRAL REVIEW See Cause and Effect lesson Unit 1, Week 3, page 73B.<br>Intervention Kit: Comprehension |
| **WRITING AND GRAMMAR**<br>Commands and Exclamations<br>Topic Development: Moment | 0–1 items correct . . . | See Topic Development lessons in Unit 1, Week 3.<br>Intervention Kit: Writing and Grammar |
| **PHONICS AND SPELLING**<br>Words with Final *e* | 0–2 items correct . . . | LOG ON Online Practice: Go to **www.macmillanmh.com**.<br>Intervention Kit: Phonics/Word Study |
| **FLUENCY** | 55–60 WCPM | AUDIO CD Fluency Solutions Audio CD |
| | 0–54 WCPM | Intervention Kit: Phonics/Word Study |

## WRITE-ON-DEMAND SCORING RUBRIC

PROMPT **How can reading make your life better? Write as much as you can as well as you can. Write for five minutes.**

| 4 Excellent | 3 Good | 2 Fair | 1 Unsatisfactory |
|---|---|---|---|
| • More than 7 sentences<br>• Almost no spelling or grammar errors<br>• Cohesive ideas, focused and organized | • 5–7 sentences<br>• A few spelling and grammar errors<br>• Well-developed ideas and facts provided | • 4–5 sentences<br>• Several spelling and grammar errors<br>• Some good information; some vague | • Fewer than 4 sentences<br>• Many spelling and grammar errors<br>• Few developed ideas or little accurate information |

## Daily Planner

| | |
|---|---|
| DAY 1 | • Prepare to Read<br>• Academic Language<br>• Vocabulary (Preteach) |
| DAY 2 | • Comprehension<br>• Practice Reader Lesson 1 |
| DAY 3 | • Phonics/Decoding<br>• Practice Reader Lesson 2 |
| DAY 4 | • Phonics/Decoding<br>• Vocabulary (Review)<br>• Practice Reader Lesson 3 |
| DAY 5 | • Self-Selected Reading<br>• Fluency |

**StudentWorks Plus**

Strategic

# Approaching Level

## Prepare to Read

**Objective** Preview *Amazing Grace*
**Materials** • **StudentWorks Plus** • self-stick notes

### PREVIEW TEXT

- Have students preview *Amazing Grace* using **StudentWorks Plus**. This version of StudentWorks contains oral summaries in multiple languages, on-line multilingual glossaries, word-by-word highlighting, and questions that assess and build comprehension.
- Remind students that listening carefully to and following along with the word-by-word reading will help them prepare for the reading of the selection with the class. Ask students to place self-stick notes on any challenging words or places that confuse them. Discuss these with students prior to the reading of the selection with the rest of the class.
- Ask students to write three or four sentences in their Writer's Notebooks telling what they learned about Grace.

## Academic Language

**Objective** Teach academic language
**Materials** • none

### PRETEACH LANGUAGE OF INSTRUCTION

Tell students that there are many important lesson words you will be using this week. You want them to become familiar with these words *before* the lessons. These words also appear in the directions of the tests they will be taking this year.

Preteach the following academic words: *realistic fiction*, *inferences*, *cause*, *effect*, *personification*.

- Define each word using student-friendly language. Tell students that *personification* is when an object, animal, or place is given the abilities or traits that humans have. For example, the wind might be described as whistling through the trees. Since only people can whistle, the wind is given the qualities of a person. Underline the word *person* in *personification* to help students remember this.
- In addition, relate each word to known words. For example, connect *realistic* to *real*, *cause* to *reason something happens*, and *stated* to *spoken* or *told*.
- Highlight these words when used throughout the week and reinforce their meanings.

Strategic

# Approaching Level

## Phonics/Decoding

**Objective** Decode words with final *e*

**Materials**
- **Approaching Reproducible,** page 21
- **Sound-Spelling WorkBoards**

TESTED SKILL

### PHONICS MAINTENANCE

- Distribute a **WorkBoard** to each student. Say a sound previously taught, including the short vowel sounds and long vowel sounds. Have students find the **Sound-Spelling Card** on the board for each sound.
- Review the spelling(s) for each sound by providing a sample word containing that spelling. Guide students to write the word on the board. Model how to segment the word and write the spelling for each sound, as needed. In addition, point out spelling rules, such as dropping the final *e* when you add a suffix that begins with a vowel to a word, as in *like—liking*. When the suffix begins with a consonant, keep the final *e*, as in *like—likely.*
- Dictate the following words for students to spell: *clam, shape, ship, twice, drive, drip, huge, club*. Write the word on the board and have students self-correct their work.

### RETEACH SKILL

**Final *e*** Point to the long *a, i, o,* and *u* Sound-Spelling Cards on the WorkBoard and review the final *e* spellings for these sounds. State each spelling and provide a sample word.

CA CONTENT STANDARD R 3.1.2 Decode regular multisyllabic words.

- Write the words below on the board. Model how to decode the first word in each row, then guide students as they decode the remaining words. For the multisyllabic words, divide the words into syllables using the syllable-scoop technique to help students read one syllable at a time.
- When completed, point to the words in random order for students to chorally read. Repeat several times.

| | | | | | |
|---|---|---|---|---|---|
| late | mate | fate | slide | hide | glide |
| rope | hope | scope | broke | smoke | spokes |
| brave | bravely | shave | describe | prescribe | subscribe |
| note | wrote | vote | wise | unwise | wisely |
| bride | decide | line | decline | recline | refine |
| wise | wisely | advertise | taste | tasteful | alone |
| divide | provide | reside | zone | cube | fuse |

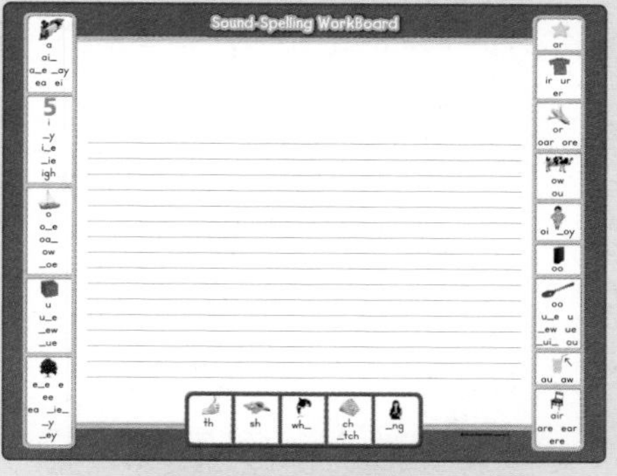

**Sound-Spelling WorkBoard**

### English Learners

UNIVERSAL ACCESS

**Minimal Contrasts** Focus on articulation. Make the long *a* and *i* sounds and point out your mouth position. Have students repeat. Use the articulation photos on the small **Sound-Spelling Cards**. Repeat for long vowel sounds *o* and *u*. Then have students say each sound together, noticing the difference in mouth position. Continue by having students read minimal contrast pairs, such as *like/lake, mole/mule, cave/cove.*

### Approaching Reproducible, page 21

When a word has a vowel that is followed by a consonant and a final silent **e**, the vowel usually has a long vowel sound. Say the following words aloud. Notice that each word has a vowel that is followed by a consonant and a final silent **e**.

| | | | |
|---|---|---|---|
| cove | plane | twice | made |
| spike | throne | flute | smile |

**Write the word that completes each sentence. Underline the vowel, and draw a box around the final silent e in each word.**

1. We played a reading game. (gum game)
2. We called out a story's name. (nest name)
3. We told about where the story takes place. (place play)
4. We said why we thought kids would like the story. (lick like)
5. We wrote our ideas on the board. (wrap wrote)
6. My team won first prize. (print prize)
7. Winning was a huge surprise. (hug huge)
8. Reading helps you become very wise. (wise wish)

Strategic

# Approaching Level

## Vocabulary

**Objective** Preteach selection vocabulary

**Materials** • **Visual Vocabulary Resources** • **Approaching Reproducible,** p. 22

### PRETEACH VOCABULARY

Use the **Visual Vocabulary Resources** to preteach the key selection words *auditions, adventure, exploring, sparkling, fantastic,* and *success*. Focus on two words per day. Use the following routine that appears in detail on the cards.

- Define the word in English and provide the example given.
- Define the word in Spanish, if appropriate, and indicate if the word is a cognate.
- Display the picture and explain how it illustrates or demonstrates the word.
- Then engage students in structured partner talk about the image, using the key word.
- Ask students to chorally say the word three times.
- Point out any known sound-spellings or focus on a key aspect of phonemic awareness related to the word.
- Distribute copies of the Vocabulary Glossary, **English Learner Resource Book**.

### REVIEW PREVIOUSLY TAUGHT VOCABULARY

Display the Vocabulary Cards from the previous week. Say the meaning of each word, one by one, and have students identify it. Then point to words in random order for students to provide definitions and related words they know.

**Approaching Reproducible,** page 22

**A. Read the vocabulary words. Write the correct word in each sentence below.**

auditions adventure exploring sparkling fantastic success

1. My favorite books are adventure stories.
2. Reading them teaches me about people who like exploring.
3. Some explorers see fantastic sights.
4. Some sail to places with clear and sparkling seas.
5. Explorers don't always have success in finding what they're looking for.
6. My friends and I hold auditions for parts in plays about adventure stories.

**B. Write two sentences. Use one of the vocabulary words in each sentence.**

7. Possible response: The stars were sparkling in the dark sky.
8. Possible response: It's fun to go exploring in a new place.

Strategic

# Approaching Level

## Vocabulary

**Objective** Review vocabulary and high-frequency words

**Materials** • **Vocabulary Cards** • **High-Frequency Word Cards**

### REVIEW VOCABULARY

**Review Words** Display the **Vocabulary Cards** *auditions, adventure, exploring, sparkling, fantastic,* and *success*. Point to each word, read it aloud, and have students chorally repeat.

Then use one of the vocabulary words to complete each sentence below.

- While _____ the deep sea, you may find unusual kinds of fish.
- The director held _____ to find the best actor for the role.
- Everyone had fun at the party. It was a great _____.
- We won the game and I felt _____.
- The diamond jewelry was _____ in the light.
- You must be careful if you go on an _____ in the wild.

### HIGH-FREQUENCY WORDS

**Top 250 Words** The ability to read accurately and effortlessly the most frequently used words in written English will help students develop reading fluency. Display **High-Frequency Word Cards 11–20**. Then do the following:

- Display one card at a time, and ask students to chorally state each word.
- Have students spell each word aloud.
- Ask students to write each word in their Writer's Notebooks as they state aloud each letter. Then have them read the word again.
- When completed, quickly flip through the word card set as students chorally read the words.
- Provide opportunities for students to use the words in speaking and writing. For example, provide sentence starters such as *I ate some* _______ for oral and written practice. Or point to a word card and ask a question such as *What word is a synonym of this word?* (when pointing to the *ask* word card).
- Continue the routine throughout the week.

### Word Webs

Have students create word webs in their Writer's Notebooks for each vocabulary word. Ask them to add related words, phrases, and illustrations to the webs.

Student Book

Strategic

# Approaching Level

## Comprehension

**Objective** Reteach make inferences and analyze and cause and effect

**Materials** • **Student Book:** "The Big Show"

### RETEACH STRATEGY: MAKE INFERENCES AND ANALYZE

CA CONTENT STANDARD
R 3.2.2
Ask questions and support answers by connecting prior knowledge with literal information found in, and inferred from, the text.

- **Define** Tell students that good readers **make inferences** by using information in the text, including the pictures, and their own experiences to reach conclusions about what happens in a story.

  Relate the word *inference* to words with similar meaning, such as *opinion* and *judgment*. An inference is an opinion that the reader forms about the story based on information in the text and personal experience.
- **Relate to Real Life** Ask students to imagine they're reading a news story about a rainstorm that flooded roads. A friend asks how the people stuck in traffic feel, but the article does not say. They have to tell the friend how they think the people stuck in traffic feel; this is an inference.
- **Set Purpose** Remind students that good readers have to make inferences when information is not directly stated in the text to help them understand why things happen. Readers must use what they know from the text and their own knowledge to come to conclusions about characters and events in a story.

### RETEACH SKILL: CAUSE AND EFFECT

- **Define** Tell students that a **cause** is why something happens. An **effect** is what happens as a result.
- **Relate to Real Life** Ask students if they have ever seen an accident. Ask, *Can you describe what happened?* Explain that when they describe what made the accident happen, they are telling the *cause*. When they describe what happened next, they are describing the *effect*.
- **Set Purpose** Remind students that good readers look for causes and effects as they read. This helps them better understand the text and make predictions about what will happen next. Authors sometimes state causes and effects by using signal words, such as *because*, *so*, and *since*. Sometimes there are no signal words, and readers must figure out the causes and effects on their own.
- **Apply** Work with students to identify the causes and effects in "The Big Show." Then use the causes and effects to retell the story. Have students retell the story in their own words. Students will apply this strategy and skill to a simpler text as they read *Puss in Boots*.

**Corrective Feedback**

Read the paragraph that starts with the line "The play sounded like fun, so all the friends came." Ask: *What caused all the friends to come? Which signal word helped you figure it out?* Ask students to listen for other causes and effects as you read and to identify any signal words they hear.

Strategic

# Approaching Level

## Practice Reader Lesson 1

**Objective** Read to apply skills and strategies

**Materials**
- **Practice Reader:** *Puss in Boots*
- **Approaching Reproducible,** p. 24

Practice Reader

### BEFORE READING

**Preview and Predict** Have students read the title and preview the first scene. Ask students to make predictions about the plot of this section. Students should note any questions they have before they read.

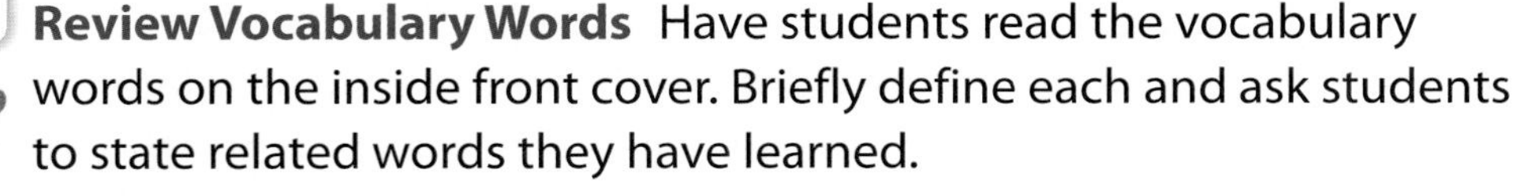

**Review Vocabulary Words** Have students read the vocabulary words on the inside front cover. Briefly define each and ask students to state related words they have learned.

**Set a Purpose for Reading** *Let's read to find out how Puss in Boots helps the miller's son.*

### DURING READING

**STRATEGY**
**MAKE INFERENCES AND ANALYZE**

Remind students that to make inferences about what is happening in a story, you use information in the text, including pictures, and your own experiences.

**SKILL**
**CAUSE AND EFFECT**

Remind students to think about causes and effects of events as they read. Read Scene 1 with students. Help students complete the graphic organizer for this week.

As you read, help students decode unknown words. In addition, ask open-ended questions to facilitate rich discussion, such as *What is the author trying to tell you about Puss's character?* Build on students' responses to develop deeper understanding of the text.

Stop after each two pages and ask students to summarize causes and effects to check their understanding before reading on. If they struggle, help students reread the difficult parts. Then model determining the main causes and effects in the scene.

### AFTER READING

Ask students to comment on what they think about Puss in Boots's behavior in the play. Ask: *Would you trick people like Puss in Boots did to help a friend? Why or why not?* Ask students to comment on what part of the play they enjoyed the most.

#### Corrective Feedback

Throughout the lessons, provide feedback based on students' responses. If the answer is correct, ask another question. If the answer is tentative, restate key information to assist the student. If the answer is wrong, provide corrective feedback such as hints or clues, refer to a visual such as a Sound-Spelling Card or story illustration, or probe with questions to help the student clarify any misunderstanding.

**Practice Reader**

Strategic

# Approaching Level

## Practice Reader Lesson 2

**Objective** Reread to apply skills and strategies and develop fluency

**Materials**
- **Practice Reader:** *Puss in Boots*
- **Approaching Reproducible,** p.25

### BEFORE READING

**Review Strategy and Skill** Review students' completed Cause and Effect Charts from the first read. Remind them that a cause is why something happens. An effect is what happens as a result.

**Review Vocabulary Words** Have students search the book for each vocabulary word. Ask them to read aloud the sentence containing the word and state the word's definition or provide related words. Point out any words that have parts that may remind students of other words they know.

**Set a Purpose for Reading** *Let's reread to check our understanding of the information in the book and to work on our reading fluency.*

### DURING READING

Reread *Puss in Boots* with students. Have them read silently two pages at a time, or read aloud to a partner. Stop and have students summarize before reading the next two pages. Model oral summaries, as needed.

### AFTER READING

**Check Comprehension** Have partners complete the Comprehension Check on page 16. Review students' answers. Help them find evidence for their answers in the text.

**Model Fluency** Model reading the fluency passage on **Approaching Reproducible** page 25. Tell students to pay close attention to your intonation as you read. Then read one sentence at a time and have students echo-read the sentences, copying your intonation.

During independent reading time, have students work with a partner using the fluency passage. One student reads aloud, while the other repeats each sentence back. If students need additional support, have them listen to the "practice speed" version of the passage on the **Fluency Solutions Audio CD**.

Strategic

# Approaching Level

## Practice Reader Lesson 3

**Objective** Build fluency

**Materials**
- **Practice Reader:** *Puss in Boots*
- **Approaching Reproducible,** p. 25

### FOCUS ON FLUENCY

**CA CONTENT STANDARD R 3.1.3** Read aloud narrative and expository text fluently and accurately and with appropriate pacing, intonation, and expression.

**Timed Reading** Tell students that they will be doing a final timed reading of the fluency passage on **Approaching Reproducible**, page 11, that they have been practicing. With each student, follow these directions:

- Place the passage facedown.
- When you say "Go," the student begins reading the passage aloud.
- When you say "Stop," the student stops reading the passage.

As they read, note words students mispronounce and their overall intonation. Stop after one minute. Help students record and graph the number of words they read correctly.

### REREAD PREVIOUSLY READ BOOKS

- Distribute copies of six **Practice Readers** from the previous grade. Have students select two to reread. Tell students that rereading these books will help them develop their skills. The more times they read the same words, the quicker they will learn these words. This will make the reading of other books easier.
- Circulate and listen in as students read. Stop students periodically and ask them how they are figuring out difficult words and how they are monitoring their comprehension. Note students who need additional work with specific decoding or comprehension skills.
- Have students read other previously read Practice Readers during independent reading time or for homework.

### Meet Grade-Level Expectations

As an alternative to this day's lesson, guide students through a reading of the On Level Practice Reader. See page 65U. Since both books contain the same vocabulary, phonics, and comprehension skills, the scaffolding you provided will help most students gain access to this more challenging text.

### Book Talk

See page 65HH. Students will work with peers of varying language abilities to discuss this week's Practice Readers.

Student Book

Student Book

## Decodable Text

Use the Reading *Triumphs* Anthology and the decodable stories in the **Teacher's Resource Book** to help students build fluency with basic decoding patterns.

Strategic

# Approaching Level

## Fluency

**Objectives** Reread selections to develop fluency; develop speaking skills

**Materials** • **Student Book:** *Amazing Grace,* "The Storytelling Stone"

### REREAD FOR FLUENCY

- Have students reread a portion of *Amazing Grace*. Suggest that they focus on two to four of their favorite pages from the selection. Work with students to read the pages with the appropriate intonation, paying particular attention to questions.
- Provide time for students to read their sections of text to you. Comment on their intonation and provide corrective feedback by modeling proper fluency.

### DEVELOP SPEAKING/LISTENING SKILLS

- Have students practice reading the first seven paragraphs of the legend "The Storytelling Stone."
- Work with students to read with appropriate intonation. Model reading a few lines at a time. Emphasize the question and dialogue with your intonation. Have students repeat.
- Provide time for students to read aloud that portion of the legend to partners. Ask them to name ways in which their partner expressed the question or dialogue with his or her voice.
- Challenge students to retell what happens when the boy meets Great Stone.

CA CONTENT STANDARD
LAS 3.1.1
Retell, paraphrase, and explain what has been said by a speaker.

Strategic

# Approaching Level

## Self-Selected Reading

**Objective** Read independently to identify causes and effects

**Materials** • **Classroom Library** • other fiction books

### APPLY SKILLS TO INDEPENDENT READING

- Have students choose a fiction book for independent reading. (See the **Theme Bibliography** on pages T8–T9 for book suggestions.) Remind them that a *cause* is why something happens. An *effect* is what happens as a result. Have students read their books and record the causes and effects on a Cause and Effect Chart.
- After reading, ask students to use their Cause and Effect Chart to write or orally state a summary of the book. Provide time for students to share their summaries and comment on their reactions to the book. Ask: *Would you recommend this book to a classmate? Why or why not?*

Classroom Library

Daily Planner

| | |
|---|---|
| DAY 1 | • Vocabulary |
| DAY 2 | • Phonics |
| DAY 3 | • Practice Reader Lesson 1 |
| DAY 4 | • Practice Reader Lesson 2<br>• Fluency |
| DAY 5 | • Self-Selected Reading |

Benchmark

# On Level

## Vocabulary

**Objective** Review vocabulary
**Materials** • **Vocabulary Cards**

TESTED SKILL

### REVIEW PREVIOUSLY TAUGHT WORDS

**Review Words** Display the **Vocabulary Cards** *auditions, adventure, exploring, sparkling, fantastic,* and *success*. Point to each word, read it aloud, and have students chorally repeat.

CA CONTENT STANDARD R 3.1.4 Use knowledge of antonyms, synonyms, homophones, and homographs to determine the meanings of words.

Then provide the following Synonym/Antonym questions. Ask students to answer each question, justifying their answer. Allow other students to respond. Use the discussions to determine each student's depth of word knowledge.

- Is *tryouts* an antonym for *auditions*?
- Is *adventure* an antonym for *swim*?
- Is *exploring* a synonym for *searching*?
- Is *sparkling* an antonym of *dull*?
- Is *fantastic* an antonym of *excellent*?
- Is *success* a synonym of *failure*?

## Phonics/Word Study

**Objective** Decode multisyllabic words with final *e*
**Materials** • **Sound-Spelling WorkBoards**

TESTED SKILL

### RETEACH SKILL

- **Final *e* Words** Point to the Long Vowels **Sound-Spelling Cards** on the **WorkBoard** and review the final *e* spellings for these sounds. State each spelling and provide a sample word.
- Write the words below on the board. If necessary, divide the words into syllables using the syllable-scoop procedure to help students read one syllable at a time. When completed, point to the words in random order for students to chorally read.

CA CONTENT STANDARD R 3.1.2 Decode regular multisyllabic words.

| | | | | |
|---|---|---|---|---|
| create | pantomime | relate | unfazed | backslide |
| firefighter | timely | bravely | probing | unwise |
| hideaway | overripe | baseball | driveway | devise |

- **Spelling** Dictate the following words for students to spell on their WorkBoards: *advise, graceful, tasteless, elevate, retire*. Guide students to use the Sound-Spelling Cards and model how to segment words, such as spelling a word syllable by syllable.

Sound-Spelling WorkBoard

Benchmark

# On Level

## Fluency

**Objectives** Reread selections to develop fluency; develop speaking skills

**Materials** • **Student Book:** *Amazing Grace*, "The Storytelling Stone"

### REREAD FOR FLUENCY

CA CONTENT STANDARD R 3.1.3 Read aloud narrative and expository text fluently and accurately and with appropriate pacing, intonation, and expression.

- Have students reread *Amazing Grace*. Work with students to read with the appropriate intonation, paying particular attention to questions. Model as needed.
- Provide time for students to read a section of text to you. Comment on their intonation, particularly when reading questions, and provide corrective feedback.

Student Book

### DEVELOP SPEAKING/LISTENING SKILLS

- Have students practice reading the legend "The Storytelling Stone."
- Work with students to read with appropriate intonation. Model reading a few lines at a time. Emphasize the question and dialogue with your intonation. Have students repeat.
- Provide time for students to read aloud the first two pages to the class. Ask students to name ways in which the reader expressed the question or dialogue with his or her voice.

CA CONTENT STANDARD LAS 3.1.6 Provide a beginning, a middle, and an end, including concrete details that develop a central idea.

- Challenge students to present orally a summary of the section students have read aloud. Have them present the events in the story in order so that their summary has a clear beginning, middle, and end.

Student Book

## Self-Selected Reading

**Objective** Read independently to identify causes and effects

**Materials** • **Classroom Library** • other fiction books

### APPLY SKILLS TO INDEPENDENT READING

- Have students choose a fiction book for independent reading. (See the **Theme Bibliography** on pages T8–T9 for book suggestions.) Have students read their books and write down the causes and effects.
- After reading, ask students to use their cause and effect list to write a summary of the book. Provide time for students to share their summaries and comment on their reactions to the book. Ask: *Would you recommend this book to a classmate? Why or why not?*

Classroom Library

Practice Reader

Benchmark

# On Level

## Practice Reader Lesson 1

**Objective** Read to apply strategies and skills

**Materials**
- **Practice Reader:** *Anansi Wins Back the World's Stories*
- **Practice Book,** p. 24

### BEFORE READING

CA CONTENT STANDARD R 3.2.4 Recall major points in the text and make and modify predictions about forthcoming information.

**Preview and Predict** Have students read the title and preview the play by looking at the illustrations. Ask them to predict what this play is about and what they might learn.

**Review Vocabulary Words** Have students read the vocabulary words on the inside front cover. Ask them to state related words they have learned. Review definitions, as needed.

**Set a Purpose for Reading** *Let's read to find out how Anansi won back the world's stories.*

### DURING READING

**STRATEGY**
**MAKE INFERENCES AND ANALYZE**

Remind students that readers use what they learn from the text, including pictures, as well as their own experiences to make inferences about a story.

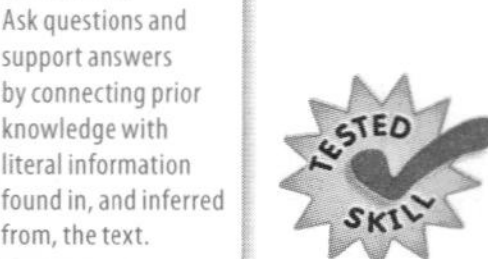

CA CONTENT STANDARD R 3.2.2 Ask questions and support answers by connecting prior knowledge with literal information found in, and inferred from, the text.

**SKILL**
**CAUSE AND EFFECT**

Remind students that a *cause* is why something happens. An *effect* is what happens as a result. Causes and their effects make up the events in a story.

Read Scene 1 with students. Ask open-ended questions to facilitate rich discussion, such as *What do you think the author wants us to know about Anansi's character?* Build on students' responses to develop deeper understanding of the text. Have students fill in the first section of the graphic organizer, then continue reading.

CA CONTENT STANDARD R 3.1.1 Know and use complex word families when reading to decode unfamiliar words.

**Word Families** As they read, have students point out this week's new vocabulary words and any parts of those words that remind them of other words.

### AFTER READING

Ask students to comment on the tasks that Anansi performed. *Why did the sky pick those three tasks? What did completing them show about Anansi?* Have students discuss their favorite parts of the play.

Benchmark

# On Level

## Practice Reader Lesson 2

**Objective** Reread to apply skills and strategies and develop fluency

**Materials**
- **Practice Reader:** *Anansi Wins Back the World's Stories*
- **Practice Book,** p. 25

Practice Reader

### BEFORE READING

**Review Strategy and Skill** Review students' completed Cause and Effect Charts from the first read. Remind students that a cause is why something happens, and an effect is the result. Sometimes the cause or effect is not stated and must be inferred.

Remind students that readers use what they learn from the text, including pictures, as well as their own experiences to make inferences about a story.

**Set a Purpose for Reading** *Let's reread to check our understanding of the information in the book and to work on our reading fluency.*

### DURING READING

Reread *Anansi Wins Back the World's Stories* with students. Have them read silently two pages at a time, or read aloud to a partner. Stop and have students summarize before reading the next two pages. Model oral summaries, as needed.

### AFTER READING

**Check Comprehension** Have partners complete the Comprehension Check on page 16. Review students' answers. Help students find evidence for their answers in the text.

**Model Fluency** Model reading the fluency passage on **Practice Book** page 25. Tell students to pay close attention to your intonation as you read. Then read one sentence at a time and have students echo-read the sentences, copying your intonation.

During independent reading time, have students work with a partner using the fluency passage. One student reads aloud, while the other repeats each sentence back. If students need additional support, have them listen to the "practice speed" version of the passage on the **Fluency Solutions Audio CD**.

### Book Talk

See page 65HH. Students will work with peers of varying language abilities to discuss this week's Practice Readers.

### Practice Book, page 25

**As I read, I will pay attention to my intonation.**

| | |
|---|---|
| | Rainforests are home to over half the world's plants |
| 9 | and animals. When the rainforest is lost, the circle of life |
| 20 | breaks down. The climate changes. The plants and animals |
| 29 | die off. |
| 31 | People have come up with many ways to address this |
| 41 | problem. One way to save the forests is to learn all about |
| 53 | them. |
| 54 | Another way is to get wood from somewhere else. Now |
| 64 | there are tree farms where wood is grown. If you can get |
| 76 | trees from a farm, then you don't need to cut down a forest. |
| 89 | Cutting a rainforest tree should only be done as a last |
| 100 | **resort.** 101 |

**Comprehension Check**

1. What happens when the rainforest is lost? **Main Idea and Details**
   The circle of life breaks down, climate changes, and plants and animals die.
2. What are ways to help save the forests? **Main Idea and Details**
   learn about them, get wood from a tree farm

| | Words Read | – | Number of Errors | = | Words Correct Score |
|---|---|---|---|---|---|
| First Read | | – | | = | |
| Second Read | | – | | = | |

## Daily Planner

| | |
|---|---|
| DAY 1 | • Practice Reader Lesson 1 |
| DAY 2 | • Practice Reader Lesson 2 |
| DAY 3 | • Phonics |
| DAY 4 | • Vocabulary<br>• Fluency |
| DAY 5 | • Self-Selected Reading |

Advanced

# Beyond Level

## Phonics/Word Study

**Objective** Decode multisyllabic words with final *e*

**Materials** • **Sound-Spelling WorkBoards**

TESTED SKILL

### EXTEND/ACCELERATE

CA CONTENT STANDARD R 3.1.2 Decode regular multisyllabic words.

- **Read Multisyllabic Words with Final *e*** Write the words below on the board. Challenge students to read the words, using known word parts. When completed, point to the words in random order for students to chorally read.

| | | | |
|---|---|---|---|
| overrate | unmistakable | dislike | disintegrate |
| driveway | recreate | replace | interstate |
| imprecise | lubricate | microwave | resume |
| celebrate | telescope | racetrack | crudely |

- **Define Words** Ask students to use word parts to find the meanings of the above words. Then have partners find the words in a dictionary and confirm or revise the meanings. Challenge students to use these words in this week's writing assignments.
- **Spell Final *e* Words** Dictate the following words for students to spell on their **WorkBoards**: *obliterate, microwave, confuse, hopefully, vibrate.* Write the words for students to self-correct.

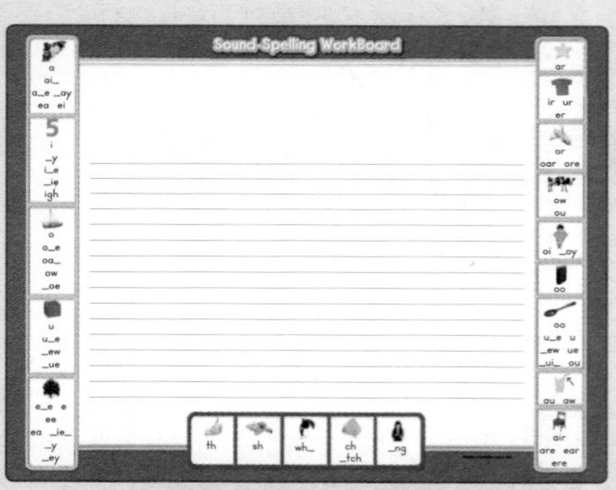

**Sound-Spelling WorkBoard**

## Vocabulary

**Objectives** Review word families; write a story

**Materials** • none

TESTED SKILL

### ENRICH VOCABULARY

CA CONTENT STANDARD R 3.1.1 Know and use complex word families when reading to decode unfamiliar words.

- **Review Word Families** Remind students that many words contain a common word part. Write the word part *audio* on the board. Explain that it comes from a Latin word that means "to hear." Ask students to discuss how *auditions* is related to this word part. Brainstorm a list of other words that belong to this word family (*audible, audience, auditorium*). Talk about the meaning of each and how its meaning is related to "to hear."
- **Write a Story** Ask students to think about the auditions in *Amazing Grace*. Have them write a story about a real or imaginary audition, using the vocabulary words they have learned in this week's selections.

Advanced

# Beyond Level

## Fluency

**Objectives** Reread selections to develop fluency; develop speaking skills
**Materials** • **Student Book:** *Amazing Grace*, "The Storytelling Stone"

### REREAD FOR FLUENCY

CA CONTENT STANDARD R 3.1.3 Read aloud narrative and expository text fluently and accurately and with appropriate pacing, intonation, and expression.

- Have students reread *Amazing Grace*. Work with students to read the book with the appropriate intonation.
- Provide time for students to read a section of text to you. Comment on their intonation and provide corrective feedback.

Student Book

### DEVELOP SPEAKING/LISTENING SKILLS

- Have students practice reading the legend "The Storytelling Stone."
- Work with students to read with appropriate pacing and intonation. Model reading a few lines at a time. Emphasize the question and dialogue with your intonation. Have students repeat.
- Provide time for students to read aloud the legend to the class. Ask students to name ways in which the reader expressed the question and dialogue with his or her voice.
- Challenge students to work with partners to present their interpretation of the dialogue between the boy and Great Stone when they first meet. Then direct another student to retell the scene using appropriate intonation and vocal patterns.

CA CONTENT STANDARD LAS 3.1.1 Retell, paraphrase, and explain what has been said by a speaker.

Student Book

## Self-Selected Reading

**Objective** Read independently to identify the causes and effects of a selection
**Materials** • **Classroom Library** • other fiction books

### APPLY SKILLS TO INDEPENDENT READING

- Have students choose a fiction book for independent reading. (See the **Theme Bibliography** on pages T8–T9 for book suggestions.) Have students read their books and write down the causes and effects.
- After reading, ask students to use their cause and effect list to write a summary of the book. Provide time for students to share their summaries and comment on their reactions to the book. Ask: *Would you recommend this book to a classmate? Why or why not?*

Classroom Library

Practice Reader

Advanced

# Beyond Level

## Practice Reader Lesson 1

**Objective** Read to apply strategies and skills

**Materials**
- **Practice Reader:** *Aladdin and His Lamp*
- **Beyond Reproducible,** p. 24

### BEFORE READING

**Preview and Predict** Have students preview the book by reading the title and looking at the illustrations. Ask them to predict what they think this book is about and what they might learn.

**Review Vocabulary Words** Have students read the vocabulary words on the inside front cover. Ask them to state each definition and any related words they have learned.

**Set a Purpose for Reading** *Let's read to find out how a genie changes Aladdin's life.*

### DURING READING

**STRATEGY**
**MAKE INFERENCES AND ANALYZE**

Ask students to define what it means to make inferences. Have them explain what tools they use to make inferences from text.

**SKILL**
**CAUSE AND EFFECT**

Ask students to define the terms *cause* and *effect*. Remind them that a *cause* is why something happens. An *effect* is what happens as a result. Causes and their effects make up the events in a story.

Read the book with students. Ask open-ended questions to facilitate rich discussion, such as *What is the author trying to tell us about the merchant? What's the big idea the author is trying to get across?* Build on students' responses to develop deeper understanding of the text. Have students fill in their graphic organizers for the week independently as they read.

### AFTER READING

Have students discuss how they would act and what they would wish for if they were Aladdin. Have them comment on their favorite part of the play. Ask students to work in pairs to write an additional scene or alternate ending to the play. Have them explain what they wrote and why it should be included in the play.

Advanced

# Beyond Level

## Practice Reader Lesson 2

**Objective** Reread to apply skills and strategies and develop fluency

**Materials**
- **Practice Reader:** *Aladdin and His Lamp*
- **Beyond Reproducible,** p. 25

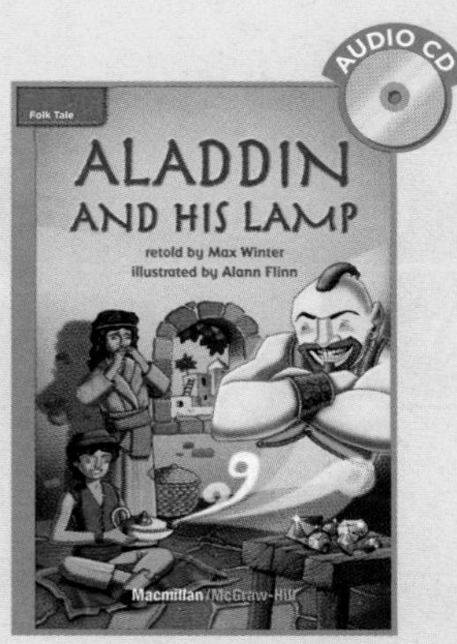

Practice Reader

### BEFORE READING

**Review Strategy and Skill** Review students' completed graphic organizers from the first read.

Remind students that a summary includes the main ideas and main causes and effects from the book. If students' summaries are incomplete, provide a model summary or use a student summary and revise it as a group. Have students copy the revised summary in their Writer's Notebooks.

**Set a Purpose for Reading** *Let's reread to check our understanding of the information in the book and work on our reading fluency.*

### DURING READING

Have students reread *Aladdin and His Lamp* silently or with a partner. If reading in pairs, prompt students to stop every two pages and summarize or ask their partner probing questions.

### AFTER READING

**Check Comprehension** Have students independently complete the Comprehension Check on page 16. Review students' answers. Help students find evidence for their answers in the text.

CA CONTENT STANDARD R 3.1.3 Read aloud narrative and expository text fluently and accurately and with appropriate pacing, intonation, and expression.

**Model Fluency** Model reading the fluency passage on **Beyond Reproducible** page 25. Tell students to pay close attention to your intonation as you read. Then read one sentence at a time and have students echo-read the sentences, copying your intonation.

During independent reading time, have students work with a partner using the fluency passage. One student reads aloud, while the other repeats each sentence back. Students can check their fluency by reading along with the "expert speed" version of the passage on the **Fluency Solutions Audio CD**.

#### Book Talk

See page 65HH. Students will work with peers of varying language abilities to discuss this week's Practice Readers.

#### Beyond Reproducible, page 25

**As I read, I will pay attention to my intonation.**

A forest is a wooded area, a place where many trees
11 grow. Forests are found on every continent except
19 Antarctica.
20 No two forests are the same. The contents of each
30 forest depends on the climate where it is found.
39 A forest can be damp or dry. It may be several centuries
51 old or as young as a few days. Its trees may keep their
64 leaves or they may drop their leaves. A forest may be
75 composed of one kind of tree. More often it is made up of
88 many different kinds of trees.
93 Forests are all different from each other. In one way,
103 though, they are all alike. All forests are shady. Little sun
114 can reach beneath the canopy of tall trees. This shade
124 limits what can grow on the ground around the trees. 134

**Comprehension Check**

1. What is the topic of this article? Main Idea and Details The topic is forests.
2. Where are forests found? Main Idea and Details Forests are found on every continent except Antarctica.

| | Words Read | – | Number of Errors | = | Words Correct Score |
|---|---|---|---|---|---|
| First Read | | – | | = | |
| Second Read | | – | | = | |

**Daily Planner**

| | |
|---|---|
| DAY 1 | • Build Background Knowledge<br>• Vocabulary |
| DAY 2 | • Vocabulary<br>• Access to Core Content<br>*Amazing Grace* |
| DAY 3 | • Vocabulary<br>• Grammar<br>• Access to Core Content<br>*Amazing Grace* |
| DAY 4 | • Vocabulary<br>• Writing/Spelling<br>• Access to Core Content<br>"The Storytelling Stone" |
| DAY 5 | • Vocabulary<br>• Practice Reader<br>• Self-Selected Reading |

StudentWorks Plus

# English Learners

## Prepare to Read

**Content Objective** Describe the power of stories
**Language Objective** Use key words to describe the power of stories
**Materials** **StudentWorks Plus** (interactive eBook)

### BUILD BACKGROUND KNOWLEDGE

CA CONTENT STANDARD R 3.1.3 Read aloud narrative and expository text fluently and accurately and with appropriate pacing, intonation, and expression.

- Have students preview *Amazing Grace* using **StudentWorks Plus**, the interactive eBook. This version of the Student Book contains oral summaries in multiple languages, online multilingual glossaries, word-by-word highlighting, and questions that assess and build comprehension.
- Students can build their word reading fluency by reading along as the text is read or by listening during the first reading and, at the end of each paragraph, returning to the beginning of the paragraph and reading along.
- Students can build their comprehension by reviewing the definitions of key words in the online glossary and by answering the comprehension questions. When appropriate, the text required to answer the question is highlighted to provide students with additional support and scaffolding.
- Following the reading, ask students to respond in writing to a question that links the story to their personal experiences, such as: *Have you ever imagined you were a character in a book? If so, describe what it was like.*

## Academic Language

**Language Objective** Use academic language in classroom conversations

- This week's academic words are **boldfaced** throughout the lesson. Define the word in context and provide a clear example from the selection. Then ask students to generate an example or a word with a similar meaning.

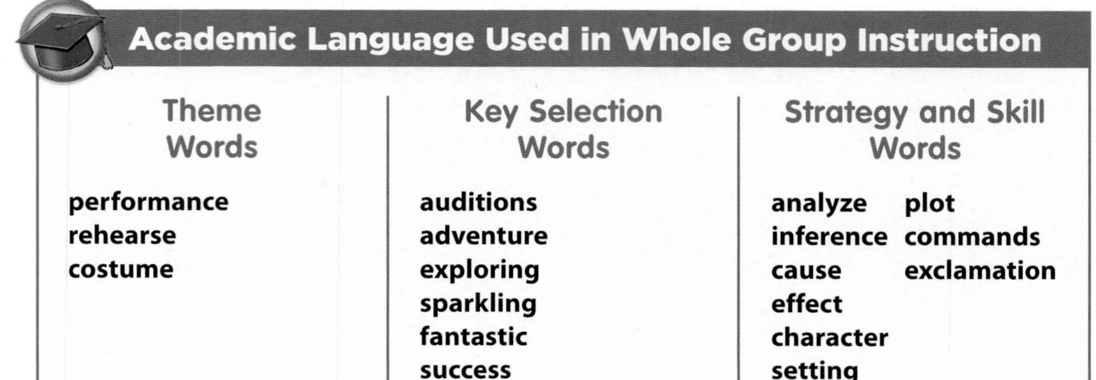

**Academic Language Used in Whole Group Instruction**

| Theme Words | Key Selection Words | Strategy and Skill Words | |
|---|---|---|---|
| **performance** | **auditions** | **analyze** | **plot** |
| **rehearse** | **adventure** | **inference** | **commands** |
| **costume** | **exploring** | **cause** | **exclamation** |
| | **sparkling** | **effect** | |
| | **fantastic** | **character** | |
| | **success** | **setting** | |

# English Learners

## Vocabulary

**Language Objective** Demonstrate understanding and use of key words by describing the power of stories

**Materials** • **Visual Vocabulary Resources** • **English Learner Resource Book**

TESTED SKILL

### PRETEACH KEY VOCABULARY

**All Language Levels** Use the **Visual Vocabulary Resources** to preteach the key selection words *auditions, adventure, exploring, sparkling, fantastic,* and *success*. Focus on 1–2 words per day. Use the following routine that appears in detail on the cards.

- Define the word in English and provide the example given.
- Define the word in Spanish, if appropriate, and indicate if the word is a cognate.
- Display the picture and explain how it illustrates or demonstrates the word. Engage students in structured partner-talk about the image, using the key word.
- Ask students to chorally say the word three times.
- Point out any known sound-spellings or focus on a key aspect of phonemic awareness related to the word.
- Distribute copies of the Vocabulary Glossary in the **English Learner Resource Book** page 28.

### PRETEACH FUNCTION WORDS AND PHRASES

**All Language Levels** Use the Visual Vocabulary Resources to preteach the function words and phrases *after it was all over, still going on, most of all,* and *when it was time*. Focus on one word per day. Use the detailed routine on the cards.

- Define the word in English and, if appropriate, in Spanish. Point out if the word is a cognate.
- Refer to the picture and engage students in talk about the word; for example, students will Partner-Talk using sentence frames or they will listen to sentences and replace a word or phrase with the new function word.
- Ask students to chorally repeat the word three times.

### TEACH BASIC WORDS

For **Beginning** and **Early Intermediate** students, use the Visual Vocabulary Resources to teach the basic words *play, theater, tickets, ballet, ballerina,* and *movie*. Teach these "theater" words using the routine provided on the card.

**Visual Vocabulary Resources**

**EL Resource Book,** page 28

**Use the word chart to study this week's vocabulary words. Write a sentence using each word in your writer's notebook.**

| Word | Context Sentence | Illustration |
|---|---|---|
| adventure | The canoe trip on rough water was a real adventure. | |
| exploring | Some people learn about caves by exploring them. | What else do people like to explore? |
| auditions | The drama teacher held auditions for the class play. | |
| sparkling | The stars were sparkling and looked like jewels. | |
| fantastic | The play was great, so we had a fantastic time. | |
| success | The book sale was a success. We sold all the books! | SALE |

Student Book

# English Learners

## Access to Core Content

**Content Objective** Read grade-level text
**Language Objective** Discuss text using key words and sentence frames
**Materials** • **English Learner Resource Book,** pp. 16–27

TESTED SKILL

### PRETEACH MAIN SELECTION (PAGES 38–57)

Use the Interactive Question-Response Guide on **English Learner Resource Book** pages 16–25 to introduce students to *Amazing Grace*. Preteach half of the selection on **Day 2** and half on **Day 3**.

- Use the prompts provided in the guide to develop meaning and vocabulary. Use the Partner-Talk and whole-class responses to engage students and increase student talk.
- When completed, have partners reread the story.

### PRETEACH PAIRED SELECTION (PAGES 60–63)

Use the Interactive Question-Response Guide on English Learner Resource Book pages 26–27 to preview the paired selection "The Storytelling Stone." Preteach the selection on **Day 4**.

English Learner Resource Book

# English Learners

## Fluency

**Content Objective** Reread selections to develop fluency; develop speaking skills
**Language Objective** Tell a partner what a selection is about
**Materials** • **Student Book:** *Amazing Grace,* "The Storytelling Stone"

### REREAD FOR FLUENCY

CA CONTENT STANDARD
R 3.1.3
Read aloud narrative and expository text fluently and accurately and with appropriate pacing, intonation, and expression.

- Have students reread a portion of *Amazing Grace*. Suggest that they focus on two to four of their favorite pages from the selection. Work with students to read the pages with appropriate intonation; for example, read each sentence of the first paragraph and have students echo the way your voice rises and falls according to the punctuation or story action. Then have students continue by chorally rereading additional paragraphs.
- Provide time for students to read their sections of text to you. Comment on their accuracy and intonation and provide corrective feedback by modeling proper fluency.

### DEVELOP SPEAKING/LISTENING SKILLS

- Have students practice reading "The Storytelling Stone." Work with them to read with accuracy and appropriate intonation.
- Provide time for students to read aloud the legend to a partner, reminding them to use appropriate intonation. Ask students to tell their partner about the legend. Provide the sentence frame: *This legend explains* _____.

Student Book

## Self-Selected Reading

**Content Objective** Read independently
**Language Objective** Orally retell information learned
**Materials** • **Classroom Library** • other fiction books

### APPLY SKILLS TO INDEPENDENT READING

- Have students choose a fiction book for independent reading. (See the **Theme Bibliography** on page T8–T9 for book suggestions.)
- After reading, ask students to orally summarize the book. Provide time for students to comment on their reactions to the book and share them with classmates. Ask: *Would you recommend this book to a classmate? Why or why not?*

Classroom Library

# English Learners

## Grammar

**Content Objective** Identify commands and exclamations
**Language Objective** Speak in complete sentences, using sentence frames

TESTED SKILL

### COMMANDS AND EXCLAMATIONS

- Review commands and exclamations with students. Remind them that a command gives an order and ends with a period, while an exclamation shows excitement and ends with an exclamation mark. Write the following example sentences on the board:

  *Take out your homework. (command)*

  *What a great job! (exclamation)*

Point out that the "you" at the beginning of a command is understood.

- Write sentences on the board, such as those provided below. Have students provide end punctuation.

  *Sit down on this rock* ____

  *How nice to see you* ____

  *What a beautiful story* ____

  *Tell me your name* ____

### PEER DISCUSSION STARTERS

- Write the following sentences on the board.

  Stories can give us ____. I learned that legends ____.

- Pair students and have them complete each sentence frame. Ask them to expand on their sentences by providing as many details as they can from this week's readings. Circulate, listen in, and take note of each student's language use and proficiency.

### English Learners

UNIVERSAL ACCESS

Build on students' responses to help move them to the next level of language acquisition; for example, if students say "Stories can give us an escape from everyday life," say "That's correct. Reading a good story can make us forget about our own world for a little while. Stories can also give us new information, or teach us a lesson. Now turn to your partner and tell more about stories."

Provide the following sentence frames orally or in writing for support.

**Beginning/Early Intermediate** A legend is ____.

**Intermediate** The legend we read explains ____.

**Early Advanced** An idea for another legend might be ____.

### Transfer Skills

**Punctuation** In Spanish, the punctuation for an exclamation includes two exclamation marks. One is placed upside down at the beginning of the exclamatory statement, and the other at the end as in English. This may make it more likely for Spanish-speaking children to try to frame exclamations in their own writing with double marks. Write additional exclamations, and have children point to the end punctuation. Point out in each case that there is no punctuation mark at the beginning of these sentences.

### Corrective Feedback

During whole group grammar lessons, follow the routine on the **Grammar Transparencies** to provide students with extra support. This routine includes completing the items with English Learners while other students work independently, having students reread the sentences with partners to build fluency, and providing a generative task such as writing a new sentence using the skill.

# English Learners

## Writing/Spelling

**Content Objective** Spell words correctly
**Language Objective** Write in complete sentences, using sentence frames

**VOCABULARY**

- Write the key vocabulary words on the board: *auditions, adventure, exploring, sparkling, fantastic, and success*. Have students copy each word on their **WorkBoards**. Then help them say each word and write sentences for each word. Provide sentence starters such as:

  *The auditions for the school _____ are today.*

  *A trip to the _____ would be a big adventure.*

  *_____ went exploring in the woods.*

  *The _____ were sparkling in the night sky.*

  *A fantastic story can help you escape to _____ worlds.*

  *_____ cheered when her performance was a success.*

- Help students spell words using their growing knowledge of English sound-spelling relationships. Model how to segment the word students are trying to spell and attach a spelling to each sound (or spellings to each syllable if a multisyllabic word). Use the **Sound-Spelling Cards** to reinforce the spellings for each English sound.
- Dictate the following words for students to spell: *lake, hope, rude, note, ripe, like, tube,* and *bake*. Guide students using the Sound-Spelling Cards as they spell each word.
- When completed, review the meanings of words that can be easily demonstrated or explained. Use actions, gestures, and available pictures.

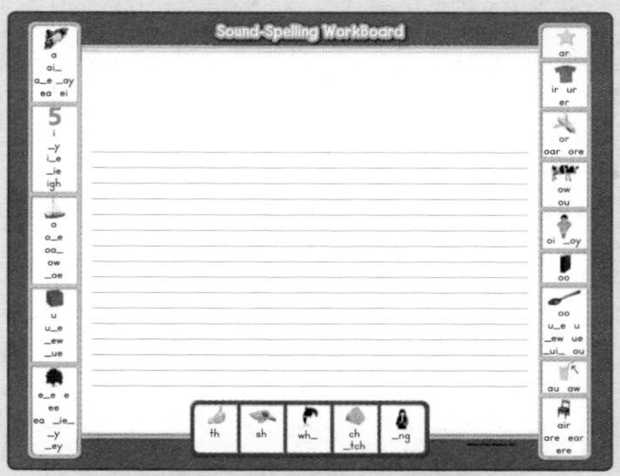

Sound-Spelling WorkBoard

### Phonics/Word Study

For English Learners who need more practice with this week's phonics/spelling skill, see the Approaching Level lesson on page 65J. Focus on minimal contrasts, articulation, and those sounds that do not transfer from the student's first language to English. For a complete listing of transfer sounds, see pages T18–T33.

Practice Reader

# English Learners

## Practice Reader

**Content Objective** Read to apply skills and strategies

**Language Objective** Retell information using complete sentences

**Materials**
- **Practice Reader:** *Anansi and the Three Tasks*
- **English Learner Resource Book,** p. 29

### BEFORE READING

CA CONTENT STANDARD R 3.2.4 Recall major points in the text and make and modify predictions about forthcoming information.

- **Preview** Read the title *Anansi and the Three Tasks*. Ask: *What's the title? Say it again.* Repeat with the author's name. Then page through the book. Use simple language to tell about each page. Immediately follow up with questions, such as: *What was the first task? What does Anansi learn?*
- **Review Skills** Use the inside front cover to review the phonics skill and vocabulary words.
- **Set a Purpose** Say: *Let's read to find out about Anansi's adventures.*

### DURING READING

- Have students whisper-read each page, or use the differentiated suggestions below. Circulate, listen in, and provide corrective feedback, such as modeling how to blend a decodable word or clarifying meaning by using techniques from the Interactive Question-Response Guides.
- **Retell** Stop after every two pages and ask students to state the main ideas they have learned so far. Reinforce language by restating students' comments when they have difficulty using story-specific words. Provide differentiated sentence frames to support students' responses and engage students in partner-talk where appropriate.

### English Learners

UNIVERSAL ACCESS

#### Beginning/Early Intermediate

**Echo-Read** Have children echo-read after you.

**Check Comprehension** Point to pictures and ask questions such as: *What does this picture show?*

#### Intermediate

**Choral-Read** Have children choral-read with you.

**Check Comprehension** Ask questions/prompts such as: *What is Anansi doing in this part of the story?*

#### Early Advanced

**Choral-Read** Have children choral-read.

**Check Comprehension** Ask: *How does Anansi complete the three tasks? What details tell about each task?*

# English Learners

## AFTER READING

CA CONTENT STANDARD
LAS 3.1.3
Respond to questions with appropriate elaboration.

**Book Talk** Write the **Book Talk Prompts** below on the board or distribute copies of **English Learner Resource Book** page 29. Students will work with peers of varying language abilities to discuss them. Form groups so that students who read the Beyond level, On level, Approaching level, and English Learner versions of *Anansi and the Three Tasks* are in the same group.

Help students determine who will be the Leader for the discussion. Then have students discuss the following:

- **Explain what you learned about fairytales.**
- **Give examples of the types of characters in fairytales.**
- **Retell what you learned about having good luck or good fortune.**
- **Tell what the castle looks like.**
- **Describe one way that people in fairytales live happily ever after.**
- **Write one question about the book to ask your group.**

**English Learner Resource Book**

**Develop Listening and Speaking Skills** Tell students to remember the following:

- Use clear and specific vocabulary to communicate ideas. Suggest they use the vocabulary words in their discussions.
- Take turns speaking and listening. Give everyone a chance to speak.
- Retell, paraphrase, and explain information shared by others.
- Clarify and enhance the discussion through the use of pictures and props. Ask, *how does the illustration on this page help you better see what is happening in this part of the story?*
- Connect and relate prior knowledge and experiences to ideas brought up in the discussion. Ask, *have you ever been in a similar situation? Explain.*

### Newcomer

**Survival Skills: Basic Requests** Teach children sentence frames for basic requests, such as *I need ______, I want ______, and Do you have ______?* In addition, teach them how to ask for permission, such as *May I use the restroom, please?* and to respond with "thank you." Provide daily opportunities to model and practice each request. Reinforce "please" and "thank you."

# The Big Question

Week 2

## Big Question Board LAS 3.1.1, LAS 3.1.3, LAS 3.1.5

**WRAP UP** Tell students to add information learned this week related to the unit theme *Personal Experiences: Let's Learn*. Students should record how *Amazing Grace* adds to their growing knowledge of the theme. Students should also record any research facts they have uncovered throughout the week or questions they want to explore as they continue reading the selections in the unit. Have students present the information they learned. Remind them of the following speaking and listening skills:

- **Speaking** Tell students that when presenting information, they should organize their ideas chronologically, or in the proper sequence. Have them write the numbers 1–5 on a sheet of paper. Then have them write their five main points in the order in which they want to present them. After presenting, prompt the student to ask for questions and answer them with appropriate elaboration.
- **Listening** Once students have listened to a presenter, ask them to turn to a partner and retell or paraphrase what they heard to check their understanding.

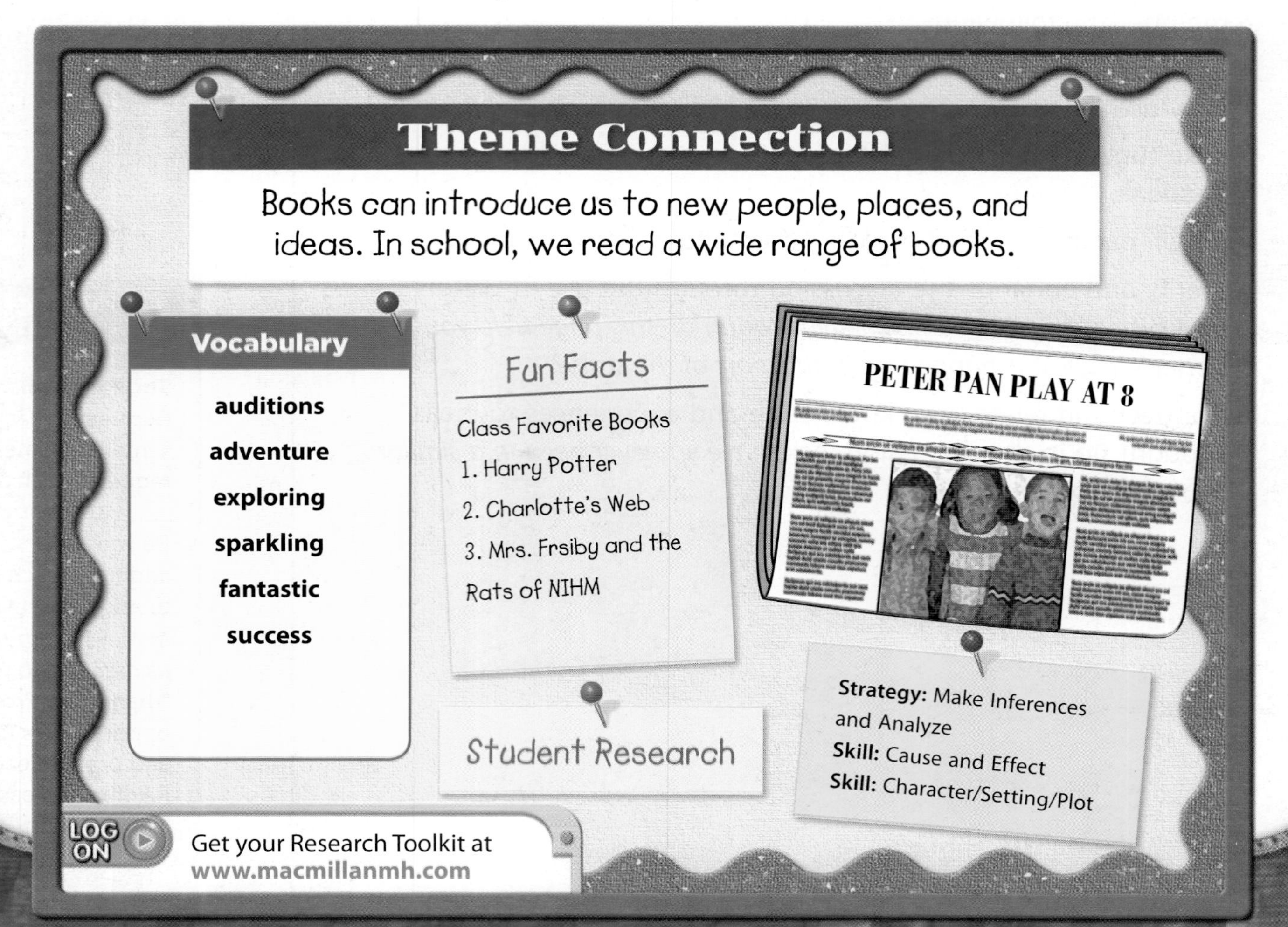

# Week 3 At a Glance

## WHOLE GROUP

### Phonics/Word Study
Long *a*, Multisyllabic Words

### Vocabulary
Robust Words: *donate, unaware, members, contribute*

Thesaurus: Synonyms

### Comprehension
Strategy: Summarize
Skill: Main Idea/Details

Skill: Cause and Effect

### Fluency
Pacing

### Spelling
Long *a*: *fail, bay, pail, ray, plain, tray, trails, may, braid, sway, gray, plays, paint, snail, great*

### Grammar/Mechanics
Subjects

Correct Sentences

### Writing
Personal Narrative: Description

### Read Aloud
Genre: Folklore

## SMALL GROUP

### Differentiated Instruction for Tested Skills

Approaching Level | On Level | Beyond Level | English Learners

## Teacher Tools

Technology to help plan and implement instruction

**PREPARE**
- Professional Development Videos
- Parent Connection

**PLAN/ORGANIZE**

Go to **www.macmillanmh.com** for Online Lesson Planner

TeacherWorks Plus™
All-In-One Planner and Resource Center

**TEACH**
- Theme Launcher Video
- Classroom Presentation Toolkit
- Vocabulary PuzzleMaker
- Sound Pronunciation CD

**ASSESS**

Assessment Online

ExamView® CD-ROM

# Weekly Literature

## Student Book

**A mix of fiction and nonfiction connected to:**

- Unit Theme
- California Content Standards

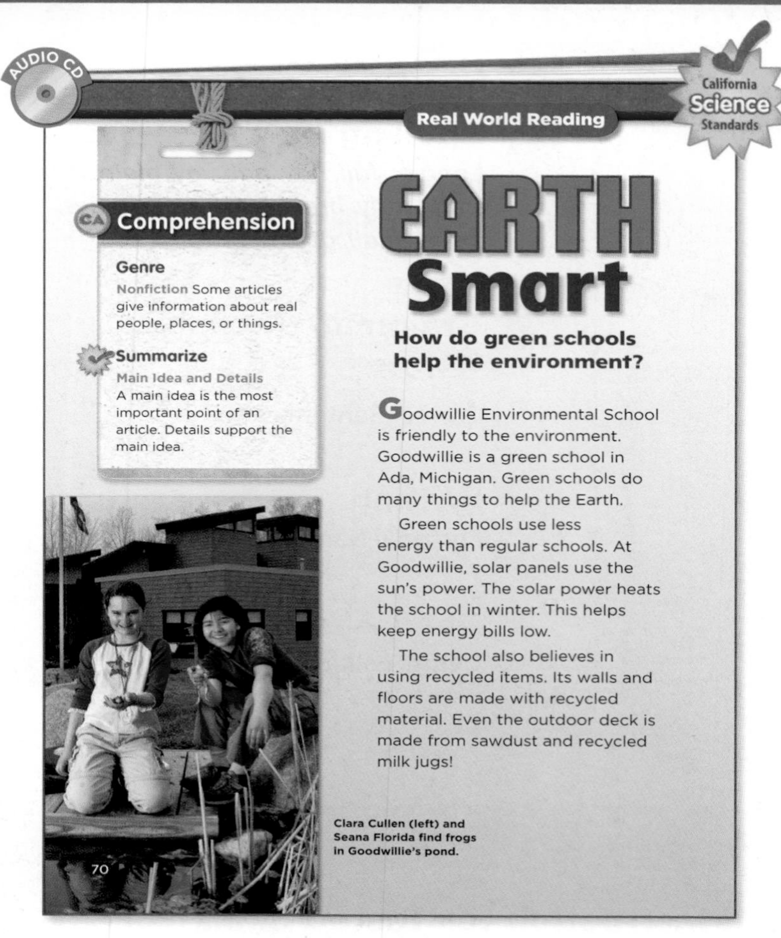
AUDIO CD

California Science Standards

Real World Reading

Comprehension

Genre

Nonfiction Some articles give information about real people, places, or things.

Summarize

Main Idea and Details

A main idea is the most important point of an article. Details support the main idea.

EARTH Smart

How do green schools help the environment?

Goodwillie Environmental School is friendly to the environment. Goodwillie is a green school in Ada, Michigan. Green schools do many things to help the Earth.

Green schools use less energy than regular schools. At Goodwillie, solar panels use the sun's power. The solar power heats the school in winter. This helps keep energy bills low.

The school also believes in using recycled items. Its walls and floors are made with recycled material. Even the outdoor deck is made from sawdust and recycled milk jugs!

Clara Cullen (left) and Seana Florida find frogs in Goodwillie's pond.

70

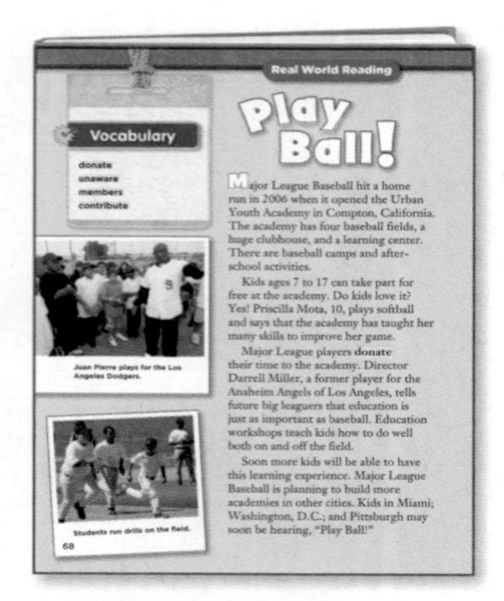
Real World Reading

Vocabulary

donate
unaware
members
contribute

Play Ball!

Major League Baseball hit a home run in 2006 when it opened the Urban Youth Academy in Compton, California. The academy has four baseball fields, a huge clubhouse, and a learning center. There are baseball camps and after-school activities.

Kids ages 7 to 17 can take part for free at the academy. Do kids love it? Yes! Priscilla Mota, 10, plays softball and says that the academy has taught her many skills to improve her game.

Major League players donate their time to the academy. Director Darrell Miller, a former player for the Anaheim Angels of Los Angeles, tells future big leaguers that education is just as important as baseball. Education workshops teach kids how to do well both on and off the field.

Soon more kids will be able to have this learning experience. Major League Baseball is planning to build more academies in other cities. Kids in Miami; Washington, D.C.; and Pittsburgh may soon be hearing, "Play Ball!"

Juan Pierre plays for the Los Angeles Dodgers.

Students run drills on the field.

68

### Preteach Vocabulary and Comprehension

**Genre** Nonfiction

### Main Selection

**Genre** Nonfiction

Show What You Know

Right There

You can put your finger on the answer. Look for key words in the questions. Then find those key words in the selection.

Summer Break?

Do you have school in summer? Students in Oxnard, California, do. That's because schools in Oxnard are year-round schools. There are 1,483 year-round schools in California. In the United States, about 2 million students attend year-round schools.

All students in the United States have to go to school for 180 days each year. In regular school, kids go to class for about ten months and get two months off in the summer. Year-round schools break up the 180 days differently. Students usually get short breaks scattered throughout the year.

What are the benefits of year-round school? Experts say that students remember more when breaks are shorter. With less vacation time, teachers spend less time on review. That can add up to better grades. As a result, some schools say year-round students score higher on tests.

Still, not everyone is happy. Some parents say year-round school cuts into vacation time. Students say they miss out on summer activities, such as camp. Change could take some getting used to, but it's clear to see that there are many different ways to get your 180 school days.

74

Go on

### Show What You Know

**Genre** Nonfiction

## Support Literature

**Resources to build robust vocabulary, fluency, and content knowledge**

### Interactive Read-Aloud Anthology

- Listening Comprehension
- Readers Theater Plays

### Content Reader

- Meets all California Science and History/Social Science Standards

## Skill-Based Practice Readers

- Same Theme
- Same Vocabulary/Phonics
- Same Comprehension Skills

Approaching Level

On Level

Beyond Level

English Learner

On Level Practice Reader sheltered for English Learners

## StudentWorks Plus

- eBook
- Use for preteaching
- Summaries in multiple languages
- Word-by-Word Reading
- Assessment

## Practice Book and Reproducibles

Also available:

Approaching Reproducible

Beyond Reproducible

## Intensive Vocabulary

Build robust vocabulary with fiction and nonfiction

**Oral Vocabulary Cards**

## Home-School Connection

- Family letters in English, Spanish, Hmong, Vietnamese, Cantonese, Khmer
- Take-Home Stories

## Intervention Kit

- Intervention Anthology
- Phonemic Awareness Teacher's Edition
- Phonics/Word Study Teacher's Edition
- Comprehension Teacher's Edition
- Vocabulary Teacher's Edition
- Fluency Teacher's Edition
- Writing and Grammar Teacher's Edition

## Visual Vocabulary Resources

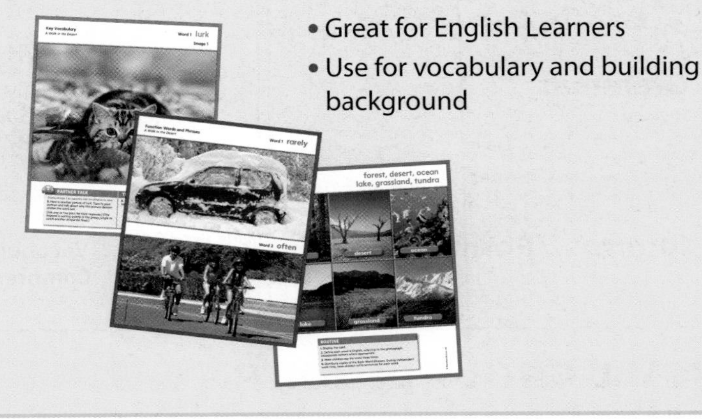


- Great for English Learners
- Use for vocabulary and building background

# LOG ON Suggested Lesson Plan

Go to www.macmillanmh.com for Online Lesson Planner

Earth Smart, pp. 70–73

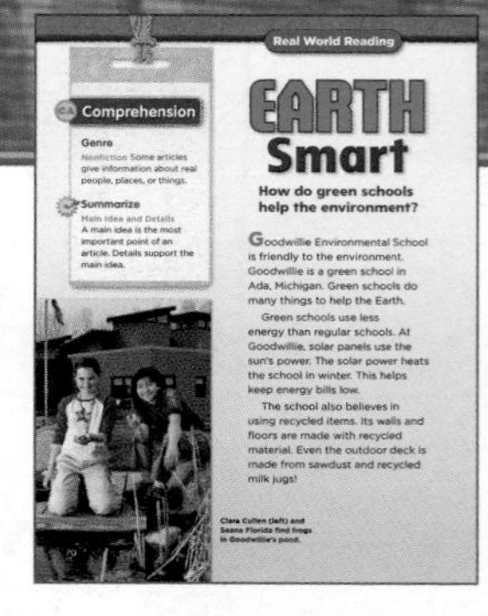


| WHOLE GROUP | DAY 1 | DAY 2 |
|---|---|---|
|  **ORAL LANGUAGE** (15–20 min)<br>• Listening Comprehension<br>• Speaking/Viewing | **Listening/Speaking/Viewing**<br>**Focus Question** What do you think a school should look like? Are all schools alike?<br>Read Aloud: "The Name of the Tree," 66L–66M<br>Build Background, 66 | **Listening/Speaking**<br>**Focus Question** How do green schools help the environment? |
|  **WORD STUDY** (30–40 min)<br>• Vocabulary<br>• Phonics/Word Study<br>• Spelling |  **Vocabulary** R 3.1.4<br>*donate, unaware, members, contribute,* 69, 77A<br>Practice Book, 34<br>**Strategy:** Thesaurus/Synonyms, 68<br> **Spelling** Pretest Words with Long a, 77C LC 3.1.8<br>Practice Book, 41 |  **Vocabulary** R 3.1.4, R 3.1.8<br>Review Words, Thesaurus/Synonyms, 70, 77A<br>Practice Book, 40<br> **Phonics**<br>Long *a*, 66N–66O R 3.1.1, R 3.1.2<br>Practice Book, 33<br>**Spelling** Word Sorts, 77C LC 3.1.8<br>Reproducible, SP7 |
|  **READING** (30–40 min)<br>• Comprehension<br>• Fluency |  Student Book<br>**Read** "Play Ball!," "Top 5 Biggest Elementary Schools," and "Freedom Fighter," 68–69<br>**Comprehension**, 69A–69B<br>**Strategy:** Summarize R 3.1.4<br>**Skill:** Main Idea and Details R 3.2.5<br>Practice Book, 35<br>**Fluency** Model Fluency, 66M R 3.1.3 | 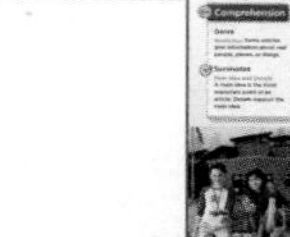 Student Book<br>**Read** *Earth Smart* 70–73<br>**Comprehension**, 70–73<br>**Strategy:** Summarize R 3.1.4<br>**Skill:** Main Ideas and Details R 3.2.5<br>Practice Book, 36<br>**Fluency** Repeated Reading: Pacing, 73A R 3.1.3 |
|  **LANGUAGE ARTS** (30–40 min)<br>• Writing<br>• Grammar | 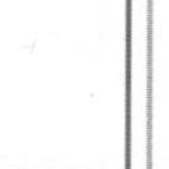 **Writing**<br>**Daily Writing Prompt** Write a paragraph describing something you like about your school.<br>Prewrite, 77G–77H W 3.1.1, W 3.2.1a, W 3.2.1b, W 3.2.1c<br>**Grammar** Daily Language Activities, 77E<br>Subjects, 77E LAS 3.1.4<br>Reproducible, GR7 |  **Writing**<br>**Daily Writing Prompt** Write a paragraph about your dream school.<br>Draft, 77H–77J W 3.1.1, W 3.2.1a, W 3.2.1b, W 3.2.1c<br>Practice Book, 45<br>**Grammar** Daily Language Activities, 77E<br>Subjects, 77E LAS 3.1.4<br>Practice Book, 43 |
| **ASSESSMENT**<br>• Informal/Formal | **Quick Check** **Vocabulary**, 69<br>**Comprehension**, 69B | **Quick Check** **Comprehension**, 73 |

**SMALL GROUP Lesson Plan** (45–60 min) — **Differentiated Instruction 77Q–77PP**

## California Standards

**Vocabulary**
Vocabulary Words
Thesaurus/Synonyms
R 3.1.4, R 3.1.8

**Comprehension**
**Strategy:** Summarize
**Skill:** Main Ideas and Details
R 3.1.4, R 3.2.5

**Writing Process**
Personal Narrative: Description
W 3.1.1, W 3.2.1a, W 3.2.1b, W 3.2.1c, W 3.1.4

**History/Social Science**
HSS 3.4.6

# DAY 3

### Listening/Speaking

**Focus Question** What are the **main ideas** in "Play Ball!" and "*Earth Smart*"? What opinion do both writers share?

### Vocabulary R 3.1.4, R 3.1.8

Review Words, Related Words, 77B

### Spelling

Word Meanings, 77D LC 3.1.8
Reproducible, SP8

### Read

*Earth Smart,* 70–73

Student Book

### Comprehension

Critical Thinking, 73
Practice Book, 39
**Skill:** Cause and Effect, 73B

### Fluency

Repeated Reading: Pacing, 73A
Practice Book, 37 R 3.1.3

### Writing

**Daily Writing Prompt** Explain whether you would like to attend Goodwillie.

Revise, Use Rubrics, 77H, 77K–77L W 3.1.1, W 3.2.1a, W 3.2.1b, W 3.2.1c

### Grammar

Daily Language Activities, 77E
Mechanics and Usage, 77F LAS 3.1.4
Reproducible, GR8

**Quick Check** Fluency, 73A

# DAY 4

### Listening/Speaking/Viewing

**Focus Question** Compare and contrast regular schools with year-round schools. How are they alike? How are they different?

### Vocabulary R 3.1.4, R 3.1.8

Review Words, Morphology, 77B

### Spelling

Proofread, 77D LC 3.1.8
Practice Book, 42

### Read

"Summer Break?" 73C–75

Student Book

### Test Strategy

**Answer Questions:** Right There

### Research and Study Skills

**Study Skill:** Using a Dictionary, 73C–73D R 3.1.7

Content Reader

### Fluency

Repeated Reading: Pacing, 73A R 3.1.3

### Writing

**Daily Writing Prompt** Write a paragraph about why recycling is important.

Write on Demand, 76–77
Revise, Proofread, 77H, 77M–77N W 3.1.1

### Grammar

Daily Language Activities, 77E
Subjects, 77F LAS 3.1.4
Practice Book, 44

**Quick Check** Vocabulary, 77B

# DAY 5 Review and Assess

### Listening/Speaking/Viewing

**Focus Question** Use details from the articles to describe how green schools differ from other schools.

Speaking and Listening Strategies, 77L

### Vocabulary R 3.1.4, R 3.1.8

**Assess Words:** Connect to Writing, 77B

### Spelling

Posttest, 77D LC 3.1.8
Reproducible, SP9

### Read

Self-Selected Reading, 66J R 3.3.2

Student Book

### Comprehension

**Strategy:** Summarize R 3.1.4
**Skill:** Main Ideas and Details R 3.2.5

### Fluency

Practice, 66J R 3.1.3

### Writing

**Daily Writing Prompt** Write a letter to your teacher explaining how you feel about going to school in the summer.

Publish, Conference, 77H, 77M–77N W 3.1.4

### Grammar

Daily Language Activities, 75E
Subjects, 77F LAS 3.1.4
Reproducible, GR9

**Weekly Assessment, 77O–77P**

# Differentiated Instruction

## What do I do in small groups?

## Focus on Skills

**IF...** **students need additional instruction and practice based on your Quick Check observations of the following skills:**

- **Phonics/Word Study**
  Long *a*
- **Vocabulary Words**
  *donate, unaware, members, contribute*
  **Strategy:** Thesaurus/Synonyms
- **Comprehension**
  **Strategy:** Summarize
  **Skill:** Main Idea and Details
- **Fluency**

**THEN...**

| | |
|---|---|
| Approaching<br>English Learners | Preteach and Reteach Skills |
| On Level | Consolidate Learning |
| Beyond | Enrich and Accelerate Learning |

## Suggested Small Group Lesson Plan

| Focus on Skills | DAY 1 | DAY 2 |
|---|---|---|
| **Phonics/Word Study**<br>• **Long *a*** | English Learners Preteach Long *a*, 77R | On Level Reteach Long *a*, 77AA |
| **Vocabulary**<br>• **Week 3 Words**  | Approaching Preteach; Academic Language, 77Q, 77S<br>On Level Review, 77AA<br>Beyond Practice Reader Lesson 1, 77GG<br>English Learners Preteach; Academic Language 77II–77JJ | Approaching Practice Reader Lesson 1, 77V<br>Beyond Practice Reader Lesson 2, 77HH<br>English Learners Preteach Vocabulary; Access to Core Content, 77JJ–77KK |
| **Comprehension**<br>• **Strategy:** Summarize<br>• **Skill:** Main Idea and Details | Approaching Prepare to Read, 77Q<br>Beyond Practice Reader Lesson 1, 77GG<br>English Learners Prepare to Read, 77II | Approaching Reteach; Practice Reader Lesson 1, 77U–77V<br>Beyond Practice Reader Lesson 2, 77HH<br>English Learners Practice Reader, 77OO |
| **Fluency**<br>• **Repeated Reading** | | Beyond Practice Reader Lesson 2, 77HH |

## Skill-Based Practice Readers

Apply skills and strategies while reading appropriate leveled books.

**Teacher's Edition** with California Content Standards instruction also available.

**Leveled Practice Database**
Go to **www.macmillanmh.com**.

## Manipulatives

Use for Hands-on Learning

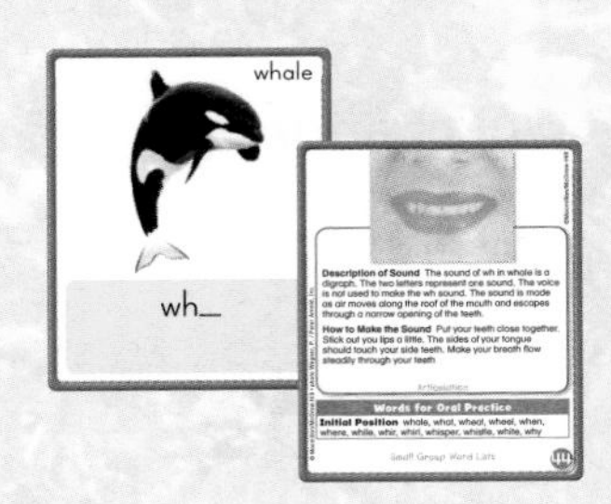


**Sound-Spelling Cards**

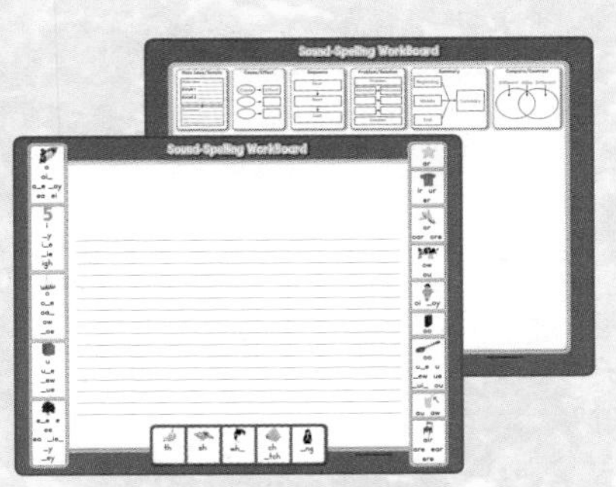

**Sound-Spelling WorkBoards**

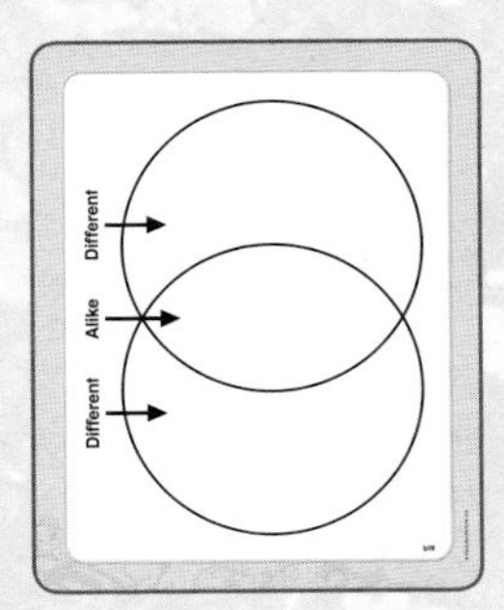


**Vocabulary/Comprehension Write-on/Wipe-off Boards**

**FOLDABLES®** Hands-on activities for reinforcing weekly skills

| DAY 3 | DAY 4 | DAY 5 |
|---|---|---|
| **Approaching** Long *a*, 77R<br>**Beyond** Extend and Accelerate, 77EE | **Approaching** Long *a*, 77R<br>**English Learners** Writing/Spelling, 77NN | **English Learners** Review Long *a*, 77R |
| **Approaching** Practice Reader Lesson 2, 77W<br>**On Level** Practice Reader Lesson 1, 77CC<br>**English Learners** Preteach Vocabulary; Access to Core Content, Grammar, 77JJ–77KK, 77MM | **Approaching** Review Vocabulary, 77T<br>**On Level** Practice Reader Lesson 2, 77DD<br>**Beyond** Enrich, 77EE<br>**English Learners** Vocabulary, 77OO–77PP | **English Learners** Vocabulary, Practice Reader, 77OO |
| **Approaching** Practice Reader Lesson 2, 77W<br>**On Level** Practice Reader Lesson 1, 77CC<br>**English Learners** Practice Reader, 77OO | **Approaching** Practice Reader Lesson 3, 77X<br>**On Level** Practice Reader Lesson 2, 77DD<br>**English Learners** Practice Reader, 77OO | **Approaching** Book Talk, 77PP<br>**On Level** Book Talk, 77PP<br>**Beyond** Book Talk, 77PP<br>**English Learners** Book Talk, 77PP |
| **Approaching** Practice Reader Lesson 2, 77W | **Approaching** Reread, Model, 77Y<br>**On Level** Reread, Model, 77BB<br>**Beyond** Reread, Model,77FF<br>**English Learners** Reread, Model, 77LL | **Approaching** Self-Selected Reading, 77Z<br>**On Level** Self-Selected Reading, 77BB<br>**Beyond** Self-Selected Reading, 77FF<br>**English Learners** Self-Selected Reading, 77LL |

# Managing the Class

## What do I do with the rest of my class?

- Literacy Workstations
- Practice Book
- Online Activities
- Classroom Library

## Classroom Management Tools

**Weekly Contract**

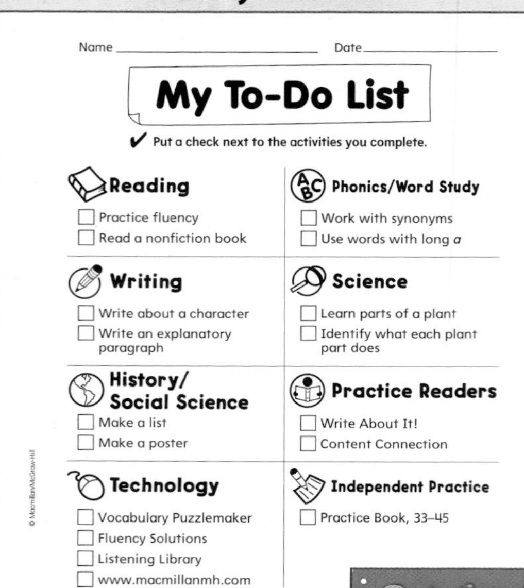

Name ____________ Date ____________

**My To-Do List**

✔ Put a check next to the activities you complete.

| Reading | Phonics/Word Study |
| --- | --- |
| ☐ Practice fluency<br>☐ Read a nonfiction book | ☐ Work with synonyms<br>☐ Use words with long *a* |
| **Writing** | **Science** |
| ☐ Write about a character<br>☐ Write an explanatory paragraph | ☐ Learn parts of a plant<br>☐ Identify what each plant part does |
| **History/ Social Science** | **Practice Readers** |
| ☐ Make a list<br>☐ Make a poster | ☐ Write About It!<br>☐ Content Connection |
| **Technology** | **Independent Practice** |
| ☐ Vocabulary Puzzlemaker<br>☐ Fluency Solutions<br>☐ Listening Library<br>☐ www.macmillanmh.com | ☐ Practice Book, 33–45 |

How-to Guide

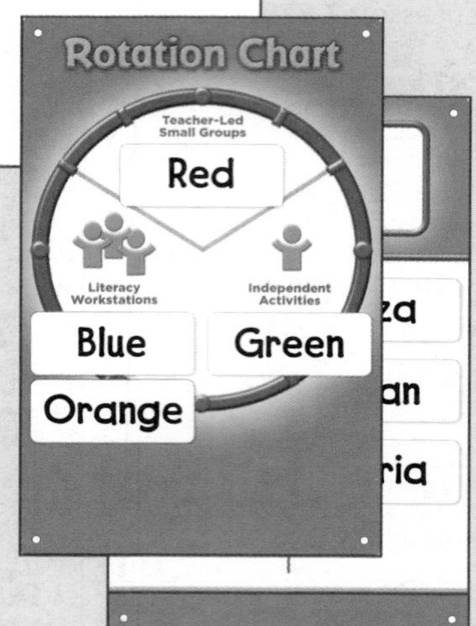


Rotation Chart

## Digital Learning

**StudentWorks Plus**

- Summaries in Multiple Languages
- Word-by-Word Reading
- Assessment

**Meet the Author/Illustrator**

**Mary Hoffman**

- Mary grew up in Manchester, England.
- Mary never wears anything blue.
- When Mary was a girl, she wanted to be a garage mechanic.

Other books written and by Mary Hoffman

- Hoffman, Mary. *Boundless Grace.* New York: Puffin, 2000.
- Hoffman, Mary. *The Color of Home.* New York: Dial, 2002.
- Hoffman, Mary. *Starring Grace.* Frances Lincoln Childrens Books, 2003.

- Read Other Books by Author or Illustrator

## Classroom Library

Use the trade books to apply skills. See lessons on pages T2–T7. See also **Theme Bibliography**, pages T8–T9, to select books for 30 minutes of daily independent reading.

Approaching

On Level

Beyond

# Independent Activities

**ONLINE INSTRUCTION** www.macmillanmh.com

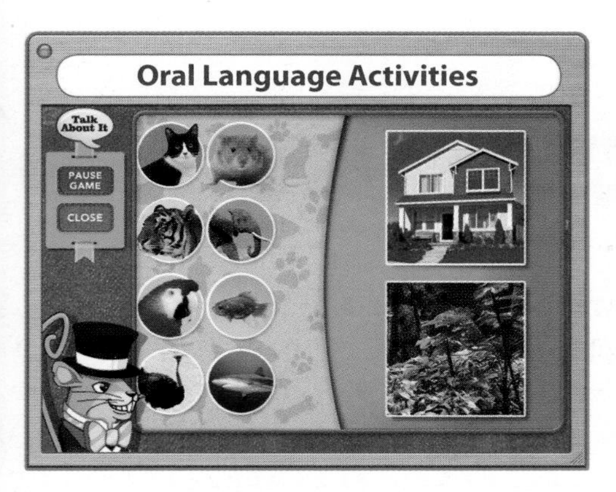

**Oral Language Activities**

- Focus on Unit Vocabulary and Concepts
- English Learner Support

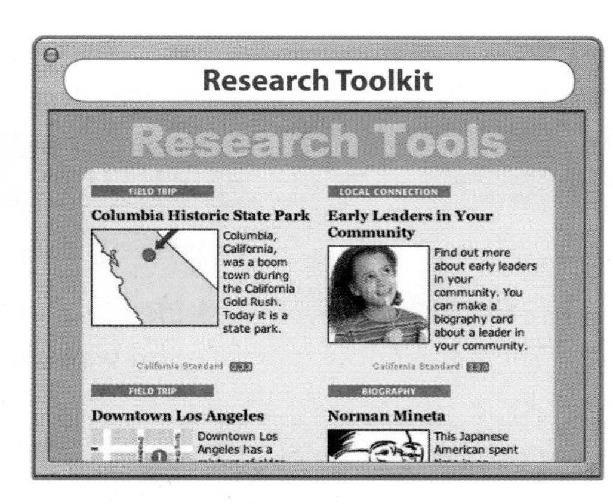


**Research Toolkit**

- Research Roadmap
- Research and Presentation Tools
- Theme Launcher Video
- Links to CA Science and History/Social Science Programs

**Computer Literacy Lessons**

- Focus on Keyboard and Internet Skills
- Media Literacy

**Vocabulary/Spelling Activities**

- Differentiated Lists and Activities

## Available on CD

**LISTENING LIBRARY**
Recordings of selections
- Main Selections
- Paired Selections
- Practice Readers
- EL Readers

**FLUENCY SOLUTIONS**
Recorded passages at two speeds for modeling and practicing fluency

## Practice Book

Also Available:
- Approaching Reproducible
- Beyond Reproducible

## Literacy Workstation Flip Charts

Daily independent and partner activities connected to the weekly skills. See pages 66J–66K.

# Managing the Class

## What do I do with the rest of my class?

## Reading

### Objectives

- Develop fluency through partner reading
- Practice pronouncing difficult words
- Create a Main Idea/Details chart for a nonfiction book

## Phonics/Word Study

### Objectives

- Identify and use synonyms in context
- Sort words with Long *a*

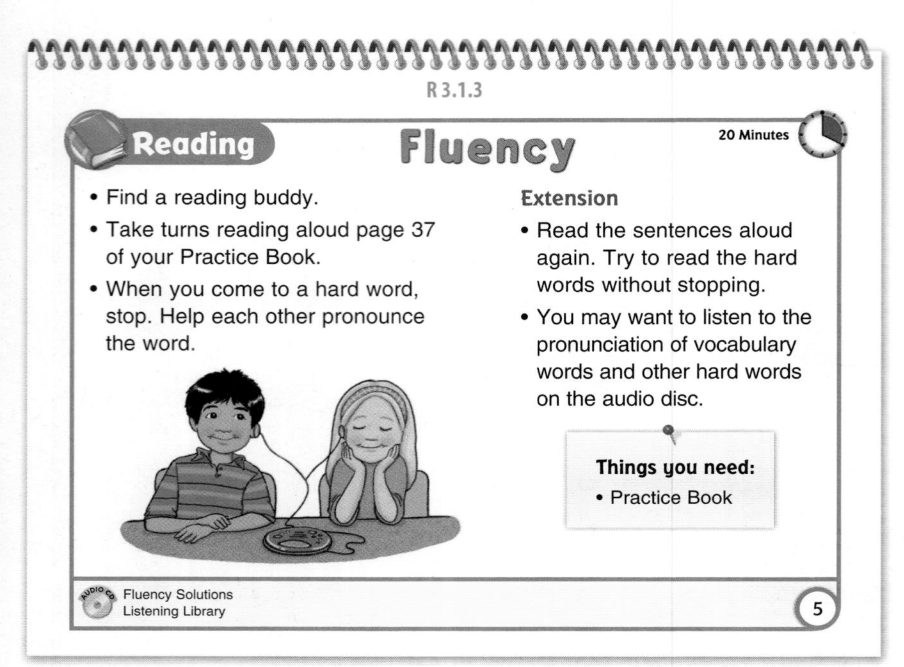

R 3.1.3

**Reading** — **Fluency** — 20 Minutes

- Find a reading buddy.
- Take turns reading aloud page 37 of your Practice Book.
- When you come to a hard word, stop. Help each other pronounce the word.

**Extension**

- Read the sentences aloud again. Try to read the hard words without stopping.
- You may want to listen to the pronunciation of vocabulary words and other hard words on the audio disc.

**Things you need:**
- Practice Book

Fluency Solutions Listening Library

5

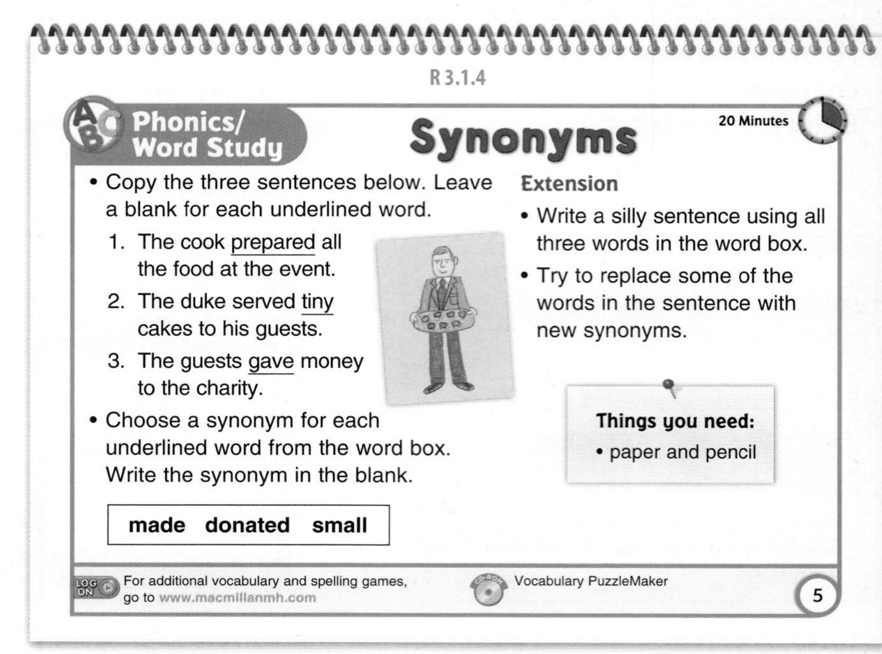

R 3.1.4

**Phonics/Word Study** — **Synonyms** — 20 Minutes

- Copy the three sentences below. Leave a blank for each underlined word.
  1. The cook prepared all the food at the event.
  2. The duke served tiny cakes to his guests.
  3. The guests gave money to the charity.
- Choose a synonym for each underlined word from the word box. Write the synonym in the blank.

**made donated small**

**Extension**

- Write a silly sentence using all three words in the word box.
- Try to replace some of the words in the sentence with new synonyms.

**Things you need:**
- paper and pencil

For additional vocabulary and spelling games, go to www.macmillanmh.com

Vocabulary PuzzleMaker

5

R 3.2.5

**Reading** — **INDEPENDENT READING** — 20 Minutes

- Read a nonfiction book.
- During your independent work time, create your own Main Idea and Details Chart. Fill it in.

| Main Idea | Details |
| --- | --- |

**Extension**

- What are some of your favorite nonfiction books? Why do you like them?
- In your response journal, list these books. Tell why you like them.

**Things you need:**
- nonfiction book
- paper and pencil
- journal

For more books about Building Communities, go to the Author/Illustrator section at www.macmillanmh.com

6

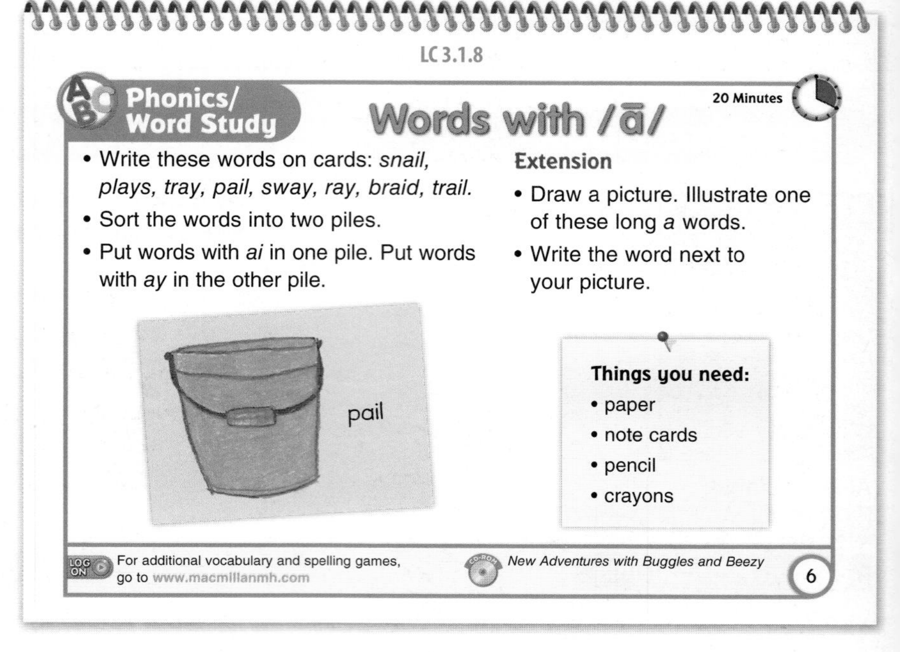

LC 3.1.8

**Phonics/Word Study** — **Words with /ā/** — 20 Minutes

- Write these words on cards: *snail, plays, tray, pail, sway, ray, braid, trail.*
- Sort the words into two piles.
- Put words with *ai* in one pile. Put words with *ay* in the other pile.

pail

**Extension**

- Draw a picture. Illustrate one of these long *a* words.
- Write the word next to your picture.

**Things you need:**
- paper
- note cards
- pencil
- crayons

For additional vocabulary and spelling games, go to www.macmillanmh.com

*New Adventures with Buggles and Beezy*

6

**Literacy Workstation Flip Charts**

## Writing

### Objectives

- Write an explanatory paragraph about natural resources
- Write a story about a character who is a good citizen

## Content Literacy

### Objectives

- Think and write about respecting nature and communities
- Research the parts of a flower
- Practice taking notes from research

W 3.1.1

**Writing** **Our Natural Resources** 20 Minutes

- Write an explanatory paragraph. Tell why air, water, sunlight, and soil are important natural resources.
- Do research if you need information.

**Extension**

- Read your paragraph to a partner.
- Ask if your explanation was clear.

**Things you need:**

- paper and pencil

5

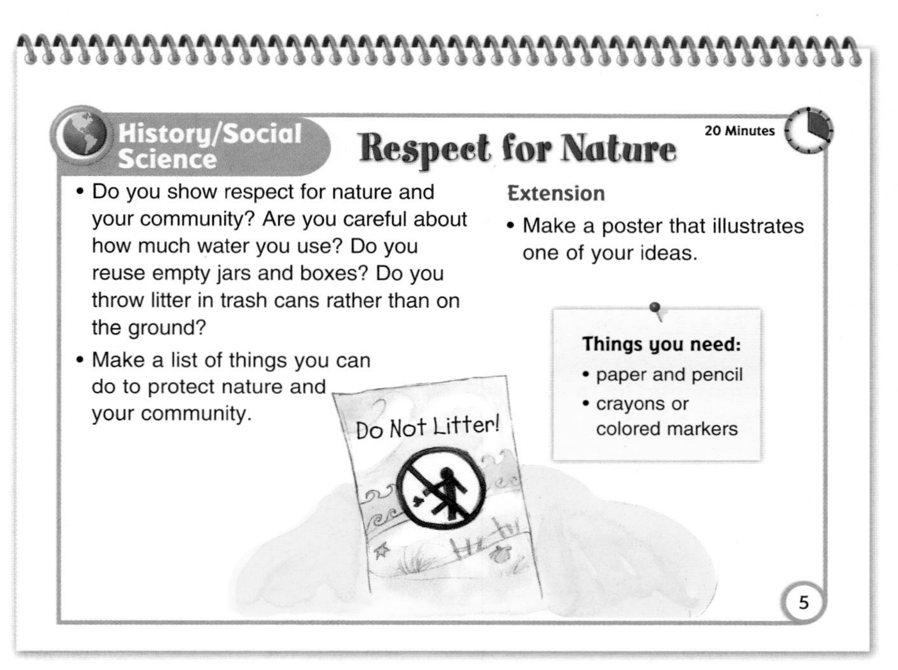

**History/Social Science** **Respect for Nature** 20 Minutes

- Do you show respect for nature and your community? Are you careful about how much water you use? Do you reuse empty jars and boxes? Do you throw litter in trash cans rather than on the ground?
- Make a list of things you can do to protect nature and your community.



**Extension**

- Make a poster that illustrates one of your ideas.

**Things you need:**

- paper and pencil
- crayons or colored markers

5

W 3.2.1

**Writing** **A Good Person** 20 Minutes

- Make up a story about a character who is a good citizen. Tell what the character does to help a person, a community, or a country. Write a story with a beginning, a middle, and an end.

**Extension**

- Draw a picture. Show how your story ends. Write a caption for your picture.

**Things you need:**

- paper and pencil
- crayons or markers

6

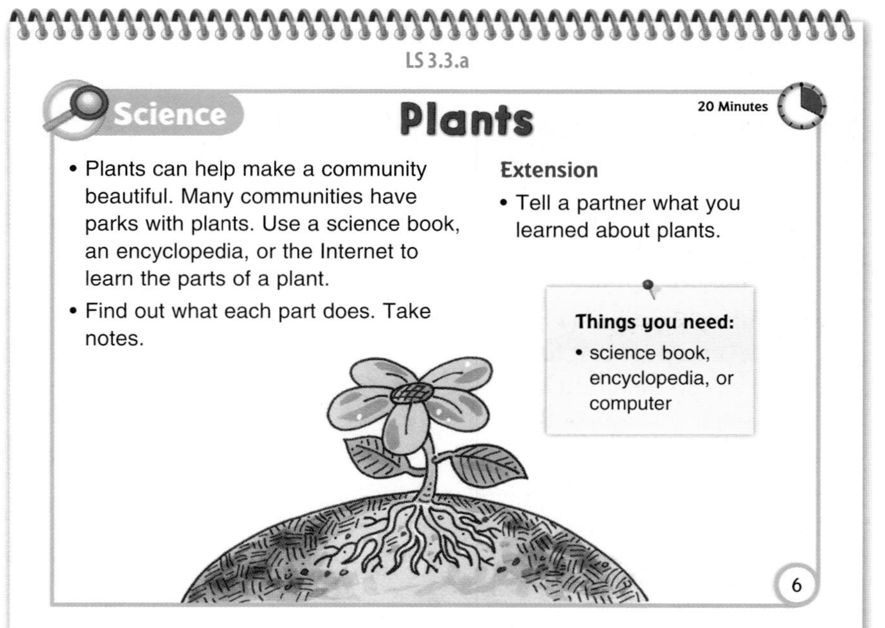

LS 3.3.a

**Science** **Plants** 20 Minutes

- Plants can help make a community beautiful. Many communities have parks with plants. Use a science book, an encyclopedia, or the Internet to learn the parts of a plant.
- Find out what each part does. Take notes.

**Extension**

- Tell a partner what you learned about plants.

**Things you need:**

- science book, encyclopedia, or computer

6

# Prepare

## WHOLE GROUP

**ORAL LANGUAGE**
- Read Aloud
- Build Background
- Connect to Theme

**PHONICS/WORD STUDY**
- Long *a* Words

**VOCABULARY**
- Teach Words in Context
- Thesaurus: Synonyms

**COMPREHENSION**
- Strategy: Summarize
- Skill: Main Idea and Details

**CONTENT STANDARDS**
R 3.1.1, R 3.1.2, R 3.1.3, R 3.1.4, R 3.3.1, LAS 3.2.2

## SMALL GROUP

- Differentiated Instruction, pp. 77Q–77PP

### Intensive Vocabulary

To provide 15–20 minutes additional vocabulary instruction, see **Oral Vocabulary Card** 5-Day Plan. The pre- and post-test for this week can be found in the **Teacher's Resource Book**, pages 270–272.

# Read Aloud

## Read "The Name of the Tree"

**Read Aloud**

**GENRE: FOLKTALE**

Share with students the following key characteristics of a **folktale**:

CA CONTENT STANDARD
R 3.3.1 Distinguish common forms of literature.

- Folktales are fictional stories that are passed down from generation to generation and reflect the life, culture, and environment of the people who first told them.
- Folktales can have animal or human characters. They often feature a clever main character who outsmarts another, stronger or more powerful, character.

**FOCUS ON VOCABULARY**

Introduce the following words, using the **Define/Example/Ask** routine. Tell students that knowing these words will help them understand the setting and actions of the characters in the story.

### Vocabulary Routine

Use the routines below to discuss the meaning of each word.

Define: A **plain** is an area of land that is very flat and has no trees.
Example: The elephants roamed the plain in search of water.
Ask: What animals might you find living on a plain?

Define: If you **strode**, you walked with very long steps.
Example: The actor strode off the stage at the end of the play.
Ask: How is strode different from walked?

Define: **Haughtily** means doing something in a very proud way.
Example: The boy haughtily waved his first place trophy at the other contestants after winning the talent competition.
Ask: When might you do something haughtily?

**LISTENING FOR A PURPOSE**

Ask students to listen carefully as you read "The Name of the Tree" in the **Read-Aloud Anthology**, pages 103–107. Use the Think Alouds and vocabulary prompts provided.

EL **Interactive Reading** Build students' oral language by engaging them in talk about the story's basic meaning.

- Point to the picture on page 103. Name each animal and have students repeat. Describe the characteristics of each animal.

- After the first three paragraphs, say, *Turn to your partner and discuss why the animals need to go across the great flat plain.*
- After the twelfth paragraph, say, *The fruit on the tree is delicious, or tastes very good. Think of something you like to eat that you would consider to be delicious. What is it and why is it delicious?*
- After the last paragraph, say, *Tell your partner how the young tortoise remembered the name of the tree. How did this inspire the other animals?*

**Think/Pair/Share** Use **Copying Master 2**, "I made a connection when . . . ," to help students figure out the main idea of the folktale. When completed, have students turn to a partner and orally summarize the story. Then have a few students share their summaries with the class.

**RESPOND TO THE FOLKTALE**

Ask students the **Think and Respond** questions on page 108. Then have students discuss and list the characteristics of the tortoise that made him successful at solving the problem. Ask them to describe how staying focused can help them accomplish difficult tasks.

## Model Fluency

Reread the folktale. Tell students that this time you want them to focus on your **pacing**, or tempo.

Point out that you speed up in sections of the text that are exciting to add drama to your reading. Model an example and have students think of words to describe the feelings you expressed, such as confidence.

**CA CONTENT STANDARD R 3.1.3** Read aloud narrative and expository text fluently and accurately and with appropriate pacing, intonation, and expression.

**Think Aloud** Listen as I read the part where the very young tortoise learns the name of the tree and is returning to the great flat plain. He falls right to the bottom of the rabbit hole. Listen to my pacing and notice how I add drama to the reading: *Even when he fell right to the bottom of that same rabbit hole, the very young tortoise just climbed out saying, "Ungalli, Ungalli, the name of the tree is Ungalli."* Did you notice how I read that part of the story a little faster to add excitement? Now you try. Repeat each sentence after me, using the same pace that I use.

**Establish Fluency Focus** Remind students that you will be listening for these same qualities in their reading throughout the week. You will help them improve their reading by adjusting their pace to add drama. Point out that good readers adjust the pace of their reading at different points in a selection according to the action of the story.

### Readers Theater

**BUILDING LISTENING AND SPEAKING SKILLS**
Distribute copies of "Take Me to Your Litter," **Read-Aloud Anthology** pages 132–145. Have students practice reading the play throughout the unit. Assign parts and have students present the play or perform it as a dramatic reading at the end of the unit.

**CA CONTENT STANDARD LAS 3.2.2** Plan and present dramatic interpretations of experiences, stories, poems, or plays with clear diction, pitch, tempo, and tone.

## Objectives

- Decode multisyllabic words with long *a* spellings

## Materials

- Sound-Spelling Cards
- Practice Book, p. 33
- Transparency 3
- Word-Building Cards
- Teacher's Resource Book, 180

### English Learners
UNIVERSAL ACCESS

**Transfer Sounds** In some languages, including **Cantonese, Vietnamese,** and **Hmong**, the transfer for the long *a* sound is only approximate. Emphasize the sound and demonstrate correct mouth position when pronouncing each word. Contrast words with the short and long *a* sounds, such as *Sam/same*. Use the Approaching Level phonics lessons for additional pronunciation/decoding practice.

HOMEWORK **Practice Book,** page 33

When a vowel says its name, it is a long vowel. When a syllable has two vowels, the letters stand for the sound of the first vowel. The letters *ai* or *ay* stand for the long *a* sound.

**A. Read each sentence. Circle the word that has the long *a* sound.**

1. My dog is (afraid) of thunderstorms.
2. I like to (paint) using watercolors.
3. The kitten (plays) with yarn until it is tired.
4. "Don't knock over that (pail!)"
5. (May) is one of the loveliest months of the year.
6. My dog (laid) by my feet during dinner.

**B. Write rhyming words for each of the words with the long *a* sound.** Possible responses below.

7. afraid paid
8. paint saint
9. plays days, stays
10. pail sail, bail, hail
11. May pay, lay, say
12. laid maid

Approaching Reproducible, page 33
Beyond Reproducible, page 33

# Phonics

## Long *a*

### EXPLAIN/MODEL

Display the *Train* **Sound-Spelling Card** for the long *a* sound. Tell students that the long *a* sound /ā/ can be spelled several different ways. Point to each spelling on the card and provide a sample word. For example, long *a* can be spelled:

- **ay** as in play
- **ai** as in tail
- **a_e** as in face
- **a** as in table
- **ea** as in great
- **ei** as in weigh

Write the sample words on the board, underline the long *a* spelling, and model blending each one.

**Think Aloud** Look at the first word I wrote: *p-l-a-y*. I see the long *a* spelling *ay*. Listen as I blend the sounds to read the word: /plā/ *play*. [Run your finger under the word as you sound it out.]

### PRACTICE/APPLY

CA CONTENT STANDARD R 3.1.1 Know and use complex word families when reading to decode unfamiliar words.

**Read Word List** Display **Phonics Transparency 3**. The first two lines include long *a* words students will encounter in the upcoming selections. Have students underline the long *a* spelling in each word. Then have them chorally read the words.

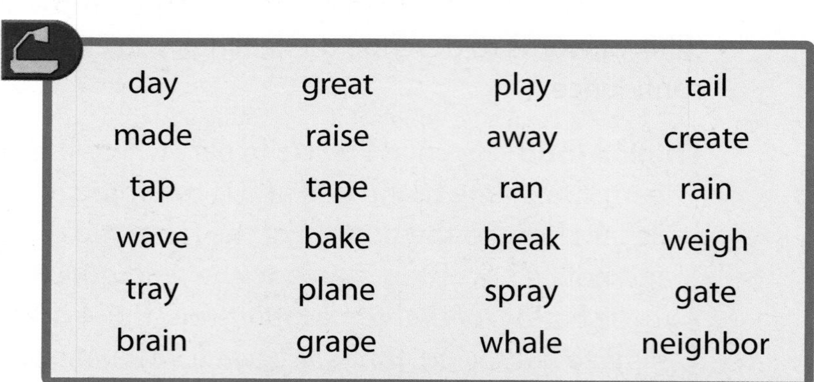

| | | | |
|---|---|---|---|
| day | great | play | tail |
| made | raise | away | create |
| tap | tape | ran | rain |
| wave | bake | break | weigh |
| tray | plane | spray | gate |
| brain | grape | whale | neighbor |

**Phonics Transparency 3**

**Sort Words** Ask students to sort the words on the board by spelling pattern. Then have them write the word sort in their Writer's Notebooks.

| ay | ai | a_e | ea | ei |
|---|---|---|---|---|
| | | | | |

## Read Multisyllabic Words

CA CONTENT STANDARD
**R 3.1.2** Decode regular multisyllabic words.

**TRANSITION TO LONGER WORDS** Help students transition from reading one-syllable to multisyllabic long *a* words. Have students read the word in the first column, then model how to read the longer word in the second column. Point out the added syllable(s), such as prefix or suffix, to help students gain awareness of these common word parts.

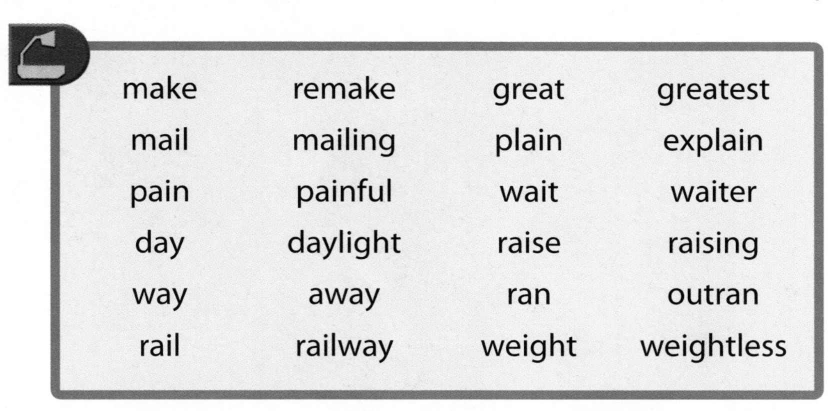

| | | | |
|---|---|---|---|
| make | remake | great | greatest |
| mail | mailing | plain | explain |
| pain | painful | wait | waiter |
| day | daylight | raise | raising |
| way | away | ran | outran |
| rail | railway | weight | weightless |

**Phonics Transparency 3**

**BUILD WORDS** Use **Word-Building Cards** *re, play, main, tain, con, enter, ing*. Display the cards. Have students use the word parts to build as many long *a* multisyllabic words as possible. These and other words can be formed: *replay, remain, retain, contain, entertain, replaying, remaining, retaining, containing, entertaining.*

**CONNECT TO 6 SYLLABLE TYPES** To further help students break apart longer words to decode them, explain the following:

- **Vowel Team Syllables** When a common vowel team, such as *ay* or *ai*, appears in a long word, the vowel team must remain in the same syllable. (re/main)
- **Final *e* Syllables** When a word or syllable ends in *e*, the vowel before it and the *e* must remain in the same syllable. They form a team. (es/cape)

**APPLY DECODING STRATEGY** Guide students to use **Decoding Strategies** to decode the following words: *complains, carefully, castaway, rainbow, eighteen, interstate, bakery, migrate.* Write each word on the board. Remind students to look for vowel team and final *e* spellings in Step 3 of the Decoding Strategy procedure.

## Build Fluency

**SPEED DRILL** Distribute copies of the long *a* Speed Drill in the **Teacher's Resource Book**. Use the Speed Drill routine to help students become fluent reading words with long *a* spelling patterns.

### Syllable Fluency

Use **Word-Building Cards 21–30.** Display one card at a time. Have students chorally read each common syllable. Repeat at varying speeds and in random order. Have students work with partners during independent time to write as many words as they can containing each syllable. Add these lists to the **Unit 1 Big Question Board**.

### Decoding Strategy

**Decoding Strategy Chart**

| Step | |
|---|---|
| Step 1 | Look for word parts (prefixes) at the beginning of the word. |
| Step 2 | Look for word parts (suffixes) at the end of the word. |
| Step 3 | In the base word, look for familiar spelling patterns. Think about the six syllable-spelling patterns you have learned. |
| Step 4 | Sound out and blend together the word parts. |
| Step 5 | Say the word parts fast. Adjust your pronunciation as needed. Ask yourself: "Is this a word I have heard before?" Then read the word in the sentence and ask: "Does it make sense in this sentence?" |

# Oral Language

## Build Background

**ACCESS PRIOR KNOWLEDGE**

Share the following information: People can learn in all kinds of environments. Look at the schoolchildren in this photograph. They are holding a discussion outdoors. Perhaps their goal is to have a discussion about a class trip or to plan a big project. They are cooperating with each other and learning something new and exciting.

**EL** Write the following words on the board and briefly define each one using the **Define/Example/Ask** routine: **discussion** (a group talk about a topic or idea) **goal** (something a person wants and tries to get), **project** (a carefully planned piece of work that people often do together).

**FOCUS QUESTION** Ask students to read "Talk About It" on **Student Book** page 66. Then have students turn to a partner and describe the photo. Ask:

- Are the students working on a project? Why do you think so?
- Why is having a discussion, or talking about a topic, a good way to learn?

**BUILD WRITING FLUENCY**

WRITE ON DEMAND

Ask students to write in their **Writer's Notebook** about the different types of schools they know about. Tell students to write as much as they can as well as they can. Students should write for five minutes without stopping. Meet with individuals during Writing Conference time to provide feedback and revision assignments. Students should self-correct any errors they notice prior to the conference.

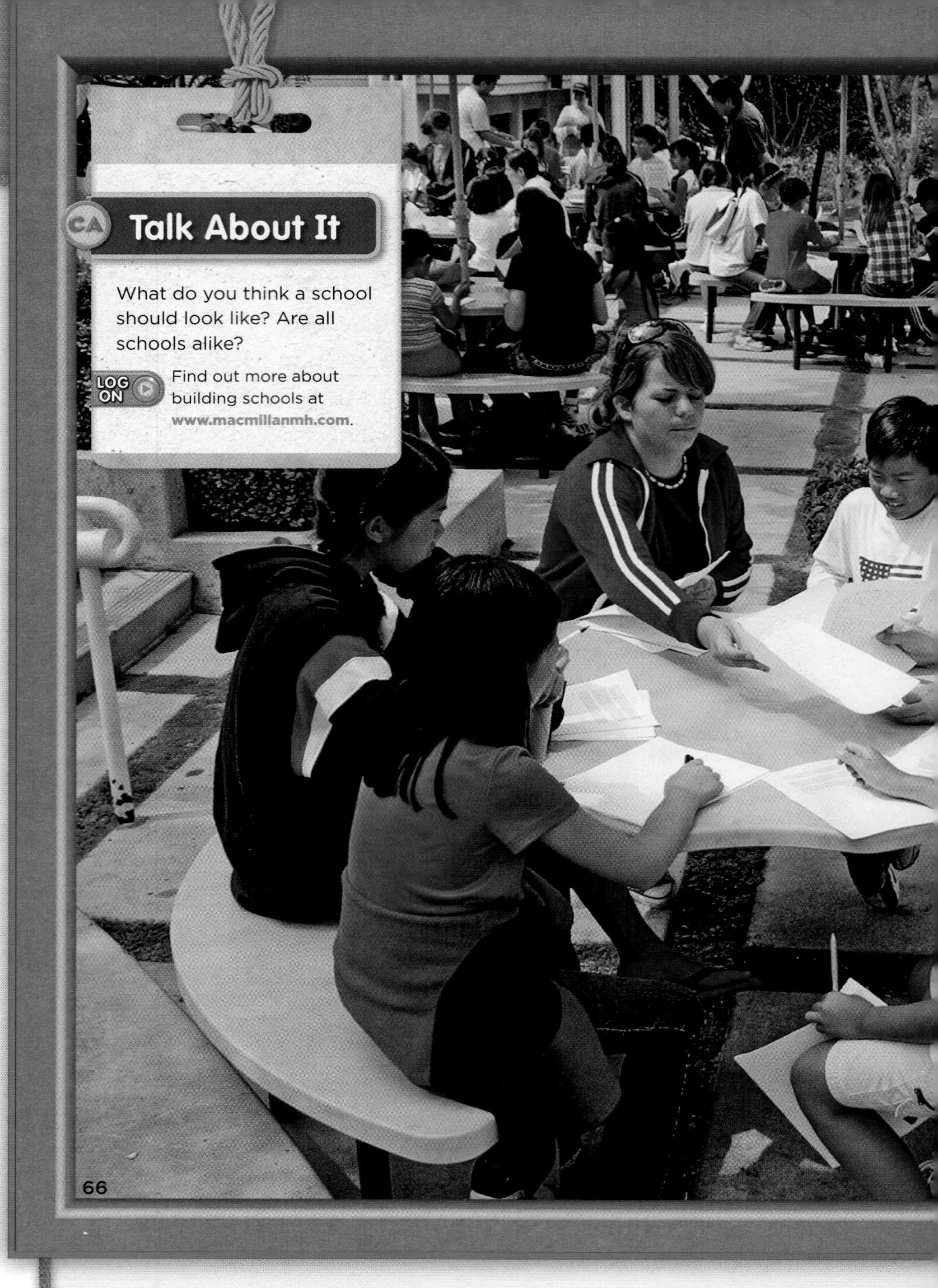


**English Learners**

UNIVERSAL ACCESS

During the discussion, build on students' responses to help them move to the next level of language acquisition. For example, if a student answers *yes* to the first question, say:
*That's correct. The students seem to be working together on a project. Now turn to your partner and tell about this picture.*
Provide the following frames orally or in writing to help students respond in complete sentences.

**Beginning/Early Intermediate** The students are ______.

**Intermediate** Students work together because ______.

**Early Advanced** Students have discussions to ______.

# Unit Theme

## Big Idea

Many people have built schools to help those in the community get an education. How do green schools help the environment?

### CONNECT TO THEME

Ask students what they have learned so far in this unit about schools.

- What do you think "green" schools" are? How do they help students learn?
- Why is it important to get an education?

### USE THEME FOLDABLES

Write the **Big Idea** statement on the board. Ask students to copy it on their Unit Theme Foldables. Remind them to add details as they complete this week's readings.

## Digital Learning

**PRETEACH** Have Approaching Level students and English Learners listen to the selection on **StudentWorks Plus**, the interactive eBook, before reading with the class. The recording contains summaries in multiple languages, word-by-word reading support, a bilingual glossary, and comprehension questions with corrective feedback.

For Web site activities for oral language development, go to **www.macmillanmh.com**.

FOLDABLES® Study Organizer

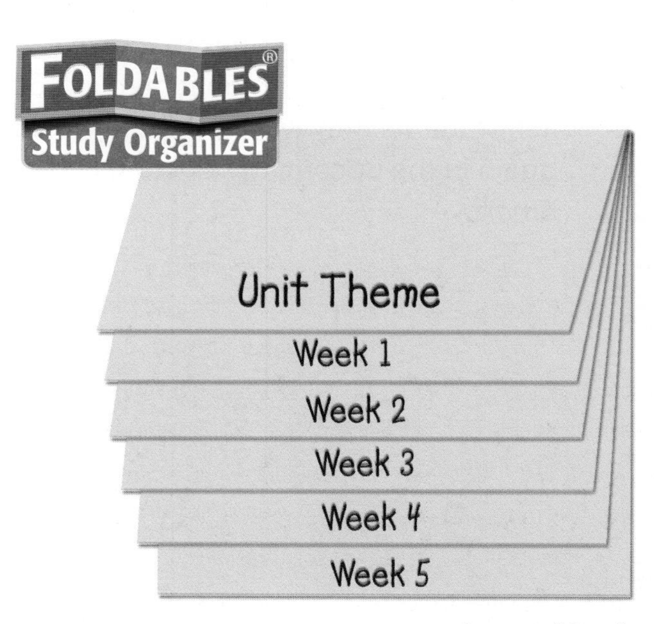


**Layered Book**

# Vocabulary

**STRATEGY**
**WORD PARTS**

CA CONTENT STANDARD
R 3.1.4
Use knowledge of antonyms, **synonyms**, homophones, and homographs to determine the meanings of words.

**Thesaurus: Synonyms** Explain to students that synonyms are words that have the same, or almost the same, meaning. The words *big* and *gigantic* are synonyms. Point out that a thesaurus is a book of synonyms. It is organized in alphabetical order, like a dictionary.

To find the meaning of an unfamiliar word, readers can look up the word in a thesaurus and look for familiar synonyms that have the same meaning.

Point to the word *dangerous* in the first paragraph of "Freedom Fighter" on **Student Book** page 69. Ask students to use a thesaurus to find synonyms to help define the word. (hazardous, harmful) Then have students define what *dangerous* must mean. (likely to cause something bad to happen)

## Read "Play Ball!"

As you read "Play Ball!" with students, ask them to identify clues that reveal the meanings of the highlighted words. Tell students they will read these words again in the upcoming selection *Earth Smart*.

Real World Reading

# Play Ball!

Major League Baseball hit a home run in 2006 when it opened the Urban Youth Academy in Compton, California. The academy has four baseball fields, a huge clubhouse, and a learning center. There are baseball camps and after-school activities.

Kids ages 7 to 17 can take part for free at the academy. Do kids love it? Yes! Priscilla Mota, 10, plays softball and says that the academy has taught her many skills to improve her game.

Major League players **donate** their time to the academy. Director Darrell Miller, a former player for the Anaheim Angels of Los Angeles, tells future big leaguers that education is just as important as baseball. Education workshops teach kids how to do well both on and off the field.

Soon more kids will be able to have this learning experience. Major League Baseball is planning to build more academies in other cities. Kids in Miami; Washington, D.C.; and Pittsburgh may soon be hearing, "Play Ball!"

Juan Pierre plays for the Los Angeles Dodgers.

Students run drills on the field.

68

HOMEWORK **Practice Book,** page 34

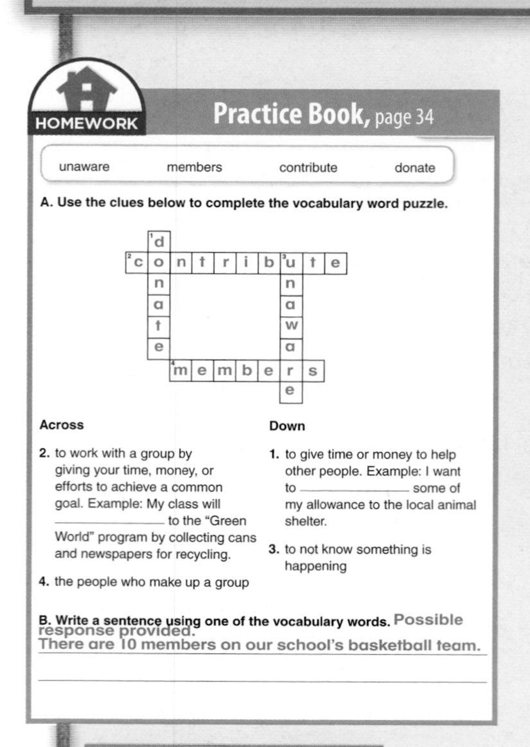

unaware members contribute donate

**A. Use the clues below to complete the vocabulary word puzzle.**



**Across**

2. to work with a group by giving your time, money, or efforts to achieve a common goal. Example: My class will ____________ to the "Green World" program by collecting cans and newspapers for recycling.
4. the people who make up a group

**Down**

1. to give time or money to help other people. Example: I want to ____________ some of my allowance to the local animal shelter.
3. to not know something is happening

**B. Write a sentence using one of the vocabulary words.** Possible response provided.
There are 10 members on our school's basketball team.

Approaching Reproducible, page 34
Beyond Reproducible, page 34

## English Learners

UNIVERSAL ACCESS

**Preteach Vocabulary**
See pages 77S and 77JJ to preteach the vocabulary words to **English Learners** and **Approaching Level** students. Activities include demonstrating the action *donate,* displaying visuals that emphasize the meaning of *members,* having students demonstrate ways they can *contribute* to their school or family, and connecting the word *contribute* to the Spanish cognate *contribuir.*

TIME FOR KIDS

## Top 5 Biggest Elementary Schools

The average United States elementary school has 400 to 600 students. Here are the elementary schools in the U.S. that have the most students.

| Rank | School/Location | Number of students |
|---|---|---|
| 1 | Miles Avenue Elementary, Huntington Park, California | 2,709 |
| 2 | Ernest R. Graham Elementary, Hialeah, Florida | 2,449 |
| 3 | Hoover Street Elementary, Los Angeles, California | 2,372 |
| 4 | Palm Springs North Elementary, Hialeah, Florida | 2,245 |
| 5 | Public School 19 Marion P. Jeantet, Corona, New York | 2,164 |

Source: National Center for Education Statistics

= 500 students

## Freedom Fighter

Craig Kielburger and friends at a new school in Ecuador

In seventh grade, Craig Kielburger discovered that many children around the world were being forced to do hard and dangerous work. He knew that most people were **unaware** of the situation. So he began an organization called Free the Children.

Today, the children's charity has one million **members**. They have built more than 450 schools around the world and helped pay for medical programs in poor communities. People help in many ways. Some give money while others volunteer overseas. It's a great way to **contribute** to children's lives around the world.

LOG ON Find out more about types of schools at www.macmillanmh.com.

69

# Vocabulary

### TEACH WORDS

Introduce each word using the **Define/Example/Ask** routine. Model reading each word using the syllable-scoop technique.

#### Vocabulary Routine

**Define:** To **donate** means you give some of your time or money to help other people.
**Example:** Our class will donate winter coats to needy children.
**Ask:** How might you donate your time to your school? EXAMPLE

- When you are **unaware** of something, you do not know that it is happening. *I was unaware that it was raining outside, so I did not take an umbrella with me.* Describe a time you were unaware of something. DESCRIPTION
- **Members** are people who are part of the same group. *The members of Mr. David's third-grade class are performing a play for the school.* How would you describe the members of your family? EXPLANATION
- When you **contribute**, you work with a group by giving your time, money, or efforts to reach a common goal. *Our class will contribute to the "Keep It Clean" program by picking up the trash on the playground.* How do you contribute to keeping your classroom clean and tidy? EXPLAIN

### Quick Check

**Do students understand word meanings?**

During **Small Group Instruction**

**If No →** Approaching Level Reteach the words using the Vocabulary lesson, pp. 77S–77T.

**If Yes →** On Level Consolidate the learning using p. 77AA.

Beyond Level Extend the learning using p. 77EE.

## Objectives

- Summarize a nonfiction text
- Identify the stated main idea and supporting details
- Use academic language: *summarize, main idea, details*

### Materials

- Transparency 3
- Practice Book, p. 35

### Skills Trace

**Main Idea and Details**

| | |
|---|---|
| **Introduce** | U1: 69A–B |
| **Practice/ Apply** | U1: 70–73; Practice Book 35–36 |
| **Reteach/ Review** | U1: 77O–P; U2: 213A–B, 214–217, 221O–JJ; Practice Book 96–97 |
| **Assess** | Weekly Tests; Unit 1, 2, 5 Tests |
| **Maintain** | U1: 105B; U2: 239B; U5: 145A–B, 193B |

### English Learners

UNIVERSAL ACCESS

**Academic Language**
As students read the selection, explain important content words such as *academy, volunteer*, and *organization*. After students read each paragraph, have them retell what they have learned. Ask questions to check comprehension, and explain information as necessary. Help students use the terms *main idea* and *supporting details* as they talk about the information.

# Reread for Comprehension

## STRATEGY
### SUMMARIZE

**What Is It?** Tell students that when they **summarize**, they tell the main ideas and the most important details of a paragraph, a section of text, or a whole article in their own words.
**Why Is It Important?** Explain that summarizing helps readers identify and remember important ideas in a paragraph or passage.

## SKILL
### MAIN IDEA AND DETAILS

CA CONTENT STANDARD R 3.2.5 Distinguish the main idea and supporting details in expository text.

**What Is It?** The **main idea** is the most important point an author makes about a topic. The main idea can be **stated** in a topic sentence, usually at the beginning of a paragraph or a section of text. **Details** give more information about the main idea.
**Why Is It Important?** Students can identify the main idea and important details in a selection as they read to check their understanding. When they have finished reading, they can summarize the main idea and details to help them remember what they have read.

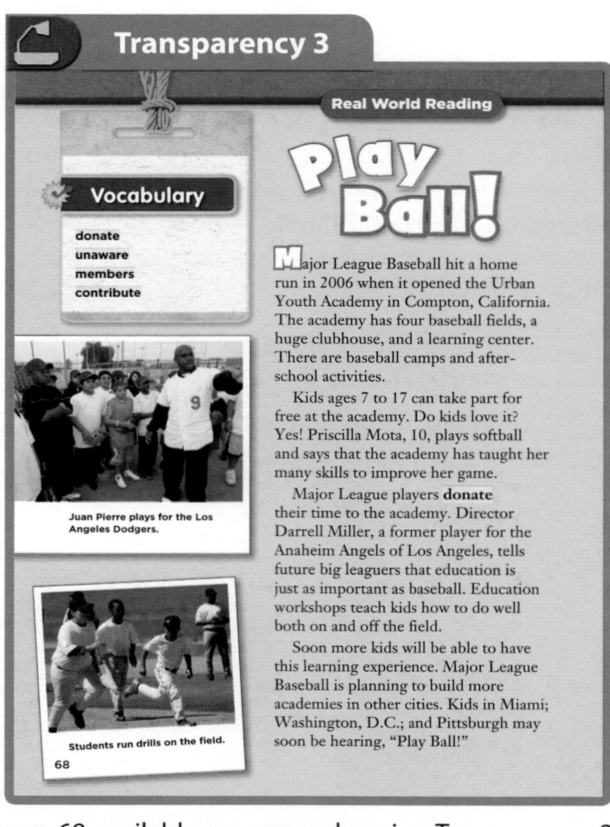

Transparency 3

Real World Reading

**Play Ball!**

Vocabulary
donate
unaware
members
contribute

Major League Baseball hit a home run in 2006 when it opened the Urban Youth Academy in Compton, California. The academy has four baseball fields, a huge clubhouse, and a learning center. There are baseball camps and after-school activities.

Kids ages 7 to 17 can take part for free at the academy. Do kids love it? Yes! Priscilla Mota, 10, plays softball and says that the academy has taught her many skills to improve her game.

Major League players **donate** their time to the academy. Director Darrell Miller, a former player for the Anaheim Angels of Los Angeles, tells future big leaguers that education is just as important as baseball. Education workshops teach kids how to do well both on and off the field.

Soon more kids will be able to have this learning experience. Major League Baseball is planning to build more academies in other cities. Kids in Miami; Washington, D.C.; and Pittsburgh may soon be hearing, "Play Ball!"

Juan Pierre plays for the Los Angeles Dodgers.

Students run drills on the field.

68

Student Book page 68 available on comprehension Transparency 3

**MODEL**

**How Do I Use It?** Read aloud the first paragraph of "Play Ball" on **Student Book** page 68. Model how to identify the main idea of this short article. Write the main idea on the board.

**Think Aloud** To identify the main idea in this article, I will reread the first paragraph and look for a sentence that tells what the entire article is about. The first sentence states that major-league baseball hit a home run when it opened the Urban Youth Academy in Compton, California. I think this sentence states the main idea of the article. As I continue to read, I will look for important details that tell about this main idea.

**GUIDED PRACTICE**

Help students identify important details in the first two paragraphs that support, or tell about, the main idea. (The first important detail tells what the academy is: The academy has baseball fields, a clubhouse, a learning center, baseball camps, and after-school activities. The second detail shows who goes to the academy: Kids ages 7 to 17 can go to the academy for free.) Write the details on the board. Guide students to see that the information about Priscilla Mota is interesting but is not an important detail.

**APPLY**

Tell students to read the rest of "Play Ball" and identify the important details in the remaining two paragraphs. Write these details on the board. (Major-league players donate their time. They hold education workshops that teach kids how to do well on and off the baseball field. Major-league baseball is planning to build more academies in Miami, Washington, D.C., and Pittsburg.)

Remind students that they can use the main idea and details to summarize what they read. A summary is a short paragraph that tells the main idea and important details in their own words. Then have students summarize the main idea and details of "Play Ball" in their own words and present their summaries to the class.

**Quick Check**

**Can students identify main ideas and supporting details?**

During **Small Group Instruction**

**If No →** **Approaching Level** Reteach the skill using the Comprehension lesson, pp. 77U–77X.

**If Yes →** **On Level** Consolidate the learning using pp. 77CC–77DD.

**Beyond Level** Extend the learning using pp. 77GG–77HH.

**Practice Book,** page 35

The **main idea** is what a paragraph or section is mostly about. The main idea is often stated. It is the most important idea the writer wants readers to know about.

**Supporting Details** are ideas that are related to the main idea. A paragraph or section may include details that don't support the main idea.

**Read the passage. Then answer the questions that follow.**
Possible responses provided.

Many people have built schools to help students in their community get an education. In California, the major league baseball organization built baseball fields, a clubhouse, and a learning center. Kids learn to play baseball, as well as reading and math. Some kids like football better than baseball. Craig Kielburger started a group called Free the Children. Free the Children has built more than 450 schools around the world.

1. What is the main idea of this paragraph? Many people have built schools to help students in their community get an education.
2. Choose two details that tell more about the main idea. The major league baseball organization built baseball fields, a clubhouse and a learning center; Free the Children has built 450 schools around the world.
3. Choose one detail that doesn't tell about the main idea. Some kids like football better than baseball.
4. Write a good title for this passage. People Care About Educating Kids.

Approaching Reproducible, page 35

Beyond Reproducible, page 35

# Read

## WHOLE GROUP

**MAIN SELECTION**
- *Earth Smart*
- Skill: Main Idea and Details

**STANDARDS PRACTICE**
- "Summer Break?"
- **Test Strategy**: Right There

**CONTENT STANDARDS**
R 3.1.3, R 3.2.3, R 3.2.4, R 3.2.5, R 3.3.1, W 3.1.3, HSS 3.4.6

## SMALL GROUP

- Differentiated Instruction, pp. 77Q–77PP

# Comprehension

**GENRE: NONFICTION**

CA CONTENT STANDARD R 3.3.1 Distinguish common forms of literature.

Have a student read the definition of nonfiction on **Student Book** page 70. Remind students to look for pictures and captions that describe different places as they read.

**STRATEGY**
**SUMMARIZE**

Remind students that they should stop and summarize by restating the main ideas and important details in their own words. This will help them monitor their understanding of the text.

**SKILL**
**MAIN IDEA AND DETAILS**

CA CONTENT STANDARD R 3.2.5 Distinguish the main idea and supporting details in expository text.

Tell students that the main idea is the most important point of a paragraph of section. The details tell about, or support, that main idea.

Real World Reading

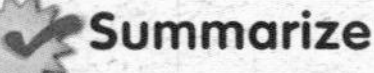

**Comprehension**

**Genre**

**Nonfiction** Some articles give information about real people, places, or things.

**Summarize**

**Main Idea and Details**

A main idea is the most important point of an article. Details support the main idea.

# EARTH Smart

## How do green schools help the environment?

Goodwillie Environmental School is friendly to the environment. Goodwillie is a green school in Ada, Michigan. Green schools do many things to help the Earth.

Green schools use less energy than regular schools. At Goodwillie, solar panels use the sun's power. The solar power heats the school in winter. This helps keep energy bills low.

The school also believes in using recycled items. Its walls and floors are made with recycled material. Even the outdoor deck is made from sawdust and recycled milk jugs!

Clara Cullen (left) and Seana Florida find frogs in Goodwillie's pond.

70

## Vocabulary

**Vocabulary Words** Review the tested words while reading: **donate, unaware, members,** and **contribute**.

**Additional Selection Words** Students may be unfamiliar with these words. Pronounce the words, give student-friendly explanations as needed, and help students use the previously taught vocabulary strategies: prefixes and word families.

**solar power** (p. 70): energy that comes from the sun and is used for electricity

**recycled** (p. 70): to have made something new from an old item

**nature** (p. 71): all the plants, animals, and natural resources in the outside world

**compost** (p. 72): a mixture of rotting matter such as leaves, grass, or straw that can be used for fertilizer

Students at green schools learn a lot about nature and the environment. The teachers and students at Goodwillie spend part of nearly every day outside, even in the freezing winter. Kids might collect sap from a tree, visit the school pond, or pick up trash along the road.

Kids tackle large projects, too. Some classmates work together to build a canoe. Others create a butterfly garden. Students also **donate** money or time to environmental groups.

**Going to the Birds**

The students at Goodwillie school also raise chickens. This farming lesson teaches kids about nature, the environment, and business. The chickens make eggs that are sold in the school store, which students run.

**Molly Gaudette and Stephen Dozeman observe a tree's bark.**

71

## Read Together

PARTNERS

If your students need support to read the Main Selection, use the prompts to guide comprehension and model how to complete the graphic organizer. Allow students time to fill in their organizers before you provide the answers.

Use **Think/Pair/Share**. When asking a question, have students *think* about their answer, then discuss it with a *partner*. Finally, have selected students *share* their answers with the group. Provide sentence frames for discussion, such as *The main idea of the paragraph is* ____ or *The details that tell about the main idea are* ____ to help students use academic language. Students should support their answers with evidence from the text.



## Preview and Predict

**QUICK WRITE** Ask students to read the title, preview the photographs, think about the genre. Have students write their predictions about the kind of information they will find in the text.

**CA CONTENT STANDARD R 3.2.4** Recall major points in the text and make and modify predictions about forthcoming information.

## Set Purposes

**FOCUS QUESTION** Discuss the question under the article title.

Point out the Main Idea Chart on **Practice Book** page 36. Explain that students will use it to identify main ideas and supporting details in this article.

## Read *Earth Smart*

**1 STRATEGY**
**SUMMARIZE**

**Teacher Think Aloud** Summarizing nonfiction by finding the main idea and details can help you understand and remember what you read. Tell how you would summarize the first three paragraphs on page 70.

Prompt students to apply the strategy in a Think Aloud.

**Student Think Aloud** I see the main idea stated in the first sentence. Goodwillie School is friendly to the environment. The details are: Goodwillie uses solar panels to heat the school in winter. They use recycled items in its walls and floors. I would summarize it this way: Goodwillie School helps the environment by using solar power in the winter and by building walls and floors with recycled materials.

# Develop Comprehension

## 2 SKILL
### MAIN IDEA AND DETAILS

What is the **main idea** of "Great Green Schools" on page 72? (Schools across the country are going green.) What **details** support the main idea? (California plans to open 150 green schools because they're better for students and the environment. Kids learn better in classrooms with sunlight. Green schools have lower energy bills. Kids travel to school in energy-saving vehicles.) Add this to your Main Idea and Details Chart.

| Main Idea | Details |
|---|---|
| Schools across the country are going green. | California plans to open 150 green schools in the next few years. |
| | Green schools are better for the environment and for students. |
| | Students learn better in rooms with natural sunlight. |
| | Green schools have lower energy bills by using solar power. |
| | In some green schools, some students ride to school in energy-saving vehicles. |

## 3 STRATEGY
### SUMMARIZE

**Summarize** "Great Green Schools." (Schools are going green. California is planning to build 150 green schools. There are many reasons to build green schools. Kids learn better in classrooms with sunlight. Green schools save energy. Some kids even ride to green school on energy-saving buses.)



**2** Everyone at Goodwillie pitches in to take care of the chickens. They **contribute** by feeding the chickens and taking turns cleaning the chicken coop. Manure that is cleaned from the coop is recycled. It makes compost for the school garden. Compost helps plants grow. Students at Goodwillie then study the plant growth in the garden.

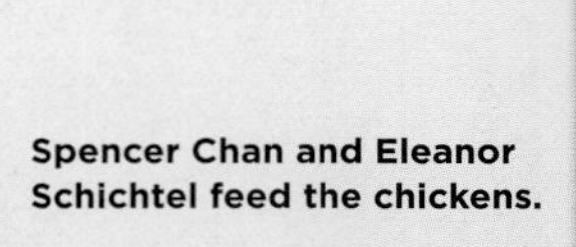
Spencer Chan and Eleanor Schichtel feed the chickens.

**3**

### Great Green Schools

Schools across the country are going green! In the next few years, Southern California alone plans to open 150 green schools. Why? Green schools are better for the environment and the people inside the schools. Students learn better in rooms that have natural sunlight. Green schools also have lower energy bills.

In Lick-Wilmerding High School in San Francisco, California, students create objects from natural and recycled materials. The cafeteria serves only healthful food. Most students ride energy-saving buses and trains to school instead of riding in cars. The school gets an A in helping the environment!



### Quick Check

**Can students identify the main idea and details?**

During **Small Group Instruction**

**If No →** Approaching Level Reteach the skill and have students apply it to a simpler text. Use the Practice Reader lesson, pp. 77V–77X.

**If Yes →** On Level Have students apply the skill to a new text to consolidate learning. Use the Practice Reader lesson, pp. 77CC–77DD.

Beyond Level Have students apply the skill to a more complex text to extend learning. Use the Practice Reader lesson, pp. 77GG–77HH.

### The Great Outdoors

As part of their studies, students at Goodwillie also study the life cycles of plants and animals. Instead of classrooms, they sometimes study in the woods and fields. "We write about some of the things we're seeing, such as the change in seasons," says Clara Cullen, 10.

Some **members** of a third-grade class are working on a project that will last about two years. They are studying the weather cycle. The students are figuring out how the weather helps or harms plants. Clara was **unaware** of what she could learn outside. Spending time in nature has opened her eyes. "It's amazing how much is out there," she says.

### Critical Thinking

1. What does the writer mean by saying Goodwillie is friendly to the environment?
2. In what ways is your school green? In what ways is it not?
3. What could you do to make your school more green?
4. What are the **main ideas** in "Play Ball!" and "Earth Smart"? What opinion about these two different types of schools do both writers share?

Anna Veltman (left) and Rachel Wallace enjoy class outdoors.

73

# Develop Comprehension

## Personal Response

Have students respond to the selection by revising or confirming their predictions and purposes for reading. Were students able to identify the main ideas in the article and the details that support them? Have students write about how they feel about green schools. Remind them to write in a clear, logical manner, using examples from the selection as well as their own experiences.

## Critical Thinking

**SUMMARIZE/WRITING FRAME**

Have students summarize the selection using the Nonfiction Text Structure Writing Frame on **Practice Book** page 39. Remind them to use their Main Idea Charts as they complete their summary.

**THINK AND COMPARE**

1. **Main Idea and Details** Goodwillie is an earth-friendly school because it teaches students how to take care of the environment.
2. **Analyze** Students may say their school recycles but does not use solar power.
3. **Text-to-Self** Students could use less electricity and more natural light or recycle more.
4. **Text-to-World** The main idea of both pieces is that education is important. Both writers feel that schools are places where children can learn and grow by trying new things and working with others.

### English Learners

**UNIVERSAL ACCESS**

The nonfiction writing frames are especially useful for English learners when speaking and writing because they focus on those key transition words. Suggest all students use these frames to organize information when orally presenting to the class.

HOMEWORK **Practice Book, page 39**

**Description Writing Frame**

**Summarize "Earth Smart."**
**Use the Description Writing Frame below.**

The Goodwillie Environmental School is a green school. The students at this green school help the environment in **many ways**.

**One way** they help is ______________________________.

**Another way** they help is ______________________________.

**They also** help by ______________________________.

Rewrite the completed summary on another sheet of paper. Keep it as a model for writing a summary of an article or selection using this text structure.

**Approaching Reproducible,** page 39
**Beyond Reproducible,** page 39

## Objectives

- Read fluently with appropriate pacing
- 61–81 WCPM

## Materials

- Transparency 3
- Practice Book, p. 37
- Fluency Solutions Audio CD

### English Learners

UNIVERSAL ACCESS

**Develop Comprehension**
Explain to students that two words together can make a phrase that means something different from what the two words on their own mean. Point to the phrase *pitches in*. Say, *pitches* means "throw" and *in* is a direction. When the words are combined, they mean "help out." Tell students to think of other phrases.

### Practice Book, page 37

**As I read, I will pay attention to pacing.**

| | |
|---|---|
| | Charlie called Emma. "I've got a problem," he told her |
| 10 | as soon as she picked up the phone. "How can I show my |
| 23 | mom I can take care of a pet?" |
| 31 | "Hmmm…," said Emma. "What if you did some |
| 39 | research on pets?" |
| 42 | "Yeah, I could do that," he said. |
| 49 | "Listen," Emma said. "Lucy needs a bath. She keeps |
| 58 | scratching her fur, and I'm worried that she has fleas. Let's |
| 69 | talk about this tomorrow, okay?" |
| 74 | Charlie called Josh. Josh said, "I can't talk. I'm feeding |
| 84 | Prince. I can't believe this dog's appetite! If I don't get this |
| 96 | food in his bowl, I'm afraid he's going to cook for himself." 108 |

**Comprehension Check**

1. What is Charlie's problem? **Problem and Solution** Charlie has to show his mom that he is responsible enough to take care of a pet.
2. Why can't Charlie's friends talk with him about his problem? **Plot** Charlie's friends are busy taking care of their pets.

| | Words Read | – | Number of Errors | = | Words Correct Score |
|---|---|---|---|---|---|
| First Read | | – | | = | |
| Second Read | | – | | = | |

**Approaching Reproducible,** page 37

**Beyond Reproducible,** page 37

# Fluency

## Repeated Reading: Pacing

CA CONTENT STANDARD
**R 3.1.3** Read aloud narrative and expository text fluently and accurately and with appropriate pacing, intonation, and expression.

**EXPLAIN/MODEL** Tell students that **pacing** is an important part of reading fluently. Good readers read words at different paces. When reading nonfiction, they might read at a slower or more moderate pace in order to figure out the meaning of unfamiliar words and information. Model reading **Transparency 3** for them at a moderate pace that is appropriate for a nonfiction article.

**Transparency 3**

Everyone at Goodwillie pitches in to take care of the chickens. They contribute by feeding the chickens and taking turns cleaning the chicken coop. Manure that is cleaned from the coop is recycled. It makes compost for the school garden. Compost helps plants grow. Students at Goodwillie then study the plant growth in the garden.

Fluency (from *Earth Smart,* page 72)

**PRACTICE** Have one student read a sentence. Then have another student join in, and a third. Repeat until all students are reading together. When students reach the end of the passage, tell them to go back to the beginning and repeat until every student has been included in the reading.

**DAILY FLUENCY** Students will practice fluency using **Practice Book** page 37 or the **Fluency Solutions Audio CD**. The passage is recorded at a slow, practice speed and a faster, fluent speed.

### Quick Check

**Can students read fluently?**

During **Small Group Instruction**

**If No** → **Approaching Level** Use the Fluency lesson and model, p. 77Y.

**If Yes** → **On Level** See Fluency, p. 77BB.

**Beyond Level** See Fluency, p. 77FF.

# Comprehension

**REVIEW SKILL**
**CAUSE AND EFFECT**

### EXPLAIN/MODEL

- A **cause** is an event that makes something else happen.
- An **effect** is something that happens because of an earlier event or action—the cause.
- When readers look for causes and effects, they can ask themselves the following questions: *What happened?* The answer to this question is the effect. *Why did it happen?* The answer to this question is the cause.
- Sometimes readers can find signal words to help them identify causes and effects. The signal words *because, due to,* and *since* usually signal causes. The signal words *so* and *as a result* usually signal effects.

Model how to identify a cause-and-effect relationship in the second and third sentences of "Freedom Fighter" on **Student Book** page 69. Ask: *What happened?* (Craig Kielburger formed an organization called Free the Children.) *Why did it happen?* (He knew most people did not know that children around the world were forced to work.) Point out that the first sentence is the cause and the second is the effect. The signal word *so* tells the reader that what follows is an effect.

### PRACTICE/APPLY

Help students identify causes and their effects in *Earth Smart on pages 70–73.* Ask:

- On page 70, what is the effect when Goodwillie Environment School uses solar panels? (The effect is that the solar power from the panels heats the school and keeps the energy bills low.)
- On page 72, what is causing California to open 150 green schools in the next few years? (Green schools are better for the environment and the people inside the schools.)

Have students work with a partner to identify cause-and-effect relationships in another nonfiction selection that they have read recently. Then have them discuss the causes and effects they found with other groups.

## Objectives

- Identify cause-and-effect relationships

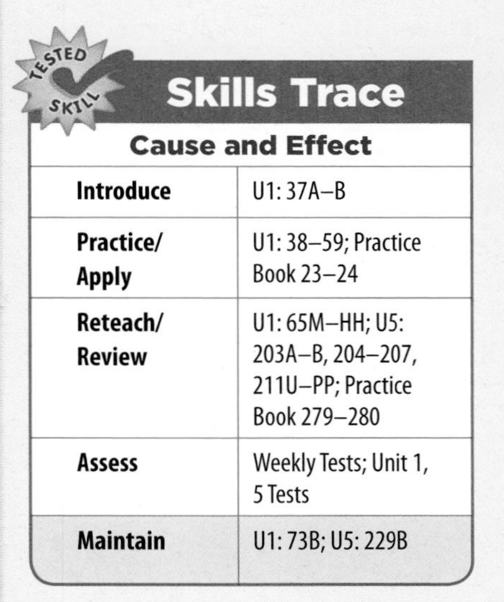


**Skills Trace**

| Cause and Effect | |
|---|---|
| **Introduce** | U1: 37A–B |
| **Practice/ Apply** | U1: 38–59; Practice Book 23–24 |
| **Reteach/ Review** | U1: 65M–HH; U5: 203A–B, 204–207, 211U–PP; Practice Book 279–280 |
| **Assess** | Weekly Tests; Unit 1, 5 Tests |
| **Maintain** | U1: 73B; U5: 229B |

**Content Reader**

For content correlated to California Science and History/Social Science standards, see pages 162–167 in the **Content Reader**.
HSS 3.4.6

## Objectives

- Identify the parts of a dictionary or glossary entry
- Discover how to learn the meanings of unknown words by using a dictionary

### Materials

- Transparency 1
- Leveled Practice Books, p. 38

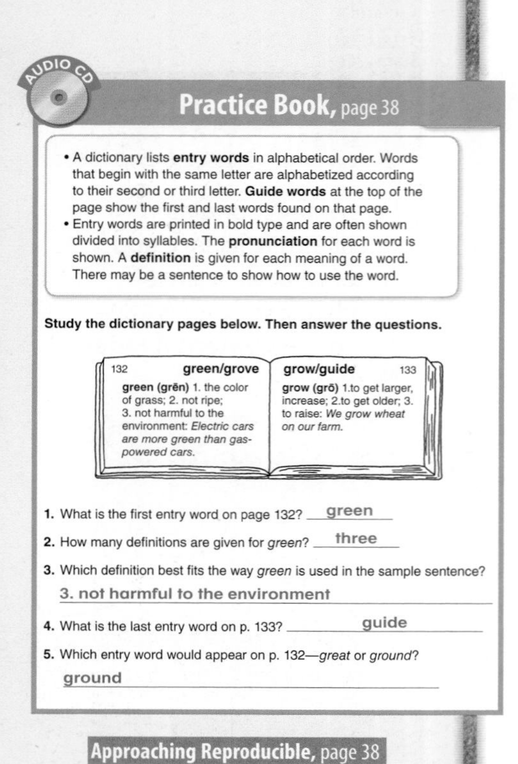
AUDIO CD

**Practice Book,** page 38

- A dictionary lists **entry words** in alphabetical order. Words that begin with the same letter are alphabetized according to their second or third letter. **Guide words** at the top of the page show the first and last words found on that page.
- Entry words are printed in bold type and are often shown divided into syllables. The **pronunciation** for each word is shown. A **definition** is given for each meaning of a word. There may be a sentence to show how to use the word.

**Study the dictionary pages below. Then answer the questions.**

132 **green/grove**
**green (grēn)** 1. the color of grass; 2. not ripe; 3. not harmful to the environment: *Electric cars are more green than gas-powered cars.*

**grow/guide** 133
**grow (grō)** 1.to get larger, increase; 2.to get older; 3. to raise: *We grow wheat on our farm.*

1. What is the first entry word on page 132? green
2. How many definitions are given for *green*? three
3. Which definition best fits the way *green* is used in the sample sentence? 3. not harmful to the environment
4. What is the last entry word on p. 133? guide
5. Which entry word would appear on p. 132—*great* or *ground*? ground

**Approaching Reproducible,** page 38

**Beyond Reproducible,** page 38

# Research
# Study Skills

## Using a Dictionary

**CA CONTENT STANDARD R 3.1.7** Use a dictionary to learn the meaning and other features of unknown words.

### EXPLAIN

Students can use a print or digital **dictionary** to look up an unfamiliar word as they read. Display a third-grade-level print dictionary. Discuss the parts of a dictionary page.

**CA CONTENT STANDARD R 3.1.3** Understand the structure and organization of various reference materials.

- A dictionary is a resource that presents words and their meanings in alphabetical order. Students can look up unfamiliar words in a dictionary.
- Words in the dictionary are called **entry words**. An entry word is printed in bold type and is sometimes divided into syllables. An entry also has a **pronunciation**, a **definition** for each meaning, and different forms of the word, such as verbs and plurals.
- Entry words beginning with the same letter are alphabetized according to the second or third letter. For example, *neon, Nepal, nerve.*
- **Guide words** at the top of each page show the first and last word on the page and help users find the words they are looking for.
- An entry will show all the meanings of a word and usually has an **example sentence** that shows how to use the word correctly.
- If a dictionary entry has a synonym or an antonym, it may be listed in the entry, too. The dictionary entry may also include homophones, words that sound the same but are spelled differently.
- Dictionaries have a **pronunciation key** that tells the user how to say the letters and symbols in an entry word's pronunciation. A pronunciation key usually appears on every spread, or two pages together in the dictionary.
- Many dictionaries have pictures with captions to illustrate entry words. Sometimes a picture can help the reader understand something more than the definition alone does.
- Like dictionaries, **glossaries** have alphabetical entries for words. Glossaries appear at the back of textbooks and nonfiction books and often contain special content-area words.

## MODEL

Display **Transparency 1**.

**Transparency 1**

**Use a Dictionary**

**neigh/Nepal**

**neigh** (nâ) n. the sound a horse makes. The horse's *neigh* got our attention. v. to make the sound that a horse makes. The horses always *neigh* when they see us. **neighs, neighed, neighing**

**neighbor** (nâ´bər) n. **1.** a person who lives near another. Our *neighbor* has a dog. **2.** a person, place, or thing located next to another. Mexico is a *neighbor* of the United States. **3.** a fellow human being. I am happy when good things happen to my neighbor. neighbors

**neon** (nē´ on) n. A gas that has no color or odor. Tubes filled with *neon* are used in electric signs.

**Nepal** (nəpôl´ or nəpäl) *n.* a country in central Asia. Maria visited Nepal.

Study Skill Transparency

**Think Aloud** I want to find *neon* in the dictionary. The guide words *neigh* and *Nepal* show the first and last words on the page. I know that *neon* comes between these guide words. I also know that *neon* will come after *neighbor* but before *Nepal* because entry words that begin with the same letter are alphabetized to the second or third letter. When I find the entry word *neon*, the pronunciation in parentheses will help me say the word. The definition tells me what the word means—"a gas that has no color or odor." An example sentence after the meaning shows how to use *neon*.

## PRACTICE/APPLY

Have students use a print or digital dictionary to look up the meanings of *alligator* and *habitat*. Have them identify the guide words that appear on the same page as each word, the pronunciation, meanings, any special word forms, and example sentences.

## Standards Practice

# Show What You Know

## Answer Questions:
### Right There

**EXPLAIN**

Good test-takers think about whether they can find the answer to a question right there in the selection.

- **Read** the question carefully.
- **Identify** the key words in the question that tell you what you need to find out.
- **Look for key words** by scanning the selection. Often the answer will be found in the sentences that include or surround key words. The answer to the question is right there on the page.

**MODEL** Remind students not to write in their books but to record their answers on a separate sheet of paper.

**Question 1** Read the question and all of the answer choices.

**Teacher Think Aloud** The question is asking me why the students in Oxnard, California, attend school in the summer. I think I can find the answer **right there** in the selection if I look for key words. The key words in the question are *school* and *summer*. I see the key words in the first sentence. As I read on, I find out that the students in Oxnard, California, go to school in the summer because the schools in their community are year-round schools. So answer B is the best choice.

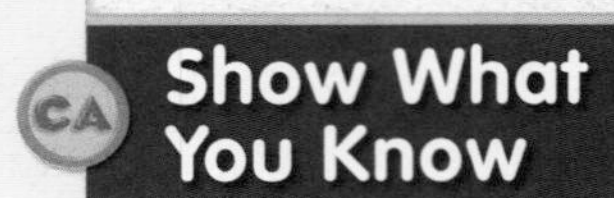


**Right There**

You can put your finger on the answer. Look for key words in the questions. Then find those key words in the selection.

# Summer Break?

Do you have school in summer? Students in Oxnard, California, do. That's because schools in Oxnard are year-round schools. There are 1,483 year-round schools in California. In the United States, about 2 million students attend year-round schools.

All students in the United States have to go to school for 180 days each year. In regular school, kids go to class for about ten months and get two months off in the summer. Year-round schools break up the 180 days differently. Students usually get short breaks scattered throughout the year.

What are the benefits of year-round school? Experts say that students remember more when breaks are shorter. With less vacation time, teachers spend less time on review. That can add up to better grades. As a result, some schools say year-round students score higher on tests.

Still, not everyone is happy. Some parents say year-round school cuts into vacation time. Students say they miss out on summer activities, such as camp. Change could take some getting used to, but it's clear to see that there are many different ways to get your 180 school days.



Go on

## CA Standards Practice

**What Students Can Do Before Reading the Passage**

**Teach/Model** Tell students that before reading a test passage, they should:

- ✓ Read the questions that follow the passage.
- ✓ Make sure they understand what each question is asking. They should restate the question in their own words.
- ✓ Note key parts of the question. Suggest that they circle or underline key words.

**Teach/Model Practice/Apply** Have students silently read the questions following "Summer Break?" Ask, *What is each question asking? What information should we look for as we read?* Have students circle important parts of each question as you chorally read them. These include bold or key words, such as **mostly about** or **cause**.

CA Standards Practice

**Directions: Now answer Numbers 1–5. Base your answers on the article "Summer Break?"**

**1. Why do students in Oxnard, California, have school in the summer?**

A The schools in Oxnard close during the winter.
B The schools in Oxnard are year-round schools.
C The schools in Oxnard are open more than 180 days a year.
D The schools in Oxnard have too many students.

**Tip**
Look for key words.

**2. What do experts say about shorter breaks in the school year?**

A Students remember less.
B Teachers spend more time on review.
C Students remember more.
D Students may score lower on tests.

**3. Why are some parents not happy about year-round school?**

A They say they will never get used to it.
B They think it doesn't help their children's grades.
C They think it costs too much money.
D They say it cuts into vacation time.

**4. Do you think year-round schools are a good idea? Why or why not? Use details from the article to support your answer.**

**5. Compare and contrast regular schools with year-round schools. How are they alike? How are they different? Use details from the article in your answer.**

**GUIDED PRACTICE**

**Question 2** After reading the question, ask students:

*What are the key words in Question 2?* (*experts, shorter breaks*) *What should you do?* (Find the key word in the selection using the test strategy **Right There**. The fourth paragraph says, "Experts say that students remember more when breaks are shorter." So the best answer is C.)

**APPLY**

**Question 3** Read Question 3 and all of the answer choices. Have students use the **Right There** strategy to choose an answer.

After they have chosen an answer, ask: *What did you think the question asks you to do?* (find out why some parents are not happy about year-round school) *What key words did you find in the question?* (parents, not happy) *Where did you find the answer?* (in the fourth paragraph) *What is the best answer?* (The best answer is D.)

Have students answer questions 4 and 5.

**Question 4** Answers will vary. Students may say that year-round schools are a good idea because teachers can spend less time reviewing and they can learn much more in that time. Plus students in year-round schools score higher on tests.

**Question 5** Year-round schools and regular schools both have 180 days in their schedules. The difference is that year-round schools break up the days differently. Year-round schools are also different in that students remember more because their breaks are shorter. Year-round students also score higher on tests.

# Writing Prompt

CA CONTENT STANDARD W 3.2.1 Write narratives.

**EXPLAIN**

Tell students that when taking a test, they often will be asked to write to a prompt. Explain that a prompt introduces or gives information about a writing topic, and then provides instructions about a specific writing assignment related to the information. Explain to students that most prompts will fall under two types of writing or writing modes: expository prompts, which ask the writer to explain something, or narrative prompts, which ask the writer to tell a story.

Before students begin to write to a prompt, they need to find the following information:

- What is the mode, or type, of writing? Is the prompt expository or narrative?
- What is the purpose for writing? What is the actual assignment?
- Does the prompt call for a specific form or format?

**Determine the Writing Mode** Read the prompt above the student model aloud. Then draw students' attention to the information in the bubbles. Review the definition of narrative writing. Point out the clue words in the bubble and the specific clue words in the prompt.

**Determine the Purpose** Ask: *What part of the prompt tells you the purpose for writing?* Point out the second and third sentences. Explain that the second sentence tells the student to think about the topic. (Think about a time you enjoyed a game or a ride.) The third sentence says to write a story. It is clear that the purpose will be to write an entertaining story about a real event.



## Write on Demand

People often enjoy games and rides.
Think about a time you enjoyed a game or ride.
Now write a story about the time you enjoyed a game or ride.

Narrative writing tells a story about a personal or fictional experience.

To figure out if a writing prompt asks for narrative writing, look for clue words, such as write a story about or tell what happened.

Below see how one student begins a response to the prompt above.

The story events are told in a sequence that makes sense.

I gave my blue ticket to the man and ran to the horse I had chosen. I climbed up and held the gold pole with both hands. Loud music started, and the carousel began to turn.

My beautiful horse galloped up and down. Its saddle was painted bright red and yellow. The horse was grayish with smoky black spots. It was the best horse on the carousel!

When the ride stopped, I looked at the other people. Everyone was smiling. I guess they all enjoyed the ride, too.

76

### Unit 1 Writing: Personal Narrative (Description)

| | |
|---|---|
| Week 1 | • Strong Sentences: Focus on Moment |
| Week 2 | • Strong Paragraphs: Focus on Moment |
| Week 3 | • **Narrative** (Guided Writing) |
| Week 4 | • Strong Sentences: Focus on Setting/Object |
| Week 5 | • Strong Paragraphs: Focus on Setting/Object |
| Week 6 | • **Narrative** (Independent Writing) |

## Writing Prompt

Respond in writing to the prompt below. Write for 5 minutes. Write as much as you can, as well as you can. Review the hints before and after you write.

Most students like to play in the playground or park. Think of a time when you played in the playground or park. Now write a story about a time you played in the playground or park.

### Writing Hints for Prompts

- ☑ Read the prompt carefully.
- ☑ Plan your writing by organizing your ideas.
- ☑ Support your ideas by telling more about each event.
- ☑ Use a variety of sentence structures.
- ☑ Choose words that help others understand what you mean.
- ☑ Review and edit your writing.

77

**4-POINT SCORING RUBRIC**

| 4 Excellent | 3 Good | 2 Fair | 1 Unsatisfactory |
|---|---|---|---|
| Writing is on topic, well developed, and based on information in the selection. Paragraphs are well organized and interesting. Writing generally shows accuracy in punctuation and capitalization. | Writing is on topic. There is an attempt at sequence of development of thought. The writing holds the reader's attention. It may have errors, but they do not interfere with understanding. | Writing is generally on topic. There is an attempt to get sentences on paper. Sentences may be simple or incomplete with limited vocabulary. Errors may make understanding difficult. | Writing may show little or no development of topic, but may contain meaningful vocabulary. There is an attempt to get words on paper. Written vocabulary is limited. Writing shows no use of writing conventions. |

**CA CONTENT STANDARD W 3.2.1.b** Include well-chosen details to develop the plot.

### PRACTICE

Work with students to read the writing prompt on **Student Book** page 77 and find the clues that determine the correct mode and purpose.

**Writing Mode** This is a narrative prompt. The student is being asked to tell a story.

**Purpose** The student is being asked to think about a time that he or she enjoyed playing in a playground or a park.

### APPLY

**Writing Prompt** Students can practice writing from the prompt, simulating a test-taking situation. After they have analyzed the prompt, tell them they will have 5 minutes to write their responses.

**Tell Students** You may use scrap paper to organize your thoughts before you begin to draft your essay. Be sure to use Writing Hints for Prompts to help you draft, revise, and edit for language conventions.

# 5-Day Vocabulary

## Connect Language Arts

**WHOLE GROUP**

**VOCABULARY**
- Tested words

**SPELLING**
- Long *a*

**GRAMMAR**
- Subjects

**CA CONTENT STANDARDS**
R 3.1.4, R 3.1.8, LC 3.1.4, LC 3.1.8, LC 3.1.9

**SMALL GROUP**
- Differentiated Instruction, pp. 77Q–77PP

ON YOUR OWN **Practice Book,** page 40

A **thesaurus** is a book of synonyms. **Synonyms** are words that have similar meanings. When you don't know the exact meaning of a word, finding words with similar meanings in a thesaurus can help you figure out the meaning of that word. Sometimes a word has more than one meaning. A thesaurus will provide synonyms for each meaning of the word.

**A. Read the thesaurus entry. Answer the questions below using information from the thesaurus entry.** Possible responses provided.

**direction 1.** leadership, guidance, control, management **2.** guideline, instruction, rule, order, command **3.** path, route, course, track, way.

1. How many different meanings of **direction** does this thesaurus entry provide? 3

**B. Use the thesaurus entry to find a synonym of *direction* that makes sense in each sentence. Write a synonym.**

2. Our school is under the *direction* of our new principal, Mrs. Jackson. leadership
3. Which *direction* do you want to take on our hike? route
4. Did you read the direction before you started the activity? instruction

**Approaching Reproducible,** page 40
**Beyond Reproducible,** page 40

# Build Robust Vocabulary

## Day 1 Teach/Practice

### CONNECT TO WORDS

- Practice this week's vocabulary words using the following prompts:
  1. Why is it a good idea to *donate* your time to help an environmental group?
  2. What might happen if you are *unaware* of weather conditions?
  3. How do *members* of a soccer team celebrate winning a game?
  4. How can you *contribute* time to a Kids Action group?

### ACADEMIC VOCABULARY

- Review the important academic vocabulary words for the week. These words include: *main idea, details, summarize, thesaurus, synonyms, cause, effect.*
- Write each word on the board. Define each using student-friendly language and ask students to select the word you are defining. Then point to words in random order for students to define.

## Day 2 Review

### CONNECT TO WORDS

- Review the definitions of this week's vocabulary words using **Student Book** pages 68–69. Then discuss each word using the following prompts:
  1. What could you *donate* to charity?
  2. What would happen if you were *unaware* of a test and didn't study?
  3. What could a club do to get more *members* to join?
  4. How can you *contribute* to taking care of our classroom?

### THESAURUS: SYNONYMS

- Remind students that synonyms are words with similar meanings and a thesaurus is a book of synonyms.
- Display **Transparency 5**. Read the first sentence and model how to use the thesaurus entries provided to figure out the meaning of the underlined word.
- Have students use a thesaurus to find synonyms for the underlined words in the remaining sentences.
- Have students identify synonyms for this and last week's vocabulary words. Have them use the vocabulary word and synonyms to write sentences in their Writer's Notebooks. The sentences must define the vocabulary word using the synonym. Model for students using the word *donate*. (Synonym: to give; *I didn't mind giving my old clothes to charity when I donated everything last week.*)

CA CONTENT STANDARD
**R 3.1.8** Use knowledge of prefixes and suffixes to determine the meaning of words.

## Day 3 Reinforce

### CONNECT TO WORDS

- Ask students to create Word Squares for each word in their Writer's Notebooks.
- In the first square, students write the word. (Example: *unaware*)
- In the second square, students write their own definition of the word and any related words, such as synonyms. (Example: *uninformed, didn't know*)
- In the third square, students draw a simple illustration that will help them remember the word. (Example: *drawing of someone looking confused, drawing of a question mark*)
- In the fourth square, students write nonexamples, including antonyms for the word. (Example: *in the know, informed*)

### RELATED WORDS

- Help students generate words related to *contribute*.
- Draw a T-chart on the board. One column is headed "To give"; the other column is headed "To take."
- Have students list words they know in each column. Ask students to use a thesaurus. Add words not included, such as (to give) *bestow, grant, present*; (to take) *capture, acquire, seize*.
- Extend the discussion by having students locate in a dictionary words with the same root as *contribute*. Discuss these and other words: *contribution, contributor*.

## Day 4 Extend

### CONNECT TO WORDS

- Review this week's vocabulary using the following sentence stems. Have students orally complete each one.

1. Our class should donate _____ because _____.
2. I was unaware that _____.
3. I think club members are _____ because _____.
4. I can contribute to making our city a better place by _____.

### MORPHOLOGY

- Use the additional selection vocabulary word *recycle* as a springboard to learn other words.
- Write the word *recycle* on the board. Underline *re-*. Explain that the prefix *re-* means "again." To *recycle* means to use over again.
- Display the words *return* and *rewrite*. Tell students to underline the prefix *re-* in each word.
- Use the word parts to define each word. Explain that *re-* means "again" and the base word is *turn*. Therefore *return* means "to turn back." Repeat with *rewrite,* which means "to write again."

## Day 5 Assess and Reteach

### POSTTEST

-  Display **Transparency 6**. Have students complete the cloze sentences using one of this week's vocabulary words.
- Note how quickly and accurately students can complete this task. Work with students who make errors or require too much time to complete this task during Small Group time.

### CONNECT TO WRITING

-  Have students write sentences in their Writer's Notebooks using this week's vocabulary. Tell students to write sentences that provide information they learned from this week's readings.
- EL Provide the Day 4 sentence stems for students needing extra support.

# 5-Day Spelling

See page T17 for **Differentiated Spelling Lists.** Pretests and Posttests available in **Teacher's Resource Book**.

## Spelling Words

| | | |
|---|---|---|
| fail | tray | gray |
| bay | trail | plays |
| pail | may | paint |
| ray | braid | snail |
| plain | sway | great* |

**Review** safe, globe, rice
**Challenge** lady, afraid

## Dictation Sentences

1. If I study, I won't fail the test.
2. We sailed in the bay.
3. Fill the pail with sand.
4. A ray of sunlight came through the window.
5. He is wearing a plain white shirt.
6. The waiter carried our food on a tray.
7. Let's walk on the trail.
8. May I use your hairbrush?
9. I like to braid my hair.
10. The trees sway in the wind.
11. Elephants are huge gray animals.
12. My sister **plays** with toys.
13. What color did you paint your room?
14. A snail moves very slowly.
15. That is a **great** book.

## Review/Challenge Words

1. Is it safe to swim here?
2. You can cook rice in a pot.
3. He sailed around the globe.
4. The young lady is my friend.
5. I am not afraid of the dark.

* Oddball words

# Long *a*

CA CONTENT STANDARD
**LC 3.1.8** Spell correctly one-syllable words that have blends, contractions, compounds, orthographic patterns and common homophones.

## Day 1 Pretest

### ASSESS PRIOR KNOWLEDGE

- Model for students how to spell the word *tray*. Segment the word sound by sound, then attach a spelling to each sound. Point out that *ay* is the long *a* spelling found at the end of a word or syllable.
- Use the Dictation Sentences. Say the underlined word, read the sentence, and repeat the word. Have students write the words.
- Have students self-correct their tests. Point out that the *ai* spelling for a long *a* never appears at the end of a word.
- Have students cut apart the Spelling Word Cards BLM on **Teacher's Resource Book** page 104 and figure out a way to sort them. Have them use the cards throughout the week.

## Day 2 Word Sorts

### SPIRAL REVIEW

Review Final *e* sound-spellings in the words *date, rice,* and *globe*. Have students find words in this week's readings with the same sound-spellings.

### WORD SORTS

- Have students take turns sorting cards and explaining how they sorted them. When students have finished the sort, discuss any words that have unexpected vowel spellings. (great)
- Review the Spelling Words, pointing out the long *a* vowel spellings. Use the cards on the Spelling Word Cards BLM. Write the key words *fail, pay,* and *oddball*. Model how to sort words by long *a* spellings. Place one or two cards beneath the correct key words.

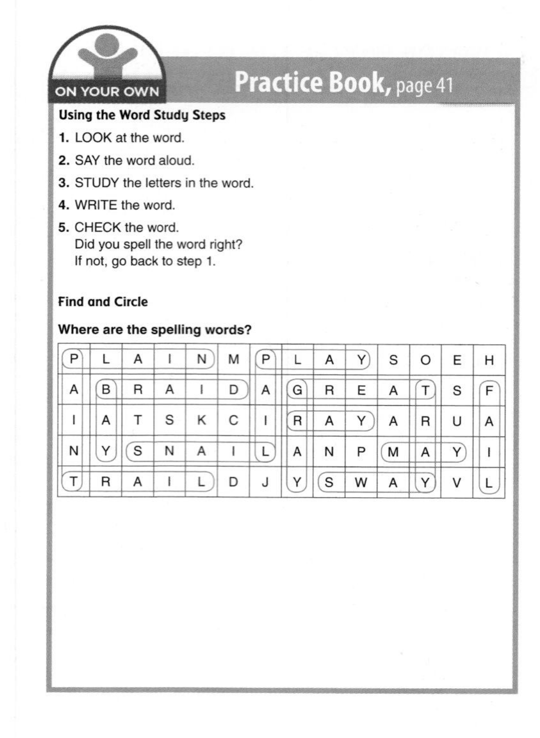
ON YOUR OWN
**Practice Book,** page 41

**Using the Word Study Steps**
1. LOOK at the word.
2. SAY the word aloud.
3. STUDY the letters in the word.
4. WRITE the word.
5. CHECK the word.
Did you spell the word right?
If not, go back to step 1.

**Find and Circle**

**Where are the spelling words?**

| | | | | | | | | | | | | | |
|---|---|---|---|---|---|---|---|---|---|---|---|---|---|
| P | L | A | I | N | M | P | L | A | Y | S | O | E | H |
| A | B | R | A | I | D | A | G | R | E | A | T | S | F |
| I | A | T | S | K | C | I | R | A | Y | A | R | U | A |
| N | Y | S | N | A | I | L | A | N | P | M | A | Y | I |
| T | R | A | I | L | D | J | Y | S | W | A | Y | V | L |

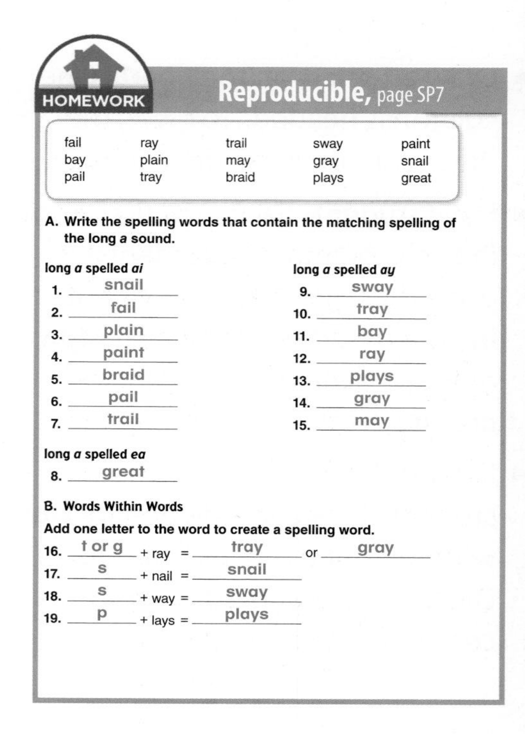
HOMEWORK
**Reproducible,** page SP7

| | | | | |
|---|---|---|---|---|
| fail | ray | trail | sway | paint |
| bay | plain | may | gray | snail |
| pail | tray | braid | plays | great |

**A. Write the spelling words that contain the matching spelling of the long *a* sound.**

**long *a* spelled *ai***
1. snail
2. fail
3. plain
4. paint
5. braid
6. pail
7. trail

**long *a* spelled *ea***
8. great

**long *a* spelled *ay***
9. sway
10. tray
11. bay
12. ray
13. plays
14. gray
15. may

**B. Words Within Words**

**Add one letter to the word to create a spelling word.**
16. t or g + ray = tray or gray
17. s + nail = snail
18. s + way = sway
19. p + lays = plays

**CA CONTENT STANDARD**
**LC 3.1.9** Arrange words in alphabetical order.

## Day 3 Alphabetize

### ALPHABETIZE

- Display the words *fail, bay, plays,* and *pail*. Model how to alphabetize. Say: *Look at the first letters. Determine which one comes first in the alphabet. If the first letters are the same, go to the second letter.*
- Put the words in ABC order: *bay, fail, pail, play.* Point out that the words *pail* and *play* begin with *p*, so it is necessary to go to the second letter in order to put these words in the correct order. Since *a* comes before *l*, the order is *pail* then *play*.
- Have students alphabetize the following words: *gray, bay, globe, snail, tray, braid*. Continue with other word sets.

## Day 4 Review and Proofread

### PROOFREAD AND WRITE

Write these sentences. Have students proofread/edit.

1. Joe filled the payl with red paynt. (pail, paint)
2. Walk on the dirt trayl to the bai. (trail, bay)
3. A snal is a grat pet! (snail, great)
4. Make your brayde sweye as you walk. (braid, sway)
5. I fale to see why grei is your favorite color. (fail, gray)

**Error Correction** Remind students that the *ai* spelling for the long *a* sound never appears at the end of a word or syllable. However, the *ay* spelling always appears at the end of a word or syllable. Use the underscore hints on the Sound-Spelling Cards (*ai_* and *_ay*) to reinforce this principle.

## Day 5 Assess and Reteach

### POSTTEST

Use the Dictation Sentences on page 75C for the Posttest.

If students have difficulty with any of the words in the lesson, have them place the words on a list called *Spelling Words I Want to Remember* in their Writer's Notebooks. Look for students' use of these words in their writings.

**Extra Support** Some students having spelling difficulties may need additional phonemic awareness instruction and practice. See the **Intervention Kit** for phoneme reversal, substitution, addition, deletion, and segmentation exercises.

Challenge students to find words for each long *a* spelling and add them to the **Unit 1 Big Question Board**.

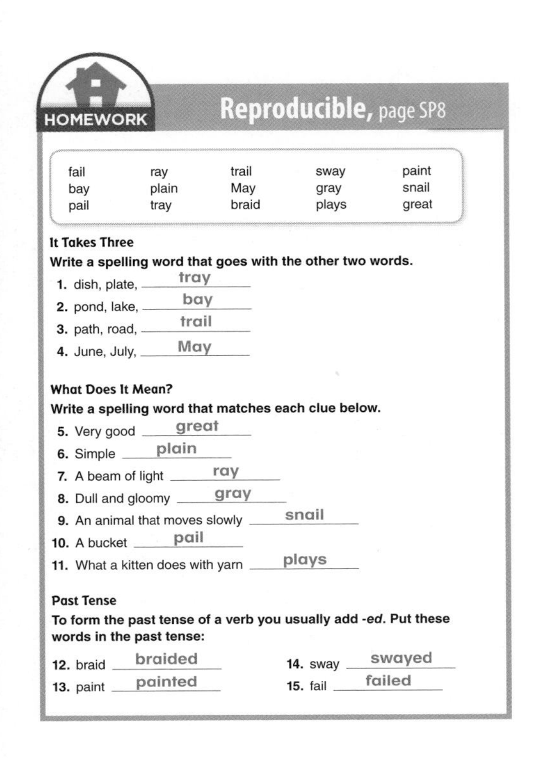

HOMEWORK **Reproducible,** page SP8

| fail | ray | trail | sway | paint |
|---|---|---|---|---|
| bay | plain | May | gray | snail |
| pail | tray | braid | plays | great |

**It Takes Three**
Write a spelling word that goes with the other two words.

1. dish, plate, tray
2. pond, lake, bay
3. path, road, trail
4. June, July, May

**What Does It Mean?**
Write a spelling word that matches each clue below.

5. Very good great
6. Simple plain
7. A beam of light ray
8. Dull and gloomy gray
9. An animal that moves slowly snail
10. A bucket pail
11. What a kitten does with yarn plays

**Past Tense**
To form the past tense of a verb you usually add *-ed*. Put these words in the past tense:

12. braid braided
13. paint painted
14. sway swayed
15. fail failed

ON YOUR OWN **Practice Book,** page 42

**There are eight spelling mistakes in this paragraph. Circle the misspelled words. Write the words correctly on the lines below.**

Every (Mai) I visit my grandma. She moved near the (bae) two years ago, but it already feels like home. It is a fun place to live. I always bring my (payl) and I fill it with sand and sometimes a (snale) gets in there. We sometimes have visitors. On nice days the seagulls fly over her house. I throw them bread crumbs and give them names.

My grandma (plase) lots of card games with me. She also teaches me a few card tricks. Sometimes we (peant) pictures of the trees in her yard.

After dinners we take walks on a (trayl) by the water. The sky is gray, the air is cool, and the sounds of the bay fill the night.

It is (grait) to visit grandma.

1. May
2. bay
3. pail
4. snail
5. plays
6. paint
7. trail
8. great

**Writing Activity**
**Write about a place you like to visit. Use at least three spelling words in your description.**

HOMEWORK **Reproducible,** page SP9

**Look at the words in each set below. One word in each set is spelled correctly. Look at Sample A. The letter next to the correctly spelled word in Sample A has been shaded in. Do Sample B yourself. Shade the letter of the word that is spelled correctly. When you are sure you know what to do, go on with the rest of the page.**

**Sample A:** Ⓐ clai Ⓑ clae Ⓒ claa Ⓓ clay

**Sample B:** Ⓔ mayl Ⓕ mail Ⓖ mael Ⓗ mayle

1. Ⓐ fayle Ⓑ fayl Ⓒ fail Ⓓ fale
2. Ⓔ bey Ⓕ baye Ⓖ bai Ⓗ bay
3. Ⓐ payle Ⓑ payl Ⓒ pail Ⓓ paile
4. Ⓔ rai Ⓕ ray Ⓖ raye Ⓗ raie
5. Ⓐ plian Ⓑ plain Ⓒ plaen Ⓓ playn
6. Ⓔ trai Ⓕ tray Ⓖ traye Ⓗ trae
7. Ⓐ trail Ⓑ trayl Ⓒ trayle Ⓓ treil
8. Ⓔ Mai Ⓕ Maye Ⓖ Mey Ⓗ May
9. Ⓐ brade Ⓑ brayd Ⓒ brayde Ⓓ braid
10. Ⓔ sway Ⓕ swaye Ⓖ swaie Ⓗ swai
11. Ⓐ grae Ⓑ grai Ⓒ graye Ⓓ gray
12. Ⓔ plaiz Ⓕ plays Ⓖ playz Ⓗ plaes
13. Ⓐ paint Ⓑ pante Ⓒ paynt Ⓓ paynte
14. Ⓔ snale Ⓕ snail Ⓖ snaile Ⓗ snayle
15. Ⓐ great Ⓑ grayt Ⓒ grait Ⓓ graite

# 5-Day Grammar

## Daily Language Activities

Write the sentences on the board.

**DAY 1**
**1.** School starts at nine **2.** I get to school on Time. **3.** i do not want to be Late! (1: nine.; 2: time.; 3: I; late.)

**DAY 2**
**1.** Who is in the class play! **2.** is maria playing an ant? **3.** i will find out (1: play?; 2: Is; Maria; 3: I; out.)

**DAY 3**
**1.** Give me toast on a trai **2.** Please put jam on the toast? **3.** who wants orange juice. (1: tray.; 2: toast.; 3: Who; juice?)

**DAY 4**
**1.** there is wet paynt on the door. **2.** do not touch anything **3.** You might get paint on your hand? (1: There; paint; 2: Do; anything.; 3: hand.)

**DAY 5**
**1.** Mai is the best month; **2.** i can hike on a trale. **3.** the trees swai in the wind. (1: May; month.; 2: I; trail.; 3: The; sway)

### English Learners

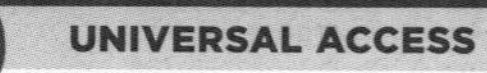

UNIVERSAL ACCESS

**Generate Sentences**
Ask students for example sentences and write them on the board. For example, *Bears steal food.* Ask: *Who steals food?* Explain that a sentence's subject answers who or what. Have students identify the subject in the other sentences.

# Subjects

CA CONTENT STANDARD
**LC 3.1.4** Identify and use subjects and verbs correctly in speaking and writing simple sentences.

## Day 1 Introduce the Concept

**INTRODUCE SUBJECTS**

Present the following:

- A **sentence** is a group of words that expresses a complete thought.
- Every complete sentence has two parts: the **subject** and the **predicate**.
- The subject of a sentence tells what or whom the sentence is about.

**Subject**
**Jacob** lived in Harlem.
**Entertainers** worked there, too.

See Grammar Transparency 11 for modeling and guided practice.

HOMEWORK **Reproducible,** page GR7

- The **subject** of a sentence is whom or what the sentence is about.
- The subject can be one word or more than one word.
  The *buildings* are tall.
  The *office buildings* are tall.

**What or whom is the sentence about? Draw a line under the subject.**

1. The city is my habitat.
2. The streets are busy.
3. The fast cars pass quickly.
4. The park has trees and grass.
5. Tired birds rest in the branches.
6. Squirrels hop through the park.
7. Summers get very hot.
8. Winters are cold and snowy.
9. People rush by quickly.
10. Large buses stop at the corner.
11. The deer runs through the park.
12. Trees lose their leaves.
13. Children play on the playground.
14. The bikes are on the grass.
15. The bus is crowded in the winter.

## Day 2 Teach the Concept

**REVIEW SUBJECTS**

Remind students what a subject is. Write a sentence on the board and have students identify the subject.

**INTRODUCE MULTI-WORD SUBJECTS**

Present the following:

- The subject of a sentence tells what or whom a sentence is about.
- The subject of a sentence can be one word, more than one word, or a **compound subject** connected by *and*.

| **Subject** | |
|---|---|
| **African Americans** | lived there. |
| **Many artists** | worked there. |
| **Artists and poets** | worked there. |

See Grammar Transparency 12 for modeling and guided practice.

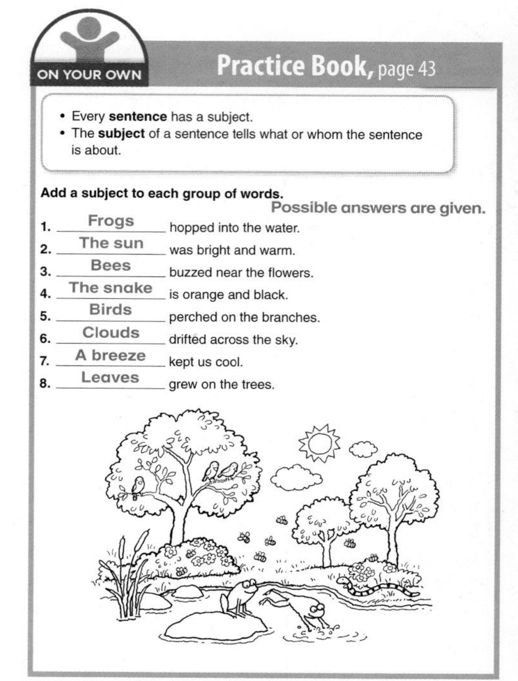

ON YOUR OWN **Practice Book,** page 43

- Every **sentence** has a subject.
- The **subject** of a sentence tells what or whom the sentence is about.

**Add a subject to each group of words.**
Possible answers are given.

1. Frogs hopped into the water.
2. The sun was bright and warm.
3. Bees buzzed near the flowers.
4. The snake is orange and black.
5. Birds perched on the branches.
6. Clouds drifted across the sky.
7. A breeze kept us cool.
8. Leaves grew on the trees.

## Day 3 Review and Practice

### REVIEW SUBJECTS

Review with students how to identify a sentence's subject.

### MECHANICS AND USAGE: CORRECT SENTENCES

Every sentence has a subject.

A fragment may be a sentence that does not have a subject. It does not express a complete thought.

Correct some sentence fragments by adding a subject.

**Fragment:** Form communities.

**Complete Sentence:** Many different people form communities.

See Grammar Transparency 13 for modeling and guided practice.

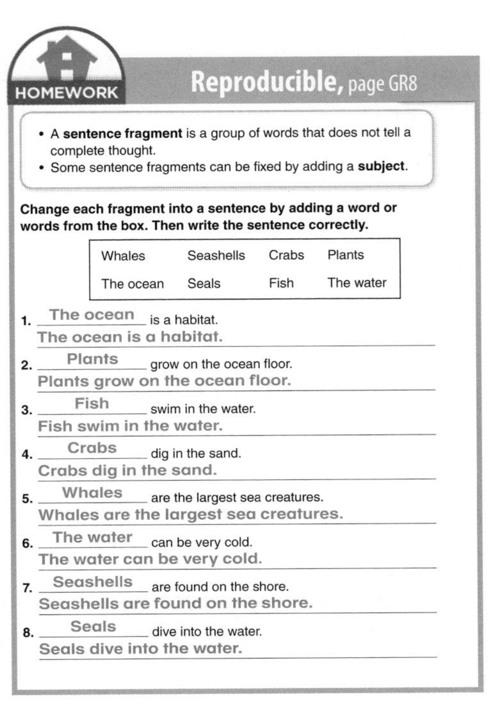

HOMEWORK **Reproducible,** page GR8

- A **sentence fragment** is a group of words that does not tell a complete thought.
- Some sentence fragments can be fixed by adding a **subject**.

**Change each fragment into a sentence by adding a word or words from the box. Then write the sentence correctly.**

| Whales | Seashells | Crabs | Plants |
|---|---|---|---|
| The ocean | Seals | Fish | The water |

1. The ocean is a habitat.
The ocean is a habitat.
2. Plants grow on the ocean floor.
Plants grow on the ocean floor.
3. Fish swim in the water.
Fish swim in the water.
4. Crabs dig in the sand.
Crabs dig in the sand.
5. Whales are the largest sea creatures.
Whales are the largest sea creatures.
6. The water can be very cold.
The water can be very cold.
7. Seashells are found on the shore.
Seashells are found on the shore.
8. Seals dive into the water.
Seals dive into the water.

## Day 4 Review and Proofread

### REVIEW CORRECT SENTENCES

Ask students to explain what a complete sentence is. Ask how to correct a sentence fragment.

### PROOFREAD

Have students correct errors in the following sentences.

1. Girls going around the block. (The girls are going around the block.)
2. Jan likes red bikes? (bikes.)
3. ted is on the phone (Ted; phone.)
4. Drank a glass of water. (She drank a glass of water.)
5. Likes funny books. (My class likes funny books.)

See Grammar Transparency 14 for modeling and guided practice.

ON YOUR OWN **Practice Book,** page 44

- The **subject** of a sentence tells what or whom the sentence is about.

**Read the paragraph below about habitat.**

My habitat each day is Lowell Elementary School. Students make up the largest group of living things in this habitat. They come in all shapes and sizes. Be very loud. They can be very quiet. Move around. Some of their food comes in brown lunch bags. Others get food from plastic containers. Other living things include the plants sitting near the window. Watered every day. The living things also include the fish in the fish tank. We can watch the fish and see how they live in their habitat. Swim around.

**Rewrite the paragraph fixing any sentence fragments you found.**

Possible answer: My habitat each day is Lowell Elementary School. Students make up the largest group of living things in this habitat. They come in all shapes and sizes. They can be very loud. They can be very quiet. They move around. Some of their food comes in brown lunch bags. Others get food from plastic containers. Other living things include the plants sitting near the window. The plants are watered every day. The living things also include the fish in the fish tank. We can watch the fish and see how they live in their habitat. They swim around in the tank.

## Day 5 Assess and Reteach

### ASSESS

Use the Daily Language Activities or **Reproducible** page GR 9 for assessment.

### RETEACH

Use Reproducible page GR 9 and selected pages from the **Grammar and Writing Handbook** for additional reteaching.

Check students' writing for use of the skill. Assign Grammar Revision Assignments in their Writer's Notebooks, as needed.

See Grammar Transparency 15 for modeling and guided practice.

HOMEWORK **Reproducible,** page GR9

**A. Write the subject of each sentence.**

1. A habitat is where living things live. habitat
2. Animals share their habitats with plants. Animals
3. People have habitats too. People
4. The climate is the weather in a habitat. climate
5. Snow is covering my habitat. snow

**B. Choose a subject from the box that best completes each sentence. Rewrite the correct sentence.**

| fish | people | bears |
|---|---|---|
| birds | everyone | |

6. _____ needs the right kind of habitat.
Everyone needs the right kind of habitat.
7. _____ live in trees.
Birds live in trees.
8. _____ find shelter in buildings.
People find shelter in buildings.
9. _____ swim in lakes and oceans.
Fish swim in lakes and oceans.
10. _____ live in the woods.
Bears live in the woods.

## Write

**WHOLE GROUP**

**WRITING**

- Personal Narrative (Description)

**CONTENT STANDARDS**

W 3.1.2, W 3.1.4, W 3.2.1, LAS 3.2.1

**SMALL GROUP**

- Differentiated Instruction, pp. 77Q–77PP

**5-Day Writing**

| | |
|---|---|
| DAY 1 | Genre Introduction |
| DAY 2 | Introduce Personal Narrative (Description) Writing Process |
| DAY 3 | Minilesson 1 Revision Assignments |
| DAY 4 | Minilesson 2 Revision Assignments |
| DAY 5 | Writing Conferences |

The Writers' Express
Immediate Impact. Lasting Transformation. wex.org

**Research Proven Writing Approach**

# Genre Introduction: Personal Narrative

**CA CONTENT STANDARD**
**W 3.2.1** Write narratives:
a. Provide a context within which an action takes place.
b. Include well-chosen details to develop the plot.
c. Provide insight into why the selected incident is memorable.

## Professional Development

### WHAT IS PERSONAL NARRATIVE?

A personal narrative is a true story about an event or situation that the writer personally experienced. It is written in the first person, using words such as *I* and *my*. In this type of essay, the writer not only explains an experience, but also shows the reader how he thinks and feels about that experience. In Grade 3, students should practice focusing on a moment, an object, a person, or a setting through detailed description as they write their personal narratives.

### WHY TEACH PERSONAL NARRATIVE?

Writing a personal narrative:

- Builds on students' own unique observations and perspectives.
- Allows a writer to tap into the power that comes from emotions associated with personal experiences.
- Is simple and supports the expression of voice.

Through writing personal narratives, students will learn:

- To focus on one event or moment and fully develop it.
- To allow personal perspective and voice to engage the reader.
- To describe the setting of their entry using specific details.

### ASSESSMENT: WHAT WILL I SEE IN MY STUDENTS' WRITING?

We suggest giving the following weight to the various elements of the third graders' first writing project.

- 60% Writing Process and understanding of genre:

  *Did the writer write about something he knows well?*

  *Did the writer revise in order to add detail?*
- 30% Skillfulness:

  *Did the writer describe the setting using specific details?*
- 10% Clarity:

  *Did the writer use grade-level appropriate technical skills to communicate clearly?*

When giving students feedback, comments are an effective teaching tool. See the conferencing pages 77M–77N for feedback tips.

## Writing Process

During this week, students will have their first chance to move through the writing process by writing a personal narrative. You will carefully guide them, step by step. At the end of the unit, they will write a personal narrative on their own.

**STEP 1: Prewrite** During the first session, have students:

- Select from two Writer's Notebook entries they have written over the past two weeks.
- Flag the entry with a self-stick note so that they (and you) can find it easily.

In between sessions one and two, read the entry each student has selected and give each student a revision assignment (see the conferencing page).

**STEP 2: Draft** During the lesson it is important to introduce the personal narrative genre and show students sample writing selections. Use the Anchor papers provided in the Teacher's Resource Book. Circulate the room for over-the-shoulder conferencing. See the conferencing page for suggestions on conferencing. If you do not have time for individual conferences, over-the-shoulder conferencing is a great way to make sure you connect with every student about their writing.

**STEP 3: Revising** In the two minilessons, students will experiment with different leads for their entry.

**STEP 4: Proofreading** During the proofreading process, students should edit their own work for spelling, grammar, and punctuation. Third graders should:

- Begin new thoughts with capital letters.
- End thoughts with ending punctuation.
- Read their writing aloud to check for errors in syntax.
- Make sure their subjects and verbs are in agreement and that correct tense was used.

**STEP 5: Publish** As students begin to polish and publish their work, it is important to post student work. Post examples of strong detailed sentences and strong lead sentences. Have students type or write a final draft. Remind them to write legibly. Model for them how to create documents with correct margins and spacing between letters in words and words in sentences.

**CA CONTENT STANDARD**
**W 3.1.2** Write legibly in cursive or joined italic, allowing margins and correct spacing between letters in a word and words in a sentence.

### Objective

- Introduce Genre: Personal Narrative

### Materials

- Writer's Notebooks

### Selecting Journal Entries

This quick classroom routine encourages students to reread their work with a purpose and make some judgments about their own writing.

1. Read each student's Writer's Notebook, select two of the strongest entries from recent student writing, and flag each of them with a sticky note.

2. Explain that you have posted a sticky note on two pieces that you thought were strong. The student's job is to reread them and choose one of the pieces for you to give an individual Revision Assignment. Give the student a basis for choosing the entry, and post the criteria. For example:

- Choose a piece in which you've really used some great detail.
- Choose a piece that you think will make someone laugh (gasp, cringe, feel sad, etc).
- After deciding on a piece, write a check (√) on the sticky note attached to the entry you want me to read.

## Objectives

- Define "personal narrative" and its characteristics
- Develop one idea in a selected journal entry

### Materials

- Writer's Notebook
- Transparencies 3-4

### Writing Professional Development Guide

See **Writing Professional Development Guide** for additional examples and research information.

# Personal Narrative

## Begin Writing Process

**TEACH/MODEL**

**Identify Audience** Tell students that a personal narrative is a story we write about ourselves. Explain that they have been writing about themselves a lot in their Writer's Notebooks already. Now they are going to turn a Writer's Notebook entry into something a reader would be interested in—something that's not just for their journals, but something that their friends, families, and even people they don't know would find entertaining.

Explain to students that to do that, they have to make sure that they describe their experiences with lots of details so that readers will be able to imagine exactly what happened. The more clearly a reader can imagine what they experienced, the more the reader will be able to share the experience with them.

Display **Transparency 3**. Have students chorally read the passage. Discuss the example, probing students for information about the details and the beginning. Ask students for opinions on the writing.

**Teacher:** *What do you think?*
**Student:** *It's really boring. It keeps saying everything tastes good.*
**Teacher:** *Right. How could this student make his writing more interesting?*
**Student:** *By describing the food he ate or putting something funny in.*
**Teacher:** *Great. The student hasn't put much thought into what other people might think about his work. We don't get any details about what makes the lobster taste so good or about how the writer ate it.*

Display **Transparency 4**. Have students chorally read it. Ask students for details they notice the writer has added or sentences they really enjoyed. Make a list on chart paper or the board. For example:

Crack. The lobster juice flew in my eye.
I tasted the meat and it was so good I had to give my mom a compliment.
I went to another dimension and when I came back to my world I gave her a compliment, too.
It was fantastic.

Ask students to help you make a list of characteristics of a Personal Narrative. Write it on chart paper so it can be posted in your classroom. Be sure to include the following:

**A Personal Narrative**

- **It is a true story about me or something I've experienced.**
- **It uses words such as *I* or *my*.**
- **It has many strong, unique, entertaining details.**
- **It reflects me and my feelings (funny if I'm funny, sad if I felt sad, etc).**

**PRACTICE/APPLY**

Point out to students that you have written comments in their Writer's Notebooks. [Be sure to have included at least two to three revision assignments for each student by this point in the unit.] Ask students to read your comments and pay careful attention to the underlined sentences.

Post the following, or explain to students:

Focus Drill
- Look at the underlined sentence.
- Re-copy the sentence at the bottom of your entry or on the back.
- Now write two more sentences about that sentence.

While students are working, you should circulate through the room and complete over-the-shoulder conferences. When completed, ask students to share their work.

**Summarize Learning** Discuss the following:

**Think Aloud** Well, what do you think? Were you able to add more specific details in your writing? Did the example help you? Over the next couple of days, we will continue to look for places to add to our writing. I'm excited to read your writing!

Each day, continue guiding students through the Writing Process. Use the minilessons and revision assignments provided.

## Objective

- Add specific details to a part of an entry to help the reader imagine the moment more clearly

### Materials

- Writer's Notebooks
- Transparencies 5–8
- Practice Book page 45

### Teacher-to-Teacher

**Structured Practice**

Daily, low-stakes writing gives students the chance to work on specific skills—and gives you a clear snapshot of what each of your students can and can't do. Use the information from this quick "dipsticking" to assign each student a short individualized revision assignment that focuses on the specific skill the student needs to get him to the next stage.

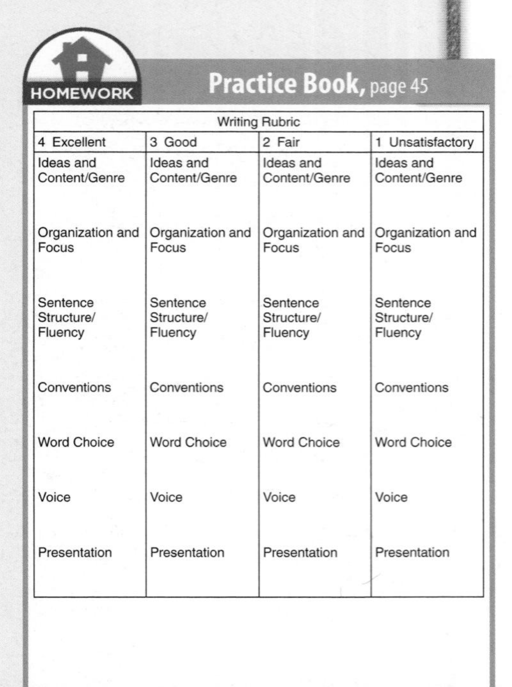

HOMEWORK **Practice Book,** page 45

Writing Rubric

| 4 Excellent | 3 Good | 2 Fair | 1 Unsatisfactory |
|---|---|---|---|
| Ideas and Content/Genre | Ideas and Content/Genre | Ideas and Content/Genre | Ideas and Content/Genre |
| Organization and Focus | Organization and Focus | Organization and Focus | Organization and Focus |
| Sentence Structure/ Fluency | Sentence Structure/ Fluency | Sentence Structure/ Fluency | Sentence Structure/ Fluency |
| Conventions | Conventions | Conventions | Conventions |
| Word Choice | Word Choice | Word Choice | Word Choice |
| Voice | Voice | Voice | Voice |
| Presentation | Presentation | Presentation | Presentation |

**Approaching Reproducible,** page 45

**Beyond Reproducible,** page 45

# Minilesson 1

**Personal Narrative** Revision Practice

### TEACH/MODEL

Explain to students that today they are going to revisit the writing they have been revising to create a personal narrative. They are going to think about adding more specific details. Yesterday they underlined a place where they thought they could add more details. Today they get to pick a place to add more details. Ask students to select a place in their entry that they want to be sure the reader can imagine clearly.

Have students reread their entries silently. Display **Transparency 5** or post the following on the board:

**Transparency 5**

**Focus Drill**

- Find a place in your writing to add details and underline it.
- Re-copy the sentence(s) at the bottom of your entry or on the back.
- Now write two more sentences about that sentence.

**Writing Transparency**

### PRACTICE/APPLY

Ask students to find a place to add details and follow the directions provided. Display **Transparencies 6** and **7**, *Strong Verbs*. Model how to replace a common verb with a stronger word. Ask students to refer to the list as they revise. Prompt them to replace overused or boring verbs with these more precise ones. Model as you circulate and provide over-the-shoulder conferences.

**Summarize Learning** When completed, ask for students to share their work. Discuss the following:

**Think Aloud** Were you able to find a place to add details? This can be challenging at first. When we are looking at our writing, we want to ask ourselves questions such as: *Can I say more about this? What did it look, smell, feel, or sound like?* The more practice we have, the more natural this will become to us as writers.

As a follow-up, display **Transparency 8**. Have students refer to **Practice Book**, page 45. Work with students to fill in the rubric for this week's writing. Tell students that you will use this rubric to evaluate their completed pieces. They should refer to the rubric as they write, revise, and proofread.

# Minilesson 2

**Revision** Practice

### TEACH/MODEL

Display **Transparency 9**, Personal Narrative Characteristics, and review it. Explain to students that now they will add some details to help the reader imagine where they were during the moment in their entry. This is also called the setting.

Using **Transparencies 3** and **4**, guide students to notice the differences between the lead in Example 1 and the lead in Example 2.

- **Example 1** *I was sitting in the kitchen eating lobster with my mom and sister.*
- **Example 2** *The smell of lobster filled my nostrils. I looked at the red and white checked tablecloth. On it, my mom had placed the red and orange plates that looked like lobsters. The eyes were staring back at me. A cup of melted butter was calling to me to soak it up with delicious lobster.*

Ask: *Which example do you find more interesting/entertaining? Why?* Explain that Example 2 is more entertaining because the writer clearly intended for us to imagine where the story was taking place by describing the setting.

### PRACTICE/APPLY

Display **Transparency 5** or post the following on the board:

**Transparency 5**

**Topic Development (Setting) Drill**

- Underline a place where you mention the setting or where you could add some details about the setting.
- Rewrite the sentence on the bottom of your entry or on the back.
- Now write 2–3 new sentences to describe the setting.

**Writing Transparency**

While students are completing the lesson, circulate around the room completing Over-the-Shoulder Conferences.

**Summarize Learning** When finished, have students share their work. Discuss the following:

**Think Aloud** Whenever reading a book in class or at home, pay attention to how that author discussed the setting. Think about how you can do this in your own writing.

## Objective

- Add details about setting to an entry

### Materials

- Writer's Notebooks with chosen journal entry
- Transparencies 3, 4, 5, 9

## Teacher-to-Teacher

**Writing for Impact**

By commenting specifically on how you've been affected by what you've read, you show students the impact they're able to make as writers. This sense of their power gives students a reason to keep writing—and a growing confidence that they have what it takes to make the world listen to what they have to say.

## Minilesson

**Narrative Presentations**

As students complete their Personal Narrative, review how to give a personal narrative presentation. Point out that students should:

- Clearly state why they selected the moment, or incident, described.
- Provide enough context so the listener will understand the moment's importance, or why it is memorable.
- Include details to create a clear image of the moment, including the setting and any people involved, in the listener's mind. LAS 3.2.1

## Objective

- Meet with the teacher to discuss writing and receive revision assignments

### Materials

- Writer's Notebooks
- Revision Assignments

### Teacher-to-Teacher

**Over-the-Shoulder Conferences**

Use these quick, focused opportunities to comment while students are writing.

- **Step 1** Quietly move close enough to a student that you can read the journal entry he or she is writing.
- **Step 2** Read part of what you see. You don't need to start from the beginning or read the entire piece.
- **Step 3** Show the student a spot in the writing where he or she is using a particular skill or describing something that piques your interest.
- **Step 4** Whisper a sentence or two about why you noticed that spot in the writing and ask a question that will nudge the student to add a detail or clarify.
- **Step 5** Move on to the next student. Select students strategically. You should see 12–15 students in a 15-minute period.

# Conferences

## Writing Journals

### DYNAMIC FEEDBACK SYSTEM

**Purpose** One of the best ways for students to develop skills is by understanding how their writing affects their readers. Your targeted comments direct students to notice the impact they've made by using a specific skill.

Comments should get students looking backward (to notice effect of particular choices they've made in the piece they've just written) and forward (to consider how they might apply what they've learned from their last piece to their next).

**Managing Conference Time** Between Days 2 and 3 set aside time to select five to seven students each day to review their Writer's Notebooks during Small Group time. During this time address proofreading goals, such as beginning an entry and new thoughts with capital letters, and ending thoughts with proper ending punctuation.

### WRITE EFFECTIVE COMMENTS ON PERSONAL NARRATIVE

**Sample Comments for Personal Narrative** At least one of your comments should highlight the way the student uses the skills related to the genre. Here are some sample comments. Use these comments to get you started. Once you're comfortable, you can craft your own comments to be more specific to a particular entry.

- *I like the way you wrote more details about [how cold the ice cream was].*
- *Wow! This detail really caught my attention. I want to read more!*
- *Will you tell me more about this?*
- *These details helped me picture your moment.*

# Revision Assignments

CA CONTENT STANDARD
**W 3.1.4** Revise drafts to improve the coherence and logical progression of ideas by using an established rubric.

## IMPROVE WRITING

**What Is It?** Revision assignments play a crucial role in the dynamic feedback system. They enable you to work with each student on one skill at a time until the student has mastered it.

Revision assignments involve marking a specific section of a student's journal entry and then asking the student to revise it in a specific way. By requiring students to put to use your feedback to revise their own writing, revision assignments show clearly how that feedback has affected what students are able to do next.

**Sample Revision Assignments for Personal Narrative** Here are some examples of effective revision assignments for personal narratives. Use them to get started. You may also use the preprinted Revision Assignment Notes or create your own revision assignments based on these.

[Write, underline, or bracket the sentence.] *I underlined a sentence that caught my interest. Write two more details that describe [how the lobster tasted].*

[Write, underline, or bracket the sentence.] *I underlined a place in your writing that left me wanting more. Write two more details about this moment.*

[Write, underline, or bracket the sentence.] *I underlined your first sentence(s). Rewrite the sentence(s) thinking about how you can get your reader's attention.*

Revise

### Revision Assignment Notes

Use the Revision Assignment Notes to focus students' rewrites.

jump drive **Available on Jump Drive**

### Daily Handwriting

Introduce students to transitioning from manuscript to cursive writing. See **Handwriting** page 12 for daily practice.
W 3.1.2

Mark students' Journal Checklists to indicate mastered skills.

**Reproducible,** page 222

**STAGE 1** Establishing Habits

☐ Write Journal Entries ☐ Practice Skill Drills ☐ Engage in Experience
☐ Respond to Feedback ☐ Develop Vocabulary ☐ Share Writing

**STAGE 2** Strengthening Voice

| |  |  |
|---|---|---|
| Expressive Skills | Topic Development | ☐ Moment ☐ Object ☐ Setting |
| | Showing | ☐ Include unique observations<br>☐ Recognize showing and telling |
| | Strong Verbs | ☐ Recognize and use strong verbs |
| | Sensory Detail | ☐ Use multiple senses<br>☐ Choose sensory detail effectively |
| | Dialogue and Evidence I | ☐ Include dialogue |
| | Character Development | ☐ Believable<br>☐ Change and growth |
| | Logical Structure I: Distinguishing Moments | ☐ Use chronological order<br>☐ Distinguish moments |
| Technical Skills | Sentence Mechanics & Usage I: The Complete Sentence | ☐ Capitals and end punctuation<br>☐ Parts of speech<br>☐ Possessives<br>☐ Commas in a series |
| | Subject/Verb Agreement I | ☐ With present tense<br>☐ With simple past tense |
| | Punctuating and Formatting Dialogue & Quotations | ☐ Quotation marks |

**Writing Journal Checklist**

# Administer the Test

## Weekly Reading Quick Check,

### Passage and questions, pages Unit 1 Week 3

**ASSESSED SKILLS**

- Vocabulary Words; Thesaurus/Synonyms
- Main Idea/Details
- Subjects; Personal Narrative/Description
- Long *a*

*Selection Test Also Available.*

**Progress Monitoring, Unit 1, Week 3**

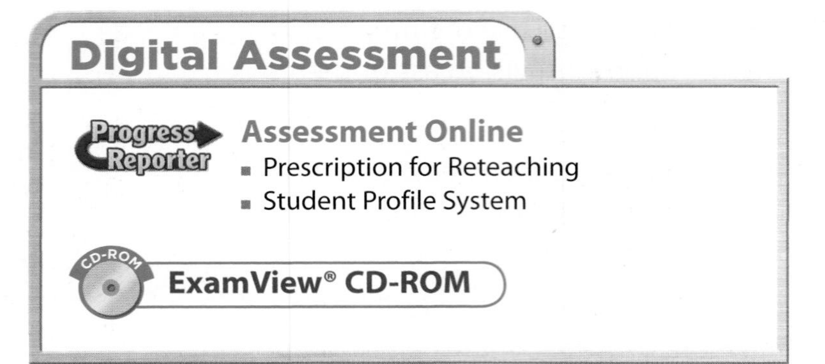

## Unit Fluency Assessment

Assess fluency for one group of students per week. Use the Oral Fluency Record Sheet to track the number of words read correctly. Fluency goal for all students: **61–81 words correct per minute (WCPM)**.

| | |
|---|---|
| Approaching Level | Weeks 1, 3, 5 |
| On Level | Weeks 2, 4 |
| Beyond Level | Week 6 |

**Diagnostic, Unit 1 Fluency**

| Diagnose | | Prescribe |
|---|---|---|
| **Review the assessment answers with students. Have them correct their errors. Then provide additional instruction as needed.** | | |
| | **IF...** | **THEN...** |
| **VOCABULARY WORDS**<br>**VOCABULARY STRATEGY**<br>Thesaurus/Synonyms | 0–2 items correct . . . | Reteach Skills: Intervention Kit<br>Online Practice: Go to **www.macmillanmh.com**.<br>Vocabulary PuzzleMaker |
| **COMPREHENSION**<br>Skill: Main Idea and Details | 0–2 items correct . . . | See Main Idea and Details lesson Unit 1, Week 4, page 105B.<br>Intervention Kit: Comprehension |
| **WRITING AND GRAMMAR**<br>Subjects<br>Personal Narrative/ Description | 0–1 items correct . . . | Review with Unit 1 Writing lesson. Use revision assignments.<br>Intervention Kit: Writing and Grammar |
| **PHONICS AND SPELLING**<br>Words with Long *a* | 0–2 items correct . . . | Online Practice: Go to **www.macmillanmh.com**.<br>Intervention Kit: Phonics/Word Study |
| **FLUENCY** | 55–60 WCPM | Fluency Solutions Audio CD |
| | 0–54 WCPM | Evaluate for Intervention |

## WRITE-ON-DEMAND SCORING RUBRIC

**PROMPT** **Why are green schools good for the environment? Write as much as you can as well as you can. Write for five minutes.**

| 4 Excellent | 3 Good | 2 Fair | 1 Unsatisfactory |
|---|---|---|---|
| • More than 7 sentences<br>• Almost no spelling or grammar errors<br>• Cohesive ideas, focused and organized | • 5–7 sentences<br>• A few spelling and grammar errors<br>• Well-developed ideas and facts provided | • 4–5 sentences<br>• Several spelling and grammar errors<br>• Some good information; some vague | • Fewer than 4 sentences<br>• Many spelling and grammar errors<br>• Few developed ideas or little accurate information |

## Daily Planner

| | |
|---|---|
| DAY 1 | • Prepare to Read<br>• Academic Language<br>• Vocabulary (Preteach) |
| DAY 2 | • Comprehension<br>• Practice Reader Lesson 1 |
| DAY 3 | • Phonics/Decoding<br>• Practice Reader Lesson 2 |
| DAY 4 | • Phonics/Decoding<br>• Vocabulary (Review)<br>• Practice Reader Lesson 3 |
| DAY 5 | • Fluency<br>• Self-Selected Reading |

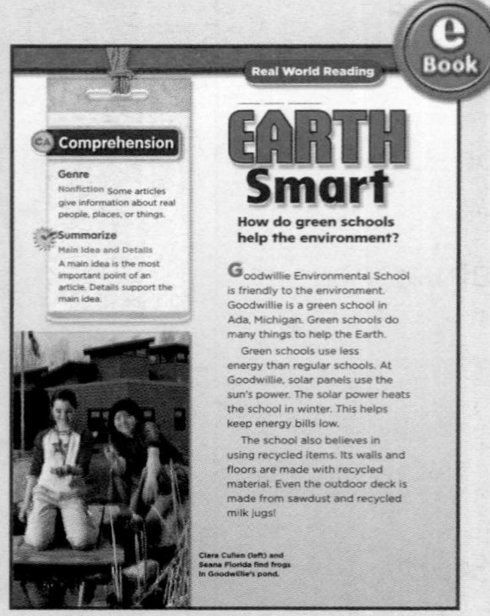


**StudentWorks Plus**

Strategic

# Approaching Level

## Prepare to Read

**Objective** Preview *Earth Smart*

**Materials** • **StudentWorks Plus** • self-stick notes

### PREVIEW TEXT

- Have students preview *Earth Smart* using **StudentWorks Plus**. This version of the Student Book contains oral summaries in multiple languages, on-line multilingual glossaries, word-by-word highlighting, and questions that assess and build comprehension.
- Remind students that listening carefully to and following along with the word-by-word reading will help them prepare for the reading of the selection with the class. Ask students to place self-stick notes on any challenging words or places that confuse them. Discuss these with students prior to the reading of the selection with the rest of the class.
- Ask students to write three or four sentences in their Writer's Notebooks telling what they learned about environmentally friendly or green schools.

## Academic Language

**Objective** Teach academic language

**Materials** • none

### PRETEACH LANGUAGE OF INSTRUCTION

Tell students that there are many important lesson words you will be using this week. You want them to become familiar with these words *before* the lessons. These words also appear in the directions of the tests they will be taking this year.

Preteach the following academic words: *main idea, details, stated, summarize, thesaurus, synonyms, cause, effect*.

- Define each word using student-friendly language. Tell students that *details* are sentences that tell more about a topic or main idea. For example, if the main idea is *Green schools are better for the environment*, a detail could be *Green schools use recycled materials to build their walls and floors.*
- In addition, relate each word to known words. For example, connect *main idea* to *point of article, summarize* to *retell, thesaurus* to *book of synonyms*, *synonyms* to *similar, cause* to *reason,* and *effect* to *result.*
- Highlight these words when used throughout the week and reinforce their meanings.

Strategic

# Approaching Level

## Phonics/Decoding

**Objective** Decode words with long *a*

**Materials**
- **Approaching Reproducible,** page 33
- **Sound-Spelling WorkBoards**

TESTED SKILL

### PHONICS MAINTENANCE

- Distribute a **WorkBoard** to each student. Say a sound previously taught, including the short vowel sounds and long *a*. Have students find the **Sound-Spelling Card** on the board for each sound.
- Review the spelling(s) for each sound by providing a sample word containing that spelling. Guide students to write the word on the board. Model how to segment the word and write the spelling for each sound, as needed. In addition, point out spelling hints, such as that the *ay* spelling for long *a* only appears at the end of a word or syllable.
- Dictate the following words for students to spell: *mat, rush, send, sick, dime, stop, tray, rain, lake*. Write the word on the board and have students self-correct their work.

### RETEACH SKILL

CA CONTENT STANDARD R 3.1.2 Decode regular multisyllabic words.

**Long *a*** Point to the long *a* Sound-Spelling Card on the WorkBoard and review the spellings for this sound. State each spelling and provide a sample word.

- Write the words below on the board. Model how to decode the first word in each row, then guide students as they decode the remaining words. For the multisyllabic words, divide the words into syllables using the syllable-scoop procedure to help students read one syllable at a time.
- When completed, point to the words in random order for students to chorally read. Repeat several times.

| | | | | | |
|---|---|---|---|---|---|
| mad | made | cap | cape | tap | tape |
| say | stay | ray | tray | gray | stray |
| gain | grain | rain | train | paint | stain |
| head | bread | steak | sleigh | weigh | weight |
| pay | paying | rain | rained | brain | brains |
| day | today | raise | raised | take | taking |

**Sound-Spelling WorkBoard**

### English Learners

UNIVERSAL ACCESS

**Minimal Contrasts** Focus on articulation. Make the /a/ sound and point out your mouth position. Have students repeat. Use the articulation photos on the small Sound-Spelling Cards. Repeat each long a sound. Then have students say each sound together, noticing the slight difference in mouth position. Continue by having students read minimal contrast word pairs, such as *ray/pray, sat/spat, Sam/same, rain/sprain, lad/laid, bat/bait*.

### Approaching Reproducible, page 33

If a vowel says its own name, it is a long vowel. If a syllable has two vowels, they make the long sound of the first vowel. So words with the letters *ai* or *ay* will make the long *a* sound.

**Put the letters *ai* or *ay* in the blanks below to finish the sentences.**

1. I followed the t r _a_ _i_ l in the woods.
2. The wooden bridge began to s w _a_ _y_.
3. I moved as slowly as a s n _a_ _i_ l.
4. Anyone who p l _a_ _y_ s in the forest must be careful.

**Review the words with the long vowel pattern from last week. Write the missing vowel in the blanks.**

5. Growing r _i_ c _e_ takes a lot of rain.
6. I looked at the g l _o_ b _e_ to find China.

Strategic

# Approaching Level

## Vocabulary

**Objective** Preteach selection vocabulary

**Materials** • **Visual Vocabulary Resources** • **Approaching Reproducible,** p. 34

TESTED SKILL

### PRETEACH VOCABULARY

Use the **Visual Vocabulary Resources** to preteach the key selection words *donate, unaware, members,* and *contribute*. Focus on two words per day. Use the following routine that appears in detail on the cards.

- Define the word in English and provide the example given.
- Define the word in Spanish, if appropriate, and indicate if the word is a cognate.
- Display the picture and explain how it illustrates or demonstrates the word.
- Then engage students in structured partner-talk about the image, using the key word.
- Ask students to chorally say the word three times.
- Point out any known sound-spellings or focus on a key aspect of phonemic awareness related to the word.
- Distribute copies of the Vocabulary Glossary, **English Learner Resource Book**.

### REVIEW PREVIOUSLY TAUGHT VOCABULARY

Display the Vocabulary Cards from the previous two weeks. Say the meaning of each word, one by one, and have students identify it. Then point to words in random order for students to provide definitions and related words they know.

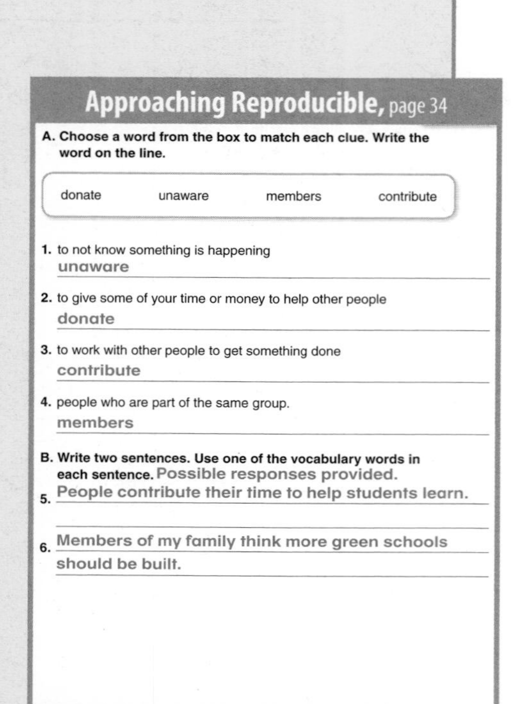
**Approaching Reproducible,** page 34

A. Choose a word from the box to match each clue. Write the word on the line.

donate unaware members contribute

1. to not know something is happening
unaware
2. to give some of your time or money to help other people
donate
3. to work with other people to get something done
contribute
4. people who are part of the same group.
members

B. Write two sentences. Use one of the vocabulary words in each sentence. Possible responses provided.

5. People contribute their time to help students learn.
6. Members of my family think more green schools should be built.

Strategic

# Approaching Level

## Vocabulary

**Objective** Review vocabulary and high-frequency words

**Materials** • **Vocabulary Cards** • **High-Frequency Word Cards**

### REVIEW VOCABULARY

**Review Words** Display the **Vocabulary Cards** *donate, unaware, members, contribute*. Point to each word, read it aloud, and have students chorally repeat.

Then complete with students the activities and questions below to provide additional practice for the vocabulary words.

- If you were raising money for a school garden project, how might you convince your family members to *donate*?
- Show us how the *members* of the writing team would look if their story won first place in the Young Author's Writing Contest.
- Describe a time you have been *unaware* of something.
- Which would be a way to *contribute*: swimming in the local pool, watching cartoons, going bowling or cleaning up trash around your neighborhood? Explain why.

### HIGH-FREQUENCY WORDS

**Top 250 Words** The ability to read accurately and effortlessly the most frequently used words in written English will help students develop reading fluency. Display **High-Frequency Word Cards 21–30**. Then do the following:

- Display one card at a time and ask students to chorally state each word.
- Have students spell each word aloud.
- Ask students to write each word in their Writer's Notebooks as they state aloud each letter. Then have them read the word again.
- When completed, quickly flip through the word card set as students chorally read the words.
- Provide opportunities for students to use the words in speaking and writing. For example, provide sentence starters such as *I like to read because* ________ for oral and written practice. Or, point to a word card and ask a question such as *What word means the opposite of this word?* (when pointing to the *big* word card).
- Continue the routine throughout the week.

### Word Webs

Have students create word webs in their Writer's Notebooks for each vocabulary word. Have students brainstorm related words. Have them add other words, phrases, and illustrations.

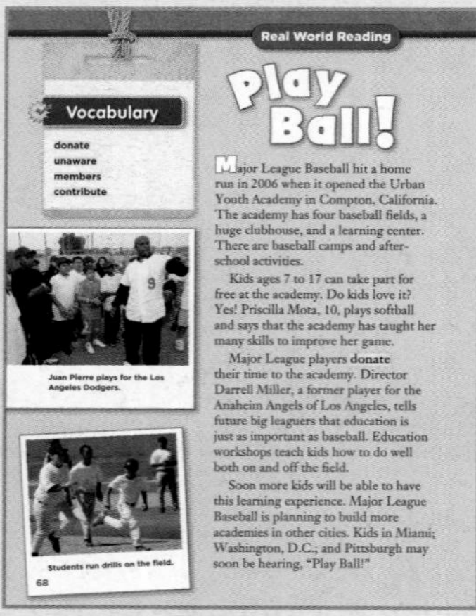
Real World Reading

Play Ball!

Vocabulary
donate
unaware
members
contribute

Major League Baseball hit a home run in 2006 when it opened the Urban Youth Academy in Compton, California. The academy has four baseball fields, a huge clubhouse, and a learning center. There are baseball camps and after-school activities.

Kids ages 7 to 17 can take part for free at the academy. Do kids love it? Yes! Priscilla Mota, 10, plays softball and says that the academy has taught her many skills to improve her game.

Major League players **donate** their time to the academy. Director Darrell Miller, a former player for the Anaheim Angels of Los Angeles, tells future big leaguers that education is just as important as baseball. Education workshops teach kids how to do well both on and off the field.

Soon more kids will be able to have this learning experience. Major League Baseball is planning to build more academies in other cities. Kids in Miami; Washington, D.C.; and Pittsburgh may soon be hearing, "Play Ball!"

Juan Pierre plays for the Los Angeles Dodgers.

Students run drills on the field.

68

**Student Book**

## Corrective Feedback

Read each paragraph aloud with students. Ask: *What is this paragraph mostly about?* Underline the details in the paragraph and circle the main idea. Guide students to understand how each detail relates to the main idea.

Strategic

# Approaching Level

## Comprehension

**Objective** Reteach summarize and main idea/details

**Materials** • **Student Book:** "Play Ball!"

STRATEGY

### RETEACH STRATEGY: SUMMARIZE

- **Define** Explain to students that a summary is a brief retelling of the most important ideas and details of a selection.

  Discuss the similarities between a *summary* and *previews* for movies. Point out that a preview briefly describes and shows the most important information about the movie. A preview usually introduces the characters and includes important scenes that tell what the movie is mostly about. In this same way, a summary tells about the most important events, facts, and ideas in a selection.
- **Relate to Real Life** Ask students to think about their favorite movie. Tell them to write a script for a movie preview. They should include only the most important information that introduces the characters and describes the movie; that is a summary.
- **Set Purpose** Remind students that good readers pay careful attention to the details in a selection. Identifying the most important message of a selection and the details that support that message helps readers better understand and remember a selection. Tell them they can use their own words to summarize.

TESTED SKILL

### RETEACH SKILL: MAIN IDEA AND DETAILS

CA CONTENT STANDARD R 3.2.5 Distinguish the main idea and supporting details in expository text.

- **Define** Tell students that the main idea is what a picture, a paragraph, or a section of text is mostly about. Details are the ideas that tell about the main idea.
- **Relate to Real Life** Choose and display a Visual Vocabulary Resource Card. Tell the main idea of the photograph or picture. Then point out the details in the picture that tell about that main idea. Display another card. Help students identify the main idea of the picture and the details that tell about the picture.
- **Set Purpose** Remind students that good readers look for the main ideas and details in text as they read. This helps them better remember the events in a selection. Point out that sometimes the main idea is stated in or near the first sentence of a paragraph.
- **Apply** Guide students to identify the main idea and the details of "Play Ball" Then help them use the main idea and details to create a summary. Explain that students should use their own words to tell summary. Tell students they will apply this strategy and skill to a simpler text in *Jay Beckwith and Julia Morgan: Two Builders.*

Strategic

# Approaching Level

## Practice Reader Lesson 1

**Objective** Read to apply skills and strategies

**Materials**
- **Practice Reader:** *Jay Beckwith and Julia Morgan: Two Builders*
- **Approaching Reproducible,** p. 36

Practice Reader

### BEFORE READING

**Preview and Predict** Have students read the title and preview the first chapter. Ask students to make predictions about the main idea of this section. Students should note any questions they have before they read.

**Review Vocabulary Words** Have students read the vocabulary words on the inside front cover. Briefly define each and ask students to state related words they have learned.

**Set a Purpose for Reading** *Let's read to find out who Jay Beckwith and Julia Morgan are, what they built, and why they're important.*

### DURING READING

**STRATEGY**
**SUMMARIZE**

Remind students that a summary is a short statement of the most important ideas in a selection.

**SKILL**
**MAIN IDEA AND DETAILS**

Remind students to think about the most important information they are learning as they read. Read Chapter 1 with students. Help students complete the Main Idea and Details Chart.

As you read, help students decode unknown words. In addition, ask open-ended questions to facilitate rich discussion, such as *What is going on in this chapter? What's the big idea the author is trying to get across about Jay Beckwith?* Build on students' responses to develop deeper understanding of the text.

Stop after each two pages and ask students to summarize the information they read to check their understanding before reading on. If they struggle, help students reread the difficult pages or passage. Then model determining the main idea of the chapter.

### AFTER READING

Ask students to compare what they know about green schools to what they just read about the two builders. *How are their designs similar to green schools? How do they differ?* Have students comment on what they found interesting about the builders.

Practice Reader

## Corrective Feedback

Throughout the lessons, provide feedback based on students' responses. If the answer is correct, ask another question. If the answer is tentative, restate key information to assist the student. If the answer is wrong, provide corrective feedback such as hints or clues, refer to a visual such as a Sound-Spelling Card or story illustration, or probe with questions to help the student clarify any misunderstanding.

Strategic

# Approaching Level

## Practice Reader Lesson 2

**Objective** Reread to apply skills and strategies and develop fluency

**Materials**
- **Practice Reader:** *Jay Beckwith and Julia Morgan: Two Builders*
- **Approaching Reproducible,** p. 37

### BEFORE READING

**Review Strategy and Skill** Review students' completed Main Idea and Details Charts from the first read. Remind students that the main idea is the most important idea in a passage or text. A summary includes the main ideas from the book.

**Review Vocabulary Words** Have students search the book for each vocabulary word. Ask students to read aloud the sentence containing the word and state the word's definition or provide related words. Ask students to use a thesaurus to generate synonyms they could use to better understand the meaning of the words.

**Set a Purpose for Reading** *Let's reread to check our understanding of the information in the book and to work on our reading fluency.*

### DURING READING

Reread *Jay Beckwith and Julia Morgan: Two Builders* with students. Have them read silently two pages at a time, or read aloud to a partner. Stop and have students summarize before reading the next two pages. Model oral summaries, as needed.

### AFTER READING

**Check Comprehension** Have partners complete the Comprehension Check on page 16. Review students' answers. Help students find evidence for their answers in the text.

**Model Fluency** Model reading the fluency passage on **Approaching Reproducible**, page 37. Tell students to pay close attention to your pacing, or speed, as you read. Then read one sentence at a time and have students echo-read the sentences, copying your pacing.

During independent reading time, have students work with a partner using the fluency passage. One student reads aloud, while the other repeats each sentence back. If students need additional support, have them listen to the "practice speed" version of the passage on the **Fluency Solutions Audio CD**.

Strategic

# Approaching Level

## Practice Reader Lesson 3

**Objective** Build fluency

**Materials** • **Practice Reader:** *Jay Beckwith and Julia Morgan: Two Builders*

### FOCUS ON FLUENCY

CA CONTENT STANDARD
R 3.1.3
Read aloud narrative and expository text fluently and accurately and with appropriate pacing, intonation, and expression.

**Timed Reading** Tell students that they will be doing a final timed reading of the fluency passage that they have been practicing. With each student, follow these directions:

- Place the passage facedown.
- When you say "Go," the student begins reading the passage aloud.
- When you say "Stop," the student stops reading the passage.

As they read, note words students mispronounce and their overall pace. Stop after one minute. Help students record and graph the number of words they read correctly.

### REREAD PREVIOUSLY READ BOOKS

- Distribute copies of the past **Practice Readers**. Have students select two to reread. Tell them that rereading these books will help them develop their skills. The more times they read the same words, the quicker they will learn these words. This will make the reading of other books easier.
- Circulate and listen in as students read. Stop students periodically and ask them how they are figuring out difficult words and how they are monitoring their comprehension. Note students who need additional work with specific decoding or comprehension skills.
- Encourage students to read other previously read Practice Readers during independent reading time or for homework.

### Meet Grade-Level Expectations

As an alternative to this day's lesson, guide students through a reading of the On Level Practice Reader. See page 77CC. Since both books contain the same vocabulary, phonics, and comprehension skills, the scaffolding you provided will help most students gain access to this more challenging text.

### Book Talk

See page 77PP. Students will work with peers of varying language abilities to discuss this week's Practice Readers.

Real World Reading

Comprehension

Genre
Nonfiction Some articles give information about real people, places, or things.

Summarize
Main Idea and Details
A main idea is the most important point of an article. Details support the main idea.

EARTH Smart

How do green schools help the environment?

Goodwillie Environmental School is friendly to the environment. Goodwillie is a green school in Ada, Michigan. Green schools do many things to help the Earth.

Green schools use less energy than regular schools. At Goodwillie, solar panels use the sun's power. The solar power heats the school in winter. This helps keep energy bills low.

The school also believes in using recycled items. Its walls and floors are made with recycled material. Even the outdoor deck is made from sawdust and recycled milk jugs!

Clara Cullen (left) and Seana Florida find frogs in Goodwillie's pond.

70

Student Book

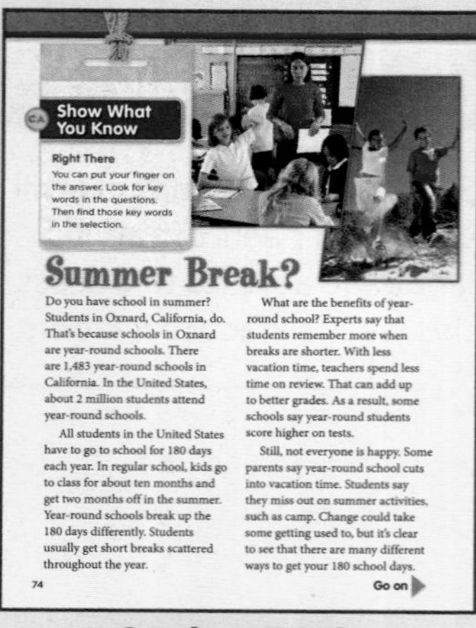
Show What You Know

Right There
You can put your finger on the answer. Look for key words in the questions. Then find those key words in the selection.

Summer Break?

Do you have school in summer? Students in Oxnard, California, do. That's because schools in Oxnard are year-round schools. There are 1,483 year-round schools in California. In the United States, about 2 million students attend year-round schools.

All students in the United States have to go to school for 180 days each year. In regular school, kids go to class for about ten months and get two months off in the summer. Year-round schools break up the 180 days differently. Students usually get short breaks scattered throughout the year.

What are the benefits of year-round school? Experts say that students remember more when breaks are shorter. With less vacation time, teachers spend less time on review. That can add up to better grades. As a result, some schools say year-round students score higher on tests.

Still, not everyone is happy. Some parents say year-round school cuts into vacation time. Students say they miss out on summer activities, such as camp. Change could take some getting used to, but it's clear to see that there are many different ways to get your 180 school days.

74

Go on

Student Book

## Decodable Text

Use the Reading *Triumphs* Anthology and the decodable stories in the **Teacher's Resource Book** to help students build fluency with basic decoding patterns.

Strategic

# Approaching Level

## Fluency

**Objectives** Reread selections to develop fluency; develop speaking skills

**Materials** • **Student Book:** *Earth Smart*, "Summer Break?"

### REREAD FOR FLUENCY

- Have students reread a portion of *Earth Smart*. Suggest that they focus on one to two of their favorite paragraphs from the selection. Work with students to read the pages with the appropriate pace.
- Provide time for students to read their sections of text to you. Comment on their pace and provide corrective feedback by modeling proper fluency.

### DEVELOP SPEAKING/LISTENING SKILLS

- Have students practice reading the last two paragraphs of the test strategy passage "Summer Break?"
- Work with students to read the prose aloud with fluency and appropriate pace. Model reading a few sentences at a time. Use expression to make the reading interesting. Ask students to repeat the sentences copying both your expression and pace.
- Have students work with a partner to take turns reading aloud the last two paragraphs of "Summer Break?" Tell them to concentrate on using appropriate speed and expression. Ask them to discuss how their partner paced the reading appropriately to add meaning to the selection.
- Tell students to work with their partners. After one student has read a paragraph, the second one retells or paraphrases what the speaker has just said.

**CA CONTENT STANDARD LAS 3.1.1** Retell, paraphrase, and explain what has been said by a speaker.

Strategic

# Approaching Level

## Self-Selected Reading

**Objective** Read independently to identify main idea and supporting details

**Materials** • **Classroom Library** • other nonfiction books

### APPLY SKILLS TO INDEPENDENT READING

- Have students choose a nonfiction book for independent reading. (See the **Theme Bibliography** on pages T8–T9 for book suggestions.) Remind them that the main idea is what the book is mostly about. The details provide more information about the main idea. Ask students to read their books and record the main idea and supporting details on a Main Idea and Details Chart.
- After reading, ask students to use their Main Idea and Details Chart to write or orally state a summary of the book. Provide time for students to share their summaries and comment on their reactions to the book. Ask: *What was the most interesting fact you learned from this selection? Would you like to learn more about this topic? Why or why not?*

Classroom Library

## Daily Planner

| | |
|---|---|
| DAY 1 | • Vocabulary |
| DAY 2 | • Phonics |
| DAY 3 | • Practice Reader Lesson 1 |
| DAY 4 | • Practice Reader Lesson 2<br>• Fluency |
| DAY 5 | • Self-Selected Reading |

Sound-Spelling WorkBoard

Benchmark

# On Level

## Vocabulary

**Objective** Review vocabulary

**Materials** • **Vocabulary Cards**

TESTED SKILL

### REVIEW PREVIOUSLY TAUGHT WORDS

**Review Words** Display the **Vocabulary Cards** *donate, unaware, members,* and *contribute*. Point to each word, read it aloud, and have students chorally repeat.

Then ask students the following questions. Have them answer to provide additional practice for the vocabulary words.

- What charity would you like to *donate* time or money to? Why?
- If one of the *members* of our class was having trouble understanding a math problem, how would you help them?
- What situations, things, or words come to mind when you think about the word *unaware*?
- What kinds of things can you do to *contribute* to your community?

## Phonics/Word Study

**Objective** Decode multisyllabic words with long *a*

**Materials** • **Sound-Spelling WorkBoards**

TESTED SKILL

### RETEACH SKILL

CA CONTENT STANDARD R 3.1.2 Decode regular multisyllabic words.

CA CONTENT STANDARD R 3.1.1 Know and use complex word families when reading to decode unfamiliar words.

- **Long *a* Words** Point to the long *a* **Sound-Spelling Card** on the **WorkBoard** and review the spellings for this sound. State each spelling and provide a sample word.
- Write the words below on the board. If necessary, divide the words into syllables using the syllable-scoop procedure to help students read one syllable at a time. When completed, point to the words in random order for students to chorally read.

| | | | | |
|---|---|---|---|---|
| maybe | away | birthday | player | always |
| playful | raindrop | painful | rainbow | braided |
| explain | escape | steakhouse | neighbor | eighteen |

- **Spelling** Dictate the following words for students to spell on their WorkBoards: *rainfall, praised, payment, became, eighty*. Guide students to use the Sound-Spelling Cards and model how to segment words, such as spelling a word syllable by syllable.

Benchmark

# On Level

## Fluency

**Objectives** Reread selections to develop fluency; develop speaking skills

**Materials** • **Student Book:** *Earth Smart*, "Summer Break?"

### REREAD FOR FLUENCY

- Have students reread *Earth Smart*. Work with students to read with the appropriate pace. Model as needed.
- Provide time for students to read a section of text to you. Comment on their pace and provide corrective feedback.

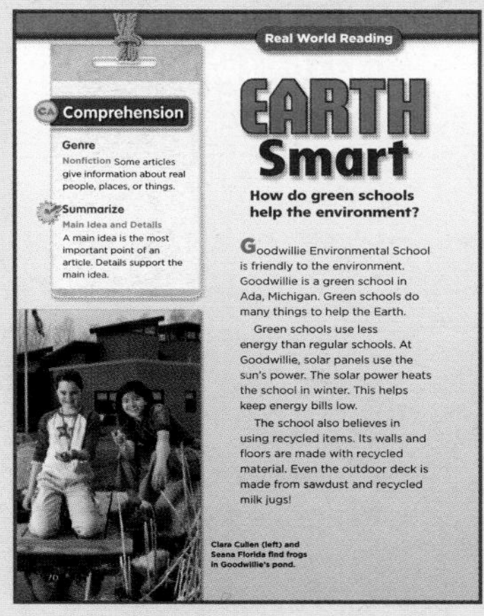

Student Book

### DEVELOP SPEAKING/LISTENING SKILLS

**CA CONTENT STANDARD LAS 3.1.1** Retell, paraphrase, and explain what has been said by a speaker. Appropriate intonation and vocal patterns to emphasize important passages of the text being read.

- Have students practice reading the first two paragraphs of "Summer Break?"
- Work with students to read with appropriate pace. Model reading a few sentences. Use expression to make the reading interesting. Ask students to copy your pace as they repeat the sentences.
- Have students work with a partner to read aloud the first two paragraphs of "Summer Break?" Tell them to concentrate on using appropriate speed and expression. Discuss how using appropriate speed helped them better understand the selection.
- After students have finished reading, have them take turns retelling or paraphrasing what the other one read, using clear and specific vocabulary to communicate ideas.

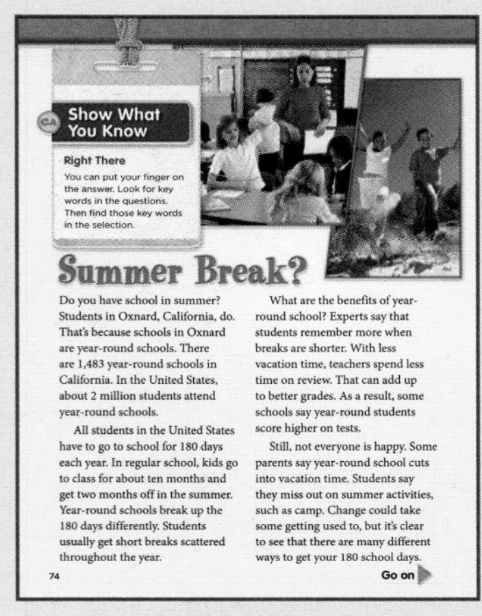

Student Book

## Self-Selected Reading

**Objective** Read independently to identify main idea and supporting details

**Materials** • **Classroom Library** • other nonfiction books

### APPLY SKILLS TO INDEPENDENT READING

- Have students choose a nonfiction book for independent reading. (See the **Theme Bibliography** on pages T8–T9 for book suggestions.) Remind them that the main idea is what the book is mostly about. Details tell more about the main idea. Ask students to read their books and record the main idea and supporting details on a Main Idea and Details Chart.
- After reading, ask students to use their Main Idea and Details Chart to write a summary of the book. Provide time for students to share their summaries with the class. Ask: *What was the most interesting fact you learned from this selection? Would you like to learn more about this topic? Why or why not?*

Classroom Library

Practice Reader

Benchmark

# On Level

## Practice Reader Lesson 1

**Objective** Read to apply strategies and skills

**Materials**
- **Practice Reader:** *Jay Beckwith and Julia Morgan: Two Builders*
- **Practice Book,** p. 36

### BEFORE READING

CA CONTENT STANDARD R 3.2.4 Recall major points in the text and make and modify predictions about forthcoming information.

**Preview and Predict** Have students read the title and preview the book by reading the chapter titles and looking at the photographs. Ask students to predict what this book is about and the types of information they might learn.

**Review Vocabulary Words** Have students read the vocabulary words on the inside front cover. Ask them to state related words they have learned. Review definitions, as needed.

**Set a Purpose for Reading** *Let's read to find out who Jay Beckwith and Julia Morgan are and what they've built.*

### DURING READING

**STRATEGY**
**SUMMARIZE**

Remind students that a summary tells the most important ideas in a passage or text.

**SKILL**
**MAIN IDEA AND DETAILS**

CA CONTENT STANDARD R 3.2.5 Distinguish the main idea and supporting details in expository text.

Remind students that the main idea in a selection is the important idea or topic that the author wants readers to focus on. The details give the reader additional information about the main idea.

Read Chapter 1 with students. Ask open-ended questions to facilitate rich discussion, such as *What is the author telling us about these two builders? What does the author want us to know about Jay Beckwith and Julia Morgan?* Build on students' responses to help them develop a deeper understanding of the text. Have them fill in the first section of the Main Idea and Details Chart. Then have them continue reading.

**Synonyms** As they read, have students generate synonyms for this week's new vocabulary words to help them better understand the meanings. Tell students they can use a thesaurus if needed.

### AFTER READING

Ask students to think about *Earth Smart* and *Jay Beckwith and Julia Morgan: Two Builders*. Ask: *How are their designs similar to the green schools mentioned in* Earth Smart*? How are they different? Explain.*

Benchmark

# On Level

## Practice Reader Lesson 2

**Objective** Reread to apply skills and strategies and develop fluency

**Materials**
- **Practice Reader:** *Jay Beckwith and Julia Morgan: Two Builders*
- **Practice Book,** p. 37

**Practice Reader**

### BEFORE READING

**Review Strategy and Skill** Review students' completed Main Idea and Details Charts from the first read. Remind them that the main idea is what a selection is mostly about. Supporting details provide additional information about the main idea.

A summary includes the main ideas from the book. If students' summaries are incomplete, provide a model summary or use a student summary and revise it as a group. Have students copy the revised summary in their Writer's Notebooks.

**Set a Purpose for Reading** *Let's reread to check our understanding of the information in the book and to work on our reading fluency.*

### DURING READING

Reread *Jay Beckwith and Julia Morgan: Two Builders* with students. Have them read silently two pages at a time, or read aloud to a partner. Stop and have students summarize before reading the next two pages. Model oral summaries as needed.

### AFTER READING

**Check Comprehension** Have partners complete the Comprehension Check on page 16. Review students' answers. Help them find evidence for their answers in the text.

**Model Fluency** Model reading the fluency passage on **Practice Book**, page 37. Tell students to pay close attention to your pace, or speed, as you read. Then read one sentence at a time and have students echo-read the sentences, copying your pace.

During independent reading time, have students work with a partner using the fluency passage. One student reads aloud while the other repeats each sentence back. If students need additional support, have them listen to the "practice speed" version of the passage on the **Fluency Solutions Audio CD**.

### Book Talk

See page 77PP. Students will work with peers of varying language abilities to discuss this week's Practice Readers.

### Practice Book, page 37

**As I read, I will pay attention to pacing.**

Charlie called Emma. "I've got a problem," he told her
10 as soon as she picked up the phone. "How can I show my
23 mom I can take care of a pet?"
31 "Hmmm…," said Emma. "What if you did some
39 research on pets?"
42 "Yeah, I could do that," he said.
49 "Listen," Emma said. "Lucy needs a bath. She keeps
58 scratching her fur, and I'm worried that she has fleas. Let's
69 talk about this tomorrow, okay?"
74 Charlie called Josh. Josh said, "I can't talk. I'm feeding
84 Prince. I can't believe this dog's appetite! If I don't get this
96 food in his bowl, I'm afraid he's going to cook for himself." 108

**Comprehension Check**

1. What is Charlie's problem? **Problem and Solution** Charlie has to show his mom that he is responsible enough to take care of a pet.
2. Why can't Charlie's friends talk with him about his problem? **Plot** Charlie's friends are busy taking care of their pets.

| | Words Read | – | Number of Errors | = | Words Correct Score |
|---|---|---|---|---|---|
| First Read | | – | | = | |
| Second Read | | – | | = | |

## Daily Planner

| | |
|---|---|
| DAY 1 | • Practice Reader Lesson 1 |
| DAY 2 | • Practice Reader Lesson 2 |
| DAY 3 | • Phonics |
| DAY 4 | • Vocabulary<br>• Fluency |
| DAY 5 | • Self-Selected Reading |

Advanced

# Beyond Level

## Phonics/Word Study

**Objective** Decode multisyllabic words with long *a*

**Materials** • **Sound-Spelling WorkBoards**

TESTED SKILL

### EXTEND/ACCELERATE

CA CONTENT STANDARD R 3.1.2 Decode regular multisyllabic words.

- **Read Multisyllabic Words with Long *a*** Write the words below on the board. Challenge students to read the words, using known word parts. When completed, point to the words in random order for students to chorally read.

| | | | |
|---|---|---|---|
| runaway | mainland | bricklayer | hurricane |
| available | undertake | underway | candidate |
| overpay | layover | weightless | neighborhood |
| holiday | investigate | entertain | faithful |

- **Define Words** Ask students to use their knowledge of word parts to figure out the meanings of the above words. Then have partners find the words in a dictionary and confirm or revise the meanings. Challenge students to use these words in this week's writing assignments.
- **Spell Long *a* Words** Dictate the following words for students to spell on their **WorkBoards**: *escape, outbreak, explaining, yesterday, safety, eighteen*. Write the words for students to self-correct.

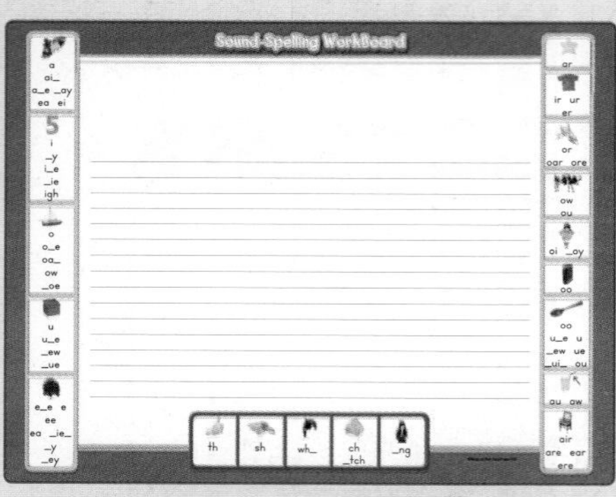

**Sound-Spelling WorkBoard**

## Vocabulary

**Objectives** Elaborate concept of helping the environment; create advertisements

**Materials** • none

TESTED SKILL

### ENRICH VOCABULARY

- **Elaborate On the Concept** Discuss with students the concept of green schools presented in *Earth Smart*. Ask them to describe how these schools help the environment. Then tell them they are going to create their own environmental group. Brainstorm a list of ways their groups can take care of the environment, such as recycling, picking up trash, or using less electricity and water.
- **Create Advertisements** Explain to students that they must recruit new members for their environmental group. Challenge them to write an advertisement that describes the purpose of their group, using clear and specific words to communicate ideas. They must also use this week's vocabulary words and descriptive language. Have them orally present their advertisements.

Advanced

# Beyond Level

## Fluency

**Objectives** Reread selections to develop fluency; develop speaking skills

**Materials** • **Student Book:** *Earth Smart*, "Summer Break?"

### REREAD FOR FLUENCY

CA CONTENT STANDARD **R 3.1.3** Read aloud narrative and expository text fluently and accurately and with appropriate pacing, intonation, and expression.

- Have students reread "Summer Break?" Work with them to read the passage with the appropriate pace.
- Provide time for students to read a section of the passage to you. Comment on their pace and provide corrective feedback.

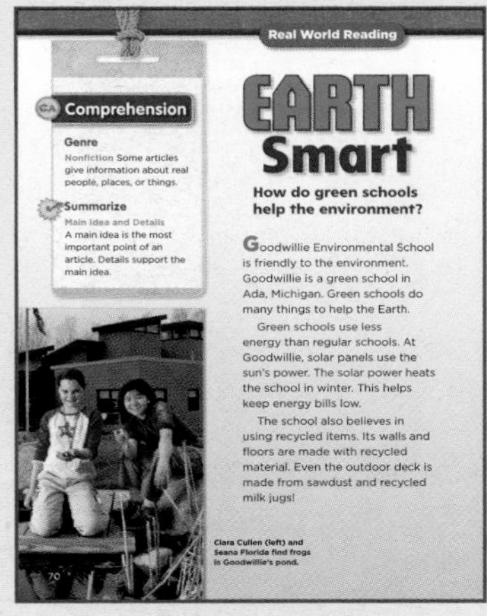
Real World Reading

Comprehension

Genre
Nonfiction Some articles give information about real people, places, or things.

Summarize
Main Idea and Details
A main idea is the most important point of an article. Details support the main idea.

EARTH Smart

How do green schools help the environment?

Goodwillie Environmental School is friendly to the environment. Goodwillie is a green school in Ada, Michigan. Green schools do many things to help the Earth.

Green schools use less energy than regular schools. At Goodwillie, solar panels use the sun's power. The solar power heats the school in winter. This helps keep energy bills low.

The school also believes in using recycled items. Its walls and floors are made with recycled material. Even the outdoor deck is made from sawdust and recycled milk jugs!

Clara Cullen (left) and Seana Florida find frogs in Goodwillie's pond.

70

**Student Book**

### DEVELOP SPEAKING/LISTENING SKILLS

- Have students practice reading the first two pages of *Earth Smart*.
- Ask them to explain the importance of pace, or speed, while reading. Have them describe times when they may increase or decrease their pace.
- Have students work with a partner to read aloud the first two pages of *Earth Smart*. Ask them to concentrate on using appropriate speed and expression. Have students discuss how their partner used appropriate pace to add meaning to the selection.
- After students have finished reading, have them take turns asking each other questions about what they read and responding to the questions with appropriate elaboration.

CA CONTENT STANDARD **LAS 3.1.3** Respond to questions with appropriate elaboration.

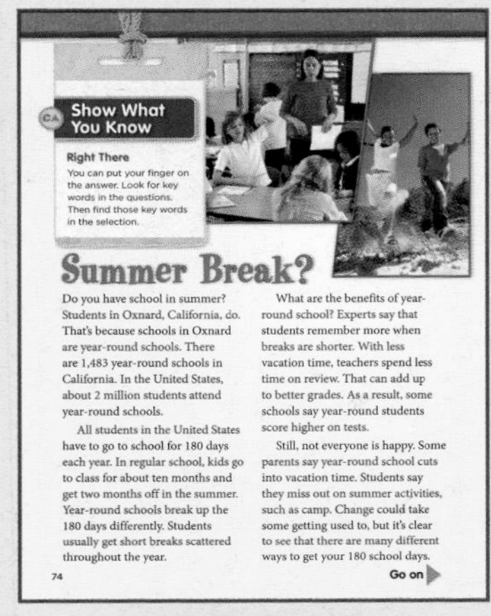
Show What You Know

Right There
You can put your finger on the answer. Look for key words in the questions. Then find those key words in the selection.

Summer Break?

Do you have school in summer? Students in Oxnard, California, do. That's because schools in Oxnard are year-round schools. There are 1,483 year-round schools in California. In the United States, about 2 million students attend year-round schools.

All students in the United States have to go to school for 180 days each year. In regular school, kids go to class for about ten months and get two months off in the summer. Year-round schools break up the 180 days differently. Students usually get short breaks scattered throughout the year.

What are the benefits of year-round school? Experts say that students remember more when breaks are shorter. With less vacation time, teachers spend less time on review. That can add up to better grades. As a result, some schools say year-round students score higher on tests.

Still, not everyone is happy. Some parents say year-round school cuts into vacation time. Students say they miss out on summer activities, such as camp. Change could take some getting used to, but it's clear to see that there are many different ways to get your 180 school days.

74

Go on

**Student Book**

## Self-Selected Reading

**Objective** Read independently to identify the main idea and supporting details of a selection

**Materials** • **Classroom Library** • other nonfiction books

### APPLY SKILLS TO INDEPENDENT READING

- Have students choose a nonfiction book for independent reading. (See the **Theme Bibliography** on pages T8–T9 for book suggestions.) Have students read their books and write down the main idea and important supporting details.
- After reading, ask students to use their main idea and details list to write a summary of the book. Provide time for students to share their summaries and comment on their reactions to the book. Ask: *What was the most interesting fact you learned from this selection? Would you like to learn more about this topic? Why or why not?*

**Classroom Library**

Practice Reader

Advanced

# Beyond Level

## Practice Reader Lesson 1

**Objective** Read to apply strategies and skills

**Materials**
- **Practice Reader:** *Jay Beckwith and Julia Morgan: Two Builders*
- **Beyond Reproducible,** p. 36

### BEFORE READING

CA CONTENT STANDARD R 3.2.4 Recall major points in the text and make and modify predictions about forthcoming information.

**Preview and Predict** Have students preview the book by reading the title and chapter titles and looking at the photographs. Ask them to predict what this book is about and the types of information they might learn.

**Review Vocabulary Words** Have students read the vocabulary words on the inside front cover. Ask them to state each definition and any related words they have learned.

**Set a Purpose for Reading** *Let's read to find out who Jay Beckwith and Julia Morgan are, what they built, and why they are important.*

### DURING READING

**STRATEGY**
**SUMMARIZE**

Ask students to explain what it means to create a *summary*. Remind them that a summary briefly restates the most important ideas in a passage or text.

**SKILL**
**MAIN IDEA AND DETAILS**

CA CONTENT STANDARD R 3.2.5 Distinguish the main idea and supporting details in expository text.

Ask students to define the terms *main idea* and *details*. Remind them that the main idea in a selection is the most important idea or topic that the writer wants to focus on. Details support and give more information about the main idea.

Read the book with students. Ask open-ended questions to facilitate rich discussion, such as *What does the author say about Playspaces? Does the author say it clearly?* Build on students' responses to help them develop a deeper understanding of the text. Have them fill in the Main Idea and Details Chart independently as they read.

### AFTER READING

Ask students to think about *Earth Smart* and *Jay Beckwith and Julia Morgan: Two Builders*. Ask: *How are Jay Beckwith's and Julia Morgan's designs similar to green schools? How are they different? Explain. Which is better for the environment? Why or why not?*

Advanced

# Beyond Level

## Practice Reader Lesson 2

**Objective** Reread to apply skills and strategies and develop fluency

**Materials**
- **Practice Reader:** *Jay Beckwith and Julia Morgan: Two Builders*
- **Beyond Reproducible,** p. 37

### BEFORE READING

**Review Strategy and Skill** Review students' completed Main Idea and Details Charts from the first read.

Remind students that a summary includes the main ideas from the book. If students' summaries are incomplete, provide a model summary or use a student summary and revise it as a group. Have students copy the revised summary in their Writer's Notebooks.

**Set a Purpose for Reading** *Let's reread to check our understanding of the information in the book and work on our reading fluency.*

### DURING READING

Have students read *Jay Beckwith and Julia Morgan: Two Builders* silently or with a partner. If reading in pairs, prompt students to stop every two pages and summarize or ask their partner probing questions.

### AFTER READING

**Check Comprehension** Have students independently complete the Comprehension Check on page 16. Review students' answers. Help students find evidence for their answers in the text.

**Model Fluency** Model reading the fluency passage on **Beyond Reproducible**, page 37. Tell students to pay close attention to your pace, or speed, as you read. Then read one sentence at a time and have students echo-read the sentences, copying your pace.

During independent reading time, have students work with a partner using the fluency passage. One student reads aloud while the other repeats each sentence back. Students can check their fluency by reading along with the "expert speed" version of the passage on the **Fluency Solutions Audio CD**.

**Practice Reader**

### Book Talk

See page 77PP. Students will work with peers of varying language abilities to discuss this week's Practice Readers.

### Beyond Reproducible, page 37

**As I read, I will pay attention to pacing.**

Dan didn't mind reading the textbook, but sometimes
8 he wished he could get out of his seat and do something.
20 In Mr. Horatio's class, the class did experiments during
29 science all the time. Dan had heard that they were going
40 to have an ant farm in their classroom this month.
50 Now Mr. Cruz was saying, "This week we are going to
61 focus on animal groups and animal adaptations. Does
69 anyone know what an adaptation is?"
75 Dan looked around the room. He could see that the
85 other kids were about as excited as he was. "If only
96 Mr. Cruz had props to make his ideas come alive," thought
107 Dan. If Dan were leading the class, he would start by
118 holding up a chameleon or something.
124 He would say, "Did you know this chameleon can
133 change the color of its skin?" 139

**Comprehension Check**

1. What is Dan's problem? **Problem and Solution** Dan wishes that Mr. Cruz would make class more interesting and have more experiments.
2. What does Dan mean when he says that the other kids are about as excited as he was? **Make Inferences** Dan means that the other students were bored.

| | Words Read | – | Number of Errors | = | Words Correct Score |
|---|---|---|---|---|---|
| First Read | | – | | = | |
| Second Read | | – | | = | |

## Daily Planner

| | |
|---|---|
| DAY 1 | • Build Background Knowledge<br>• Vocabulary |
| DAY 2 | • Vocabulary<br>• Access to Core Content<br>*Earth Smart* |
| DAY 3 | • Vocabulary<br>• Grammar<br>• Access to Core Content<br>*Earth Smart* |
| DAY 4 | • Vocabulary<br>• Writing/Spelling<br>• Access to Core Content<br>"Summer Break?" |
| DAY 5 | • Vocabulary<br>• Practice Reader<br>*Jay Beckwith: Artist, Inventor, Builder*<br>• Self-Selected Reading |

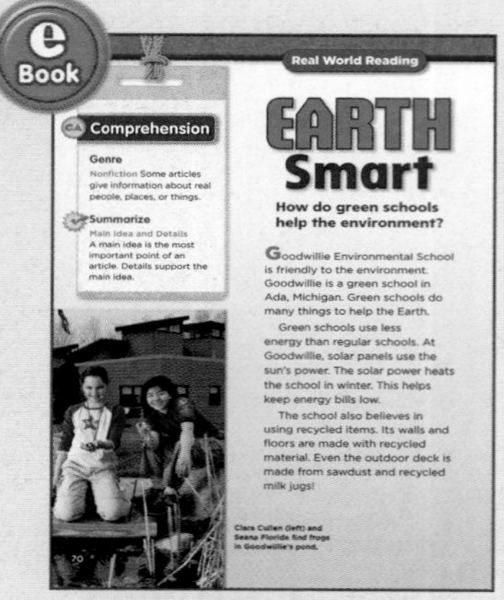

StudentWorks Plus

# English Learners

## Prepare to Read

**Content Objective** Describe how green schools help the environment

**Language Objective** Use key words to describe how green schools help the environment

**Materials** **StudentWorks Plus** (interactive eBook)

### BUILD BACKGROUND KNOWLEDGE

**CA CONTENT STANDARD R 3.1.3** Read aloud narrative and expository text fluently and accurately and with appropriate pacing, intonation, and expression.

- Have students preview "Earth Smart" using **StudentWorks Plus**, the interactive eBook. This version of the Student Book contains oral summaries in multiple languages, on-line multilingual glossaries, word-by-word highlighting, and questions that assess and build comprehension.
- Students can build their word reading fluency by reading along as the text is read or by listening during the first reading and, at the end of each paragraph, returning to the beginning of the paragraph and reading along.
- Students can build their comprehension by reviewing the definitions of key words in the on-line glossary and by answering the comprehension questions. When appropriate, the text required to answer the question is highlighted to provide students with additional support and scaffolding.
- Following the reading, ask students to respond in writing to a question that links the story to their personal experiences, such as: *What kinds of things do you do to help the environment? Explain.*

## Academic Language

**Language Objective** Use academic language in classroom conversations

- This week's academic words are **boldfaced** throughout the lesson. Define the word in context and provide a clear example from the selection. Then ask students to generate an example or a word with a similar meaning.

### Academic Language Used in Whole Group Instruction

| Theme Words | Key Selection Words | Strategy and Skill Words |
|---|---|---|
| **discussion** | **donate** | **summarize** |
| **goal** | **unaware** | **main idea** |
| **project** | **members** | **details** |
| | **contribute** | **cause** |
| | | **effect** |
| | | **predicates** |

# English Learners

## Vocabulary

**Language Objective** Demonstrate understanding and use of key words by describing how green schools help the environment

**Materials** • **Visual Vocabulary Resources** • **English Learner Resource Book**

TESTED SKILL

### PRETEACH KEY VOCABULARY

**All Language Levels** Use the **Visual Vocabulary Resources** to preteach the key selection words *donate, unaware, members,* and *contribute*. Focus on 1–2 words per day. Use the following routine that appears in detail on the cards.

- Define the word in English and provide the example given.
- Define the word in Spanish, if appropriate, and indicate if the word is a cognate.
- Display the picture and explain how it illustrates or demonstrates the word. Engage students in structured partner-talk about the image, using the key word.
- Ask students to chorally say the word three times.
- Point out any known sound-spellings or focus on a key aspect of phonemic awareness related to the word.
- Distribute copies of the Vocabulary Glossary in the **English Learner Resource Book** page 32.

### PRETEACH FUNCTION WORDS AND PHRASES

**All Language Levels** Use the Visual Vocabulary Resources to preteach the function words and phrases *tackle a project, spend part of a day, get an A,* and *have off from*. Focus on one word per day. Use the detailed routine on the cards.

- Define the word in English and, if appropriate, in Spanish. Point out if the word is a cognate.
- Refer to the picture and engage students in talk about the word; for example, students will Partner Talk using sentence frames or they will listen to sentences and replace a word or phrase with the new function word.
- Ask students to chorally repeat the word three times.

### TEACH BASIC WORDS

For **Beginning** and **Early Intermediate** students, use the Visual Vocabulary Resources to teach the basic words *solar power, solar panel, trash, compost, sunlight,* and *cleanup*. Teach these "Earth Day" words using the routine provided on the card.

**Visual Vocabulary Resources**

**EL Resource Book,** page 32

Use the word chart to study this week's vocabulary words.
Write a sentence using each word in your writer's notebook.

| Word | Context Sentence | Illustration |
|---|---|---|
| donate | We donate canned food to help hungry people. | HELP THE FOOD BANK. What else can people donate to help others? |
| unaware | The dog was unaware of the traffic. | |
| members | The members of the ecology club picked up trash. | |
| contribute | I contribute money to help save the whales. | SAVE THE WHALES What is another word that means "contribute"? |

Real World Reading

Comprehension

Genre
Nonfiction Some articles give information about real people, places, or things.

Summarize
Main Idea and Details
A main idea is the most important point of an article. Details support the main idea.

EARTH Smart

How do green schools help the environment?

Goodwillie Environmental School is friendly to the environment. Goodwillie is a green school in Ada, Michigan. Green schools do many things to help the Earth.

Green schools use less energy than regular schools. At Goodwillie, solar panels use the sun's power. The solar power heats the school in winter. This helps keep energy bills low.

The school also believes in using recycled items. Its walls and floors are made with recycled material. Even the outdoor deck is made from sawdust and recycled milk jugs!

Clara Cullen (left) and Seana Florida find frogs in Goodwillie's pond.

70

Student Book

English Learner Resource Book

# English Learners

## Access to Core Content

**Content Objective** Read grade-level text
**Language Objective** Discuss text using key words and sentence frames
**Materials** • **English Learner Resource Book,** pp. 30–31

TESTED SKILL

### PRETEACH MAIN SELECTION (PAGES 70–73)

Use the Interactive Question-Response Guide on **English Learner Resource Book pages 30–31** to introduce students to *Earth Smart*. Preteach half of the selection on **Day 2** and half on **Day 3**.

- Use the prompts provided in the guide to develop meaning and vocabulary. Use the Partner Talk and whole-class responses to engage students and increase student talk.
- When completed, have partners reread the story.

### PRETEACH STANDARDS PRACTICE SELECTION (PAGES 74–75)

Use the Interactive Question-Response Guide on **English Learner Resource Book pages 30–31** to preview the standards practice selection "Summer Break?" Preteach the selection on **Day 4**.

# English Learners

## Fluency

**Content Objective** Reread selections to develop fluency; develop speaking skills
**Language Objective** Tell a partner what a selection is about
**Materials** • **Student Book:** "Earth Smart," "Summer Break?"

### REREAD FOR FLUENCY

CA CONTENT STANDARD R 3.1.3 Read aloud narrative and expository text fluently and accurately and with appropriate pacing, intonation, and expression.

- Have students reread a portion of "Earth Smart." Suggest that they focus on two to four of their favorite pages from the selection. Work with students to read the pages with appropriate pacing; for example, read each sentence of the first paragraph and have students echo your pacing, or speed, as you read. Then have students continue by chorally rereading additional paragraphs.
- Provide time for students to read their sections of text to you. Comment on their pacing and provide corrective feedback by modeling proper fluency.

### DEVELOP SPEAKING/LISTENING SKILLS

- Have students practice reading "Summer Break?" Work with them to read with appropriate pacing.
- Provide time for students to read aloud the informational article to a partner, and then have partners discuss the topic of the article. Provide the sentence frame: *I think year-round schools are a good/bad idea because _____.*

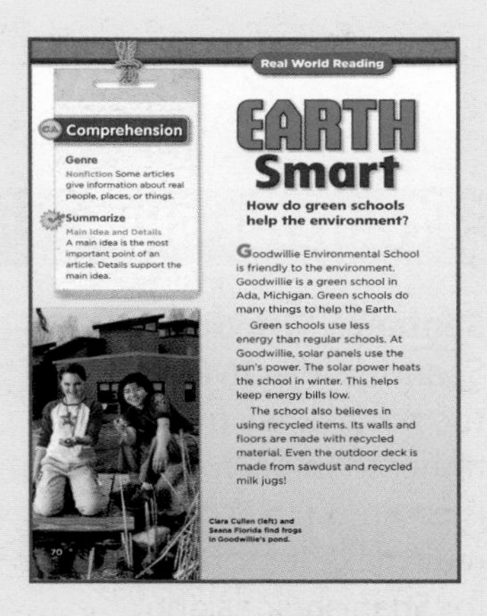

Student Book

## Self-Selected Reading

**Content Objective** Read independently
**Language Objective** Orally retell information learned
**Materials** • **Classroom Library** • other informational books

### APPLY SKILLS TO INDEPENDENT READING

- Have students choose an informational book for independent reading. (See the **Theme Bibliography** on pages T8–T9 for book suggestions.)
- After reading, ask students to orally summarize the book. Provide time for students to comment on their reactions to the book and share them with classmates. Ask: *Would you recommend this book to a classmate? Why or why not?*

Classroom Library

## Transfer Skills

**Sentence Structure** In Spanish, adjectives follow the nouns they modify, rather than precede them as is common in English. This may make it more difficult for Spanish-speaking students to separate the subject and predicate. Therefore, have these students identify the simple subject (*schools*) before identifying the complete subject (*Green schools*).

## Corrective Feedback

During whole group grammar lessons, follow the routine on the **Grammar Transparencies** to provide students with extra support. This routine includes completing the items with English Learners while other students work independently, having students reread the sentences with partners to build fluency, and providing a generative task such as writing a new sentence using the skill.

# English Learners

## Grammar

**Content Objective** Identify the subject of a sentence
**Language Objective** Speak in complete sentences, using sentence frames

TESTED SKILL

### SUBJECTS

- Review subjects. Write the following on the board: *Green schools help the environment*. Underline the subject. (*Green schools*) Tell students that this is the subject; it is what the sentence is about.
- Write sentences on the board, such as those provided below. Have students underline the subject in each sentence. Have them say: *The subject is ____.*

  *Goodwillie Elementary teaches students to protect the environment.*

  *Some students have science class outdoors.*

  *A school year is 180 days.*

  *Year-round schools do not have summer vacation.*

### PEER DISCUSSION STARTERS

- Write the following sentences on the board.

  Green schools have ____. I learned that year-round schools ____.
- Pair students and have them complete each sentence frame. Ask them to expand on their sentences by providing as many details as they can from this week's readings. Circulate, listen in, and take note of each student's language use and proficiency.

### English Learners

UNIVERSAL ACCESS

Build on students' responses to help move them to the next level of language acquisition; for example, if students say "I learned that year-round schools do not have summer vacation," say "That's correct. Year-round schools do not have two months off in the summer like most schools do. But they do have more breaks throughout the year. Some think this helps students at year-round schools do better on tests. Now turn to your partner and tell more about year-round schools."

Provide the following sentence frames orally or in writing for support.

**Beginning/Early Intermediate** A green school is ____.

**Intermediate** Green schools are interesting because ____.

**Early Advanced** Some green schools, such as Goodwillie Elementary, ____.

# English Learners

## Writing/Spelling

**Content Objective** Spell words correctly
**Language Objective** Write in complete sentences, using sentence frames

**VOCABULARY**

- Write the key vocabulary words on the board: *donate, unaware, members, contribute*. Have students copy each word on their **Sound-Spelling WorkBoards**. Then help them say each word and write sentences for each word. Provide sentence starters such as:

  *Students at green _____ donate time to help the environment.*

  *Many _____ are unaware that these schools exist.*

  *Some members of the staff teach _____ outdoors.*

  *Taking buses to _____helps contribute to saving the environment.*

- Help students spell words using their growing knowledge of English sound-spelling relationships. Model how to segment the word students are trying to spell and attach a spelling to each sound (or spellings to each syllable if a multisyllabic word). Use the Sound-Spelling Cards to reinforce the spellings for each English sound.
- Dictate the following words for students to spell: *day, stay, bait, ai, cake,* and *lake, eat, teach, weigh, eight*. Guide students using the Sound-Spelling Cards as they spell each word.
- When completed, review the meanings of words that can be easily demonstrated or explained. Use actions, gestures, and available pictures.

**Sound-Spelling WorkBoard**

### Phonics/Word Study

For English Learners who need more practice with this week's phonics/spelling skill, see the Approaching Level lesson on page 77R. Focus on minimal contrasts, articulation, and those sounds that do not transfer from the student's first language to English. For a complete listing of transfer sounds, see pages T18–T33.

# English Learners

## Practice Reader

**Practice Reader**

**Content Objective** Read to apply skills and strategies

**Language Objective** Retell information using complete sentences

**Materials** • **Practice Reader:** *Two Builders*
• **English Learner Resource Book,** p. 33

### BEFORE READING

CA CONTENT STANDARD R 3.2.4 Recall major points in the text and make and modify predictions about forthcoming information.

- **Preview** Read the title *Two Builders*. Ask: *What's the title? Say it again.* Repeat with the author's name. Then page through the book. Use simple language to tell about each page. Immediately follow up with questions, such as: *Who is in this picture? What do you think the children are doing?*
- **Review Skills** Use the inside front cover to review the phonics skill and vocabulary words.
- **Set a Purpose** Say: *Let's read to find out about these builders.*

### DURING READING

- Have students whisper-read each page, or use the differentiated suggestions below. Circulate, listen in, and provide corrective feedback, such as modeling how to blend a decodable word or clarifying meaning by using techniques from the Interactive Question-Response Guides.
- **Retell** Stop after every two pages and ask students to state the main ideas they have learned so far. Reinforce language by restating students' comments when they have difficulty using story-specific words. Provide differentiated sentence frames to support students' responses and engage students in partner-talk where appropriate.

### English Learners

UNIVERSAL ACCESS

#### Beginning/Early Intermediate

**Echo-Read** Have children echo-read after you.

**Check Comprehension** Point to pictures and ask questions such as: *Do you see the playspaces? Point to them.*

#### Intermediate

**Choral-Read** Have children choral-read with you.

**Check Comprehension** Ask questions/prompts such as: *Describe what you see in this photo. What did the author tell us about this playground?*

#### Early Advanced

**Choral-Read** Have children choral-read.

**Check Comprehension** Ask: *What did you learn about the Jay Beckwith on this page? Read sentences that tell how he invented playspaces.*

# English Learners

## AFTER READING

CA CONTENT STANDARD LAS 3.1.3 Respond to questions with appropriate elaboration.

**Book Talk** Write the **Book Talk Prompts** below on the board or distribute copies of **English Learner Resource Book** page 33. Students will work with peers of varying language abilities to discuss them. Form groups so that students who read the Beyond Level, On Level, Approaching Level, and English Learner versions of *Two Builders* are in the same group.

Help students determine who will be the Leader for the discussion. Then have students discuss the following:

- **Tell what Jay Beckwith does for a living.**
- **Describe Jay's experience as a young boy in school.**
- **Explain how Jay's playgrounds are different from other playgrounds.**
- **Tell what people help Jay build his playgrounds.**
- **Describe the difference between a FingerPark and a Playspace.**
- **Write one question about the book to ask your group.**

**Develop Listening and Speaking Skills** Tell students to remember the following:

- Use clear and specific vocabulary to communicate ideas. Suggest they use a thesaurus to look for related words to use in their discussions.
- Take turns speaking and listening. Give everyone a chance to speak.
- Retell, paraphrase, and explain information shared by others. Tell the main idea and important details in each section.
- Clarify and enhance the discussion through the use of pictures and props. Ask, *how does this photograph help you better understand this section of the article?*
- Connect and relate prior knowledge and experiences to ideas brought up in the discussion. Ask, *what did you know about this topic before reading this section? What have you learned?*

CA CONTENT STANDARD LAS 3.1.2 Connect and relate prior experiences, insights, and ideas to those of a speaker.

**English Learner Resource Book**

### Newcomer

**Survival Skills: Classroom Items** Teach children the names of commonly used classroom items, such as pencil, paper, book, chair, and desk. Reinforce each using the sentence frames *This is my* ______, *That is your* ______ and *This is a* ______. These sentence frames focus on possession. Provide daily practice; for example, *This is my book. That is your book.*

The Big Question

## Big Question Board LAS 3.1.7, LAS 3.1.11

**WRAP UP** Tell students to add information learned this week related to the unit theme *Personal Experiences: Let's Learn*. Students should record how *Earth Smart* adds to their growing knowledge of the theme. Students should also record any research facts they have uncovered throughout the week or questions they want to explore as they continue reading the selections in the unit. Have students present the information they learned. Remind them of the following speaking and listening skills:

- **Speaking** Tell students that when presenting information, they should use clear and specific vocabulary to clearly communicate their ideas. Model an example, using academic vocabulary from the selection. Tell students that their word choice can also affect the tone of the presentation. If the presentation is informative, they will choose more academic words and use more formal sentences.
- **Listening** Once students have listened to a presenter, ask them to distinguish the speaker's opinion on the topic from facts that can be found in a reference book.

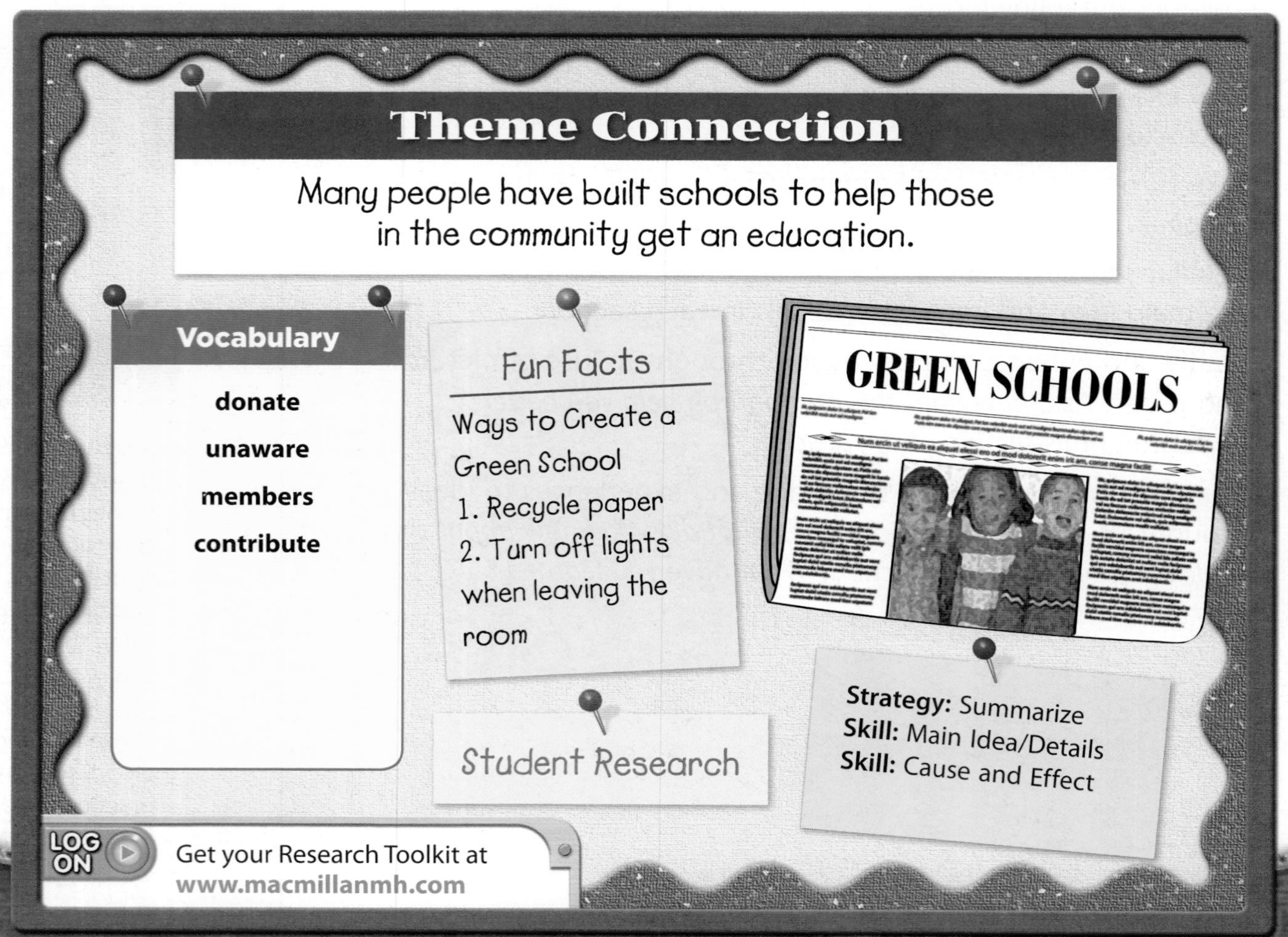

# Week 4 At a Glance

## WHOLE GROUP

### Phonics/Word Study
Long *o*, Multisyllabic Words

### Vocabulary
Robust Words: *passion, bothering, admire, concentrate, ached, splendid*

Dictionary: Multiple-Meaning Words

### Comprehension
Strategy: Generate Questions
Skill: Compare and Contrast

Skill: Main Idea/Details

### Fluency
Expression

### Spelling
Long *o*: *gold, bowl, soak, sold, snow, loaf, roast, coast, scold, coal, slow, grows, show, float, blow*

### Grammar/Mechanics
Predicates

Complete Sentences

### Writing
Topic Development: Object, Setting

### Read Aloud
Genre: Nonfiction

## SMALL GROUP

### Differentiated Instruction for Tested Skills

Approaching Level | On Level | Beyond Level | English Learners

## Teacher Tools

Technology to help plan and implement instruction

**PREPARE**
- Professional Development Videos
- Parent Connection

**PLAN/ORGANIZE**

Go to
**www.macmillanmh.com**
for Online Lesson Planner

TeacherWorks Plus
All-In-One Planner and Resource Center

**TEACH**
- Theme Launcher Video
- Classroom Presentation Toolkit
- Vocabulary PuzzleMaker
- Sound Pronunciation CD

**ASSESS**

Assessment Online

ExamView® CD-ROM

# Weekly Literature

## Student Book

**A mix of fiction and nonfiction connected to:**

- Unit Theme
- California Content Standards

**Main Selection**

**Genre** Fantasy

**Preteach Vocabulary and Comprehension**

**Genre** Folktale

**Paired Selection**

**Genre** Nonfiction

## Support Literature

**Resources to build robust vocabulary, fluency, and content knowledge**

**Interactive Read-Aloud Anthology**

- Listening Comprehension
- Readers Theater Plays

**Content Reader**

- Meets all California Science and History/Social Science Standards

# Resources for Differentiated Instruction

## Skill-Based Practice Readers

- Same Theme
- Same Vocabulary/Phonics
- Same Comprehension Skills

Approaching Level

On Level

Beyond Level

English Learner

On Level Practice Reader sheltered for English Learners

## Intensive Vocabulary

Build robust vocabulary with fiction and nonfiction

Oral Vocabulary Cards

## Intervention Kit

- Intervention Anthology
- Phonemic Awareness Teacher's Edition
- Phonics/Word Study Teacher's Edition
- Comprehension Teacher's Edition
- Vocabulary Teacher's Edition
- Fluency Teacher's Edition
- Writing and Grammar Teacher's Edition

## StudentWorks Plus

- eBook
- Use for preteaching
- Summaries in multiple languages
- Word-by-Word Reading
- Assessment

## Practice Book and Reproducibles

Also available:

Approaching Reproducible

Beyond Reproducible

## Home-School Connection

- Family letters in English, Spanish, Hmong, Vietnamese, Cantonese, Khmer
- Take-Home Stories

## Visual Vocabulary Resources

- Great for English Learners
- Use for vocabulary and building background

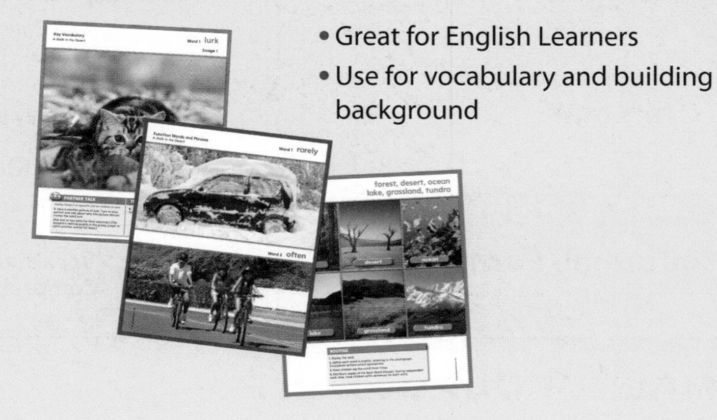

# Suggested Lesson Plan

Go to www.macmillanmh.com for Online Lesson Planner

**Wolf! pp. 82–103**

| WHOLE GROUP | DAY 1 | DAY 2 |
|---|---|---|
|  15–20 min **ORAL LANGUAGE** • Listening Comprehension • Speaking/Viewing | **Listening/Speaking/Viewing** **Focus Question** Wolves are beautiful, wild creatures. Why do you think they are not kept as pets? Read Aloud: "The Wolves of Winter," 78L–78M Build Background, 78 | **Listening/Speaking** **Focus Question** Why does the wolf go to school? |
|  20–30 min **WORD STUDY** • Vocabulary • Phonics/Word Study • Spelling |  **Vocabulary** R 3.1.7 *passion, bothering, admire, concentrate, ached, splendid,* 81, 109A Practice Book, 47 **Strategy:** Dictionary/Multiple-Meaning Words, 80 **Spelling** Pretest, 109C Practice Book, 53 LC 3.1.8 |  **Vocabulary** R 3.1.7 Review Words, Multiple-Meaning Words, 109A Practice Book, 52  **Phonics** Decode Words with Long *o*, 78N Practice Book, 46 R 3.1.1, R 3.1.2 **Spelling** Words with Long *o*, 109C Reproducible, SP10 LC 3.1.8 |
| 20–30 min **READING** • Comprehension • Fluency |  **Read** "The Boy Who Cried Wolf," 80–81  Student Book  **Comprehension**, 81A–81B **Strategy:** Generate Questions **Skill:** Compare and Contrast Practice Book, 48 **Fluency** Model Fluency, 78M R 3.1.3 | 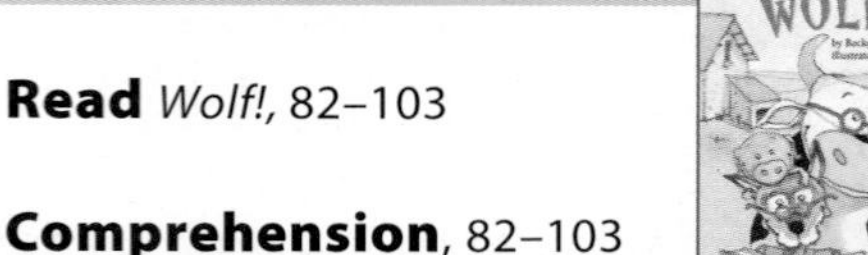 **Read** *Wolf!*, 82–103 Student Book **Comprehension**, 82–103 **Strategy:** Generate Questions **Skill:** Compare and Contrast Practice Book, 49 **Fluency** Repeated Reading: Expression, 105A R 3.1.3 |
|  20–30 min **LANGUAGE ARTS** • Writing • Grammar | **Writing**  **Daily Writing Prompt** Write a paragraph describing how it feels to stand face to face with a wolf. Topic Development: Object, Setting, 110–111B W 3.2.2 **Grammar** Daily Language Activities, 109E Predicates, 109E Reproducible, GR10 LC 3.1.2, LC 3.1.4 |  **Writing** **Daily Writing Prompt** If you could talk with a wolf, what would you say? Write a short dialogue between the two of you. Topic Development: Object, Setting, 111C W 3.2.2 **Grammar** Daily Language Activities, 109E Predicates, 109E Practice Book, 55 LC 3.1.2, LC 3.1.4 |
| **ASSESSMENT** • Informal/Formal | **Quick Check** **Vocabulary**, 80 **Comprehension**, 81B | **Quick Check** **Comprehension**, 103 |

 45–60 min **SMALL GROUP Lesson Plan** — **Differentiated Instruction 111K–111JJ**

## California Standards

| Vocabulary | Comprehension | Writing | Science |
|---|---|---|---|
| Vocabulary Words<br>Dictionary/Multiple-Meaning Words<br>R 3.1.7 | **Strategy:** Generate Questions<br>**Skill:** Compare and Contrast | **Topic Development: Object Setting**<br>W 3.2.2, W 3.1.4 | Living things have structures for everyday living<br>LS 3.3.a, LS 3.3.e |

## DAY 3

**Listening/Speaking**

**Focus Question** Compare "The Boy Who Cried Wolf" to *Wolf!* In which story do the animal characters act more like real people?

Retell, 105

**Vocabulary** R 3.1.5, R 3.1.7, R 3.1.8
Review Words, Related Words, 109B

**Spelling** Word Meanings, 109D
Reproducible, SP11 LC 3.1.8

Student Book

**Read** *Wolf!* 82–103

**Comprehension**
Critical Thinking, 105
**Review Skill:** Main Idea and Details, 105B R 3.2.5

**Fluency** Repeated Reading: Expression, 105A
Practice Book, 50 R 3.1.3

**Writing**
**Daily Writing Prompt** Write a brief article describing wolves for an encyclopedia for very young children.
**Topic Development: Object, Setting,** 111D
W 3.2.2

**Grammar** Daily Language Activities, 109E
Mechanics and Usage, 109F
Reproducible, GR11 LC 3.1.2, LC 3.1.4

**Quick Check** **Fluency**, 105A

## DAY 4

**Listening/Speaking/Viewing**

**Focus Question** Use information in this article to tell how the main character in *Wolf!* is different from a real wolf.

**Vocabulary** R 3.1.5, R 3.1.7, R 3.1.8
Content Vocabulary: *reputation, offspring, den, communicate,* 106
Review Words, Morphology, 109B

**Spelling** Proofread, 109D
Practice Book, 54 LC 3.1.8

Student Book

**Read** "The Truth About Wolves," 106–109

**Comprehension**
**Nonfiction:** Informational Text
Headings, Pronunciations, Boldface, and Italics, 106
Practice Book, 51 R 3.2.1

Content Reader

**Fluency** Repeated Reading: Expression, 105A R 3.1.3

**Writing**
**Daily Writing Prompt** Write a paragraph describing a wild animal that you have seen or read about.
**Reading/Writing Connections,** 111E–111F
W 3.2.2

**Grammar** Daily Language Activities, 109E
Predicates, 109F
Practice Book, 56 LC 3.1.2, LC 3.1.4

**Quick Check** **Vocabulary**, 109A–109B

## DAY 5 Review and Assess

**Listening/Speaking/Viewing**

**Focus Question** Read "The Boy Who Cried Wolf" and *Wolf!* Which story is more of a fantasy than a reality?

**Vocabulary** R 3.1.5, R 3.1.7, R 3.1.8
Assess Words, Connect to Writing, 109B

**Spelling** Posttest, 109D
Reproducible, SP12 LC 3.1.8

Student Book

**Read** Self-Selected Reading
R 3.3.2

**Comprehension**
Critical Thinking, 109

**Fluency** Practice, 105A R 3.1.3

**Writing**
**Daily Writing Prompt** Imagine you are a teacher with a wolf in your class. Write about the kind of student the wolf is.
**Conferences/Revision (Assignments),** 111G–111H W 3.1.4, W 3.2.2

**Grammar** Daily Language Activities, 109E
Predicates, 109F
Reproducible, GR12 LC 3.1.2, LC 3.1.4

**Weekly Assessment, 111I–111J**

# Differentiated Instruction

## What do I do in small groups?

## Focus on Skills

**IF...** **students need additional instruction and practice based on your Quick Check observations of the following skills:**

**Phonics/Word Study**
Long *o*

**Vocabulary Words**
*passion, bothering, admire, concentrate, ached, splendid*
**Strategy:** Multiple-Meaning Words

**Comprehension**
**Strategy:** Generate Questions
**Skill:** Compare and Contrast

**Fluency**

**THEN...**

| | |
|---|---|
| Approaching<br>English Learners | Preteach and Reteach Skills |
| On Level | Consolidate Learning |
| Beyond | Enrich and Accelerate Learning |

## Suggested Small Group Lesson Plan

| Focus on Skills | DAY 1 | DAY 2 |
|---|---|---|
| **Phonics/Word Study**<br>• **Long *o*** | **English Learners** Preteach Long *o*, 111DD | **On Level** Reteach Long *o*, 111U |
| **Vocabulary**<br>• **Week 4 Words**  | **Approaching** Preteach; Academic Language, 111K, 111M<br>**On Level** Review, 111U<br>**Beyond** Practice Reader Lesson 1, 111AA<br>**English Learners** Preteach; Academic Language, 111CC–111DD | **Approaching** Practice Reader Lesson 1, 111P<br>**Beyond** Practice Reader Lesson 2, 111BB<br>**English Learners** Preteach Vocabulary; Access to Core Content, 111DD-111EE |
| **Comprehension**<br>• **Strategy:** Generate Questions<br>• **Skill:** Compare and Contrast | **Approaching** Prepare to Read, 111K<br>**Beyond** Practice Reader Lesson 1, 111AA<br>**English Learners** Prepare to Read, 111CC | **Approaching** Reteach, Practice Reader Lesson 1, 111O–111P<br>**Beyond** Practice Reader Lesson 2, 111BB<br>**English Learners** Practice Reader,111II |
| **Fluency**<br>• **Repeated Reading** | | |

## Skill-Based Practice Readers

Apply skills and strategies while reading appropriate leveled books.

**Leveled Practice Database**
Go to **www.macmillanmh.com**.

## Manipulatives

Use for Hands-on Learning

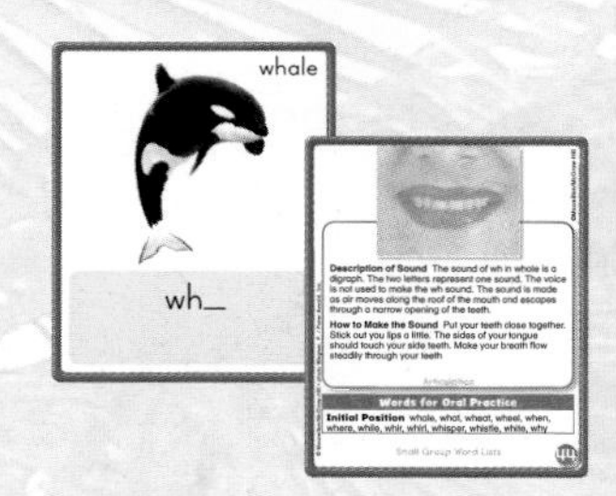


**Sound-Spelling Cards**

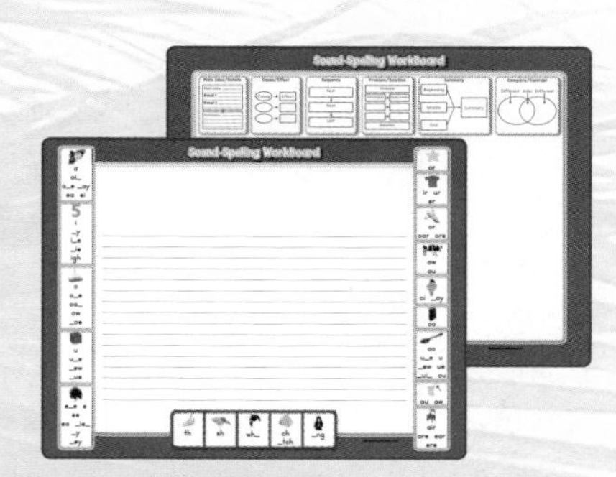

**Sound-Spelling WorkBoards**

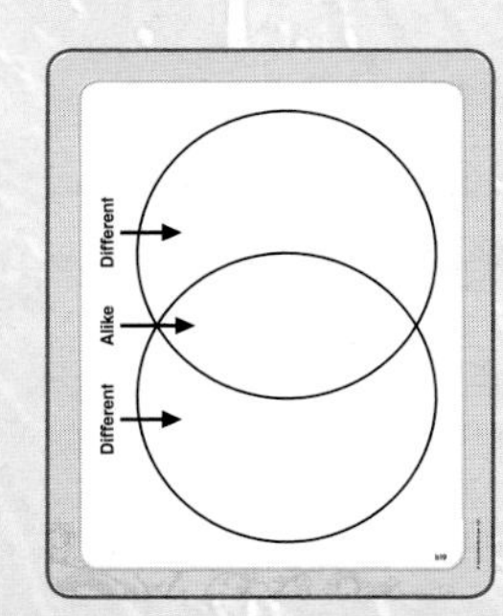


**Vocabulary/Comprehension Write-on/Wipe-off Board**

**FOLDABLES®** Hands-on activities for reinforcing weekly skills

| DAY 3 | DAY 4 | DAY 5 |
|---|---|---|
| **Approaching** Long *o*, 111L<br>**Beyond** Enrich and Accelerate, 111Y | **English Learners** Grammar, 111GG | **Approaching** Long *o*, 111L |
| **Approaching** Practice Reader Lesson 2, 111Q<br>**On Level** Practice Reader Lesson 1, 111W<br>**English Learners** Preteach Vocabulary; Access to Core Content, Grammar, 111DD–111EE, 111GG | **Approaching** Review Vocabulary, 111N<br>**On Level** Practice Reader Lesson 2, 111X<br>**English Learners** Vocabulary, 111II–111JJ<br>**Beyond** Enrich, 111Y | **English Learners** Vocabulary, Practice Reader, 111II |
| **Approaching** Practice Reader Lesson 2, 111Q<br>**On Level** Practice Reader Lesson 1, 111W<br>**English Learners** Practice Reader, 111II | **Approaching** Practice Reader Lesson 3, 111R<br>**On Level** Practice Reader Lesson 2, 111X<br>**English Learners** Practice Reader, 111II | **Approaching** Book Talk, 111JJ<br>**On Level** Book Talk, 111JJ<br>**Beyond** Book Talk, 111JJ<br>**English Learners** Book Talk, 111JJ |
| | **Approaching** Reread, Model, 111S<br>**On Level** Reread, Model, 111V<br>**Beyond** Reread, Model, 111Z<br>**English Learners** Reread, Model, 111FF | **Approaching** Self-Selected Reading, 111T<br>**On Level** Self-Selected Reading, 111V<br>**Beyond** Self-Selected Reading, 111Z |

# Managing the Class

## What do I do with the rest of my class?

- Literacy Workstations
- Practice Book
- Online Activities
- Classroom Library

## Classroom Management Tools

**Weekly Contract**

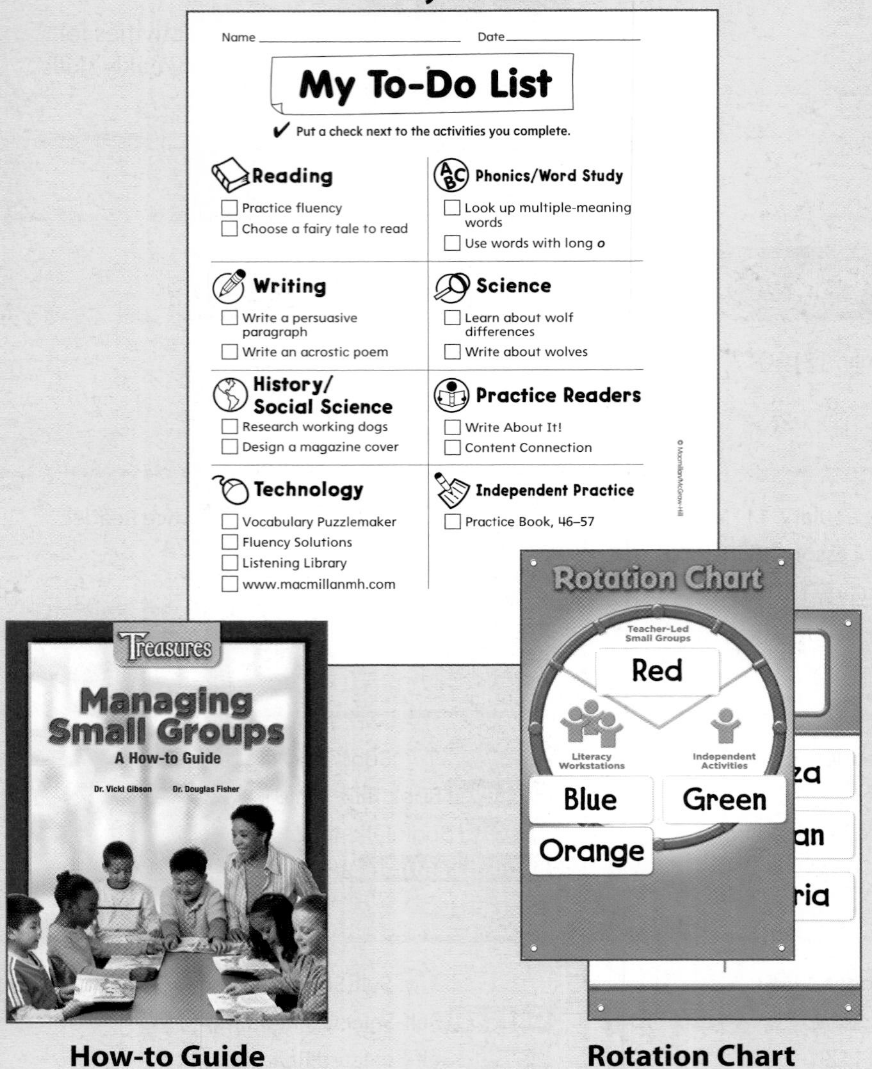

Name ______ Date ______

**My To-Do List**

✔ Put a check next to the activities you complete.

| Reading | Phonics/Word Study |
| --- | --- |
| ☐ Practice fluency<br>☐ Choose a fairy tale to read | ☐ Look up multiple-meaning words<br>☐ Use words with long *o* |
| **Writing** | **Science** |
| ☐ Write a persuasive paragraph<br>☐ Write an acrostic poem | ☐ Learn about wolf differences<br>☐ Write about wolves |
| **History/ Social Science** | **Practice Readers** |
| ☐ Research working dogs<br>☐ Design a magazine cover | ☐ Write About It!<br>☐ Content Connection |
| **Technology** | **Independent Practice** |
| ☐ Vocabulary Puzzlemaker<br>☐ Fluency Solutions<br>☐ Listening Library<br>☐ www.macmillanmh.com | ☐ Practice Book, 46–57 |

© Macmillan/McGraw-Hill



**How-to Guide** **Rotation Chart**

## Digital Learning

**StudentWorks Plus**
- Summaries in Multiple Languages
- Word-by-Word Reading
- Assessment

- Read Other Books by Author or Illustrator

## Classroom Library

Use the trade books to apply skills. See lessons on pages T2–T7. See also **Theme Bibliography**, pages T8–T9, to select books for 30 minutes of daily independent reading.

Approaching

On Level

Beyond

**ONLINE INSTRUCTION** www.macmillanmh.com

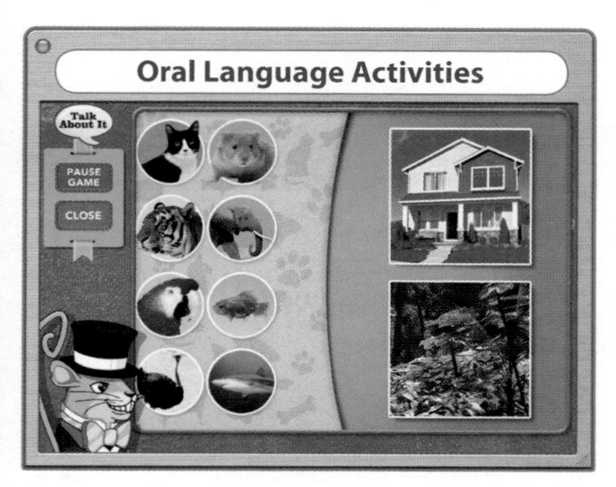


- Focus on Unit Vocabulary and Concepts
- English Learner Support

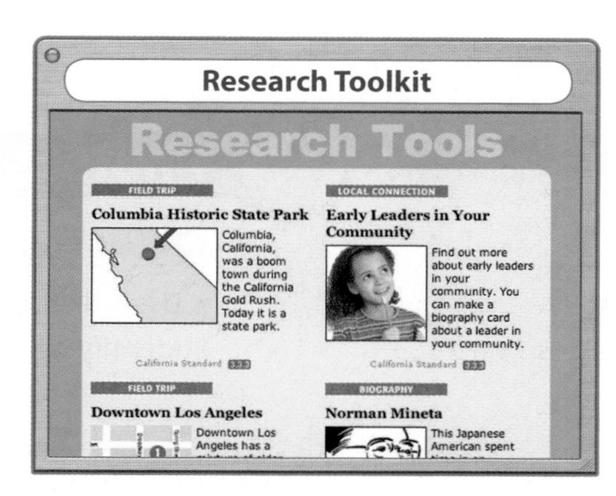


- Research Roadmap
- Research and Presentation Tools
- Theme Launcher Video
- Links to CA Science and History/Social Science Programs

- Focus on Keyboard and Internet Skills
- Media Literacy

- Differentiated Lists and Activities

## Available on CD

**LISTENING LIBRARY**
Recordings of selections

- Main Selections
- Paired Selections
- Practice Readers
- EL Readers

**FLUENCY SOLUTIONS**
Recorded passages at two speeds for modeling and practicing fluency

## Practice Book

Also Available:

**Approaching Reproducible**

**Beyond Reproducible**

## Literacy Workstation Flip Charts

Daily independent and partner activities connected to the weekly skills. See pages 78J–78K.

# Managing the Class

## What do I do with the rest of my class?

## Reading

### Objectives

- Read aloud text to a partner fluently and accurately
- Read to comprehend basic plots of classic fairy tales
- Read independently daily

## Phonics/Word Study

### Objectives

- Use a dictionary to figure out the meaning of words
- Identify sounds in words and sort them

R 3.1.3

**Reading** **Fluency** 20 Minutes

- Find a reading buddy.
- Take turns reading aloud page 50 of your Practice Book.
- Pause for a short time at commas. Pause for a longer time at periods.

**Extension**

- Read the page aloud again. Have your partner guess the punctuation by clapping once for commas and twice for periods.

**Things you need:**

- Practice Book

Fluency Solutions
Listening Library

7

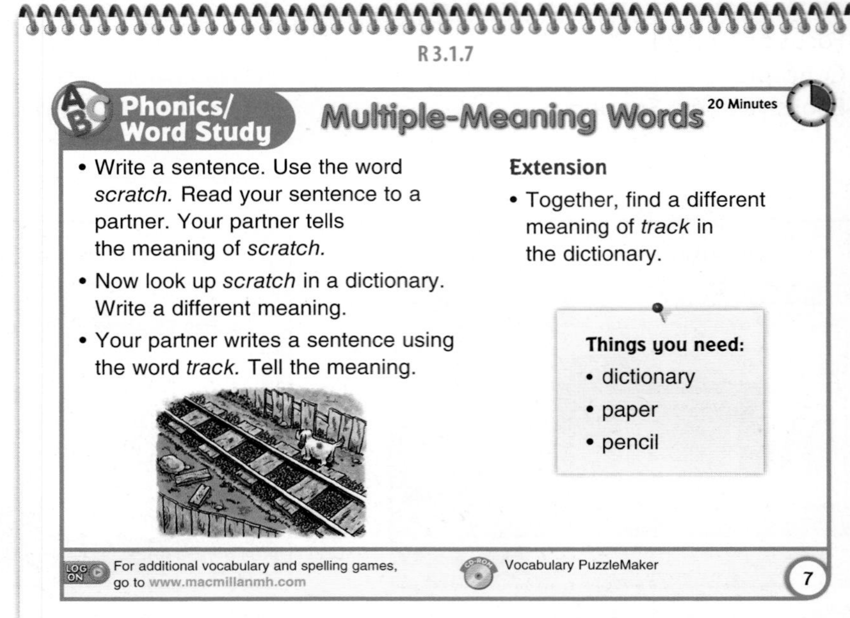

R 3.1.7

**Phonics/ Word Study** **Multiple-Meaning Words** 20 Minutes

- Write a sentence. Use the word *scratch.* Read your sentence to a partner. Your partner tells the meaning of *scratch.*
- Now look up *scratch* in a dictionary. Write a different meaning.
- Your partner writes a sentence using the word *track.* Tell the meaning.

**Extension**

- Together, find a different meaning of *track* in the dictionary.

**Things you need:**

- dictionary
- paper
- pencil

For additional vocabulary and spelling games, go to www.macmillanmh.com

Vocabulary PuzzleMaker

7

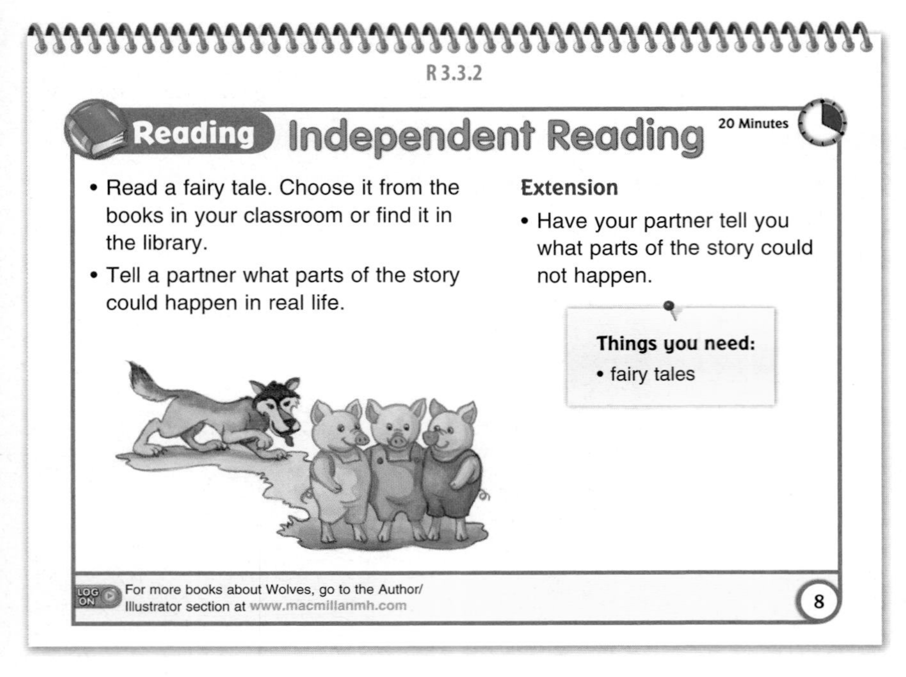

R 3.3.2

**Reading** **Independent Reading** 20 Minutes

- Read a fairy tale. Choose it from the books in your classroom or find it in the library.
- Tell a partner what parts of the story could happen in real life.

**Extension**

- Have your partner tell you what parts of the story could not happen.

**Things you need:**

- fairy tales

For more books about Wolves, go to the Author/ Illustrator section at www.macmillanmh.com

8

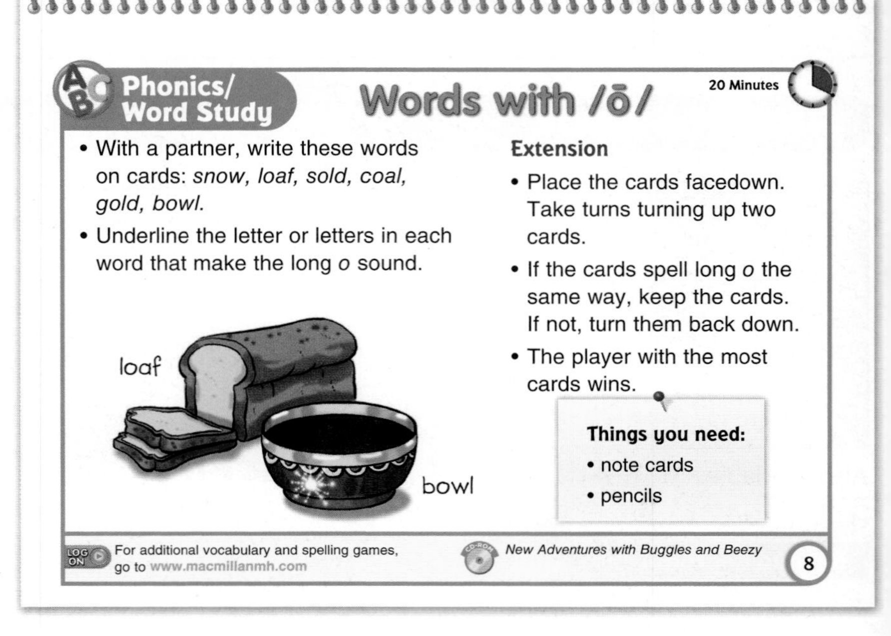

**Phonics/ Word Study** **Words with /ō/** 20 Minutes

- With a partner, write these words on cards: *snow, loaf, sold, coal, gold, bowl.*
- Underline the letter or letters in each word that make the long *o* sound.

loaf

bowl

**Extension**

- Place the cards facedown. Take turns turning up two cards.
- If the cards spell long *o* the same way, keep the cards. If not, turn them back down.
- The player with the most cards wins.

**Things you need:**

- note cards
- pencils

For additional vocabulary and spelling games, go to www.macmillanmh.com

*New Adventures with Buggles and Beezy*

8

**Literacy Workstation Flip Charts**

## Writing

### Objectives

- Write a persuasive paragraph with a topic sentence and supporting details
- Create an acrostic poem with descriptions that use concrete sensory details

## Content Literacy

### Objectives

- Research information about wolves to understand they have different structures that serve different functions in life
- Understand and use different reference materials to research

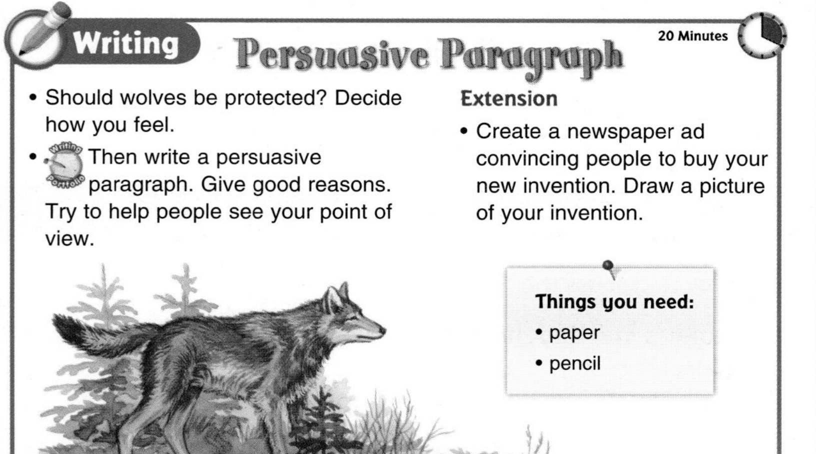


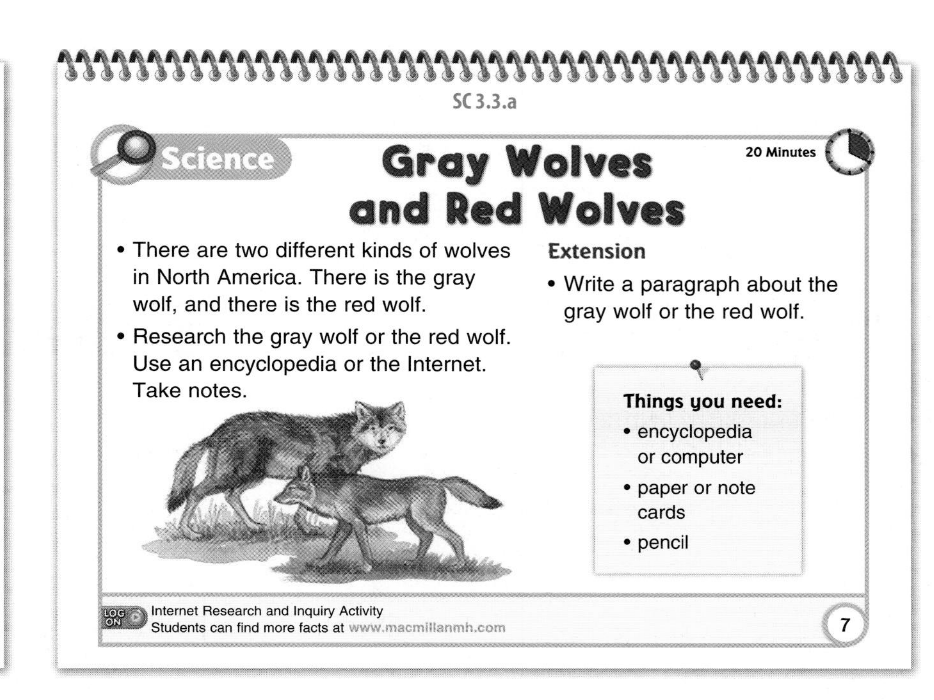


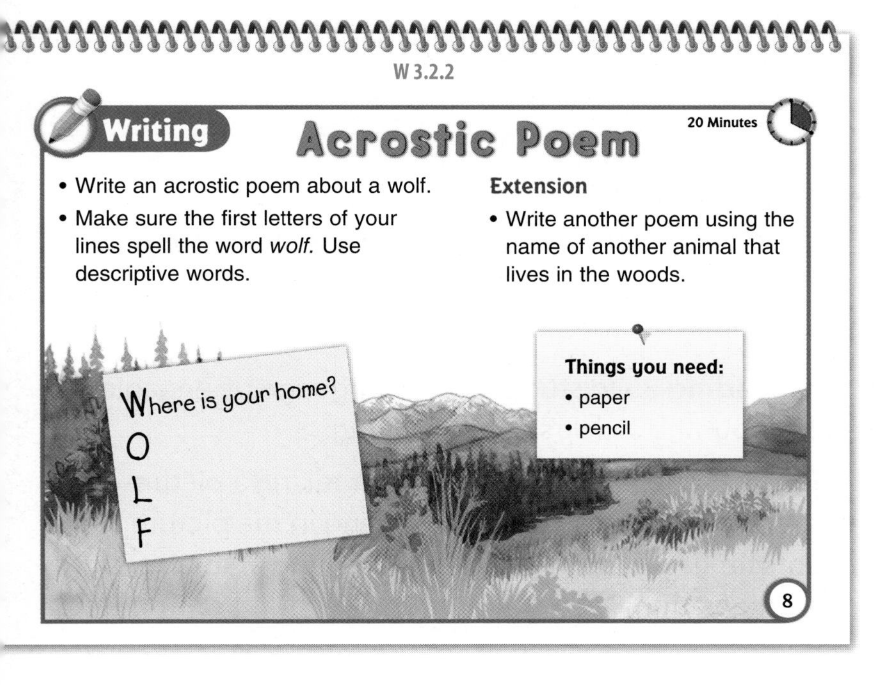


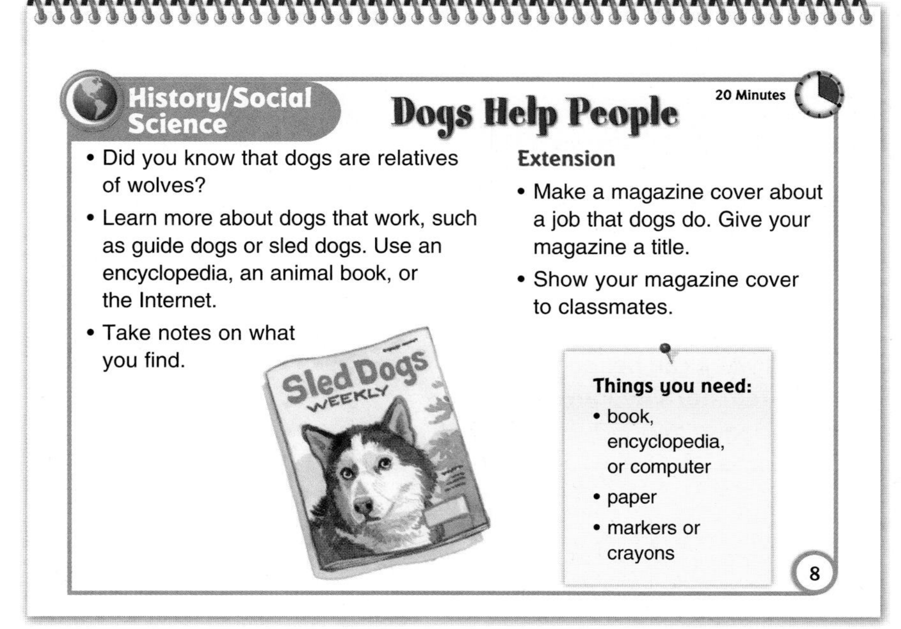

# Prepare

## WHOLE GROUP

**ORAL LANGUAGE**
- Read Aloud
- Build Background
- Connect to Theme

**PHONICS/WORD STUDY**
- Read Words with Long *o*

**VOCABULARY**
- Teach Words in Context
- Dictionary: Multiple-Meaning Words

**COMPREHENSION**
- Strategy: Generate Questions
- Skill: Compare and Contrast

**CA CONTENT STANDARDS**
R 3.1.1, R 3.1.2, R 3.1.3, R 3.1.7, R 3.2.2, R 3.3.1, LAS 3.1.9

## SMALL GROUP

- Differentiated Instruction, pp. 111K–111JJ

### Intensive Vocabulary

To provide 15–20 minutes additional vocabulary instruction, see **Oral Vocabulary Cards** 5-Day Plan. The pre- and posttests for this week can be found in the **Teacher's Resource Book**, pages 269–272.

# Read Aloud

## Read "The Wolves of Winter"

**Read Aloud**

**GENRE: NONFICTION**

Share with students the following key characteristics of a **nonfiction** article:

- The purpose of a nonfiction article is to present information about a topic.
- Information in nonfiction articles can be checked in other sources, such as encyclopedias.
- Nonfiction articles tell about real people, animals, places, or events.

**FOCUS ON VOCABULARY**

Introduce the following words, using the **Define/Example/Ask** routine. Tell students that knowing these words will help them understand the information in the article as you read.

### Vocabulary Routine

Use the routines below to discuss the meaning of each word.

**Define:** When someone is **startled**, he or she is suddenly frightened or surprised by something.
**Example:** The deer was startled by the sound of approaching footsteps.
**Ask:** What is the difference between startled and scared?

**Define:** **Prey** is an animal that is hunted by another for food.
**Example:** A mouse is often a hungry snake's prey.
**Ask:** What other animals are considered prey?

**Define:** To **peek** is to take a brief look.
**Example:** Our dad told us not to peek inside the box, but I had to look!
**Ask:** What is the difference between taking a peek and staring?

**LISTENING FOR A PURPOSE**

Ask students to listen carefully as you read "The Wolves of Winter" on **Read-Aloud Anthology** pages 34–37. Use the Think Alouds and Genre Study prompts provided.

EL
- **Interactive Reading** Build students' oral language by engaging them in talk about the article's basic meaning.
- Point to the illustration of the photographer taking a picture of a wolf mother and her pups. Name each thing in the picture and have students repeat. Describe what the man and animals are doing in the illustration.

- After the introductory section, say, *Turn to a partner and discuss what you thought about Jim Brandenburg's story about the wolf.*
- After "Big, Bad Wolf," say, *How are wolves important? Explain using details from the article.*
- After "Wolves Are Smart," say, *How did Jim Brandenburg photograph wolves? What did he do to get them to come out?*

**Think/Pair/Share** Use **Copying Master 5**, "I noticed the author used . . . ," to help students talk about the descriptive text structure in "Winter Hunters." Remind students that in a descriptive text structure, the author uses examples or details that describe the topic. Then have students turn to a partner and discuss how description works as a text structure in the section titled "Wolves Are Smart."

**RESPOND TO THE NONFICTION ARTICLE**

Ask students the Think and Respond questions on page 37. Then have them generate a short list of questions they would like to ask the author about wolves. Have students read their lists aloud to the class. Try and answer as many questions as you can.

## Model Fluency

Reread the article. Tell students that this time you want them to focus on an aspect of how you read the story—your expression.

CA CONTENT STANDARD **R 3.1.3** Read aloud narrative and expository text fluently and accurately and with appropriate pacing, intonation, and expression.

Point out to students that in order to read a passage fluently, they must pay attention to their expression. Remind students that when they read dialogue, they should read it the way the character or person would say it, showing surprise, happiness, and so on.

**Think Aloud** Listen as I read the part where Jim Brandenburg tries to sneak up on the wolf to take his picture. Listen to how I express what the wolf is thinking: "Maybe it's a dead moose for dinner." Now listen to how I express what Jim says about the wolf: "The wolf simply walked away," Jim said. "He looked at me over his shoulder once like, 'Oh no! I can't believe it!'" Did you notice how I said the wolf's words in a curious way? Did you notice how I used a matter-of-fact tone when I repeated what Jim said about the wolf? Now you try. Repeat each sentence after me, using the same expression that I do.

**Establish Fluency Focus** Remind students that you will be listening for this same quality in their reading throughout the week. You will help them improve their reading through their use of expression.

### Readers Theater

**BUILDING LISTENING AND SPEAKING SKILLS**
Distribute copies of "Take Me to Your Litter," **Read-Aloud Anthology** pages 132–145. Have students practice reading the play throughout the unit. Assign parts and have students present the play or perform it as a dramatic reading at the end of the unit.

CA CONTENT STANDARD **LAS 3.1.9** Read prose and poetry aloud with fluency, rhythm, and pace, using appropriate intonation and vocal patterns to emphasize important passages of the text being read.

## Objectives

- Decode multisyllabic words with long *o*

## Materials

- Sound Spelling Cards
- Practice Book, p. 46
- Transparency 4
- Word-Building Cards
- Teacher's Resource Book, 181

### English Learners

UNIVERSAL ACCESS

**Transfer Sounds** Students speaking **Cantonese** and **Hmong** will have difficulties pronouncing and perceiving the long *o* sound. Emphasize the sound and demonstrate correct mouth position when pronouncing each word. Contrast words with the short and long *o* sounds, such as *not/note*. Use the Approaching level phonics lessons for additional pronunciation/decoding practice.

HOMEWORK **Practice Book,** page 46

Here are several spelling patterns that stand for the long *o* sound:

The letters oa stand for the long *o* sound. (coat)
The letters ow stand for the long *o* sound. (row)
When the letter o comes before the letters **ld**, the letter stands for the long *o* sound.

**A. Fill in the missing letter or letters so that the following words have the long *o* sound. Check the rules above if you have questions.**

| | |
|---|---|
| **1.** s _o_ _a_ k | **9.** kn _o_ _w_ |
| **2.** sn _o_ _w_ | **10.** fl _o_ _a_ t |
| **3.** bl _o_ _w_ | **11.** m _o_ _a_ t |
| **4.** c _o_ _a_ st | **12.** sh _o_ _w_ |
| **5.** g _o_ ld | **13.** b _o_ _a_ st |
| **6.** l _o_ _a_ f | **14.** fl _o_ _w_ |
| **7.** sc _o_ ld | **15.** l _o_ _a_ n |
| **8.** r _o_ _a_ st | **16.** gr _o_ _w_ |

**B. Follow the directions above to review these words with the long *a* sound.**

| | |
|---|---|
| **17.** gr _a_ _y_ | **19.** str _a_ _i_ ght |
| **18.** pl _a_ _i_ n | **20.** del _a_ _y_ |

**Approaching Reproducible,** page 46

**Beyond Reproducible,** page 46

# Phonics

## Long *o*

boat
o oa_ ow
o_e _oe

**EXPLAIN/MODEL**

Display the *Boat* **Sound-Spelling Card** for the long *o* sound. Tell students that long *o* can be spelled in different ways. Point to the spelling on the card, provide a sample word, and discuss the spelling hint on the card. For example, the spelling *oa* never appears at the end of a word or syllable. That is why the underscore follows the spelling on the card (*oa_*). The long *o* sound can be spelled:

- **o** as in *no* and *cold*
- **ow** as in *low*
- **o_e** as in *note*
- **oa** as in *boat*
- **oe** as in *toe*

Write the sample words on the board, underline the long *o* spelling, and model blending each one.

**Think Aloud** Look at this word. It is spelled *b-o-a-t*. I see the long *o* spelling *oa* in this word. Listen and watch as I sound out the word /bōt/, *boat*. (Run your finger under the word as you sound it out.)

**PRACTICE/APPLY**

CA CONTENT STANDARD
**R 3.1.1** Know and use complex word families when reading to decode unfamiliar words.

**Read Word List** Display **Transparency 4**. The first two lines include words with the long *o* sound that students will encounter in the upcoming selections. Have students underline the long *o* spelling in each word. Then have them chorally read the words.

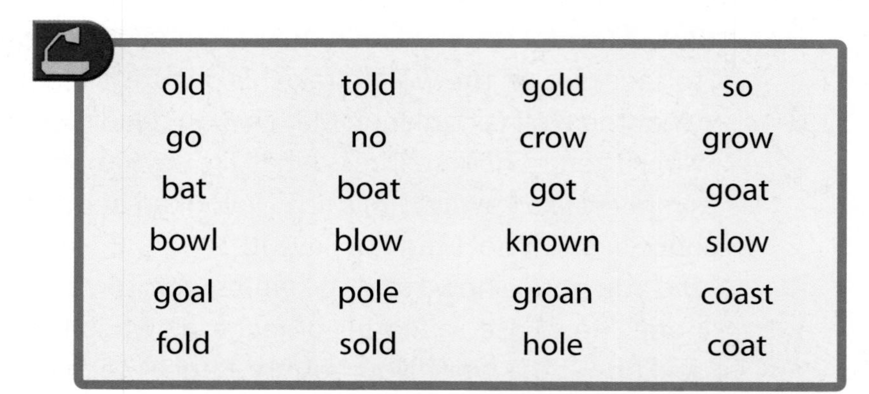

| | | | |
|---|---|---|---|
| old | told | gold | so |
| go | no | crow | grow |
| bat | boat | got | goat |
| bowl | blow | known | slow |
| goal | pole | groan | coast |
| fold | sold | hole | coat |

**Phonics Transparency 4**

**Sort Words** Ask students to sort the words by spelling pattern. Then have them write the sort in their Writer's Notebooks.

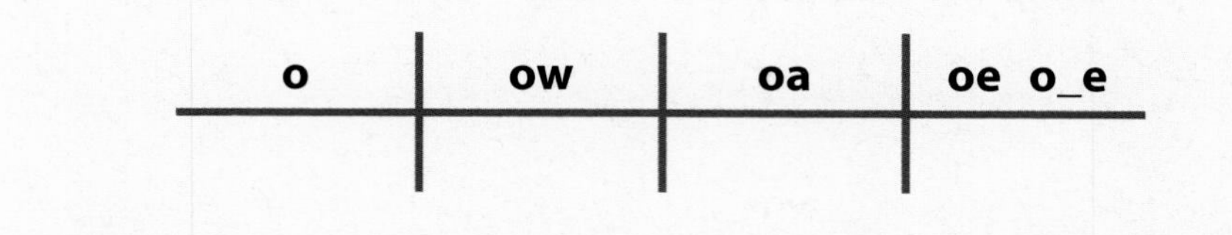

# Read Multisyllabic Words

CA CONTENT STANDARD
**R 3.1.2** Decode regular multisyllabic words.

**TRANSITION TO LONGER WORDS** Help students transition from reading one-syllable to multisyllabic long *o* words. Have students read a word in the first column, then model how to read the longer word in the second column. Point out the added syllable(s), such as a prefix or suffix, to help students gain awareness of these common word parts.

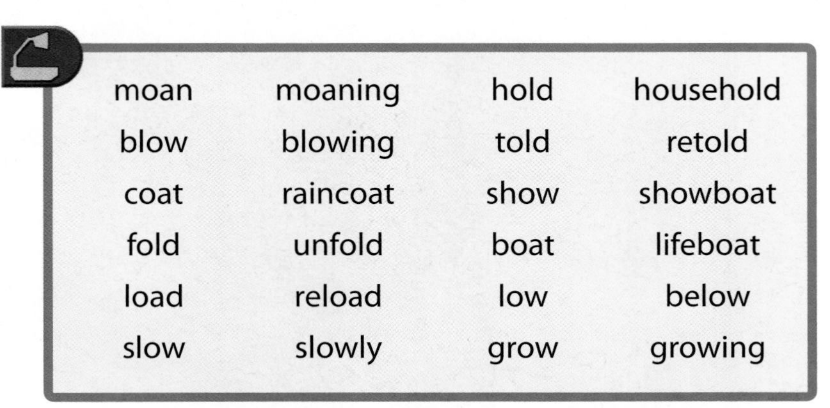

| | | | |
|---|---|---|---|
| moan | moaning | hold | household |
| blow | blowing | told | retold |
| coat | raincoat | show | showboat |
| fold | unfold | boat | lifeboat |
| load | reload | low | below |
| slow | slowly | grow | growing |

**Phonics Transparency 4**

**BUILD WORDS** Use **Word-Building Cards** *over, flow, load, re, un, told, sold, ed*. Display the cards. Have students use the word parts to build as many long *o* multisyllabic words as possible. These and other words can be formed: *overflow, overload, retold, untold, resold, unload, overflowing, overflowed, overloaded, unloading, unloaded*.

**CONNECT TO 6 SYLLABLE TYPES** To further help students break apart longer words to decode them, explain the following:

- **Vowel Team Syllables** When a common vowel team, such as *ow* or *oa*, appears in a long word, the vowel team must remain in the same syllable. This is because the two letters in the vowel team stand for one vowel sound. (el/bow; roam/ing)

**APPLY DECODING STRATEGY** Guide students to use the Decoding Strategy to decode the following words: *soaking, buffalo, Mexico, pillow, oatmeal, freeload, slowly, microphone*. Remind students to look for vowel teams in step 3 of the Decoding Strategy procedure.

# Build Fluency

**SPEED DRILL** Distribute copies of the **Long o Speed Drill** in the **Teacher's Resource Book**. Use the Speed Drill routine to help students become fluent reading words with long *o* spelling patterns.

## Syllable Fluency

Use **Word-Building Cards 31-40**. Display one card at a time. Have students chorally read each common syllable. Repeat at varying speeds and in random order. Have students work with partners during independent time to write as many words as they can containing each syllable. Add these lists to the **Unit 1 Big Idea Board**.

## Decoding Strategy

**Decoding Strategy Chart**

| Step | |
|---|---|
| Step 1 | Look for word parts (prefixes) at the beginning of the word. |
| Step 2 | Look for word parts (suffixes) at the end of the word. |
| Step 3 | In the base word, look for familiar spelling patterns. Think about the six syllable-spelling patterns you have learned. |
| Step 4 | Sound out and blend together the word parts. |
| Step 5 | Say the word parts fast. Adjust your pronunciation as needed. Ask yourself: "Is this a word I have heard before?" Then read the word in the sentence and ask: "Does it make sense in this sentence?" |

# Oral Language

## Build Background

**ACCESS PRIOR KNOWLEDGE**

Share the following information:

Look at the illustration of the wolf and the little girl. This picture is from the story *Little Red Riding Hood*. In this story, the wolf is the villain. Wolves appear in all kinds of books and stories and are usually shown as the "bad guys." When students first learn to read, chances are they will read a story with a wolf in it!

EL Write the following words on the board and briefly define each one using the **Define/Example/Ask** routine: **villain** (bad guy), **realistic** (showing people or animals as they are in everyday life), **frightening** (scary).

**FOCUS QUESTION** Ask students to read "Talk About It" on **Student Book** page 79. Then have them turn to a partner and describe the photo. Ask:

- Why do you think wolves are often shown as villains, or bad guys, in stories? Explain.
- Based on this photo, why do you think the wolf is realistic, or like a real wolf?

WRITE ON DEMAND

**BUILD WRITING FLUENCY**

Ask students to write in their Writer's Notebook what they know about wolves. Tell students to write as much as they can as well as they can. Students should write for 5 minutes without stopping. Meet with individuals during Writing Conference time to provide feedback and revision assignments. Students should self-correct any errors they notice prior to the conference.

### English Learners

**UNIVERSAL ACCESS**

During the discussion, build on students' responses to help them move to the next level of language acquisition. For example, if a student answers that the wolf looks like the villain, say: *That's correct. The wolf looks like he is planning something bad. He looks sneaky. Say it with me.* (Students repeat the sentence.) *Now turn to your partner and tell about this picture.*
Provide the following frames to help students respond in complete sentences orally or in writing.

**Beginning/Early Intermediate** This wolf is ______.

**Intermediate** The wolf is a villain because ______.

**Early Advanced** Wolves are ______ animals because ______.

# Unit Theme

## Big Idea

Learning to read is the first step in learning about the world around you through books.

**CONNECT TO THEME**

Ask students what they have learned so far in this unit about how books, schools, and teachers help enrich various learning experiences.

- What have we read about so far? What new things did we learn about teachers, books, and schools?
- How does reading books help students learn?

**USE THEME FOLDABLES**

Write the **Big Idea** statement on the board. Ask students to copy it on their Unit Theme Foldables. Remind them to add details as they complete this week's readings.

## Digital Learning

**PRETEACH** Have Approaching Level students and English Learners listen to the selection on **StudentWorks Plus**, the interactive eBook, before reading with the class. The recording contains summaries in multiple languages, word-by-word reading support, a bilingual glossary, and comprehension questions with corrective feedback.

For Web site activities for oral language development, go to www.macmillanmh.com.

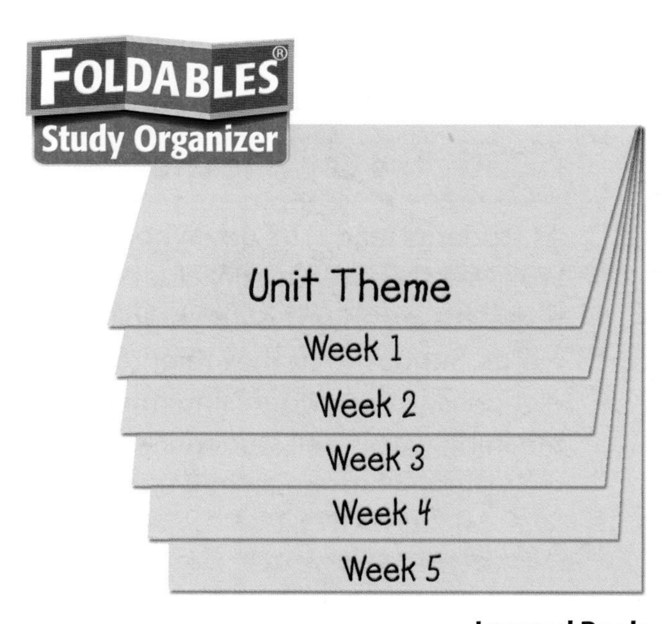


Layered Book

# Vocabulary

**STRATEGY**
**USE A DICTIONARY**

CA CONTENT STANDARD R 3.1.7
Use a dictionary to learn the meaning and other features of unknown words.

**Multiple-Meaning Words** Some words have more than one meaning. To figure out the meaning that fits in a sentence, sometimes you need to look up the word in a dictionary and choose the meaning that makes sense in the context of that sentence. Have students read "Dictionary" in the bookmark on **Student Book** page 80. Then model for students how to use a dictionary to correctly use the multiple meanings of the word *concentrate*.

**Think Aloud** The dictionary lists two meanings for the word *concentrate*. One meaning is "to think very carefully about what you are doing." The other meaning is "to bring together into one place." When I read the sentence in the passage, the author mentions that the boy's mind wanders while he watches the sheep. The word mind helps me figure out the meaning for the word *concentrate* in this story. It means to "think very carefully about what you are doing."

## Read "The Boy Who Cried Wolf"

As students read "The Boy Who Cried Wolf," ask them to identify clues that reveal the meanings of the highlighted words. Suggest that they refer to a dictionary for any confusing multiple-meaning words. Tell students they will read these words again in *Wolf!*

**Vocabulary**

| | |
|---|---|
| passion | splendid |
| admire | bothering |
| concentrate | ached |

**Dictionary**
**Multiple-Meaning Words** have more than one meaning. Use a dictionary to find the meanings of *concentrate*.

# THE BOY WHO CRIED WOLF

*retold by Carole Bartell*

There was once a young shepherd who lived in a village. This boy loved looking after his sheep. He did his job with **passion**. The villagers always told him what a good job he was doing. His work was easy to **admire**.

**HAVING SOME FUN**

One day the boy was bored. His mind wandered. He couldn't **concentrate** on watching the sheep. Then he thought of something wonderful to do. He thought it was a **splendid** idea.

80

**Quick Check**

**Do students understand word meanings?**

During **Small Group Instruction**

**If No →** Approaching Level Reteach the words using the Vocabulary lesson, p. 111M.

**If Yes →** On Level Consolidate the learning using, p. 111U.

Beyond Level Extend the learning using, p. 111Y.

He yelled, "Help! Wolf! A wolf is chasing the sheep!"

The villagers came running.

"Where is it?" one man asked.

"There's no wolf," the boy laughed. "I was just having fun."

"We are all busy working. You shouldn't be **bothering** us when there's no wolf!" he said.

Far away, a wolf looked at his watch and waited. He chuckled at his plot to fool the boy and the villagers.

### THE NEXT DAY

The next day the boy was bored again. "Wolf!" he cried.

Once again the villagers ran up the hill but saw no wolf.

"Wolves are dangerous! They can harm you and the sheep!" they shouted angrily.

### ONE DAY LATER

The next day the boy saw the wolf. He cried out, "Wolf! Wolf!"

"Time to run," said the wolf as he chased the sheep.

The villagers didn't come. When they saw the boy next, he was crying. His throat **ached** from crying for help.

"Why didn't you come when I called?" he asked. "A wolf chased all the sheep away."

"No one believes a liar, even if he is telling the truth," they said.

## Reread for Comprehension

**Generate Questions**

**Compare and Contrast** Generating, or asking, questions as you read can help you compare and contrast characters, things, and events. To compare and contrast characters, tell how characters are **alike** and **different**. Reread the selection. As you read, look for character actions, traits, and feelings that you can **compare**. Use your Compare and Contrast Chart to help you determine how characters are alike and different.

| Alike | Different |
| --- | --- |
| | |
| | |
| | |



## English Learners

UNIVERSAL ACCESS

**Preteach Vocabulary**
See pages 111M and 111DD to preteach the vocabulary words to **English Learners** and **Approaching Level** students. Use the **Visual Vocabulary Resources** to demonstrate and discuss each word. Use the Interactive Question-Response Guide to preteach the content in "The Boy Who Cried Wolf" and develop meaning.

HOMEWORK **Practice Book, page 47**

A. Write the correct word from the word box on each line.

| passion | splendid | ached |
| --- | --- | --- |
| bothering | admire | concentrate |

1. The exciting games made the party the most splendid ever!
2. I admire the paintings of a good artist.
3. The wolf's paw ached after he stepped on a sharp rock.
4. A person who has a strong feeling has passion.
5. The buzzing bee kept bothering me when I picked the flowers.
6. I had to concentrate while I read a hard part of the story.

B. Use the words from the box to answer the questions.

7. Which word from the box has one syllable? ached
8. Write the words from the box that are two-syllable words. passion admire splendid
9. Write the words from the box that are three-syllable words. concentrate bothering

Approaching Reproducible, page 47

Beyond Reproducible, page 47

# Vocabulary

## TEACH WORDS

Introduce each word using the **Define/Example/Ask** routine. Model reading each word using the syllable-scoop technique.

### Vocabulary Routine

**Define:** If you have **passion** for something, you have a strong feeling for it.
**Example:** Miss Jung has a passion for teaching.
**Ask:** What do you have a passion for? EXAMPLE

- When you **admire** a person, you respect or think well of him or her. *I admire my teacher, who helps me learn.* Who is someone you admire? EXAMPLE
- When you **concentrate**, you think very carefully about what you are doing. *Students concentrate when they take a test.* Why is it important to concentrate when you take a test? EXPLANATION
- Something that is **splendid** is very good or excellent. *I think spring is a splendid time of the year.* What is a synonym for *splendid*? SYNONYM
- If you are **bothering** people, you are annoying them, or making them feel slightly unhappy with you. *Bothering* can also mean "to take time to do something." What does *bothering* mean in the following sentence? *Jamie is not bothering to clean her room today.* MULTIPLE-MEANING WORDS
- **Ached** means "hurt with a constant or dull pain." *My feet ached after I went on a long hike.* Have you ever had something that ached? What was it? EXAMPLE

## Objectives

- Generate questions
- Compare and contrast similarities and differences in characters, settings, and plots
- Use academic language: *compare, contrast*

### Materials

- Transparencies 4a, 4b, 5
- Practice Book, p. 48

## Skills Trace

**Compare and Contrast**

| | |
|---|---|
| **Introduce** | U1: 81A–B |
| **Practice/ Apply** | U1: 82–105; Practice Book 48-49 |
| **Reteach/ Review** | U1: 1110–JJ; U5: 237A–B, 238-261, 267M–HH; Practice Book 304–305 |
| **Assess** | Weekly Tests; Unit 1, 5, 6 Tests |
| **Maintain** | U1: 139B; U6: 303B, 339A–B , 351A–B |

## English Learners

UNIVERSAL ACCESS

**Academic Language**
Preteach the following academic language words to English Learners and Approaching Level students during Small Group time: *compare, contrast, generate, questions.*
See page 111K.

# Reread for Comprehension

## STRATEGY
### GENERATE QUESTIONS

CA CONTENT STANDARD R 3.2.2 Ask questions and support answers by connecting prior knowledge with literal information found in, and inferred from, the text.

**What Is It?** Explain that good readers **generate**, or ask themselves, **questions** about a story as they read. The questions may be about something that is not clear or is confusing in the story.

**Why Is It Important?** Point out that as students continue reading, they should try to answer the questions. Generating questions can help students monitor their understanding and compare and contrast story elements such as the setting, characters, and events.

## SKILL
### COMPARE AND CONTRAST

**EXPLAIN**

**What Is It?** When you **compare** two characters, settings, or events, you tell their **similarities,** how they are alike**.** When you contrast characters, settings, or events, you explain their differences.

**Why Is It Important?** Point out that being able to compare and contrast different characters, settings, and events in a story gives readers a better understanding of the plot. It can also help show how the same character, setting, or event changes during the story.

**Transparency 4a**

Vocabulary
passion splendid
admire bothering
concentrate ached

Dictionary
Multiple-Meaning Words have more than one meaning. Use a dictionary to find the meanings of *concentrate*.

THE BOY WHO CRIED WOLF

*retold by Carole Bartell*

There was once a young shepherd who lived in a village. This boy loved looking after his sheep. He did his job with **passion**. The villagers always told him what a good job he was doing. His work was easy to **admire**.

HAVING SOME FUN

One day the boy was bored. His mind wandered. He couldn't **concentrate** on watching the sheep. Then he thought of something wonderful to do. He thought it was a **splendid** idea.

80

**Transparency 4b**

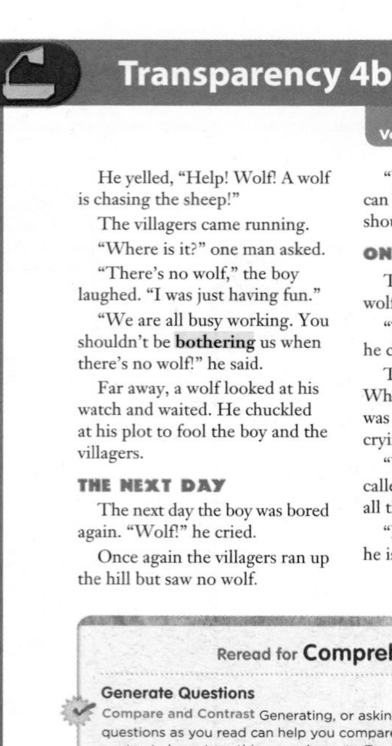

Vocabulary and Comprehension

He yelled, "Help! Wolf! A wolf is chasing the sheep!"

The villagers came running.

"Where is it?" one man asked.

"There's no wolf," the boy laughed. "I was just having fun."

"We are all busy working. You shouldn't be **bothering** us when there's no wolf!" he said.

Far away, a wolf looked at his watch and waited. He chuckled at his plot to fool the boy and the villagers.

THE NEXT DAY

The next day the boy was bored again. "Wolf!" he cried.

Once again the villagers ran up the hill but saw no wolf.

"Wolves are dangerous! They can harm you and the sheep!" they shouted angrily.

ONE DAY LATER

The next day the boy saw the wolf. He cried out, "Wolf! Wolf!"

"Time to run," said the wolf as he chased the sheep.

The villagers didn't come. When they saw the boy next, he was crying. His throat **ached** from crying for help.

"Why didn't you come when I called?" he asked. "A wolf chased all the sheep away."

"No one believes a liar, even if he is telling the truth," they said.

Reread for Comprehension

Generate Questions

Compare and Contrast Generating, or asking, questions as you read can help you compare and contrast characters, things, and events. To compare and contrast characters, tell how characters are **alike** and **different**. Reread the selection. As you read, look for character actions, traits, and feelings that you can **compare**. Use your Compare and Contrast Chart to help you determine how characters are alike and different.

| Alike | Different |
|---|---|
| | |
| | |
| | |

81

Student Book pages 80–81 available on Comprehension Transparencies 4a and 4b

### MODEL

**How Do I Use It?** Read pages 80 and 81 of "The Boy Who Cried Wolf." Display **Transparency 5** and model for students how to complete the first box. Remind students that a Compare and Contrast Chart can help them identify how parts of a story are alike and different.

**Think Aloud** In the story's beginning, the shepherd cries "Help, Wolf!" because he is bored, even though the sheep are not in danger from the wolf. All the villagers come running and are angry that they have been fooled. At the end of the story, the boy cries for help again. This time the sheep are in danger, but the villagers don't come to help because they don't believe him. The two events are alike because the boy calls for help at the beginning and end of the story. The events are different because the second time that the boy calls for help, no one comes to help.

**Transparency 5**

| Alike | Different |
|---|---|
| The boy cries for help at the beginning and end of the story. | Villagers come to help at the beginning of the story, but not at the end. No one comes to help at the end of the story. |
| The wolf is like a real wolf because he chases sheep. | The wolf is different from a real wolf because he wears a watch and talks. |

**Graphic Organizer Transparency**

### GUIDED PRACTICE

Now ask students to think about the wolf. Ask: *How is the wolf like a real wolf? How is the wolf different from a real wolf?* (The wolf is like a real wolf because it chases sheep. It is different from a real wolf because it has a watch and talks.)

### APPLY

Work with students to use their answers to complete the next part of the Compare and Contrast Chart by showing how the wolf is like a real wolf and different from a real wolf. Then ask students to compare the wolf and the boy. (They are different because the boy is a person who cares for the sheep, and the wolf is an animal who wants to eat the sheep. They are alike because both can talk.) By comparing and contrasting, students develop a deeper understanding of the characters, setting, and events in the plot.

**Quick Check**

**Can students compare and contrast characters, setting, and plot events?**

During **Small Group Instruction**

**If No →** **Approaching Level** Reteach the skill using the Comprehension lesson, p. 111O–111R.

**If Yes →** **On Level** Consolidate learning using pp. 111W–111X.

**Beyond Level** Extend the learning using pp. 111AA–111BB.

HOMEWORK **Practice Book,** page 48

When you **compare** characters, settings, or events, you tell how they are alike.
When you **contrast** characters, settings, or events, you tell how they are different.

**Read the following paragraph and answer the questions below.**
Possible responses provided.

Sally and Mike are students in Mrs. Stine's classroom. They both like to read. On Friday they both went to the library to choose a book for a report. Sally chose a sports book about basketball. Mike chose a sports book about baseball. Sally wrote a long report. Mike's report was short. Mike went back to the library to check out two extra books about baseball.

1. How are Sally and Mike alike?

Both Sally and Mike are in Mrs. Stine's classroom. They both like to read and went to the library to find a book. Sally and Mike both chose a sports book.

2. How are Sally and Mike different?

Sally chose a book about basketball. Mike's book was about baseball. Sally wrote a long report and Mike's report was short.

**Approaching Reproducible,** page 48
**Beyond Reproducible,** page 48

# Read

## WHOLE GROUP

**MAIN SELECTION**

- *Wolf!*
- Skill: Compare and Contrast

**PAIRED SELECTION**

- "The Truth About Wolves"
- Text Features

**CONTENT STANDARDS**

R 3.1.3, R 3.1.7, R 3.1.8, R 3.2.1, R 3.2.2, R 3.2.3, R 3.2.4, R 3.2.5, R 3.2.6, R 3.3.1, R 3.3.2, R 3.3.3, R 3.3.4, R 3.3.5, LS 3.3a, LS 3.3e

## SMALL GROUP

- Differentiated Instruction, pp. 111K–111JJ

# Main Selection

CA CONTENT STANDARD
R 3.3.1
Distinguish common forms of literature.

**GENRE: FANTASY**

Have a student read the definition of Fantasy on **Student Book** page 82. Remind students to look for characters, settings, or events that cannot be found in real life.

**STRATEGY**
**GENERATE QUESTIONS**

Good readers **generate questions** about something in the story that is not clear or is confusing. Answering these questions will help them better understand what happens in the story.

**SKILL**
**COMPARE AND CONTRAST**

To **compare** characters, settings, or events, a reader tells how they are alike. To **contrast** story elements, a reader tells how they are different.

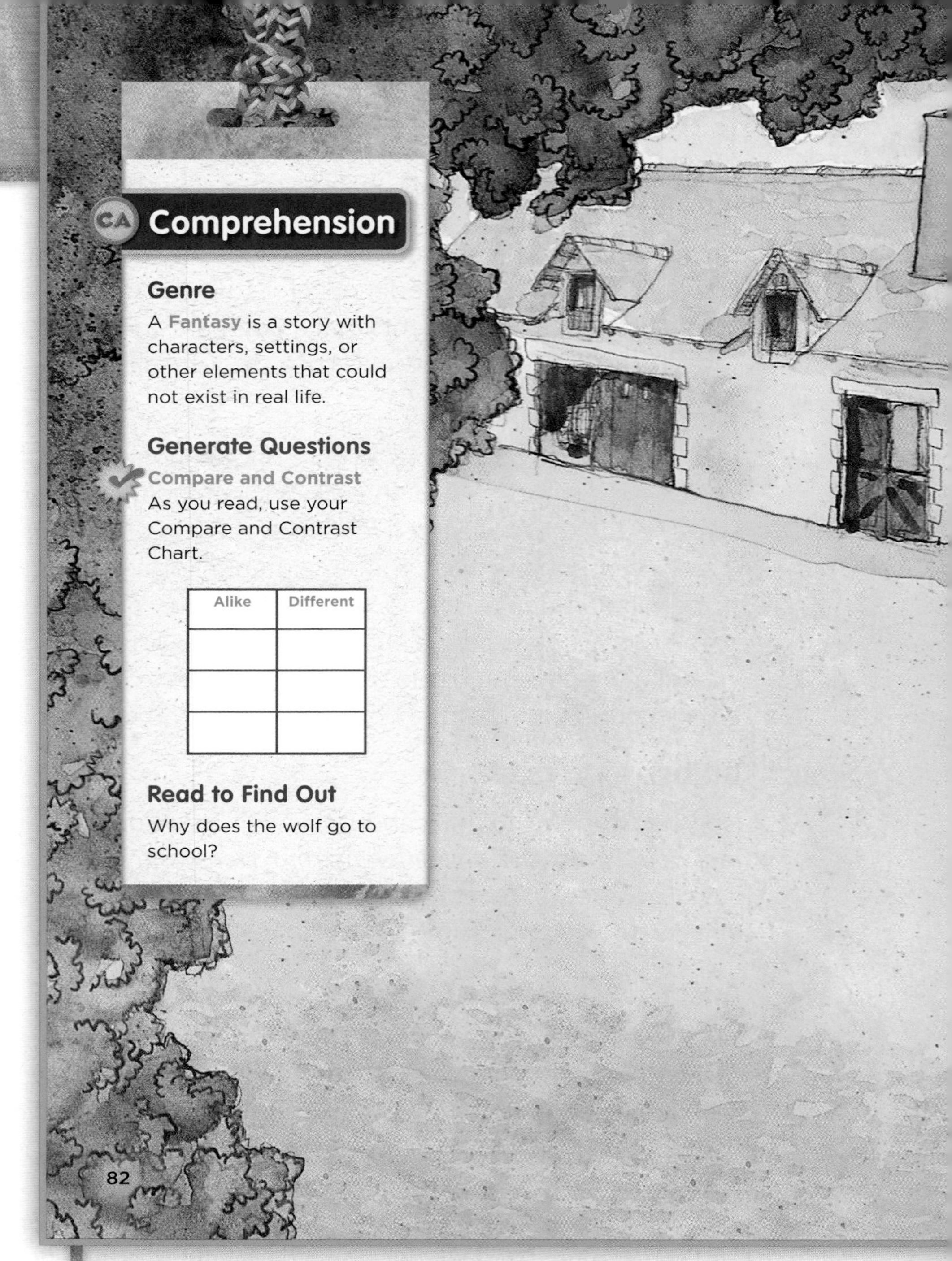

## Comprehension

**Genre**

A **Fantasy** is a story with characters, settings, or other elements that could not exist in real life.

**Generate Questions**

**Compare and Contrast**
As you read, use your Compare and Contrast Chart.

| Alike | Different |
|---|---|
| | |
| | |
| | |

**Read to Find Out**

Why does the wolf go to school?

82

## Vocabulary

**Vocabulary Words** Review the tested vocabulary words: **passion, admire, concentrate, splendid, bothering,** and **ached**.

**Additional Selection Words** Students may be unfamiliar with these words. Pronounce the words, give student-friendly explanations as needed, and help students use the previously taught vocabulary strategies: word families and prefixes.

**ignore** (p. 88): to pay no attention to something

**educated** (p. 91): to be taught something, to have knowledge

**satisfied** (p. 94): a feeling of happiness after fulfilling a need

**emerging** (p. 101): rising from

## Preview and Predict

CA CONTENT STANDARD R 3.2.4 Recall major points in the text and make and modify predictions about forthcoming information.

**QUICK WRITE** Ask students to read the title, preview the illustrations, think about the genre, and write their predictions about what will happen in the story. Students may also include information they already know about stories with wolves.

## Set Purpose

CA CONTENT STANDARD R 3.2.3 Demonstrate comprehension by identifying answers in the text.

**FOCUS QUESTION** Discuss the "Read to Find Out" question on **Student Book** page 82. Remind students to look for the answer as they read.

Point out the Compare and Contrast Chart in the Student Book and on **Practice Book** page 49. Explain that students will fill it in as they read.

## Read *Wolf!*

Use the questions and Think Alouds to support instruction about the comprehension strategy and skill.

**Practice Book,** page 49

As you read *Wolf!*, fill in the Compare and Contrast Chart.

| Alike | Different |
|---|---|
| | |
| | |
| | |

How does the information you wrote in the Compare and Contrast Chart help you generate questions about *Wolf!*?

**Approaching Reproducible,** page 49

**Beyond Reproducible,** page 49

PARTNERS

### Read Together

If your students need support to read the Main Selection, use the prompts to guide comprehension and model how to complete the graphic organizer. Allow students time to fill in their organizers before you provide the answers.

Use **Think/Pair/Share.** When asking a question, have students *think* about their answer, then discuss it with a *partner*. Finally, have selected students *share* their answers with the group. Provide sentence frames for discussion, such as *The farm animals in this story are alike because ____. They are different because____*, to help students use academic language. Students should support their answers with evidence from the text.

# Develop Comprehension

## 1 GENRE: FANTASY

CA CONTENT STANDARD R 3.3.1 Distinguish common forms of literature.

Look at the illustration on pages 84–85 and read page 85. What clues so far tell you that this story is a **fantasy**? What other elements of a fantasy do you think you will find? (The illustrator pictures the wolf walking upright, like a person, and carrying a bag over his shoulder. On page 85 the wolf thinks like a person. These clues tell me this story is a fantasy, because a fantasy is a story in which the characters could not exist in real life. I think that as I continue to read, I'll find events that can't happen in real life and other characters that wouldn't exist in real life.)

# Develop Comprehension

**2 SKILL**
**COMPARE AND CONTRAST**

**Compare and contrast** the wolf in the story to a real wolf. How is the wolf like a real wolf? How is he different? (The wolf in the story is the same as a real wolf because he is hungry and thinks of hunting to find food. But the wolf in the story does not act like a real wolf. Wolves don't carry money. They don't think human thoughts, and they don't walk on two legs.)

## Phonics/Word Study

**APPLY DECODING SKILLS** While reading, point out words with the sound/spelling patterns, syllable types, and word parts students have recently learned. Help students blend these words. You may wish to focus on words from this and future selections with long *o* spelling patterns, such as *so, go, old, told, gold, no, crow, glow, know, cold,* and *grow.*

## English Learners

**UNIVERSAL ACCESS**

Prepare students to read the story *prior* to the whole class reading. Use the Interactive Question-Response Guide on page 111EE to preteach the story content, build language, and develop meaning. This will enable students to participate successfully in the whole class reading and discussion.

**Beginning/Early Intermediate** Emphasize those questions and responses marked Beginning/Early Intermediate. In addition, focus on Key Words, Basic Words, and Function Words/Phrases.

**Intermediate** Use all the questions and prompts in the Interactive Question-Response Guide.

**Early Advanced** Extend language by using more complex sentence frames in the Interactive Question-Response Guide.

# Develop Comprehension

**3 PLOT**

Think about the events in the **plot** in this part of the story. What does the wolf see and how does he feel about what he sees? (The wolf sees a cow, duck, and pig reading in the sun. He is surprised because he has never seen animals read before.)

As he peered over the farm fence, he saw a pig, a duck, and a cow reading in the sun.

The wolf had never seen animals read before. "I'm so hungry that my eyes are playing tricks on me," he said to himself. But he really was very hungry and didn't stop to think about it for long. **3** **4**

87

# Develop Comprehension

**4 SKILL**
## COMPARE AND CONTRAST

**Compare and contrast** the farm in the story to a real farm. How is the farm like a real farm? How is it different? Add these clues to your Compare and Contrast Chart. (The farm is like a real farm because it has a house that looks real. It also has farm animals—a cow, a duck, and a pig. It is different from a real farm because the farm animals are reading books.)

| Alike | Different |
|---|---|
| The farm is like a real farm because it has a real house and farm animals. | The farm is different from a real farm because it has animals that read books. |

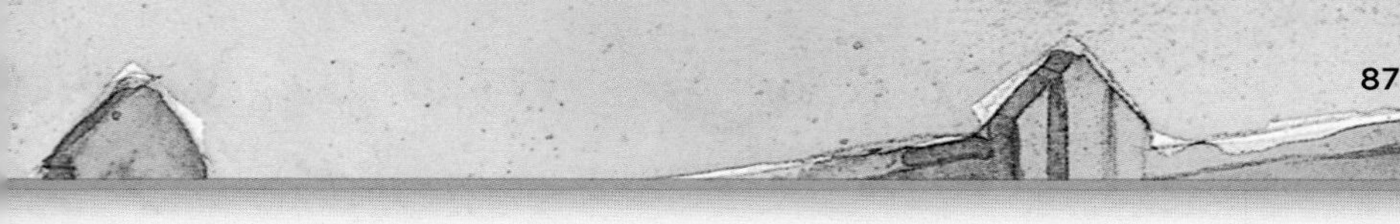

## English Learners
UNIVERSAL ACCESS

### STRATEGIES FOR EXTRA SUPPORT

**Question 4 COMPARE AND CONTRAST**
Review the meaning of the terms compare and contrast. Ask: *Is a talking dog real or fantasy?* Explain. *Is a dog that is barking real or fantasy?* Explain. Have students look at the illustrations in the story. Write these sentence frames on the board to help students talk about their ideas: (The farmhouse) seem(s) real because (I've seen farmhouses that look like that). (The pig) isn't real because (pigs can't talk). (The pig) is a fantasy.

# Develop Comprehension

**5 STRATEGY**
**GENERATE QUESTIONS**

**Teacher Think Aloud** Asking myself **questions** is one way to better understand what I read. In this part of the story, I see that the farm animals don't budge when the wolf howls at them. They should be running away. My question is: Why aren't the farm animals afraid of the wolf? I think that the way the farm animals act will be important later on in the story. I will continue reading and try to answer my question, so I will better understand the story.

**CA CONTENT STANDARD R 3.2.2** Ask questions and support answers by connecting prior knowledge with literal information found in, and inferred from, the text.

**6 SKILL**
**COMPARE AND CONTRAST**

**Compare and contrast** the chickens and the duck. How are they alike? How are they different? Add this information to your Compare and Contrast Chart. (The chickens and the duck are both farm animals and birds. However, the chickens run away from the wolf, and the duck does not budge.)

| Alike | Different |
|---|---|
| The chickens and the duck are alike because they are all birds and they all live on the farm. | The chickens and the duck are different because the chickens run away from the wolf and the duck does not budge. |

The wolf stood up tall, took a deep breath …
and leaped at the animals with a howl—

**5** "AaaOOOOOooo!"

Chickens and rabbits ran for their lives, but the duck, the pig, and the cow didn't budge.

**6** "What is that awful noise?" complained the cow. "I can't **concentrate** on my book."

"Just ignore it," said the duck.

**7**

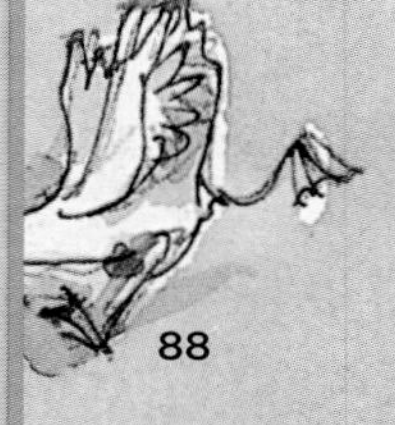

88

## Monitor Comprehension

### Monitor and Clarify: *Visualize*

**Explain** One technique students can use to better understand what they are reading is to visualize the author's words. They can do this by using the author's words to create a picture in their minds. Some authors make visualizing easy by using sensory language that helps readers see images.

**Discuss** Ask: *What sensory words or images on page 88 of the **Student Book** help you visualize what the wolf looks like when he howls at the animals?* (Students should mention the phrases *stood up tall* and *took a deep breath* and the word *leaped.*)

**Apply** As students read, ask them to practice visualizing, using phrases such as *In my mind, I see* and *I have a picture of*. Have them choose one image from the text and write a description of what they visualized when they first read the passage.

# Develop Comprehension

**7 MONITOR AND CLARIFY: VISUALIZE**

Read the author's description of how the animals reacted to the wolf growling. **Visualize** the scene in your head. How do the other animals react when the wolf howls and runs towards them? What do the cow, duck, and pig do? (The author uses the phrase *ran for their lives*, which makes me visualize animals running away looking petrified. The author then says the duck, cow, and pig did not budge. The author then has the cow say she can't concentrate on her book and the duck says to ignore the noise. This helps me visualize the animals calmly reading their books while the wolf is howling at them.)

# Develop Comprehension

**8** **ONOMATOPOEIA**

CA CONTENT STANDARD R 3.3.5 Recognize the similarities of **sounds in words** and rhythmic patterns in a selection.

Remind students that **onomatopoeia** is a word that sounds like the sound it names. The word *buzz* in the phrase *the buzz of a bee* is an example of onomatopoeia. Then read the following sentence aloud: *"What's wrong with you?" growled the wolf.* Which word in the sentence is an onomatopoeia, or sound word? (The word *growled* is an onomatopoeia, or sound word. It sounds like the actual sound a wolf might make when it is angry.)

90

## Comprehension

CA CONTENT STANDARD R 3.2.6 Extract appropriate and significant information from the text, including problems and solutions.

### Problem and Solution

**Explain** In a story, the **problem** is something that a character wants or needs to do. The **solution** is the way that the problem is solved.

**Discuss** Ask: *What is the problem between the wolf and the pig on page 91?* (The wolf wants the pig to be afraid of him, but the pig isn't afraid. He just wants to read and pushes the wolf away. The problem is that the wolf doesn't want to be ignored.) Ask students to predict how the problem will be solved.

**Apply** As students continue reading, ask them whether the problem remains the same or changes. (At first the wolf wants the other animals to be afraid of him; later he wants them to admire him.) At the end of the story, discuss how the wolf finally solved his problem. (He learned to read and became the animals' friend.)

The wolf did not like to be ignored.

"What's wrong with you?" growled the wolf. "Can't you see I'm a big and dangerous wolf?" **8**

"I'm sure you are," replied the pig. "But couldn't you be big and dangerous somewhere else? We're trying to read. This is a farm for educated animals. Now be a good wolf and go away," said the pig, giving him a push.

**9** **10**

91



# Develop Comprehension

**9 GENRE: FANTASY**

What has happened so far that tells you this story is a **fantasy**? (A fantasy is a story that could not happen in real life. Although the setting is like a real place, the characters are animals that talk and walk upright. So far in the story, the wolf has seen farm animals reading. The pig tells him it's a farm for educated animals. This tells me that this is a fantasy, because animals being able to talk and read would never happen in real life.)

**10 PLOT AND CHARACTER**

CA CONTENT STANDARD R 3.3.3 Determine what characters are like by what they say or do and by how the author or illustrator portrays them.

Think about this part of the story's **plot**. Why does the pig push the wolf and tell him to go away? (The wolf is bothering the cow, the duck, and pig with all the noise he is making and is keeping them from reading their books.)

# Develop Comprehension

**11 CHARACTER**

Why does the wolf decide to go to school? What does this tell you about his **character**? (The wolf cares what the animals think about him and he wants them to like him. He thinks that if he goes to school and learns how to read they will like him. The wolf's actions show that he is clever and can solve problems because he figures out a way to become an educated animal, too.)

**12 SKILL**
**COMPARE AND CONTRAST**

**Compare** the wolf to the students in class. How is he like the other students in the class? (The wolf goes to school to learn how to read and write, just like the other students. He sits in the classroom and works hard.)

The wolf had never been treated like this before.

"Educated animals ... educated animals!" the wolf repeated to himself. "This is something new. Well then! I'll learn how to read too." And off he went to school. **11**

The children found it strange to have a wolf in their class, but since he didn't try to eat anyone, they soon got used to him. The wolf was serious and hardworking, and after much effort he learned to read and write. Soon he became the best in the class. **12**

**Compare and Contrast**
Compare the wolf with the other students in the class. How is he the same? How is he different?

92

## English Learners

UNIVERSAL ACCESS

**STRATEGIES FOR EXTRA SUPPORT**

**Question 13 COMPARE AND CONTRAST**
Discuss what a classroom is like. Say: *A classroom has* ______. Have students complete the sentence. Have them look at pages 92 and 93. Help them understand that having a wolf in the classroom is different. Say: *A classroom does not have* _________. Point out that this classroom is different from their classroom because the wolf is a student.

# Develop Comprehension

**13 SKILL**
**COMPARE AND CONTRAST**

How is the schoolroom in this story like a schoolroom in a real school? How is it different? Add this information to your **Compare and Contrast** Chart. (The room has a teacher, students, desks, and a board, just like in a real school. In a real school, a talking wolf would never be a student.)

| Alike | Different |
|---|---|
| The schoolroom is like a real schoolroom because it has a real teacher, students, and a board. | The schoolroom is not like a real schoolroom because one of the students is a talking wolf. |

**14 SELF-SELECTED STRATEGY USE**

What strategies have you used so far to help you understand the selection? Where did you use them? Why? How did they help?

**RETURN TO PREDICTIONS AND PURPOSES**

Have students respond to the selection in their Writer's Notebooks by confirming or revising their predictions and purposes for reading. Encourage them to revise or write additional questions to help focus their attention as they continue to read the selection.

## Extra Support

**Compare and Contrast**

Check that students can compare and contrast story elements. Ask: *What do you notice about the schoolroom?* (It is a regular schoolroom with children, a teacher, a board, and desks. However, there is a wolf there, too.) *How is this schoolroom like a real schoolroom? How is it different?* Help students see that they can compare this schoolroom with their schoolroom. (It is alike because there is a teacher and students. It is different because there is a wolf learning to read.)

If students have difficulty, model how to compare and contrast two things. Ask them how the wolf and the pig are alike and how they are different on pages 91 and 92. (Both can talk, but the pig is educated and likes to read. The wolf does not.)

Stop here if you wish to read this selection over two days.

# Develop Comprehension

**15 SUMMARIZE**

What has the wolf done so far in the story? What have the farm animals done? **Summarize** what has happened. (The wolf wandered into a quiet little town, saw farm animals reading books, tried to scare the animals, and learned that the animals are too busy reading to be afraid of him. The farm animals told the wolf to go away. Then he went to school to learn to read and became the best in the class.)

**16 CHARACTER**

How do you think the wolf feels when the duck tells him that he has a long way to go? Use details from the story that describe the wolf's **character** in your answer. (The wolf probably feels bad because he has worked so hard to impress the animals. He had become the best reader in his reading class.)

15

Feeling quite satisfied, the wolf went back to the farm and jumped over the fence. I'll show them, he thought.

He opened his book and began to read:

*"Run, wolf! Run!*
*See wolf run."*

"You've got a long way to go," said the duck, without even **bothering** to look up. And the pig, the duck, and the cow went on reading their own books, not the least impressed.

16

17

94

## Comprehension

CA CONTENT STANDARD R 3.3.2
Comprehend basic plots of classic fairy tales, myths, folktales, legends, and fables from around the world.

### Compare Wolf Stories Around the World

A common literature theme from various cultures and times is a good character's stuggle against a bad character. Wolves appear as the "bad guy" in tales in many cultures, such as "The Rabbit and the Tar Wolf" (Native American, Chinese), "Lon Po Po" (Chinese), "Little Red Riding Hood" (European), "The Boy Who Cried Wolf" (Scandinavian), and "The Wolf and the Seven Little Kids" (German).

Have students read illustrated fairy tales, folk tales, legends, and fables that are stories about wolves. Have students compare the setting, characters, and problems to those in *Wolf!*. Have them tell how the two stories are alike and different in plot, character, and theme. Have students compare illustrations and tell what they liked and disliked about the way the illustrators presented their ideas.

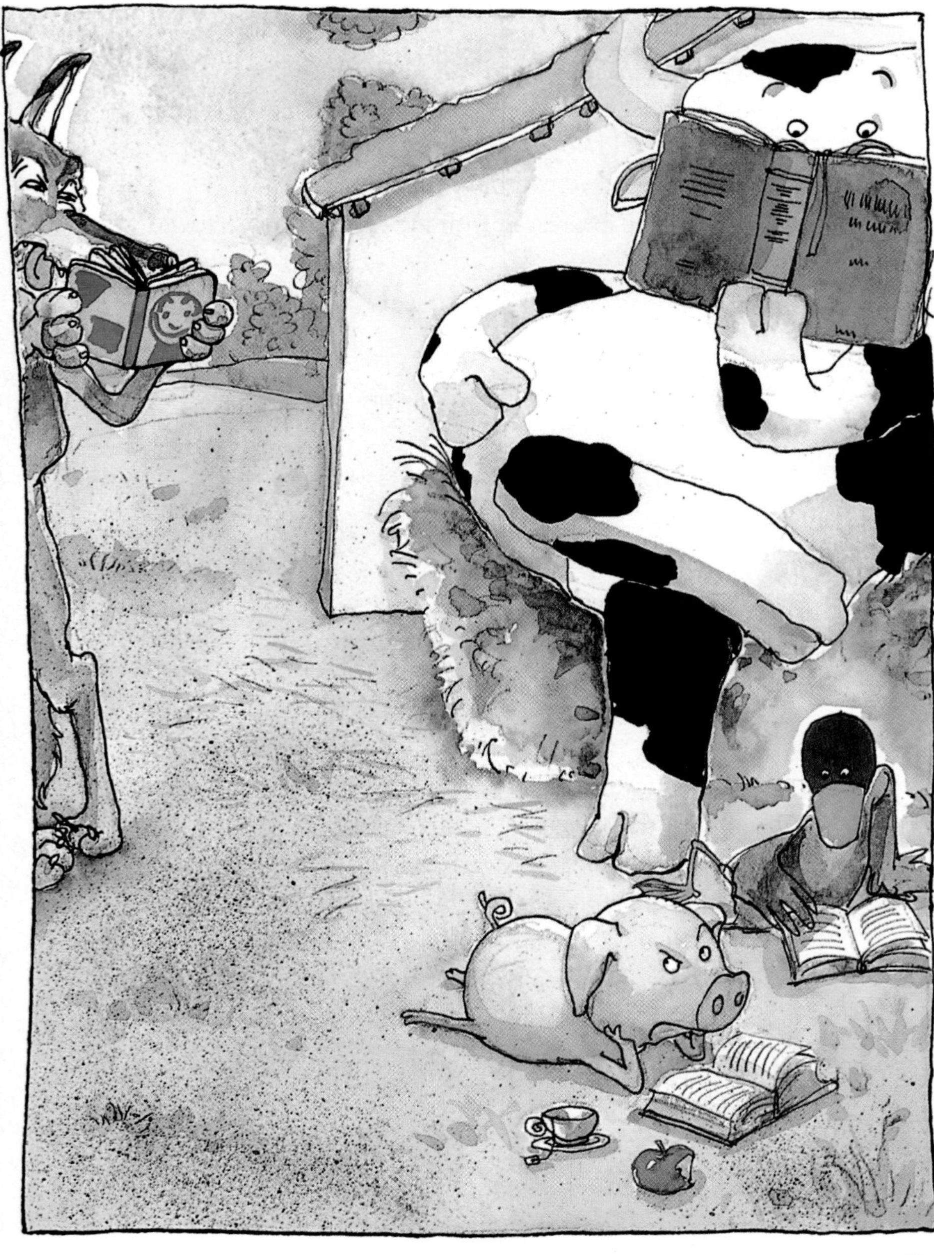
95

# Develop Comprehension

17 STRATEGY
GENERATE QUESTIONS

**Teacher Think Aloud** As I read I can ask **questions** about parts of the story that confuse or surprise me. This helps me understand the story better. On this page I'm surprised by the animals' response to the wolf when he reads. I will ask a question: Why weren't the animals impressed with the wolf? As I continue reading, I'll try to find the answer to my question. Now it's your turn. What question do you have about the story? Explain how you will find the answer.

Guide students to apply the strategy in a Think Aloud.

**Student Think Aloud** I wonder what the wolf will have to do to impress the farm animals and get them to pay attention to him. To answer my question, I will pay attention to what happens in the story as I continue to read.

# Develop Comprehension

**18** **SKILL**
**COMPARE AND CONTRAST**

**Compare** the wolf's actions at the beginning of the story with how he is now. How has he changed? (In the beginning of the story, the wolf could not read. He went to school to learn how. At first he wanted to scare the farm animals and maybe eat them, but now he wants to impress them.)

**19** **STRATEGY**
**GENERATE QUESTIONS**

What **question** could you ask yourself here that would help you better understand the story? Explain your thinking.

**Student Think Aloud** Here is one question I have: How does the wolf feel? I also want to know why he feels this way. As I read I see that he tucks his tail between his legs. I do not think he feels proud of himself. I think he feels bad because the animals are still ignoring him. As I continue to read, I will pay attention to the wolf's actions and find out what he does to feel better.

The wolf jumped back over the fence and ran straight to the public library. He studied long and hard, reading lots of dusty old books, and he practiced and practiced until he could read without stopping.

"They'll be impressed with my reading now," he said to himself.

**18**

The wolf walked up to the farm gate and knocked. He opened *The Three Little Pigs* and began to read:

*"Onceuponatimetherewerethreelittlepigsonedaytheir mothercalledthemandtoldthem—"*

"Stop that racket," interrupted the duck.

**19**

"You have improved," remarked the pig, "but you still need to work on your style."

The wolf tucked his tail between his legs and slunk away.

96

## Comprehension

**CA CONTENT STANDARD R 3.3.3** Determine what characters are like by what they say or do and by how the author or illustrator portrays them.

### Character Development

**Explain** A reader can understand a character by looking at what they do and say. The feelings, actions, and traits of a character may change during a story. Understanding a character's development can help readers understand what happens in a story and why.

**Discuss** Discuss the wolf's behavior at the beginning. Point out that he wanted to eat the farm animals and couldn't read. Then help students see how he has changed. (He has learned to read and wants to impress the animals.)

**Apply** Have students continue to look at the wolf's behavior to the end of the story and identify other ways he changes. They can identify how his actions and his words have changed.

97



# Develop Comprehension

20 SKILL
COMPARE AND CONTRAST

**Compare** the wolf's attitude towards reading in the beginning of the story and this part of the story. What has changed? What has stayed the same? Explain. (In the beginning of the story, the wolf didn't like the fact that the farm animals were ignoring him in order to read their books. He only learned how to read in order to impress the other animals. But as the story progresses, we see a change in the wolf. He still wants to impress the animals with his reading, but he starts to like reading. He works hard to make sure he's a good reader. It seems that reading is something he wants to do well because he is starting to appreciate it.)

# Develop Comprehension

**21 CHARACTER**

CA CONTENT STANDARD R 3.2.3
Demonstrate comprehension by identifying answers in the text.

How does the wolf feel about buying the book? What details in the story tell you about this **character's** feelings? (He is very excited. The book is described as "splendid" and "his first very own book!")

But the wolf wasn't about to give up. He counted the little money he had left, went to the bookshop, and bought a **splendid** new storybook. His first very own book! 21

He was going to read it day and night, every letter and every line. He would read so well that the farm animals would **admire** him. 22 23

99



# Develop Comprehension

**22 CHARACTER**

Think about the wolf's **character**. Which of the wolf's actions show that he is a hard worker? (He decides to learn how to read; he goes to school, where he works hard to do his best; he does not get discouraged when the pig tells him he needs to work on his style; he buys a storybook, and then he reads the storybook over and over.)

**23 PLOT**

Look at the **plot** event on page 98. What does the wolf do after the pig tells him that he still needs to improve? (The wolf buys another book and says he will practice day and night until he reads so well that the farm animals will admire him.)

# Develop Comprehension

## 24 STRATEGY
### DICTIONARY

How can you figure out the meaning of the **multiple-meaning** word *confidence*? (It is not a compound word. There are no word parts, suffixes, or endings that can help me figure out the meaning. Also, there are no context clues in the sentence or paragraph. The only way to figure out the meaning is to use a dictionary and try each meaning until I find the one that makes sense in the sentence.)

**CA CONTENT STANDARD R 3.1.7**
Use a dictionary to learn the meaning and other features of unknown words.

*Ding-dong,* rang the wolf at the farm gate.

He lay down on the grass, made himself comfortable, took out his new book, and began to read.

He read with confidence and **passion**, and the pig, the cow, and the duck all listened and said not one word.

Each time he finished a story, the pig, the duck, and the cow asked if he would please read them another. **24**

So the wolf read on, story after story.

**25**

One minute he was Little Red Riding Hood,

the next a genie emerging from a lamp,

and then a swashbuckling pirate.

101



# Develop Comprehension

**25** **PLOT**

Look at the **plot** events in this part of the story. Why do the animals ask the wolf to read another story? (They enjoy listening to the stories he reads, and they think he reads them well. They might also be proud of him because he can finally read.)

## Comprehension

CA CONTENT STANDARD R 3.3.4 Determine the underlying theme or author's message in fiction and nonfiction text.

### Theme

**Explain/Discuss** The theme of a story is the author's message. Sometimes the message is stated. Sometimes it is implied, or unstated. Analyzing events, characters, and main ideas can help readers identify a story's theme or implied message. Point out the theme of the story "The Three Little Pigs": "It's better to be clever than strong."

**Apply** Talk about the events on **Student Book** p. 101. (The animals listen with pleasure as the wolf reads.) Discuss how the relationship between the wolf and the farm animals has changed. (The animals now get along well.) Based on these facts, help students identify the story's theme. (Having the same interests can build friendships.)

# Develop Comprehension

**26** **SKILL**
**COMPARE AND CONTRAST**

**Compare** the wolf's first meeting with the farm animals with their meeting at the end of the story. How is it different? (The first time the wolf met the animals, they told him to go away because he was bothering them. At the story's end, the animals tell the wolf he is a master storyteller and ask him to join them in a picnic. At the end of the story, they are friends because they all can read.)

**27** **PLOT**

CA CONTENT STANDARD
R 3.2.6
Extract appropriate and significant information from the text, including problems and solutions.

Think about the story's **plot**. What was the wolf's problem at the beginning of the story? How did he solve it? (The wolf wanted the animals to like him. To solve his problem, he learned to read so they all had something they could enjoy together.)

"This is so much fun!" said the duck.

"He's a master," said the pig.

"Why don't you join us on our picnic today?" offered the cow.

26
27

102

## Vocabulary

CA CONTENT STANDARD
R 3.1.8
Use knowledge of prefixes and suffixes to determine the meaning of words.

### Word Structure Clues: *Suffixes*

**Explain** A suffix is a word part added to the end of a root word, or base word, that changes the word's meaning. When readers see a suffix and know the meaning of the root word, they can figure out the word's meaning. The suffixes *-er* and *-or* often mean "a person who" or "someone who." Write *teacher* on the board.

**Think Aloud** I see the root word *teach* and the suffix *-er*. This suffix means "a person who," so a *teacher* is someone who teaches.

**Practice/Apply** Display the nouns *reader* and *singer*. Have students identify the suffix and root word in each and use the suffix's meaning to tell the word's meaning. Then have them tell the meaning of *storyteller* on page 103 using their knowledge of the prefix *-er*. (a person who tells stories)

And so they all had a picnic—the pig, the duck, the cow, and the wolf. They lay in the tall grass and told stories all the afternoon long.

"We should all become storytellers," said the cow suddenly.

"We could travel around the world," added the duck.

"We can start tomorrow morning," said the pig.

The wolf stretched in the grass. He was happy to have such wonderful friends.

103

## Quick Check

**Can students compare characters, settings, and events?**

During **Small Group Instruction**

**If No →** **Approaching Level** Reteach the skill and have students apply it to a simpler text. Use Practice Reader lessons, pp. 111P–111R.

**If Yes →** **On Level** Have students apply the skill to a new text to consolidate learning. Use Practice Reader lesson, pp. 111W–111X.

**Beyond Level** Have students apply the skill to a more complex text to extend learning. Use Practice Reader lesson, pp. 111AA–111BB.



# Develop Comprehension

**CA CONTENT STANDARD R 3.2.4** Recall major points in the text and make and modify predictions about forthcoming information.

### RETURN TO PREDICTIONS AND PURPOSES

Review students' predictions and purposes for reading. Did students find out why the wolf goes to school? (to learn how to read to impress the other animals) What questions do they have now that they have finished reading the story?

### REVIEW READING STRATEGIES

- **Compare and Contrast** In what ways did comparing and contrasting story elements help you understand the selection?
- **Monitor and Clarify: Visualize** Do you understand the strategy of visualizing to help you better understand the story?
- **Decoding** What difficult words did you encounter? How did the Reading Multisyllabic Words strategy help you sound out these words?
- **Self-Selected Strategy Use** What strategies did you use to make sense of what you read? Where? How were these strategies helpful?

### PERSONAL RESPONSE

Ask students to think about the wolf why he wants to learn how to read. How did reading change his life? Then have students write about why learning to read is important and how the wolf's story showed the advantages of being able to read.

## Author and Illustrator

**READ ALONG WITH BECKY AND PASCAL**

Have students read the biographies of the author and the illustrator. Ask:

- How do you think Becky Bloom's children helped her write this story?
- How do Pascal Biet's illustrations help show how the characters change from the beginning to the end of the story?

**WRITE ABOUT IT**

**Figurative Language: Idioms**
Remind students how the author uses idioms to interject humor into the story. Have students write a short, humorous story involving one of the characters from the story. Tell them they may include idioms in their writing.

### Author's Purpose

Discuss whether the story's events could happen. Point out that this is a made-up story about talking animals. The author does not give facts or try to persuade someone to do something. Help students conclude that the author's purpose is to write a funny story about how a wolf learns to read.

## Read Along with Becky and Pascal

**Author**
**Becky Bloom** was born in Greece but has traveled to many countries to work and go to school. She studied architecture at the University of California at Berkeley and now lives in the south of France with her husband and children. She has many different animals around her home, but no wolf.

**Other books** by Becky Bloom and Pascal Biet: *Leo and Lester* and *Mice Make Trouble*

**Illustrator**
**Pascal Biet** has lived in France his whole life. He was born in Saint-Laurent, in the north of France. He studied visual communication and design in Blois, France, and now he lives in Paris.

Find out more about Becky Bloom and Pascal Biet at **www.macmillanmh.com**.

**Author's Purpose**
*Wolf!* mixes fantasy with reality. Did Becky Bloom want to inform or entertain her readers? What clues help you to understand her purpose?

104

### Author's Craft

**Figurative Language: Idioms**

Author Becky Bloom uses **idioms** in *Wolf!* An idiom is a phrase or expression whose meaning cannot be understood from the ordinary meanings of the separate words. For example: When the wolf sees the farm animals reading in the sun, he says, "I'm so hungry my eyes are playing tricks on me" (page 81). He means that he is so hungry he is seeing things that aren't really happening. His hunger is causing him to imagine things.

Discuss how idioms add to the humorous tone of the story and make the plot and characters more appealing. Have students look for and discuss other idioms in the story and paired selection, such as *ran for their lives* and *set the record straight*.

## Critical Thinking

### Retell the Story

Retell the events in *Wolf!* Then use your Compare and Contrast Chart to help you compare and contrast the characters and events.

| Alike | Different |
|---|---|
| | |
| | |
| | |

### Think and Compare

1. **Compare and contrast** the wolf with the pig in the beginning of the story. How are they alike and different? Use story details. **Generate Questions: Compare and Contrast**
2. Explain the steps the wolf takes to make friends with the cow, pig, and duck. Use story details in your answer. **Synthesize**
3. The animals in the story have a **passion** for reading and learning. Tell about a passion you have. **Apply**
4. Why did the animals like the wolf after he learned to read well? Explain your answer. **Analyze**
5. Read "The Boy Who Cried Wolf" on pages 80–81. Compare it with *Wolf!* In which story do the animal characters act more like real people? Use details from both selections in your answer. **Reading/Writing Across Texts**

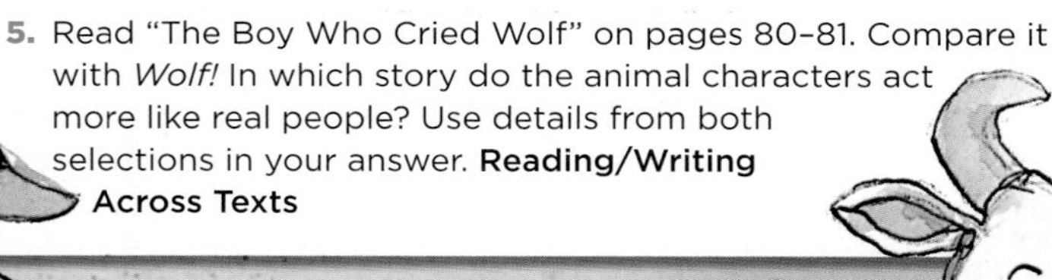

105

## Answering Questions

CA CONTENT STANDARD
R 3.2.3
Demonstrate comprehension by identifying answers in the text.

### Think and Search

Model the Think and Search strategy with question 2.

Students will find the answers to Think and Search questions in the story in several different places. they will need to reread the story to find all the parts of the answers.

**Question 2 Think Aloud** I will find the answer to this story by rereading and searching for the steps that the wolf took to make friends with the farm animals. First he learns to read but they tell him he has a long way to go. Then he practices reading, but they tell him to work on his style. Finally, he practices and practices until he reads really well. Then the farm animals admired him and they became friends. By thinking and searching, I found the answer to this question.

## Critical Thinking

### RETELL

Have partners retell *Wolf!* Remind students to use their Compare and Contrast Charts to help them organize their summaries.

### THINK AND COMPARE

Sample answers are given.

1. **Compare and Contrast** The pig and wolf are different because the wolf can't read and is dangerous and the pig is calm and can read. They are alike because they are both animals, And after the wolf meets the pig, he becomes interested in reading, too
2. **Synthesize** The wolf knows that the farm animals will like him if he can read, so he learns how to read. When they tell him to work on his style, he buys a new book and practices reading. At the end he says he's happy to have such wonderful friends.
3. **Text-to-Self** Answers may vary. Students may say they have a passion for writing, drawing, or playing a favorite sport. USE ON MY OWN
4. **Text-to-World** The animals like him because they now have the same interests. The animals act like people, and when people have the same hobbies or interests, they often enjoy spending time together.

### FOCUS QUESTION

5. **Text-to-Text** Both wolves act like real people because they talk and make plans. The wolf in *Wolf!* does even more human things. He goes to school, learns how to read, and buys books in a store.

### Objectives

- Read fluently with expression
- Rate: 61–81 WCPM

### Materials

- Transparency 4
- Practice Book, p. 50
- Fluency Solutions Audio CD

### English Learners
UNIVERSAL ACCESS

**Develop Comprehension**
Break the passage into small phrase units and discuss each paragraph so that students understand what they will read. Use gestures and board sketches to convey meaning. Then read each phrase aloud and have students repeat.

**Practice Book,** page 50

**As I read, I will pay attention to my expression.**

| | |
|---|---|
| | "You haven't eaten any lunch, Katie," my grandmother |
| 8 | said. She was right. The pile of mashed potatoes was a |
| 19 | round ball. My broccoli pieces still looked like perfect |
| 28 | little trees. And I had eaten only a spoonful of bean chili. |
| 40 | The next day, Granny was leaving on a trip to Europe. |
| 51 | She was staying on a sheep farm in Ireland for a month. |
| 63 | Traveling the world was Granny's passion, but I was |
| 72 | worried. |
| 73 | "With all those sheep, there might be wolves," I told |
| 83 | her. "It could be dangerous." |
| 88 | "You've been reading too many fairy tales," Granny |
| 96 | said. |
| 97 | I had read plenty of fairy tales. But I had also read a lot |
| 111 | of nonfiction. 113 |

**Comprehension Check**

1. Why is Katie worried? **Plot** Katie is worried about her grandmother spending time on a sheep farm where there may be lots of wolves.
2. What does Granny think of Katie's fear about the wolves? **Make Inferences** Granny thinks Katie has read too many fairy tales and she does not need to be worried.

| | Words Read | – | Number of Errors | = | Words Correct Score |
|---|---|---|---|---|---|
| First Read | | – | | = | |
| Second Read | | – | | = | |

**Approaching Reproducible,** page 50
**Beyond Reproducible,** page 50

# Fluency

## Repeated Reading: Expression

CA CONTENT STANDARD
**R 3.1.3** Read aloud narrative and expository text fluently and accurately and with appropriate pacing, intonation, and expression.

**EXPLAIN/MODEL** Explain to students that they will echo-read, or read aloud phrase by phrase after hearing a model. Read aloud the dialogue on **Transparency 4** with expression—making a howling sound when the wolf howls and showing anger in a growling tone when reading the sentence *"What's wrong with you?" growled the Wolf.*

**Transparency 4**

The wolf stood up tall, took a deep breath and leaped at the animals with a howl—**"AaaOOOOOooo!"**

Chickens and rabbits ran for their lives, but the duck, the pig, and the cow didn't budge.

"What is that awful noise?" complained the cow. "I can't concentrate on my book."

"Just ignore it," said the duck.

The wolf did not like to be ignored. "What's wrong with you?" growled the wolf. "Can't you see I'm a big and dangerous wolf?"

"I'm sure you are," replied the pig. "But couldn't you be big and dangerous somewhere else?"

from *Wolf!,* pages 82–105

**PRACTICE** Divide students into two groups. The first group reads the passage a sentence at a time. The second group echo-reads. Then groups switch roles until they have completed the passage.

**DAILY FLUENCY** Students will practice fluency using **Practice Book** page 50 or the **Fluency Solutions Audio CD**. The passage is recorded at a slow practice speed and a faster fluent speed.

### Quick Check

**Can students read fluently?**

During **Small Group Instruction**

**If No** → **Approaching Level** Use the Fluency lesson and model, p. 111S.

**If Yes** → **On Level** See Fluency, p. 111V.

**Beyond Level** See Fluency, p. 111Z.

# Comprehension

REVIEW SKILL
**MAIN IDEA AND DETAILS**

CA CONTENT STANDARD R 3.2.5
Distinguish the main idea and supporting details in expository text.

### EXPLAIN/MODEL

- The **main idea** is the most important point the author makes about a subject in a nonfiction text. It may be **stated** in a topic sentence at the beginning or end of the paragraph.
- **Details** tell more about the main idea and help to explain, describe, or support it. Readers need to recognize the difference between important details that tell about the main idea and unimportant details that do not.

Model how to identify the main idea and supporting details in the first paragraph of the paired piece "The Truth About Wolves" on page 106. Help students see that the main idea of the paragraph is stated in the first sentence, "For years wolves have been feared and misunderstood." Guide them to see that all the sentences in the paragraph tell about wolves being feared and misunderstood—they are villains in folktales, they have a bad reputation, people think they are sneaky.

### PRACTICE/APPLY

Ask students the questions below about the main idea and details in the paired selection "The Truth About Wolves." For comprehension practice, use Graphic organizer on page 293 in the **Teacher's Resource Book**.

Have students read the third paragraph on **Student Book** page 107.

- What is the sentence that tells the main idea? (Wolves often help each other.)
- What details in this paragraph support, or tell about, this main idea? (Wolves live, hunt, and raise pups together. They work together to hunt deer or moose.)

Look at Student Book page 109.

- Is the main idea stated in this paragraph? What is the main idea? (Yes, the main idea is stated. The main idea is: Wolves communicate, or give information to each other in different ways.)
- What details in this paragraph support the main idea? (Sometimes wolves use body movements to show their feelings. They also use different howls to communicate with the pack.)

## Objectives

- Identify the main idea and supporting details in a text
- Use academic language: *main idea, stated, supporting details*

TESTED SKILL

## Skills Trace

| Main Idea and Details | |
|---|---|
| **Introduce** | U1: 69A–B |
| **Practice/Apply** | U1: 70–73; Practice Book 35–36 |
| **Reteach/Review** | U1: 77O–P; U2: 213A–B, 214–217, 221O–JJ; Practice Book 96–97 |
| **Assess** | Weekly Tests; Unit 1, 2, 5 Tests |
| **Maintain** | U1: 105B; U2: 239B; U5: 145A–B, 193B |

## Content Reader

For content correlated to California Science and History/Social Science standards, see pages 72–77 in the **Content Reader**.
LS 3.3.e

# Paired Selection

**GENRE: NONFICTION**

Have students read the bookmark on **Student Book** page 106. Explain that a nonfiction article

- gives facts about a topic
- can contain headings, pronunciations, and italic, boldface, or colored type to help readers organize and interpret information for tasks such as writing a report, taking a test, or performing a task

## Text Features:
### Headings, Pronunciations, Bold Type, Italics

CA CONTENT STANDARD R 3.2.1 Use titles, tables of contents, **chapter headings**, glossaries, and indexes to locate information in text.

**EXPLAIN** Point out the box with text features on page 107. Explain that these features help readers understand and interpret nonfiction.

- **Headings** tell the topic, or main idea, of the section that follows.
- **Italic**, **bold**, and **colored type** are special kinds of type that help readers identify important words. Italics are often used for scientific words or terms, such as *alpha*. Bold words are in darker type and usually highlight important vocabulary. The definitions of words in bold type often appear in the text.
- **Pronunciations** show readers how to say difficult words correctly.

**APPLY** Have students identify the headings and italics in this selection and tell how these features help them read and understand the article.

CA **Science**

**Genre**

**Nonfiction Articles** give information about real people, places, or things.

**Text Features**

**Headings, Pronunciations, Italics**, and **Bold** or **Colored Type** help you understand important information in the text.

**Content Vocabulary**

**reputation** **den**
**offspring** **communicate**

1

# The Truth About WOLVES

by Paul Netcher

For years wolves have been feared and misunderstood. They are the villains in many folk tales. How did these furry animals get such a bad **reputation**? It's because people think they're sneaky and always hunting for food.

The wolf's bad reputation is not truly deserved. It's time to set the record straight. Here is the truth about *Canis lupus*—the gray wolf.

106

### Content Vocabulary

**Science Words** Explain the words using the **Define/Example/Ask** routine. Definitions are provided below.

**reputation** (p. 106): the opinion that people have about someone or something because of what has happened in the past

**offspring** (p. 107): babies or children of a person, animal, or plant

**den** (p. 108): a place where wild animals rest or sleep

**communicate** (p. 109): to share or pass along information

### Life in a Pack

**2**

Wolves do not like to live near humans. They prefer the company of other wolves. They live in groups called packs. A pack is made up of two parents and their newest **offspring**, or young. Sometimes other wolves become part of a pack, too.

Most packs have six to eight wolves. Some packs can have as many as 30 members!

Wolves often help each other. They live, hunt, and raise pups together. In fact, members of a pack always work together to hunt deer or moose.

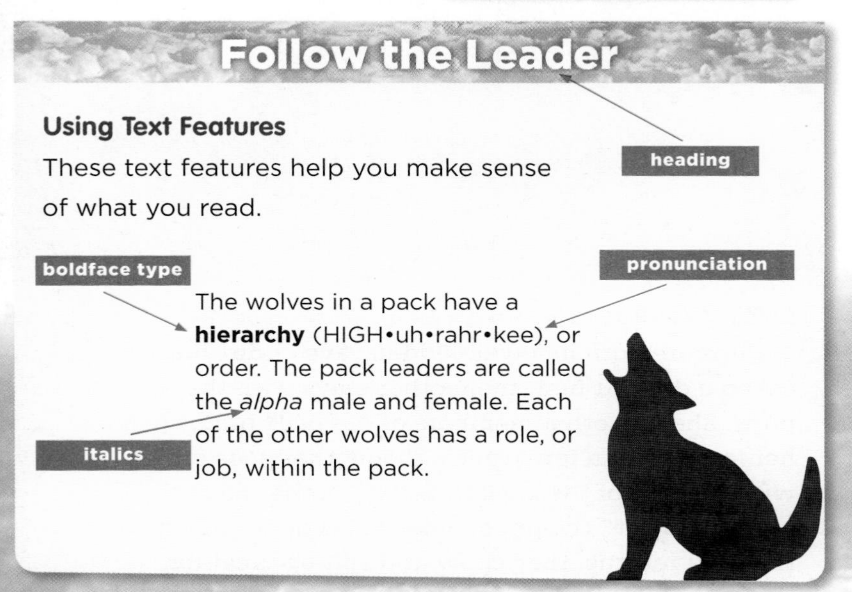




## Digital Learning

**Internet Research and Inquiry** Students can continue their unit research using the Research Toolkit on **www.macmillanmh.com**.

# Read

## Paired Selection

## Read "The Truth About Wolves"

Remind students to apply what they have learned about text features. Also have them identify clues to the meanings of the highlighted words.

### 1 TEXT FEATURES: ITALICS

Why does *Canis lupus* on page 106 appear in **italics**? (Italics tells me that it is a special and important word or term. *Canis lupus* is a scientific name for the gray wolf. Italics help readers who might not have seen the words before.)

### 2 TEXT FEATURE: HEADINGS

How can **headings** help readers find what they are looking for as they read a nonfiction article? (Headings tell readers the topic or main idea of the information in the sections that follow.)

**CA CONTENT STANDARD R 3.2.1** Use titles, tables of contents, **chapter headings**, glossaries, and indexes to locate information in text.

# Develop Comprehension

### 3 TEXT FEATURES: HEADINGS

How can the **heading** help you figure out the main idea of the text on page 108? How can a heading like this help you while you are taking a test or writing a report? (The heading is "Raising the Pups." This tells me that the main idea of this section—or what it is mainly about—is how a wolf pup is raised. It can help me take a test or write a report because I know what the section of the article with the heading is about without having to read it. Headings can help me find information I am looking for quickly.)

### 4 MAIN IDEA AND DETAILS

What is the stated **main idea** of "Talking Like a Wolf"? (Wolves communicate with one another in different ways.) What are **details** that tell about it? (Sometimes wolves use body movements to show other wolves how they feel. They also have different howls—one that calls the pack together, and one that warns other packs to stay away.)

CA CONTENT STANDARD R 3.2.5
Distinguish the main idea and supporting details in expository text.

**Raising the Pups**

Pups are born in a well-hidden cave or dirt hole called a **den**. At first, the mother stays with the pups. She lets other members of the pack bring her food. After a few weeks, the mother goes off with the rest of the pack to hunt. Another adult may "baby-sit" the pups while she is gone. When the pack returns, they chew and spit up meat for the pups.

Young wolves learn how to hunt by playing. They also learn by watching other pack members.

108

ON YOUR OWN

**Practice Book, page 51**

**Boldface type, headings, italics,** and **pronunciation** can help you better understand important information in the text.

**Look at the numbered parts of the article. Identify each text feature from the list below. Write the correct feature on each line.**

boldface type
heading
italics
pronunciation key

(1) Animals in the Wild
Animals living in the wild know they must take care of themselves. Animals know this because they were born with (2)**instinct** (3)(in´ • stingkt´) and don't have to learn how to do things. For example, wolves know to make their home in a place called a (4)*den*. They know that the den must be well hidden to keep the young wolves safe.

1. heading
2. boldface type
3. pronunciation key
4. italics
5. Based on the information in the article, what is the definition of instinct? animals knowing how to take care of themselves because they were born knowing how

**Approaching Reproducible, page 51**
**Beyond Reproducible, page 51**

## English Learners

UNIVERSAL ACCESS

**Use Visuals** Point to the photos and describe them using simple language. Have students repeat. Point out Spanish cognates to Spanish speakers: *reputation/ reputación; members/ miembros; to communicate/ comunicar; movements/ movimientos.*

**Talking Like a Wolf**

4

Wolves **communicate**, or give information to each other in different ways. Sometimes they use body movements to let other wolves know how they feel. Different howls also have different meanings. One howl calls the pack together. Another howl warns other packs to stay away. Even though many pictures show wolves howling during a full moon, wolves never howl at the moon! They are just communicating with the pack.

## CA Critical Thinking

1. How can the heading and the word in boldface type on page 209 help you find information quickly? **Using Text Features**
2. What is your opinion of wolves after reading this article? Use details from the article in your answer. **Evaluate**
3. Use information in this article to tell how the main character in *Wolf!* is different from a real wolf. **Reading/Writing Across Texts**

### Science Activity

Do more research about wolves. On the computer, write an article for younger students that tells what you learned. Use text features such as *italics*, *headings*, and *bold* or *colored type* to highlight important parts of your article.

Find out more about wolves at **www.macmillanmh.com**.

109

# Critical Thinking

## SUGGESTED ANSWERS

1. The heading tells the topic of the section so I know what it is about. I know that the boldface word is an important vocabulary word so I will look for a definition about its meaning in the text. USING TEXT FEATURES
2. Wolves help each other hunt and raise their offspring. When they howl, they are just talking to each other. This shows me that wolves are not as frightening as I thought they were. EVALUATE

3. **FOCUS QUESTION** The main character in *Wolf!* is different from a real wolf because he doesn't live in a pack or hunt with other wolves. Instead, he talks, wears clothes, goes to school, and learns to read. READING/WRITING ACROSS TEXTS

### Science Activity

Remind students to include facts about how wolves live and survive. Discuss how using text features and beginning new paragraphs for new topics help readers find information and understand what they will read in each section of the articles.

## CA Connect to Standards

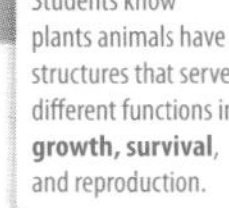

CA CONTENT STANDARD
LS 3.3.a
Students know plants animals have structures that serve different functions in **growth, survival,** and reproduction.

### How Wolves Live and Survive

Share with students that wolves have special physical structures that help them grow, survive, and have offspring. Point out that wolves live in the northern United States and Canada.

Discuss with students different wolf habitats—forests and the Arctic—and physical structures, such as strong jaws, sharp teeth, heavy fur coats, that help them hunt deer and moose. Have small groups research wolves and find other ways they have adapted to survive. Students can present their findings orally to the class and answer questions.

# 5-Day Vocabulary

## Connect Language Arts

### WHOLE GROUP

**VOCABULARY**
- Tested Words

**SPELLING**
- Long *o*

**GRAMMAR**
- Predicates

**CONTENT STANDARDS**
R 3.1.5, R 3,1,7, R 3.1.8 , LC 3.1.4, LC 3.1.8,

### SMALL GROUP

- Differentiated Instruction, pp. 111K–111JJ

ON YOUR OWN

**Practice Book,** page 52

Suppose you find a word you don't understand as you are reading. You look up the word in the dictionary and find it has more than one meaning. How do you know which meaning is correct?
- Read the definitions.
- Try each meaning in the sentence to see if it makes sense.

**Read the dictionary entry. Then write the letter of the correct meaning on the line next to each sentence below.**

**load** *noun* 1. something carried: *There is a load of hay in the wagon.*
2. the amount that can be carried: *One load of stones will fill in the ditch.*
3. something that weighs on the mind: *Leaving the dentist's office took a load off my mind.*
*verb* 4. to put a load in or on something: *Let's load the hay into the wagon.*
5. to put something into a device: *Do you know how to load film into that camera?*

a. Finishing his book report took a load off Justin's mind. 3
b. Ms. Gomez will show us how to load that program into the computer. 5
c. Will one load of bricks be enough to build the wall? 2
d. The truck carried a load of fresh fruit to the market. 1
e. Tomorrow morning we will load the car and start our trip. 4

**Approaching Reproducible,** page 52

**Beyond Reproducible,** page 52

# Build Robust Vocabulary

## Day 1 Teach/Practice

### CONNECT TO WORDS

- Practice this week's vocabulary words using the following prompts:

1. What subject in school do you have a *passion* for?
2. What do you do if someone is *bothering* you?
3. Who is someone you *admire*? Why?
4. Why is it important for students to *concentrate* in class?
5. What part of you body might *ache* after running a race? Explain.
6. What are some antonyms for the word *splendid*?

### ACADEMIC VOCABULARY

- Review the important academic vocabulary words for the week. These words include: *multiple-meaning words, dictionary, generate questions, compare and contrast, italics, heading, pronunciations, bold* or *colored type.*
- Write each word on the board. Define each using student-friendly language and ask students to select the word you are defining. Then point to words in random order for students to define.

## Day 2 Review

### CONNECT TO WORDS

- Review the definitions of this week's vocabulary words using **Student Book** pages 8–9. Then discuss each word using the following prompts:

1. Why do artists need to have a *passion* for their work? Explain.
2. What kind of things *bother* you?
3. Why is honesty a quality we all *admire*?
4. How do you make yourself *concentrate*?
5. What would you do if a part of your body *ached*?
6. Which season do you think is the most *splendid* time of year?

### DICTIONARY: MULTIPLE-MEANING WORDS

- Remind students that some words have more than one meaning. If a student is unsure what a word means, they can use a dictionary.
- Display **Transparency 7**. Read the definition of *confidence*. Model for students how to figure out its meaning in the first sentence. Point out the word *secret*. This means the third meaning is the answer.
- Have students identify the correct meanings for the remaining sentences on the transparency.
- Have students write their own sentences for each meaning of the multiple-meaning word *confidence* in their Writer's Notebooks.

CA CONTENT STANDARD
R 3.1.8 Use knowledge of prefixes and suffixes to determine the meaning of words.

## Day 3 Reinforce

### CONNECT TO WORDS

- Ask students to create word squares for each word in their Writer's Notebooks.
- In the first square, students write the word. (Example: *splendid*)
- In the second square, students write their own definitions of the word and any related words, such as synonyms. (Example: *great, wonderful, terrific*)
- In the third square, students draw a simple illustration that will help them remember the word. (Example: *drawing of a person who is dressed in very fancy clothes*)
- In the fourth square, students write nonexamples, including antonyms. (Example: *horrible, terrible, yucky*)

### RELATED WORDS

- Help students see the relationships among words related to *offspring*.
- Write the words *wolf pup, baby, child, offspring, family* on the board in that order. Discuss the meanings of the words and help students see the relationships and levels of specificity. Guide students to see that a wolf pup is a kind of baby, a baby is a very young child, a child is a specific name for offspring, and an offspring is part of a family.
- Have students think of other baby animals they could substitute for wolf cub, such as kitten and calf, and explain the relationships.

## Day 4 Extend

### CONNECT TO WORDS

- Review this week's vocabulary using the following sentence stems. Have students orally complete each one.

1. I have a passion for _____ .
2. One person I admire is _____ because _____.
3. I can't concentrate when _____.
4. The weather is splendid only when it is______.
5. It really bothers me when _____.
6. My head aches when______.

### MORPHOLOGY

- Use the additional selection vocabulary word *educated* as a springboard to learn other words.
- Write the word *educated* on the board. Underline *-ed*. Explain that the suffix *-ed* is attached to a verb to show the action happened in the past. The word *educated* indicates that someone got an education in the past.
- Write the words *helped* and *painted* on the board. Have students underline *-ed* in each word.
- Use the word parts to define each word. Explain that *-ed* indicates an action that occurred in the past. Therefore, *helped* means someone got help in the past. *Painted* means something was painted in the past.

CA CONTENT STANDARD
R 3.1.5 Demonstrate knowledge of levels of specificity among grade-appropriate words and explain the importance of these relations.

## Day 5 Assess and Reteach

### POSTTEST

- Display **Transparency 8**. Have students complete the cloze sentences using one of this week's vocabulary words.
- Note how quickly and accurately students can complete this task. Work with students who make errors or require too much time to complete this task during Small Group time.

### CONNECT TO WRITING

- Have students write sentences in their Writer's Notebooks using this week's vocabulary. Tell students to write sentences that provide information they learned from this week's readings.
- EL Provide the Day 4 sentence stems for students needing extra support.

# 5-Day Spelling

Go to pages T17 for **Differentiated Spelling Lists**. Pretest and Posttest available in Teacher's Resource Book.

### Spelling Words

| | | |
|---|---|---|
| gold | loaf | slow |
| bowl | roast | grows |
| soak | coast | show |
| sold | scold | float |
| snow | coal | blow |

**Review** snail, gray, plain
**Challenge** window, program

### Dictation Sentences

1. The metal was a gold color.
2. Fill the dog's bowl with water.
3. Water will soak through the soil.
4. The store sold fish.
5. The snow is deep.
6. We bought a loaf of bread.
7. I ate roast chicken for dinner.
8. The penguin swam along the coast.
9. She will scold the bad dog.
10. Some people burn coal for heat.
11. A penguin is slow when it walks.
12. A chick grows quickly.
13. Please **show** me your new book.
14. Ice can float on water.
15. Did you hear the wind blow?

### Review/Challenge Words

1. A snail does not move fast.
2. A plain is a flat stretch of land.
3. The clouds were dark gray.
4. I looked out the window.
5. What program do you like most?

Words in **bold** are from this week's selections.

## Long *o*

CA CONTENT STANDARD
**LC 3.1.8** Spell correctly one-syllable words that have blends, contractions, compounds, orthographic patterns, and common homophones.

### Day 1 Pretest

#### ASSESS PRIOR KNOWLEDGE

- Model for students how to spell the word *bowl*. Segment the word sound by sound, then attach a spelling to each sound. Point out that *ow* is the long *o* spelling that can be found in the middle or at the end of a word or in a syllable.
- Use the Dictation Sentences. Say the underlined word, read the sentence, and repeat the word. Have students write the words.
- Have students self-correct their tests. Point out that the *oa* spelling for a long *o* never appears in the beginning or end of a word.
- Have students cut apart the **Spelling Word Cards BLM** on **Teacher's Resource Book** page 105 and figure out a way to sort them. Have students save the cards for use throughout the week.

### Day 2 Word Sorts and Review

#### SPIRAL REVIEW

Review the long a sound in the words *snail*, *gray*, and *plain*. Have students identify the long *a* spelling pattern. (ai, ay) Then have them find words in this weeks' readings with the same sounds.

#### WORD SORTS

- Have students take turns sorting words and explaining how they sorted them. When students have finished the sort, discuss any words that might have been difficult for them to sort.
- Review the spelling words, pointing out the long *o* vowel spellings. Use the cards on the Spelling Word Cards BLM. Write the key words *old, low,* and *foam* to a bulletin board. Model how to sort words by long *o* spellings. Place the cards beneath the correct key words.

ON YOUR OWN **Practice Book,** page 53

**Using the Word Study Steps**
1. LOOK at the word.
2. SAY the word aloud.
3. STUDY the letters in the word.
4. WRITE the word.
5. CHECK the word.
Did you spell the word right?
If not, go back to step 1.

**Fill in the missing letters of each word to create a spelling word.**
1. s h _o_ _w_
2. r _o_ _a_ s t
3. s c _o_ l d
4. b l _o_ _w_
5. f l _o_ _a_ t
6. g _o_ l d
7. g r _o_ _w_ s
8. c _o_ _a_ s t
9. s _o_ l d
10. b _o_ _w_ l
11. c _o_ _a_ l
12. s l _o_ _w_
13. l _o_ _a_ f
14. s n _o_ _w_
15. s _o_ _a_ k

**Choose the spelling word that best completes the sentence.**
1. The boat will _float_ on the lake.
2. _Snow_ fell all night and covered the ground.
3. I like to have a _bowl_ of ice cream for dessert.

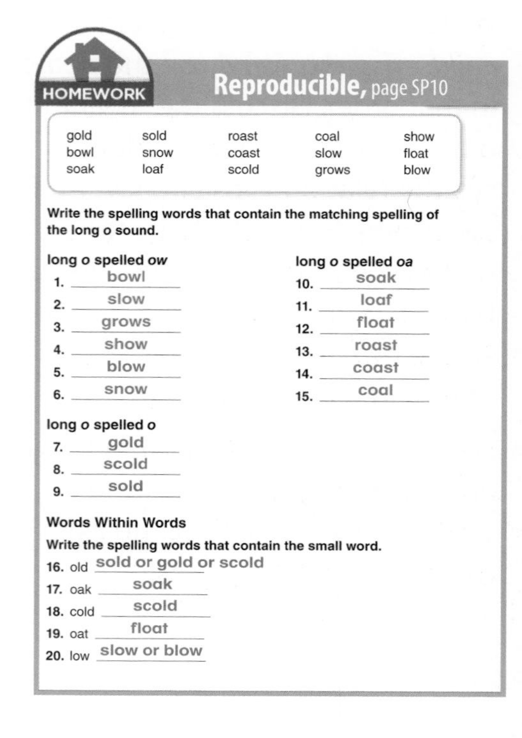
HOMEWORK **Reproducible,** page SP10

| | | | | |
|---|---|---|---|---|
| gold | sold | roast | coal | show |
| bowl | snow | coast | slow | float |
| soak | loaf | scold | grows | blow |

**Write the spelling words that contain the matching spelling of the long *o* sound.**

**long *o* spelled *ow***
1. bowl
2. slow
3. grows
4. show
5. blow
6. snow

**long *o* spelled *o***
7. gold
8. scold
9. sold

**long *o* spelled *oa***
10. soak
11. loaf
12. float
13. roast
14. coast
15. coal

**Words Within Words**
**Write the spelling words that contain the small word.**
16. old sold or gold or scold
17. oak soak
18. cold scold
19. oat float
20. low slow or blow

## Day 3 Word Meanings

### ANTONYMS

Have students copy the words below into their Writer's Notebooks. Have them complete each pair by adding the spelling word that is the antonym.

1. bought, not ____ (sold)
2. fast, not ____ (slow)
3. sink, not ____ (float)
4. dry, not ____ (soak)
5. praise, not ____ (scold)

Challenge students to come up with sentences for spelling words, review words, or challenge words.

Have students do a word hunt for the words in weekly reading or other materials. They should identify the definition of the spelling word being used in context.

## Day 4 Proofread

### PROOFREAD AND WRITE

Write the sentences below on the board. Have students circle and correct each misspelled word.

1. I watched the sno flowt down. (snow, float)
3. Jan sowld a lowf of bread. (sold, loaf)
4. There is goald on the California cowst! (gold, coast)
5. Please sho me your best boal. (show, bowl)

**Error Correction.** Remind students that the *oa* spelling for the long *o* sound never appear at the end of a word. Use the underscore hints on the Sound-Spelling Card to reinforce this principle (oa_).

## Day 5 Assess and Reteach

### POSTTEST

Use the Dictation Sentences on page 109C for the Posttest.

If students have difficulty with any of the words in the lesson, have students place them on a list called *Spelling Words I Want to Remember* in their writer's notebooks. Look for students' use of these words in their writings.

Challenge students to find words for each long *o* spelling and add them to the **Unit 1 Big Question Board.**

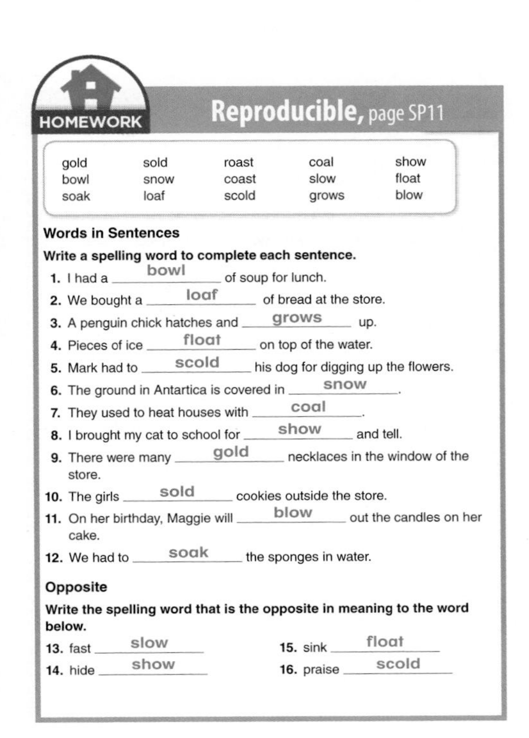

HOMEWORK **Reproducible,** page SP11

| gold | sold | roast | coal | show |
|---|---|---|---|---|
| bowl | snow | coast | slow | float |
| soak | loaf | scold | grows | blow |

**Words in Sentences**

**Write a spelling word to complete each sentence.**

1. I had a ___bowl___ of soup for lunch.
2. We bought a ___loaf___ of bread at the store.
3. A penguin chick hatches and ___grows___ up.
4. Pieces of ice ___float___ on top of the water.
5. Mark had to ___scold___ his dog for digging up the flowers.
6. The ground in Antartica is covered in ___snow___.
7. They used to heat houses with ___coal___.
8. I brought my cat to school for ___show___ and tell.
9. There were many ___gold___ necklaces in the window of the store.
10. The girls ___sold___ cookies outside the store.
11. On her birthday, Maggie will ___blow___ out the candles on her cake.
12. We had to ___soak___ the sponges in water.

**Opposite**

**Write the spelling word that is the opposite in meaning to the word below.**

13. fast ___slow___
14. hide ___show___
15. sink ___float___
16. praise ___scold___

ON YOUR OWN **Practice Book,** page 54

**There are seven spelling mistakes in this postcard. Circle the misspelled words. Write the words correctly on the lines below.**

Dear Paula,

I told you I would send you a postcard! You sure do need to come here next summer. We had so much fun on our family vacation. We would sit on beaches that had sand the color of solid golde. The other penguins and I would play on the beach, flowte in the water, and soke up the sun. At night we would stay up late to listen to the singing of the whales while eating a big boal of ice cream.

I am sad that we have to leave the coste in a few days and go home to Antarctica. I hope there isn't too much sno at home. I will shoe you pictures when I get home.

See you soon,
Peter

1. gold
2. float
3. soak
4. bowl
5. coast
6. snow
7. show

**Writing Activity**

**Write about what you like to do on a cold or snowy day. Use at least three spelling words in your description.**

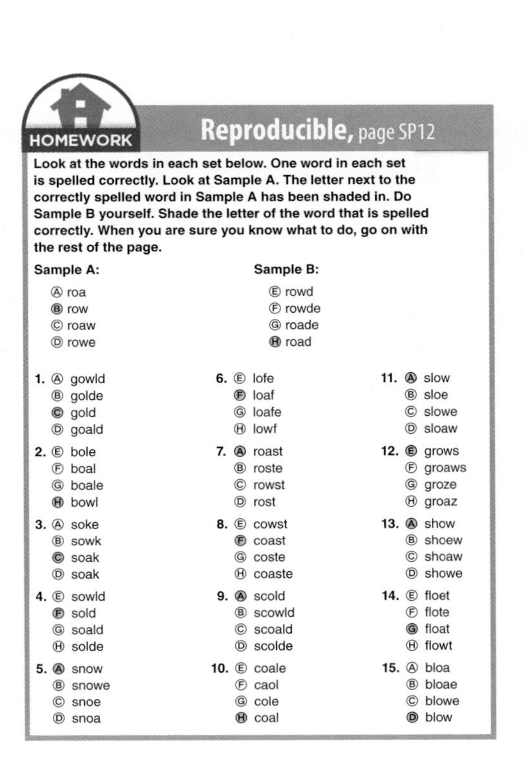

HOMEWORK **Reproducible,** page SP12

**Look at the words in each set below. One word in each set is spelled correctly. Look at Sample A. The letter next to the correctly spelled word in Sample A has been shaded in. Do Sample B yourself. Shade the letter of the word that is spelled correctly. When you are sure you know what to do, go on with the rest of the page.**

**Sample A:** (A) roa (B) row (C) roaw (D) rowe

**Sample B:** (E) rowd (F) rowde (G) roade (H) road

1. (A) gowld (B) golde (C) gold (D) goald
2. (E) bole (F) boal (G) boale (H) bowl
3. (A) soke (B) sowk (C) soak (D) soak
4. (E) sowld (F) sold (G) soald (H) solde
5. (A) snow (B) snowe (C) snoe (D) snoa
6. (E) lofe (F) loaf (G) loafe (H) lowf
7. (A) roast (B) roste (C) rowst (D) rost
8. (E) cowst (F) coast (G) coste (H) coaste
9. (A) scold (B) scowld (C) scoald (D) scolde
10. (E) coale (F) caol (G) cole (H) coal
11. (A) slow (B) sloe (C) slowe (D) sloaw
12. (E) grows (F) groaws (G) groze (H) groaz
13. (A) show (B) shoew (C) shoaw (D) showe
14. (E) floet (F) flote (G) float (H) flowt
15. (A) bloa (B) bloae (C) blowe (D) blow

# 5-Day Grammar

## Daily Language Activities

Use these activities to introduce each day's lesson. Write the day's activities on the board.

**DAY 1**
**1.** come with me to the game **2.** Can you score a goal **3.** what fun it is to play (1: Come; game.; 2: goal?; 3: What; play!)

**DAY 2**
**1.** the iceberg has melted **2.** where is Antarctica **3.** We reed about penguins (1: The; melted.; 2: Where; Antarctica?; 3: read; penguins.)

**DAY 3**
**1.** some people read about seals **2.** did you see the seals **3.** Do you have a map of Antarctica (1: Some; seals.; 2: Did; seals?; 3: Antarctica?)

**DAY 4**
**1.** i like winter **2.** Do you like to ply in the snow **3.** my ears get cold in the winter (1: I; winter.; 2: play; snow?; 3: My; winter.)

**DAY 5**
**1.** dave and Jack made a snowman? **2.** They used cole for the nose. **3.** dave named the snowman Frosty (1: Dave; snowman.; 2: coal; 3: Dave; Frosty.)

### English Learners
UNIVERSAL ACCESS

**Elaborate** Write on the board: *Don talked on the phone.* Circle the subject and underline the predicate. Ask: *Who talked on the phone? What did Don do?* Give other examples such as *Kim is tired and cold.* Then write sentences and have students identify the subjects and predicates.

# Predicates

CA CONTENT STANDARD
LC 3.1.4 Identify and use subjects and verbs correctly in speaking and writing simple sentences.

## Day 1 Introduce the Concept

### INTRODUCE PREDICATES

- Every complete **sentence** is made up of two parts: the **subject** and the **predicate**.
- The subject tells who or what the sentence is about.
- The predicate tells what the subject does or is. Predicates can be one word or more than one word.
- Two predicates joined by the word *and* form a **compound predicate**.

**Examples:**
Antarctica is cold.
Penguins dive and swim.

| **Subject** | **Predicate** |
|---|---|
| Antarctica | is cold |
| Penguins | dive and swim |

See Grammar Transparency 16 for modeling and guided practice.

HOMEWORK **Reproducible,** page GR10

- Every sentence has two parts.
- Every sentence has a subject and a predicate.
- The **predicate** of a sentence tells what the subject does or is.
  The penguins walked across the snow.
  The predicate is walked across the snow.

**Which word or words tell what the subject does or is? Draw a line under the predicate.**

1. Penguins live in cold climates.
2. A layer of fat keeps penguins warm.
3. Penguins shed their feathers.
4. They grow new feathers.
5. Penguins gather in large groups.
6. They settle along the shore.
7. We watch them hop over the rocks.
8. They like to slide along the snow.
9. I love when penguins dive into the water.
10. Penguins swim very quickly.

## Day 2 Teach the Concept

### REVIEW PREDICATES

Review with students what a subject is and what a predicate is. Write a sentence on the board and have students identify the subject and the predicate.

Present the following:

- There are two parts in every sentence: a subject and a predicate.
- The predicate identifies what the subject does or is.
- A predicate can be one word or more than one word.

**Examples:**
Penguins **swim**.
Penguins **swim in the ocean**.

See Grammar Transparency 17 for modeling and guided practice.

ON YOUR OWN **Practice Book,** page 55

- Every sentence has two parts.
- Every sentence has a predicate.
- The **predicate** of a sentence tells what the subject does or is.

**Match each group of words in the first column with its predicate in the second column. Write the predicate.**

1. Ice and snow cover Antarctica.
2. The ice is millions of years old.
3. Temperatures stay below freezing.
4. Cold wind blows across the land.
5. Giant icebergs float in the sea.
6. Seals and penguins live in the cold.
7. Few plants grow in Antarctica.
8. Tourists like to see Antarctica.

stay below freezing.
float in the sea.
like to see Antarctica.
grow in Antarctica.
cover Antarctica.
blows across the land.
live in the cold.
is millions of years old.

## Review and Practice

### REVIEW PREDICATES

Review with students how to identify a sentence's subject and predicate.

### MECHANICS AND USAGE: COMPLETE SENTENCES

- A sentence fragment does not have a subject and a predicate. Correct a sentence fragment by adding a subject or predicate. For example:

**Sentence Fragment:** Clear and blue.
**Complete Sentence:** The sky was clear and blue.

- A run-on sentence joins two sentences that should be separate. Correct a run-on sentence by separating two complete ideas into two sentences.

**Run-on:** The sky is clear it is blue.
**Correct:** The sky is clear. It is blue.

## Review and Proofread

### REVIEW COMPLETE SENTENCES

Review what a subject is and what a predicate is. Explain how to correct a sentence fragment and a run-on sentence.

### PROOFREAD

Have students correct errors in the following sentences.

1. the penguin father. (The penguin father keeps his egg warm.)
2. We slide on the ice  penguins slide too? (ice. Penguins)
3. Winter is a cold season it snows often (season. It; often.)
4. Live in Antarctica. (Penguins live in Antarctica.)

## Assess and Reteach

### ASSESS

Use the Daily Language Activity or the Reproducible page GR12 for assessment.

### RETEACH

Use Reproducible page GR12 and selected pages from the **Grammar and Writing Handbook** for additional reteaching.

Check students' writing for use of the skill. Assign Grammar Revision Assignments in their Writer's Notebooks, as needed.

See Grammar Transparency 18 for modeling and guided practice.

ON YOUR OWN **Reproducible,** page GR11

- A sentence is a group of words that tells a complete thought.
- A sentence begins with a capital letter and has an end mark.
- A run-on sentence is a sentence that tells more than one thought.
  Run-on sentence: It is cold we put on our coats.
  Two sentences: It is cold. We put on our coats.

**Read the sentences. Rewrite each sentence and fix any run-on sentences.**

1. I think snow is beautiful I can't wait for the first snowfall each year!
   I think snow is beautiful. I can't wait for the first snowfall each year!
2. Then it's time to go skiing I also like to skate.
   Then it's time to go skiing. I also like to skate.
3. Skating outside is fun it's better than skating indoors.
   Skating outside is fun. It's better than skating indoors.
4. I don't mind the cold it makes me feel wide awake.
   I don't mind the cold. It makes me feel wide awake.
5. I really like to build snowmen we dress them in funny clothes.
   I really like to build snowmen. We dress them in funny clothes.
6. I also like to make snow angels I make them all over the grass.
   I also like to make snow angels. I make them all over the grass.

See Grammar Transparency 19 for modeling and guided practice.

HOMEWORK **Practice Book,** page 56

- The **predicate** of a sentence tells what the subject does or is.

**Rewrite the paragraphs below. Be sure to correct each run-on sentence.**

My mom loves to visit Antarctica. She goes there every winter she wants me to go with her one day. She travels there for work she is an animal doctor who works with penguins. My mom helps sick penguins feel better she also works with the local animal doctors to help find cures for diseases

One time, my mom got stuck in Antarctica. She could not fly home for a week. I was worried about her, but she called me everyday to tell me that she was okay. Maybe I will go to Antarctica one day with my mom I just do not want to get stuck

My mom loves to visit Antarctica. She goes there every winter. She wants me to go with her one day. She travels there for work. She is an animal doctor who works with penguins. My mom helps sick penguins feel better. She also works with the local animal doctors to help find cures for diseases.

One time, my mom got stuck in Antarctica. She could not fly home for a week. I was worried about her, but she called me everyday to tell me that she was okay. Maybe I will go to Antarctica one day with my mom. I just do not want to get stuck!

See Grammar Transparency 20 for modeling and guided practice.

HOMEWORK **Reproducible,** page GR12

**A. Decide which part of the sentence is the predicate. Circle your answer.**

1. The penguin on the shore lost clumps of feathers.
   **A.** lost clumps of feathers (circled)
   **B.** on the shore
   **C.** The penguin
2. New feathers quickly filled in the patches.
   **A.** New feathers
   **B.** quickly
   **C.** filled in the patches (circled)
3. The guide at the zoo showed us the penguins.
   **A.** showed us the penguins (circled)
   **B.** at the zoo
   **C.** The guide
4. The penguins in the pool slid down ice hills.
   **A.** in the pool
   **B.** slid down ice hills (circled)
   **C.** The penguins

**B. Choose a predicate from the box that best completes each sentence.**

| | |
|---|---|
| is called the South Pole | dive for food |
| raced to the South Pole | is very cold |

5. The water around Antarctica is very cold.
6. Seabirds of Antarctica dive for food.
7. The center of Antarctica is called the South Pole.
8. Groups of explorers raced to the South Pole.

**Write**

**WHOLE GROUP**

**WRITING**
- Focus on Object and Setting

**CA CONTENT STANDARDS**
W 3.1.2, W 3.1.4, W 3.2.2, LAS 3.1.3

**SMALL GROUP**
- Differentiated Instruction, pp. 111K–111JJ

**5-Day Writing**

| | |
|---|---|
| DAY 1 | Skill Introduction |
| DAY 2 | Minilesson 1<br>Revision Assignments |
| DAY 3 | Minilesson 2<br>Revision Assignments |
| DAY 4 | Reading/Writing Connection<br>Focus on Object/Setting |
| DAY 5 | Writing Conferences |

The Writers' Express
Immediate Impact. Lasting Transformation. wex.org

**Research Proven Writing Approach**

# Topic Development: Focus on Object/Setting

## Professional Development

**WHAT IS TOPIC DEVELOPMENT (FOCUS)?**

**Focus is a writer's ability to stick with and develop one central moment, place, or object.**

**WHY TEACH TOPIC DEVELOPMENT (FOCUS)?**

Focus is the first skill in the writing scope and sequence because research has shown that it drives students to develop a set of abilities that are fundamental to powerful writing.

Below are a few of the common problems that students overcome as they learn to focus.

- listing without including any detail or development
- touching on a subject without really developing it
- including some detail without developing a theme or message

**WHAT HAPPENS WHEN STUDENTS FOCUS ON AN OBJECT OR A SETTING?**

Focusing on an object or a setting helps students hone their abilities to both observe and describe what is around them. When writers focus on objects or settings, they may struggle at first—listing descriptions rather than integrating concrete, sensory details into their writing. With practice they will incorporate these descriptions more naturally to create vivid images and a sense of context.

**ASSESSMENT: WHAT WILL I SEE IN MY STUDENTS' WRITING?**

Focusing on where they are and who or what is around them in a given moment develops students' unique perspective on the world.

We haven't taken the trash out in days. It stunk so bad. It was full of banana peels, wasted chips, peanut butter, all kinds of stuff. It kinda smelled like skunk and beans.

By using specific details to describe the trash, this student provided the reader with information about the setting.

**TARGETING FOCUS: USING OVER-THE-SHOULDER CONFERENCES**

You can use an Over-the-Shoulder Conference to let a student know that he has done a great job with focus or to remind him why focus is so important. For example,

- You might recognize how well the student has focused.
  *This is great! You've included four details about the playground. I can picture that!*
- You might remind the student to focus.
  *That sounds like a fun birthday party. Can you describe what the fancy cake looked like?*

**POST STUDENT EXCERPTS**

While students are working on focus, you should post strong student examples of focus, and make sure to discuss briefly how these excerpts demonstrate the skill particularly well.

**Think Aloud** We've spent lots of time this week talking about why focusing on an object or a place is an important writing skill. Let's read the writing I hung up today. Does anyone see a great example of how focused writing helps you picture a specific object? How it lets you imagine where this moment happened?

**SHARING CIRCLE**

Sharing plays a vital role in the writing process because of what it teaches students about community, as well as writing. In Sharing Circle, students repeat a protocol that lets them appreciate each other's work, pinpoint the impact their writing is making on their readers, and gain confidence in their skills.

When you and your students target the skill of Focusing on an Object or a Setting, you might begin Sharing Circle by saying:

**Think Aloud** During sharing today, I want everyone to listen carefully for details that really help you picture [an object/place].

## Objective

- Introduce Skill: Focus on Object and Setting

### Materials

- none

## Objective

- Focus on a single object in writing

### Materials

- Writer's Notebook
- Objects that fit in your hand and can be passed around
- Transparency 10

**Writing Professional Development Guide**

See **Writing Professional Development Guide** for student examples and additional research information.

# Writer's Craft

## Strong Sentences: Describing a Single Object

**TEACH/MODEL**

**CA CONTENT STANDARD W 3.2.2** Write descriptions that use concrete sensory details to present and support unified impressions of people, places, things, or experiences.

Display **Transparency 10** or post the following chart where everyone can see it. Model aloud how to describe an object such as lip balm.

**Teacher:** *I brought in this cherry lip balm and we're going to describe it using this chart. I want to think about how it smells (take off cap). Like cherries! Mmm! I'm going to write that in the chart. What noise did you hear when I took off the cap?*
**Students:** *It pops!*
**Teacher:** *Exactly. Now I can write that in the sounds category. I bet you normally wouldn't think of lip balm sounding like anything, but when we really stop and think about it, it definitely makes a noise doesn't it?*

Continue to fill in the chart for the lip balm with student input. Encourage students to use creative vocabulary such as "gooey" or "sticky" to describe how it feels.

**Transparency 10**

| Item | Smells | Tastes | Looks | Feels | Sounds |
|---|---|---|---|---|---|
| Lip balm | sweet<br><br>like cherries | like cherries | red | gooey<br><br>sticky | pops when the top comes off |
| Tooth-brush | | | | | |

**Writing Transparency**

## Teacher Write Aloud

Show the objects to the group. Tell students that you have collected these objects from your house. They just helped you describe the [tube of lip balm]. Next they are going to work together to describe the toothbrush. Pass it around so everyone has a chance to feel it and see it up close.

Record students' answers in the proper categories on the transparency. Point out that there are many ways to describe one object and that different people were able to observe different aspects of it. For example:

**Teacher:** *What does the toothbrush feel like?*
**Students:** *The shiny part is smooth, but the bristles are rough.*
**Teacher:** *Good. Now we have some details about what it looks like and feels like.*

Continue to fill in the chart with the rest of the details about the toothbrush. If time permits, allow students to create a chart for another object you brought in or one they have at their desks.

**Summarize Learning** Explain the following to students:

**Think Aloud** What do you think? Did we stay focused on our objects? There were so many ways to describe our objects. You did a fantastic job pointing out all of the details about the [toothbrush, lip balm, ball, toy, etc]. In a moment you will get to choose one of the items and describe a moment when you were once using it or wearing it.

Ask students to take out their Writer's Notebooks. Pass the rest of the objects around silently. Tell students that they will need to choose one of the objects to complete the following Writing Prompt.

- Raise your hand if you have ever used lip balm.
- Raise your hand if you love to brush your teeth.
- Raise your hand if you love to eat fruits and vegetables.

**Transparency 10**

Focus on a moment when you were using, wearing, or playing with the object you selected. Describe the object using your senses and describe how you used it.

**Writing Transparency**

### Daily Journal Prompts

**Focus on Object**

Use these and other prompts for independent daily journal writing.

- Write about a moment when you were helping to make dinner. Describe the objects you used using your senses and describe how you used them.
- Write about a time you were playing a sport/game. Describe the objects you used using your senses and describe how you used them.
- Write about a moment when you were in art class. Describe the objects you used using your senses and describe how you used them.
- Write about a moment when you were playing outside in the sand or dirt. Describe the objects you used using your senses and describe how you used them.

## Objective

- Select a single object and write four sentences describing it

## Materials

- Writer's Notebooks
- Practice Book, p. 20

### Teacher-to-Teacher

**Show Them What They Did Well**

Being explicit and honest about what students accomplished can motivate them to write again, and will help to create a writing community in which everyone believes they have a contribution to make.

**Practice Book, page 57**

1. Look carefully at one of your arms.
2. Write 4 sentences only about your arm. Focus on the object and describe exactly how it looks.

**Example:** My right arm looks pale sticking out of my dark blue t-shirt. Freckles make it look like the map of constellations that hangs in our classroom. If I look hard enough, I think I can make out Orion's belt near my wrist. It's right next to the jagged, white scar that my cat, George, gave me when I tried to put him in a doll's dress last year.

**Extra Practice:** Do the same exercise describing one of your feet.

**Approaching Reproducible,** page 57
**Beyond Reproducible,** page 57

# Minilesson 1

**Strong Sentences** Describing a Single Object

### TEACH/MODEL

**Write Strong Sentences** Write the following on the board, or have students use **Practice Book** page 57.

> Look carefully at one of your arms.
> Write four sentences about only your arm. Focus on the object and describe exactly how it looks.

Explain that by focusing on an object, the writer can describe it in detail and create a picture for the reader.

**Think Aloud** It might seem like you don't have a lot to write about your arm, but think about any little details you see that you could write a sentence about. Consider any marks you have on your skin like moles or freckles. Is your skin rough or smooth?

### PRACTICE/APPLY

Students work independently. Ask for students to share their work. Circulate and provide Over-the-Shoulder Conferences.

**Summarize Learning** Explain the following to students:

**Think Aloud** Were you able to write just about your arm? What good examples of focus do you recall from today's writing? I liked the way [Juan] described the freckles on his arm. As you write, remember that focus is picking one thing and writing a lot about it. You are working hard to develop this skill. I can see it already.

# Minilesson 2

**Strong Sentences** Describing a Single Object

**TEACH/MODEL**

**Write Strong Sentences** Explain to students the goal of the lesson.

**Think Aloud** We've been examining the skill of focus and why it's so important. So far most of our discussion as a class has been devoted to focusing on a moment in time. You are really getting the hang of it. Today we're going to talk about how writers focus on a single object. After that we're going to write and share. As always I'm excited to see what everyone comes up with, and you'll have a chance to share at least an excerpt of your piece at the end of the period.

Display **Transparency 10** or write the following on the board.

**Transparency 10**

Choose an object from somewhere in the classroom.
Write three sentences about that object alone. Focus on the object and describe it using specific details. Try to create a picture of the object in the reader's mind.

**Writing Transparency**

**PRACTICE/APPLY**

List some possible objects students can choose, then lead thirty seconds of modeling the exercise for students. When you see that students get the idea, have them choose an object and begin to work independently. Ask for students to share their work.

**Summarize Learning** Explain the following:

**Think Aloud** Who can remind us of some strong examples of focus from today's writing and sharing? You did an outstanding job picking one object and focusing your writing on it. In other words you picked one object and wrote a lot about it. This is what focus is all about. You are really getting the hang of this.

## Objective

- Describe a single object using details

### Materials

- Writer's Notebooks

## Teacher-to-Teacher

**Authorizing Students**

As students become comfortable using the tools of a writer, they become increasingly able to identify the specific parts of a text in which an author is using those tools. You can encourage this transfer by, for example, asking students to find a passage in their reading in which the author uses focus to describe an object in detail.

## English Learners

UNIVERSAL ACCESS

**Provide Language** Have students select their object, then say or write all the words they know to describe it. Provide additional words and explain each. List the words on the student's paper. Prompt them to use some of the new words in their description.

# Reading and Writing Connection

## Writer's Craft

### STRONG SENTENCES: FOCUS ON OBJECT/SETTING

Use the example from *Wolf!* to show the author's skilled use of focus.

- Ask: *When have you read aloud to someone else?*
- Have students read aloud the excerpt from *Wolf!* Ask: *What details stand out to you in this moment? Why do you think the author wanted us to be able to imagine this small moment in time?*

### USE FOCUS TO WRITE ABOUT TEXT

Remind students to use the skill of focus when they write about *Wolf!* so that they can help the reader see or understand clearly.

CA CONTENT STANDARD LAS 3.1.3 Respond to questions with appropriate elaboration.

**Engagement Prompt** These prompts have been designed to help students deepen their connection to the text and to discover their own perspective on it.

- *Focus on a moment when you bought something. Describe the object you bought in detail.*

**Response Prompt** These prompts have been designed to help students explore more deeply their reactions to particular passages in the reading.

- *Focus on a moment in the story when you thought an animal was doing something strange.*

CA **Writing**

**Focus on Moment**
Good writers **slow down a moment** in time by describing character details.

# Reading and Writing Connection

Read the passage below. Notice how author Becky Bloom focuses on a moment in her story.

An excerpt from *Wolf!*

Ding-dong, rang the wolf at the farm gate.

He lay down on the grass, made himself comfortable, took out his new book, and began to read.

He read with confidence and passion, and the pig, the cow, and the duck all listened and said not one word.

The author focuses the moment when the wolf finally gets the other animals to pay attention to his reading. By using focus, the author can include details about what each character does as the wolf starts reading.

110

| Unit 1 Writing: Personal Narrative (Description) | |
|---|---|
| Week 1 | • Strong Sentences: Focus on Moment |
| Week 2 | • Strong Paragraphs: Focus on Moment |
| Week 3 | • Personal Narrative (Guided Writing) |
| Week 4 | • Strong Sentences: Focus on Setting/Object |
| Week 5 | • Strong Paragraphs: Focus on Setting/Object |
| Week 6 | Personal Narrative (Independent Writing) |

## Read and Find

Read Robert's writing below. What did he do to focus on a character and an object? Use the tips below to help you.

### My Best Catch Ever

by Robert R.

Read about when I caught the ball.

Crack! I heard the batter smash the ball with her bat. The ball flew up into the air, soaring higher and higher. I lost sight of it for a second when it passed the sun, but then I saw it coming right toward me! I locked my eyes on the ball and lifted my glove over my head. Thump! It dropped right in!

### Writer's Checklist

Does the writer pick one **moment** and write a lot about it?

Does the writer use specific details about what happened in the moment

Do you get a clear picture in your mind of how Bob experienced this moment?

111

# Write

**Literary Analysis Prompt** These prompts have been designed to help students deepen their connection to the text and discover their own perspective on it.

- *Focus on a place in the story where you think the author was trying to make the wolf seem hardworking.*

## Use Student Model

Have students chorally read the student sample at the top of **Student Book** page 111. Discuss what this student writer did to focus on a moment in time (or object/setting). Use the Writer's Checklist.

Write the following journal prompt on the board:

**Think about a book you enjoyed reading. Select one moment, setting, or object in the book. Write three to five sentences about it.**

Tell students that you will be reading and commenting on their writing during Writing Conference time.

Model how to use the Writer's Checklist to write and revise their work.

- What is the moment you chose?
- What sentences did you add to tell about that moment? Will readers be able to clearly picture that moment? If not, what details could you add?

## Objective

- Meet with the teacher to discuss writing and receive revision assignments

**Materials**

- Writer's Notebooks
- Revision Assignments

### Teacher-to-Teacher

**Over-the-Shoulder Conferences**

Use these quick, focused opportunities to comment while students are writing.

- **Step 1** Quietly move close enough to a student that you can read the journal entry he or she is writing.
- **Step 2** Read part of what you see. You don't need to start from the beginning or read the entire piece.
- **Step 3** Show the student a spot in the writing where he or she is using a particular skill or describing something that piques your interest.
- **Step 4** Whisper a sentence or two about why you noticed that spot in the writing and ask a question that will nudge the student to add a detail or clarify.
- **Step 5** Move on to the next student. Select students strategically. You should see 12–15 students in a 15-minute period.

# Conferences

## Writing Journals

**DYNAMIC FEEDBACK SYSTEM**

**Purpose** One of the best ways for students to develop skills is by understanding how their writing affects their readers. Your targeted comments direct students to notice the impact they've made by using a specific skill. Your comments should aim to:

- Engage and encourage students by showing them your appreciation for what they've written.
- Focus students' attention on developing one particular skill.

**Steps in the Dynamic Feedback System**

1. Read and appreciate the writing.
2. Notice how the student uses the targeted skill. (e.g. focus: Ask: *For how many sentences does the student stay on a topic?)*
3. Write comments in which you show how the writing has an impact on you. Direct your comments to those places in the piece where the student has used the targeted skill.
4. Meet with and give the student a revision assignment.

**WRITE EFFECTIVE COMMENTS ON FOCUS**

**Sample Comments for Focus** At least one of your comments should highlight the way the student uses the skill of focus. Here are some sample comments. Use these comments to get you started.

- *The tiny details you used really help me see the [baseball game] you are describing.*
- *You made me want to know more about [the scrapbook you made].*
- *Wow! This is a great description of (your house). Can you tell me more about it?*
- *I'm curious about (that setting or object). Can you tell me more about it?*

# Revision Assignments

CA CONTENT STANDARD
**W 3.1.4** Revise drafts to improve the coherence and logical progression of ideas by using an established rubric.

## IMPROVE WRITING

**What Is It?** Revision assignments play a crucial role in the dynamic feedback system. They enable you to work with each student on one skill at a time until the student has mastered it.

Revision assignments involve marking a specific section of a student's journal entry and then asking the student to revise it in a specific way. By requiring students to put to use your feedback to revise their own writing, revision assignments show clearly how that feedback has affected what students are able to do next.

**Sample Revision Assignments for Focus** Here are some examples of effective revision assignments for focus. Use them to get started. You may also use the preprinted Revision Assignment Notes or create your own revision assignments based on these.

*I underlined a sentence in your entry that names a place that I wanted to know more about. Write two more sentences that describe exactly what the place looked like.*

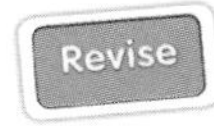
*I would love to know more about [insert object from entry]. Write two sentences about it as if you were looking at it through a magnifying glass.*

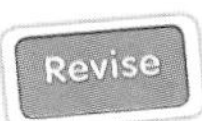
*I was curious to know about where you were when [insert event from entry]. Pretend you took a picture of the place where you were and write two sentences that describe that picture.*

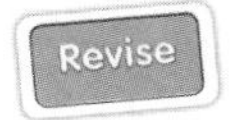
*Underline a sentence in your entry that you like. Write two more sentences about the person/setting/object in the sentence.*

Revise

### Revision Assignment Notes

Use the Revision Assignment Notes to focus students' rewrites.

 **Available on Jump Drive**

### Daily Handwriting

Introduce the cursive alphabet. See Handwriting page 14 for daily practice.
W 3.1.2

Mark students' Journal Checklists to indicate mastered skills.

**Reproducible,** page 222

| STAGE 1 Establishing Habits | | |
|---|---|---|
| ☐ Write Journal Entries | ☐ Practice Skill Drills | ☐ Engage in Experience |
| ☐ Respond to Feedback | ☐ Develop Vocabulary | ☐ Share Writing |

| STAGE 2 Strengthening Voice | | |
|---|---|---|
| Expressive Skills | Topic Development | ☐ Moment ☐ Object ☐ Setting |
| | Showing | ☐ Include unique observations<br>☐ Recognize showing and telling |
| | Strong Verbs | ☐ Recognize and use strong verbs |
| | Sensory Detail | ☐ Use multiple senses<br>☐ Choose sensory detail effectively |
| | Dialogue and Evidence I | ☐ Include dialogue |
| | Character Development | ☐ Believable<br>☐ Change and growth |
| | Logical Structure I: Distinguishing Moments | ☐ Use chronological order<br>☐ Distinguish moments |
| Technical Skills | Sentence Mechanics & Usage I: The Complete Sentence | ☐ Capitals and end punctuation<br>☐ Parts of speech<br>☐ Possessives<br>☐ Commas in a series |
| | Subject/Verb Agreement I | ☐ With present tense<br>☐ With simple past tense |
| | Punctuating and Formatting Dialogue & Quotations | ☐ Quotation marks |

**Writing Journal Checklist**

# Administer the Test

## Weekly Reading Quick Check,

### Passage and questions, Unit 1 Week 4

**ASSESSED SKILLS**

- Dictionary: Multiple-Meaning Words
- Compare and Contrast
- Predicates, Focus on: Object, Setting
- Long *o*

*Selection Test Also Available.*

**Progress Monitoring, Unit 1 Week 4**

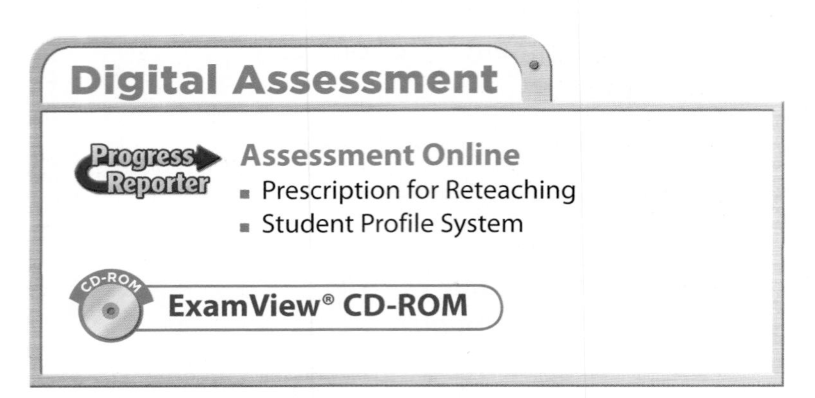

## Unit Fluency Assessment

Assess fluency for one group of students per week. Use the Oral Fluency Record Sheet to track the number of words read correctly. Fluency goal for all students: **61–81 words correct per minute (WCPM)**.

| | |
|---|---|
| Approaching Level | Weeks 1, 3, 5 |
| On Level | Weeks 2, 4 |
| Beyond Level | Week 6 |

**Diagnostic, Unit 1 Fluency**

| Diagnose | | Prescribe |
|---|---|---|
| **Review the assessment answers with students. Have them correct their errors. Then provide additional instruction as needed.** | | |
| | **IF...** | **THEN...** |
| **VOCABULARY WORDS**<br>**VOCABULARY STRATEGY**<br>Dictionary: Multiple-Meaning Words | 0–2 items correct . . . | LOG ON Online Practice: Go to **www.macmillanmh.com**.<br>CD-ROM Vocabulary Puzzlemaker |
| **COMPREHENSION**<br>Skill: Compare and Contrast | 0–2 items correct . . . | SPIRAL REVIEW See Compare and Contrast lessons Unit 1, Week 5, page 139B. |
| **WRITING AND GRAMMAR**<br>Predicates, Focus on: Object, Setting | 0–1 items correct . . . | See Focus Lesson in Unit 1 Week 5. |
| **PHONICS AND SPELLING**<br>Words with Long *o* | 0–1 items correct . . . | LOG ON Online Practice: Go to **www.macmillanmh.com**.<br>Intervention Anthology: Phonics/Word Study |
| **FLUENCY** | 55–60 WCPM | AUDIO CD Fluency Solutions Audio CD |
| | 0–54 WCPM | Evaluate for Intervention |

## WRITE-ON-DEMAND SCORING RUBRIC

**PROMPT** **How can a person learn about the world around them through books? Write as much as you can as well as you can. Write for 5 minutes.**

| 4 Excellent | 3 Good | 2 Fair | 1 Unsatisfactory |
|---|---|---|---|
| • More than 7 sentences<br>• Almost no spelling or grammar errors<br>• Cohesive ideas, focused and organized | • 5–7 sentences<br>• A few spelling and grammar errors<br>• Well-developed ideas and facts provided | • 4–5 sentences<br>• Several spelling and grammar errors<br>• Some good information; some vague | • Fewer than 4 sentences<br>• Many spelling and grammar errors<br>• Few developed ideas; little accurate information |

**Daily Planner**

| | |
|---|---|
| DAY 1 | • Prepare to Read<br>• Academic Language<br>• Vocabulary (Preteach) |
| DAY 2 | • Comprehension<br>• Practice Reader Lesson 1 |
| DAY 3 | • Phonics/Decoding<br>• Practice Reader Lesson 2 |
| DAY 4 | • Phonics/Decoding<br>• Vocabulary (Review)<br>• Practice Reader Lesson 3 |
| DAY 5 | • Fluency<br>• Self-Selected Reading |

**StudentWorks Plus**

**Corrective Feedback**

Many speakers of African American Vernacular English drop the /l/ sound and letter in words, such as in words with *-oal* spelling patterns, such as *coal*. Provide additional articulation support prior to reading and spelling these words.

Strategic

# Approaching Level

## Prepare to Read

**Objective** Preview *Wolf!*

**Materials** • **StudentWorks Plus** • self-stick notes

### PREVIEW TEXT

- Have students preview *Wolf!* using **StudentWorks Plus**. This version of the Student Book contains oral summaries in multiple languages, on-line multilingual glossaries, word-by-word highlighting, and questions that assess and build comprehension.
- Remind students that listening carefully to and following along with the word-by-word reading will help them prepare for the reading of the selection with the class. Ask students to place self-stick notes on any challenging words or places that confuse them. Discuss these with students prior to the reading of the selection with the rest of the class.
- Ask students to write three or four sentences in their Writer's Notebooks telling what they learned about reading.

## Academic Language

**Objective** Teach academic language

**Materials** • none

### PRETEACH LANGUAGE OF INSTRUCTION

Tell students that there are many important lesson words you will be using this week. You want them to become familiar with these words *before* the lessons. These words also appear in the directions of the tests they will be taking this year.

Preteach the following academic words: *fantasy, compare, contrast, multiple-meaning words, headings, colored type, pronunciations.*

- Define each word using student-friendly language. Tell students that *multiple-meaning words* are words that have more than one meaning. For example, the word *light* can mean "something that is not heavy" or it can mean "a color that isn't dark." To help students remember the concept, underline the prefix *multi-* in *multiple* and explain that *multi-* means "many."
- In addition, relate each word to known words. For example, connect *fantasy* to *dream*; *compare* to *same*; *contrast* to *different*; *headings* to *labels*; *pronunciations* to *intonation*.
- Highlight these words when used throughout the week and reinforce their meanings.

Strategic

# Approaching Level

## Phonics/Decoding

**Objective** Decode words with long *o*

**Materials**
- **Approaching Reproducible,** p. 46
- **Sound-Spelling WorkBoards**

TESTED SKILL

### PHONICS MAINTENANCE

- Distribute a **WorkBoard** to each student. Say a sound previously taught, including final *e* and long *a*. Have students find the **Sound-Spelling Card** on the board for each sound.
- Review the spelling(s) for each sound by providing a sample word containing that spelling. Guide students to write the word on the board. Model how to segment the word and write the spelling for each sound, as needed. In addition, point out spelling hints, such as the *e* at the very end of a word is almost always silent.
- Dictate the following words for students to spell: *raise, straight, stays, playing, hunt, packs, spit, hole, coat, show, sold*. Write each word on the board and have students self-correct their work.

### RETEACH SKILL

CA CONTENT STANDARD R 3.1.2 Decode regular multisyllabic words.

**Long *o*** Point to the long *o* Sound-Spelling Card on the WorkBoard and review the spellings for this sound. State each spelling and provide a sample word.

CA CONTENT STANDARD R 3.1.2 Decode regular multisyllabic words.

- Write the words below on the board. Model how to decode the first word in each row, then guide students as they decode the remaining words. For the multisyllabic words, divide the words into syllables using the syllable scoop procedure to help students read one syllable at a time.
- When completed, point to the words in random order for students to chorally read. Repeat several times.

| | | | | | |
|---|---|---|---|---|---|
| hop | hope | rope | road | cod | coldly |
| boat | boast | hole | hold | sow | sown |
| snow | snowed | moat | most | grow | growable |
| low | loan | load | loaded | float | floatable |
| sole | stole | sold | foal | fold | folding |
| low | lower | flow | flowing | hoe | homerun |

Sound-Spelling WorkBoard

### English Learners

UNIVERSAL ACCESS

**Minimal Contrasts** Focus on articulation. Make the /o/ sound and point to your mouth position. Repeat for the /ō/ sound. Then have students say each sound together, noticing the slight difference in mouth position. Continue by having students read minimal-contrast word pairs, such as *choose/chose; close/close; ton/tone; hop/hope; not/note; rob/robe.*

### Approaching Reproducible, page 46

If a vowel says its own name, it is a long vowel. Here is a rule to help you remember: "When two vowels go out walking, the first does all the talking." That means the first vowel is a long vowel and the second vowel is silent. Sometimes the letter *w* acts as a vowel.

**A. Circle the word that has a long o sound in each sentence.**

1. The (snow, crowd) covered the car.
2. I like to (pop, float) at the pool.
3. We will (roast, spool) marshmallows at the camp fire.
4. He (sold, enjoyed) the most candy in the school sale.
5. The (gallon, bowl) on the table is glass.
6. Pirates sailed the seas looking for (gold, world).

**B. Follow the directions above to review these words with the long a sound.**

7. My new sweater is (gray, yarn).
8. I like my ice cream (candle, plain).
9. We had to (stand, wait) for the bus.
10. He had a (stain, cat) on his shirt.

Strategic

# Approaching Level

## Vocabulary

**Objective** Preteach selection vocabulary

**Materials** • **Visual Vocabulary Resources** • **Approaching Reproducible,** p. 47

### PRETEACH VOCABULARY

Use the **Visual Vocabulary Resources** to preteach the key selection words: *passion, bothering, admire, concentrate, ached, splendid*. Focus on two words per day. Use the following routine that appears in detail on the cards.

- Define the word in English and provide the example given.
- Define the word in Spanish, if appropriate, and indicate if the word is a cognate.
- Display the picture and explain how it illustrates or demonstrates the word.
- Then engage students in structured partner talk about the image, using the key word.
- Ask students to chorally say the word three times.
- Point out any known sound-spellings or focus on a key aspect of phonemic awareness related to the word.
- Distribute copies of the Vocabulary Glossary, **English Learners Resource Book**.

### REVIEW PREVIOUSLY TAUGHT VOCABULARY

Display the Vocabulary Cards from the previous three weeks. Say the meaning of each word, one by one, and have students identify it. Then point to words in random order for students to provide definitions and related words they know.

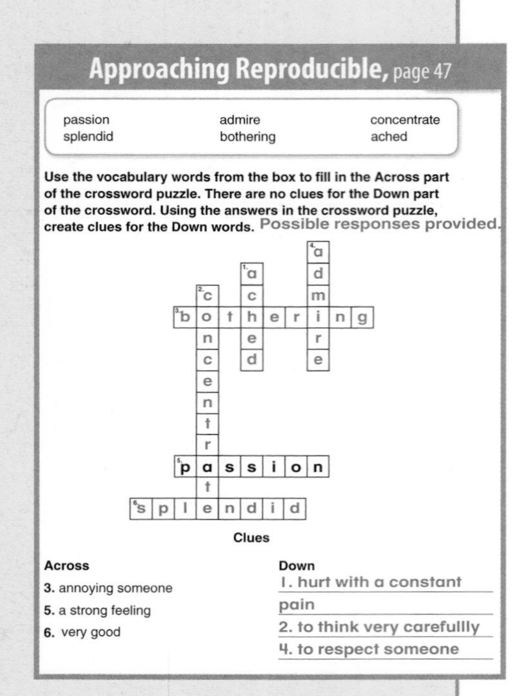
**Approaching Reproducible,** page 47

| passion | admire | concentrate |
|---|---|---|
| splendid | bothering | ached |

**Use the vocabulary words from the box to fill in the Across part of the crossword puzzle. There are no clues for the Down part of the crossword. Using the answers in the crossword puzzle, create clues for the Down words.** Possible responses provided.



**Clues**

**Across**
3. annoying someone
5. a strong feeling
6. very good

**Down**
1. hurt with a constant pain
2. to think very carefullly
4. to respect someone

Strategic

# Approaching Level

## Vocabulary

**Objective** Review vocabulary and high-frequency words

**Materials** • **Vocabulary Cards** • **High-Frequency Word Cards**

### REVIEW VOCABULARY

**Review Words** Display the **Vocabulary Cards** for *passion, bothering, admire, concentrate, ached,* and *splendid*. Point to each word, read it aloud, and have students chorally repeat.

Then have students describe a time when:

- they did something for which they felt a *passion*
- someone was *bothering* them
- they met someone they *admire*
- they had to *concentrate*
- some part of their body *ached*
- they read a *splendid* book

### HIGH-FREQUENCY WORDS

**Top 250 Words** The ability to read accurately and effortlessly the most frequently used words in written English will help students develop reading fluency. Display **High-Frequency Word Cards 31–40**. Then do the following:

- Display one card at a time and ask students to chorally state each word.
- Have students spell each word aloud.
- Ask students to write each word in their Writer's Notebooks as they state aloud each letter. Then have them read the word again.
- When completed, quickly flip through the word card set as students chorally read the words.
- Provide opportunities for students to use the words in speaking and writing. For example, provide sentence starters such as *I like to* ________ for oral and written practice. Or point to a word card and ask a questions such as *What word means the same thing as this word?* (when pointing to the *bring* word card).
- Continue the routine throughout the week.

### Word Webs

Have students create word webs in their Writer's Notebooks for each vocabulary word. Write the related words provided and ask students to add other words, phrases, and illustrations.

Student Book

Strategic

# Approaching Level

## Comprehension

**Objective** Reteach generate questions and compare and contrast

**Materials** • **Student Book:** "The Boy Who Cried Wolf"

STRATEGY

### RETEACH STRATEGY: GENERATE QUESTIONS

- **Define** Tell students that asking questions before, during, and after reading and then looking for answers in the story helps readers think about the most important ideas in a text and figure out parts that might have been confusing.

  Help students relate the word *generate* to the machine *generator*. Show a picture of a *generator* and explain that it makes electricity. Tell students that when they *generate questions*, they are making questions, like the generator makes electricity.
- **Relate to Real Life** Ask students to imagine they have the opportunity to interview someone they admire. To get information they most want to learn, they need to think of some questions. Answers to their questions will give them the most important facts about the person.
- **Set Purpose** Remind students that good readers generate questions to find important information or to make confusing ideas clear. As they read, they try to answer the questions in order to better understand the story.

TESTED SKILL

### RETEACH SKILL: COMPARE AND CONTRAST

- **Define** Tell students that when you compare characters, settings, or events, you tell how they are the same. Authors use signal words such as *both, also, too,* and *same* to compare. When you contrast, you tell how things are different. Words such as *instead of, yet, different from,* and *however* signal contrast.
- **Relate to Real Life** Ask students to compare two friends. Encourage them to think about a way they are alike, such as height, eye color, or special interests or talents. Then ask them to contrast them, or think about a way in which they differ.
- **Set Purpose** Remind students that good readers compare and contrast story characters, settings, and events as they read. This helps them predict what may happen next.
- **Apply** Work with students to compare and contrast the story characters in "The Boy Who Cried Wolf." Have students restate your comparisons and contrasts in their own words. Students will apply this strategy and skill to a simpler text as they read "Running with Wolves."

### Corrective Feedback

Read the passage with students. Ask: *What is the boy like in the beginning of the story? What is the boy like at the end of the story? Does he change or stay the same? Explain.* Have students underline details in the passage to support their comparisons and contrasts.

Strategic

# Approaching Level

## Practice Reader Lesson 1

**Objective** Read to apply skills and strategies

**Materials**
- **Practice Reader:** "Running with Wolves"
- **Approaching Reproducible,** p. 49

Practice Reader

### BEFORE READING

CA CONTENT STANDARD R 3.2.4 Recall major points in the text and make and modify predictions about forthcoming information.

**Preview and Predict** Have students read the title and preview the first chapter. Ask students to predict what this portion of the story is about. Then have them generate questions about this section before they begin reading.

**Review Vocabulary Words** Have students read the vocabulary words on the inside front cover. Briefly define each and ask students to state related words they have learned.

**Set a Purpose for Reading** *Let's read to find out the answers to the questions we generated about the wolves in this book.*

### DURING READING

**STRATEGY**
**GENERATE QUESTIONS**

Remind students that the answers to questions you generate help you focus on important story ideas and events. They also make clear any ideas that may be confusing.

**SKILL**
**COMPARE AND CONTRAST**

Remind students to compare and contrast the most important characters, settings, and events as they read. Read pages 2–5 with students. Help students complete the Venn Diagram.

As you read, help students decode unknown words. In addition, ask open-ended questions to facilitate rich discussion, such as *How does Evan feel about reading the book? In what ways are Evan and the wolf similar?* Build on students' responses to develop deeper understanding of the text.

Stop after each two pages and ask students to compare and contrast the story characters and events to check their understanding before reading on. If they struggle, help students generate questions that will help them find the important ideas and clarify confusing ideas.

### AFTER READING

Ask students to contrast Evan's attitude at the beginning of the book with his attitude at the end. How is it different? Have students comment on the reason for the change.

Strategic
SMALL GROUP

Practice Reader

Strategic

# Approaching Level

## Practice Reader Lesson 2

**Objective** Reread to apply skills and strategies and develop fluency

**Materials**
- **Practice Reader:** "Running with Wolves"
- **Approaching Reproducible,** p. 50

### BEFORE READING

**Review Strategy and Skill** Review students' completed Venn Diagram from the first read. Remind students that when you compare, you tell how things are the same. When you contrast, you tell how things are different.

**Review Vocabulary Words** Have students search the book for each vocabulary word. Ask students to read aloud the sentence containing the word and state the word's definition or provide related words. Point out any words that have multiple meanings.

**Set a Purpose for Reading** *Let's reread to check our understanding of the story and to work on our reading fluency.*

### DURING READING

Reread "Running with Wolves" with students. Have them read silently two pages at a time, or read aloud to a partner. Stop and have students generate questions before they read the next two pages. Model generating questions, as needed.

### AFTER READING

**Check Comprehension** Have partners complete the Comprehension Check on page 16. Review students' answers. Help students find evidence for their answers in the text.

**Model Fluency** Model reading the Practice Reader fluency passage on **Approaching Reproducible** page 50. Tell students to pay close attention to your expression, the way you raise and lower your voice to show a character's emotions and how he or she would speak. Point out quotation marks that tell you when a character is speaking. Then read one sentence at a time and have students echo-read the sentences, copying your expression.

During independent reading time, have students work with a partner using the fluency passage. One student reads aloud, while the other repeats each sentence back. If students need additional support, have them listen to the "practice speed" version of the passage on the **Fluency Solutions Audio CD**.

**Approaching Reproducible,** page 50

As I read, I will pay attention to phrasing.

Evan's mother walked into the living room.
7 She turned off the TV set.
13 "Time to stop watching TV," she told him. "You need to
24 do your schoolwork now."
28 Evan had to write a report about wolves. But he really
39 wanted to hang out with his older brother, Toby. "But this
50 show is about wolves," Evan told her.
57 "That's fiction. It's not real," his mother said. "You
66 need to read some nonfiction books or magazines."
74 "I'm tired. I played soccer all day," he told her. 84

Comprehension Check

1. What is Evan's problem? **Problem and Solution** Evan has to write a report about wolves, but he would rather hang out with his brother.
2. What excuses does Evan give to his mother? **Main Idea and Details** He is doing research by watching a fictional show about wolves. He is too tired because he played soccer all day.

| | Words Read | – | Number of Errors | = | Words Correct Score |
|---|---|---|---|---|---|
| First Read | | – | | = | |
| Second Read | | – | | = | |

Strategic

# Approaching Level

## Practice Reader Lesson 3

**Objective** Build fluency
**Materials** • **Practice Reader:** "Running with Wolves"

### FOCUS ON FLUENCY

CA CONTENT STANDARD R 3.1.3 Read aloud narrative and expository text fluently and accurately and with appropriate pacing, intonation, and expression.

**Timed Reading** Tell students that they will be doing a final timed reading of the fluency passage from "Running with Wolves" that they have been practicing. With each student, follow these directions:

- Place the passage facedown.
- When you say "Go," the student begins reading the passage aloud.
- When you say "Stop," the student stops reading the passage.

As they read, note words students mispronounce and their overall expression. Stop after one minute. Help students record and graph the number of words they read correctly.

### REREAD PREVIOUSLY READ BOOKS

- Distribute copies of the past six **Practice Readers**. Have students select two to reread. Tell students that rereading these books will help them develop their skills. The more times they read the same words, the quicker they will learn these words. This will make the reading of other books easier.
- Circulate and listen in as students read. Stop students periodically and ask them how they are figuring out difficult words and how they are monitoring their comprehension. Note students who need additional work with specific decoding or comprehension skills.
- Encourage students to read other previously read Practice Readers during independent reading time or for homework.

### Meet Grade-Level Expectations

As an alternative to this day's lesson, guide students through a reading of the On Level Practice Reader. See page 111W. Since both books contain the same vocabulary, phonics, and comprehension skills, the scaffolding you provided will help most students gain access to this more challenging text.

### Book Talk

See page 111JJ. Students will work with peers of varying language abilities to discuss this week's Practice Readers.

Student Book

Student Book

**Decodable Text**

Use the Reading *Triumphs* Anthology and the decodable stories in the **Teacher's Resource Book** to help students build fluency with basic decoding patterns.

Strategic

# Approaching Level

## Fluency

**Objectives** Reread selections to develop fluency; develop speaking skills

**Materials** • **Student Book:** *Wolf!,* "The Truth About Wolves"

### REREAD FOR FLUENCY

- Have students reread a portion of "The Truth About Wolves." Tell that they focus on two of their favorite pages from the selection. Work with students to read the pages with the appropriate expression.
- Provide time for students to read their sections of text to you. Comment on their pace and intonation and provide corrective feedback by modeling proper fluency.

### DEVELOP SPEAKING/LISTENING SKILLS

- Have students practice reading two pages of *Wolf!*
- Work with students to read with appropriate expression. Model reading a few sentences at a time. Emphasize how you raise and lower your voice to show a character's emotions and how they would speak. Have students repeat.
- Provide time for students to read aloud their chosen pages to partners. Ask students to identify when their partner used his or her voice to show expression.
- Challenge students to retell the portion of the story that their partner read aloud, using proper expression.

**CA CONTENT STANDARD LAS 3.1.1** Retell, paraphrase, and explain what has been said by a speaker.

Strategic

# Approaching Level

## Self-Selected Reading

**Objective** Read independently to compare and contrast

**Materials** • **Classroom Library** • other informational books

### APPLY SKILLS TO INDEPENDENT READING

- Have students choose a fiction book for independent reading. (See the **Theme Bibliography** on pages T8–T9 for book suggestions.) Remind them that when you compare, you tell how things are the same or similar. *Like, both*, and *also* signal that things are being compared. When you contrast, you tell how things are different. Contrast signal words include *but, different from,* and *however*. Have students read their books and record their comparisons and contrasts on a Venn Diagram.
- After reading, ask students to use their Venn Diagram to write or orally state a summary of the book. Provide time for students to share their summaries and comment on their reactions to the book. Ask: *Did you enjoy reading this book? Why or why not?*

Classroom Library

## Daily Planner

| | |
|---|---|
| DAY 1 | • Vocabulary |
| DAY 2 | • Phonics |
| DAY 3 | • Practice Reader Lesson 1 |
| DAY 4 | • Practice Reader Lesson 2<br>• Fluency |
| DAY 5 | • Self-Selected Reading |

Benchmark

# On Level

## Vocabulary

**Objective** Review vocabulary
**Materials** • **Vocabulary Cards**

TESTED SKILL

### REVIEW PREVIOUSLY TAUGHT WORDS

**Review Words** Display the **Vocabulary Cards** for *passion, bothering, admire, concentrate, ached,* and *splendid*. Point to each word, read it aloud, and have students chorally repeat.

Then provide the following Yes/No questions. Ask students to answer each question, justifying their answer. Allow other students to respond. Use the discussions to determine each student's depth of word knowledge.

- When you have a *passion* for something, do you hate doing it?
- When someone is *bothering* you, do you thank them?
- When people are good students, do you *admire* them?
- Did you feel good when your tooth *ached*?
- If you saw a *splendid* movie, would you tell your friends not to watch it?

## Phonics/Word Study

**Objective** Decode multisyllabic words with long *o*
**Materials** • **Sound-Spelling WorkBoards**

TESTED SKILL

### RETEACH SKILL

CA CONTENT STANDARD R 3.1.2 Decode regular multisyllabic words.

- **Long *o* Words** Point to the long *o* **Sound-Spelling Card** on the **WorkBoard** and review the spellings for this sound. State each spelling and provide a sample word.

CA CONTENT STANDARD R 3.1.2 Decode regular multisyllabic words.

- Write the words below on the board. If necessary, divide the words into syllables using the syllable-scoop procedure to help students read one syllable at a time. When completed, point to the words in random order for students to chorally read.

| | | | | |
|---|---|---|---|---|
| flowing | snowball | lowest | owner | rowboat |
| toaster | boastful | roasted | coldest | coastline |
| bolder | golden | molding | holder | scolded |

- **Spelling** Dictate the following words for students to spell on their WorkBoards: *snowflake, floated, blowing, speedboat, holding*. Guide students to use the Sound-Spelling Cards and model how to segment words, such as spelling a word syllable by syllable.

Sound-Spelling WorkBoard

Benchmark

# On Level

## Fluency

**Objectives** Reread selections to develop fluency; develop speaking skills

**Materials** • **Student Book:** "The Boy Who Cried Wolf", *Wolf!*

### REREAD FOR FLUENCY

- Have students reread "The Boy Who Cried Wolf." Work with students to read with the appropriate expression. Model as needed.
- Provide time for students to read a section of text to you. Comment on their expression and provide corrective feedback.

Student Book

### DEVELOP SPEAKING/LISTENING SKILLS

- Have students practice reading four to six pages of *Wolf!*
- Work with students to read with appropriate expression. Model reading a few lines at a time. Point out quotation marks that indicate dialogue. Then emphasize how you raise and lower your voice to show a character's emotions and how he or she would speak. Have students repeat.
- Provide time for students to read aloud their chosen pages to partners. Ask students to identify when their partner used his or her voice to show expression.
- Challenge students to retell the portion of the story they chose, using proper expression, and then to use examples to explain why they chose that portion.

**CA CONTENT STANDARD R 3.1.3** Read aloud narrative and expository text fluently and accurately and with appropriate pacing, intonation, and expression.

Student Book

## Self-Selected Reading

**Objective** Read independently to compare and contrast

**Materials** • **Classroom Library** • other informational books

### APPLY SKILLS TO INDEPENDENT READING

- Have students choose a fiction book for independent reading. (See the **Theme Bibliography** on pages T8–T9 for book suggestions.) Remind them that when you compare, you tell how things are the same. Like, both, also, and too are signal words that the author uses to compare two or more things. Contrast signal words include but, different, from, and however. Have students read their books and record any comparisons and contrast on a Venn Diagram.
- After reading, ask students to use their Venn Diagram to write or orally state a summary of the book. Provide time for students to share their summaries and comment on their reactions to the book. Ask: *Did you enjoy reading this book? Why or why not?*

Classroom Library

Practice Reader

Benchmark

# On Level

## Practice Reader Lesson 1

**Objective** Read to apply strategies and skills

**Materials**
- **Practice Reader:** *Katie and the Wolf*
- **Practice Book,** p. 49

### BEFORE READING

CA CONTENT STANDARD R 3.2.4 Recall major points in the text and make and modify predictions about forthcoming information.

**Preview and Predict** Have students read the title and preview the book by browsing the pages and looking at the illustrations. Ask students to predict what they think this book is about. Encourage them to generate questions that will help them understand the most important ideas.

**Review Vocabulary Words** Have students read the vocabulary words on the inside front cover. Ask students to look for multiple-meaning words. Review definitions, as needed.

**Set a Purpose for Reading** *Let's read to find out about characters and events in this story.*

### DURING READING

**STRATEGY**
**GENERATE QUESTIONS**

Remind students that generating questions helps you understand the most important ideas and events in a story that are confusing.

**SKILL**
**COMPARE AND CONTRAST**

Remind students that when you compare, you tell how characters, setting, and story events are the same. When you contrast, you tell how these story elements are different.

Read the first few chapters of the book with students. Ask open-ended questions to facilitate rich discussion, such as: *What's the author trying to say about Katie? What's the big idea the author is trying to get across?* Build on students' responses to develop deeper understanding of the text. Have students fill in the first section of the Venn Diagram, then continue reading.

CA CONTENT STANDARD R 3.1.7 Use a dictionary to learn the meaning and other features of unknown words.

**Dictionary: Multiple-Meaning Words** As they read, have students point out this week's new vocabulary words. Have them tell how to look those words up in a dictionary and how to find the meaning.

### AFTER READING

Ask students to compare and contrast the events in the story. Have students comment on how generating questions helped them understand the most important story ideas.

Benchmark

# On Level

## Practice Reader Lesson 2

**Objective** Reread to apply skills and strategies and develop fluency

**Materials**
- **Practice Reader:** *Katie and the Wolf*
- **Practice Book,** p. 50

Practice Reader

### Book Talk

See page 111JJ. Students will work with peers of varying language abilities to discuss this week's Practice Readers.

### BEFORE READING

**Review Strategy and Skill** Review students' completed Venn Diagram from the first read. Remind students that when you compare, you tell how things are alike. When you contrast, you tell how things are different.

Generating questions helps readers focus on the most important ideas and events in a text and clear up confusing ideas. If students have trouble generating questions, provide model questions or use a student's questions to revise them as a group. Have students copy the revised questions in their Writer's Notebooks.

**Set a Purpose for Reading** *Let's reread to check our understanding of the information in the book and to work on our reading fluency.*

### DURING READING

Reread *Katie and the Wolf* with students. Have them read silently two pages at a time, or read aloud to a partner. Stop and have students summarize before reading the next two pages. Model oral summaries as needed.

### AFTER READING

**Check Comprehension** Have partners complete the Comprehension Check on page 16. Review students' answers. Help students find evidence for their answers in the text.

**Model Fluency** Model reading the Practice Reader fluency passage on **Practice Book** page 50. Tell students to pay close attention to your expression, the way you raise and lower your voice to show a character's emotions and how he or she would speak. Point out quotation marks that indicate when a character is talking. Then read one sentence at a time and have students echo-read the sentences, copying your expression.

During independent reading time, have students work with a partner using the fluency passage. One student reads aloud, while the other repeats each sentence back. If students need additional support, have them listen to the "practice speed" version of the passage on the **Fluency Solutions Audio CD**.

### Practice Book, page 50

**As I read, I will pay attention to my expression.**

"You haven't eaten any lunch, Katie," my grandmother
8 said. She was right. The pile of mashed potatoes was a
19 round ball. My broccoli pieces still looked like perfect
28 little trees. And I had eaten only a spoonful of bean chili.
40 The next day, Granny was leaving on a trip to Europe.
51 She was staying on a sheep farm in Ireland for a month.
63 Traveling the world was Granny's passion, but I was
72 worried.
73 "With all those sheep, there might be wolves," I told
83 her. "It could be dangerous."
88 "You've been reading too many fairy tales," Granny
96 said.
97 I had read plenty of fairy tales. But I had also read a lot
111 of nonfiction. 113

**Comprehension Check**

1. Why is Katie worried? **Plot** Katie is worried about her grandmother spending time on a sheep farm where there may be lots of wolves.
2. What does Granny think of Katie's fear about the wolves? **Make Inferences** Granny thinks Katie has read too many fairy tales and she does not need to be worried.

| | Words Read | – | Number of Errors | = | Words Correct Score |
|---|---|---|---|---|---|
| First Read | | – | | = | |
| Second Read | | – | | = | |

| Daily Planner | |
|---|---|
| DAY 1 | • Practice Reader Lesson 1 |
| DAY 2 | • Practice Reader Lesson 2 |
| DAY 3 | • Phonics |
| DAY 4 | • Vocabulary<br>• Fluency |
| DAY 5 | • Self-Selected Reading |

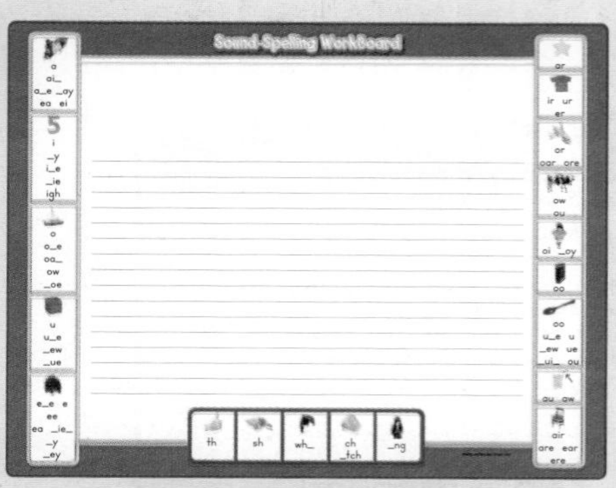
**Sound-Spelling WorkBoard**

Advanced

# Beyond Level

## Phonics/Word Study

**Objective** Decode multisyllabic words with long *o*

**Materials** • **Sound-Spelling WorkBoards**

### EXTEND/ACCELERATE

CA CONTENT STANDARD R 3.1.2 Decode regular multisyllabic words.

- **Read Multisyllabic Words with Long *o*** Write the words below on the board. Challenge students to read the words, using known word parts. When completed, point to the words in random order for students to chorally read.

| | | | |
|---|---|---|---|
| snowboard | snowstorm | outgrowing | embolden |
| snowmobile | shadowing | roadrunner | goldenrod |
| speedboat | totally | overcoat | refolding |
| toenail | soapiest | stowaway | refrozen |

- **Define Words** Ask students to use their knowledge of word parts to figure out the meanings of the above words. Then have partners find the words in a dictionary and confirm or revise the meanings. Challenge students to use these words in this week's writing assignments.
- **Spell Long *o* Words** Dictate the following words for students to spell on their **WorkBoards**: *boastful, boldface, lowering, scolded, ownership.* Write the words for students to self-correct.

## Vocabulary

**Objectives** Review genre; write a nonfiction paragraph

**Materials** • none

### ENRICH VOCABULARY

CA CONTENT STANDARD R 3.3.1 Distinguish common forms of literature (e.g., poetry, drama, fiction, nonfiction).

- **Review Vocabulary Words** Review the week's vocabulary words (*passion, admire, concentrate, splendid, bothering, ached.*) Point out that they are all strong words that help build a picture for the reader. Have students brainstorm other strong words that have similar meanings. They may wish to use a thesaurus to help them.
- **Write Colorful Descriptions** Ask students to write a descriptive paragraph about someone they know using one of the vocabulary words and as many strong synonyms as possible. For example, *My brother Will is a splendid soccer player. He has the most wonderful way to kicking the ball. He is a fantastic runner, too. He is a terrific player.* Have students share their descriptions with classmates who identify which words are synonyms.

Advanced

# Beyond Level

## Fluency

**Objectives** Reread selections to develop fluency; develop speaking skills
**Materials** • **Student Book:** "The Boy Who Cried Wolf," *Wolf!*

### REREAD FOR FLUENCY

CA CONTENT STANDARD R 3.1.3 Read aloud narrative and expository text fluently and accurately and with appropriate pacing, intonation, and expression.

- Have students reread "The Boy Who Cried Wolf." Work with students to read the book with the appropriate expression.
- Provide time for students to read a section of text to you. Comment on their expression and provide corrective feedback by modeling proper fluency.

Student Book

### DEVELOP SPEAKING/LISTENING SKILLS

- Have students practice reading several pages of *Wolf!*
- Work with students to read with appropriate expression. Model reading a few lines at a time. Point out quotation marks that indicate when a character is speaking. Then emphasize how you raise and lower your voice to show how a character would express emotions. Have students repeat.
- Provide time for students to read aloud their chosen pages to partners. Ask students to identify when their partner used his or her voice to show expression.
- Challenge students to retell the portion of the story they chose, using proper expression. Have them add gesture and movement that express each character's words.

Student Book

## Self-Selected Reading

**Objective** Read independently to identify to compare and contrast
**Materials** • **Classroom Library** • other fiction books

### APPLY SKILLS TO INDEPENDENT READING

- Have students choose a fiction book for independent reading. (See the **Theme Bibliography** on pages T8–T9 for book suggestions.) Remind them that when you compare, you tell how things are the same. Signal words such are *like, both, also*, and *too*. When you contrast, you tell how things are different. Some contrast signal words are *but, different from*, and *however*. Have students read and record comparisons and contrasts on a Venn Diagram.
- After reading, ask students to use their Venn Diagram to write a summary of the book. Provide time for students to share their summaries and comment on the book. Ask: *Did you enjoy reading this book? Why or why not?*

Classroom Library

Practice Reader

Advanced

# Beyond Level

## Practice Reader Lesson 1

**Objective** Read to apply strategies and skills

**Materials**
- **Practice Reader:** *A Dog's Life*
- **Beyond Reproducible,** p. 49

### BEFORE READING

**Preview and Predict** Have students preview the book by reading the title and chapter titles and looking at the illustrations. Ask students to predict what they think this book is about and to generate questions to help them focus on the important ideas.

**Review Vocabulary Words** Have students read the vocabulary words on the inside front cover. Ask students to state each definition and any related words they have learned.

**Set a Purpose for Reading** *Let's read to find out the important ideas in this story.*

### DURING READING

**STRATEGY**
**GENERATE QUESTIONS**

Ask students to discuss how generating questions helps them understand what they read. Remind students that the answers to their questions can help them compare and contrast story elements, such as characters, setting, and events.

**SKILL**
**COMPARE AND CONTRAST**

Ask students to define the terms *compare* and *contrast*. Remind students that when you compare, you tell how things are the same or similar. When you contrast, you tell how things are different.

Read the book with students. Ask open-ended questions to facilitate rich discussion, such as *What is the author trying to say about a dog's life? What do you think the author wants us to know from this?* Build on students' responses to develop deeper understanding of the text. Have students fill in the Venn Diagram independently as they read.

### AFTER READING

Ask students to compare story events with events that could happen in real life. How are they different? Have students comment on whether and why they think the wolf made a mistake when he gave up looking for another wolf pack. Prompt them to make suggestions about what else he might have done.

Advanced

# Beyond Level

## Practice Reader Lesson 2

**Objective** Reread to apply skills and strategies and develop fluency

**Materials**
- **Practice Reader:** *A Dog's Life*
- **Beyond Reproducible,** p. 50

### BEFORE READING

**Review Strategy and Skill** Review students' completed Venn Diagrams from the first read.

Remind students that generating questions helps readers compare and contrast characters, ideas, and events in a story. If students' questions are not useful, provide a model question or use a student question and revise it as a group. Have students copy the revised question in their Writer's Notebooks.

**Set a Purpose for Reading** *Let's reread to check our understanding of the information in the book and work on our reading fluency.*

### DURING READING

Have students reread *A Dog's Life* silently or with a partner. If reading in pairs, prompt students to stop every two pages and summarize or ask their partner probing questions.

### AFTER READING

**Check Comprehension** Have students independently complete the Comprehension Check on page 16. Review students' answers. Help students find evidence for their answers in the text.

**Model Fluency** Model reading the Practice Reader fluency passage on **Beyond Reproducible** page 50. Tell students to pay close attention to your expression as you read. Then read one sentence at a time and have students echo-read the sentences, copying your expression.

During independent reading time, have students work with a partner using the fluency passage. One student reads aloud, while the other repeats each sentence back. Students can check their fluency by reading along with the "expert speed" version of the passage on the **Fluency Solutions Audio CD**.

**Practice Reader**

### Book Talk

See page 111JJ. Students will work with peers of varying language abilities to discuss this week's Practice Readers.

**Beyond Reproducible,** page 50

**As I read, I will pay attention to punctuation and intonation.**

You see, I'm a lone wolf. I used to be in a wolf pack,
14 but they threw me out. Ever since then, I've been roaming
25 the forest and looking for a new group of friends.
35 Unfortunately, that's turned out to be more difficult
43 than I'd anticipated. Wolf packs prefer to keep outsiders
52 out. After a long, cold winter, I hadn't found a pack to
64 join, and I was very lonely.
70 Then I realized there might be another possibility. I
79 hadn't been hanging out with any other animals. From
88 what I saw as I went roaming, there were many different
99 kinds. So what if I hadn't found a pack of wolves? Maybe
111 I'd be happier in a gaggle of geese, a herd of elephants, a
124 pride of lions, or a school of fish.
132 I crossed through the forest, looking everywhere for
140 new friends. 142

**Comprehension Check**

1. Why is Wolf having a difficult time finding a new pack to join? **Plot** Wolves keep outsiders out so no packs would let Wolf join their group.
2. What plan does Wolf come up with? **Problem and Solution** to make friends with other animals

| | Words Read | – | Number of Errors | = | Words Correct Score |
|---|---|---|---|---|---|
| First Read | | – | | = | |
| Second Read | | – | | = | |

**Daily Planner**

| | |
|---|---|
| DAY 1 | • Build Background Knowledge<br>• Vocabulary |
| DAY 2 | • Vocabulary<br>• Access to Core Content *Wolf!* |
| DAY 3 | • Vocabulary<br>• Grammar<br>• Access to Core Content *Wolf!* |
| DAY 4 | • Vocabulary<br>• Writing/Spelling<br>• Access to Core Content "The Truth about Wolves" |
| DAY 5 | • Vocabulary<br>• Practice Reader *The Wolf*<br>• Self-Selected Reading |

**StudentWorks Plus**

# English Learners

## Prepare to Read

**Content Objective** Describe how reading helps you learn about the world

**Language Objective** Use key words to describe how reading helps you learn about the world

**Materials** **StudentWorks Plus** (interactive eBook)

### BUILD BACKGROUND KNOWLEDGE

CA CONTENT STANDARD R 3.1.3 Read aloud narrative and expository text fluently and accurately and with appropriate pacing, intonation, and expression.

- Have students preview *Wolf!* using **StudentWorks Plus,** the interactive eBook. This version of the Student Book contains oral summaries in multiple languages, online multilingual glossaries, word-by-word highlighting, and questions that assess and build comprehension.
- Students can build their word reading fluency by reading along as the text is read or by listening during the first reading and, at the end of each paragraph, returning to the beginning of the paragraph and reading along.
- Students can build their comprehension by reviewing the definitions of key words in the online glossary and by answering the comprehension questions. When appropriate, the text required to answer the question is highlighted to provide students with additional support and scaffolding.
- Following the reading, ask students to respond in writing to a question that links the story to their personal experiences, such as: *What is something you have learned more about from reading a book? Describe what you learned.*

## Academic Language

**Language Objective** Use academic language in classroom conversations

- This week's academic words are **boldfaced** throughout the lesson. Define the word in context and provide a clear example from the selection. Then ask students to generate an example or a word with a similar meaning.

### Academic Language Used in Whole Group Instruction

| Theme Words | Key Selection Words | Strategy and Skill Words | |
|---|---|---|---|
| **villain** | **passion** | **generate** | **predicates** |
| **realistic** | **bothering** | **compare** | **sentences** |
| **frightening** | **admire** | **contrast** | **expression** |
| | **concentrate** | **main idea** | |
| | **ached** | **details** | |
| | **splendid** | **multiple-meaning** | |

# English Learners

## Vocabulary

**Language Objective** Demonstrate understanding and use of key words by describing how books help you learn about the world

**Materials** • **Visual Vocabulary Resources** • **English Learner Resource Book**

**Visual Vocabulary Resources**

TESTED SKILL

### PRETEACH KEY VOCABULARY

**All Language Levels** Use the **Visual Vocabulary Resources** to preteach the key selection words *passion, bothering, admire, concentrate, ached,* and *splendid.* Focus on 1–2 words per day. Use the following routine that appears in detail on the cards.

- Define the word in English and provide the example given.
- Define the word in Spanish, if appropriate, and indicate if the word is a cognate.
- Display the picture and explain how it illustrates or demonstrates the word. Engage students in structured partner-talk about the image, using the key word.
- Ask students to chorally say the word three times.
- Point out any known sound-spellings or focus on a key aspect of phonemic awareness related to the word.
- Distribute copies of the Vocabulary Glossary in the **English Learner Resource Book** page 48.

### PRETEACH FUNCTION WORDS AND PHRASES

**All Language Levels** Use the Visual Vocabulary Resources to preteach the function words and phrases *my eyes are playing tricks, strange, to read with confidence,* and *outside*. Focus on one word per day. Use the detailed routine on the cards.

- Define the word in English and, if appropriate, in Spanish. Point out if the word is a cognate.
- Refer to the picture and engage students in talk about the word; for example, students will Partner Talk using sentence frames or they will listen to sentences and replace a word or phrase with the new function word.
- Ask students to chorally repeat the word three times.

### TEACH BASIC WORDS

For **Beginning** and **Early Intermediate** students, use the Visual Vocabulary Resources to teach the basic words *word, story, public library, bookshop, school,* and *class.* Teach these "reading" words using the routine provided on the card.

**EL Resource Book,** page 48

Use the word chart to study this week's vocabulary words.
Write a sentence using each word in your writer's notebook.

| Word | Context Sentence | Illustration |
|---|---|---|
| passion | I love to watch birds. It is my passion. | |
| admire | We admire the beautiful garden. | |
| concentrate | It is hard to concentrate when it is noisy. | When do you need to concentrate? |
| splendid | We had a splendid meal. The food was delicious. | |
| bothering | The fly was bothering the horse. | |
| ached | His side ached from running so quickly. | |

# English Learners

## Access to Core Content

**Content Objective** Read grade-level text
**Language Objective** Discuss text using key words and sentence frames
**Materials** • **English Learner Resource Book,** pp. 34–47

TESTED SKILL

### PRETEACH MAIN SELECTION (PAGES 82–103)

Use the Interactive Question-Response Guide on **English Learner Resource Book pages 34–45** to introduce students to *Wolf!* Preteach half of the selection on **Day 2** and half on **Day 3**.

- Use the prompts provided in the guide to develop meaning and vocabulary. Use the Partner-Talk and whole-class responses to engage students and increase student talk.
- When completed, have partners reread the story.

### PRETEACH PAIRED SELECTION (PAGES 106–109)

Use the Interactive Question-Response Guide on English Learner Resource Book pages 46–47 to preview the paired selection "The Truth about Wolves." Preteach the selection on **Day 4**.

Student Book

English Learner Resource Book

# English Learners

## Fluency

**Content Objective** Reread selections to develop fluency; develop speaking skills
**Language Objective** Tell a partner what a selection is about
**Materials** • **Student Book:** *Wolf!,* "The Truth about Wolves"

### REREAD FOR FLUENCY

CA CONTENT STANDARD R 3.1.3 Read aloud narrative and expository text fluently and accurately and with appropriate pacing, intonation, and expression.

- Have students reread a portion of *Wolf!* Suggest that they focus on two to four of their favorite pages from the selection. Work with students to read the pages with the appropriate expression; for example, read each sentence of the first paragraph, emphasizing how you raise and lower your voice to show a character's emotions. Have students echo your expression. Then have students continue by chorally rereading additional paragraphs.
- Provide time for students to read their sections of text to you. Comment on their expression and provide corrective feedback by modeling proper fluency.

### DEVELOP SPEAKING/LISTENING SKILLS

- Have students practice reading "The Truth about Wolves." Work with students to read with expression.
- Provide time for students to work on using appropriate expression by reading to a partner. Then have partners discuss the nonfiction article. Provide the sentence frame: *The truth about wolves is _____.*

Student Book

## Self-Selected Reading

**Content Objective** Read independently
**Language Objective** Orally retell information learned
**Materials** • **Classroom Library** • other informational books

### APPLY SKILLS TO INDEPENDENT READING

- Have students choose an informational book for independent reading. (See the **Theme Bibliography** on pages T8–T9 for book suggestions.)
- After reading, ask students to orally summarize the book. Provide time for students to comment on their reactions to the book and share them with classmates. Ask: *Would you recommend this book to a classmate? Why or why not?*

Classroom Library

# English Learners

## Grammar

**Content Objective** Identify predicates
**Language Objective** Speak in complete sentences, using sentence frames

TESTED SKILL

### PREDICATES

- Review predicates. Write the following on the board: *The wolf looked for food*. Underline the predicate. (*looked for food*) Tell students that this is the predicate; it is the part of the sentence containing the verb. It tells what the subject is or does. If necessary, remind students that the subject is who or what the sentence is about.
- Write sentences on the board, such as those provided below. Have students underline the predicate in each sentence. Have them say: *The predicate is ____.*

  *The pig read a book.*

  *The wolf counted his money.*

  *Wolves live in packs.*

  *A baby wolf is called a pup.*

### PEER DISCUSSION STARTERS

- Write the following sentences on the board.

  Wolves in fantasy stories are ____. I learned that real wolves ____.
- Pair students and have them complete each sentence frame. Ask them to expand on their sentences by providing as many details as they can from this week's readings. Circulate, listen in, and take note of each student's language use and proficiency.

### English Learners

UNIVERSAL ACCESS

Build on students' responses to help move them to the next level of language acquisition; for example, if students say, "I learned that real wolves live in packs," say, "That's correct. Wolves live in packs with other wolves. They do not like to live near humans. The members of a wolf pack take very good care of their pups. Now turn to your partner and tell more about wolves."

Provide the following sentence frames orally or in writing for support.

**Beginning/Early Intermediate** A wolf pack is made up of ____.

**Intermediate** Wolf packs are interesting because ____.

**Early Advanced** Wolf packs take care of their pups by ____.

### Transfer Skills

**Pronunciation** The English letters *w, f, l*, and *v* all present difficulties in pronunciation to speakers of Cantonese. The subject matter of this week, with frequent repetition of the words *wolf* and *wolves*, may offer a potential source of frustration for Cantonese-speaking students, but also an excellent opportunity for practice. Make a game of it to avoid anxiety, and ask these students to take turns reading aloud the words containing problem letters, chorally and with a partner.

### Corrective Feedback

During whole group grammar lessons, follow the routine on the **Grammar Transparencies** to provide students with extra support. This routine includes completing the items with English Learners while other students work independently, having students reread the sentences with partners to build fluency, and providing a generative task such as writing a new sentence using the skill.

# English Learners

## Writing/Spelling

**Content Objective** Spell words correctly
**Language Objective** Write in complete sentences, using sentence frames

**VOCABULARY**

- Write the key vocabulary words on the board: *passion, bothering, admire, concentrate, ached, splendid*. Have students copy each word on their **WorkBoards**. Then help them say each word and write sentences for each word. Provide sentence starters such as:

  *The wolf has a passion for ____.*

  *The wolf kept bothering the other ____.*

  *The animals began to admire the ____.*

  *The pig could not concentrate on his ____.*

  *The wolf's ____ ached from walking.*

  *The wolf told splendid ____.*

- Help students spell words using their growing knowledge of English sound-spelling relationships. Model how to segment the word students are trying to spell and attach a spelling to each sound (or spellings to each syllable if a multisyllabic word). Use the **Sound-Spelling Cards** to reinforce the spellings for each English sound.
- Dictate the following words for students to spell: *coat, note, spoke, tone, loan, rope, phone*. Guide students using the Sound-Spelling Cards as they spell each word.
- When completed, review the meanings of words that can be easily demonstrated or explained. Use actions, gestures, and available pictures.

**Sound-Spelling WorkBoard**

**Phonics/Word Study**

For English Learners who need more practice with this week's phonics/spelling skill, see the Approaching Level lesson on page 111L. Focus on minimal contrasts, articulation, and those sounds that do not transfer from the student's first language to English. For a complete listing of transfer sounds, see pages T18–T33.

# English Learners

## Practice Reader

Practice Reader

**Content Objective** Read to apply skills and strategies
**Language Objective** Retell information using complete sentences
**Materials** • **Practice Reader:** *The Wolf* • **English Learner Resource Book,** p. 49

### BEFORE READING

CA CONTENT STANDARD R 3.2.4 Recall major points in the text and make and modify predictions about forthcoming information.

- **Preview** Read the title *The Wolf*. Ask: *What's the title? Say it again*. Repeat with the author's name. Then page through the book. Use simple language to tell about each page. Immediately follow up with questions, such as: *This is a girl and her grandmother. What are they doing? What is the girl wearing? Why? What animals do you see in this book?*
- **Review Skills** Use the inside front cover to review the phonics skill and vocabulary words.
- **Set a Purpose** Say: *Let's read to find out about the wolf in this story.*

### DURING READING

- Have students whisper-read each page, or use the differentiated suggestions below. Circulate, listen in, and provide corrective feedback, such as modeling how to blend a decodable word or clarifying meaning by using techniques from the Interactive Question-Response Guides.
- **Retell** Stop after every two pages and ask students to state the main ideas they have learned so far. Reinforce language by restating students' comments when they have difficulty using story-specific words. Provide differentiated sentence frames to support students' responses and engage students in partner-talk where appropriate.

### English Learners

UNIVERSAL ACCESS

**Beginning/Early Intermediate**

**Echo-Read** Have children echo-read after you.

**Check Comprehension** Point to pictures and ask questions such as: *Do you see a computer? Point to it.*

**Intermediate**

**Choral-Read** Have children choral-read with you.

**Check Comprehension** Ask questions/prompts such as: *Describe what you see in this illustration. Why is Katie working on the computer?*

**Early Advanced**

**Choral-Read** Have children choral-read.

**Check Comprehension** Ask: *What does Katie learn about the e-mail she is reading? Read sentences that tell who is writing to Katie.*

# English Learners

## AFTER READING

**CA CONTENT STANDARD LAS 3.1.3** Respond to questions with appropriate elaboration.

**Book Talk** Write the **Book Talk Prompts** below on the board or distribute copies of **English Learner Resource Book** page 49. Students will work with peers of varying language abilities to discuss them. Form groups so that students who read the Beyond Level, On Level, Approaching Level, and English Learner versions of *The Wolf* are in the same group.

Help students determine who will be the Leader for the discussion. Then have students discuss the following:

- **Describe what a wolf looks like.**
- **Explain what you learned about wolves and where they live.**
- **Tell the differences and similarities between wolves and dogs. Remember that they are from the same animal family.**
- **Give examples of why people are afraid of wolves.**
- **Retell what wolves like to eat.**
- **Write one question about the book to ask your group.**

**Develop Listening and Speaking Skills** Tell students to remember the following:

- Use clear and specific vocabulary to communicate ideas.
- Take turns speaking and listening. Give everyone a chance to speak.
- Retell, paraphrase, and explain information shared by others.
- Clarify and enhance the discussion through the use of pictures and props.
- Connect and relate prior knowledge and experiences to ideas brought up in the discussion.

**CA CONTENT STANDARD LAS 3.1.2** Connect and relate prior experiences, insights, and ideas to those of a speaker.

**English Learner Resource Book**

### Newcomer

**Survival Skills: School People and Places** Take children on a tour of the school. Teach the names of important people and places. Use sentence frames such as, *Hello, Mrs. Sanchez. How are you?* Also verbalize these people and place names throughout the day; for example, *We are going to the library. Mrs. Gonzalez works there. She is our librarian.*

The Big Question

## Big Question Board LAS 3.1.1, LAS 3.1.3, LAS 3.1.8

**WRAP UP** Tell students to add information learned this week related to the unit theme *Personal Experiences: Let's Learn*. Students should record how *Wolf!* adds to their growing knowledge of the theme. Students should also record any research facts they have uncovered throughout the week or questions they want to explore as they continue reading the selections in the unit. Have students present the information they learned. Remind them of the following speaking and listening skills:

- **Speaking** Tell students that when presenting information, they should use use props, such as pictures, photos, found objects, charts, and other graphics. This will help their listeners understand the ideas presented.
- **Listening** Once students have listened to a presenter, ask them to turn to a partner and retell, paraphrase, or explain what the speaker has said to check their understanding. They should also follow up with questions for the presenter to clarify or elaborate on information provided.

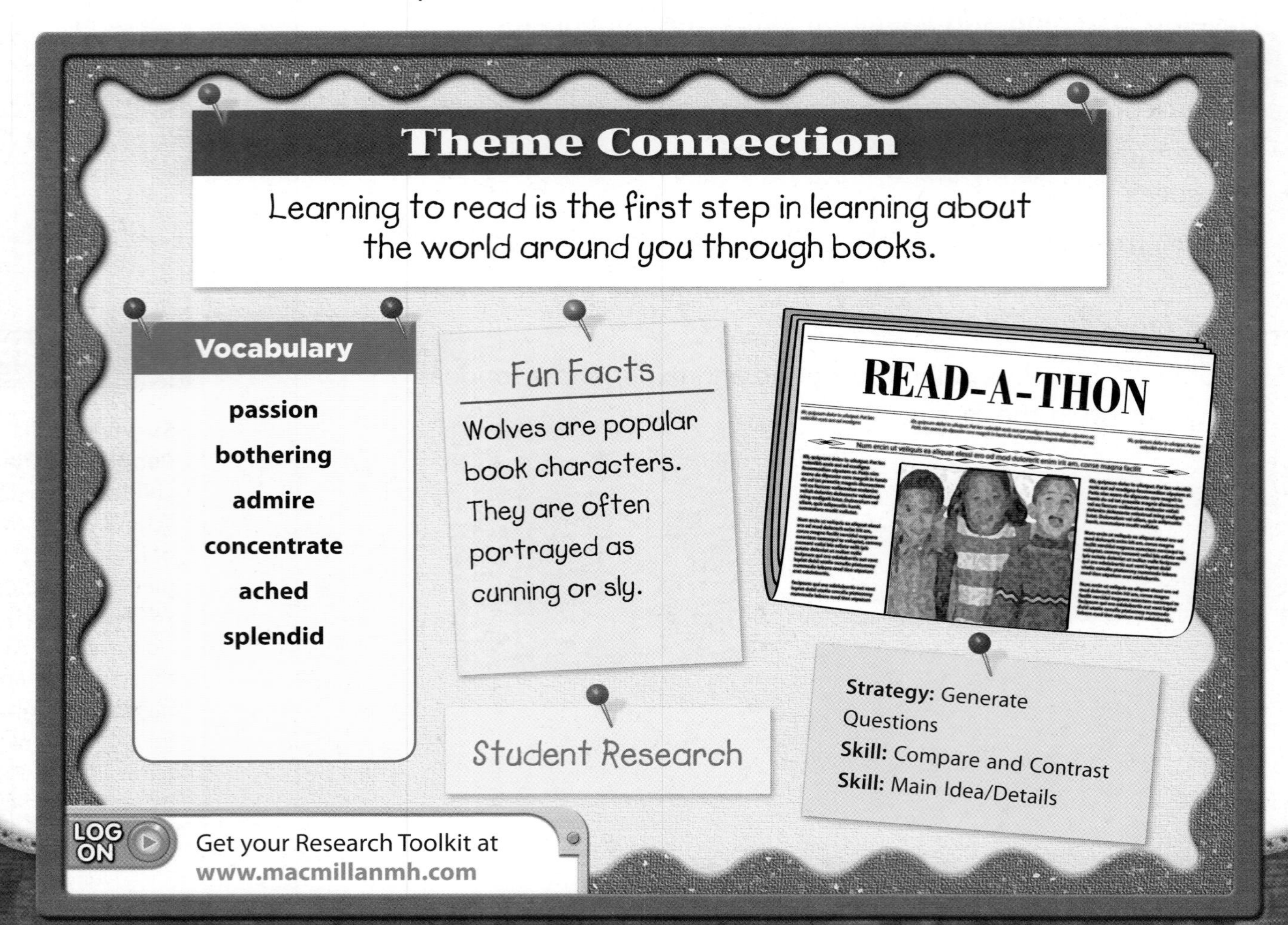

# Week 5 At a Glance

## WHOLE GROUP

### Phonics/Word Study
Long *i*, Multisyllabic Words

### Vocabulary
Robust Words: *separate, determination, storage, exact, ruined, luckiest*

Word Parts: Suffixes *-er, -est*

### Comprehension
Strategy: Monitor Comprehension
Skill: Make and Confirm Predictions

Skill: Compare and Contrast

### Fluency
Phrasing

### Spelling
Long *i*: *mild, sky, pie, might, find, fight, tied, right, fry, tight, child, flight, bright, buy, dye*

### Grammar/Mechanics
Compound Sentences

Punctuate Compound Sentences

### Writing
Topic Development: Object, Setting

### Read Aloud
Genre: Poetry

## SMALL GROUP

### Differentiated Instruction for Tested Skills

Approaching Level | On Level | Beyond Level | English Learners

## Teacher Tools

**Technology to help plan and implement instruction**

**PREPARE**
- Professional Development Videos
- Parent Connection

**PLAN/ORGANIZE**

Go to **www.macmillanmh.com** for Online Lesson Planner

TeacherWorks Plus
All-In-One Planner and Resource Center

**TEACH**
- Theme Launcher Video
- Classroom Presentation Toolkit
- Vocabulary PuzzleMaker
- Sound Pronunciation CD

**ASSESS**

Assessment Online

# Weekly Literature

## Student Book

**A mix of fiction and nonfiction connected to:**

- Unit Theme
- California Content Standards

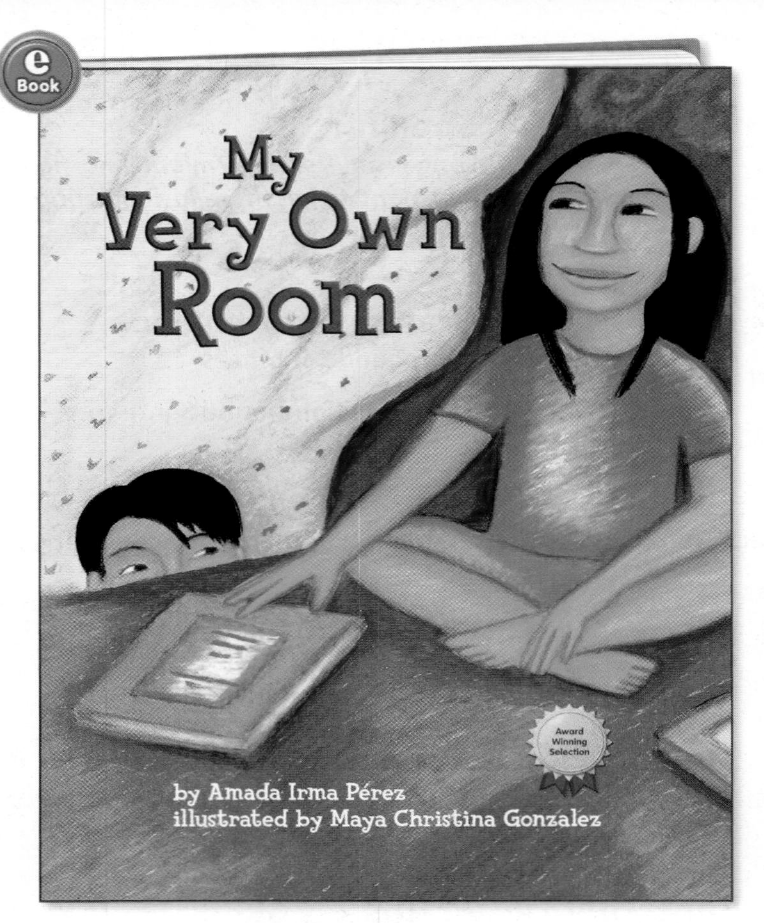


**Main Selection**

**Genre** Realistic Fiction

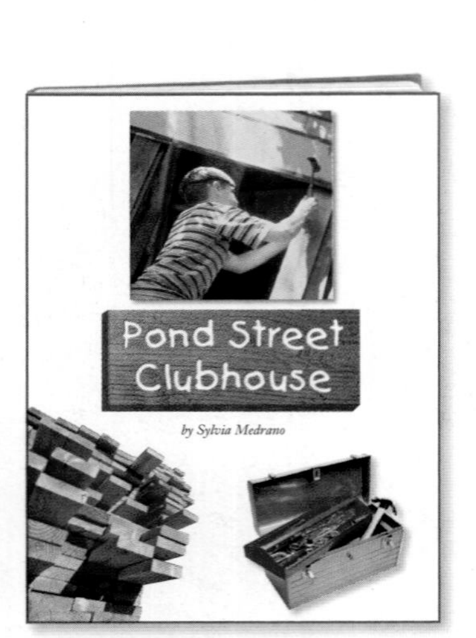


**Preteach Vocabulary and Comprehension**

**Genre** Fiction

**Paired Selection**

**Genre** Biography

## Support Literature

**Resources to build robust vocabulary, fluency, and content knowledge**

**Interactive Read-Aloud Anthology**

- Listening Comprehension
- Readers Theater Plays

**Content Reader**

- Meets all California Science and History/Social Science Standards

# Resources for Differentiated Instruction

## Skill-Based Practice Readers

- Same Theme
- Same Vocabulary/Phonics
- Same Comprehension Skills

Approaching Level

On Level

Beyond Level

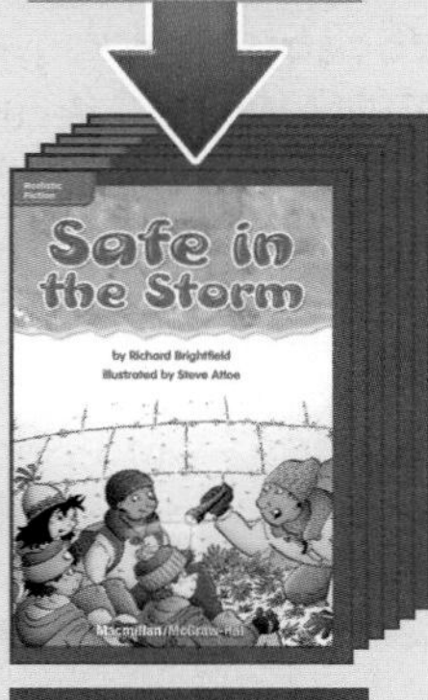


English Learner

On Level Practice Reader sheltered for English Learners

## StudentWorks Plus

- eBook
- Use for preteaching
- Summaries in multiple languages
- Word-by-Word Reading
- Assessment

## Practice Book and Reproducibles

Also available:

Approaching Reproducible

Beyond Reproducible

## Intensive Vocabulary

Build robust vocabulary with fiction and nonfiction

**Oral Vocabulary Cards**

## Home-School Connection

- Family letters in English, Spanish, Hmong, Vietnamese, Cantonese, Khmer
- Take-Home Stories

## Intervention Kit

- Intervention Anthology
- Phonemic Awareness Teacher's Edition
- Phonics/Word Study Teacher's Edition
- Comprehension Teacher's Edition
- Vocabulary Teacher's Edition
- Fluency Teacher's Edition
- Writing and Grammar Teacher's Edition

## Visual Vocabulary Resources

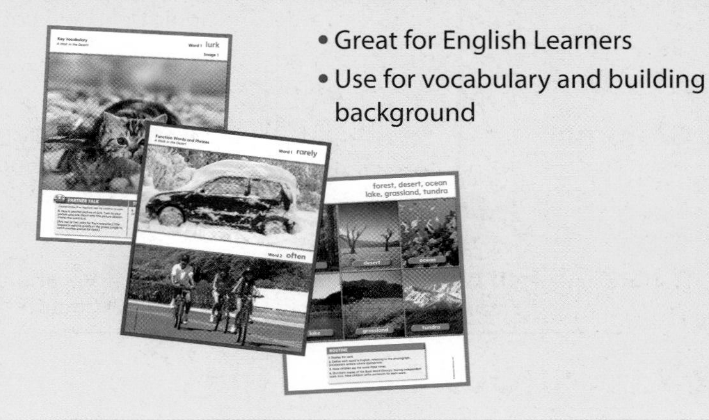


- Great for English Learners
- Use for vocabulary and building background

# Suggested Lesson Plan

Go to www.macmillanmh.com for Online Lesson Planner

My Very Own Room, pp. 116–137

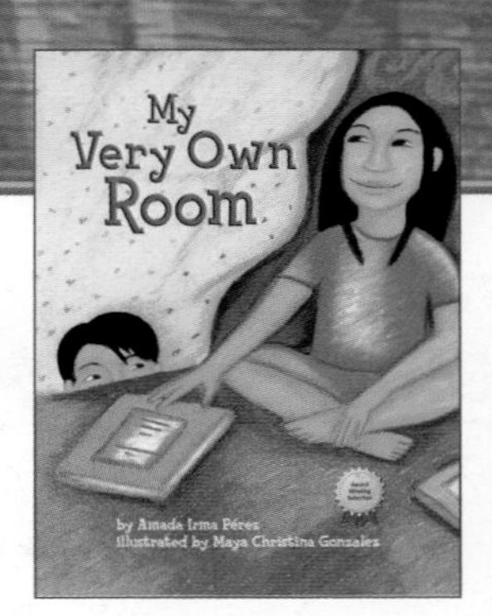


| WHOLE GROUP | DAY 1 | DAY 2 |
|---|---|---|
| **ORAL LANGUAGE** (15–20 min)<br>• Listening Comprehension<br>• Speaking/Viewing | **Listening/Speaking/Viewing**<br>Focus Question If you could have a place of your own, where would it be and what would it look like?<br>Read Aloud: "Under the Back Porch," 112L–112M<br>Build Background, 112 | **Listening/Speaking**<br>Focus Question How does the girl get her own room? |
|  **WORD STUDY** (30–40 min)<br>• Vocabulary<br>• Phonics/Word Study<br>• Spelling |  **Vocabulary** R 3.1.8<br>*separate, determination, storage, exact, ruined, luckiest*, 115, 143A<br>Practice Book, 59<br>**Strategy:** Word Parts/Suffixes *-er, -est*, 114<br> **Spelling** Pretest, 143C<br>Practice Book, 65 W 3.1.8 |  **Vocabulary** R 3.1.4, R 3.1.8<br>Review Words, Inflectional Endings, 143A<br>Practice Book, 64<br> **Phonics**<br>Decode Words with Long *i*, 112N<br>Practice Book, 58 R 3.1.1<br> **Spelling** Words Sorts, 143C<br>Reproducible, SP13 W 3.1.8 |
|  **READING** (30–40 min)<br>• Comprehension<br>• Fluency |  **Read** "Pond Street Clubhouse," 114–115<br>Student Book<br> **Comprehension**, 115A–115B<br>**Strategy:** Monitor Comprehension<br>**Skill:** Make and Confirm Predictions R 3.2.4<br>Practice Book, 60<br>**Fluency** Model Fluency, 112M R 3.1.3 | 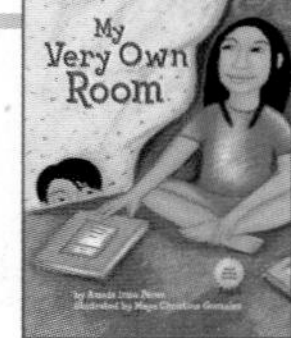 Student Book<br> **Read** *My Very Own Room*, 116–137<br>**Comprehension**, 116–137<br>**Strategy:** Monitor Comprehension<br>**Skill:** Make and Confirm Predictions R 3.2.4<br>Practice Book, 61<br>**Fluency** Repeated Reading: Attention to Punctuation, 139A R 3.1.3 |
|  **LANGUAGE ARTS** (30–40 min)<br>• Writing<br>• Grammar |  **Writing**<br>Daily Writing Prompt Write a description of an ideal place of your own.<br>Topic Development: Object, Setting, 144–145 W 3.2.2<br>**Grammar** Daily Language Activities, 143E<br>Compound Sentences, 143E<br>Reproducible, GR13 LC 3.1.2 |  **Writing**<br>Daily Writing Prompt Think of a place where you spend a lot of time. Write a paragraph about it and what you do there.<br>Topic Development: Object, Setting, 145A<br>Practice Book, 69 W 3.2.2<br>**Grammar** Daily Language Activities, 143E<br>Compound Sentences, 143E<br>Practice Book, 67 LC 3.1.2 |
| **ASSESSMENT**<br>• Informal/Formal | Quick Check **Vocabulary**, 114<br>**Comprehension**, 115B | Quick Check **Comprehension**, 137 |

 (45–60 min)

**SMALL GROUP Lesson Plan** — **Differentiated Instruction 145I–145HH**

## California Standards

**Vocabulary**
**Vocabulary Words**
**Word Parts/Suffixes *-er* and *-est***
R 3.1.8

**Comprehension**
**Strategy: Monitor Comprehension**
**Skill: Make and Confirm Predictions**
R 3.2.4

**Writing**
**Topic Development: Object, Setting**
W 3.1.4, W 3.2.2

**Social Science**
Biography
HSS 3.4.3, HSS 3.4.b

## DAY 3

**Listening/Speaking**

**Focus Question** Think about how the main character in "Pond Street Clubhouse" is like the girl in *My Very Own Room*. Why is determination an important character trait in both characters?

Summarize, 139

**Vocabulary** R 3.1.4, R 3.1.8
Review Words, Related Words, 143B

**Spelling** Word Meanings, 143D
Reproducible, SP14 W 3.1.8

**Read** *My Very Own Room*, 116–137

Student Book

**Comprehension**
Critical Thinking, 139

**Skill Review:** Compare and Contrast, 139B

**Fluency** Repeated Reading: Attention to Punctuation, 139A
Practice Book, 62 R 3.1.3

**Writing**

**Daily Writing Prompt** Write a paragraph about how you would build a place of your own. What materials would you use? Who would help you?

Topic Development: Object, Setting, 145B
W 3.2.2

**Grammar** Daily Language Activities, 143E
Mechanics and Usage, 143F
Reproducible, GR14 LC 3.1.2

**Quick Check** **Fluency**, 139A

## DAY 4

**Listening/Speaking**

**Focus Question** Think about this article and *My Very Own Room*. Why might the narrator of the story enjoy learning about Frank Lloyd Wright?

**Vocabulary** R 3.1.4, R 3.1.8

**Content Vocabulary:** *influenced, form, function, geometric, preserved*, 140
Review Words, Morphology, 143B

**Spelling** Proofread, 143D
Practice Book, 66 W 3.1.8

**Read** "Frank Lloyd Wright," 140–143

Student Book

**Comprehension**
**Genre: Biography**

**Text Features:** Encyclopedia Article, 140 R 3.2.1

Practice Book, 63

Content Reader

**Fluency** Repeated Reading: Attention to Punctuation, 139A
R 3.1.3

**Writing**

**Daily Writing Prompt** Describe the form and function of things you see around you.

Reading/Writing Connection, 145C–145D
W 3.2.2

**Grammar** Daily Language Activities, 143E
Compound Sentences, 143F
Practice Book, 68 LC 3.1.2

**Quick Check** **Vocabulary**, 143A–143B

## DAY 5 Review and Assess

**Listening/Speaking/Viewing**

**Focus Question** Describe the different types of architecture found in "Pond Street Clubhouse" and *My Very Own Room*.

**Vocabulary** R 3.1.4, R 3.1.8
**Assess Words,** Connect to Writing, 143B

**Spelling** Posttest, 143D
Reproducible, SP15 W 3.1.8

**Read** Self-Selected Reading
R 3.3.2

Student Book

**Comprehension**
Critical Thinking, 143

**Fluency** Practice, 139A R 3.1.3

**Writing**

**Daily Writing Prompt** Pretend you are one of the brothers in the story *My Very Own Room*. Write how you feel about your sister getting a room of her own.

Conferences/Revision (Assignments), 145E–F
W 3.1.4, W 3.2.2

**Grammar** Daily Language Activities, 143E
Compound Sentences, 143F
Reproducible, GR15 LC 3.1.2

**Weekly Assessment, 145G–145H**

# Differentiated Instruction

## What do I do in small groups?

## Focus on Skills

**IF...** students need additional instruction and practice based on your  **Quick Check** observations of the following skills:

**Phonics/Word Study**
Long *i*

**Vocabulary Words**
*separate, determination, storage, exact, ruined, luckiest*
**Strategy:** Word Parts

**Comprehension**
**Strategy:** Monitor Comprehension
**Skill:** Make and Confirm Predictions

**Fluency**

**THEN...**

| | |
|---|---|
| Approaching<br>English Learners | Preteach and Reteach Skills |
| On Level | Consolidate Learning |
| Beyond | Enrich and Accelerate Learning |

## Suggested Small Group Lesson Plan

| Focus on Skills | DAY 1 | DAY 2 |
|---|---|---|
| **Phonics/Word Study**<br>• **Long *i*** | English Learners Preteach Long *i*, 145BB | On Level Reteach Long *i*, 145S |
| **Vocabulary**<br>• **Week 5 Words**  | Approaching Preteach; Academic Language, 145I, 145K<br>On Level Review, 145S<br>Beyond Practice Reader Lesson 1, 145Y<br>English Learners Preteach; Academic Language, 145AA–145BB | Approaching Practice Reader Lesson 1, 145N<br>Beyond Practice Reader Lesson 2, 145Z<br>English Learners Vocabulary; Access to Core Content, 145BB–145CC |
| **Comprehension**<br>• **Strategy:** Monitor Comprehension<br>• **Skill:** Make and Confirm Predictions | Approaching Prepare to Read, 145I<br>Beyond Practice Reader Lesson 1, 145Y<br>English Learners Prepare to Read, 145AA | Approaching Reteach; Practice Reader Lesson 1, 145M–145N<br>Beyond Practice Reader Lesson 2, 145Z<br>English Learners Practice Reader, 145GG |
| **Fluency**<br>• **Repeated Reading** | | |

## Skill-Based Practice Readers

Apply skills and strategies while reading appropriate leveled books.

Leveled Practice Database
Go to www.macmillanmh.com.

## Manipulatives

Use for Hands-on Learning

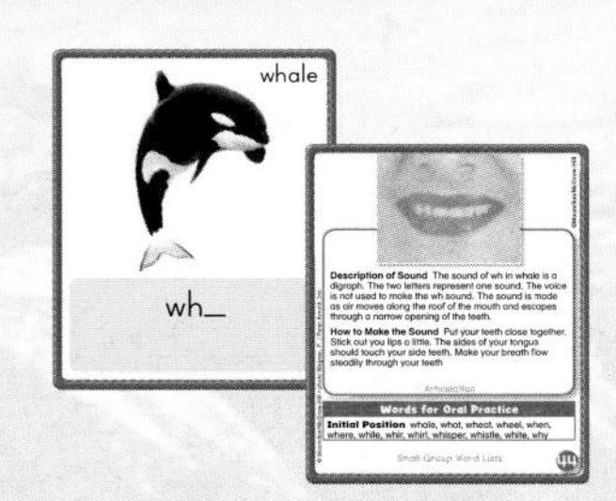
Sound-Spelling Cards

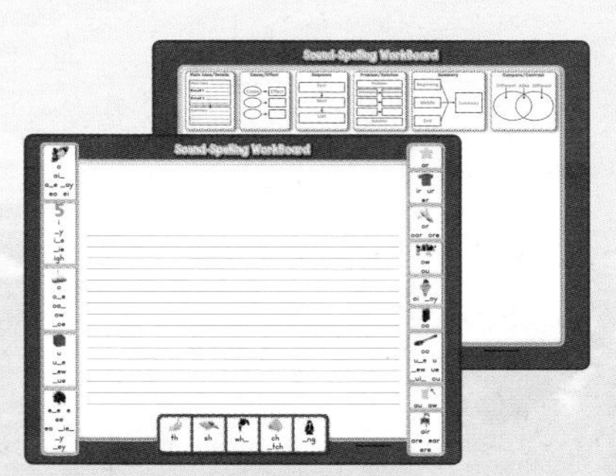
Sound-Spelling WorkBoards

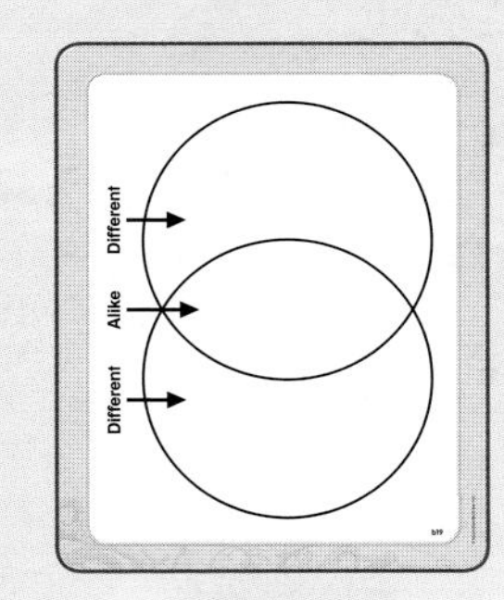

Vocabulary/Comprehension Write-on/Wipe-off Board

Hands-on activities for reinforcing weekly skills

| DAY 3 | DAY 4 | DAY 5 |
|---|---|---|
| **Approaching** Long *i*, 145J<br>**Beyond** Extend and Accelerate, 145W | **English Learners** Grammar, 145EE | **Approaching** Long *i*, 145J |
| **Approaching** Practice Reader Lesson 2, 145O<br>**On Level** Practice Reader Lesson 1, 145U<br>**English Learners** Preteach Vocabulary; Access to Core Content, Grammar, 145BB–145CC, 145EE | **Approaching** Review Vocabulary, 145L<br>**On Level** Practice Reader Lesson 2, 145V<br>**Beyond** Enrich, 145W<br>**English Learners** Vocabulary, 145GG–145HH | **English Learners** Vocabulary, Practice Reader 145GG |
| **Approaching** Practice Reader Lesson 2, 145O<br>**On Level** Practice Reader Lesson 1, 145U<br>**English Learners** Practice Reader, 145GG | **Approaching** Practice Reader Lesson 3, 145P<br>**On Level** Practice Reader Lesson 2, 145V<br>**English Learners** Practice Reader, 145GG | **Approaching** Book Talk, 145HH<br>**On Level** Book Talk, 145HH<br>**Beyond** Book Talk, 145HH<br>**English Learners** Book Talk, 145HH |
| | **Approaching** Reread, Model, 145Q<br>**On Level** Reread, Model, 145T<br>**Beyond** Reread, Model, 145X<br>**English Learners** Reread, Model, 145DD | **Approaching** Self-Selected Reading, 145R<br>**On Level** Self-Selected Reading, 145T<br>**Beyond** Self-Selected Reading, 145X |

# Managing the Class

## What do I do with the rest of my class?

- Literacy Workstations
- Practice Book
- Online Activities
- Classroom Library

## Classroom Management Tools

### Weekly Contract

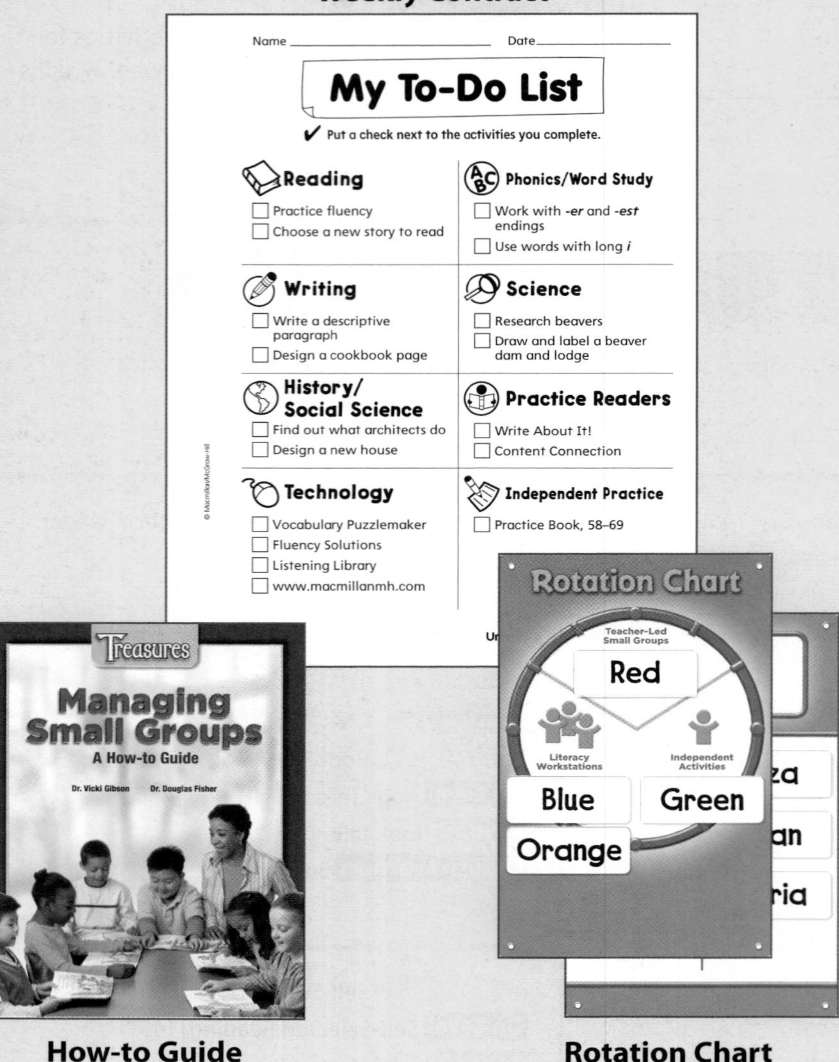

Name ______________ Date ______________

**My To-Do List**

✔ Put a check next to the activities you complete.

**Reading**
- ☐ Practice fluency
- ☐ Choose a new story to read

**Phonics/Word Study**
- ☐ Work with *-er* and *-est* endings
- ☐ Use words with long *i*

**Writing**
- ☐ Write a descriptive paragraph
- ☐ Design a cookbook page

**Science**
- ☐ Research beavers
- ☐ Draw and label a beaver dam and lodge

**History/Social Science**
- ☐ Find out what architects do
- ☐ Design a new house

**Practice Readers**
- ☐ Write About It!
- ☐ Content Connection

**Technology**
- ☐ Vocabulary Puzzlemaker
- ☐ Fluency Solutions
- ☐ Listening Library
- ☐ www.macmillanmh.com

**Independent Practice**
- ☐ Practice Book, 58–69



How-to Guide

Rotation Chart

# Digital Learning

**StudentWorks Plus**
- Summaries in Multiple Languages
- Word-by-Word Reading
- Assessment

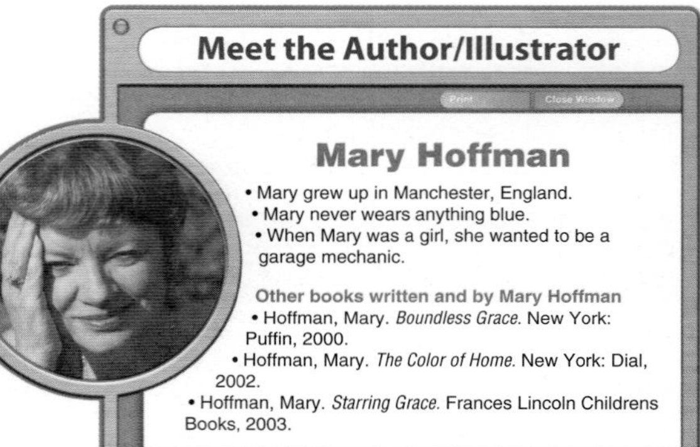


- Read Other Books by Author or Illustrator

## Classroom Library

Use the trade books to apply skills. See lessons on pages T2–T7. See also **Theme Bibliography**, pages T8–T9, to select books for 30 minutes of daily independent reading.

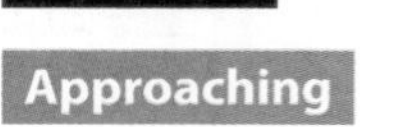

Beyond

# Independent Activities

**ONLINE INSTRUCTION** www.macmillanmh.com

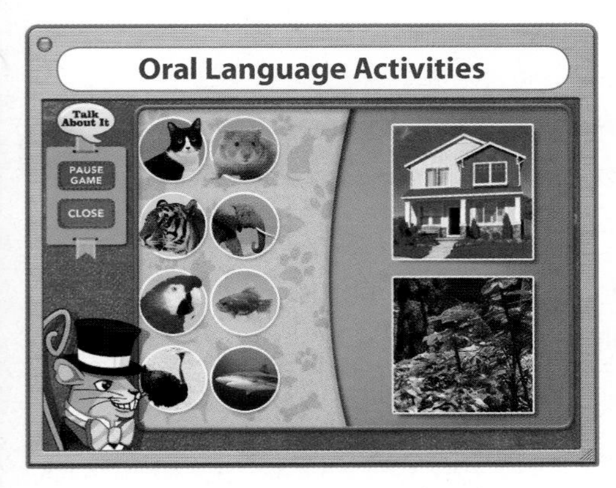


- Focus on Unit Vocabulary and Concepts
- English Learner Support

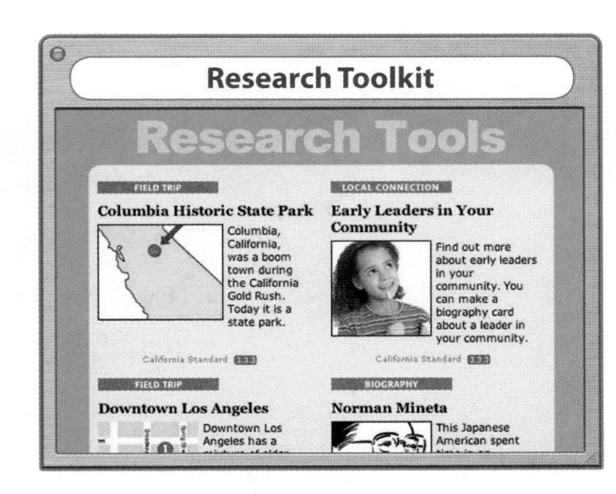


- Research Roadmap
- Research and Presentation Tools
- Theme Launcher Video
- Links to CA Science and History/Social Science Programs

- Focus on Keyboard and Internet Skills
- Media Literacy

- Differentiated Lists and Activities

## Available on CD

**LISTENING LIBRARY**
Recordings of selections

- Main Selections
- Paired Selections
- Practice Readers
- EL Readers

**FLUENCY SOLUTIONS**
Recorded passages at two speeds for modeling and practicing fluency

## Practice Book

Also Available:

**Approaching Reproducible**

**Beyond Reproducible**

## Literacy Workstation Flip Charts

Daily independent and partner activities connected to the weekly skills. See pages 112J–112K.

# Managing the Class

## What do I do with the rest of my class?

## Reading

### Objectives

- Read aloud fluently with expression
- Predict what will happen next in a story
- Select literature for daily reading enjoyment

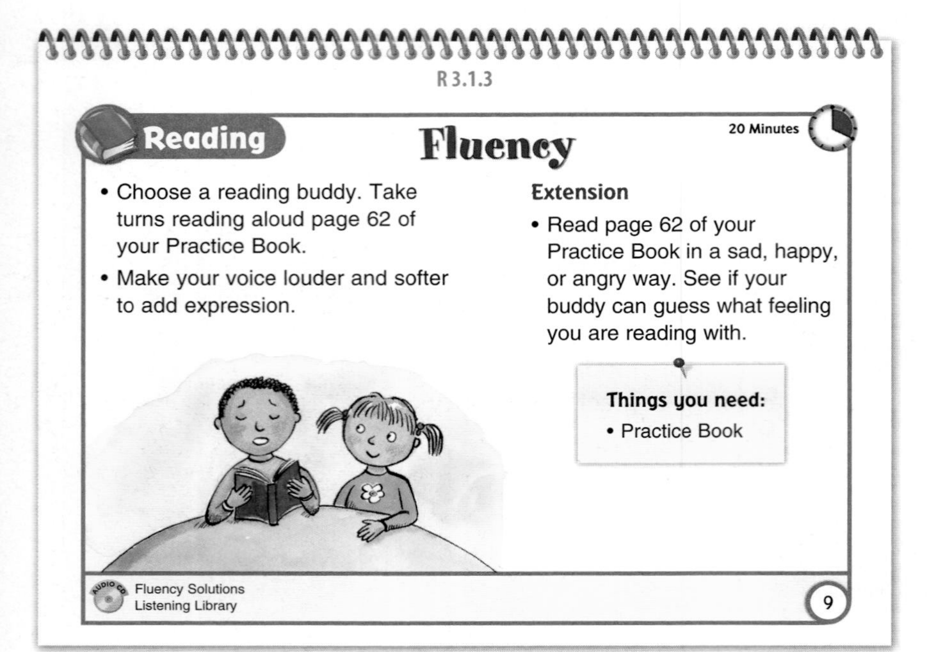

R 3.1.3

**Reading** — **Fluency** — 20 Minutes

- Choose a reading buddy. Take turns reading aloud page 62 of your Practice Book.
- Make your voice louder and softer to add expression.

**Extension**

- Read page 62 of your Practice Book in a sad, happy, or angry way. See if your buddy can guess what feeling you are reading with.

**Things you need:**
- Practice Book

Fluency Solutions
Listening Library

9

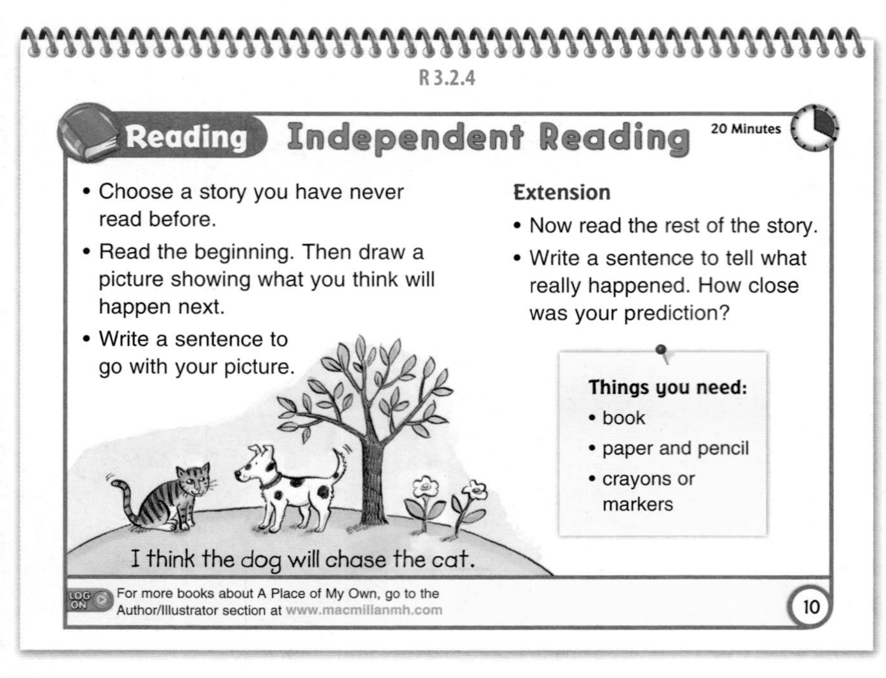

R 3.2.4

**Reading** — **Independent Reading** — 20 Minutes

- Choose a story you have never read before.
- Read the beginning. Then draw a picture showing what you think will happen next.
- Write a sentence to go with your picture.

I think the dog will chase the cat.

**Extension**

- Now read the rest of the story.
- Write a sentence to tell what really happened. How close was your prediction?

**Things you need:**
- book
- paper and pencil
- crayons or markers

For more books about A Place of My Own, go to the Author/Illustrator section at www.macmillanmh.com

10

## Phonics/Word Study

### Objectives

- Use suffixes to change meaning of words
- Identify plural endings of words

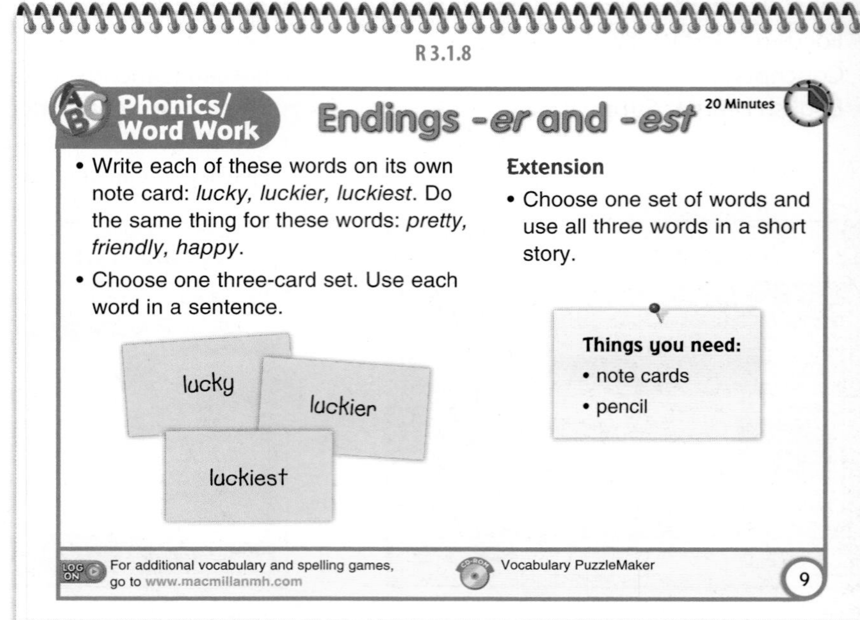

R 3.1.8

**Phonics/Word Work** — **Endings -*er* and -*est*** — 20 Minutes

- Write each of these words on its own note card: *lucky, luckier, luckiest*. Do the same thing for these words: *pretty, friendly, happy*.
- Choose one three-card set. Use each word in a sentence.

lucky
luckier
luckiest

**Extension**

- Choose one set of words and use all three words in a short story.

**Things you need:**
- note cards
- pencil

For additional vocabulary and spelling games, go to www.macmillanmh.com

Vocabulary PuzzleMaker

9

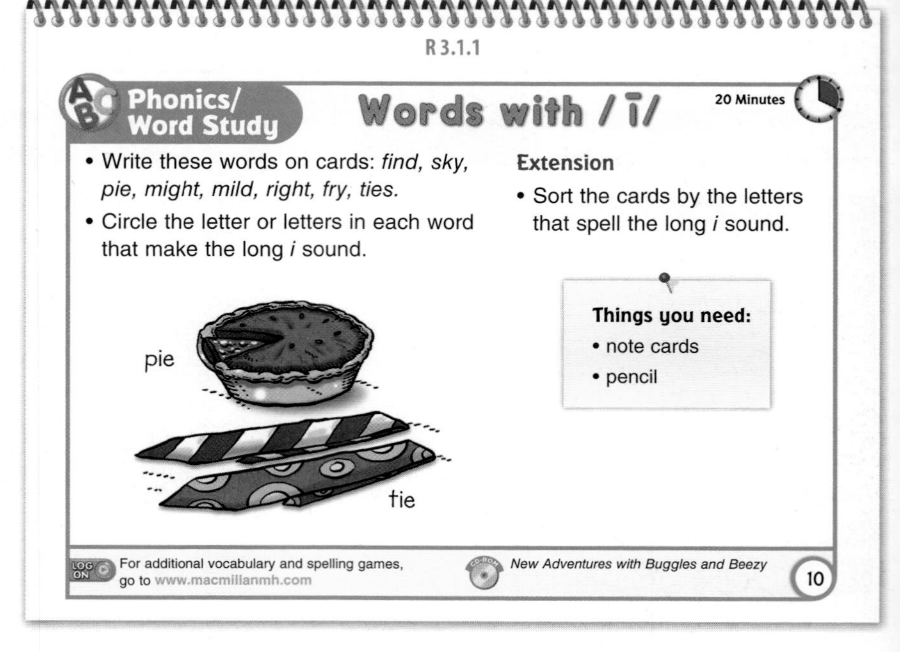

R 3.1.1

**Phonics/Word Study** — **Words with /ī/** — 20 Minutes

- Write these words on cards: *find, sky, pie, might, mild, right, fry, ties.*
- Circle the letter or letters in each word that make the long *i* sound.

pie
tie

**Extension**

- Sort the cards by the letters that spell the long *i* sound.

**Things you need:**
- note cards
- pencil

For additional vocabulary and spelling games, go to www.macmillanmh.com

*New Adventures with Buggles and Beezy*

10

# Literacy Workstations

**Literacy Workstation Flip Charts**

## Writing

### Objectives

- Write a paragraph about an activity
- Write step-by-step instructions
- Design an instructional page of information

## Content Literacy

### Objectives

- Research information about physical geography
- Describe how people modify their physical environment

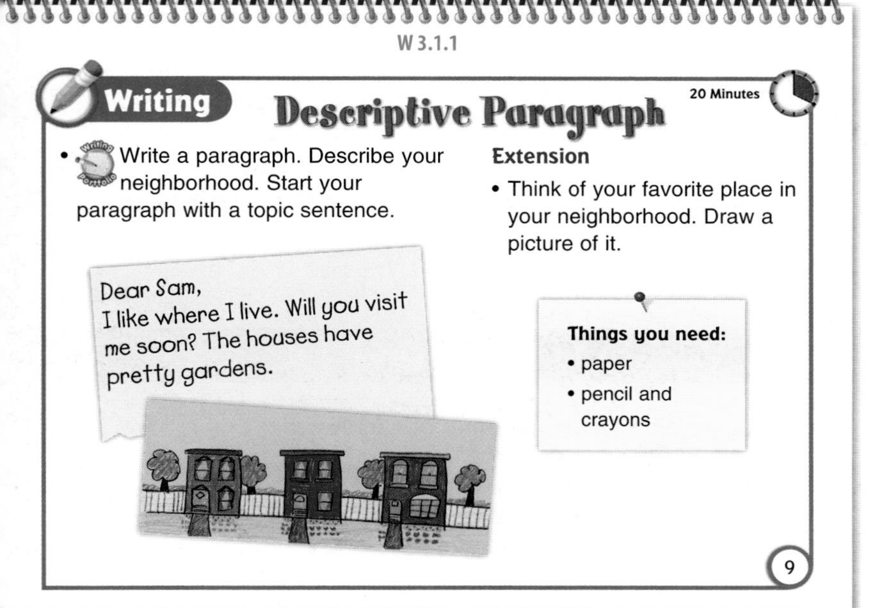

W 3.1.1

**Writing** — **Descriptive Paragraph** — 20 Minutes

- Write a paragraph. Describe your neighborhood. Start your paragraph with a topic sentence.

Dear Sam,
I like where I live. Will you visit me soon? The houses have pretty gardens.

**Extension**

- Think of your favorite place in your neighborhood. Draw a picture of it.

**Things you need:**
- paper
- pencil and crayons

9

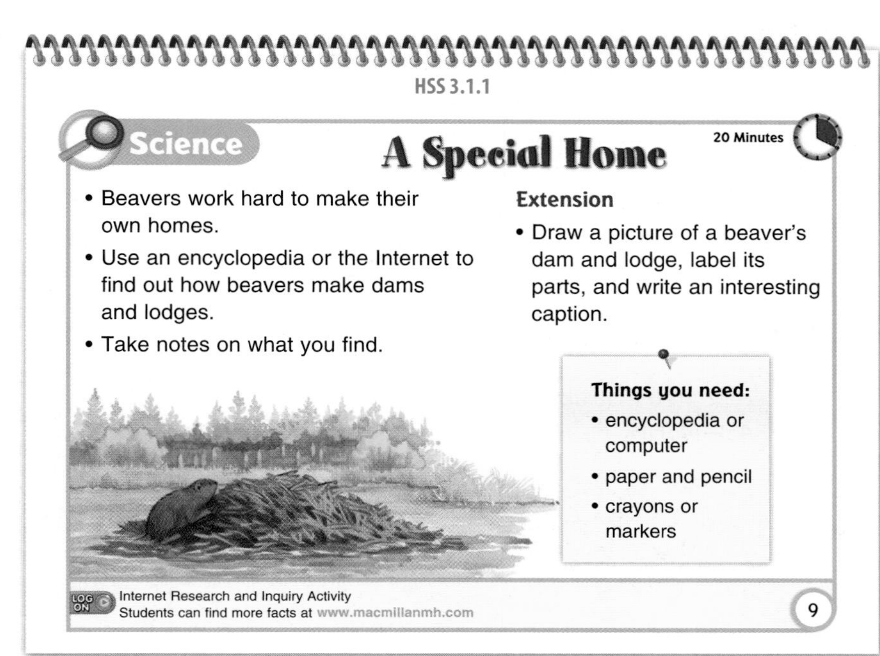

HSS 3.1.1

**Science** — **A Special Home** — 20 Minutes

- Beavers work hard to make their own homes.
- Use an encyclopedia or the Internet to find out how beavers make dams and lodges.
- Take notes on what you find.

**Extension**

- Draw a picture of a beaver's dam and lodge, label its parts, and write an interesting caption.

**Things you need:**
- encyclopedia or computer
- paper and pencil
- crayons or markers

Log On: Internet Research and Inquiry Activity
Students can find more facts at www.macmillanmh.com

9

W 3.1.0

**Writing** — **My Favorite Snack** — 20 Minutes

- Think of a favorite snack you know how to make, such as a tuna fish sandwich.
- Design a cookbook page. Tell others how to make the snack. List the ingredients and number the steps in order. Add a picture.

**Extension**

- Gather other cookbook pages from your classmates. Design a cover and make a class cookbook.

**Things you need:**
- paper and pencil
- crayons or markers

10

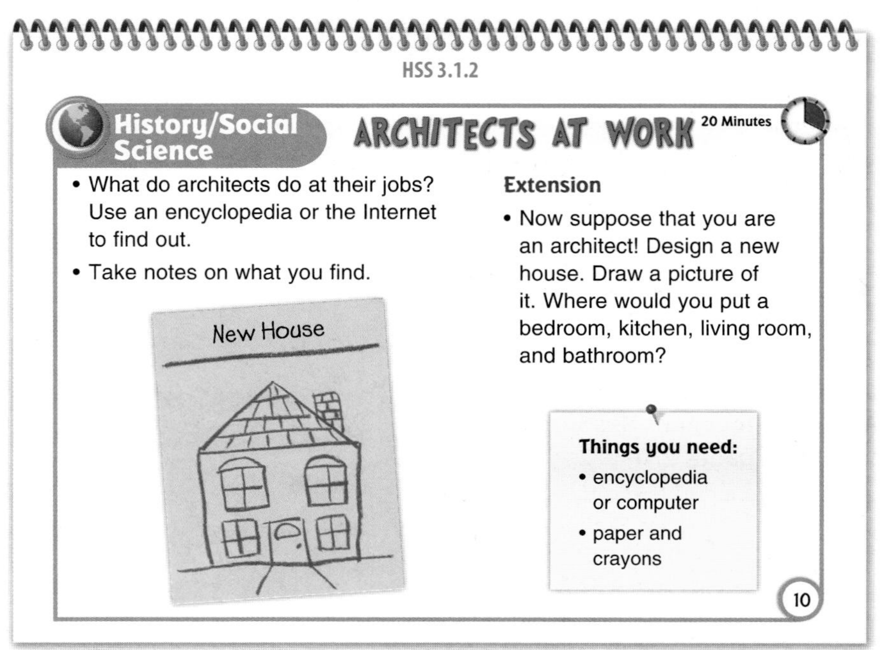

HSS 3.1.2

**History/Social Science** — **ARCHITECTS AT WORK** — 20 Minutes

- What do architects do at their jobs? Use an encyclopedia or the Internet to find out.
- Take notes on what you find.

New House

**Extension**

- Now suppose that you are an architect! Design a new house. Draw a picture of it. Where would you put a bedroom, kitchen, living room, and bathroom?

**Things you need:**
- encyclopedia or computer
- paper and crayons

10

## Prepare

### WHOLE GROUP

**ORAL LANGUAGE**
- Read Aloud
- Build Background
- Connect to Theme

**PHONICS/WORD STUDY**
- Long *i*

**VOCABULARY**
- Teach Words in Context
- Word Parts: Suffixes *-er, -est*

**COMPREHENSION**
- Strategy: Monitor Comprehension
- Skill: Make and Confirm Predictions

**CA CONTENT STANDARDS**
R 3.1.1, R 3.1.2, R 3.1.6, R 3.1.8, R 3.2.4, R 3.3.1, R 3.3.5, LAS 3.1.4, LAS 3.1.9, LAS 3.2.2

### SMALL GROUP

- Differentiated Instruction, pp. 145I–145HH

### Intensive Vocabulary

To provide 15–20 minutes additional vocabulary instruction, see **Oral Vocabulary Cards** 5-Day Plan. The pre- and posttests for this week can be found in the **Teacher's Resource Book**, pages 270–272.

# Read Aloud

## Read "Under the Back Porch"

Read Aloud

CA CONTENT STANDARD
R 3.3.1 Distinguish common forms of literature.
R 3.3.5 Recognize the similarities of sounds in words and rhythmic patterns in a selection.

**GENRE: POEM**

Share with students the following key characteristics of a **poem**:

- A poem expresses a thought or a strong feeling. The words in a poem are often placed in a rhythmic pattern.
- Poetry may include sound patterns, such as alliteration. Alliteration means that two or more words begin with the same sounds, such as the beginning /m/ sound in *moist moss*.
- Free verse poems don't rhyme.

**FOCUS ON VOCABULARY**

Introduce the following words, using the **Define/Example/Ask** routine. Tell students that knowing these words will help them understand the poem.

### Vocabulary Routine

Use the routines below to discuss the meaning of each word.

**Define:** If something is **damp**, it is wet.
**Example:** I dried my damp hair with a towel.
**Ask:** What are some things that are damp after it rains?

**Define:** When something **slants**, it comes through at an angle.
**Example:** The bright moonlight slants through the tree branches.
**Ask:** What is it like to walk on a road that slants upward?

**Define:** If something is **moist**, it is a little bit wet.
**Example:** The air was moist after the rain.
**Ask:** How is moist different from damp?

**LISTENING FOR A PURPOSE**

Ask students to listen carefully as you read "Under the Back Porch" on **Read-Aloud Anthology** pages 87–89. Use the Think Alouds and vocabulary prompts provided.

EL **Interactive Reading** Build students' oral language by engaging them in talk about the story's basic meaning.

- Point to the picture of the girl under the porch. Name each part of the picture (girl, boy, porch, slats) and have students repeat.

CA CONTENT STANDARD **LAS 3.1.4** Identify the musical elements of literary language.

**LAS 3.2.2** Plan and present dramatic interpretations of experiences, stories, poems, or **plays** with clear diction, pitch, tempo, and tone.

- After the first stanza, say *What does the house look like? Draw a picture of the house. With your hands show me where the yard and the porch are.*
- After the second stanza, say *Turn to your partner and discuss how the porch looks and smells. Draw how the sunlight slants.*
- In the second stanza, slowly read the line "Sunlight only slants through the slats" and emphasize the initial /s/ sound in *sunlight, slants,* and *slats. Tell which words begin with the /s/ sound. Now let's say the words together,* sunlight, slants, slats.
- After the last stanza, say *Tell your partner where you like to go when you want to be alone. Explain why you like going there.*

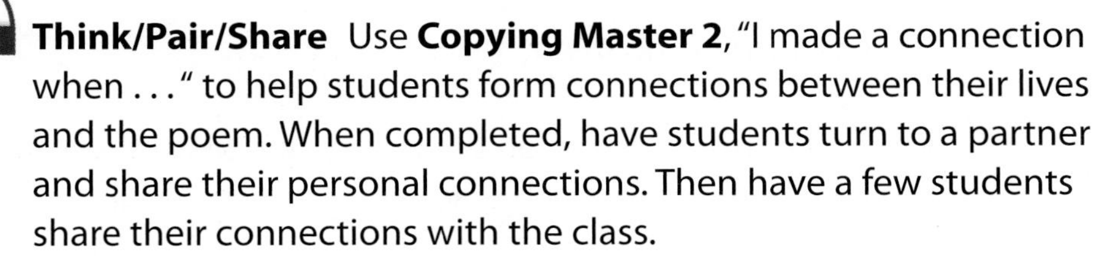

**Think/Pair/Share** Use **Copying Master 2**, "I made a connection when . . ." to help students form connections between their lives and the poem. When completed, have students turn to a partner and share their personal connections. Then have a few students share their connections with the class.

**RESPOND TO THE POEM**

Ask students the Think and Respond questions on page 89. Then ask students to think of all the special places that people can go to be alone. Have them generate a list of reasons why people like to spend time alone.

## Model Fluency

Reread the poem. Tell students that this time you want them to focus on two aspects of how you read the story—your pacing and phrasing.

CA CONTENT STANDARD **R 3.1.1** Read aloud narrative and expository text fluently and with appropriate pacing, intonation, and expression.

Point out that you pause when you come to a comma. You also stop when you come to a period. Model reading the poem with proper pauses and stops.

**Think Aloud** Listen as I read the poem, paying special attention to my pacing and phrasing. As I come to a period at the end of "shaped like a white box," I stop before moving on to the next line. As I come to a comma at the end of "in long strips of light," I pause slightly before moving on to the next line. Notice that I don't read too fast because in poetry, every word is important. Now try it with me. I will read a few lines at a time. I want you to repeat, using the same pacing and phrasing.

**Establish Fluency Focus** Remind students that you will be listening for these same qualities in their reading throughout the week. You will help them improve their reading by adjusting their pace as needed and using phrasing to make proper pauses and stops.

### Readers Theater

**BUILDING LISTENING AND SPEAKING SKILLS**
Distribute copies of "Take Me to Your Litter" **Read-Aloud Anthology**, pages 132–145. Have students practice reading the play throughout the unit. Assign parts and have students present the play or perform it as a dramatic reading at the end of the unit.

CA CONTENT STANDARD **LAS 3.1.9** Read prose and poetry aloud with fluency, rhythm, and pace, using appropriate intonation and vocal patterns to emphasize important passages of text being read.

CA CONTENT STANDARD **LAS 3.2.2** Plan and present dramatic interpretations of experiences, stories, poems, or **plays** with clear diction, pitch, tempo, and tone.

## Objectives

- Decode multisyllabic words with long *i* spellings

### Materials

- Sound-Spelling Cards
- Practice Book, p. 58
- Transparency 5
- Word-Building Cards
- Teacher's Resource Book, p. 182

### English Learners

UNIVERSAL ACCESS

**Transfer Sounds** Students speaking **Cantonese** will have difficulties pronouncing and perceiving the long *i* sound. Emphasize the sound and demonstrate correct mouth position when pronouncing each word. Use the Approaching level phonics lessons for additional pronunciation/ decoding practice.

HOMEWORK **Practice Book,** page 58

Remember the following common spellings for the long *i* sound: *i, ie, y,* and *igh.*

**A. Find the two words in each sentence that have the long *i* sound and write them in the spaces provided.**

1. Why is the sky so blue? Why sky
2. The child got into a fight. child fight
3. Dad went to buy a tie at the store. buy tie
4. I might ask the cook to fry the food. might fry
5. Can you find a bright red paint for the barn? find bright

**B. Write the word in each sentence that has the long *i* sound. Underline the letter or letters that stand for the sound.**

6. Did you know that pilot fish swim near blue sharks? pilot
7. A bear once walked in front of my dad's car. my
8. We need to pry open this box. pry
9. The lights went out during the storm. lights
10. What is your favorite pie? pie
11. The pesky fly almost ruined our picnic. fly
12. Sam eats only mild food. mild

Approaching Reproducible, page 58
Beyond Reproducible, page 58

# Phonics

## Long *i*

five
5
i y i_e igh ie

**EXPLAIN/MODEL**

Display the **Five-Sound-Spelling Cards** for the long *i* sound. Tell students that long *i* can be spelled in different ways. Point to each spelling on the card and provide a sample word. For example, the long *i* sound can be spelled:

- **igh** as in *night*
- **ie** as in *pie*
- **i** as in *child* and *mind*
- **i_e** as in *ride*
- **y** as in *fly*

Write the sample words on the board, underline the long *i* spelling, and model blending each one.

**Think Aloud** Look at this word. It is spelled *n-i-g-h-t.* I see the long *i* spelling *igh* in this word. Listen and watch as I sound out the word /nīt/, *night.* (Run your finger under the word as you sound it out.)

**PRACTICE/APPLY**

CA CONTENT STANDARD **R 3.1.1** Know and use complex word families when reading to decode unfamiliar words.

**Read the Word List** Display **Transparency 5**. The first line includes long *i* words students will encounter in the upcoming selections. Have students underline the long *i* spelling in each word. Then have them chorally read the words.

| | | | |
|---|---|---|---|
| light | my | I | bright |
| find | sky | ties | by |
| sit | sight | kid | kind |
| tie | why | wild | blind |
| fly | spy | like | pie |
| shy | fright | grind | cries |

**Phonics Transparency 5**

**Sort Words** Ask students to sort the words by spelling pattern. Then have them write the word sort in their Writer's Notebooks.

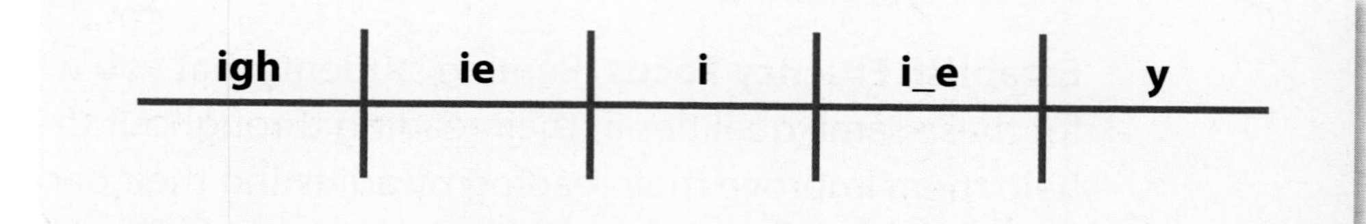

# Read Multisyllabic Words

CA CONTENT STANDARD
R 3.1.2 Decode regular multisyllabic words.

**TRANSITION TO LONGER WORDS** Help students transition from reading one-syllable to multisyllabic long *i* words. Have students read a word in the first column, then model how to read the longer word in the second column. Point out the added syllable(s), such as a prefix or suffix, to help students gain awareness of these common word parts.

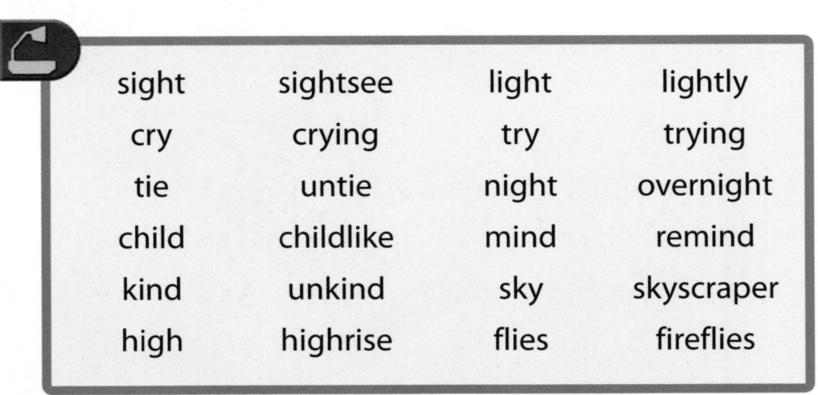

| | | | |
|---|---|---|---|
| sight | sightsee | light | lightly |
| cry | crying | try | trying |
| tie | untie | night | overnight |
| child | childlike | mind | remind |
| kind | unkind | sky | skyscraper |
| high | highrise | flies | fireflies |

**Phonics Transparency 5**

**BUILD WORDS** Use **Word-Building Cards** *light, fright, bright, wild, kind, ly, ness, ful, un*. Display the cards. Have students use the cards to build as many multisyllabic long *i* words as possible. These and other words can be formed: *lightly, lightness, frightful, brightness, brightly, wildly, kindness, kindly, unkindly*.

**CONNECT TO 6 SYLLABLE TYPES** To further help students break apart longer words to decode them, explain the following:

- **Vowel Team Syllables** When a common vowel team, such as *ie*, appears in a long word, the vowel team must remain in the same syllable. (un/tie)

**APPLY DECODING STRATEGY** Guide students to use the Decoding Strategy to decode the following words: *necktie, lightning, tonight, frightening, airtight, bullfight, foresight*. Write each word on the board. Remind students to look for vowel team syllables in step 3 of the Decoding Strategy procedure.

# Build Fluency

**SPEED DRILL** Distribute copies of the **Long i Speed Drill** in the **Teacher's Resource Book**. Use the Speed Drill routine to help students become fluent reading words with long *i* spelling patterns.

## Syllable Fluency

Use Word-Building Cards 41–50. Display one card at a time. Have students choral-read each common syllable. Repeat at varying speeds and in random order. Have students work with partners during independent time to write as many words as they can containing each syllable. Add these lists to the **Unit 1 Big Question Board.**

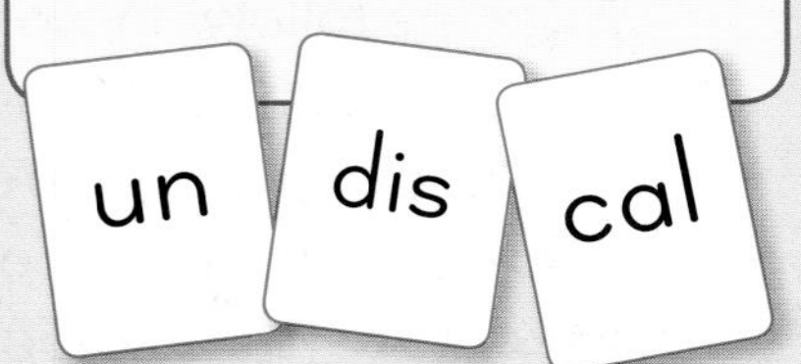


## Decoding Strategy

**Decoding Strategy Chart**

| Step | |
|---|---|
| Step 1 | Look for word parts (prefixes) at the beginning of the word. |
| Step 2 | Look for word parts (suffixes) at the end of the word. |
| Step 3 | In the base word, look for familiar spelling patterns. Think about the six syllable-spelling patterns you have learned. |
| Step 4 | Sound out and blend together the word parts. |
| Step 5 | Say the word parts fast. Adjust your pronunciation as needed. Ask yourself: "Is this a word I have heard before?" Then read the word in the sentence and ask: "Does it make sense in this sentence?" |

# Oral Language

## Build Background

**ACCESS PRIOR KNOWLEDGE**

Share the following information:
Look at the picture. It looks like the girl is reading a book she enjoys. It might tell about an adventure or a mystery or even a book about real animals. The most enjoyable books are the ones that tell interesting and exciting stories

Write the following words on the board and briefly define each one using the **Define/Example/Ask** routine:
**enjoyable** (giving joy or happiness)
**adventure** (a story about exciting events).

**FOCUS QUESTION** Ask students to read "Talk About It" on **Student Book** page 113. Then have students turn to a partner and describe the photo. Ask:

- Do you think the girl is reading an enjoyable book? What books do you think are enjoyable?
- Do you like to read adventure books? What are your favorite adventure books?

**BUILD WRITING FLUENCY**

WRITE ON DEMAND

Ask students to write in their Writer's Notebook what they know about the theme "Those Special Books." Tell students to write as much as they can as well as they can. Students should write for five minutes without stopping. Meet with individuals during Writing Conference time to provide feedback and revision assignments. Students should self-correct any errors they notice prior to the conference.

### English Learners

**UNIVERSAL ACCESS**

During the discussion, build on students' responses to help them move to the next level of language acquisition. For example, if a student answers *Yes* to the first question, say:

*That's right. The girl is reading an enjoyable book in her bedroom. Now turn to your partner and tell about this picture.* Provide the following frames to help students respond in complete sentences.

**Beginning/Early Intermediate** I see a ________.

**Intermediate** She is reading a book about ________.

**Early Advanced** People enjoy reading books because ________.

# Unit Theme

## Big Idea

We fill our homes with books that are enjoyable, have taught us something, or have special meaning.

### CONNECT TO THEME

Ask students what they have learned so far in this unit about the theme of learning.

- What books have you read that deal with the theme of learning? What lessons did the characters learn?
- What are some important lessons you've learned through books?

### USE THEME FOLDABLES

Write the **Big Idea** statement on the board. Ask students to copy it on their Unit Theme Foldables. Remind them to add details as they complete this week's readings.

## Digital Learning

**PRETEACH** Have Approaching Level students and English Learners listen to the selection on **StudentWorks Plus**, the interactive eBook, before reading with the class. The recording contains summaries in multiple languages, word-by-word reading support, a bilingual glossary, and comprehension questions with corrective feedback.

For Web site activities for oral language development, go to **www.macmillanmh.com**.

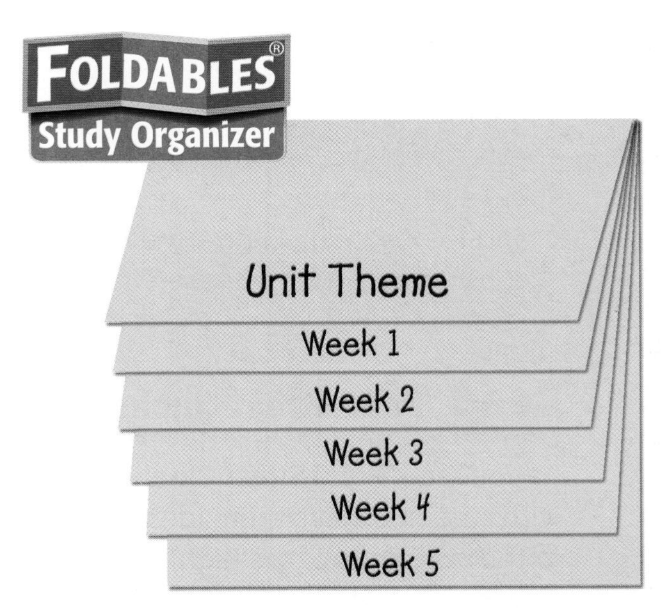


Layered Book

# Vocabulary

**STRATEGY**
**WORD PARTS**

CA CONTENT STANDARD R 3.1.8
Use knowledge of prefixes and suffixes to determine the meaning of words.

**Suffixes *-er* and *-est*** Explain to students that a suffix is a word part added to the end of a base word that changes the word's meaning.

The suffix *-er* means "more" when it is added to a base word that is an adjective. The suffix *-est* means "most" when it is added to a base word that is an adjective. Explain that when *-er* or *-est* is added to a word that ends in a vowel and a consonant, the consonant doubles. When *-er* and *-est* are added to a base word that ends in consonant *y*, the *y* changes to *i*.

Ask students to read "Word Parts" in the bookmark on **Student Book** page 114. Then model for students how to use word parts to determine the meaning of the word *bigger*.

**Think Aloud** I see the suffix *-er* at the end of *bigger*. I also see the base word *big*. I know that when *-er* is added to an adjective that is a base word, it means "more." When I put the meaning of the suffix *-er* with the meaning of the base word *big*, I get "more big." Because the word big ends in a consonant vowel and a consonant, I know that the consonant *g* doubled when the suffix *-er* was added.

## Read "Pond Street Clubhouse"

As you read "Pond Street Clubhouse" with students, have them identify clues to the meanings of the highlighted words. Tell students they will read these words again in *My Very Own Room.*

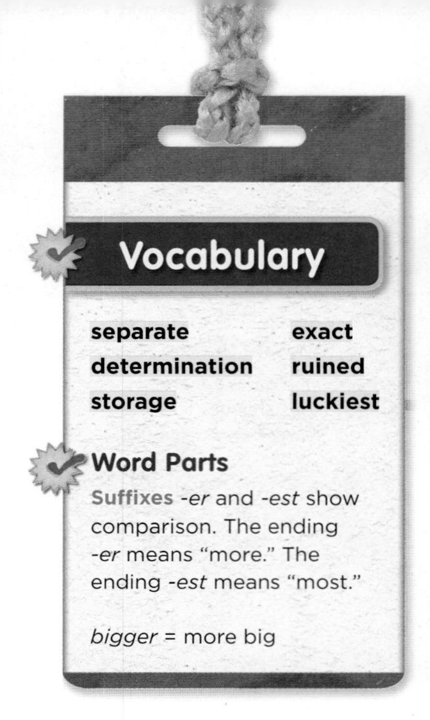

**Vocabulary**

| | |
|---|---|
| **separate** | **exact** |
| **determination** | **ruined** |
| **storage** | **luckiest** |

**Word Parts**
**Suffixes** *-er* and *-est* show comparison. The ending *-er* means "more." The ending *-est* means "most."

*bigger* = more big

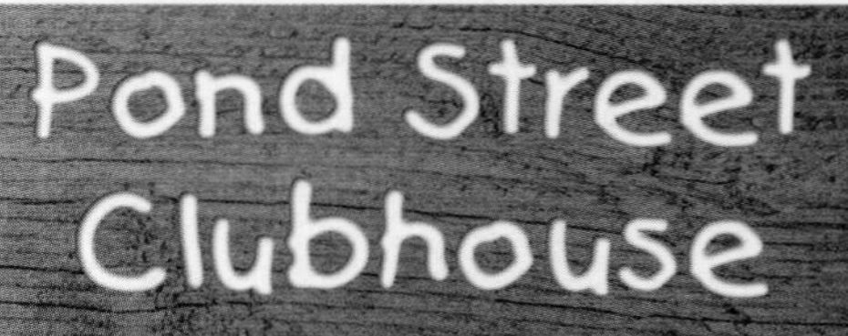


*by Sylvia Medrano*

On Saturday I went to the lumberyard with Dad to order lumber for the new garage. I saw the wood and got an idea.

"Hey, Dad," I said. "Could we build a clubhouse?"

"Probably not," said Dad. "I'll be too busy with the garage."

"But, Dad," I said, "you had a clubhouse when you were young."

Dad smiled and said, "I know, but first we have to build the garage."

I had to think of a way to get Dad to agree. "We can **separate** the clubhouse into two rooms," I said with **determination**. "The bigger one can be used as a **storage** room."

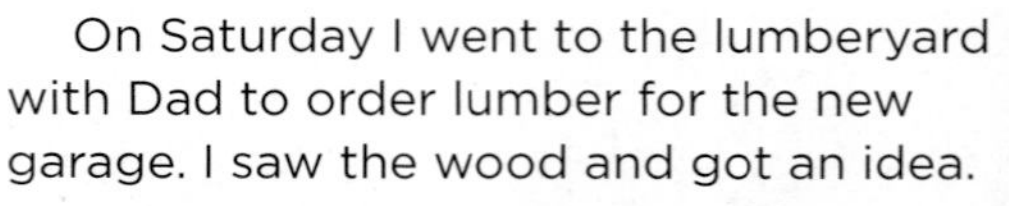

114

**Quick Check**

**Can students identify word meanings?**

During **Small Group Instruction**

**If No →** Approaching Level Reteach the words using the Vocabulary Lesson, pp. 145K–145L.

**If Yes →** On Level Consolidate the learning using p. 145S.

Beyond Level Extend the learning using p. 145W.

Dad thought about it for a moment. Then he said, "Let's wait to see if there is enough extra wood."

The garage supplies came the following weekend. There were huge piles of wood and a big box. It was a crate of nails and shingles for the roof. It looked like more than enough. When the truck left, Dad said, "Good news! We'll be able to build your clubhouse with the leftover wood when the garage is finished."

After a few weeks, it was time to start. A bunch of neighborhood kids came to help.

Dad let us measure the wood. Measuring has to be **exact** or else the pieces won't fit together. If Dad cut the wood too long or too short, our plans could be **ruined**. I knew we couldn't buy any extra wood.

When the clubhouse was finally finished, I was so thrilled. I made a sign and nailed it on the door. It said, "Pond Street Clubhouse—Welcome!" Now I have a great place to play. Am I the **luckiest** kid in town, or what?

## Reread for Comprehension

### Monitor Comprehension

**Make and Confirm Predictions** You can monitor your comprehension of a story by **making predictions** about what characters might do or what events might happen. Reread the selection. Use your Predictions Chart to keep track of your predictions about characters and events. Then check to see if your predictions were correct by writing **what happens**.

| What I Predict | What Happens |
|---|---|
| | |
| | |
| | |

115

# Vocabulary

### TEACH WORDS IN CONTEXT

Introduce each word using the **Define/Example/Ask** routine. Model reading each word using the syllable-scoop technique.

#### Vocabulary Routine

**Define:** If you **separate** things, you keep them apart.
**Example:** Fences separate the soccer field from the playground.
**Ask:** How do people usually separate the rooms of a house? EXPLANATION

CA CONTENT STANDARD R 3.1.6 Use sentence and word context to find the meaning of unknown words.

- Someone who has **determination** has decided to do something even though it may be difficult. *The girl's determination to do well on a test made her study hard.* What have you done with determination? EXAMPLE
- Things that people don't need every day are put in **storage** areas. *Basements are often used for storage.* What other places are used for storage? EXAMPLE
- If something is **exact**, it is completely correct . *To get the exact measurement of a room, you can use a tape measure.* How can you find the exact weight of something? PRIOR KNOWLEDGE
- If something is **ruined**, you can no longer use it. *The homes were ruined by a hurricane.* What is a synonym for ruined? (*destroyed*) SYNONYM
- The **luckiest** person has the most luck of anyone. *Ted thought he was the luckiest boy alive when his parents gave him a puppy.* What would make you feel like the luckiest person alive? DESCRIPTION

#### English Learners

UNIVERSAL ACCESS

**PRETEACH VOCABULARY**
See pages 145BB and 145K to preteach the vocabulary words to **English Learners** and **Approaching Level** students. Use the **Visual Vocabulary Resources** to demonstrate and discuss each word. Use the Interactive Question-Response Guide to preteach the content in "Pond Street Clubhouse" and develop meaning.

#### HOMEWORK Practice Book, page 59

determination, exact, ruined, separate, storage, luckiest, crate

**A. Fill in the blank with the word from the box that best completes each sentence.**

1. Rose's family had planned their trip with great determination.
2. Rose wrapped a few boxes and packed them in a wooden crate.
3. The family's furniture was put into a room for storage on the ship.
4. The ship sailed at the exact time it was supposed to leave.
5. Rose used a sheet to separate her space from the rest of her family.
6. She thought she was the luckiest person on the ship. She had her own quiet space to write in her journal.
7. Rose unpacked at her new home. Some boxes had been squashed. Nothing had been broken or ruined during the move.

**B. Write a sentence using one of the vocabulary words.** Possible response provided.

8. I was so happy to have my own room because I could put my stuff in the exact spot I wanted it.

Approaching Reproducible, page 59
Beyond Reproducible, page 59

## Objectives

- Monitor comprehension
- Make and confirm predictions
- Use academic language: *predictions*

## Materials

- Transparencies, 5, 5a, 5b
- Practice Book, p. 60

### Skills Trace

| Make and Confirm Predictions | |
|---|---|
| **Introduce** | U1: 115A–B |
| **Practice/ Apply** | U1: 116–139; Practice Book, 60–61 |
| **Reteach/ Review** | U1: 145M–HH |
| **Assess** | Weekly Tests; Unit 1 Test |
| **Maintain** | U2: 183B, 255–256; U3: 329–330; U4: 23, 24 |

### English Learners

UNIVERSAL ACCESS

**ACADEMIC LANGUAGE**
Preteach the following academic language words to **English Learners** and **Approaching Level** students during Small Group time: *predictions, confirm, revise*. See page 145I.

# Reread for Comprehension

## STRATEGY
### MONITOR COMPREHENSION

**What Is It?** Explain that students can monitor their comprehension by stopping regularly and asking themselves if they understand what they are reading. If they do not understand, they can self-correct by rereading, reading ahead, asking questions, paraphrasing, visualizing, adjusting their reading rate, or seeking help.

**Why Is It Important?** By monitoring their comprehension, students can figure out independently whether they understand what they are reading and then decide what to do when they do not understand. Monitoring comprehension can help students make, confirm, and revise predictions.

## SKILL
### MAKE AND CONFIRM PREDICTIONS

**CA CONTENT STANDARD**
**R 3.2.4** Recall major points in the text and make and modify predictions about forthcoming information.

#### EXPLAIN

- **What Is It?** To **make predictions**, good readers use their experiences and story clues—including story title, characters' actions, story events, and illustrations—to tell what is going to happen later on in the story.

Transparency 5a

Vocabulary

separate, exact
determination, ruined
storage, luckiest

Word Parts
Suffixes *-er* and *-est* show comparison. The ending *-er* means "more." The ending *-est* means "most."

*bigger* = more big

Pond Street Clubhouse

*by Sylvia Medrano*

On Saturday I went to the lumberyard with Dad to order lumber for the new garage. I saw the wood and got an idea.

"Hey, Dad," I said. "Could we build a clubhouse?"

"Probably not," said Dad. "I'll be too busy with the garage."

"But, Dad," I said, "you had a clubhouse when you were young."

Dad smiled and said, "I know, but first we have to build the garage."

I had to think of a way to get Dad to agree. "We can **separate** the clubhouse into two rooms," I said with **determination**. "The bigger one can be used as a **storage** room."

114

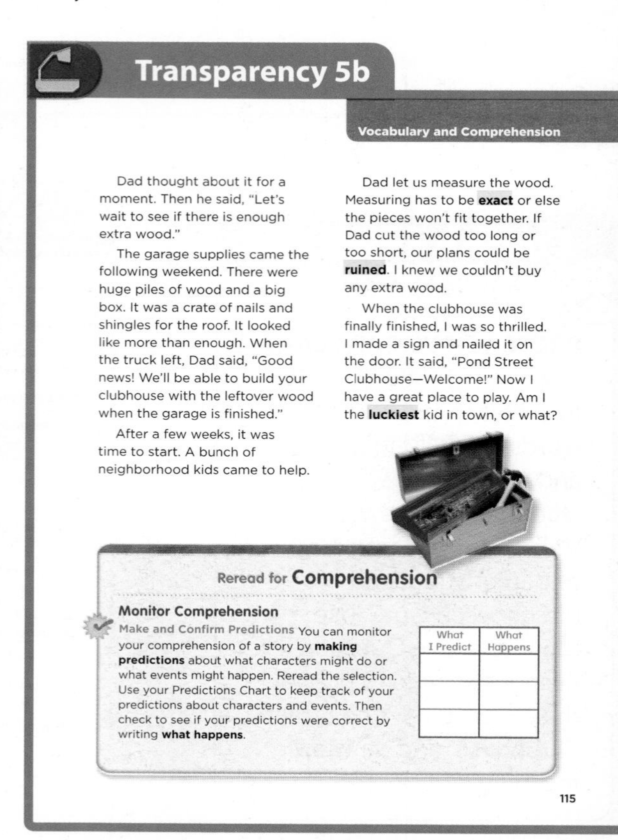
Transparency 5b

Vocabulary and Comprehension

Dad thought about it for a moment. Then he said, "Let's wait to see if there is enough extra wood."

The garage supplies came the following weekend. There were huge piles of wood and a big box. It was a crate of nails and shingles for the roof. It looked like more than enough. When the truck left, Dad said, "Good news! We'll be able to build your clubhouse with the leftover wood when the garage is finished."

After a few weeks, it was time to start. A bunch of neighborhood kids came to help.

Dad let us measure the wood. Measuring has to be **exact** or else the pieces won't fit together. If Dad cut the wood too long or too short, our plans could be **ruined**. I knew we couldn't buy any extra wood.

When the clubhouse was finally finished, I was so thrilled. I made a sign and nailed it on the door. It said, "Pond Street Clubhouse—Welcome!" Now I have a great place to play. Am I the **luckiest** kid in town, or what?

Reread for Comprehension

**Monitor Comprehension**
**Make and Confirm Predictions** You can monitor your comprehension of a story by **making predictions** about what characters might do or what events might happen. Reread the selection. Use your Predictions Chart to keep track of your predictions about characters and events. Then check to see if your predictions were correct by writing **what happens**.

| What I Predict | What Happens |
|---|---|
| | |
| | |
| | |

115

Student Book pages 114–115 available on Comprehension Transparencies 5a and 5b

- After students, have made their predictions, they can read on in the story to confirm their predictions, or find out if they are correct. If they are wrong, they can **revise**, or correct, their predictions—or make a new prediction.

**Why Is It Important?** By making predictions, readers show that they understand the characters' actions and story's events.

### MODEL

**How Do I Use It?** Read aloud the first page of "Pond Street Clubhouse" on **Student Book** page 114. Use **Transparency 5** to record predictions and to confirm or revise them.

**Think Aloud** After reading the first page, I predict that the boy's father will build a clubhouse. To make this prediction, I can use the story title, what happened so far, and my own experience. The title is "Pond Street Clubhouse." This tells me that there might be a clubhouse in the story. The boy gives his father several reasons why they should build the clubhouse. I know that good reasons can help persuade someone to do something. From my own experience, I also think that the father will want to make his son happy. I will read on to see if my prediction is correct.

### GUIDED PRACTICE

- Continue by helping students record the prediction in the What I Predict column. Then have students read on to confirm or revise their prediction and record that information the under the What Happens column.

### APPLY

Have students make another prediction about whether or not there will be enough lumber to build the clubhouse. Ask them to make inferences about what will happen using clues from the story and their own experiences. Then have them add this second prediction to the Predictions Chart. After they have read further in the story, they can confirm or revise their prediction and add it to the chart, too.

**Quick Check**

**Can students make and confirm predictions about the story?**

During **Small Group Instruction**

**If No** → Approaching Level Reteach the skill using the Comprehension Lesson, pp. 145M-145P.

**If Yes** → On Level Consolidate the learning using pp. 145U-145V.

Beyond Level Extend the learning using pp. 145Y-145Z.

**Transparency 5**

**PREDICTIONS CHART**

| What I Predict | What Happens |
| --- | --- |
| The narrator's father will agree to build a clubhouse. | The narrator's father agrees to build a clubhouse. |
| There will not be enough extra wood. | There was enough extra wood. |

**Graphic Organizer Transparency**

**Practice Book,** page 60

When you make a **prediction**, you tell what will probably happen next. As you continue reading, you can **confirm** your prediction, or find out if you were right.

**Each poem tells about characters who spend time in a place of their own. Read the poem. Read the title of the poem to help you predict what will happen. Choose the words that tell what will probably happen next and write the words on the line.**

1. **Finally We Can Play**
Rain has fallen for days and days.
We've been bored in many ways.
The sun is finally out today.
We can't wait to run out and play.
**a.** for the sky to turn gray.
**b.** to run out and play.

2. **The Tired Queen**
The queen went to sleep late last night.
She stayed up almost 'til dawn.
When she wakes up late this morning,
You'll probably see her yawn.
**a.** find her mowing her lawn.
**b.** probably see her yawn.

**Approaching Reproducible,** page 60
**Beyond Reproducible,** page 60

# Read

## WHOLE GROUP

**MAIN SELECTION**
- *My Very Own Room*
- Skill: Make and Confirm Predictions

**PAIRED SELECTION**
- Biography: "Frank Lloyd Wright"
- Text Feature: Encyclopedia Article

**CONTENT STANDARDS**
R 3.1.3, R 3.1.4, R 3.2.1, R 3.2.3, R 3.2.4, R 3.2.5, R 3.3.1, R 3.3.5, W 3.1.1, HSS 3.4.3, HSS 3.4.6

## SMALL GROUP

- Differentiated Instruction, pp. 145I–145HH

# Main Selection

CA CONTENT STANDARD R 3.3.1 Distinguish common forms of literature.

**GENRE: REALISTIC FICTION**

Have a student read the definition of Realistic Fiction on **Student Book** page 116. Students should look for characters that are like real people and events that could happen in real life.

**STRATEGY**
**MONITOR COMPREHENSION**

Good readers **monitor comprehension** by stopping often as they read to make sure they understand. If something is unclear, they reread or read ahead to find answers to their questions.

**SKILL**
**MAKE, CONFIRM, REVISE, PREDICTIONS**

CA CONTENT STANDARD R 3.2.4 Recall major points in the text and make and modify predictions about forthcoming information.

To make a prediction, readers use text features, story clues, and their own experiences to make inferences about what will happen in a story.

**Comprehension**

**Genre**
**Realistic Fiction** is an invented story that could have happened in real life.

**Monitor Comprehension**
**Make and Confirm Predictions**
As you read, use your Predictions Chart

| What I Predict | What Happens |
|---|---|
| | |
| | |
| | |

**Read to Find Out**
How does the girl get her own room?

116

## Vocabulary

**Vocabulary Words** Review the tested words while reading: **separate, determination, storage, exact, ruined,** and **luckiest.**

**Additional Selection Words** Students may be unfamiliar with these words. Pronounce the words, give student-friendly explanations as needed, and help students use the previously taught vocabulary strategies: word parts and using a dictionary.

**curtain** (p. 122) a hanging cloth panel sometimes used to divide a room

**dainty** (p. 133) small and beautiful

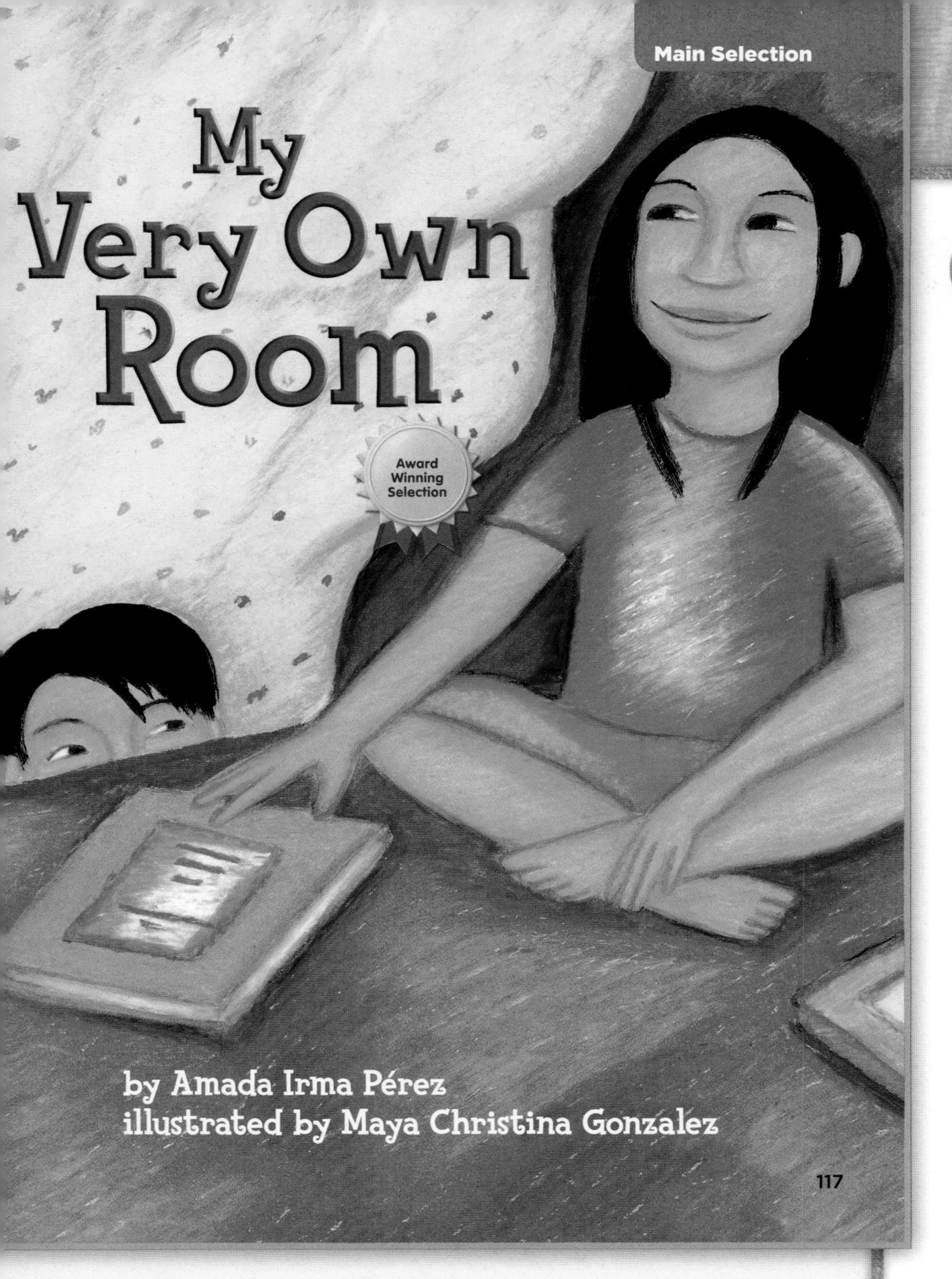

## Preview and Predict

**QUICK WRITE** Ask students to read the title, preview the illustrations, and write their predictions about the kind of information they will find in the text.

## Set Purposes

**FOCUS QUESTION** Discuss the "Read to Find Out" question on **Student Book** page 116. Remind students to look for the answer as they read.

Point out the Predictions Chart in the **Student Book and on Practice Book** page 61. Explain that students will complete it in as they read.

## Read *My Very Own Room*

Use the questions and Think Alouds to support instruction about the comprehension strategy and skill.

**Practice Book,** page 61

As you read *My Very Own Room*, fill in the Predictions Chart.

| What I Predict | What Happens |
|---|---|
| | |
| | |
| | |

How does the information you wrote in this Predictions Chart help you understand plot development in *My Very Own Room*?

**Approaching Reproducible,** page 61

**Beyond Reproducible,** page 61

PARTNERS

### Read Together

If your students need support to read the Main Selection, use the prompts to guide comprehension and model how to complete the graphic organizer. Allow students time to fill in their organizers before you provide the answers.

Use **Think/Pair/Share**. When asking a question, have students *think* about their answer, then discuss it with a *partner*. Finally, have selected students share their answers with the group. Provide sentence frames for discussion, such as *I predict ______ because ______*, to help students use academic language. Students should support their answers with evidence from the text.

# Develop Comprehension

**1 GENRE: REALISTIC FICTION**

What elements of **realistic fiction** can you expect to find in this story? (I know that realistic fiction contains characters that are like real people and events that could happen in real life. So far, from what I have read and the illustrations, I know that the main character is young girl who is nine years old and wants a room of her own. This is something that could happen in real life. As I continue to read, I expect the girl to try to solve her problem in the same way that a real kid would.)

**2 MONITOR AND CLARIFY: SELF-CORRECT**

What strategy can you do to make sure you understand why the girl wants a room of her own? (After reading this part of the story, I will stop and **ask** myself **questions**. I think that the girl might not like her brothers, but I'm not sure that's correct. So I will ask myself questions about the story and then reread and try to answer these questions. I know that the main character wakes up in a crowded room. How and what does she feel? She feels unhappy and tired of sharing her room. Why does she feel this way? She thinks she is too old to share a room. Now that I have answered my questions, I have more information. My first idea was wrong so I will correct it. The girl wants a room because she is too old to share.)

I woke up one morning on a crowded bed in a crowded room. Víctor's elbow was jabbing me in the ribs. Mario had climbed out of his crib and crawled in with us. Now his leg lay across my face and I could hardly breathe. In the bed next to ours my three other brothers were sleeping.

I was getting too big for this. I was almost nine years old, and I was tired of sharing a room with my five little brothers. More than anything in the whole world I wanted a room of my own.

118 **1** **2**

## Monitor Comprehension

**Monitor and Clarify:** *Self-Correct*

**Explain** Good readers stop and check their understanding. To make sure their ideas about a story are correct, they can ask *why, what,* and *how*, questions By answering these questions, they can correct any misunderstandings, or self-correct.

**Discuss** Use question 2 to model using the self-correct strategy. Ask *what* and *why* questions: *What is the girl feeling? Why does she feel this way?* Point out the girl is feeling very unhappy because she is sharing a room. Explain that by answering these questions, you have checked your comprehension and corrected misunderstandings.

**Apply** As students continue to read, have them demonstrate how they use the self-correct strategy to make sure they understand what they are reading.

A little space was all I wanted, but there wasn't much of it. Our tiny house was shared by eight of us, and sometimes more when our friends and relatives came from Mexico and stayed with us until they found jobs and places to live.

Once a family with eight kids (mostly boys!) lived with us for two months. It was noisy and a lot of fun. There was always a long line to use the bathroom, but the toilet seat was always warm.

3

119

# Develop Comprehension

**3 SKILL**
**MAKE PREDICTIONS**

Make a **prediction**. Do you think the girl will get her own room? Why or why not? (I predict that the girl will probably get her own room because she says that is what she wants more than anything in the whole world. I know that when I want something, I usually work very hard to get it, and I am usually successful. Also, the title of the story, *My Very Own Room*, gives a clue that she will get her own room.)

Put your **prediction** on your Predictions Chart under What I Predict.

| What I Predict | What Happens |
|---|---|
| The girl will get her own room. | |
| | |

## English Learners

**UNIVERSAL ACCESS**

Prepare students to read the story prior to the whole class reading. Use the Interactive Question-Response Guide on page 145CC to preteach the story content, build language, and develop meaning. This will enable students to participate successfully in the whole class reading and discussion.

**Beginning/Early Intermediate** Emphasize those questions and responses marked Beginning/Early Intermediate. In addition, focus on Key Words, Basic Words, and Function Words/Phrases.

**Intermediate** Use all the questions and prompts in the Interactive Question-Response Guide.

**Early Advanced** Extend language by using more complex sentence frames in the Interactive Question-Response Guide.

## Phonics/Word Study

**APPLY DECODING SKILLS** While reading, point out words with the sound/spelling patterns, syllable types, and word parts students have recently learned. Help students blend these words. You may wish to focus on selection words with the long *i* spelling pattern, such as *light, my, I, bright,* and *goodnight.*

# Develop Comprehension

**4 STRATEGY**
**MONITOR COMPREHENSION**

**Teacher Think Aloud** I am going to stop here and see if I understand what is happening in the story. I am not sure why the girl is sitting in the tree, so I'll try to figure it out. First, I will **reread** page 119. The very first sentence begins with, "A little space was all I wanted." This page also tells me that her house is very crowded. I can picture the crowded house and I know how I would feel. I would want to get away and sit in a tree, too. Now I understand why she is in the tree. She just wants some time to be by herself. **Rereading and visualizing** helped me **monitor my comprehension** of this part of the story. Now I understand what is happening.

Sometimes very early in the morning while everyone was still sleeping, I would climb up the crooked ladder that leaned against the elm tree in our backyard. I would sit on a little board, pretending it was a bench, and just think. I could hear my father snoring. He worked all night at the factory and went to bed just before dawn. **4** **5**

I loved my brothers. It wasn't that I didn't want to be near them. I just needed a place of my own.



# Develop Comprehension

## 5 COMPARE AND CONTRAST

**Compare** sitting in the elm tree to being inside of the house. How is sitting in the tree different from being inside the house? Why does the girl like the elm tree better? (The elm tree is a quiet and peaceful place where the girl goes when she wants to be alone. It is different from the house, which she describes as being crowded and noisy. The elm tree is a quiet place where she can think.)

# Develop Comprehension

**6 SKILL**
**MAKE PREDICTIONS**

What do you think the girl will try to do with the storage closet? Explain your **prediction**. (I predict that the girl will ask her mother to make the storage closet into a bedroom. I predict this because she thinks the closet will make a good room and is already imagining how it would look. It is also the only place in the house where she can make a room. From my own experience, I know that I would also ask to use the closet as a room.)

Add this to prediction to your Predictions Chart.

| What I Predict | What Happens |
| --- | --- |
| The girl will get her own room. | |
| The girl will try to make the storage closet into a bedroom. | |

I tiptoed around our tiny, two bedroom house. I peeked behind the curtain my mother had made from flour sacks to **separate** our living room from the **storage** closet.

6 "Aha! This is it! This could be my room." I imagined it with my own bed, table, and lamp—a place where I could read the books I loved, write in my diary, and dream.

I sat down among the boxes. My mother must have heard me because she came in from the kitchen.

**Make and Confirm Predictions**
What will the girl try to do with the storage closet?

122

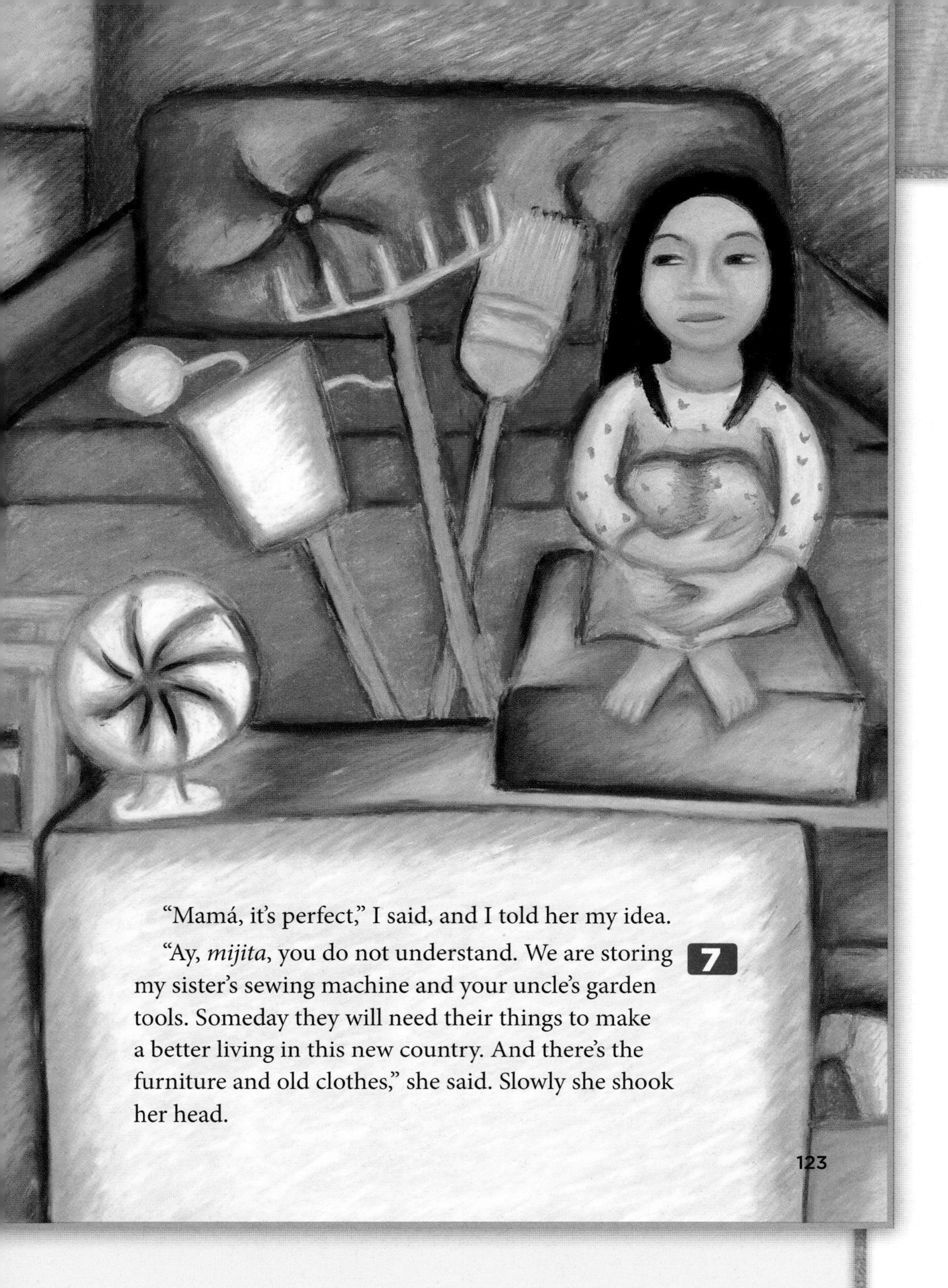


# Develop Comprehension

**7 MONITOR AND CLARIFY: SELF-CORRECT**

Do you know why the mother says *no* to her daughter? How does asking questions and **self-correcting** help you to understand the mother's reply?
(I don't understand why the mother says *no* to the girl. Using the storage closet seems like a good idea. To find out why the mother says *no*, I can ask myself questions: What does the mother say? She says they are storing things in the closet for the girl's aunt and uncle. Why does she say it? She wants the girl to know that it is important to keep these things safe. How does the mother react to the girl's question? She seems worried about where to move the things in storage. Now I have more information. I will correct my idea. The mother doesn't think the storage room is a good place for a bedroom, because it is being used to store things belonging to the girl's aunt and uncle.)

# Develop Comprehension

**8 STRATEGY**
**MONITOR COMPREHENSION**

**Teacher Think Aloud** When I don't understand something in a story, I stop reading and try to figure out what is happening. In this part of the story, it isn't clear why Mamá has changed her mind about letting the girl have her own room. How can you find out why the mother does this?

*(Prompt students to apply the strategy in a Think Aloud.)*

**Student Think Aloud** I need to **reread** this part of the story to find out why Mamá changed her mind. Mamá sees the determination on her daughter's face and the tears in her eyes. The daughter's face shows how important having her own room is to her. The look on her daughter's face makes Mamá think hard about where to move the things in the storage closet to make a bedroom for her daughter.

8 Then she saw the **determination** on my face and the tears forming in my eyes. "Wait," she said, seriously thinking. "Maybe we could put these things on the back porch and cover them with old blankets."

"And we could put a tarp on top so nothing would get **ruined**," I added.

9 "Yes, I think we can do it. Let's take everything out and see how much space there is."

I gave her a great big hug and she kissed me.

124

# Develop Comprehension

**9 SKILL**
**CONFIRM PREDICTIONS**

What does the girl persuade her mother to do with the storage closet? Was your **prediction** correct? (The girl persuades her mother to move the things in the storage closet somewhere else and turn the closet into a bedroom for her. This confirms that my prediction was correct.) Add this to your Predictions Chart.

| What I Predict | What Happens |
|---|---|
| The girl will get her own room. | |
| The girl will try to make the storage closet into a bedroom. | The girl persuades her mother to make storage closet into a bedroom. |

# Develop Comprehension

## 10 FIGURATIVE LANGUAGE: ALLITERATION

CA CONTENT STANDARD R 3.3.5 Recognize the similarities of sounds in words and rhythmic patterns in a selection.

**Alliteration** is a type of figurative language in which two or more words word begin with the same sound. Which two words in the second sentence of the second paragraph are an example of alliteration? How does this special language help you understand what is happening in this part of the story? (The two words are *bulging* and *bags*. These words help me picture how much stuff the family has to move to clean out the room.)

After breakfast we started pushing the old furniture out to the back porch. Everyone helped. We were like a mighty team of powerful ants.

We carried furniture, tools, and machines. **10** We dragged bulging bags of old clothes and toys. We pulled boxes of treasures and overflowing junk. Finally, everything was out except for a few cans of leftover paint from the one time we had painted the house.

126

## Vocabulary

CA CONTENT READER R 3.1.4 Use knowledge of antonyms, synonyms, homophones, and homographs, to determine the meanings of words.

### Context Clues: *Antonyms*

**Explain/Model** Explain that antonyms are words that have opposite meanings— *short* and *tall* are antonyms. Sometimes readers can use antonyms as context clues to figure out a word. On the board write: *My hands were cold, but my feet were toasty.*

**Think Aloud** I see *cold* and *toasty* in this sentence. I know what *cold* means—"not warm." I think *toasty* means the opposite of *cold*. So knowing what *cold* means helps me figure out the meaning *toasty—toasty* means "warm."

**Practice/Apply** On page 126, point out the sentence, "We pulled boxes of treasures and overflowing junk." Have students identify the antonyms. (*treasures, junk*). Then have them explain how knowing one of the antonyms helps them figure out the meaning of the other.

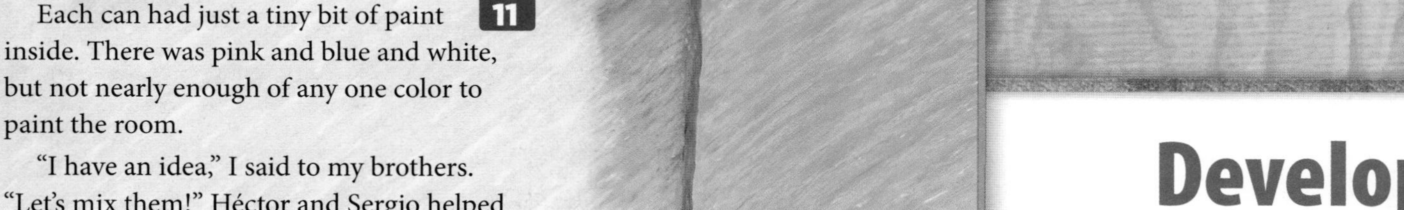

Each can had just a tiny bit of paint **11** inside. There was pink and blue and white, but not nearly enough of any one color to paint the room.

"I have an idea," I said to my brothers. "Let's mix them!" Héctor and Sergio helped me pour one can into another and we watched the colors swirl together. A new color began to appear, a little like purple and much stronger than pink. Magenta!

We painted and painted until we ran out **12** of paint.

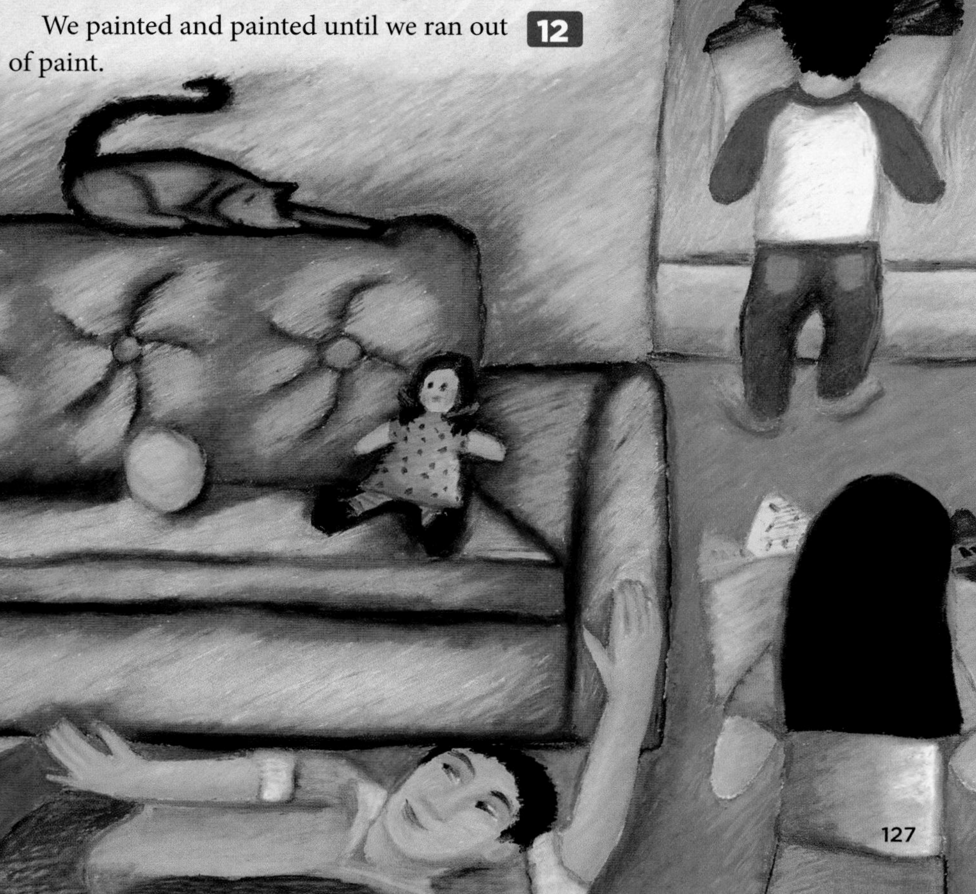

127

# Develop Comprehension

**11 SKILL**
**CONFIRM PREDICTIONS**

At the beginning of the story, you made a **prediction** about whether the girl would get her own room. What happens here? Was your prediction correct? (The girl and her family work hard to turn the storage closet into a bedroom by cleaning and painting it. My prediction was correct. The girl does get her own room.) Fill in the right column of the Predictions Chart.

| What I Predict | What Happens |
| --- | --- |
| The girl will get her own room. | The girl does get her own room. |
| The girl will try to make the storage closet into a bedroom. | The girl persuades her mother to make the storage closet into a bedroom. The family cleans out the room and paints it. |

**12 SELF-SELECTED STRATEGY USE**

What strategies have you used so far to help you understand the selection? Where did you use them? Why? How did they help?

**RETURN TO PREDICTIONS AND PURPOSES**

Have students respond to the selection by confirming or revising their predictions and purposes for reading. Encourage them to revise or write additional questions to help focus their attention as they continue to read the selection.

Stop here if you wish to read this selection over two days.

## Extra Support

**Make and Confirm Predictions**

Tell students: *A prediction is what you think will happen next. You can use what you know and what is in the story to make a prediction.* Then you can read on and find out if your prediction is correct. If students have difficulty confirming their prediction when they answer question 11, have them reread pages 124–127. Ask: *What do you think will happen after the mother says the girl can use the room?* (I think the girl will clean up the room and move into it.) *What clue appears on page 124?* (The mother talks about moving things from the room to the porch.) *What will happen next?* Why do you think this? (I think the girl will clean up the room. I think this because the mother seems nice and wants to help her daughter) Was your prediction correct? Point out that students need to revise their original predictions if they were wrong.

# Develop Comprehension

**13 SUMMARIZE**

How would you **summarize** what has happened so far in the story? What important events have happened? (A young girl wants a room of her own. She looks around the house for a space that can become her room. She asks her mother if she can move into a storage closet. At first her mother does not like the idea, but then she changes her mind. The family moves the old furniture out of the storage closet. Then they use leftover paint to paint the girl's new room.)

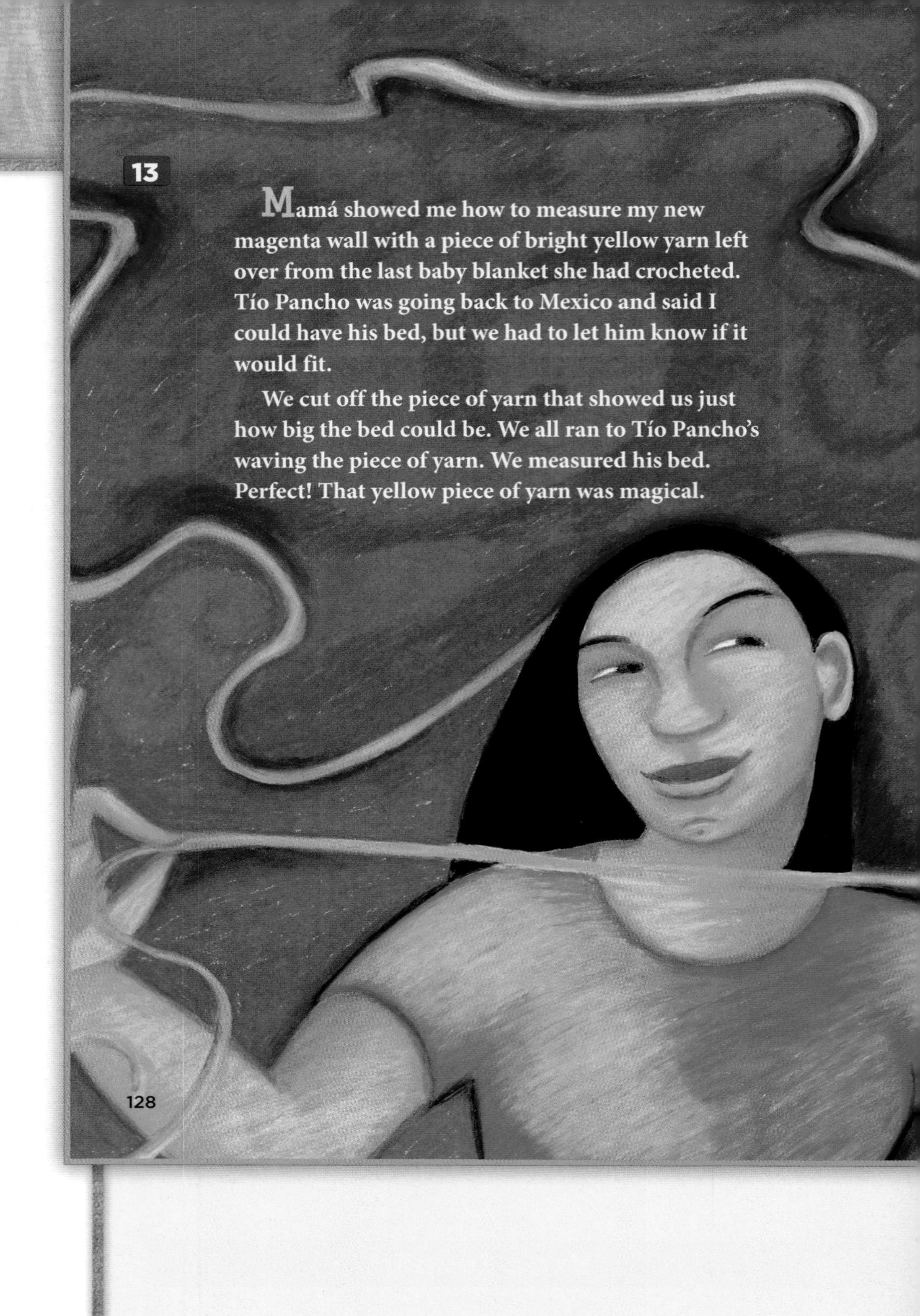

13

Mamá showed me how to measure my new magenta wall with a piece of bright yellow yarn left over from the last baby blanket she had crocheted. Tío Pancho was going back to Mexico and said I could have his bed, but we had to let him know if it would fit.

We cut off the piece of yarn that showed us just how big the bed could be. We all ran to Tío Pancho's waving the piece of yarn. We measured his bed. Perfect! That yellow piece of yarn was magical.

128

# Develop Comprehension

**14 GENRE: REALISTIC FICTION**

Think about what you've read so far. How do you know that this story is **realistic fiction**? (The events in the story could happen in real life. Many children share a room with brothers or sisters and want their own rooms. The characters in the story act and feel like real people. They talk just like real people, too.)

# Develop Comprehension

**15** **COMPARE AND CONTRAST**

**Compare and contrast** Blue Chip stamps to money. How is using Blue Chip stamps like spending money? How is using the stamps different from using money? (Using stamps is like spending money because people can use them to buy things. They are different because the stamps can only be used in special stores and money can be spent anywhere.)

She brought out a shoe box stuffed with Blue Chip stamps she had been collecting for years. Mamá and Papá got them for free when they bought food or gas. They were like little prizes that could be used as money at special stores. But before we could spend them, we had to **15** paste them into special stamp books.

130

# Develop Comprehension

**16 SKILL**
**MAKE PREDICTIONS**

What will the girl do with the Blue Chip stamps? Add this **prediction** to your Predictions Chart. (The girl's room is very important to her. It makes sense that she would use the stamps to buy something for the room. She knows that the room needs a lamp so she will probably use the Blue Chip stamps to buy one.)

| What I Predict | What Happens |
|---|---|
| The girl will get her own room. | The girl does get her own room. |
| The girl will try to make the storage closet into a bedroom. | The girl persuades her mother to make the storage closet into a bedroom. The family cleans out the room and paints it. |
| The girl will buy a lamp with the stamps. | |

## English Learners

UNIVERSAL ACCESS

### STRATEGIES FOR EXTRA SUPPORT

**Question 15 MAKE, CONFIRM, AND REVISE PREDICTIONS**

Have students read Student Book page 130. Ask: *What do people do with money?* (They buy things with it.) *What does the girl need in her room?* (She needs a lamp.) *How will the girl get the lamp?* (She will use the stamps to get a lamp.) Help students see that using the stamps to get a lamp is like using money to buy a lamp. Then have students answer the question: *Why are the Blue Chip stamps like money?*

# Develop Comprehension

**17 SKILL**
**CONFIRM PREDICTIONS**

Look at the illustration. Read page 133. Was your **prediction** about the lamp correct? (Yes. The girl used the stamps to purchase a lamp for her new room.) Add this information to the What Happens column of your Predictions Chart.

| What I Predict | What Happens |
|---|---|
| The girl will get her own room. | The girl does get her own room. |
| The girl will try to make the storage closet into a bedroom. | Mamá lets her daughter use the storage closet for a bedroom. The family cleans out the room and paints it. |
| The girl will buy a lamp with the stamps. | The girl buys a pretty lamp for her room. |

I saw the lamp I wanted right away. It was as dainty as a beautiful ballerina, made of white ceramic glass with a shade that had ruffles around the top and bottom. **17**

I shut my eyes. I was so excited yet so afraid we wouldn't have enough stamps to get it. Then I heard my mother's voice. "Yes, *mijita*. We have enough."

When we got home, I carefully set the new lamp on my bedside table. Then I lay on my new bed and stared at the ceiling, thinking. Something was still missing, the most important thing …

**18**



# Develop Comprehension

**18** **SKILL**
**MAKE PREDICTIONS**

Something is still missing from the girl's room. What do you think it is? What do you **predict** the girl will do? Why do you think this? (I think that the girl is missing a desk for writing because at the beginning of the story she said she liked to write in her diary. I think she will find a way to get the missing desk. So far, she has found everything else that she needs for the room.)

# Develop Comprehension

19 **SKILL**
**CONFIRM AND REVISE PREDICTIONS**

What did the girl do about the one thing that was missing from her room? Was your **prediction** correct? (Books were missing so the girl went to the library and checked out six of them. My prediction about what the girl would do was correct because I knew that she would find a way to get what was missing. My prediction about what she still needed was wrong. She was missing books, not a desk. So now I can revise my prediction. I know that books were missing from her room, but she found a way to get them.)

## Books!

19 The next day I went to our public library and rushed home with my arms full of books, six to be **exact**. It was my lucky number because there were six children in my family.

134

That evening, I turned on my new lamp and read and read. My two littlest brothers, Mario and Víctor, stood in the doorway holding back the flour-sack curtain. I invited them in. They cuddled up on my **20** new bed and I read them a story. Then we said goodnight and they went back to their room.

135

# Develop Comprehension

**20 STRATEGY**
**MONITOR COMPREHENSION**

At the beginning of the story, the girl doesn't want to be around her brothers. How does she feel about them now? Use the **monitor comprehension** strategy to help you figure out how she feels.

**Student Think Aloud** I will reread pages 134 and 135 to see what I can learn. I see that her little brothers wait at the doorway until they are invited in. They stay to listen to the girl read them a story. Then they say good-bye and leave. The girl seems to enjoy being with them more now that she has her own room. Her feelings toward her brothers are getting better. This makes sense, because I miss my family more when I don't see them all the time. I think the girl really loves her brothers. Rereading these pages helped me figure out how she feels.

# Develop Comprehension

**21 COMPARE AND CONTRAST**

How is the girl different at the end of the story? **Compare and contrast** how she felt at the beginning with how she felt at the end. Make sure to use evidence from the text. (At the beginning of the story, the girl was unhappy. She was tired of sharing a room and felt crowded in her own house. She longed for some place quiet where she could think and be alone. After she gets her own room, she calls herself "the luckiest, happiest little girl in the whole world." She suddenly has an urge to read lots of books. She invites her brothers to join her and no longer minds their company. She sleeps peacefully in her own room.)

**22 STRATEGY**
**WORD PARTS**

What does the word *luckiest* mean? Use what you know about base words and the meaning of the **suffix** *-est* to help you figure it out. (The word *luckiest* has the base word *lucky* and the suffix *-est, which means "most." By putting together the meanings of the base word and the suffix, I can figure out that luckiest means "most lucky."*)

# Develop Comprehension

CA CONTENT STANDARD R 3.2.4 Recall major points in the text and make and modify predictions about forthcoming information.

### RETURN TO PREDICTIONS AND PURPOSES

Review students' **predictions** and purposes for reading. Did students find clues that helped them predict how the main character would get a room of her own?

### REVIEW READING STRATEGIES

- **Monitor Comprehension** How did monitoring comprehension help you to read this story? What are some ways in which you monitored your comprehension?
- **Monitor and Clarify: Self-Correct** Do you understand the strategy of self-correcting? How does it help you to understand a story better?
- **Decoding** What difficult words did you encounter? How did the Reading Multisyllabic Words strategy help you sound out these words?
- **Self-Selected Strategy Use** What strategies did you use to make sense of what you read? Where? How were these strategies helpful?

### PERSONAL RESPONSE

Ask students to write a paragraph about why it is important to have a place of their own. After students have finished writing, they can read their paragraphs to partners, or to the class.

**Quick Check**

**Can students make and confirm predictions?**

During **Small Group Instruction**

**If No** → **Approaching Level** Reteach the skill and have students apply it to a simpler text. Use Practice Reader lessons, pp. 145N–145P.

**If Yes** → **On Level** Have students apply the skill to a new text to consolidate learning. Use Practice Reader lessons, pp. 145U–145V.

**Beyond Level** Have students apply the skill to a more complex text to extend learning. Use Practice Reader lessons, pp. 145Y–145Z.

## Author and Illustrator

**AMADA AND MAYA'S ROOM**

Have students read the biographies of the author and illustrator. Ask:

- How was Amada Irma Pérez's childhood like that of the girl in the story?
- Why do you think Maya Christina Gonzalez became an illustrator?

**WRITE ABOUT IT**

**Author's Craft: Figurative Language**
Discuss the main character's favorite new place. Then have each student write about his or her favorite place and tell why it is special. Remind students to make good word choices and use figurative language, such as similes to make their writing more colorful and interesting.

### Author's Purpose

Discuss how the author does not give facts and details about a nonfiction topic and does not explain how to do something. Help students conclude that the author's purpose was to write an entertaining story about a girl who wanted a special place of her own.

# Amada and Maya's Room

Author Amada Irma Pérez grew up in a family just like the one in this story. Because her parents were unable to get the family a bigger house, there was not much room for Amada and her five brothers. But they did give Amada and her brothers lots of love and encouraged them to study and work hard.

Another book by Amada Irma Pérez:
*My Diary from Here to There/Mi diario de aquí hasta allá*

Illustrator Maya Christina Gonzalez has always loved to draw and paint. She has also always been very proud of being Mexican. In fact, as a child, Maya would draw her face on the blank page in the back of books because she wanted someone in the books to look like her.

LOG ON Find out more about Amada Irma Pérez and Maya Christina Gonzalez at **www.macmillanmh.com**.

### Author's Purpose

What was the author's purpose for writing *My Very Own Room*? Did Amada Irma Pérez want to entertain or inform? Use details from the story in your answer.

138

### Author's Craft

**Figurative Language: Simile**

Amada Irma Pérez uses similes to make her writing more interesting.

- Similes are special comparisons that use the words *like* or *as* to compare two things that are very different. For example: *We were like a mighty team of powerful ants.* (p. 126) The family is like a team of ants because they work together. This simile helps readers understand that the family is large and hardworking, like the ants in an ant colony.

Have students find another simile on page 133. (The new lamp is "as dainty as a beautiful ballerina.")

## Critical Thinking

### Retell the Story

| What I Predict | What Happens |
|---|---|
| | |
| | |
| | |

Use your Predictions Chart to help you retell *My Very Own Room*. Tell about events in the story that you predicted and then tell what actually happens.

### Think and Compare

1. What story details help you **predict** whether the girl will get a room of her own? Use your Predictions Chart to help you answer. **Monitor Comprehension: Make and Confirm Predictions**
2. Reread pages 119–123 of *My Very Own Room*. What kind of relationship does the girl have with her family? How do you know? Use story details to support your answer. **Analyze**
3. What are some reasons why you might want a quiet space of your own? **Evaluate**
4. Why is it good for a whole family to help one family member with a problem? **Apply**
5. Reread "Pond Street Clubhouse" on pages 114–115. Think about how the main character is like the girl in *My Very Own Room*. Why is **determination** an important character trait in both characters? **Reading/Writing Across Texts**

139

## Answering Questions

CA CONTENT STANDARD R 3.2.3 Demonstrate comprehension by identifying answers in the text.

### Think and Search

Model the Think and Search strategy with question 5. The answer can be found in the story but will require students to look in more than one place.

**Question 5 Think Aloud** I need to look in both stories to find the answer. I know that both of the main characters are determined to make their own special place, but each wants the special place for different reasons. On page 118, I see that the girl *My Very Own Room* wants more space because she is tired of sharing a room with her brothers. In the last paragraph of page 115, I see that the boy in "Pond Street Clubhouse" wants a place where he can play. I had to look in several places to find this information, but it was right there in both stories.

## Critical Thinking

### SUMMARIZE

Have partners summarize in their own words *My Very Own Room*. Remind students that their Predictions Charts can help them organize their summaries.

### THINK AND COMPARE

Sample answers are given.

1. **Make and Confirm Predictions** The girl finds a closet that she can turn into a room. She shows her mother how much she wants a room of her own. She works hard to move the furniture, paint the walls, and measure the space for the bed.
2. **Analyze** The girl has a very close relationship with her family. I know this because they are all willing to pitch in and help her turn the closet into a room that is just for her.
3. **Text-to-Self** Students may say they like a quiet space to read, draw, or study.
4. **Text-to-World** Students may say that it is easier to solve a problem when several people help out. It is also important for people to help, because when a problem is solved, everyone in the family feels good about it.

### FOCUS QUESTION

5. **Text-to-Text** The boy in "Pond Street Clubhouse" wants a place of his own to play and be with friends. The girl in *My Very Own Room* wants her own room where she can read, think, and be by herself. Both characters' determination help them get what they want. USE THINK AND SEARCH

# Fluency

## Repeated Reading: Phrasing

### Objectives

- Read fluently with good phrasing
- 61–81 WCPM

### Materials

- Transparency 5
- Fluency Solutions Audio CD
- Practice Book, p. 62

**CA CONTENT STANDARD R 3.1.3** Read aloud narrative and expository text fluently and accurately and with appropriate pacing, intonation, and expression.

**EXPLAIN/MODEL** Explain that good readers learn to read groups of words together in phrases. Point out that the text on **Transparency 5** has been marked with slashes to show pauses and stops. A single slash shows a pause, usually at a comma. A double slash indicates a full stop, usually at a period at the end of a sentence. Model reading the passage aloud and have the class listen carefully. Reread the passage, one sentence at a time, and have students echo-read.

**Transparency 5**

After breakfast we started pushing the old furniture out to the back porch.// Everyone helped.// We were like a mighty team of powerful ants.//

We carried furniture,/ tools,/ and machines.// We dragged bulging bags of old clothes and toys.// We pulled boxes of treasures and overflowing junk.// Finally, / everything was out except for a few cans of leftover paint from the one time we had painted the house.//

Fluency (from *My Very Own Room,* p. 126)

**PRACTICE** Divide students into two groups. Have groups alternate echo-reading sentences. Remind students to pay attention to the pauses and stops, as indicated by the slash marks.

**DAILY FLUENCY** Students will practice fluency using **Practice Book** page 62 or the **Fluency Solutions Audio CD.** The passage is recorded at a slow, practice speed and a faster, fluent speed.

### Quick Check

**Can students read fluently with good phrasing?**

During **Small Group Instruction**

**If No** → **Approaching Level** Use the Fluency lesson and model, p. 145P–145Q.

**If Yes** → **On Level** See Fluency, p. 145T.

**Beyond Level** See Fluency, p. 145X.

### English Learners

UNIVERSAL ACCESS

**Develop Comprehension**
Break the passage into smaller phrase units and discuss each paragraph so that students understand what they will read. Use gestures and board sketches to convey meaning. Then read each phrase aloud and have students repeat.

### Practice Book, page 62

AUDIO CD

**As I read, I will pay attention to phrasing.**

| | |
|---|---|
| | "What are your plans for today?" Mr. Sanchez asked his |
| 10 | son Carlo. |
| 12 | "I'm hiking with my nature club," Carlo said, "from |
| 21 | the state park entrance to Turtle Lake. Jimmy's father, |
| 30 | Mr. Gordon, is going with us." |
| 36 | "It's colder than yesterday," his mother said. "Please |
| 44 | take your warmest jacket and your gloves." |
| 51 | "Hold on," Carlo's father said. "I need to get your warm |
| 62 | blue jacket from the storage box in the attic. Then I'll |
| 73 | drop you off." |
| 76 | A short time later, Carlo met up with Mr. Gordon and |
| 87 | the other members of the club, Jimmy, Julie, and Tyrone. |
| 97 | Mr. Gordon packed them in his van and drove them to |
| 108 | the state park. |
| 111 | When they arrived he checked his compass. "The |
| 119 | old logging trail is somewhere directly west of here," |
| 128 | he said. 130 |

**Comprehension Check**

1. What are Carlo's plans? **Main Idea and Details** Carlo is going hiking in the state park with his nature club.
2. What is the weather like? **Plot Development** The weather is very cold.

| | Words Read | – | Number of Errors | = | Words Correct Score |
|---|---|---|---|---|---|
| First Read | | – | | = | |
| Second Read | | – | | = | |

**Approaching Reproducible,** page 62

**Beyond Reproducible,** page 62

# Comprehension

**REVIEW SKILL**
**COMPARE AND CONTRAST**

### EXPLAIN/MODEL

- To **compare** characters, settings, or events, readers tell how they are alike.
- To **contrast** characters, settings, or events, readers tell how they are different.

Model how to compare and contrast the characters in "Pond Street Playhouse" on pages 114–115. Point out how the narrator and his father are different: The father wants to build a garage. The narrator wants to build a clubhouse. Then discuss how the two are alike: At the end of the story, the narrator has a clubhouse, just like the father did when he was a boy.

### PRACTICE/APPLY

Help students compare and contrast characters, settings, and events in *My Very Own Room* using the following questions

- What did the storage closet look like before the family worked on it? How did it look when the girl moved in? (At first, the storage closet was filled with tools, furniture, and old clothes. After the family worked on it, it was a small bedroom for a young girl, with newly painted walls, a bed, a bedside table, and a reading lamp.)
- How is the girl like her mother? How is she different (Both the girl and her mother are resourceful and creative in solving problems. We know the mother has made a curtain out of flour sacks and measures the walls using yarn. The girl has the idea to change the closet into a bedroom and mixes leftover paint to create a new color for her room.)

Have students form a literature circle and discuss the story events in *My Very Own Room*. Then ask students to work in pairs to identify the similarities and differences between the girl's family and the boy's father in "Pond Street Clubhouse." Students may wish to use a Venn Diagram to make the comparisons. Then have them compare their findings with other students.

## Objectives

- Identifies similarities and differences among characters, settings, and events
- Use academic language: *compare, contrast*

## Skills Trace

TESTED SKILL

| Compare Characters, Settings, Events | |
|---|---|
| **Introduce** | U1: 81A–B |
| **Practice/ Apply** | U1: 82–105; Practice Book 48-49 |
| **Reteach/ Review** | U1: 1110–JJ; U5: 237A–B, 238-261, 267M–HH; Practice Book 304–305 |
| **Assess** | Weekly Tests; Unit 1, 5, 6 Tests |
| **Maintain** | U1: 139B; U6: 303B, 339A–B, 351A–B |

## Content Reader

For content correlated to California Science and History/Social Science standards, see page 168–173 in the **Content Reader**.
HSS 3.4.6

# Paired Selection

**GENRE: BIOGRAPHY**

Have students read the bookmark on **Student Book** page 140. Explain that a biography gives facts and information about a real person's life.

## Text Features: Encyclopedia Article

CA CONTENT STANDARD R 3.2.1 Use titles, tables of contents, headings, glossaries, and indexes to locate information in text.

**EXPLAIN** Point out the encyclopedia article on page 142.

- A print **encyclopedia** is a set of books that contains information on many subjects. Each book in a set is called a **volume.** Volumes are arranged in alphabetical order.
- Most print encyclopedias have a volume that contains the index. The index lists topics covered in the encyclopedia in alphabetical order and guides one to the volumes which contain the information.
- Encyclopedia volumes contain **guide words** at the top of each page to help readers locate information.
- **Encyclopedia articles** appear in alphabetical order in each volume. The articles' **text features** that make them easy to read include **headings**, subheadings, and **illustrations with captions**.
- Electronic encyclopedias can be found on CD-ROMs or online.

**APPLY** Have students identify the topic of the encyclopedia article on page 142 and the volume in which it is found. (Topic: Architecture. Volume: A.)

CA History/Social Science

**Genre**

A **Biography** is the true story of a person's life written by another person.

**Text Features**

**Guide Words**, **Headings**, and **Captions** are features of an encyclopedia. Topics in an encyclopedia are listed in alphabetical order.

**Content Vocabulary**

**influenced**
**form**
**function**
**geometric**
**preserved**

# FRANK LLOYD WRIGHT

by Karen O'Malley

Frank Lloyd Wright was one of America's most famous architects. His building designs **influenced**, or had an effect on, many other architects. Wright's buildings include homes, office buildings, and one of the most famous museums in the world, the Guggenheim Museum in New York City. Frank Lloyd Wright believed that a building's **form**, or how it looks, should match its **function**, or how it is used.

1

### Early Years

Wright was born in Wisconsin in 1867. When he was young, his mother gave him a set of wooden blocks, which helped him learn about **geometric** shapes, such as cubes, spheres, and cylinders. He also noticed the same shapes in nature. Wright went to the University of Wisconsin and then moved to Chicago to find work as an architect.

140

## Content Vocabulary

**History/Social Science Words** Explain the words using the **Define/Example/Ask** routine. Use the definitions provided below:

- **influenced** (p. 140): persuaded to feel or think a certain way
- **form** (p. 140): the shape or way it looks
- **function** (p. 140): how something is used or the job that someone or something does
- **geometric** (p. 140): having a certain shape, such as a square, circle, or triangle
- **preserved** (p. 143): protected from harm, kept safe

The Johnson Wax Company Building has many geometric shapes.

### The Prairie Style

Frank Lloyd Wright believed that buildings should fit the places where they are built. The prairie style homes he built in the 1800s and early 1900s had low, straight lines that blended in with the prairie land where they stood.

### The 1930s

In the 1930s Wright worked with architecture students who wanted to build the way he did. He designed one of his most famous houses, *Fallingwater*, in Pennsylvania. *Fallingwater* was built over a waterfall. During the 1930s Wright also designed the Johnson Wax Company Building in Wisconsin.

*Fallingwater* in Bear Run, Pennsylvania

## Digital Learning

**Internet Research and Inquiry** Students can continue their unit research using the Research Toolkit on **www.macmillanmh.com**.



# Read "Frank Lloyd Wright"

As students read, remind them to apply what they have learned about encyclopedia articles. Also have them identify clues to the meanings of the highlighted words.

**1 MAIN IDEA AND DETAILS**

CA CONTENT STANDARD R 3.2.5 Distinguish the main idea and supporting details in expository text.

What is the stated **main idea** of the first paragraph on page 140? What **details** tell about the main idea? (The main idea of the first paragraph is that Frank Lloyd Wright was one of the America's most famous architects. The details are: his building designs influenced other architects. His famous buildings include the Guggenheim Museum in New York City.)

**2 USE PHOTOGRAPHS**

Look at the **photograph** of *Fallingwater* on the bottom of page 141. What geometric shapes can you see in the design of this house? Do you think the form of this house fits or matches its function? Why or why not? (The house has a lot of rectangles and cube shapes. Yes, I think the form matches the function because the house fits perfectly over the top of the waterfall.)

**Read**
**Paired Selection**

# Develop Comprehension

**3** **ALPHABETIZING**

Being able to **alphabetize** to the third letter can help you find an encyclopedia entry. Suppose you wanted to look up the Guggenheim Museum in an encyclopedia. Would the encyclopedia entry for Guggenheim Museum come before or after an entry on Guinea? How do you know? (Guggenheim Museum would come before Guinea, because *g,* the third letter in Guggenheim, comes before *i*, the third letter in Guinea.)

**4** **TEXT FEATURES: ENCYCLOPEDIA ARTICLE**

What is the guide word for this **encyclopedia article**? What is the purpose of guide words? (The guide word is "Architecture." Guide words are arranged alphabetically and tell the first subject on that page.)

**5** **TEXT FEATURES: ENCYCLOPEDIA ARTICLE**

What are the two headings in this **encyclopedia article**? What do the headings tell you? Why do you think they are important? (The main heading is "Architecture" and the subheading is "Early architecture." The main heading tells the topic of the whole entry. The subheading tells the topic of the information that appears below it. They both help readers easily find the information they need.)

# An Encyclopedia Article

**Reading an Encyclopedia Article**

Encyclopedia articles are arranged alphabetically in each volume, or book.

page number | guide word | caption | heading

**3** **4** 503 Architecture

## Architecture

Architecture is the art of designing buildings. An architect is a person who designs buildings and checks to make sure they are built correctly. Architects build many different kinds of buildings, including homes, schools, office buildings, skyscrapers, and monuments.

The Guggenheim Museum was designed by the architect Frank Lloyd Wright (1867-1959).

**5**

### Early Architecture

Architecture began when people built the first homes. The architecture of the ancient Egyptians included giant pyramids that were built for kings. Ancient Greeks were known for the beautiful stone columns of their early temples and monuments.

This article is from Volume A of an encyclopedia.

142

ON YOUR OWN

**Practice Book,** page 63

An encyclopedia is a set of books filled with articles. The articles are in alphabetical order and give information about many subjects. On the top of each page is a **guide word** that tells the reader what will be on that page. Some articles have **headings** and subheadings in boldface type to summarize information and make it easy to find. Sometimes there are pictures with **captions,** which explain the pictures.

210 Painters

**Vincent van Gogh's Life**
Vincent van Gogh was born

**Early paintings** Van Gogh's early paintings were

Vincent van Gogh painted beautiful pictures.

**Answer the following questions about the encyclopedia article above.**

1. What page is it on? 210
2. What is the guide word? Painters
3. What is the heading? Vincent van Gogh's Life
4. What is the subheading? Early paintings
5. What is the caption? Vincent van Gogh painted beautiful pictures.

**English Learners**
UNIVERSAL ACCESS

**Use Academic Vocabulary**
Write the word *encyclopedia* on the board. Explain that an encyclopedia is a group of books that has information about a lot of topics. Have students complete the sentence frame: *I can use an encyclopedia to* ____. Then discuss with them when to use an encyclopedia.

**Approaching Reproducible,** page 63
**Beyond Reproducible,** page 63

### Later Years

Wright designed both the Guggenheim Museum in New York City and the Marin County Civic Center in California at the end of his career. He died in Arizona in 1959 before either of the buildings opened.

The ideas and work of Frank Lloyd Wright are **preserved**, or kept, by The Frank Lloyd Wright Foundation. The Foundation watches over his designs, drawings, writings, and his homes in Arizona and Wisconsin.

**The Frank Lloyd Wright Foundation is located in Arizona.**

### Critical Thinking

1. Look at the encyclopedia article on Architecture on page 142. What do you think the numbers in parentheses mean? **Reading an Encyclopedia Article**
2. If you could travel back to the early 1900s to meet Frank Lloyd Wright, what questions would you ask him? **Apply**
3. Think about this article and *My Very Own Room*. Why might the narrator of the story enjoy learning about Frank Lloyd Wright? **Reading/Writing Across Texts**

#### History/Social Science Activity

Find out more about a famous building such as the Eiffel Tower or the Sydney Opera House. Find out who the architect was and when the building was built.

Find out more about architecture at **www.macmillanmh.com**.



## CA Connect to Standards

**CA CONTENT STANDARD HSS 3.4.3** Know the histories of important local and national landmarks, symbols, and essential documents.

### Local and National Monuments

Frank Lloyd designed buildings that became local landmarks in California, such as the Marin County Civic Center. Other famous California landmarks include the Golden Gate Bridge in San Francisco.

Have students discuss state and national landmarks they would like to know more about,—the Golden Gate Bridge, White House, or Lincoln Monument. Have them work in pairs to research the monument's history using an encyclopedia and other resources. Have students present their findings to the class, using clear and specific vocabulary to communicate their ideas and to set the tone. They may also wish to use photos or drawings to enhance their presentations.



## Critical Thinking

### SUGGESTED ANSWERS

1. The numbers in parentheses are in the photo caption. They show the year Frank Lloyd Wright was born and the year he died. READING AN ENCYCLOPEDIA ARTICLE
2. Students might ask Mr. Wright what project he was most proud of and why. APPLY

### FOCUS QUESTION

3. The narrator of *My Very Own Room* thought about what her room would look like and how she would use it. She also had to take measurements and move items around in the room until they fit. These are things that architects do, too. READING/WRITING ACROSS TEXTS

### History/Social Science Activity

Have students create encyclopedia articles about famous buildings they researched. Remind them to write the information in their own words. Have students collect their articles alphabetically in an Encyclopedia of Famous Buildings. Ask them to include an index.

# 5-Day Vocabulary

# Connect Language Arts

## WHOLE GROUP

**VOCABULARY**
- Tested Words

**SPELLING**
- Words with Long *i*

**GRAMMAR**
- Compound Sentences

**CONTENT STANDARDS**
R 3.1.4, R 3.1.8, W 3.1.1, LC 3.1.8

## SMALL GROUP

- Differentiated Instruction, pp. 145I–145HH

ON YOUR OWN **Practice Book,** page 64

The **inflectional endings** *-er* and *-est* show comparison. The ending *-er* means "more." The ending *-est* means "most."

A. **Fill in the blank with the correct form of the adjective that follows each sentence. Use *-er* or *-est* to compare the items.**

1. The giraffe was the ___tallest___ (tall) of all the giraffes in the zoo.
2. She had the ___longest___ (long) neck of all of the animals in the zoo.
3. She was even ___bigger___ (big) than her brother.
4. She thought that the leaves at the very tops of the trees were the ___sweetest___ (sweet).
5. She shared the ___largest___ (large) of the three spaces in their home with two other giraffes.
6. The breezes were ___cooler___ (cool) at night than in the day.
7. When the giraffe grew a little ___older___ (old), she got a big surprise. She got her own space!

Possible response provided.

B. **Add *-er* or *-est* to the word *great* and use it in a sentence.**

8. This is the greatest apple pie I have ever eaten.

**Approaching Reproducible,** page 64

**Beyond Reproducible,** page 64

# Build Robust Vocabulary

## Day 1 Teach/Practice

### CONNECT TO WORDS

- Practice this week's vocabulary words using the following prompts:
  1. What is one way to *separate* two rooms?
  2. When did you feel *determination* to finish something?
  3. Why might people put things into *storage*?
  4. How is an *exact* amount different from an approximate amount?
  5. What are some reasons that books get *ruined*?
  6. Who is the *luckiest* person in your family?

### ACADEMIC VOCABULARY

- Review the important academic vocabulary words for the week. These words include: *word parts, contractions, monitor comprehension, make predictions, simile, Venn diagram, synonym, biography, guide words, heading, caption.*
- Write each word on the board. Define each using student-friendly language and ask students to select the word you are defining. Then point to words in random order for students to define.

## Day 2 Review

### CONNECT TO WORDS

- Review the definitions of this week's vocabulary words using **Student Book** pages 114–115. Then discuss each word using the following prompts:
  1. What are some things you can *separate* into different colors?
  2. When was a time that you had *determination*?
  3. What kinds of things are in *storage* in your home?
  4. How do you measure the *exact* length of something?
  5. What would you do if your favorite toy was *ruined*?
  6. Describe a time when you felt like the *luckiest* person.

### WORD PARTS

- Remind students that they can use word parts to figure out the meaning of a word. Word parts include root words, prefixes, and suffixes.
- Display **Transparency 9**. Read the first pair of sentences and model identifying the root word and suffixes *-er* and *-est*. Discuss what the words mean.
- Have students identify any word parts they recognize in this week's vocabulary words and write them down in their Writer's Notebooks. Discuss what these word parts mean and how they contribute to the overall meaning of the word.

CA CONTENT STANDARD
**R 3.1.8** Use knowledge of prefixes and suffixes to determine the meaning of words.

## Day 3 Reinforce

### CONNECT TO WORDS

- Ask students to create Word Squares for each word in their Writer's Notebooks.
- In the *first square*, students write the word. (Example: *separate*)
- In the *second square*, students write their own definition of the word and any related words, such as synonyms. (Example: *divide, split up, break apart, sections, different parts*)
- In the *third square*, students draw a simple illustration that will help them remember the word. (Example: *drawing of three groups of people with lines separating them*)
- In the *fourth square*, students write nonexamples, including antonyms for the word. (Example: *join, combine, unite, bring together*)

### RELATED WORDS

- Help students generate synonyms related to *ruined*.
- Create a word web on the board. Begin by drawing a circle with the word *ruined* written inside it.
- Help students come up with other words that relate to *ruined*, and write them around the circle. For example, *damaged, hurt, destroyed, decayed*. Ask students to use a thesaurus to find more synonyms. Then have students order the synonyms by meaning from the most ruined to the least ruined. For example, *hurt, ruined, damaged, destroyed.*

## Day 4 Extend

### CONNECT TO WORDS

- Review this week's vocabulary using the following sentence stems. Have students orally complete each one.

1. It is a good idea to separate ______ ______.
2. Betty showed determination when ______________.
3. Our storage closet is used for _____ ________.
4. We tried to measure the exact length of _____________.
5. Things usually get ruined because ____________.
6. He felt luckiest when __________.

### MORPHOLOGY

- Use the Additional Selection Vocabulary word *overflowing* as a springboard to learn other words.
- Write the word *overflowing* on the board. Underline *over* and explain that it's a prefix that means "too much." *Overflowing* means "to be so full that the contents flow, or spill, over."
- Write the words *overjoyed* and *oversleep* on the board. Have students underline *over-* in each word.
- Use the word parts to define each word. Help students figure out that *overjoyed* means "extremely happy" and *oversleep* means "to sleep longer than one meant to."

## Day 5 Assess and Reteach

### POSTTEST

- Display **Transparency 10**. Have students complete the cloze sentences using one of this week's vocabulary words.
- Note how quickly and accurately students can complete this task. Work with students who make errors or require too much time to complete this task during Small Group time.

### CONNECT TO WRITING

- Have students write sentences in their Writer's Notebooks using this week's vocabulary. Tell students to write sentences that provide information they learned from this week's readings.
- EL Provide the Day 4 sentence stems for students needing extra support.

### PERIODIC REVIEW

- Check students mastery of all the words from Unit 1. Use the Day 1 prompts from each week. Continue to use these words during classroom discussions to reinforce their meanings and usage.

# 5-Day Spelling

Go to pages T17 for **Differentiated Spelling Lists**. Pretest and Posttest available in Teacher's Resource Book.

## Spelling Words

| | | |
|---|---|---|
| mild | fight | child |
| sky | **tied** | flight |
| pie | **right** | **bright** |
| **might** | fry | buy* |
| find | tight | dye* |

**Review** soak, bowl, gold

**Challenge** wind, **children**

## Dictation Sentences

1. The weather was warm and mild.
2. The sky is blue today.
3. Melissa ate a piece of pie.
4. We **might** go to the zoo.
5. Did you find your book?
6. My cats fight over their food.
7. The boy **tied** the shoelace on his sneaker.
8. This is the **right** answer.
9. She will fry the potatoes.
10. My jacket is too small and tight.
11. The child is five years old.
12. The flight went from China to Japan.
13. The **bright** light hurt my eyes.
14. I will buy food for my cat.
15. We will dye the shirt red.

## Review/Challenge Words

1. I will soak my feet in a tub of water.
2. I put the dog's food in a bowl.
3. She wore a gold ring.
4. Please wind the string into a ball.
5. The **children** played with their cat.

Words in **bold** are from this week's selections.

# Words with Long *i*

## Day 1 Pretest

### ASSESS PRIOR KNOWLEDGE

- Model for students how to spell the word *right*. Segment the word sound by sound, then attach a spelling to each sound. Point out that *igh* is one way to spell the long *i* sound.
- Use the Dictation Sentences. Say the underlined word, read the sentence, and repeat the word. Have students write the words.
- Have students self-correct their tests. Point out that long *i* can also be spelled as *i*, *y*, and *ie*.
- Have students cut apart the Spelling Word Cards BLM on **Teacher's Resource Book** page 118 and figure out a way to sort them. Have them save the cards for use throughout the week. *Oddball* is for words that don't follow the pattern.

## Day 2 Word Sorts and Review

### SPIRAL REVIEW

Review the long *o* spelling pattern in the words *soak, bowl,* and *gold*. Have students find words in this week's readings with the same sounds.

### WORD SORTS

- Have students take turns choosing cards, sorting them, and explaining how they sorted them. When students have finished the sort, discuss any words that have unexpected vowel spellings. (*tied, sky, buy, dye*).
- Review the Spelling Words, pointing out the long *i* vowel spellings. Use the cards on the Spelling Word Cards BLM. Write the key words *lie, wild, my, sigh*, and the category *oddball* to the board. Model how to sort the words by long *i* spellings. Place one or two cards beneath the correct key words.

ON YOUR OWN

**Practice Book,** page 65

**Using the Word Study Steps**

1. LOOK at the word.
2. SAY the word aloud.
3. STUDY the letters in the word.
4. WRITE the word.
5. CHECK the word.
   Did you spell the word right?
   If not, go back to step 1.

**Crossword Puzzle**

**Read the clues. Then use the spelling words to complete the sentences.**

ACROSS

1. I use my _____ to think.
2. The plane _____ was long.
4. I ___ milk for my new kitten.
5. The pants were too _____.
6. David _____ his shoes.
8. I cannot _____ my winter coat.
10. My answer was _____.
11. She uses ____ to color her hair.

DOWN

1. He closed the door with all his _____.
2. Let's _____ fish for dinner.
3. The _____ missed his mother.
4. The sun is very _____.
7. The bird flew up high in the _____.
8. The two angry dogs got into a _____.
9. We ate apple _____.

HOMEWORK

**Reproducible**, page SP13

| | | | | |
|---|---|---|---|---|
| mild | might | ties | tight | bright |
| sky | find | right | child | buy |
| pie | fight | fry | flight | dye |

**Write the spelling words that contain the matching spelling of the long *i* sound.**

**long *i* spelled *ie***

1. ties
2. pie

**long *i* spelled *igh***

3. flight
4. fight
5. right
6. might
7. bright
8. tight

**long *i* spelled *y***

9. buy
10. fry
11. sky
12. dye

**long *i* spelled *i***

13. mild
14. child
15. find

**CA CONTENT STANDARD**
**LC 3.1.8** Spell correctly one-syllable words that have blends, contractions, compounds, orthographic patterns, and common homophones.

## Day 3 Word Meanings

### CONTEXT CLUES

Have students copy the three sentences below into their Writer's Notebooks. Say the sentences aloud and ask students to fill in the missing blanks with a Spelling Word.

1. The sweater felt _____ when he wore it because it had shrunk in the wash. (tight)
2. The games were on sale so she decided to _____ two sets. (buy)
3. She knew her answer was _______ when the teacher nodded. (right)

Challenge students to come up with other sentences for spelling words, review words, or challenge words.

Have students do a word hunt for the words in weekly reading or other materials. They should identify the definition of the spelling word being used in context.

## Day 4 Proofread

### PROOFREAD AND WRITE

Write these sentences on the board. Have students circle and correct each word.

1. The skye is brite. (sky, bright)
2. The chighld ate py. (child, pie)
3. I went to the store to bigh some die. (buy, dye)
4. You mite fynd it here. (might, find)
5. She tyes it too tite. (ties, tight)

**Error Correction** Reinforce the spelling hints on the **Sound-Spelling Cards**. For example, the _y spelling for the long i sound never appears at the beginning of a word or syllable. Rather, it appears at the end of a word or syllable as indicated by the underscore that precedes the letter y.

## Day 5 Assess and Reteach

### POSTTEST

Use the Dictation Sentences on page 143C for the Posttest.

If students have difficulty with any words in the lesson, have them place them on a list called *Spelling Words I Want to Remember* in their Writer's Notebooks. Look for students' use of these words in their writings.

Challenge students to find words for each long *i* spelling and add them to the **Unit 1 Big Question Board**.

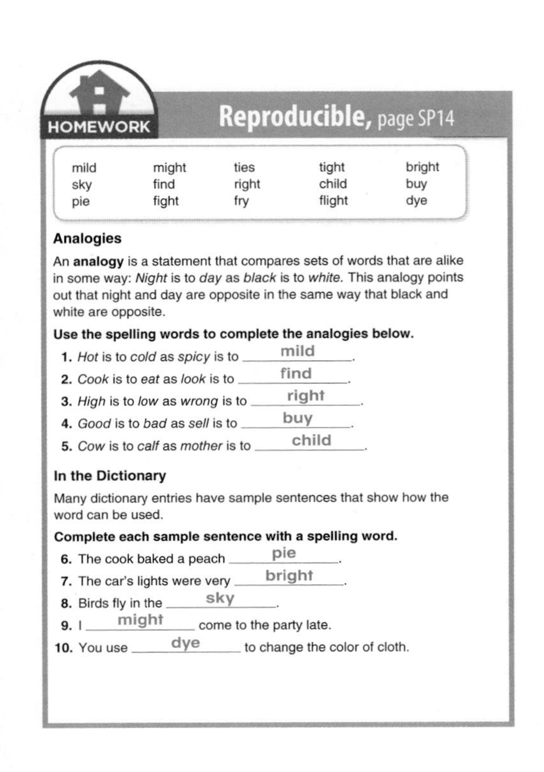

HOMEWORK **Reproducible,** page SP14

| mild | might | ties | tight | bright |
|---|---|---|---|---|
| sky | find | right | child | buy |
| pie | fight | fry | flight | dye |

**Analogies**

An **analogy** is a statement that compares sets of words that are alike in some way: *Night* is to *day* as *black* is to *white*. This analogy points out that night and day are opposite in the same way that black and white are opposite.

**Use the spelling words to complete the analogies below.**

1. *Hot* is to *cold* as *spicy* is to ___mild___.
2. *Cook* is to *eat* as *look* is to ___find___.
3. *High* is to *low* as *wrong* is to ___right___.
4. *Good* is to *bad* as *sell* is to ___buy___.
5. *Cow* is to *calf* as *mother* is to ___child___.

**In the Dictionary**

Many dictionary entries have sample sentences that show how the word can be used.

**Complete each sample sentence with a spelling word.**

6. The cook baked a peach ___pie___.
7. The car's lights were very ___bright___.
8. Birds fly in the ___sky___.
9. I ___might___ come to the party late.
10. You use ___dye___ to change the color of cloth.

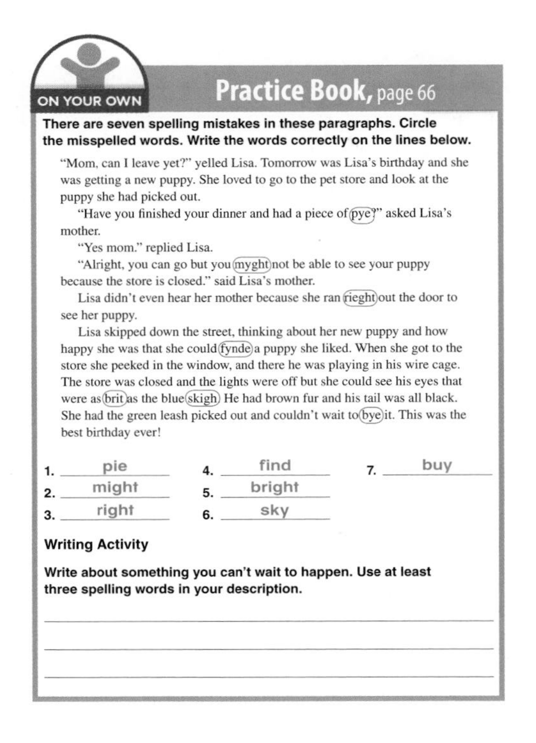

ON YOUR OWN **Practice Book,** page 66

**There are seven spelling mistakes in these paragraphs. Circle the misspelled words. Write the words correctly on the lines below.**

"Mom, can I leave yet?" yelled Lisa. Tomorrow was Lisa's birthday and she was getting a new puppy. She loved to go to the pet store and look at the puppy she had picked out.

"Have you finished your dinner and had a piece of pye?" asked Lisa's mother.

"Yes mom." replied Lisa.

"Alright, you can go but you myght not be able to see your puppy because the store is closed." said Lisa's mother.

Lisa didn't even hear her mother because she ran rieght out the door to see her puppy.

Lisa skipped down the street, thinking about her new puppy and how happy she was that she could fynde a puppy she liked. When she got to the store she peeked in the window, and there he was playing in his wire cage. The store was closed and the lights were off but she could see his eyes that were as brit as the blue skigh He had brown fur and his tail was all black. She had the green leash picked out and couldn't wait to bye it. This was the best birthday ever!

1. ___pie___
2. ___might___
3. ___right___
4. ___find___
5. ___bright___
6. ___sky___
7. ___buy___

**Writing Activity**

**Write about something you can't wait to happen. Use at least three spelling words in your description.**

HOMEWORK **Reproducible ,** page SP15

**Look at the words in each set below. One word in each set is spelled correctly. Look at Sample A. The letter next to the correctly spelled word in Sample A has been shaded in. Do Sample B yourself. Shade the letter of the word that is spelled correctly. When you are sure you know what to do, go on with the rest of the page.**

**Sample A:**
(A) cind
(B) kind
(C) kynd
(D) kynd

**Sample B:**
(E) light
(F) lyte
(G) liet
(H) lyght

1. (A) mild (B) myld (C) mighld (D) mield
2. (E) skie (F) sky (G) skye (H) skigh
3. (A) pye (B) pigh (C) py (D) pie
4. (E) might (F) myte (G) myght (H) mayt
5. (A) find (B) fynd (C) finde (D) fighnd
6. (E) fite (F) fyte (G) fight (H) fight
7. (A) tyde (B) tighd (C) tiyed (D) tied
8. (E) ryte (F) riyt (G) right (H) right
9. (A) frie (B) frye (C) fry (D) fright
10. (E) tight (F) tite (G) tyte (H) tighte
11. (A) chyld (B) child (C) childe (D) chylde
12. (E) flyte (F) fliet (G) flight (H) flite
13. (A) bryte (B) bryt (C) bryght (D) bright
14. (E) bie (F) buy (G) bigh (H) buye
15. (A) digh (B) dye (C) diegh (D) dygh

# 5-Day Grammar

## Daily Language Activities

Write the sentences on the board.

**DAY 1**
**1.** My brother loves goldfish? **2.** he wants to buy more **3.** Will fifty goldfish satisfy him. (1: goldfish.; 2: He; more.; 3: him?)

**DAY 2**
**1.** My sister wants the hamster and i want the pet iguana **2.** The iguana iz very healthy (1: hamster, and I; iguana.; 2: is; healthy.)

**DAY 3**
**1.** Is your pet okay **2.** I don't know what is the matter **3.** maybe he has the flu. (1: okay?; 2: matter.; 3: Maybe)

**DAY 4**
**1.** I lik the zoo. **2.** I went last week? **3.** It was a class trip and I had lots of fun (1: like; 2: week.; 3: trip, and; fun.)

**DAY 5**
**1.** mie cat is a lot of work but I really like her. **2.** Her name is Spot? **3.** she is wighld. (1: My; work, but; 2: Spot.; 3: She; wild.)

### English Learners
UNIVERSAL ACCESS

**Guided Practice** Students may have difficulty finding the clauses in an English compound sentence. Write compound sentences on the board, such as those from the Practice Book. Guide students to find the subject and predicate of each independent clause. Then circle the word *and*.

# Compound Sentences

## Day 1 Introduce the Concept

### INTRODUCE SENTENCE COMBINING

- **Combining sentences** can add variety to writing.
- Two related sentences can be combined with a comma and the word *and*.

**Example:**
I like cats. My sister likes dogs.
I like cats, and my sister likes dogs.

- Use the **Teach/Practice/Apply** routine and the English Learner supports on the transparency to provide additional instruction and practice.

See Grammar Transparency 21 for modeling and guided practice.

**HOMEWORK** **Reproducible,** page GR 13

- Two related sentences can be joined with a comma and the word *and*.
  Separate: A bird has wings. It has feathers.
  Joined: A bird has wings, and it has feathers.

**Combine each pair of sentences. Use a comma and the word *and*.**

1. There are yellow birds. There are blue and green birds.
   There are yellow birds, and there are blue and green birds.
2. Tame birds eat special bird food. Wild birds eat insects.
   Tame birds eat special bird food, and wild birds eat insects.
3. Most birds can sing. Some birds can learn words.
   Most birds can sing, and some birds can learn words.
4. Birds can escape from their cage. They can fly around a room.
   Birds can escape from their cage, and they can fly around a room.
5. A small bird can sit on your finger. It can even ride on your shoulder.
   A small bird can sit on your finger, and it can even ride on your shoulder.

## Day 2 Teach the Concept

### REVIEW SENTENCE COMBINING

Review how to combine related sentences. Show students how to combine sentences using a comma and the word *and*.

### INTRODUCE COMPOUND SENTENCES

- A **compound sentence** contains two related sentences joined by *and* or *but*.
- Place a comma before *and* or *but* in a compound sentence.

**Example:**
Champ is a good pet. Sometimes he is a little wild.
Champ is a good pet, but sometimes he is a little wild.

See Grammar Transparency 22 for modeling and guided practice.

**ON YOUR OWN** **Practice Book,** page 67

- A sentence that contains two sentences joined by *and* is called a **compound sentence.**

**Write a compound sentence by joining each pair of sentences. Use a comma and the word *and*.**

1. Hamsters are fun. They are easy to care for.
   Hamsters are fun, and they are easy to care for.
2. Hamsters are small. They are quiet.
   Hamsters are small, and they are quiet.
3. Some hamsters have long hair. Some have short hair.
   Some hamsters have long hair, and some have short hair.
4. Hamsters are small. They can fit in your pocket.
   Hamsters are small, and they can fit in your pocket.
5. They stuff food in their cheeks. They carry it that way.
   They stuff food in their cheeks, and they carry it that way.

**CA CONTENT STANDARD**
**LC 3.1.1** Understand and be able to use complete and correct declarative, interrogative, imperative, and exclamatory sentences in writing and speaking.

## Day 3 Review and Practice

### REVIEW COMPOUND SENTENCES

Review how to combine sentences using a comma and *and* or *but*.

### MECHANICS AND USAGE: PUNCTUATE COMPOUND SENTENCES

- Use a comma before the words *and* and *but* when joining two sentences to form a compound sentence.
- Begin a compound sentence with a capital letter: *My mother likes to dance, and my father likes to sing*.
- End a compound sentence with the correct punctuation. If it is a declarative compound sentence end it with a period. If it is a compound question, or interrogative, end it with a question mark. If it is a compound exclamation, end it with an exclamation point.

See Grammar Transparency 23 for modeling and guided practice.

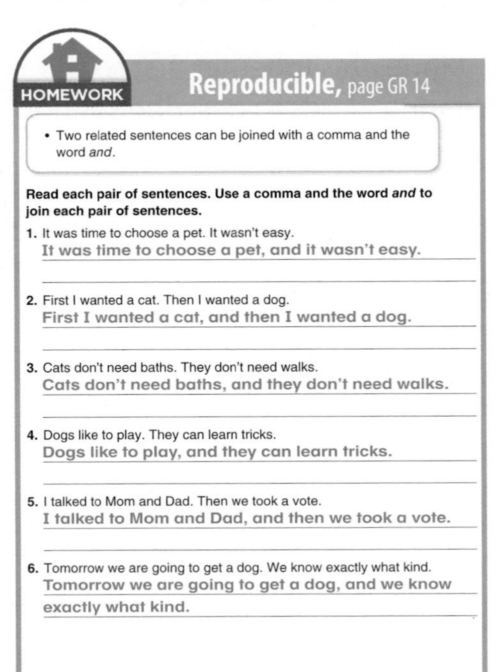

HOMEWORK **Reproducible,** page GR 14

- Two related sentences can be joined with a comma and the word *and*.

**Read each pair of sentences. Use a comma and the word *and* to join each pair of sentences.**

1. It was time to choose a pet. It wasn't easy.
   It was time to choose a pet, and it wasn't easy.
2. First I wanted a cat. Then I wanted a dog.
   First I wanted a cat, and then I wanted a dog.
3. Cats don't need baths. They don't need walks.
   Cats don't need baths, and they don't need walks.
4. Dogs like to play. They can learn tricks.
   Dogs like to play, and they can learn tricks.
5. I talked to Mom and Dad. Then we took a vote.
   I talked to Mom and Dad, and then we took a vote.
6. Tomorrow we are going to get a dog. We know exactly what kind.
   Tomorrow we are going to get a dog, and we know exactly what kind.

## Day 4 Review and Proofread

### REVIEW COMBINING SENTENCES

Ask students to show how to combine two related sentences with the words *and* or *but*. Ask what punctuation mark goes before *and* or *but*.

### PROOFREAD

Have students correct the errors in the following sentences.

1. Sue has a goldfish and Tim has a gerbil. (goldfish, and)
2. Hamsters are fun pets but rabbits are more fun (pets, but; fun.)
3. jack and Sue went to the pet store and they saw the perfect pet. (Jack; store, and)
4. Do you like cats or do you prefer dogs as pets. (cats, pets?)

See Grammar Transparency 24 for modeling and guided practice.

ON YOUR OWN **Practice Book,** page 68

- A sentence that contains two sentences joined by *and* is called a **compound sentence.**
- Use a comma before *and* when you join two sentences to form a compound sentence.

**Read the paragraph and look for sentences you can combine. Then rewrite the paragraph.**

I observed my cat, Eddie. Then I studied my dog, Belle. Eddie is orange. He weighs twenty pounds. Belle is white. She weighs twelve pounds. Both like to sleep. Both like to be in the sun. Eddie likes to chase birds. He likes to climb. Belle likes to dig. She plays fetch. Eddie sleeps on my bed. Belle sleeps on my floor. They are both good. They make great pets.

I observed my cat, Eddie, and then I studied my dog, Belle. Eddie is orange, and he weighs twenty pounds. Belle is white, and she weighs twelve pounds. Both like to sleep, and both like to be in the sun. Eddie likes to chase birds, and he likes to climb. Belle likes to dig, and she plays fetch. Eddie sleeps on my bed, and Belle sleeps on my floor. They are both good, and they make great pets.

## Day 5 Assess and Reteach

### ASSESS

Use the Daily Language Activities and the Reproducible page GR15 in the **Teacher's Resource Book** for assessment.

### RETEACH

Use Reproducible page GR15 and selected pages from the **Grammar and Writing Handbook** for additional reteaching.

Check students' writing for use of the skill. Assign Grammar Revision Assignments in their Writer's Notebooks, as needed.

See Grammar Transparency 25 for modeling and guided practice.

HOMEWORK **Reproducible,** page GR 15

**A. Write *yes* if two sentences have been combined. Write *no* if two sentences have not been combined.**

1. Some people like having pets, and some people do not want pets. yes
2. I would like to have more than two cats. no
3. I ride my horse each day in the corral. no
4. I call my dog, and then he comes to me. yes

**B. If the sentence is a compound sentence, write *compound*. If it is not a compound sentence, write *no*.**

5. I have an aquarium and several beautiful fish. no
6. I have two orange fish, and I have a zebra-striped fish. compound

**C. Use *and* to combine each pair of sentences. Write the new sentence on the line.**

7. I feed my fish. I clean the aquarium.
   I feed my fish, and I clean the aquarium.
8. I observe my fish. I learn how they live.
   I observe my fish, and I learn how they live.

Write

WHOLE GROUP

**WRITING**
- Focus on Setting

CA CONTENT STANDARDS
W 3.1.1, W 3.1.2, W 3.1.4, W 3.2.2, LAS 3.1.3

SMALL GROUP

- Differentiated Instruction, pp. 145I–145HH

5-Day Writing

| | |
|---|---|
| DAY 1 | Skill Introduction |
| DAY 2 | Minilesson 1<br>Revision Assignments |
| DAY 3 | Minilesson 2<br>Revision Assignments |
| DAY 4 | Reading/Writing Connection<br>Focus on Setting/Object |
| DAY 5 | Writing Conferences |



# Writer's Craft

## Strong Paragraphs: Describing Setting

CA CONTENT STANDARD
W 3.2.2 Write descriptions that use concrete sensory details to present and support unified impressions of people, places, things, or experiences.

**TEACH/MODEL**

**Set Purpose** Tell students that you are going to continue working on focus this week. They have spent lots of time noticing and writing about tiny moments and small details. Today they're going to think about setting and sound. Point out that including details about sounds helps readers picture the setting more clearly.

For example, if you describe the rumbles of car engines, the whine of sirens, and honking horns, what might your reader imagine about the setting? (*There are roads nearby. The story takes place in the city.*)

**Observations** Have students spread out on the floor with their Writer's Notebooks and pens. They should be within your earshot, but not too close to each other.

- Give students a few minutes simply to look at the setting around them. Tell them to observe silently the space they are in and its inhabitants.
- After one to two minutes of silent observation, ask them to close their eyes for a few minutes and concentrate on the sounds around them. Have them spend two to three minutes of listening to the sounds of the setting.

## Teacher Write Aloud

Ask students to open their eyes and jot down all the sounds they heard. Even if they heard sounds that they don't recognize, they should attempt to describe them. Model this together first so the students have some practice generating words to describe sounds. For example:

**Teacher:** *How would you describe that sound?*
**Student:** *It was weird. It sounded squeaky.*
**Teacher:** *It did. I'm going to put that on my list of sounds we might hear. Let's think of some others. What are your ideas?*
**Students:** *Rumble, growl, bang, thud, swoosh, etc.*

**Share Observations** Next, give students a couple of minutes on their own to jot down the sounds they heard.

Gather the group together and ask students to share what they heard. Go around the circle and have each student share one noise. For example:

**Teacher:** *Did you all hear that noise too?*
**Student:** *Yes. I wrote about it and described it as "loud and rumbling and it sounded like a truck passing by."*
**Teacher:** *Great. I'm glad to hear you describing the noise you heard.*

**Summarize Learning** Ask: *How does this listening activity help our ability to focus?* (By reminding us that we are surrounded by interesting details, and by giving us a strategy for noticing them and describing them.) Make the connection *again* to focus in writing.

Ask students to take out their Writer's Notebooks. Ask the following questions to spark writing ideas and focus students. Then display the Writing Prompt on **Transparency 11**.

- Raise your hand if you heard a sound you couldn't identify.
- Raise your hand if you heard the sound of a machine.
- Raise your hand if you heard the sound of an animal.
- Raise your hand if you heard the sound of something that's always there, but that you never notice.

**Transparency 11**

Describe a place that is spooky or scary. What noises do you hear? What do you see, smell, and feel?

**Writing Transparency**

## Objective

- Focus on setting and write to a prompt

### Materials

- Writer's Notebook
- Transparency 11

## Daily Journal Prompts

**Focus on Setting**

Use these and other prompts for independent daily journal writing.

- Describe your bedroom at home. What noises do you hear? What do you see, smell, and feel?
- Describe the cafeteria. What noises do you hear? What do you see, smell, and feel?
- Describe what your bus ride (or trip) to school is like. What noises do you hear? What do you see, smell, and feel?
- Describe a place you've been that has made you really happy. What noises do you hear? What do you see, smell, and feel?

# Write

## Objective

- Select a single setting and write four sentences to expand it

### Materials

- Writer's Notebooks
- Practice Book, p. 69

### Teacher-to-Teacher

**Foundational Habit: Experimenting with Vocabulary**

The writing strand includes numerous opportunities for students to generate vocabulary lists (or word walls) to describe their own experiences. These word walls are shared with the whole class, so students have an immediate opportunity to use new vocabulary words in their writing.

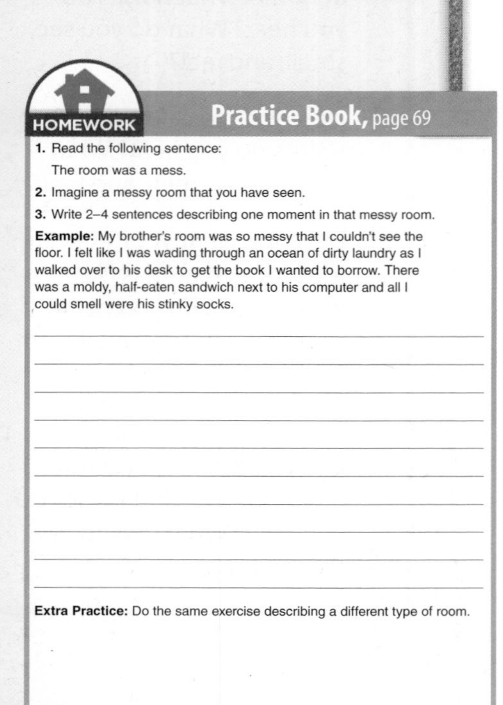

HOMEWORK **Practice Book,** page 69

1. Read the following sentence:
   The room was a mess.
2. Imagine a messy room that you have seen.
3. Write 2–4 sentences describing one moment in that messy room.

**Example:** My brother's room was so messy that I couldn't see the floor. I felt like I was wading through an ocean of dirty laundry as I walked over to his desk to get the book I wanted to borrow. There was a moldy, half-eaten sandwich next to his computer and all I could smell were his stinky socks.

**Extra Practice:** Do the same exercise describing a different type of room.

**Approaching Reproducible,** page 69

**Beyond Reproducible,** page 69

# Minilesson 1

**Strong Paragraphs** | Describing Setting

**CA CONTENT STANDARD**
**W 3.1.1** Create a single paragraph: (a) Develop a topic sentence. (b) Include simple supporting facts and details.

### TEACH/MODEL

**Write Strong Paragraphs** Write the following on the board. Have students copy the passage into their Writer's Notebooks.

> **The room was a mess.**

Have students write two to four more sentences that describe the messy room. Tell students to use detail to create a picture in the reader's head.

**Think Aloud** We want to start to think about what was messy about the room. Was it a bedroom? A classroom? A kitchen? Once you've decided what type of room you are writing about, then you can describe what you see, smell, hear, and feel as you think about what it would be like to be in the room you are describing.

### PRACTICE/APPLY

Explain that by focusing on setting, the writer can help readers picture where and when their story is taking place. Students work independently. Circulate and provide Over-the-Shoulder Conferences. Ask for students to share their work.

**Summarize Learning** Explain the following to students:

**Think Aloud** How did we do? Did we stay focused on our setting? How many of you described how messy your own room is when you were writing? Remember, the writer can help readers focus on where and when their story is taking place.

# Minilesson 2

**Strong Paragraphs** Describing Setting

### TEACH/MODEL

**Write Strong Paragraphs** Write the following on the board:

**In art class I had fun. Janice got in trouble during lunch. Carl acted silly in the gym.**

Have students choose one sentence from the passage above and write three to four more sentences about the setting in the sentence they chose. Tell them to think carefully about details that would help the reader imagine the setting.

**Think Aloud** You probably noticed that there are three different settings to choose from. I really want you to think about what happens in those settings and how you can describe them to make your reader feel like she/he is there. Think about what the setting would smell, feel, sound, or look like and use these ideas to write your sentences.

### PRACTICE/APPLY

Students work independently to write about one of the sentences. Circulate and provide Over-the-Shoulder Conferences. Ask for students to share their work. If possible, try to find one student for each of the three sentences.

**Summarize Learning** Explain the following:

**Think Aloud** Was it easier to imagine the setting when you narrowed it down to one? You provided excellent focused examples of writing today. When you are doing your own writing, remember to focus on one setting and tell the reader everything you can about it. The reader will get a much better picture of your setting.

## Objective

- Select a single setting and write three or four sentences to describe it

### Materials

- Writer's Notebooks

## Teacher-to-Teacher

**Reading Like a Writer; Writing Like a Reader**

Encourage students to experiment with their own use of language in their effort to be precise and descriptive. Instruction focuses on helping students notice and feel confident playing with the language they encounter in their reading. Reinforce places where students could use this week's (and previous weeks') vocabulary words to build facility in using **academic language**.

## Minilesson

### Thesaurus

Model for students how to use a thesaurus to replace over-used words or add variety to their word choice. Highlight that a thesaurus shows synonyms, or words that mean the same or nearly the same. Emphasize that these words have shades of meaning and students have to be careful to select the correct word for the context. W 3.1.3

# Reading and Writing Connection

## Writer's Craft

**STRONG PARAGRAPHS: FOCUS ON MOMENT/SETTING/OBJECT**

Use the example from *My Very Own Room* to show the author's skilled use of focusing on an object/setting.

- Ask: *What's one thing you do to enjoy yourself?*
- Have students read aloud the excerpt from *My Very Own Room*. Ask: *What details did the author use to describe the girl and the setting? How did the author focus on the setting?*

**USE FOCUS TO WRITE ABOUT TEXT**

Remind students to use the skill of focusing when they write about *My Very Own Room* so that they can use specific details to describe moments, objects, and setting.

CA CONTENT STANDARD LAS 3.1.3 Respond to questions with appropriate elaboration.

**Engagement Prompt** These prompts have been designed to help students deepen their connection to the text and to discover their own perspective on it.

- *Focus on a moment when you went someplace new.*

**Response Prompt** These prompts have been designed to help students explore more deeply their reactions to particular passages in the reading.

- *Focus on a moment in the text when the girl did or said something that surprised you.*

# Reading and Writing Connection

Read the passage below. Notice how author Amada Irma Pérez focuses on an object, in this case, a crowded bed.

An excerpt from *My Very Own Room*

I woke up one morning on a crowded bed in a crowded room. Victor's elbow was jabbing me in the ribs. Mario had climbed out of his crib and crawled in with us. Now his leg lay across my face and I could hardly breath.

The author focuses in on the brothers' positions on the bed. We are able to picture the scene through the use of specific details.

| Unit 1 Writing: Personal Narrative (Description) | |
|---|---|
| Week 1 | • Strong Sentences: Focus on Moment |
| Week 2 | • Strong Paragraphs: Focus on Moment |
| Week 3 | • Personal Narrative (Guided Writing) |
| Week 4 | • Strong Sentences: Focus on Setting/Object |
| Week 5 | • Strong Paragraphs: Focus on Setting/Object |
| Week 6 | Personal Narrative (Independent Writing) |

## Read and Find

Read Max's writing below. What did he do to focus on the object? Use the tips below to help you.

### Taking Care of Layla

by Max G.

When my friend was in the hospital, I helped take care of her dog, Layla. Boy, was she a project! She loved to dig through the garbage, tearing apart my microwave popcorn bag to eat the butter and unpopped kernels. She was in dog heaven in the mud puddle in our backyard, which she rolled around in every chance she had.

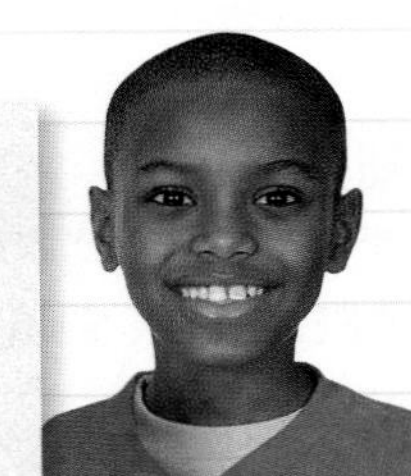

Read about my dogsitting experience.

### Writer's Checklist

 Did the writer write about one **object**?

 Did the writer include specific details about that object?

Can the reader picture the object the way Max experienced it?





**Literary Analysis Prompt** These prompts have been designed to help students deepen their connection to the text and discover their own perspective on it.

- *Focus on a place in the text where the author used details to show that the girl was satisfied with her new room.*

## Use Student Model

Have students chorally read the student sample at the top of **Student Book** page 145. Discuss what this student writer did to focus on a moment in time. Use the Writer's Checklist.

Write the following journal prompt on the board:

**Think about your room. Select one object. Write a brief paragraph about that object.**

Tell students that you will be reading and commenting on their writing during Writing Conference time.

Model how to use the Writer's Checklist to write and revise their work.

- What is the object you chose?
- What sentences did you add to tell about that object? Will readers be able to clearly picture that object? If not, what details could you add?

## Objective

- Students will meet with the teacher to discuss writing and receive revision assignments

### Materials

- Writer's Notebooks
- Revision Assignments

### Teacher-to-Teacher

**Over-the-Shoulder Conferences**

Use these quick, focused opportunities to comment while students are writing.

- **Step 1** Quietly move close enough to a student that you can read the journal entry he or she is writing.
- **Step 2** Read part of what you see. You don't need to start from the beginning or read the entire piece.
- **Step 3** Show the student a spot in the writing where he or she is using a particular skill or describing something that piques your interest.
- **Step 4** Whisper a sentence or two about why you noticed that spot in the writing and ask a question that will nudge the student to add a detail or clarify.
- **Step 5** Move on to the next student. Select students strategically. You should see 12–15 students in a 15-minute period.

# Conferences

## Writing Journals

### DYNAMIC FEEDBACK SYSTEM

**Purpose** One of the best ways for students to develop skills is by understanding how their writing affects their readers. Your targeted comments direct students to notice the impact they've made by using a specific skill. Your comments should aim to:

- Engage and encourage students by showing them your appreciation for what they've written.
- Focus students' attention on developing one particular skill.

**Steps in the Dynamic Feedback System**

1. Read and appreciate the writing.
2. Notice how the student uses the targeted skill. (e.g. focus: Ask: *For how many sentences does the student stay on a topic?)*
3. Write comments in which you show how the writing has an impact on you. Direct your comments to those places in the piece where the student has used the targeted skill.
4. Meet with and give the student a revision assignment.

### WRITE EFFECTIVE COMMENTS ON FOCUS

**Sample Comments for Focus** At least one of your comments should highlight the way the student uses the skill of focus. Here are some sample comments. Use these comments to get you started.

- *I feel like I'm in [your house] from your detailed description of the setting.*
- *I can picture [San Diego] from the details you used to describe the setting.*
- *Can you tell me more about where [you won the jump rope contest]?*
- *I'm curious to know more about the setting. Tell me about it.*

## Revision Assignments

**CA CONTENT STANDARD**
**W 3.1.4** Revise drafts to improve the coherence and logical progression of ideas by using an established rubric.

### IMPROVE WRITING

**What Is It?** Revision assignments play a crucial role in the dynamic feedback system. They enable you to work with each student on one skill at a time until the student has mastered it.

Revision assignments involve marking a specific section of a student's journal entry and then asking the student to revise it in a specific way. By requiring students to put to use your feedback to revise their own writing, revision assignments show clearly how that feedback has affected what students are able to do next.

**Sample Revision Assignments for Focus** Here are some examples of effective revision assignments for focus. Use them to get started. You may also use the preprinted Revision Assignment Notes or create your own revision assignments based on these.

Revise *I underlined the place in your writing where you've started to describe the setting. Write two more sentences that describe it in more detail so your reader can picture where this is all happening.*

*I'm wondering if you can tell me more about [the inside of the cabin where you stayed]. This will help me picture [your trip skiing].*

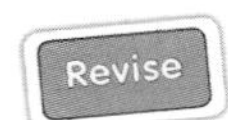
*I was curious to know about where you were when [insert event from entry]. Pretend you took a picture of the place where you were and write two sentences that describe that picture.*

Revise

### Revision Assignment Notes

Use the Revision Assignment Notes to focus students' rewrites.

**Available on Jump Drive**

### Daily Handwriting

Have students focus on the size and shape of letters. See Handwriting pages 15–16 for daily practice.
W 3.1.2

Mark students' Journal Checklists to indicate mastered skills.

**Reproducible,** page 222

| STAGE 1 Establishing Habits | | |
|---|---|---|
| ☐ Write Journal Entries | ☐ Practice Skill Drills | ☐ Engage in Experience |
| ☐ Respond to Feedback | ☐ Develop Vocabulary | ☐ Share Writing |

| STAGE 2 Strengthening Voice | | |
|---|---|---|
| Expressive Skills | Topic Development | ☐ Moment ☐ Object ☐ Setting |
| | Showing | ☐ Include unique observations<br>☐ Recognize showing and telling |
| | Strong Verbs | ☐ Recognize and use strong verbs |
| | Sensory Detail | ☐ Use multiple senses<br>☐ Choose sensory detail effectively |
| | Dialogue and Evidence I | ☐ Include dialogue |
| | Character Development | ☐ Believable<br>☐ Change and growth |
| | Logical Structure I: Distinguishing Moments | ☐ Use chronological order<br>☐ Distinguish moments |
| Technical Skills | Sentence Mechanics & Usage I: The Complete Sentence | ☐ Capitals and end punctuation<br>☐ Parts of speech<br>☐ Possessives<br>☐ Commas in a series |
| | Subject/Verb Agreement I | ☐ With present tense<br>☐ With simple past tense |
| | Punctuating and Formatting Dialogue & Quotations | ☐ Quotation marks |

**Writing Journal Checklist**

End-of-Week Assessment

# Administer the Test

## Weekly Reading Quick Check,

### Passage and questions, Unit 1, Week 5

**ASSESSED SKILLS**

- Vocabulary Words; Word Parts/Suffixes, *-er, -est*
- Make and Confirm Predictions
- Compound Sentences, Focus on: Object, Setting
- Words with Long *i*

*Selection Test Also Available.*

**Progress Monitoring, Unit 1, Week 5**

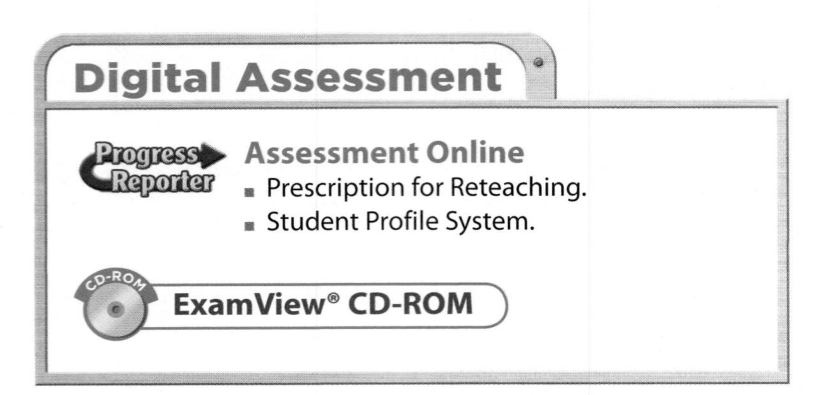

## Unit Fluency Assessment

Assess fluency for one group of students per week. Use the Oral Fluency Record Sheet to track the number of words read correctly. Fluency goal for all students: **61–81 words correct per minute (WCPM)**.

| | |
|---|---|
| Approaching Level | Weeks 1, 3, 5 |
| On Level | Weeks 2, 4 |
| Beyond Level | Week 6 |

**Diagnostic, Unit 1 Fluency**

| Diagnose | | Prescribe |
|---|---|---|
| **Review the assessment answers with students. Have them correct their errors. Then provide additional instruction as needed.** | | |
| | **IF...** | **THEN...** |
| **VOCABULARY WORDS**<br>**VOCABULARY STRATEGY**<br>Word Parts/Suffixes *-er, -est* | 0–2 items correct . . . | LOG ON Online Practice: Go to **www.macmillanmh.com**.<br>CD-ROM Vocabulary PuzzleMaker |
| **COMPREHENSION**<br>Skill: Make and Confirm Predictions | 0–2 items correct . . . | SPIRAL REVIEW See Make and Confirm Predictions lessons Unit 2, Week 1, page 183B. |
| **WRITING AND GRAMMAR**<br>Compound Sentences<br>Focus on Object, Setting | 0–1 items correct . . . | Review with Unit 1 Writing Workshop lesson. Use revision assignments. |
| **PHONICS AND SPELLING**<br>Words with Long *i* | 0–2 items correct . . . | LOG ON Online Practice: Go to **www.macmillanmh.com**.<br>Intervention Anthology: Phonics/Word Study |
| **FLUENCY** | 55–60 WCPM | AUDIO CD Fluency Solutions Audio CD |
| | 0–54 WCPM | Evaluate for Intervention. |

## WRITE-ON-DEMAND SCORING RUBRIC

**PROMPT** **What is one special book you have read? Why is it important to you? Write as much as you can as well as you can. Write for 5 minutes.**

| 4 Excellent | 3 Good | 2 Fair | 1 Unsatisfactory |
|---|---|---|---|
| • More than 7 sentences<br>• Almost no spelling or grammar errors<br>• Cohesive ideas, focused and organized | • 5–7 sentences<br>• A few spelling and grammar errors<br>• Well-developed ideas and facts provided | • 4–5 sentences<br>• Several spelling and grammar errors<br>• Some good information; some vague | • Fewer than 4 sentences<br>• Many spelling and grammar errors<br>• Few developed idea or little accurate information |

### Daily Planner

| | |
|---|---|
| DAY 1 | • Prepare to Read<br>• Academic Language<br>• Vocabulary (Preteach) |
| DAY 2 | • Comprehension<br>• Practice Reader Lesson 1 |
| DAY 3 | • Phonics/Decoding<br>• Practice Reader Lesson 2 |
| DAY 4 | • Phonics/Decoding<br>• Vocabulary (Review)<br>• Practice Reader Lesson 3 |
| DAY 5 | • Self-Selected Reading |

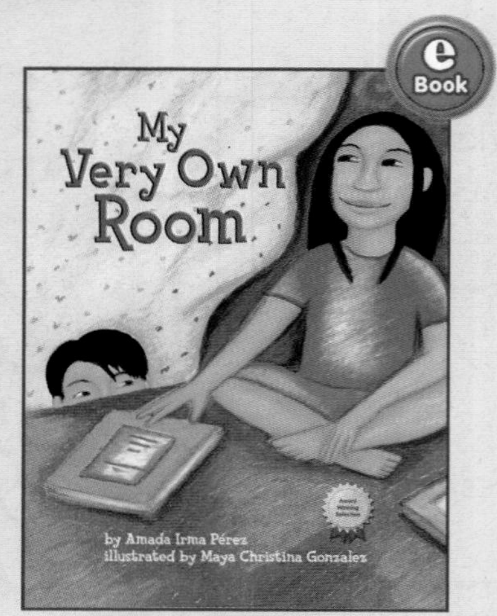

**StudentWorks Plus**

Strategic

# Approaching Level

## Prepare to Read

**Objective** Preview *My Very Own Room*

**Materials** • **StudentWorks Plus** • self-sticking notes

### PREVIEW TEXT

- Have students preview *My Very Own Room* using **StudentWorks Plus**. This version of the Student Book contains vocabulary preteaching, oral summaries in multiple languages, story recording, word-by-word highlighting, Think Aloud prompts, and comprehension monitoring questions.
- Remind students that listening carefully to and following along with the word-by-word reading will help them prepare for the reading of the selection with the class. Ask students to place self-sticking notes on any challenging words or places that confuse them. Discuss the confusing items with students prior to the reading of the selection with the rest of the class.
- Ask students to write three or four sentences in their Writer's Notebooks telling what they learned about the girl and her room.

## Academic Language

**Objective** Teach academic language

**Materials** • none

### PRETEACH LANGUAGE OF INSTRUCTION

Tell students that there are many important lesson words you will be using this week. You want them to become familiar with these words *before* the lessons. These words also appear in the directions of the tests they will be taking this year.

Preteach the following academic words: *realistic fiction, monitor, comprehension, prediction, biography, guide words, encyclopedia.*

- Define each word using student-friendly language. Tell students that *genre* is the category into which a piece of writing can be grouped. For example, this story is realistic fiction, because it is a made-up story that could have happened in real life. A story about a family of pioneers in the American West would be called historical fiction because it is a made-up story that takes place during a real historical time period.
- In addition, relate each word to known words. For example, connect *prediction* to *thinking ahead* or *guessing.*
- Highlight these words when used throughout the week and reinforce their meanings.

Strategic

# Approaching Level

## Phonics/Decoding

**Objective** Decode words with Long *i*

**Materials**
- **Approaching Reproducible,** p. 58
- **Sound-Spelling WorkBoard**

TESTED SKILL

### PHONICS MAINTENANCE

CA CONTENT STANDARD R 3.1.2 Decode regular multisyllabic words.

- Distribute a WorkBoard to each student. Say a sound previously taught, including the short vowel sounds *e* and *i* and long *a*, *o*, and *i*. Have students find the **Sound-Spelling Card** on the board for each sound.
- Review the spelling(s) for each sound by providing a sample word containing that spelling. Guide students to write the word on the board. Model how to segment the word and write the spelling for each sound, as needed. In addition, point out spelling hints, such as that the Long *i* sound can be spelled in several different ways, including *i*, *ie*, *y*, *i_e*, and *igh*.
- Dictate the following words for students to spell: *fly, fit, set, fight, boat, kite, pig, plate*. Write each word on the board and have students self-correct their work.

### RETEACH SKILL

**Long *i*** Point to the Long *i* Sound-Spelling Card on the WorkBoard and review the spellings for this sound. State each spelling and provide a sample word.

- Write the words below on the board. Model how to decode the first word in each row, then guide students as they decode the remaining words. For the multisyllabic words, divide the words into syllables using the syllable scoop procedure to help students read one syllable at a time.
- When completed, point to the words in random order for students to chorally read. Repeat several times.

| | | | | | |
|---|---|---|---|---|---|
| bit | bite | lit | light | sit | sight |
| sigh | sight | night | tight | fry | fright |
| mint | might | ripe | right | bride | brighter |
| ice | slice | slide | ice | tight | slight |
| dry | tribe | tribe | dried | light | lighten |
| cry | cried | tried | lied | scribe | sighing |

Sound-Spelling WorkBoard

## English Learners

UNIVERSAL ACCESS

**Minimal Contrasts** Focus on articulation. Make the /i/ sound and point to the position of your mouth. Have students repeat. Use the articulation photos on the small **Sound-Spelling Cards**. Repeat for the long *i* sound, then have students say each sound together, noticing the slight difference in mouth position. Continue by having students read minimal contrast word pairs, such as lit/light, pin/pine, slid/slide.

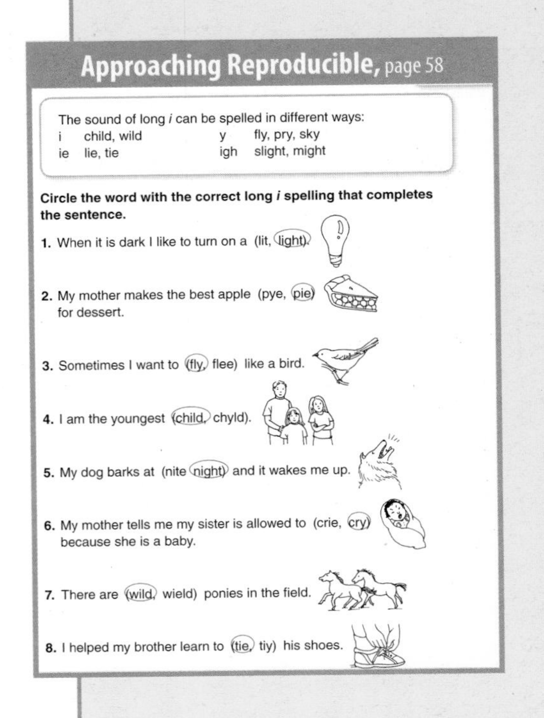
**Approaching Reproducible,** page 58

The sound of long *i* can be spelled in different ways:
i child, wild
ie lie, tie
y fly, pry, sky
igh slight, might

**Circle the word with the correct long *i* spelling that completes the sentence.**

1. When it is dark I like to turn on a (lit, light).
2. My mother makes the best apple (pye, pie) for dessert.
3. Sometimes I want to (fly, flee) like a bird.
4. I am the youngest (child, chyld).
5. My dog barks at (nite, night) and it wakes me up.
6. My mother tells me my sister is allowed to (crie, cry) because she is a baby.
7. There are (wild, wield) ponies in the field.
8. I helped my brother learn to (tie, tiy) his shoes.

Strategic

# Approaching Level

## Vocabulary

**Objective** Preteach Selection Vocabulary

**Materials** • **Visual Vocabulary Resources** • **Approaching Reproducible,** p. 59

TESTED SKILL

### PRETEACH VOCABULARY

Use the **Visual Vocabulary Resources** to preteach the key selection words *separate, determination, storage, exact, ruined,* and *luckiest*. Focus on two words per day. Use the following routine that appears in detail on the cards.

- Define the word in English and provide the example given.
- Define the word in Spanish, if appropriate, and indicate if the word is a cognate.
- Display the picture and explain how it illustrates or demonstrates the word.
- Then engage students in structured partner talk about the image, using the key word.
- Ask students to chorally say the word three times.
- Point out any known sound-spellings or focus on a key aspect of phonemic awareness related to the word.
- Distribute copies of the Vocabulary Glossary, **English Learners Resource Book**.

### REVIEW PREVIOUSLY TAUGHT VOCABULARY

Display the Vocabulary Cards from the previous four weeks. Say the meaning of each word, one by one, and have students identify it. Then point to words in random order for students to provide definitions and related words they know.

**Approaching Reproducible,** page 59

**Write whether the sentence could be true or false.**

1. Sue's determination to make friends made her not want to meet new people. false
2. To make bread you need exact amounts of ingredients, but it is fine to add extra sugar to your mixing bowl. false
3. April put her toys in storage when she got older because she did not use them. true
4. If you trip and twist your ankle, you probably feel like one of the luckiest people at school. false
5. Before you wash your clothes, you should separate the dark colors from the light colors. true
6. Our new table was shipped in a large crate to our address. true
7. The slide ruined my new pants by making them cleaner. false

**The vocabulary word letters are mixed up below. Use the words in the box and the clues to help you identify the correct word.**

exact determination ruined storage separate luckiest crate

8. Our treehouse door was made from an old (A T R E C) crate.
9. If your shoes don't fit, they are not your (C A E T X) exact size.
10. After she found her lost kitten, she felt like the (U I T C E L K S) luckiest and most grateful girl ever.

Strategic

# Approaching Level

## Vocabulary

**Objective** Review vocabulary and high-frequency words

**Materials** • **Vocabulary Cards** • **High-Frequency Word Cards**

### REVIEW VOCABULARY

**Review Words** Display the Vocabulary Cards for *separate, determination, storage, exact, ruined*, and *luckiest*. Point to each word, read it aloud, and have students chorally repeat.

Then ask students to answer the following questions.

- What is an example of something you need to separate?
- What is an example of a time you had a lot of determination?
- What is an example of something you might want to put in storage?
- When do you need an exact measurement?
- What is an example of a time your day was ruined?
- What is an example of a time you felt like the luckiest person around?

### HIGH-FREQUENCY WORDS

**Top 250 Words** The ability to read accurately and effortlessly the most frequently used words in written English will help students develop reading fluency. Display **High-Frequency Word Cards 1–40**. Then do the following:

- Display one card at a time and ask students to chorally state each word.
- Have students spell each word aloud.
- Ask students to write each word in their Writer's Notebooks as they state aloud each letter. Then have them read the word again.
- When completed, quickly flip through the word card set as students chorally read the words.
- Provide opportunities for students to use the words in speaking and writing. For example, provide sentence starters such as *I like to buy* ________ for oral and written practice. Or point to a word card and ask a questions such as What word means the same as this word? (when pointing to the *big* word card).
- Continue the routine throughout the week.

### Word Webs

Have students create word webs in their Writer's Notebooks for each vocabulary word. Write the related words provided and ask students to add other words, phrases, and illustrations.

Student Book

## Corrective Feedback

Read each paragraph with students. Ask: *What predictions can you make about the story?* Underline the details in the paragraph that support your prediction. Model how to develop predictions. After reading the story, review predictions and confirm (see if they are correct) or revise them (correct a wrong prediction).

Strategic

# Approaching Level

## Comprehension

**Objective** Reteach monitor comprehension and make predictions

**Materials** • **Student Book:** "Pond Street Clubhouse"

### RETEACH STRATEGY: MONITOR COMPREHENSION

CA CONTENT STANDARD R 3.3.4 Determine the underlying theme or author's message in fiction and nonfiction text.

- **Define** Tell students that they can monitor their comprehension of a story by making sure they understand what they read. As students read, they should stop and ask themselves what the story is all about.

  Relate the word *comprehension* to the word *understand*. When you understand something, you know what it is about. When you know what a story is about, your comprehension of the story is on target.

- **Relate to Real Life** Ask students to imagine that they are traveling in a country where they don't speak the language. At first, they walk around looking confused and feeling lost. In a few days, though, they have learned how to say hello and goodbye in this new language. They are learning to comprehend, or understand, the language.

- **Set Purpose** Remind students that good readers stop to monitor their comprehension as they read. If the reader knows what the story is about, he or she reads on. If not, he or she must go back and reread.

### RETEACH SKILL: MAKE AND CONFIRM PREDICTIONS

- **Define** Tell students that making predictions means guessing about what will happen next in a story. Once the story is over, students can ask themselves if their predictions were correct.

- **Relate to Real Life** Ask students to name their favorite movie. Ask, At the end of the movie, did you say to yourself "I knew that was going to happen!"? If so, they understood the story of the movie so well that they were able to predict what would happen at the end.

- **Set Purpose** Remind students that good readers predict what will happen next as they read. This helps the reader better understand the selection.

- **Apply** Work with students to form predictions about "Pond Street Clubhouse" as they read. Then have students confirm their predictions after reading the story.

Strategic

# Approaching Level

## Practice Reader Lesson 1

**Objective** Read to apply skills and strategies

**Materials**
- **Practice Reader:** *The Slightly Tipping Tree House*
- **Approaching Reproducible,** p. 61

Practice Reader

### BEFORE READING

**Preview and Predict** Have students read the title and preview the first chapter. Ask students to make predictions about the section. Students should note any questions they have before they read.

**Review Vocabulary Words** Have students read the vocabulary words on the inside front cover. Briefly define each and ask students to state related words they have learned.

**Set a Purpose for Reading** *Let's read to find out if these children can build a tree house.*

### DURING READING

**STRATEGY**
**MONITOR COMPREHENSION**

Remind students that monitoring their comprehension of a story means stopping to ask themselves questions about the plot as they read and then rereading or reading ahead if they need to find answers.

**SKILL**
**MAKE AND CONFIRM PREDICTIONS**

CA CONTENT STANDARD R 3.2.4 Recall major points in the text and make and modify predictions about forthcoming information.

Remind students to make predictions about what might happen next as they read. Read Chapter 1 with students. Help students complete the Predictions Chart.

As you read, help students decode unknown words. In addition, ask open-ended questions to facilitate rich discussion, such as *What is the author telling us about building a tree house?* Build on students' responses to develop deeper understanding of the text.

Stop after each two pages and ask students to make predictions in order to check their understanding before reading on. If they struggle, help students reread the difficult pages or passage. Then model determining the main idea of the chapter.

### AFTER READING

Ask students to compare the story of the tree house to something in their own lives. Have students tell stories about something that has happened to them that is very similar to or different from the events in this story.

Strategic

# Approaching Level

## Practice Reader Lesson 2

**Objective** Reread to apply skills and strategies and develop fluency

**Materials**
- **Practice Reader:** *The Slightly Tipping Tree House*
- **Approaching Reproducible,** p. 62

Practice Reader

### BEFORE READING

**Review Strategy and Skill** Review students' completed Predictions Charts from the first read. Remind students that a prediction is when you guess what might happen next in a story.

**Review Vocabulary Words** Have students search the book for each vocabulary word. Ask students to read aloud the sentence containing the word and state the word's definition or provide related words. Point out any context clues provided, such as surrounding words.

**Set a Purpose for Reading** *Let's reread to check our understanding of the information in the book and to work on our reading fluency.*

### DURING READING

Reread *The Slightly Tipping Tree House* with students. Have them read silently two pages at a time, or read aloud to a partner. Stop and have students summarize before reading the next two pages. Model oral summaries as needed.

### AFTER READING

**Check Comprehension** Have partners complete the Comprehension Check on page 16. Review students' answers. Help students find evidence for their answers in the text.

**CA CONTENT STANDARD LAS 3.1.9** Read prose and poetry aloud with fluency, rhythm, and pace, using appropriate intonation and vocal patterns to emphasize important passages of the text being read.

**Model Fluency** Model reading the Practice Reader fluency passage on **Approaching Reproducible** page 62. Tell students to pay close attention to your phrasing, or how you group words together, as you read. Then read one sentence at a time and have students echo-read the sentences, copying your phrasing.

During independent reading time, have students work with a partner using the fluency passage. One student reads aloud, while the other repeats each sentence back. If students need additional support, have them listen to the "practice speed" version of the passage on the **Fluency Solutions Audio CD**.

**Approaching Reproducible,** page 62

**As I read, I will pay attention to phrasing.**

Shatima and Jamal were on their back porch looking at
10 magazines.
11 "I really like these pictures of tree houses," Shatima
20 said. "I wish we had one."
26 "We have a tree," Jamal said. "I'll bet we could build a
38 tree house."
40 "Mom and Dad won't let us," Shatima said.
48 "You are probably right," said Jamal. "They'll come up
57 with some reason we can't do it."
64 Katrina, their friend who lived next door, came over.
73 "What are you reading about?" she asked.
80 "Tree houses," Shatima said.
84 "We want to build one, but Mom and Dad won't go for
96 it," Jamal said.
99 "Try them," Katrina said. "You'll never know unless
107 you ask." 109

**Comprehension Check**

1. What do Shatima and Jamal want to build? **Main Idea and Details** Shatima and Jamal want to build a tree house.
2. What advice does Katrina give Shatima and Jamal? **Main Idea and Details** to ask their parents about building a tree house and not assume they will say no

| | Words Read | – | Number of Errors | = | Words Correct Score |
|---|---|---|---|---|---|
| First Read | | – | | = | |
| Second Read | | – | | = | |

Strategic

# Approaching Level

## Practice Reader Lesson 3

**Objective** Build fluency

**Materials** • **Practice Reader:** *The Slightly Tipping Tree House*

### FOCUS ON FLUENCY

**Timed Reading** Tell students that they will be doing a final timed reading of the fluency passage from *The Slightly Tipping Tree House* that they have been practicing. With each student, follow these directions:

- Place the passage facedown.
- When you say "Go," the student begins reading the passage aloud.
- When you say "Stop," the student stops reading the passage.

As they read, note words students mispronounce and their overall phrasing. Stop after one minute. Help students record and graph the number of words they read correctly.

### REREAD PREVIOUSLY READ BOOKS

- Distribute copies of the past four **Practice Readers**. Have students select two to reread. Tell students that rereading these books will help them develop their skills. The more times they read the same words, the quicker they will learn these words. This will make the reading of other books easier.
- Circulate and listen in as students read. Stop students periodically and ask them how they are figuring out difficult words and how they are monitoring their comprehension. Note students who need additional work with specific decoding or comprehension skills.
- Encourage students to read other previously read Practice Readers during independent reading time or for homework.

Practice Reader

### Meet Grade-Level Expectations

As an alternative to this day's lesson, guide students through a reading of the On Level Practice Reader. See page 145U. Since both books contain the same vocabulary, phonics, and comprehension skills, the scaffolding you provided will help most students gain access to this more challenging text.

### Book Talk

See page 145HH. Students will work with peers of varying language abilities to discuss this week's Practice Readers.

Student Book

Student Book

## Decodable Text

Use the Reading *Triumphs* Anthology and the decodable stories in the **Teacher's Resource Book** to help students build fluency with basic decoding patterns.

Strategic

# Approaching Level

## Fluency

**Objectives** Reread selections to develop fluency; develop speaking skills

**Materials** • **Student Book:** *My Very Own Room,* "Pond Street Clubhouse"

TESTED SKILL

### REREAD FOR FLUENCY

- Have students reread a portion of *My Very Own Room*. Suggest that they focus on two to four of their favorite pages from the selection. Work with students to read the pages with the appropriate phrasing.
- Provide time for students to read their sections of text to you. Comment on their phrasing and provide corrective feedback by modeling proper fluency.

### DEVELOP SPEAKING/LISTENING SKILLS

- Have students practice reading the story "Pond Street Clubhouse."
- Work with students to read with appropriate phrasing. Model reading a few lines at a time. Point out that you pause at commas and group certain words together. Have students repeat.
- Provide time for students to read a few paragraphs of the story aloud to partners. Ask students to explain why they grouped certain words together, and what was the overall effect.
- Ask students to reread the same section from the story, this time not pausing for commas or grouping words together, but speaking only in a monotone. What is the effect of this reading?

Strategic

# Approaching Level

## Self-Selected Reading

**Objective** Read independently to make and confirm predictions

**Materials** • **Classroom Library** • other realistic fiction books

### APPLY SKILLS TO INDEPENDENT READING

- Have students choose a realistic fiction book for independent reading. (See the **Theme Bibliography** on pages T8–T9 for book suggestions.) Remind them that making predictions is guessing about what might happen next. When they have finished reading, they can confirm their predictions to see if they were right. Have students read their books and record their predictions on a Predictions Chart.
- After reading, ask students to use their Predictions Chart to write or orally state a summary of the book. Provide time for students to share their summaries and comment on their reactions to the book. Ask: *Would you recommend this book to a classmate? Why or why not?*

Classroom Library

### Daily Planner

| | |
|---|---|
| DAY 1 | • Vocabulary |
| DAY 2 | • Phonics |
| DAY 3 | • Practice Reader Lesson 1 |
| DAY 4 | • Practice Reader Lesson 2<br>• Fluency |
| DAY 5 | • Self-Selected Reading |

Benchmark

# On Level

## Vocabulary

**Objective** Review vocabulary

**Materials** • **Vocabulary Cards**

TESTED SKILL

### REVIEW PREVIOUSLY TAUGHT WORDS

**Review Words** Display the **Vocabulary Cards** for *separate, determination, storage, exact, ruined*, and *luckiest*. Point to each word, read it aloud, and have students chorally repeat.

Then provide the following Yes/No questions. Ask students to answer each question, justifying their answer. Allow other students to respond. Use the discussions to determine each student's depth of word knowledge.

- When poured in the same glass, does water *separate* from oil?
- Do you need *determination* to do well in school?
- Can you put winter coats in *storage*?
- Do you know the *exact* time you were born?
- Does a rainstorm always mean the day is *ruined*?
- Is the *luckiest* person always the happiest person?

## Phonics/Word Study

**Objective** Decode multisyllabic words with Long *i*

**Materials** • **Sound-Spelling WorkBoards**

TESTED SKILL

### RETEACH SKILL

CA CONTENT STANDARD R 3.1.2 Decode regular multisyllabic words.

CA CONTENT STANDARD R 3.1.1 Know and use complex word families when reading to decode unfamiliar words.

- **Long *i* Words** Point to the Long *i* **Sound-Spelling Card** on the **WorkBoard** and review the spellings for this sound. State each spelling and provide a sample word.
- Write the words below on the board. If necessary, divide the words into syllables using the syllable scoop procedure to help students read one syllable at a time. When completed, point to the words in random order for students to chorally read.

| | | | | |
|---|---|---|---|---|
| frighten | brightly | lightly | higher | spying |
| nighttime | whiten | delight | highlight | trying |
| brighten | crying | lighter | signing | refry |

- **Spelling** Dictate the following words for students to spell on their WorkBoards: *icing, icy, nightly, whiteness, rising*. Guide students to use the Sound-Spelling Cards and model how to segment words, such as spelling a word syllable by syllable.

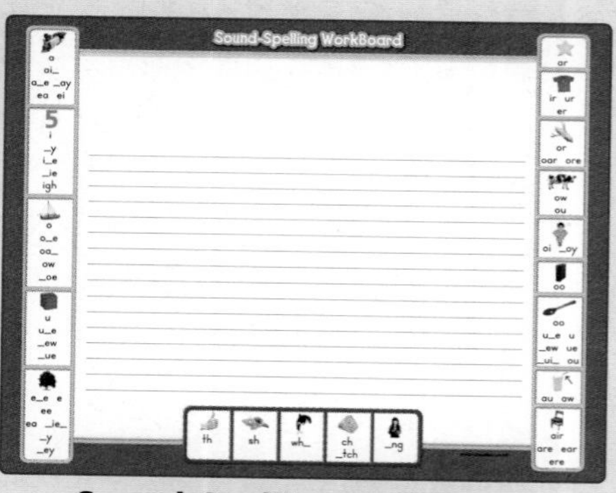

Sound-Spelling WorkBoard

Benchmark

# On Level

## Fluency

**Objectives** Reread selections to develop fluency; develop speaking skills

**Materials** • **Student Book:** *My Very Own Room*, "Pond Street Clubhouse"

### REREAD FOR FLUENCY

**CA CONTENT STANDARD R 3.1.3** Read aloud narrative and expository text fluently and accurately and with appropriate pacing, intonation, and expression.

- Have students reread *My Very Own Room*. Work with students to read with the phrasing. Model as needed.
- Provide time for students to read a section of text to you. Comment on their phrasing and provide corrective feedback.

### DEVELOP SPEAKING/LISTENING SKILLS

**CA CONTENT STANDARD LAS 3.1.9** Read prose and poetry aloud with fluency, rhythm, and pace, using appropriate intonation and vocal patterns to emphasize important passages of the text being read.

- Have students practice reading the story "Pond Street Clubhouse."
- Work with students to read with appropriate phrasing. Model reading a few sentences at a time. Point out that you pause at commas and group certain words together. Have students repeat.
- Provide time for students to read a page of the story aloud to partners. Ask students to explain why they grouped certain words together and what the overall effect was.
- Ask students to reread the same section from the story, this time not pausing for commas or grouping words together, but speaking only in a monotone. What is the effect of this reading?

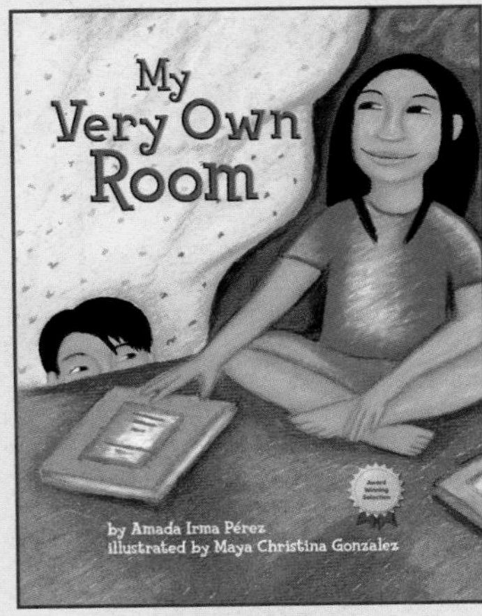

Student Book

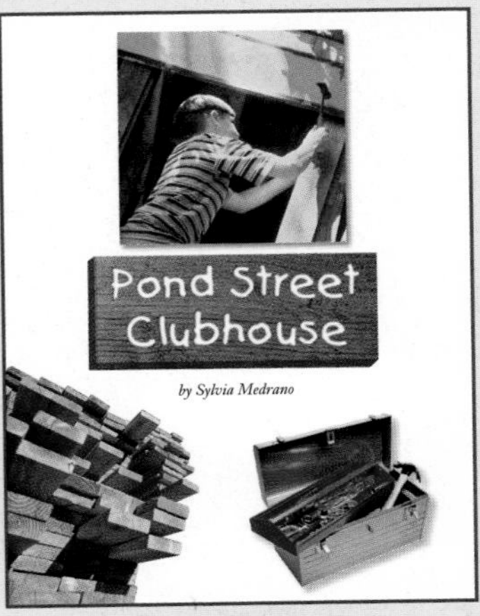

Student Book

## Self-Selected Reading

**Objective** Read independently to make and confirm predictions

**Materials** • **Classroom Library** • other realistic fiction books

### APPLY SKILLS TO INDEPENDENT READING

- Have students choose a realistic fiction book for independent reading. (See the **Theme Bibliography** on pages T8–T9 for book suggestions.) Have students read their books and write down their predictions.
- After reading, ask students to use their predictions list to write a summary of the book. Provide time for students to share their summaries and comment on their reactions to the book. Ask: *Would you recommend this book to a classmate? Why or why not?*

Classroom Library

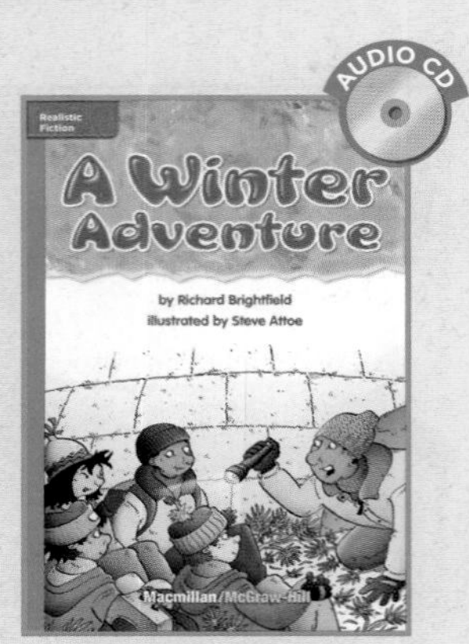


Practice Reader

Benchmark

# On Level

## Practice Reader Lesson 1

**Objective** Read to apply strategies and skills

**Materials**
- **Practice Reader:** *A Winter Adventure*
- **Practice Book,** p. 61

### BEFORE READING

**Preview and Predict** Have students read the title and preview the book by reading the chapter titles and looking at the illustrations. Ask students to predict what they think this book is about and the types of information they might learn.

**Review Vocabulary Words** Have students read the vocabulary words on the inside front cover. Ask students to state related words they have learned. Review definitions, as needed.

**Set a Purpose for Reading** *Let's read to find out how the campers deal with a sudden snowfall.*

### DURING READING

**STRATEGY**
**MONITOR COMPREHENSION**

Remind students that monitoring their comprehension means they keep track of how well they understand it as they read.

**SKILL**
**MAKE AND CONFIRM PREDICTIONS**

**CA CONTENT STANDARD R 3.2.4** Recall major points in the text and make and modify predictions about forthcoming information.

Remind students that making predictions as they read will help them understand the story better. When they have completed the book, they can confirm their predictions.

**Read** Chapter 1 with students. Ask open-ended questions to facilitate rich discussion, such as *What is the author telling us about camping and snowfalls? What does the author want us to know about these characters?* Build on students' responses to develop deeper understanding of the text. Have students fill in the first section of the Predictions Chart, then continue reading.

**Context Clues** As they read, have students point out this week's new vocabulary words and any context clues the author provides, such as nearby words with similar meanings.

### AFTER READING

Ask students to compare this story about winter to their own winter experiences. *What activities do they do in the winter? How are they the same or different from camping?* Have students comment on the tips they learned about camping in the winter.

Benchmark

# On Level

## Practice Reader Lesson 2

**Objective** Reread to apply skills and strategies and develop fluency

**Materials**
- **Practice Reader:** *A Winter Adventure*
- **Practice Book,** p. 62

### BEFORE READING

**Review Strategy and Skill** Review students' completed Predictions Charts from the first read. Remind students that a prediction is a guess about what will happen next in the story.

A prediction is created from the main ideas of the book. If students' predictions are incomplete, provide a model prediction or use a student prediction and revise it as a group. Have students copy the revised predictions in their Writer's Notebooks.

**Set a Purpose for Reading** *Let's reread to check our understanding of the information in the book and to work on our reading fluency.*

### DURING READING

Reread *A Winter Adventure* with students. Have them read silently two pages at a time or read aloud to a partner. Stop and have students summarize before reading the next two pages. Model oral summaries as needed.

### AFTER READING

**Check Comprehension** Have partners complete the Comprehension Check at the end of the book. Review students' answers. Help students find evidence for their answers in the text.

**Model Fluency** Model reading the Practice Reader fluency passage on **Practice Book** page 62. Tell students to pay close attention to your phrasing, or how you group words together, as you read. Then read one sentence at a time and have students echo-read the sentences, copying your phrasing.

During independent reading time, have students work with a partner using the fluency passage. One student reads aloud, while the other repeats each sentence back. If students need additional support, have them listen to the "practice speed" version of the passage on the **Fluency Solutions Audio CD**.

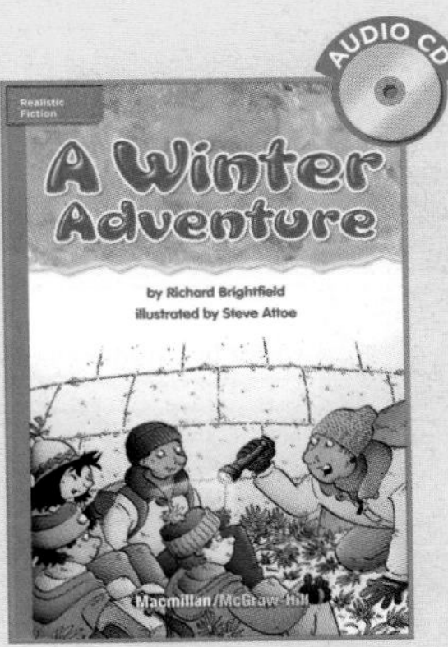


Practice Reader

**Book Talk**

See page 145HH. Students will work with peers of varying language abilities to discuss this week's Practice Readers.

**Practice Book,** page 62

**As I read, I will pay attention to phrasing.**

"What are your plans for today?" Mr. Sanchez asked his
10 son Carlo.
12 "I'm hiking with my nature club," Carlo said, "from
21 the state park entrance to Turtle Lake. Jimmy's father,
30 Mr. Gordon, is going with us."
36 "It's colder than yesterday," his mother said. "Please
44 take your warmest jacket and your gloves."
51 "Hold on," Carlo's father said. "I need to get your warm
62 blue jacket from the storage box in the attic. Then I'll
73 drop you off."
76 A short time later, Carlo met up with Mr. Gordon and
87 the other members of the club, Jimmy, Julie, and Tyrone.
97 Mr. Gordon packed them in his van and drove them to
108 the state park.
111 When they arrived he checked his compass. "The
119 old logging trail is somewhere directly west of here,"
128 he said. 130

**Comprehension Check**

1. What are Carlo's plans? **Main Idea and Details** Carlo is going hiking in the state park with his nature club.
2. What is the weather like? **Plot Development** The weather is very cold.

| | Words Read | – | Number of Errors | = | Words Correct Score |
|---|---|---|---|---|---|
| First Read | | – | | = | |
| Second Read | | – | | = | |

## Daily Planner

| | |
|---|---|
| DAY 1 | • Practice Reader Lesson 1 |
| DAY 2 | • Practice Reader Lesson 2 |
| DAY 3 | • Phonics |
| DAY 4 | • Vocabulary<br>• Fluency |
| DAY 5 | • Self-Selected Reading |

Advanced

# Beyond Level

## Phonics/Word Study

**Objective** Decode multisyllabic words with Long *i*

**Materials** • **Sound-Spelling WorkBoards**

TESTED SKILL

### EXTEND/ACCELERATE

CA CONTENT STANDARD R 3.1.2 Decode regular multisyllabic words.

- **Read Multisyllabic Words with Long *i*** Write the words below on the board. Challenge students to read the words, using known word parts. When completed, point to the words in random order for students to chorally read.

| | | | | |
|---|---|---|---|---|
| tightness | inspiring | dryer | rewriting | nightingale |
| flightless | skylight | inviting | untying | rehired |
| highlight | fryer | relying | slighter | revising |

- **Define Words** Ask students to use their knowledge of word parts to figure out the meanings of the above words. Then have partners find the words in a dictionary and confirm or revise the meanings. Challenge students to use these words in this week's writing assignments.
- **Spell Long *i* Words** Dictate the following words for students to spell on their **WorkBoards:** *invited, compiled, slider, refining, frighten.* Write the words for students to self-correct.

Sound-Spelling WorkBoard

## Vocabulary

**Objectives** Review compare and contrast; write a letter

**Materials** • none

TESTED SKILL

### ENRICH VOCABULARY

- **Brainstorm Building Words** Write the word *geometric shape* on the board. Have students create a concept of definition map with the term written in a circle in the middle and the following categories written around it—What it is? What is it like? What are some examples? Help students come up with a simple definition and then identify kinds of shapes (squares, circles, triangles, and so on) and then tell what it is like (may have angles, created by straight or curved lines).
- **Write a Letter** Ask students to think about spending a day with Frank Lloyd Wright. Challenge them to write a letter to him, using the vocabulary words they have learned in this week's selections and making sure to use comparison and contrast in their letter.

Advanced

# Beyond Level

## Fluency

**Objectives** Reread selections to develop fluency; develop speaking skills

**Materials** • **Student Book:** *My Very Own Room,* "Pond Street Clubhouse"

### REREAD FOR FLUENCY

- Have students reread *My Very Own Room.* Work with students to read the book with the appropriate phrasing.
- Provide time for students to read a section of text to you. Comment on their phrasing and provide corrective feedback.

Student Book

### DEVELOP SPEAKING/LISTENING SKILLS

CA CONTENT STANDARD LAS 3.1.9 Read prose and poetry aloud with fluency, rhythm, and pace, using appropriate intonation and vocal patterns to emphasize important passages of the text being read.

- Have students practice reading the story "Pond Street Clubhouse."
- Work with students to read with appropriate phrasing. Model reading a few lines at a time. Point out that you pause at commas and group certain words together. Have students repeat.
- Provide time for students to read aloud the story to the class. Ask students to explain why they grouped certain words together and what the overall effect was.
- Ask students to reread the same section from the story, this time not pausing for commas or grouping words together, but speaking only in a monotone. What is the effect of this reading?

Student Book

## Self-Selected Reading

**Objective** Read independently to make and confirm predictions in a selection

**Materials** • **Classroom Library** • other realistic fiction books

### APPLY SKILLS TO INDEPENDENT READING

- Have students choose a realistic fiction book for independent reading. (See the **Theme Bibliography** on pages T8–T9 for book suggestions.) Have students read their books and write down their predictions.
- After reading, ask students to use their predictions list to write a summary of the book. Provide time for students to share their summaries and comment on their reactions to the book. Ask: *Would you recommend this book to a classmate? Why or why not?*

Classroom Library

Practice Reader

Advanced

# Beyond Level

## Practice Reader Lesson 1

**Objective** Read to apply strategies and skills

**Materials**
- **Practice Reader:** *The Science Fair*
- **Beyond Reproducible,** p. 61

### BEFORE READING

**Preview and Predict** Have students preview the book by reading the title and chapter titles and looking at the illustrations. Ask students to predict what they think this book is about and the types of information they might learn.

**Review Vocabulary Words** Have students read the vocabulary words on the inside front cover. Ask students to state each definition and any related words they have learned.

**Set a Purpose for Reading** *Let's read to find out how these students worked together in a science fair.*

### DURING READING

**STRATEGY**
**MONITOR COMPREHENSION**

Ask students to define the word *comprehension*. Remind students that *comprehension* and *understand* have related meanings.

**SKILL**
**MAKE AND CONFIRM PREDICTIONS**

**CA CONTENT STANDARD R 3.2.4** Recall major points in the text and make and modify predictions about forthcoming information.

Ask students to define the term *prediction*. Remind students that a prediction is a guess about what will happen next.

Read the book with students. Ask open-ended questions to facilitate rich discussion, such as *What is the author telling us about this science fair and these students? What does the author want us to know about this team of students?* Build on students' responses to develop deeper understanding of the text. Have students fill in the Predictions Chart independently as they read.

### AFTER READING

Ask students to compare this science fair to a fair or other school-wide activity. *How were they the same? Different*? Have students comment on the most interesting facts they learned about science. Prompt them to develop questions about science that they would like to research on the Internet during independent time.

Advanced

# Beyond Level

## Practice Reader Lesson 2

**Objective** Reread to apply skills and strategies and develop fluency

**Materials**
- **Practice Reader:** *The Science Fair*
- **Beyond Level Reproducible,** p. 62

Practice Reader

### Book Talk

See page 145HH. Students will work with peers of varying language abilities to discuss this week's Practice Readers.

### BEFORE READING

**Review Strategy and Skill** Review students' completed Predictions Charts from the first read.

Remind students that a prediction is informed by the main ideas from the book. If students' predictions are incomplete, provide a model prediction or use a student prediction and revise it as a group. Have students copy the revised prediction in their Writer's Notebooks.

**Set a Purpose for Reading** *Let's reread to check our understanding of the information in the book and work on our reading fluency.*

### DURING READING

Have students reread *The Science Fair* silently or with a partner. If reading in pairs, prompt students to stop every two pages and summarize or ask their partner questions.

### AFTER READING

**Check Comprehension** Have students independently complete the Comprehension Check at the end of the book. Review students' answers. Help students find evidence for their answers in the text.

**Model Fluency** Model reading the Practice Reader fluency passage on **Beyond Reproducible** page 62. Tell students to pay close attention to your phrasing as you read. Then read one sentence at a time and have students echo-read the sentences, copying your phrasing.

During independent reading time, have students work with a partner using the Fluency passage. One student reads aloud, while the other repeats each sentence back. Students can check their fluency by reading along with the "expert speed" version of the passage on the **Fluency Solutions Audio CD**.

### Beyond Reproducible, page 62

**As I read, I will pay attention to phrasing.**

"It's time to get ready for the science fair," Ms. Thomas, the
12 science teacher, announced to the science club. "But this year, we'll
23 work in teams, rather than each on your own."
32 "How many teams?" Erin asked.
37 "Let's see," Ms. Thomas said. "There will be five teams, each with
49 three members."
51 "That's only five exhibits," said Ari.
57 "How are we going to pick the teams?" Tanya asked.
67 "We'll pick names out of a hat," Ms. Thomas said.
77 Soon everyone was part of a team.
84 "The fair is in two weeks," Ms. Thomas said. "With hard work and
97 determination, you'll all be done in time. There will be a prize for the
111 best exhibit."
113 "What's the prize?" Ari asked.
118 "I'll keep that as a surprise," Ms. Thomas said. "I predict that this
131 year's fair will be our best yet."
138 Tanya, Erin, and Ari, who were on the same team, met in
150 the school cafeteria.
153 "Who has an idea for the exhibit?" Tanya asked. 162

**Comprehension Check**

1. What is the science club preparing for? **Main Idea and Details** the science fair
2. How many students will participate in the science fair? **Plot Development** 15 students

| | Words Read | – | Number of Errors | = | Words Correct Score |
|---|---|---|---|---|---|
| First Read | | – | | = | |
| Second Read | | – | | = | |

## Daily Planner

| | |
|---|---|
| DAY 1 | • Build Background Knowledge<br>• Vocabulary |
| DAY 2 | • Vocabulary<br>• Access to Core Content<br>*My Very Own Room* |
| DAY 3 | • Vocabulary<br>• Grammar<br>• Access to Core Content<br>*My Very Own Room* |
| DAY 4 | • Vocabulary<br>• Writing/Spelling<br>• Access to Core Content<br>"Frank Lloyd Wright" |
| DAY 5 | • Vocabulary<br>• Practice Reader<br>*Safe in the Storm*<br>• Self-Selected Reading |

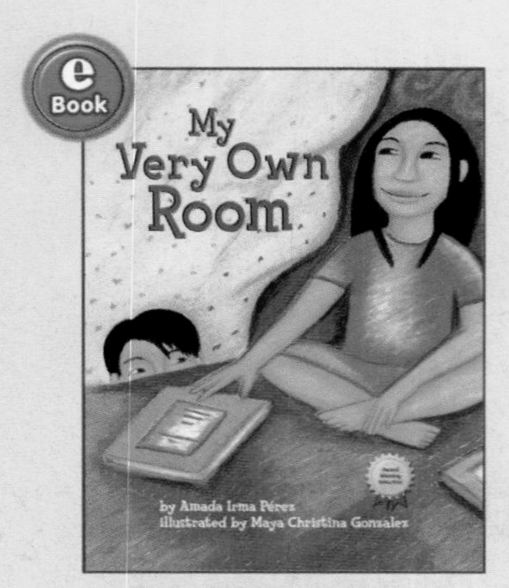


**StudentWorks Plus**

# English Learners

## Prepare to Read

**Content Objective** Describe a special place
**Language Objective** Use key words to describe a special place
**Materials** **StudentWorks Plus** (interactive eBook)

### BUILD BACKGROUND KNOWLEDGE

CA CONTENT STANDARD
R 3.1.3
Read aloud narrative and expository text fluently and accurately and with appropriate pacing, intonation, and expression.

- Have students preview *My Very Own Room* using **StudentWorks Plus**, the interactive eBook. This version of the Student Book contains oral summaries in multiple languages, online multilingual glossaries, word-by-word highlighting, and questions that assess and build comprehension.
- Students can build their word reading fluency by reading along as the text is read or by listening during the first reading and, at the end of each paragraph, returning to the beginning of the paragraph and reading along.
- Students can build their comprehension by reviewing the definitions of key words in the online glossary and by answering the comprehension questions. When appropriate, the text required to answer the question is highlighted to provide students with additional support and scaffolding.
- Following the reading, ask students to respond in writing to a question that links the story to their personal experiences, such as: *Have you ever had a special place that was just for you? If so, describe what it looked like. What did it feel like?*

## Academic Language

**Language Objective** Use academic language in classroom conversations

- This week's academic words are **boldfaced** throughout the lesson. Define the word in context and provide a clear example from the selection. Then ask students to generate an example or a word with a similar meaning.

### Academic Language Used in Whole Group Instruction

| Theme Words | Key Selection Words | Strategy and Skill Words |
|---|---|---|
| **enjoyable**<br>**adventure** | **separate**<br>**determination**<br>**storage**<br>**exact**<br>**ruined**<br>**luckiest** | **suffix** **compare**<br>**compound sentence**<br>**punctuate** **contrast**<br>**monitor** **phrasing**<br>**comprehension**<br>**prediction** |

# English Learners

## Vocabulary

**Language Objective** Demonstrate understanding and use of key words by describing a special place.

**Materials** • **Visual Vocabulary Resources** • **English Learner Resource Book**

### PRETEACH KEY VOCABULARY

**All Language Levels** Use the **Visual Vocabulary Resources** to preteach the key selection words *separate, determination, storage, exact, ruined,* and *luckiest*. Focus on 1–2 words per day. Use the following routine that appears in detail on the cards.

- Define the word in English and provide the example given.
- Define the word in Spanish, if appropriate, and indicate if the word is a cognate.
- Display the picture and explain how it illustrates or demonstrates the word. Engage students in structured partner-talk about the image, using the key word.
- Ask students to chorally say the word three times.
- Point out any known sound-spellings or focus on a key aspect of phonemic awareness related to the word.
- Distribute copies of the Vocabulary Glossary in the **English Learner Resource Book** page 64.

### PRETEACH FUNCTION WORDS AND PHRASES

**All Language Levels** Use the Visual Vocabulary Resources to preteach the function words and phrases *peacefully, cuddle up on, stuffed with,* and *run out of*. Focus on one word per day. Use the detailed routine on the cards.

- Define the word in English and, if appropriate, in Spanish. Point out if the word is a cognate.
- Refer to the picture and engage students in talk about the word; for example, students will Partner-Talk using sentence frames or they will listen to sentences and replace a word or phrase with the new function word.
- Ask students to chorally repeat the word three times.

### TEACH BASIC WORDS

For **Beginning** and **Early Intermediate** students, use the Visual Vocabulary Resources to teach the basic words *ladder, closet, sewing machine, curtain, furniture,* and *ceiling*. Teach these "household" words using the routine provided on the card.

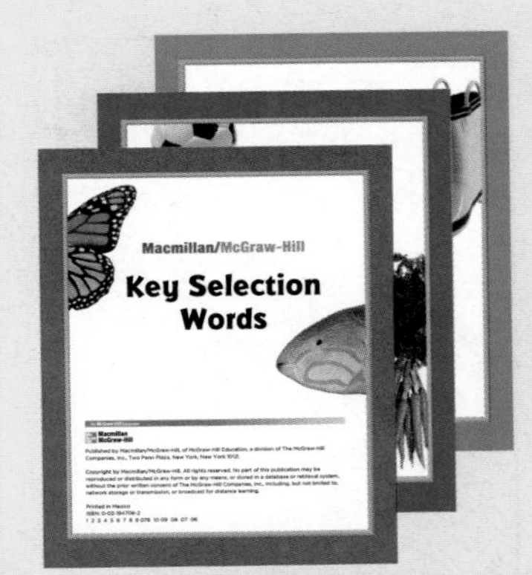


**Visual Vocabulary Resources**

**EL Resource Book,** page 64

Use the word chart to study this week's vocabulary words.
Write a sentence using each word in your writer's notebook.

| Word | Context Sentence | Illustration |
|---|---|---|
| separate | We can separate the nails by size. | |
| determination | His determination helped him build a birdhouse. | When have you showed determination? |
| storage | Items we don't often use are in storage boxes in the attic. | |
| exact | I knew the exact place I wanted to build my tree house. | |
| ruined | A fire ruined the cabin. | |
| luckiest | When I found the money I thought this was my lucki-est day ever. | |

Student Book

English Learner Resource Book

# English Learners

## Access to Core Content

**Content Objective** Read grade-level text
**Language Objective** Discuss text using key words and sentence frames
**Materials** • **English Learner Resource Book,** pp. 50–63

TESTED SKILL

### PRETEACH MAIN SELECTION (PAGES 116–137)

Use the Interactive Question-Response Guide on **English Learner Resource Book pages 50–61** to introduce students to *My Very Own Room*. Preteach half of the selection on **Day 2** and half on **Day 3**.

- Use the prompts provided in the guide to develop meaning and vocabulary. Use the Partner-Talk and whole-class responses to engage students and increase student talk.
- When completed, have partners reread the story.

### PRETEACH PAIRED SELECTION (PAGES 140–143)

Use the Interactive Question-Response Guide on English Learner Resource Book pages 62–63 to preview the paired selection "Frank Lloyd Wright." Preteach the selection on **Day 4**.

# English Learners

## Fluency

**Content Objective** Reread selections to develop fluency; develop speaking skills
**Language Objective** Tell a partner what a selection is about
**Materials** • **Student Book:** *My Very Own Room,* "Frank Lloyd Wright"

### REREAD FOR FLUENCY

CA CONTENT STANDARD R 3.1.3 Read aloud narrative and expository text fluently and accurately and with appropriate pacing, intonation, and expression.

- Have students reread a portion of *My Very Own Room*. Suggest that they focus on two to four of their favorite pages from the selection. Work with students to read the pages with appropriate phrasing; for example, read one sentence at a time, pointing out how you follow punctuation such as commas to group certain words together as you read. Have students echo-read the sentences, copying your phrasing.
- Provide time for students to read their sections of text to you. Comment on their phrasing and provide corrective feedback by modeling proper fluency.

### DEVELOP SPEAKING/LISTENING SKILLS

- Have students practice reading "Frank Lloyd Wright." Work with them to read with appropriate phrasing.
- Provide time for students to read aloud to a partner. Ask them to tell their partner about the encyclopedia article. Provide the sentence frame: *This encyclopedia article is about ____.*

Student Book

## Self-Selected Reading

**Content Objective** Read independently
**Language Objective** Orally retell information learned
**Materials** • **Classroom Library** • other fiction books

### APPLY SKILLS TO INDEPENDENT READING

- Have students choose a fiction book for independent reading. (See the **Theme Bibliography** on pages T8–T9 for book suggestions.)
- After reading, ask students to orally summarize the book. Provide time for students to comment on their reactions to the book and share them with classmates. Ask: *Would you recommend this book to a classmate? Why or why not?*

Classroom Library

# English Learners

## Grammar

**Content Objective** Identify compound sentences
**Language Objective** Speak in complete sentences, using sentence frames

TESTED SKILL

### COMPOUND SENTENCES

- Remind students that a compound sentence contains two related sentences joined by *and* or *but*. Review how to combine sentences using a comma followed by *and* or *but*. Write the following sentences on the board: *I want my own room. I have to share with my brothers.* Show students how to combine them into a compound sentence. (*I want my own room, but I have to share with my brothers.)*
- Write sentences on the board, such as those provided below. Have students decide if they should use *and* or *but* to combine the sentence pairs. Have them read the two sentences separately. Then have them say the compound sentence.

  *I was in bed. I could not sleep.*

  *My family helped me clean. They helped me move the furniture.*

  *I got books from the library. I put them in my new room.*

  *It's fun to live here. It gets noisy.*

### PEER DISCUSSION STARTERS

- Write the following sentences on the board.

  Sharing a small house is ____. I learned Frank Lloyd Wright ____.
- Pair students and have them complete each sentence frame. Ask them to expand on their sentences by providing as many details as they can from this week's readings. Circulate, listen in, and take note of each student's language use and proficiency.

### English Learners

UNIVERSAL ACCESS

Build on students' responses to help move them to the next level of language acquisition; for example, if students say, "Sharing a small house is difficult," say, "That's correct. Sharing a small house with many people can be noisy. It can be hard to concentrate on homework or read books. But you always have people to help you and keep you company. Now turn to your partner and tell more about sharing a small house."

Provide the following sentence frames orally or in writing for support.

**Beginning/Early Intermediate** Frank Lloyd Wright was ____.

**Intermediate** Frank Lloyd Wright was an interesting person because ____.

**Early Advanced** Some of Frank Lloyd Wright's designs include ____.

### Transfer Skills

**Sentence Structure** In Hmong, verbs can be connected without *and, but,* or any other conjunction. Students who speak Hmong will therefore often use two or more main verbs in one clause without any connectors; for example, *I want my own room have to share with my brothers.* Write several compound sentences that use *and* or *but* for additional practice. Have students circle the connector and read the sentences aloud.

### Corrective Feedback

During whole group grammar lessons, follow the routine on the **Grammar Transparencies** to provide students with extra support. This routine includes completing the items with English Learners while other students work independently, having students reread the sentences with partners to build fluency, and providing a generative task such as writing a new sentence using the skill.

# English Learners

## Writing/Spelling

**Content Objective** Spell words correctly
**Language Objective** Write in complete sentences, using sentence frames

### VOCABULARY

- Write the key vocabulary words on the board: *separate, determination, storage, exact, ruined, and luckiest*. Have students copy each word on their **WorkBoards**. Then help them say each word and write sentences for each word. Provide sentence starters such as:

  *I had to separate my dog from ____.*

  *She ____ with determination.*

  *We use ____ for storage.*

  *We used a scale to find the exact ____.*

  *The rain ruined ____.*

  *I felt like the luckiest person when ____.*

- Help students spell words using their growing knowledge of English sound-spelling relationships. Model how to segment the word students are trying to spell and attach a spelling to each sound (or spellings to each syllable if a multisyllabic word). Use the **Sound-Spelling Cards** to reinforce the spellings for each English sound.
- Dictate the following words for students to spell: *my, fly, pie, right, like, might, lie, stripe, cry,* and *tight*. Guide students using the Sound-Spelling Cards as they spell each word.
- When completed, review the meanings of words that can be easily demonstrated or explained. Use actions, gestures, and available pictures.

**Sound-Spelling WorkBoard**

### Phonics/Word Study

For English Learners who need more practice with this week's phonics/spelling skill, see the Approaching Level lesson on page 145J. Focus on minimal contrasts, articulation, and those sounds that do not transfer from the student's first language to English. For a complete listing of transfer sounds, see pages T18–T33.

Practice Reader

# English Learners

## Practice Reader

**Content Objective** Read to apply skills and strategies
**Language Objective** Retell information using complete sentences
**Materials**
- **Practice Reader:** *Safe in the Storm*
- **English Learner Resource Book,** p. 65

### BEFORE READING

CA CONTENT STANDARD R 3.2.4 Recall major points in the text and make and modify predictions about forthcoming information.

- **Preview** Read the title *Safe in the Storm*. Ask: *What's the title? Say it again.* Repeat with the author's name. Then page through the book. Use simple language to tell about each page. Immediately follow up with questions, such as: *Where is this family sitting? What time of day do you think it is? Why do you think this man is making a phone call? What are these children building?*
- **Review Skills** Use the inside front cover to review the phonics skill and vocabulary words.
- **Set a Purpose** Say: *Let's read to find out about how to stay safe in a storm.*

### DURING READING

- Have students whisper-read each page, or use the differentiated suggestions below. Circulate, listen in, and provide corrective feedback, such as modeling how to blend a decodable word or clarifying meaning by using techniques from the Interactive Question-Response Guides.
- **Retell** Stop after every two pages and ask students to state the main ideas they have learned so far. Reinforce language by restating students' comments when they have difficulty using story-specific words. Provide differentiated sentence frames to support students' responses and engage students in partner-talk where appropriate.

### English Learners

UNIVERSAL ACCESS

#### Beginning/Early Intermediate

**Echo-Read** Have children echo-read after you.

**Check Comprehension** Point to pictures and ask questions such as: *Do you see the snow? Point to it.*

#### Intermediate

**Choral-Read** Have children choral-read with you.

**Check Comprehension** Ask questions/prompts such as: *Describe what you see in this picture. What is happening on the mountain?*

#### Early Advanced

**Choral-Read** Have children choral-read.

**Check Comprehension** Ask: *What did you learn about staying safe during a blizzard? Read sentences that tell how the hikers kept warm and dry.*

# English Learners

## AFTER READING

CA CONTENT STANDARD LAS 3.1.3 Respond to questions with appropriate elaboration.

**Book Talk** Write the **Book Talk Prompts** below on the board or distribute copies of **English Learner Resource Book** page 65. Students will work with peers of varying language abilities to discuss them. Form groups so that students who read the Beyond Level, On Level, Approaching Level, and English Learner *Safe in the Storm* are in the same group.

Help students determine who will be the Leader for the discussion. Then have students discuss the following:

- **Tell how it is important to work together as a team.**
- **Describe ways in which you can use math to build something.**
- **Explain what you learned about using nature to build something.**
- **Give examples of things kids can build together.**
- **Describe one way that teamwork leads to success.**
- **Write one question about the book to ask your group.**

**Develop Listening and Speaking Skills** Tell students to remember the following:

- Use clear and specific vocabulary to communicate ideas. Suggest they use the weekly vocabulary words in their discussions.
- Take turns speaking and listening. Give everyone a chance to speak.
- Retell, paraphrase, and explain information shared by others.
- Clarify and enhance the discussion through the use of pictures and props. Ask, *how does this picture help you better understand the story?*
- Connect and relate prior knowledge and experiences to ideas brought up in the discussion. Ask, *Have you ever been in a storm? How did you feel?*

CA CONTENT STANDARD LAS 3.1.2 Connect and relate prior experiences, insights, and ideas to those of a speaker.

English Learner Resource Book

### Newcomer

**Survival Skills: Commands and Imperatives** Teach and reinforce basic classroom commands, such as *Sit down; Stand up; Listen, please; Line up; Stop!; Be careful;* and *Take out a pencil.* Model each and have children repeat. Use hand gestures as appropriate; for example, cup your ear when you say *Listen, please.*

# The Big Question

## Big Question Board LAS 3.1.2, LAS 3.1.3, LAS 3.1.5

**WRAP UP** Tell students to add information learned this week related to the unit theme *Personal Experiences: Let's Learn*. Students should record how *My Very Own Room* adds to their growing knowledge of the theme. They should also record any research facts they have uncovered throughout the week or questions they want to explore as they continue reading the selections in the unit. Remind them of the following speaking and listening skills:

- **Speaking** Tell students that when presenting information, they should organize their ideas chronologically, or in the proper sequence. Have them write the numbers 1–5 on a sheet of paper. Then have them write their five main points in the order in which they want to present them. After presenting, prompt the student to ask for questions and answer them with appropriate elaboration.
- **Listening** Tell students to listen carefully and try to connect what they hear to their prior experiences. Provide time for them to share any thoughts or insights that can add to the information shared.

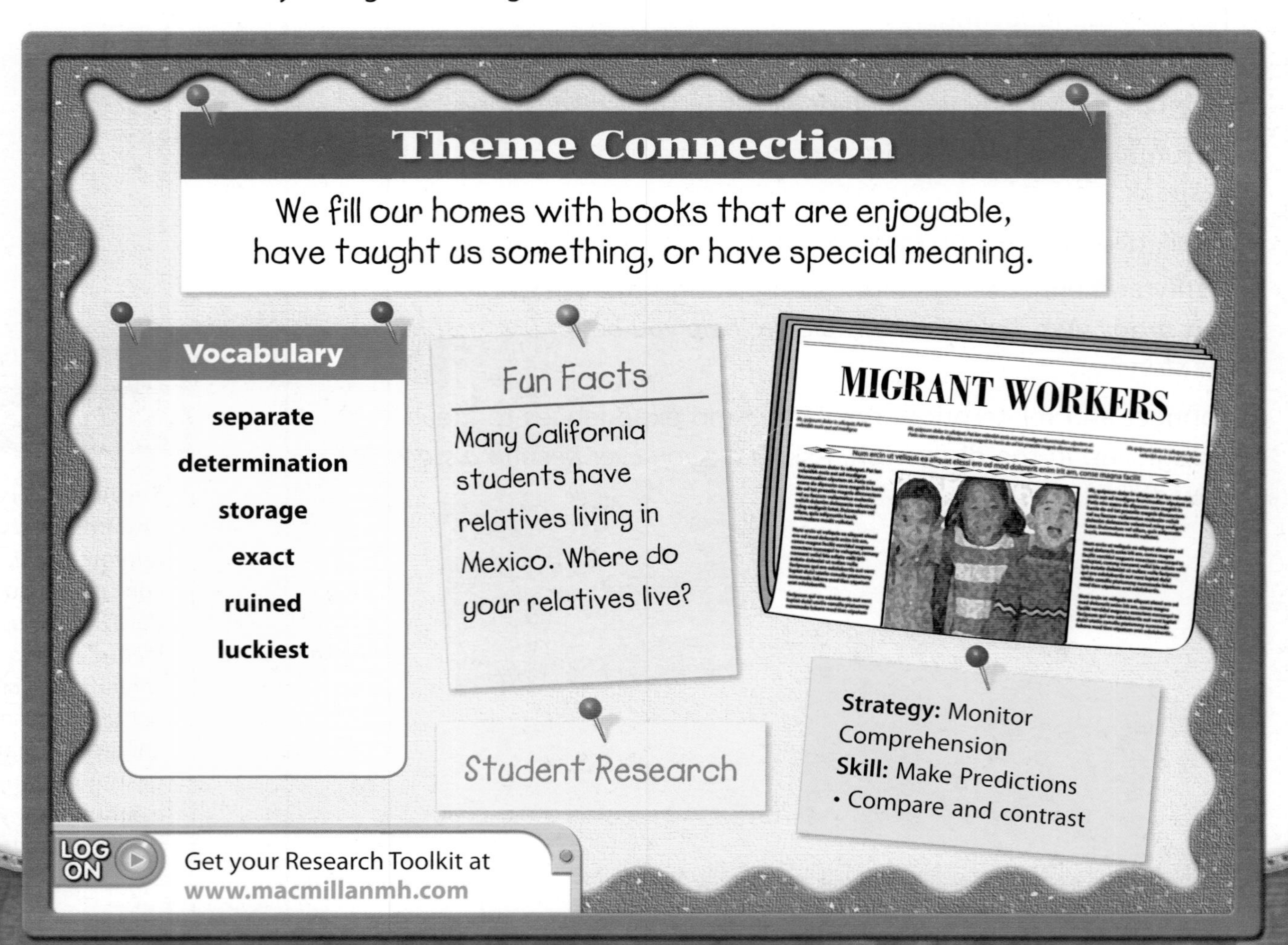

# Week 6 At a Glance

## Review and Assess

### Writing Project
Personal Narrative: Description

Use a Dictionary

### Theme Project
Group Biographical Presentation

Research Strategy: Cite and Record Sources

Listening/Speaking

### Computer Literacy
Using the Internet

Keyboarding Techniques

### Assessment
Show What You Know

## Teacher Tools

Technology to help plan and implement instruction

**PREPARE**
- Professional Development Videos
- Parent Connection

**PLAN/ORGANIZE**

Go to **www.macmillanmh.com** for Online Lesson Planner

**TEACH**
- Unit Launcher Video
- Classroom Presentation Toolkit
- Vocabulary PuzzleMaker
- Sound Pronunciation CD

**ASSESS**

Assessment Online

ExamView® CD-ROM

# Show What You Know

## Spiral Review

CA CONTENT STANDARD R 3.2.3 Demonstrate comprehension by identifying answers in the text.

*Show What You Know* provides a spiral review of selected skills and strategies through Unit 1. After reading fiction and nonfiction selections, students will take short tests that assess reading comprehension in the context of skills and strategies that have been taught.

Before students read, review with them the tips for **Before Reading a Passage** and **Write on Demand** on pages 150 and 151. Then have students read the passages independently on pages 146–149 Have them turn to page 146 in the Student Book and read "Evan's Welcome." Have students complete the **Critical Thinking** questions and record their answers on a separate sheet of paper. Remind them to use the strategies they have learned for answering questions.

## Share Your Thinking

CA CONTENT STANDARD R 3.2.3 Demonstrate comprehension by identifying answers in the text.

After students have completed the assessment, model your own thinking to show them how they can use test-taking and comprehension, vocabulary, and study skills and strategies to arrive at correct answers.

**Question 1 Setting**

*The SETTINGS in this passage are?*

Students can find the answers throughout the story. The story settings are the hallway of the school, a classroom, and a lunchroom. (D)

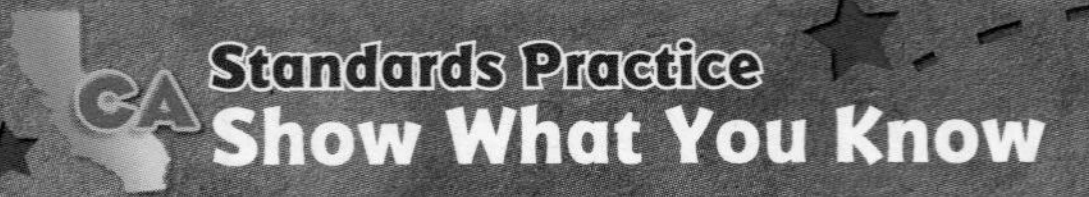

Character, Setting, Plot
Cause and Effect
Main Idea and Details
Prefixes
Bar Graph

# Evan's Welcome

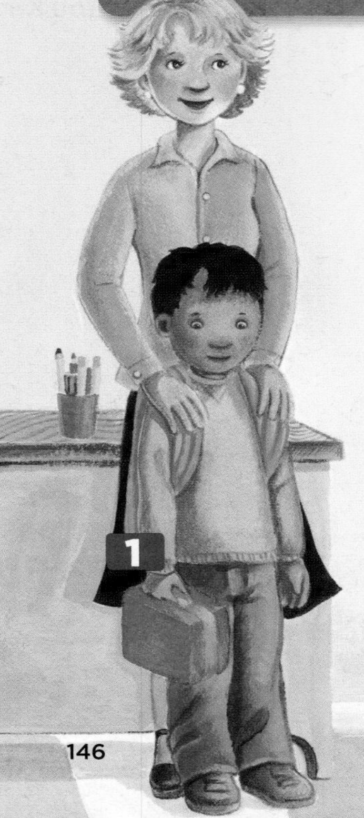


One morning at Northside School, a friendly woman greeted children in the front hallway. Right before classes began, a shy boy walked up to her. She asked the boy his name.

"My name is Evan," he replied as he looked at the ground.

The woman smiled and said, "Welcome to Northside. I'm the principal, Mrs. Bordoni."

"Good morning," said Evan, looking sad.

"I know you are new, but you will like it here," said Mrs. Bordoni. "I will show you the way to your new classroom."

"I didn't want to move … and leave my friends," whispered Evan.

Mrs. Bordoni responded, "I know. You will have friends here, too. You'll see."

She walked him to Room 106 and introduced him to his teacher, Mr. Cortez.

146

### Genre

**Fiction**

Fiction is a made-up story that comes from the author's imagination.

**Setting:** The setting is when and where the story takes place.

**Characters:** The characters are the people, animals, or things that appear in the story.

**Plot:** The plot includes the events, or what happens, in the story. The plots in most stories have a beginning, middle, and an end.

**Theme:** The theme of a story is the central idea or message that the author wants to tell the reader.

“Welcome to our class,” said Mr. Cortez. “We were talking about a story we just read. Who can tell Evan what it was about?”

One of the girls raised her hand and answered, “This family moves to a new state. It’s a funny and sad story.”

Evan seemed to cheer up a bit. He asked, “Did they like the new place?” **3**

Marco answered, “Not at first. But by the end, they made lots of new friends.”

Tom added, “The girl from next door said she needed help. When they got to her house, there was a party and a sign that read *Welcome!*”

“The neighbors really made the family feel welcome,” Mr. Cortez stated.

Later, Mrs. Bordoni returned to walk Evan to lunch. As they entered the lunchroom, Evan spotted a sign inside reading *Welcome Evan!* **1**

Evan smiled. “I can’t believe you did this for me,” he said. Three students in costumes came in carrying a cake that read *Welcome Evan!* Evan asked, “Why are the kids dressed in costumes?”

Mr. Cortez answered, “They are characters in a play. I believe they still need another cat.”

“Could I be the cat?” asked Evan.

“That’s exactly what we were hoping. That way you’ll fit right in!” answered Mrs. Bordoni.

Evan cried, “That’s great! My biggest fear was that I wouldn’t fit in. Thanks!”

Mrs. Bordoni responded, “You’re welcome. Now let’s eat the cake!” **2** **4**

147

## Standards Practice

**Question 2 Plot**

*What happens at the END of the story?*

At the end of the story, Evan says he is excited because he has just gotten the part of a cat in the classroom play with his new classmates. (A)

**Question 3 Cause and Effect**

*What CAUSES Evan to cheer up a bit in the middle of the passage?*

Evan hears about a story that tells how a family moves to a new place and find that they like living there. Evan is interested in the story because he is a new student in this school. It shows him that he can be happy. (C)

**For Question 4, see the Short Response Rubric on Teacher’s Resource Book page 223.**

# Standards Practice

## Share Your Thinking

Have students turn to page 148 in the Student Book and read "Snakes" independently. Have them complete the **Critical Thinking** questions and record their answers on a separate sheet of paper. Remind students to use the strategies they have learned for answering questions.

After students have completed the assessment, model your own thinking to show students how they can use test-taking and comprehension, vocabulary, and study skills and strategies to arrive at correct answers.

CA CONTENT STANDARD R 3.2.5 Distinguish the main idea and supporting details in expository text.

**Question 1 Main Idea and Details**
*When might a rattlesnake shake its tail?*

Help students find the main idea of the third paragraph to answer this question. Point out that it says that the rattlesnake shakes its tail to make a noise as a warning. (C)

**Question 2 Bar Graphs**
*According to the bar graph, about how many species of snakes in California are poisonous?*

Show students how to find the bar in the bar graph that shows the number of poisonous snakes species in California. (C)

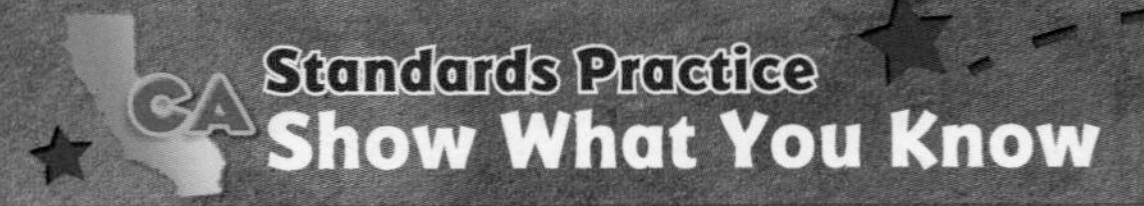


# Snakes!

When you think of a rattle, you probably picture a cute baby toy. However, there is another type of rattle that no one should play with. This is the kind of rattle that you find on a rattlesnake's tail.

Many different kinds of rattlesnakes live in the United States. They live as far north as Maine and Washington State, and as far south as southern Florida. They come in different colors and designs. Most rattlesnakes eat small rodents or lizards. Some types of rattlesnakes can grow to be seven feet long!

If you're on a walk in the desert and you hear a rattle, get moving. The rattler may bite you! Luckily, you probably

A rattlesnake forms a new rattle each time it sheds its skin.

148

### Genre

**Nonfiction**

A nonfiction passage may tell about an event, a person, or a place.

**Introduction** The introduction tells what a nonfiction passage is about.

**Body** The body is the main text of a nonfiction passage. It gives more detail about the topic.

**Conclusion** The conclusion tells the author's ideas about what is the most important lesson in a nonfiction passage.

**Text Features** Text features, such as graphs, directions, pictures and captions, and titles and headings help present information in clear, organized formats that are easy to understand.

California Snake Species

35
30
25
20
15
10
5

Total Number of Species | Poisonous Species

All of California's poisonous snakes are rattlesnakes. Rattlesnake species include the sidewinder and the Mohave rattlesnake. **2**

will never meet a rattlesnake. Rattlers try to avoid humans. In fact, these snakes only attack us if they feel cornered. When a rattlesnake thinks it is in danger, it shakes its tail, or rattle. The noise is a warning sign for others to go away! **1**

Rattlesnakes are only one type of snake. Around the world, there are about 3,000 species of snakes. Unlike rattlesnakes, most are not poisonous. However, even nonpoisonous snakes can be harmful to other animals. Some snakes, such as boa constrictors, are dangerous in other ways. Boa constrictors wind around their prey and squeeze until their prey stops breathing. Other snakes swallow small animals whole. **3**

Snakes have good qualities, too! For example, snakes eat many rats and mice. Rats and mice can spread diseases to humans. If there were no snakes, many more people could get sick from diseases spread by these rodents. So next time you see a snake, remember to respect its qualities, both good and bad! **4**





CA CONTENT STANDARD
R 3.1.8
Use knowledge of **prefixes** and suffixes to determine the meaning of words.

### Question 3 Prefixes

*Read the sentences from paragraph 4 of the article and determine the meaning of the prefix* non- *in the word* nonpoisonous.

Have students reread the fourth paragraph and consider the word nonpoisonous in context. Remind them that a prefix is found at the beginning of a word. Ask them to underline the prefix non- in the word nonpoisonous and to consider what each word part means. The sentences say that most snakes are not poisonous but can still be harmful. The prefix non- means "not." (A)

### Question 4 Cause and Effect

*What is one positive EFFECT snakes have on humans?*

Help students find the paragraph that tells about the good qualities of snakes. Point out the sentences in that paragraph that tell how snakes help humans. Snakes eat many rats and mice, rodents that could make humans sick by spreading diseases. (B)

**For the Write on Demand prompt, see the 4-Point Scoring Rubric on page 151.**

# Critical Thinking

## Before Reading a Passage

**Teach/Model** Before students read the passages in their books, remind them to read the **Critical Thinking** questions. This will help them know what information to look for.

Tell students what they should do the following before they read. Say:

- Read the questions that follow the passage.
- Make sure you understand what each question is asking. You should restate the question your own words.
- Note key parts of the question. Identify key words.

**Practice/Apply** Have students silently read the questions for "Evan's Welcome." Ask: *What is each question asking? What information should you look for as you read?* Guide students to write down important parts of each question as you chorally read them. These include bold or key words, such as **settings** or **cause**. Follow the same routine for "Snakes."

## Critical Thinking

**Now answer numbers 1 through 4. Base your answers on the passage "Evan's Welcome."**

**1. The SETTINGS in this passage are**

A a car, a classroom, and a lunchroom.
B Evan's house and his new school.
C Evan's old school and his new school.
D a school hallway, a classroom, and a lunchroom.

**2. What happens at the END of the story?**

A Evan is excited to be in a play with the other students.
B Evan feels like he doesn't fit in, and wishes he were back in his old school.
C The principal greets Evan.
D His new classmates tell him about a story they read.

**3. What CAUSES Evan to cheer up a bit in the middle of the passage?**

A He sees someone he knows from his old school.
B His mom comes to pick him up early.
C He is interested in the story that the class has just read.
D He gets to eat cake.

**4. How does the principal, Mrs. Bordoni, try to make Evan feel welcome? Use DETAILS and information from the passage to support your answer.**

150

REVIEW

Now answer numbers 1 through 4. Base your answers on the article "Snakes!"

**1.** **When might a rattlesnake shake its tail?**

A When it goes to sleep.
B When it sees a bird.
C When it wants to warn another animal.
D When it recognizes another snake.

**2.** **According to the bar graph, about how many species of snakes in California are poisonous?**

A 50 B 33
C 6 D None

**3.** **Read these sentences from paragraph 4 of the article.**

> Unlike rattlesnakes, most are not poisonous. However, even nonpoisonous snakes can be harmful to other animals.

**In the sentences above, the PREFIX non- means**

A not B very
C against D again

**4.** **What is one positive EFFECT snakes have on humans?**

A They fertilize soil, which helps farmland.
B They eat rodents, which helps stop the spread of disease.
C They entertain us with their dancing.
D Their venom makes tasty drinks.

### Write on Demand

**PROMPT** Should people fear snakes? Why or why not? Use details from the article to support your answer. Write for 5 minutes. Write as much as you can, as well as you can.

151

| WRITE ON DEMAND | | | |
|---|---|---|---|
| 4 Excellent | 3 Good | 2 Fair | 1 Unsatisfactory |
| Writing has more than 7 sentences, almost no spelling or grammar errors, cohesive ideas, is focused and organized. | Writing has 5–7 sentences, a few spelling errors and grammar errors and well developed ideas. | Writing has 4–5 sentences, several spelling and grammar errors, some good information and some vague. | Writing has less than 4 sentences, many spelling and grammar errors, and few developed ideas, or accurate information. |

# Standards Practice

## Write on Demand

Tell students that on some writing tests they will have a limited time to respond to a prompt.

**Prepare to Write** Explain to students that to do well on a timed writing test they should follow these guidelines as they prepare to write.

- Read the prompt carefully and pay attention to what it is asking.
- Organize your writing. You may use a graphic organizer to organize your ideas.
- Use complete sentences that include a subject and a verb. Use correct punctuation.
- Use a variety of sentences.

**After Writing** When students are finished writing, have them use the following questions to evaluate their work:

- Does your writing show an understanding of the selection?
- Did you include examples from the selection to support your response?
- Did you proofread to check for complete sentences and correct grammar and punctuation?
- Did you use a variety of sentences?

## Objectives

- Identify features of a personal narrative
- Plan and organize ideas for a personal narrative
- Draft and revise a personal narrative
- Proofread, publish, and present a personal narrative

### Materials

- Unit Writing Transparencies 12–17

### Features of a Personal Narrative

- It tells about something that happened in the **writer's life**.
- It tells **when** and **where** the event takes place.
- It is written in the **first person,** using words such as *I, us, we,* and *our.*
- It includes **important details** about the topic of the story.
- It expresses the **writer's personal feelings** and tells why the event was memorable.



# Personal Narrative

## Read Like A Writer

CA CONTENT STANDARD
W 3.2.1
Write narratives.

Read aloud the excerpt below from *Pond Street Clubhouse* on **Student Book** page 115. The writer, Sylvia Medrano, talks about building a clubhouse with her father. Explain to students that this story is a personal narrative—a true story a writer tells about a real experience or observation. Ask students to listen for

- **important details** about what happened in **the writer's life**;
- the way the story is told in the **first person**, using words such as *I, us, we,* and *our;*
- **time-order words** the writer uses to tell the order of events;
- the **personal feelings** of the writer.

Pond Street Clubhouse

When the truck left, Dad said, "Good news! We'll be able to build your clubhouse with the leftover wood when the garage is finished."

After a few weeks, it was time to start. A bunch of neighborhood kids came to help.

Dad let us measure the wood. Measuring has to be exact or else the pieces won't fit together. if Dad cut the wood too long or too short, our plans could be ruined. I knew we couldn't buy any extra wood.

When the clubhouse was finally finished, I was so thrilled. I made a sign and nailed it on the door. It said, "Pond Street Clubhouse—Welcome!" Now I have a great place to play. Am I the luckiest kid in town, or what?

## Discuss the Features

After reading, discuss the following questions with students:

- **Who tells the story?** (a first-person narrator who, in this case, is the writer)
- **How do you know?** (the words *I, us, we,* and *our*)
- **What words or phrases does the writer use to show his feelings?** (*thrilled, great place, luckiest kid in town*)
- **How does the writer describe building the clubhouse?** (She describes how the wood had to be cut perfectly.)

# Prewrite

**Set a Purpose** Remind students that one purpose or reason for writing a personal narrative is to share thoughts and feelings about an experience they have had. Another purpose is to entertain the reader.

**Know the Audience** Have students think about who will read their narratives, such as friends, family members, or neighbors. Ask: *Why do you want to share this experience with readers?*

**Choose a Topic** Have students brainstorm ideas about a memorable family trip or self-select a topic. Ask the following questions to help generate story details:

CA CONTENT STANDARD
W 3.2.1.a
Provide a context within which an action takes place.

- Who went on the trip? When and where does your story take place? What happened first? Next? Last?
- How did you feel about the experience? Why do you remember it?
- Remind students to plan and focus their writing by choosing one clear event and details that tell about it.

**Minilesson** Organization and Focus

Display **Transparency 12**. Explain that you will follow Carmen J.'s progress as she develops a personal narrative. With students, point out the following elements on Carmen's Sequence Chart:

- Carmen J. is going to write about something that happened in **her life**. Her narrative includes a clear **main idea**: a family camping trip. She uses **details** that tell about this trip.
- She includes the **first-person words** *I*, *my*, and *me*.
- She uses the **time-order words** *last summer*, *then*, and *next morning* to show the order in which events happened.

**Organize Ideas** Have students create their own Sequence Charts to plan their personal narratives. Use Transparency 12 to demonstrate how to organize ideas.

**Peer Review**

**Think, Pair, Share** Have students discuss their story ideas with partners. As they share their Sequence Charts, ask students to suggest time-order words to strengthen a partner's writing.

**Flexible Pairing Option** Consider pairing each student with a partner who has chosen to write about a similar type of family trip.

**Writing Prompt**
Write about an event that happened in your own life. You might write about a trip you took with your family. Include details about how you felt during your trip. Remember to tell events in the order in which they happened.

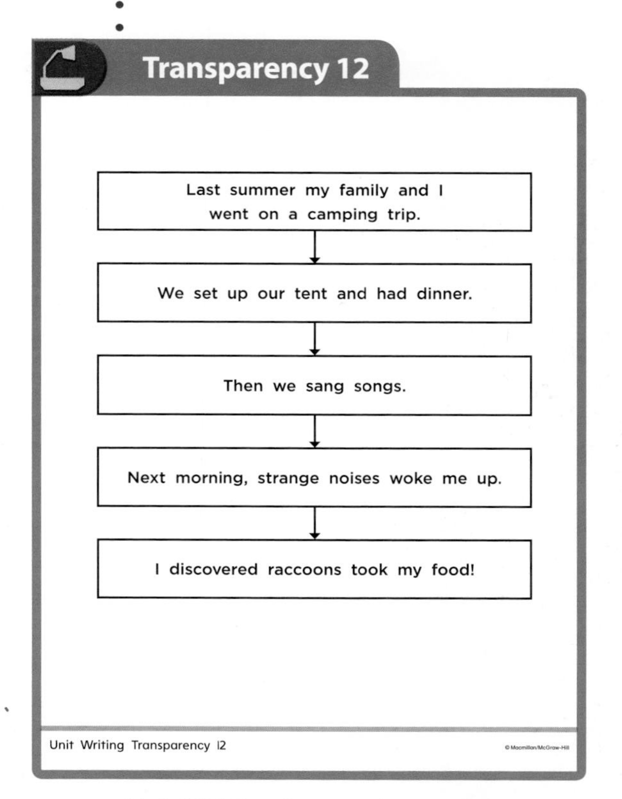


**Unit Writing Process Transparency 12**

# Draft

CA CONTENT STANDARD W 3.2.1.b Include well chosen details to develop the plot.

**Minilesson** Sequence

Display **Transparency 13** and read it with students. As you discuss Carmen J.'s draft, point out the following features:

- When I read this draft, I know that this experience happened in **the writer's life**. Carmen J. writes about *my family and I*.
- The words *I*, *me*, and *my* make it clear that this happened to Carmen. She is writing in the **first person**.
- The **time-order words** *last summer*, *then*, *next morning*, and *finally* help the reader understand what happened and when.
- The words *fun* and *tired* express some of Carmen's **feelings**.

Note that Carmen J. will have the chance to revise and proofread her draft in later stages.

**Review Your Sequence Chart** Have students review their Sequence Charts. Ask them to look back at their charts regularly as they write to help keep their ideas in order.

**Write the Draft** Remind students that their goal in writing a first draft is to get their thoughts on paper. They will have time to revise and proofread their work later. Share the following tips as students begin to write:

CA CONTENT STANDARD W 3.2.1.a Provide a context within which an action takes place.

- Include a clear topic sentence. Tell where and when the story takes place. Choose only important details that tell about this topic.
- Write from the first-person point of view, using the words *I* and *my*.
- Use time-order words to clarify sequence.
- Include words and details that show feelings.

## English Learners

UNIVERSAL ACCESS

**Interactive Writing** Before students write, model the thinking process of writing. Write: *We went on a camping trip. We swam in a lake. We went fishing. It rained. We slept in the car.* Discuss with students how to expand and connect the ideas. Ask questions to prompt them and encourage creative answers: *When did I go? Who did I go with? What happened first? When did it start raining?* Explain your thinking process as you choose sequence words and transition words (*after a while, suddenly, later*) and write the story.

## Transparency 13

**A Camping Surprise**

*by Carmen J.*

Last summer, my family and I went on our first camping trip. we visited a beautiful lake near our town.

We set up our tent and ate dinner. Then, we sang songs. Told stories. I had so much fun! I was really tired when I went to sleep.

The next morning, strange noises woke me up. I saw squirels were dropping acorns on the roof of the tent. Finally, I walked outside. A minute later, I tripped over my backpack. I had left it out by mistake? The raccoons had opened it in the night. They took nuts, fruit, and potato chips.

Unit Writing Transparency 13 © Macmillan/McGraw-Hill

**Unit Writing Transparency 13**

CA CONTENT STANDARD W 3.1.3 Understand the structure and organization of various reference materials.

## Writer's Resources

**Use a Dictionary** Tell students that they can check a word's spelling and meaning in a dictionary. Review the ABC order of a dictionary and the information in a word's entry to help students look up a word. Ask students to brainstorm words that relate to their topics. Then have them look up five of these words in the dictionary to confirm their meanings and spellings.

As students draft, they may wish to circle words they are unsure of and then look them up in a dictionary. They can use this method to correct the spelling or choose a better word, if necessary, when they edit.

## Revise

**Minilesson** Support

CA CONTENT STANDARD W 3.1.4 Revise drafts to improve the coherence and logical progression of ideas by using an established rubric.

Display **Transparency 14** and point out how Carmen J. revises a good story to make it excellent.

- She adds a detail in the first paragraph to focus on her feelings at a particular moment. (Ideas and Content/Genre)
- She ends with an exclamatory sentence to show her feelings in the last paragraph. (Sentence Fluency/Structure)
- She adds the time-order word *first* to make the sequence clear. She also changes general words such as *took* to more precise words such as *stole* to help readers picture events. (Organization and Focus)
- She rearranges a sentence to clarify the order of events. (Organization and Focus)

You may want to note that Carmen will need to proofread her personal narrative to make final corrections.

Have students think about the following writing elements as they evaluate and revise their personal narratives in response to peer and teacher feedback:

CA CONTENT STANDARD W 3.2.1.c Provide insight into why the selected incident is memorable.

**Organization and Focus** Did you write about something that happened in **your own life**? Did you write a clear **topic sentence**? Did you tell why the event you wrote about was memorable? Did you tell events in the correct **sequence**? Does each sentence fit into a **good paragraph**?

**Support** Did you tell your **personal feelings** about the experience? Did you include **time-order words** to help readers understand when events happened? Have you used **first-person words** such as *I* and *my*?

**Conventions** Did you use a **dictionary** to look up definitions and spellings? Are all your sentences complete thoughts with **end punctuation**?

### Peer Review

**Think, Pair, Share** Ask students to read their revised drafts aloud to partners. Suggest that listeners close their eyes and picture the stories. Then listeners should describe the parts they found easy to visualize and hard to visualize.

**Flexible Pairing Option** Consider pairing students who have written a minimal amount with those who have written lengthier stories.

### English Learners

UNIVERSAL ACCESS

**Model Words That Show Emotion** Ask students to identify words and expressions in the model that show the emotions of the author (*excited, fun, tired*). Discuss their meanings. Discuss other expressions and words related to those emotions. Then write emotions that are in students' stories. List and discuss words and expressions related to each emotion. Encourage students to use the new language in their work.

### Transparency 14

**A Camping Surprise**

*by Carmen J.*

Last summer, my family and I went on our first camping trip. we visited a beautiful lake near our town. I was excited about hiking and swimming.

First, We set up our tent and ate dinner. Then, we sang songs. Told stories. I had so much fun! I was really tired when I went to sleep.

The next morning, strange noises woke me up. I saw squirels were dropping acorns on the roof of the tent. Finally, I walked outside. A minute later, I tripped over my backpack. I had left it out by mistake? The raccoons had ~~opened it~~ ripped it open in the night. They ~~took~~ stole nuts, fruit, and potato chips. I will never make that mistake again!

Unit Writing Transparency 14

Unit Writing Transparency 14

Unit 1 Writing

## Speaking and Listening

Have students read their personal narratives aloud. Share these strategies.

**SPEAKING STRATEGIES**

- Present a narrative with context for the event, give insight into the event's importance, and include well chosen details. LAS 3.2.1.a, LAS 3.2.1.b, LAS 3.2.1.c
- Use sensory details to communicate ideas and establish the tone. LAS 3.2.3

**LISTENING STRATEGIES**

- Retell, paraphrase, and explain what has been said by a speaker. LAS 3.1.1
- Connect and relate prior experiences, insights, and ideas to those of the speaker. LAS 3.1.2

# Proofread/Edit

**CA CONTENT STANDARD LC 3.1.1** Understand and be able to use complete and correct declarative, interrogative, imperative, and exclamatory sentences in writing and speaking.

**Minilesson** Conventions

Display **Transparency 15** to point out examples of Carmen J.'s proofreading corrections.

- She capitalizes the word *We* because it begins a sentence and corrects an incomplete sentence by combining it with another sentence. Her sentences are correct and complete.
- She corrects the spelling of the word *squirrels*.
- She changes a question mark to a period to complete an interrogative sentence.

Have students read and reread their narratives to find and correct mistakes. Review the use of proofreading marks on **Teacher's Resource Book** page 224. Have students apply them as they proofread. Remind students to indent the first line in a paragraph.

### Peer Review

**Think, Pair, Share** Have partners review each other's edited drafts to look for errors. Encourage students to pay particular attention to correcting sentence fragments.

**TEACHER CONFERENCE**

Address individual students with the following questions to foster self-assessment. Ask: *How did you show your feelings in your story? How did you let readers know that this experience happened in your own life? What time-order words have you included?*

## Transparency 15

**A Camping Surprise**

*by Carmen J.*

Last summer, my family and I went on our first camping trip. we visited a beautiful lake near our town. I was excited about hiking and swimming.

First, We set up our tent and ate dinner. Then, we sang songs. and Told stories. I had so much fun! I was really tired when I went to sleep.

The next morning, strange noises woke me up. I saw squirels were dropping acorns on the roof of the tent. Finally, I walked outside. A minute later, I tripped over my backpack. I had left it out by mistake? The raccoons had opened it ripped it open in the night. They took stole nuts, fruit, and potato chips. I will never make that mistake again!

Unit Writing Transparency 15



**Unit Writing Transparency 15**

# Publish

**CA CONTENT STANDARD W 3.1.2** Write legibly in cursive or joined italic, allowing margins and correct spacing between letters in a word and words in a sentence.

Ask students to write legibly in cursive or type a final copy of their personal narratives. Remind students, if they write in cursive, to use appropriate margins and spacing between letters in a word and words in a sentence. Encourage students to publish one of their other weekly writing assignments.

**PRESENTATION** Ask students to bring print or digital photographs, home video recordings, or slides to share during presentations.

**Author's Chair** Invite students who have written strong narratives to read from the Author's Chair.

# Raising Scores

CA CONTENT STANDARD W 3.1.4 Revise drafts to improve the coherence and logical progression of ideas by using an established rubric.

**READ AND SCORE**

Display **Transparency 16** and invite a volunteer to read it aloud. Then have students use the student rubric for Personal Narrative on **Teacher's Resource Book** page 225 to assess the writing sample. Guide students to understand that this personal narrative is only a fair writing sample, which would score only a 2, and that they will work together in groups to improve it.

**RAISE THE SCORE**

Point out the following shortfalls in the writing sample:

**Organization and Focus** The writer has attempted to tell a story about a car trip, but the key events lack focus. Some details belong in a different story. Since this is a narrative, the writer needs to include more details about his feelings. Several events are told out of order.

**Ideas and Content** The writer could use more time-order words to clarify the sequence of events. The writer also needs to use precise words about his experience to help readers picture events.

Ask students to work in small groups to revise the personal narrative to raise the score. Remind them to refer to the student rubric.

**SHARE AND COMPARE**

Have groups share their revised versions with the class, explaining how they improved the writing. Then display **Transparency 17** to show the same story written at an excellent level. Have each group compare its revised version with the transparency. Remind students that although the two versions vary, they may both be considered excellent papers. Then have students review their own personal narratives to raise their scores.

## Objective

- **Revise a personal narrative to raise the writing score from a 2 to 4**

**CREATE A RUBRIC**

Distribute copies of the blank rubric form on page 232 in the Teacher's Resource Book. Remind students that the rubric should assess whether or not the personal narrative focuses on the topic, is logically organized, includes ample development of supporting ideas, and demonstrates a strong command of language and conventions.

**Transparency 17**

**Jen's Car Trip**

*by Larry C.*

During Thanksgiving, my family drove to Springfield to visit my Grandpa. I was sitting in the back seat with Jen, my baby sister. I knew there would be trouble. She hates her car seat!

First, she cried. I tried singing and playing her favorite tapes. She just kept on crying. Next she threw her stuffed toys at me. A frog landed on my head! Nothing my parents said could get Jen to stop throwing things.

Finally, Dad climbed in the back seat with us. I was amazed! Jen fell asleep right away. After that, I had a great trip! Mom, Dad, and I talked the whole way. I gave Jen a big kiss when she woke up.

Unit Writing Transparency 17

**Unit Writing Transparency 17**

# 4-Point Narrative Writing Rubric

Use this four-point rubric to assess student writing.

| SCORING RUBRIC FOR PERSONAL NARRATIVE | | | |
|---|---|---|---|
| 4 Excellent | 3 Good | 2 Fair | 1 Unsatisfactory |
| **Ideas and Content/ Genre** Creates a clear account of a personal experience; includes the writer's thoughts and feelings | **Ideas and Content/ Genre** Relates a personal experience; includes some thoughts and feelings about the events | **Ideas and Content/ Genre** Relates a personal experience; includes few if any thoughts and feelings about the event | **Ideas and Content/ Genre** Does not share a personal experience; includes no thoughts or feelings about the event |
| **Organization and Focus** Details unfold in a logical easy-to-follow way; transitions are effective; maintains a consistent focus throughout | **Organization and Focus** Details unfold in a logical way; most transitions are effective; maintains a focus throughout | **Organization and Focus** Few details told in a logical order; little use of transitions; focus is inconsistent | **Organization and Focus** Details are not logical; there is no organization or focus, no use of transitions |
| **Voice** Relates events in the first person; clearly expresses the writer's personality, thoughts, and feelings | **Voice** Events told mostly in the first person; somewhat expresses the writer's personality, thoughts, and feelings | **Voice** Strays from the first person; conveys insufficient amount of feeling | **Voice** Not in first person; does not express the feelings or personality of the writer |
| **Word Choice** Uses time-order words; and precise and colorful words to add sensory details | **Word Choice** Uses time-order and space-order words; includes precise words | **Word Choice** Does not use enough time-order or clarify the order of events; does not use precise words | **Word Choice** Uses words that do not fit the order of events or are confusing to the reader |
| **Sentence Structure/ Fluency** Writes complete sentences; ideas flow logically and cohesively | **Sentence Structure/ Fluency** Writes complete sentences; ideas follow a logical pattern | **Sentence Structure/ Fluency** Writes mostly complete sentences; reader may have to reread in order to follow the meaning | **Sentence Structure/ Fluency** Constructs incomplete, rambling, or confusing sentences; text is hard to follow |
| **Conventions** Narrative is mostly free of errors; uses proper end punctuation and capitalization | **Conventions** Some errors in spelling, capitalization, punctuation, or usage; little or no errors in end punctuation and capitalization | **Conventions** Numerous errors interfere with a smooth reading of the text; needs significant editing | **Conventions** Makes severe errors in most or all conventions; some parts of the text are impossible to follow or understand |
| **Presentation** Text is easy to read whether word-processed or handwritten; white space is uniform | **Presentation** Text is readable; spacing is mostly uniform | **Presentation** Text is readable but variations in size slant, or font are distracting | **Presentation** Text is difficult to read due to slant, font, or size; spacing is uneven |

**Portfolio**

Tell students to place their finished narratives in their portfolios. Remind students that portfolios should include more than just finished work. Then have them review and evaluate their personal collection of work to determine progress and set goals for improvement. They can also discuss their work with teachers and parents/ caregivers. Have them jot down ideas for future writing assignments or what they learned about personal narrative to include in their portfolios.

## Write-on-Demand Rubric

Use this rubric to assess short and extended responses.

### WRITE-ON-DEMAND SCORING RUBRIC

**PROMPT** **Why is important for people to tell about their personal experiences? Write as much as you can as well as you can. Write for 5 minutes.**

| 4 Excellent | 3 Good | 2 Fair | 1 Unsatisfactory |
|---|---|---|---|
| • More than 7 sentences<br>• Almost no spelling or grammar errors<br>• Cohesive ideas, focused and organized | • 5–7 sentences<br>• A few spelling and grammar errors<br>• Well-developed ideas and facts provided | • 4–5 sentences<br>• Several spelling and grammar errors<br>• Some good information; some vague | • 1–3 sentences<br>• Many spelling and grammar errors<br>• Few developed ideas or accurate information |

## Anchor Papers

Use these Anchor Pages in the **Teacher's Resource Book** to evaluate student writing.

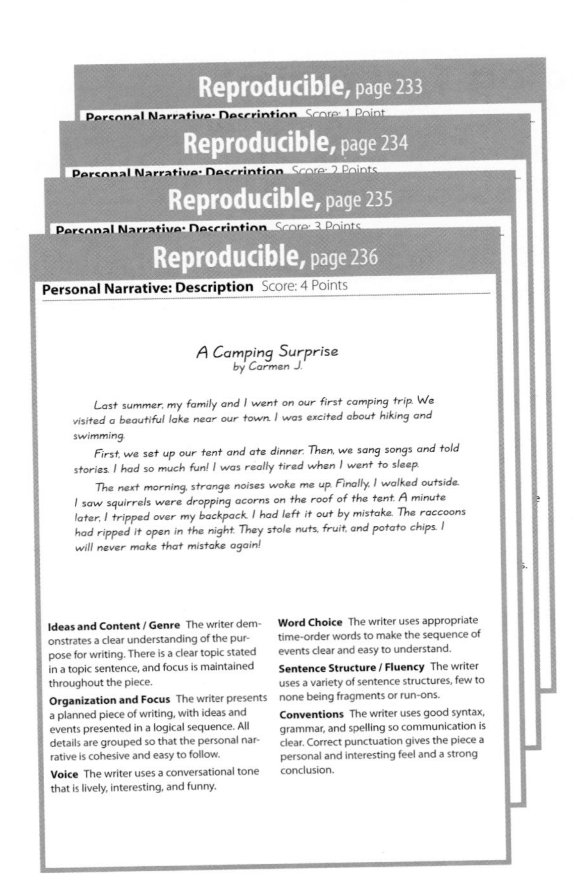

**Reproducible,** page 233

**Personal Narrative: Description** Score: 1 Point

**Reproducible,** page 234

**Personal Narrative: Description** Score: 2 Points

**Reproducible,** page 235

**Personal Narrative: Description** Score: 3 Points

**Reproducible,** page 236

**Personal Narrative: Description** Score: 4 Points

*A Camping Surprise*
*by Carmen J.*

*Last summer, my family and I went on our first camping trip. We visited a beautiful lake near our town. I was excited about hiking and swimming.*

*First, we set up our tent and ate dinner. Then, we sang songs and told stories. I had so much fun! I was really tired when I went to sleep.*

*The next morning, strange noises woke me up. Finally, I walked outside. I saw squirrels were dropping acorns on the roof of the tent. A minute later, I tripped over my backpack. I had left it out by mistake. The raccoons had ripped it open in the night. They stole nuts, fruit, and potato chips. I will never make that mistake again!*

**Ideas and Content / Genre** The writer demonstrates a clear understanding of the purpose for writing. There is a clear topic stated in a topic sentence, and focus is maintained throughout the piece.

**Organization and Focus** The writer presents a planned piece of writing, with ideas and events presented in a logical sequence. All details are grouped so that the personal narrative is cohesive and easy to follow.

**Voice** The writer uses a conversational tone that is lively, interesting, and funny.

**Word Choice** The writer uses appropriate time-order words to make the sequence of events clear and easy to understand.

**Sentence Structure / Fluency** The writer uses a variety of sentence structures, few to none being fragments or run-ons.

**Conventions** The writer uses good syntax, grammar, and spelling so communication is clear. Correct punctuation gives the piece a personal and interesting feel and a strong conclusion.

# Using the Internet

## Objectives

- Learn about the Internet and other digital tools
- Access Web pages by entering URLs, using links, and using search engines
- Practice keyboarding techniques

### Materials

- www.macmillanmh.com

## Vocabulary

**Web browser** a program that allows a person to explore and view documents on the World Wide Web

**home page** a Web page that acts like the table of contents in a book to introduce a Web site

**URL (Uniform Resource Locator)** the location or address of a Web page that starts with the abbreviation http://

**hypertext link** an electronic link from a point in one document to a point in another

**home keys** on the keyboard are A, S, D, and F for the left hand and J, K, L, for the right hand

### ACCESS PRIOR KNOWLEDGE

Discuss with students:

- What is the Internet? (a network of computers that electronically connects people around the world)
- How have you used the Internet?

### EXPLAIN

Introduce the lesson vocabulary by writing each word on the board and asking for its definition.

- Tell students that a **Web browser** is used to enter the World Wide Web and a **home page** is the first Web page of a site.
- The address at the top of the home page is a **URL**. URLs start with the abbreviation http:// followed by the address.

### MODEL

- Show students how to open the home page of their Internet browser.
- Then show them how to link to a new Web page using a **hypertext link**.

## Keyboarding Techniques

- Explain that a keyboard is a device used to key or type information into a computer.
- The most effective way to type is by keeping the fingers on the **home keys**. Have students place their fingers on the home keys.
- Practice having students key in a sentence. Point out that they should use their little finger to hold down the shift key for capital letters.

**GUIDED PRACTICE**

Have students connect to **www.macmillanmh.com** and go to **Computer Literacy Lesson Grade 3 Unit 1**.

The online practice lesson is an excerpt from SRA TechKnowledge. For information about the full SRA TechKnowledge program, go to **www.sratechknowledge.com**

## Students with Instructional Needs

There are a variety of ways for students with special instructional needs to use materials and demonstrate their competence (e.g., physically forming letters for students who have dyslexia or who have difficulties writing legibly or spelling words). Modifications can be made so students have access to the materials. Examples of modifications might include student use of computers to complete pencil and paper tasks, use of on-screen scanning keyboards, enlarged keyboards, word prediction, and spellcheckers.

Remind students never to give their names, addresses, phone numbers, or e-mail addresses to anyone on the Internet.

# Theme Project Wrap-Up

## Research and Inquiry

**CA CONTENT STANDARD LAS 3.2.2** Plan and present dramatic interpretations of experiences, stories, poems, or plays with clear diction, pitch, tempo, and tone.

After students complete Step 1, Step 2, Step 3, and Step 4 of their projects, have them work on the following:

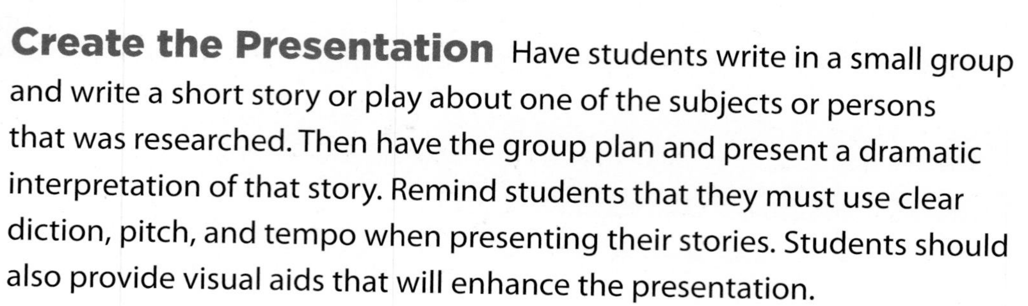

**Step 5 Create the Presentation** Have students write in a small group and write a short story or play about one of the subjects or persons that was researched. Then have the group plan and present a dramatic interpretation of that story. Remind students that they must use clear diction, pitch, and tempo when presenting their stories. Students should also provide visual aids that will enhance the presentation.

**Step 6 Review and Evaluate** Use these questions to help you and students evaluate their research and presentations.

## Teacher's Checklist

### Assess the Research Process

**Planning the Project**

✔ Participated in identifying a subject to research.

✔ Identified places to find resources.

✔ Identified information sources.

**Doing the Project**

✔ Used electronic and print text sources.

✔ Cited sources correctly.

✔ Helped to create a short story or play about the topic.

### Assess the Presentation

**Speaking**

✔ Used clear and specific vocabulary to communicate ideas and establish a tone.

✔ Used complete sentences.

✔ Enhance the presentation through the use of props.

**Representing**

✔ Organized ideas chronologically or around major points of information.

✔ Delivered information with a clear beginning, middle, and end.

### Assess the Listener

**Listening**

✔ Listened quietly and politely.

✔ Retold what happened in the presentation.

✔ Held questions and comments until the speaker had finished.

## Student's Checklist

### Research Process

✔ Where did you find the most helpful information?

✔ Did you give credit to all your sources?

### Presenting

**Speaking**

✔ Did you use clear and specific vocabulary to communicate?

✔ Did you speak loudly enough for everyone to hear you?

**Representing**

✔ Did you choose appropriate visual props?

✔ Did you use visuals to help your audience understand your ideas?

| SCORING RUBRIC FOR THEME PROJECT | | | |
|---|---|---|---|
| 4 Excellent | 3 Good | 2 Fair | 1 Unsatisfactory |
| The student<br>• presents information or ideas clearly.<br>• includes lively and relevant details.<br>• may make sophisticated observations. | The student<br>• presents information or ideas adequately.<br>• provides adequate details.<br>• makes relevant observations. | The student<br>• attempts to present information or ideas.<br>• may offer few or vague details.<br>• may make few or irrelevant personal observations. | The student<br>• may not grasp the task.<br>• may present irrelevant information.<br>• may have extreme difficulty with research or presentation. |

### Home-School Connection

Invite family members, adult friends, and other students to the performances of the plays.

- Introduce guests to the school by name and describe their relationship to the students.
- Videotape the performances for family members to borrow or to show at parent/teacher conferences. Have students view and evaluate the videos, including how well the production works on film and determine what kind of message it sends.

# Monitoring Progress

## Administer the Test

| UNIT 1 UNIT ASSESSMENT |
|---|
| **TESTED SKILLS AND STRATEGIES** |
| **READING COMPREHENSION** |
| • Strategies: Analyze story structure, make inferences and analyze, summarize, generate questions, monitor comprehension<br>• Skills: cause and effect, main idea and details, compare and contrast, make and confirm predictions |
| **LITERARY RESPONSE AND ANALYSIS** |
| • Character, Setting, Plot |
| **WORD ANALYSIS/VOCABULARY** |
| • Short vowels, Final *e*, Long *a*, Long *o*, Long *i* |
| • Word parts; prefixes *un-*, *non-* and suffixes *-er*, *-est*, word families, thesaurus: synonyms, dictionary: multiple-meaning words |
| • Spelling |
| • Selection vocabulary |
| **WRITTEN USAGE/CONVENTIONS** |
| • Statements and questions: capitalization and punctuation in statements and questions |
| • Commands and exclamations: punctuation in commands and exclamations |
| • Subjects: correct sentences (sentence fragments) |
| • Predicates: complete sentences (sentence fragments and run-ons) |
| • Compound sentences: punctuate compound sentences |
| **WRITING STRATEGIES** |
| • Personal Narrative |
| **ORAL FLUENCY** |
| • Words read correct per minute (WCPM) |

## Using Multiple Assessments for Instructional Planning

To create instructional profiles for your students, look for patterns in the results from any of the following assessments.

### Progress Monitoring Unit Assessment

This test covers all domains and strands in the content standards. Multiple questions and next-step information are provided. Use the results for regrouping decisions.

### Unit Fluency Assessment

Gather results from the fluency tests administered throughout the unit to plan appropriate fluency-building activities and practice.

### Summative Assessment

Administer tests two times a year as an additional measure of both student progress and the effectiveness of the instructional program.

Progress Reporter

**Assessment Online**
- Administer the **Unit Assessment** electronically.
- Score all tests electronically.
- Prescriptions for Reteaching
- Student Profile System

**ExamView® CD-ROM**

| Diagnose | | Prescribe |
|---|---|---|
| **Review the assessment answers with students. Have them correct their errors. Then provide additional instruction as needed.** | | |
| | **IF...** | **THEN...** |
| **READING COMPREHENSION** | 0–7 items correct . . . | Reteach skills: **Intervention Kit**<br>Online Practice: Go to **www.macmillanmh.com**. |
| **LITERARY RESPONSE AND ANALYSIS** | 0–7 items correct . . . | Reteach skills: **Intervention Kit** |
| **WORD ANALYSIS/ VOCABULARY WORD** | 0–7 items correct . . . | Reteach skills: **Intervention Kit**<br>Online Practice: Go to **www.macmillanmh.com**. |
| **WRITTEN USAGE/ CONVENTIONS**<br><br>**WRITING STRATEGIES** | 0–7 items correct . . . | Reteach skills: **Intervention Kit** |
| **FLUENCY** | 55-60 WCPM<br><br>0–54 WCPM | Fluency Solutions Audio CD |

## WRITE-ON-DEMAND SCORING RUBRIC

**PROMPT** **What kinds of things can you learn from books? Use what you learned in the unit to answer the prompt. Write as much as you can as well as you can. Write for 15 minutes.**

| 4 Excellent | 3 Good | 2 Fair | 1 Unsatisfactory |
|---|---|---|---|
| • More than 7 sentences<br>• Proper capitalization and end punctuation<br>• Most words spelled correctly<br>• Clear ideas presented | • 5–7 sentences<br>• Proper capitalization and end punctuation<br>• A few spelling errors<br>• Ideas fairly clear | • 4–5 sentences<br>• Missing capitalization and end punctuation<br>• Some spelling errors<br>• Ideas somewhat clear | • 1–3 sentences<br>• Missing both capitalization and end punctuation<br>• Many spelling errors<br>• No clear ideas presented |

CA CONTENT STANDARD
W 3.1.3
Understand the structure and organizaiton of various reference materials.

# Glossary

Introduce students to the Glossary by reading through the introduction and looking over the pages with them. Ask the class to talk about what they see.

Words in a glossary, like words in a dictionary, are listed in **alphabetical order**. Point out the **guide words** at the top of each page that tell the first and last words appearing on that page.

## ENTRIES

Point out examples of **main entries**, or entry words, and entries. Read through a sample entry with the class, identifying each part. Have students note the order in which information is given: entry word(s), syllable division, pronunciation respelling, part of speech, definition(s), example sentence(s).

Note if more than one definition is given for a word, the definitions are numbered. Note the format used for a word that is more than one part of speech.

Review the **parts of speech** by identifying each in a sentence:

| ***Inter.*** | ***article*** | ***n.*** | ***conj.*** | ***adj.*** | ***n.*** |
|---|---|---|---|---|---|
| Wow! | A | dictionary | and | useful | glossary |

| ***v.*** | ***adv.*** | ***pron.*** | ***prep.*** | ***n.*** |
|---|---|---|---|---|
| tell | almost | everything | about | words! |

## HOMOGRAPHS/HOMOPHONES/HOMONYMS

Point out that some entries are for multiple-meaning words called **homographs**. Homographs have the same spellings but have different origins and meanings, and, in some cases, different pronunciations.

Explain that students should not confuse homographs with **homophones** or **homonyms**. Homophones are words that have the same pronunciation but have different spellings and meanings. Homonyms are words that have the same pronunciation and spelling but have different meanings. Provide students with examples.

## PRONUNCIATION KEY

Explain the use of the pronunciation key (either the short key, at the bottom of every other page, or the long key, at the beginning of the Glossary). Demonstrate the difference between primary stress and secondary stress by pronouncing a word with both. Pronounce the words both correctly and incorrectly to give students a clearer understanding of the proper pronunciations.

## WORD HISTORY

The Word History feature explains the **etymology** of select words. Explain that etymology is the history of a word from its origin to its present form. A word's etymology explains which language it comes from and what changes have occurred in its spelling and/or meaning. Many English words are derivatives of words from other languages, such as Latin or Greek. Derivatives are formed from base or root words.

# Glossary

## What Is a Glossary?

A glossary can help you find the **meanings** of words in this book that you may not know. The words in the glossary are listed in **alphabetical order**. **Guide words** at the top of each page tell you the first and last words on the page.

Each word is divided into syllables. The way to pronounce the word is given next. You can understand the pronunciation respelling by using the **pronunciation key** at the right. A shorter key appears at the bottom of every other page. When a word has more than one syllable, a dark accent mark (ˊ) shows which syllable is stressed. In some words, a light accent mark (ˊ) shows which syllable has a less heavy stress. Sometimes an entry includes a second meaning for the word.

potential

equipment



**Guide Words**
First word on the page — Last word on the page

## Sample Entry

Main entry & Syllable division — Pronunciation — Part of speech — Definition — Example sentence

**sketch•es** (skech´əz) *plural noun.* Simple drawings that are done quickly. *I made several* ***sketches*** *before finally painting the tree.*

## Pronunciation Key

| Phonetic Spelling | Examples | Phonetic Spelling | Examples |
|---|---|---|---|
| a | at, bad, plaid, laugh | d | dear, soda, bad |
| ā | ape, pain, day, break | f | five, defend, leaf, off, cough, elephant |
| ä | father, calm | g | game, ago, fog, egg |
| âr | care, pair, bear, their, where | h | hat, ahead |
| e | end, pet, said, heaven, friend | hw | white, whether, which |
| ē | equal, me, feet, team, piece, key | j | joke, enjoy, gem, page, edge |
| i | it, big, give, hymn | k | kite, bakery, seek, tack, cat |
| ī | ice, fine, lie, my | l | lid, sailor, feel, ball, allow |
| îr | ear, deer, here, pierce | m | man, family, dream |
| o | odd, hot, watch | n | not, final, pan, knife, gnaw |
| ō | old, oat, toe, low | ng | long, singer |
| ô | coffee, all, taught, law, fought | p | pail, repair, soap, happy |
| ôr | order, fork, horse, story, pour | r | ride, parent, wear, more, marry |
| oi | oil, toy | s | sit, aside, pets, cent, pass |
| ou | out, now, bough | sh | shoe, washer, fish, mission, nation |
| u | up, mud, love, double | t | tag, pretend, fat, dressed |
| ū | use, mule, cue, feud, few | th | thin, panther, both |
| ü | rule, true, food, fruit | th | these, mother, smooth |
| u̇ | put, wood, should, look | v | very, favor, wave |
| ûr | burn, hurry, term, bird, word, courage | w | wet, weather, reward |
| ə | about, taken, pencil, lemon, circus | y | yes, onion |
| b | bat, above, job | z | zoo, lazy, jazz, rose, dogs, houses |
| ch | chin, such, match | zh | vision, treasure, seizure |





# Aa

**ac•cept•ance** (ak sep´təns) *noun.* An agreement to take something given or offered. *My sister learned of her* ***acceptance*** *to college yesterday.*

**ached** (ākt) *verb.* To have had a dull and steady pain. *Hannah's tooth* ***ached*** *all day, so she went to the dentist.*

**ad•mire** (ad mīr´) *verb.* To respect or think well of someone or something. *The team had to* ***admire*** *the coach for never giving up.*

**ad•ven•ture** (ad ven´chər) *noun.* An exciting, unusual, or risky experience. *Lisa and her mom went on a camping* ***adventure*** *this past summer.*

**Word History**
**Adventure** comes from Latin *adventura*, meaning "a thing about to happen."

**an•ces•tors** (an´ses tərz) *plural noun.* People who lived before you in your family. *Jorge's* ***ancestors*** *once lived in an old castle in Spain.*

**an•i•ma•tors** (an´ə mā´tərz) *plural noun.* Artists or technicians who draw and produce cartoons. *Many* ***animators*** *today use computers to bring their drawings to life.*

**an•nounced** (ə nounst´) *verb.* Told something in a loud or official way. *The winners of the writing contest were* ***announced*** *at the assembly.*

**an•nu•al** (an´ū əl) *adjective.* Happening once a year. *Every July 4, my family holds an* ***annual*** *family reunion.*

**ap•pli•ances** (ə plī´əns əz) *plural noun.* Small machines or devices that have particular uses, such as toasters, refrigerators, and washing machines. *The store was crowded because of the sale on kitchen* ***appliances***.

**au•di•tions** (ô dish´ənz) *plural noun.* Trial performances. *The actor had three* ***auditions*** *before being rewarded with the part.*





# Bb

**batch•es** (bach´əz) *plural noun.* Groups of things prepared or gathered together. *Tracey and Darryl made several* ***batches*** *of cookies for the bake sale at the library.*

**blos•somed** (blos´əmd) *verb.* Grew or developed. *The student kept practicing until she* ***blossomed*** *into a wonderful violinist.*

**both•er•ing** (both´ər ing) *verb.* 1. Giving people trouble or annoying them. 2. Taking the time to do something. *1. Henry's need to talk while watching TV was* ***bothering*** *Maria. 2. My dad said no without even* ***bothering*** *to look up from the paper.*

**busi•ness** (biz´nis) *noun.* 1. The work a person does to earn a living. 2. The buying and selling of things; trade. *1. Kenneth worked in the fashion* ***business*** *for eight years. 2. The kite shop does good* ***business*** *in the summer.*

# Cc

**cap•ture** (kap´chər) *verb.* To catch and hold a person, animal, or thing. *The park rangers were trying to* ***capture*** *the bear that was roaming the picnic area.*

**chuck•led** (chuk´əld) *verb.* Laughed in a quiet way. *When the plan worked, Calvin* ***chuckled*** *to himself.*

**cit•i•zen** (sit´ə zən) *noun.* A person who lives in a community and has rights and duties. *Each* ***citizen*** *in our town has the right to vote for a mayor.*

**civ•i•li•za•tions** (siv´ə lə zā´shənz) *plural noun.* Groups of people sharing a way of life in a specific place or time. *Historians study ancient* ***civilizations*** *to learn how people lived in the past.*

at; āpe; fär; câre; end; mē; it; īce; pîerce; hot; ōld; sông; fôrk; oil; out; up; ūse; rüle; pu̇ll; tûrn; chin; sing; shop; thin; this; hw in white; zh in treasure.

The symbol ə stands for the unstressed vowel sound in about, taken, pencil, lemon, and circus.



# Glossary

Glossary



**com•mu•ni•cate** (kə mū′ni kāt′) *verb.* To pass along or exchange information, thoughts, or ideas. *It is difficult to **communicate** with people who do not listen.*

**com•mu•ni•ty** (kə mū′ni tē) *noun, pl.* **com•mu•ni•ties.** 1. A group of people who live together in the same place. 2. A group of people who share a common interest. *1. Our **community** voted to build a new library. 2. The scientific **community** is involved in important research projects.*

**con•cen•trate** (kon′sən trāt′) *verb.* To pay attention or think very carefully about something being done. *If the radio is on, I find it hard to **concentrate** on anything else.*

**con•struc•tion** (kə n struk′shən) *noun.* The act or process of building something. *It was interesting to watch the **construction** of our town's new grocery store.*

**con•trib•ute** (kən trib′yūt) *verb.* To give, or supply along with others. *The club organizers asked members to **contribute** several hours of their time, to help with the special event.*

**crack•le** (krak′əl) *verb.* To make a series of small, sharp snapping noises. *I like to hear the burning wood **crackle** in the fireplace.*

**cul•ture** (kul′chər) *noun.* Characteristics, beliefs, and behaviors of a social group. *The travelers were excited to experience the country's **culture**.*

## Dd

**de•mand** (di mand′) *noun.* An urgent requirement or need. *Katie knew there was a **demand** for blankets at the dog shelter.*

**den** (den) *noun.* 1. A place, often underground or in a cave, where wild animals live. 2. A small, cozy room for reading or studying. *1. The bears crawl into their **den** each winter for a long sleep. 2. Jane studies at her computer in the **den**.*





**de•serve** (di zûrv′) *verb.* To have a right to something. *I believe I **deserve** to be on the soccer team because I practiced after school and on weekends.*

**de•ter•mi•na•tion** (di tûr′mə nā′shən) *noun.* A firm purpose. *Miguel's **determination** made him study very hard to get the best test score in the class.*

**dis•ap•pear** (dis′ə pîr′) *verb.* To stop existing or become extinct. *Elephants began to **disappear** because so many people hunted them for their tusks.*

**do•nate** (dō′nāt) *verb.* To give or offer. *Every winter my family will **donate** winter clothes we no longer wear.*

## Ee

**en•clo•sure** (en klō′zhər) *noun.* A place that is surrounded by a fence or wall on all sides. *The animals were kept in an **enclosure** until their owners came to pick them up.*

**e•quip•ment** (i kwip′mənt) *noun.* Anything that is provided for a special purpose or use. *The firefighters showed the class all the different **equipment** they have and how it is used.*

**es•tab•lished** (i stab′lishd) *verb.* To have set up permanently. *The colony was **established** in 1734.*

**es•ti•mate** (es′ tə māt′) *verb.* To approximate. *Greg asked the sailmaker to **estimate** the amount of canvas that would be needed to sew a new sail.*

**ex•act** (eg zakt′) *adjective.* Very accurate. *I need to know the **exact** time because I can't be one minute late.*

at; āpe; fär; câre; end; mē; it; īce; pîerce; hot; ōld; sông; fôrk; oil; out; up; ūse; rüle; pu̇ll; tûrn; chin; sing; shop; thin; th͟is; hw in white; zh in treasure.

The symbol ə stands for the unstressed vowel sound in about, taken, pencil, lemon, and circus.





**ex•cite•ment** (ek sīt′mənt) *noun.* A feeling of being happy because something good has happened or will happen. *The class was full of **excitement** before the show began.*

**ex•pen•sive** (ek spen′siv) *adjective.* Costing a lot of money. *A wonderful gift does not have to be **expensive**.*

**ex•plor•ing** (ik splôr′ing) *verb.* Searching for purpose of discovery. *Amy has been **exploring** her new neighborhood since her family moved.*

## Ff

**fan•tas•tic** (fan tas′tik) *adjective.* 1. Very unusual. 2. Splendid. *1. The artist's favorite drawings were of mythical and **fantastic** animals. 2. Emily's flute playing was **fantastic**.*

**fo•cus** (fō′kəs) *verb.* 1. An adjustment to produce a clear image. 2. A point of attention. *1. A good photographer will always **focus** carefully before snapping the picture. 2. My coach always reminds me to **focus** on the ball before swinging.*

**form** (fôrm) *noun.* 1. A body or figure. 2. The state in which something exists. 3. A document that requires information to be added. *1. Although it was foggy, the **form** of a tall figure could be seen. 2. Jello is meant to be eaten in its solid **form**, not liquid. 3. Before the dentist would see me, I had to fill in a **form**.*

**fum•bled** (fum′bəld) *verb.* Tried to get hold of or handled in a clumsy way. *I **fumbled** around in the dark for my glasses.*





**func•tion** (fungk′shən) *noun.* The proper action or purpose of something. *The **function** of the heart is to pump blood through the body.*

## Gg

**ge•o•met•ric** (jē′ə met′rik) *adjective.* 1. Of or relating to geometry. 2. Made up or decorated with lines, angles, triangles. *1. The triangle is a **geometric** form. 2. The rug had **geometric** patterns.*

**Word History**

**Geometric** is a combination of *ge* "earth, land" and *metria,* from Greek *metrein,* "to measure."

**grum•bled** (grum′bəld) *verb.* Complained in a low voice. *The class **grumbled** when the teacher gave them a lot of homework to do over the holiday.*

## Hh

**harm•ing** (här′ming) *verb.* Doing damage to or hurting. *The construction company was told that it was **harming** the environment, because it cut down so many trees.*

## Ii

**il•lus•trate** (il′ə strāt′) *verb.* To draw a picture or diagram; to explain or decorate something written. *The art teacher helped me **illustrate** my story.*

at; āpe; fär; câre; end; mē; it; īce; pîerce; hot; ōld; sông; fôrk; oil; out; up; ūse; rüle; pu̇ll; tûrn; chin; sing; shop; thin; th͟is; hw in white; zh in treasure.

The symbol ə stands for the unstressed vowel sound in about, taken, pencil, lemon, and circus.

**im•ages** (im'ijz) *plural noun.* Pictures of persons or things. *I still have **images** in my head of the beautiful sunset at the beach.*

**Word History**

Image comes from the Latin *imago*, or *imitari*, "to imitate."

**im•mi•grants** (im'i grənts) *plural noun.* People who move from one country to live in another. *Most **immigrants** to the United States passed through Ellis Island.*

**im•proved** (im prüvd') *verb.* Made or became better. *Her singing ability has greatly **improved** since last year.*

**Word History**

Improve is from the Middle English *improwen*, "to enclose land for farming," and from Anglo-Norman *emprouwer*, "to turn to profit."

**in•flu•enced** (in'flü ənsd) *verb.* Changed or affected behavior or thought. *Sam **influenced** his sister to read the same comic book.*

**in•no•cent** (in'ə sənt) *adjective.* Not guilty; harmless. *The puppy looked **innocent**, but we knew she knocked over the cup.*

**in•stance** (in'stəns) *noun.* An occurance. *The witness recalled an **instance** when the door was left unlocked.*

## Ll

**laws** (lôz) *plural noun.* Sets of rules that tell people in a community how to behave. *Drivers must obey certain safety **laws**.*

**leak•y** (lē'kē) *adjective.* Having a hole or small opening that water, light, or air can pass through. *The **leaky** hose caused a big puddle whenever I tried to water the plants.*

**lone•some** (lōn'səm) *adjective.* Not often visited by people; deserted. *The **lonesome** house in the swamp was a sad sight.*

**luck•i•est** (luk'ē est) *adjective.* Having or bringing the most good luck. *Of all the contest winners, James was the **luckiest**; he won the grand prize.*

## Mm

**mem•bers** (mem'bərz) *plural noun.* Persons, animals, or things belonging to a group. *The **members** of the basketball team met at the park every Thursday to practice.*

## Nn

**na•tion** (nā'shən) *noun.* A group of people who live in one land and share the same government, laws, and language. *Our **nation** celebrates a national holiday on July 4.*

**need•y** (nē'dē) *adjective.* Being in a position of want. *My family adopted the **needy** kitten that appeared on our door step.*

**nerv•ous** (nûr'vəs) *adjective.* Not able to relax; tense or fearful. *Barking dogs make my aunt **nervous**.*

**Word History**

Nervous comes from the Latin word *nervosus*, meaning "sinewy" or "containing nerves."

**non•sense** (non'sens) *noun.* Words or actions that are silly and make no sense. *The talk about a monster in the closet was **nonsense**.*

at; āpe; fär; câre; end; mē; it; īce; pîerce; hot; ōld; sông; fôrk; oil; out; up; ūse; rüle; pull; tûrn; chin; sing; shop; thin; this; hw in white; zh in treasure. The symbol ə stands for the unstressed vowel sound in about, taken, pencil, lemon, and circus.





**no•ticed** (nō'tisd) *verb.* Became aware of. *Keith was not **noticed** until he raised his hand to ask the question.*

## Oo

**off•spring** (ôf'spring') *plural noun.* The young of a person, animal, or plant. *A lioness and her three **offspring** approached the water hole, frightening off the other animals.*

**or•gan•i•za•tion** (ôr'gən i zā'shən) *noun.* A group of persons united for a particular purpose. *Katheryn joined that **organization** because she believed in their goal for a cleaner environment.*

**own•ers** (ō'nərz) *plural noun.* People who possess something. *The **owners** of the new store put out a sign to advertise.*

## Pp

**pas•sion** (pash'ən) *noun.* A very strong feeling or liking for something. *Love is a **passion**, and so is anger.*

**po•lite•ly** (pə līt'lē) *adverb.* In a way that shows good manners or consideration for others' feelings. *When my friend arrived, he greeted my parents **politely**.*

**po•ten•tial** (pə ten'shəl) *noun.* The possibility to become something more. *The runners had great **potential**, but they would have to practice more.*

**pre•served** (pri zûrvd') *verb.* Protected from harm. *Mr. Smith built a fence around the sapling so it would be **preserved**.*

**proj•ect** (proj'ekt') *noun.* A plan or proposal. *The class **project** took several weeks to complete.*

**prop•er** (prop'ər) *adjective.* Correct or suitable for a certain purpose. *My brother showed me the **proper** way to tie a necktie.*

**pro•tect** (prə tekt') *verb.* To defend from harm. *Mr. Trang used an umbrella to **protect** himself from the rain.*





## Rr

**re•cord**[1] (ri kôrd') *verb.* To preserve. *The audio technician prepared to **record** the musician's new song.*

**re•cord**[2] (re kərd') *noun.* An account preserved. *The accountant kept a **record** of the company's transactions.*

**rent** (rent) *1. noun. 2. verb.* 1. Payment for the use of property. 2. To lease. *1. Henry and Mike split the **rent** evenly. 2. When we go on vacation this year, we will **rent** a cabin rather than stay in a hotel.*

**rep•u•ta•tion** (rep'yə tā'shən) *noun.* What most people think of a person or thing. *Micheline's **reputation** as a speller has gotten better since she won the spelling bee.*

**ru•ined** (rü'ind) *verb.* Damaged greatly or harmed. *The flood **ruined** all our carpets in the basement.*

## Ss

**script** (skript) *noun.* 1. The text of a play, movie, or television show. 2. A style of writing using cursive characters. *1. The **script** wasn't very long, so it would be easy for her to memorize the lines. 2. The boy had not learned how to write **script**, so he printed the words instead.*

**Word History**

Script comes from Latin *scribere*, meaning "to write."

**sep•a•rate** (sep'ə rāt') *verb.* To set apart or place apart. *After the big fight, we had to **separate** the cat and the dog and put them in different rooms.*

**ser•vi•ces** (sûr'vis əz) *plural noun.* A variety of tasks or acts done for others, usually for pay. *The car wash provided other **services**, such as dusting and vacuuming inside the car.*

at; āpe; fär; câre; end; mē; it; īce; pîerce; hot; ōld; sông; fôrk; oil; out; up; ūse; rüle; pull; tûrn; chin; sing; shop; thin; this; hw in white; zh in treasure. The symbol ə stands for the unstressed vowel sound in about, taken, pencil, lemon, and circus.

**side•walks** (sīd′wôks) *plural noun.* Paths by the side of the street or road, usually made of cement. *Vladimir and Bill were paid to shovel snow off the* ***sidewalks*** *around their apartment building.*

**sin•gle** (sing′gəl) *adjective.* One. *Not a* ***single*** *person knew about the event.*

**sketch•es** (skech′əz) *plural noun.* Simple drawings that are done quickly. *I made several* ***sketches*** *before finally painting the tree.*

**slo•gan** (slō′gən) *noun.* A phrase, statement, or motto. *Today our teacher asked us to think up a* ***slogan*** *for our science club.*

**soared** (sôrd) *verb.* Flew high in the air. *The hawk* ***soared*** *above the meadow.*

**spar•kling** (spär′ kəl ing) *verb.* Shining or giving off sparks. *The water was* ***sparkling*** *in the sunlight.*

**splen•did** (splen′did) *adjective.* Very good or beautiful. *Some birds have* ***splendid*** *feathers of many colors.*

> **Word History**
>
> The word **splendid** comes from the Latin *splendere*, "to shine."

**star•ry** (stär′ē) *adjective.* Full of stars or heavenly bodies that shine by their own light. *The* ***starry*** *sky made the nighttime seem bright.*

**stor•age** (stôr′ij) *noun.* A place for keeping things for future use. *Mr. Chen used his garage mainly for* ***storage****.*

**sto•ry•board** (stôr′ē bôrd′) *noun.* A series of drawings or sketches that shows how the action of a film or video will be shot. *According to the* ***storyboard****, there would be a lot of special effects in the next scene.*

**style** (stīl) *noun.* A particular way of saying or doing something. *Every singer has his or her own* ***style****.*

> **Word History**
>
> A long time ago, the word **style** meant "a pen," which came from the Latin *stylus*, "a pointed instrument used for writing."

**suc•cess** (sək ses′) *noun.* A favorable achievement. *The rocket launch was a complete* ***success****.*

**sug•ges•tions** (səg jes′chənz) *plural noun.* Ideas or plans offered for others to think about. *The artist made* ***suggestions*** *for ways to improve Arthur's painting.*

**sup•ply** (sə plī′) *noun.* An amount of something needed or available for use. *We had a* ***supply*** *of candles and batteries in the closet in case of an emergency.*

## Tt

**tal•ent•ed** (tal′ən tid) *adjective.* Having a natural ability or skill. *I didn't know Curtis was such a* ***talented*** *pianist.*

**tech•nol•o•gy** (tek nol′ə jē) *noun.* 1. The use of science for practical purposes, especially in engineering and industry. 2. Methods, machines, and devices that are used in doing things in a science or profession. *1. Medical* ***technology*** *has helped doctors to diagnose illnesses. 2. The artist used new* ***technology*** *to improve her computer graphics.*

at; āpe; fär; câre; end; mē; it; īce; pîerce; hot; ōld; sông; fôrk; oil; out; up; ūse; rüle; pu̇ll; tûrn; chin; sing; shop; thin; <u>th</u>is; hw in white; zh in treasure.

The symbol ə stands for the unstressed vowel sound in about, taken, pencil, lemon, and circus.





**tex•tures** (teks′chərz) *plural noun.* The way a surface looks or how it feels when you touch it. *Fabrics have many* ***textures****, from silky to rough.*

**3-D** (thrē′dē′) *adjective.* Three-dimensional. *The images on the computer created the illusion of being* ***3-D****.*

**thrilled** (thrild) *verb.* Filled with pleasure or excitement. *The team members were* ***thrilled*** *when they heard they had won the championship.*

**tour** (tôr) *noun.* A trip or journey in which many places are visited or many things are seen. *The guide led a* ***tour*** *through the museum and explained all the famous artwork.*

**trad•ers** (trā′dərz) *plural noun.* People who buy and sell things as a business. *The* ***traders*** *went to the settlers to sell them blankets and clothes.*

**tra•di•tion•al** (trə dish′ ə nəl) *adjective.* Coming from established customs. *On holidays, it is* ***traditional*** *for the Lee family to wear nice clothing at dinner.*

**trudged** (trujd) *verb.* Walked slowly and with effort. *The children* ***trudged*** *up the snowy hill to go sledding.*

## Uu

**un•a•ware** (un′ə wâr′) *adjective.* Not conscious of. *The bird was* ***unaware*** *of the cat watching it.*

**use•ful** (ūs′fəl) *adjective.* Helpful; serving a good use or purpose. *My mom always tells me to make myself* ***useful*** *by helping others.*

## Vv

**vol•un•teers** (vol′ən tîrz′) *plural noun.* People who offer to do things by choice and often without pay. *Several* ***volunteers*** *showed up to help clean up the park and paint the fence.*





## Ww

**wailed** (wāld) *verb.* Made a long and sad cry, especially to show grief or pain. *The baby* ***wailed*** *when she dropped her toy.*

**wrap•ping** (rap′ing) *noun.* Paper or other material used to cover or protect something. *Aunt Marie likes to see pretty* ***wrapping*** *on a present.*

at; āpe; fär; câre; end; mē; it; īce; pîerce; hot; ōld; sông; fôrk; oil; out; up; ūse; rüle; pu̇ll; tûrn; chin; sing; shop; thin; <u>th</u>is; hw in white; zh in treasure.

The symbol ə stands for the unstressed vowel sound in about, taken, pencil, lemon, and circus.

# Additional Resources

Additional Resources

Additional Resources

# Contents

# Instructional Routines

## Professional Development

- Read the routine prior to using *California Treasures*. Use the Routine QuickNotes as a reminder of key routine steps throughout Unit 1, or as needed.
- View the online classroom video clip through **TeacherWorks Plus**. Watch master teachers use these routines.

1. **Phonological Awareness/ Phonemic Awareness**
   Rhyme
   Oddity Tasks
   Sound Categorization
   Oral Blending
   Oral Segmentation
   Manipulation
2. **Phonics**
   Blending
   Introducing Sound-Spelling Cards
   Letter Recognition
   Building Words
   Building Fluency
   Reading Decodables
   Multisyllabic Words/Routine
3. **Fluency**
   Strategies
4. **Vocabulary**
   Define/Example/Ask Routine
   Strategies
5. **High-Frequency Words**
   Read/Spell/Write Routine
   Reading Pre-decodables
6. **Spelling**
   Dictation
7. **Comprehension**
   Strategies
   Skills
   Reading Big Books
   Reading Student Book
8. **Grammar, Usage, and Mechanics**
   AAVE Modifications
9. **Writing**
   Conferences
   Revision Assignments
   Writing Process
   Using Rubrics
   Using Anchor Papers
   Writers' Express Sequence
10. **Research Process**
    Big Question Board
11. **Classroom Management**
    Workstation Flip Charts
    Contracts
    Centers
    Small Groups
12. **Listening/Speaking/Viewing**
13. **Assessment**

Classroom Library

## Objectives

- Monitor comprehension
- Identify main ideas and details
- Identify cause and effect

**Genre** Biography

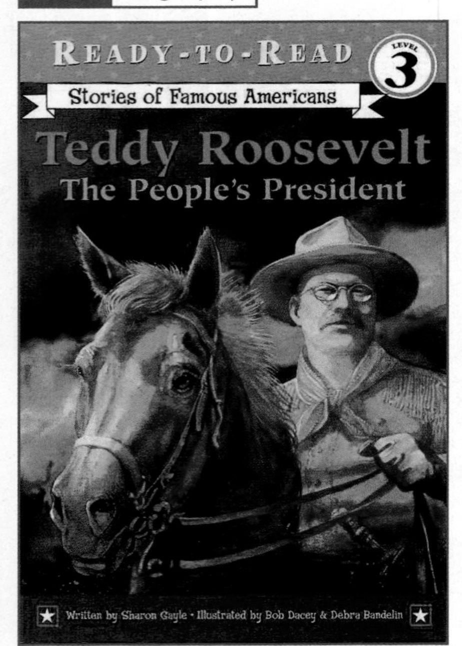


Approaching Level

## Summary

This biography profiles the life of Teddy Roosevelt, the twenty-sixth President of the United States. Readers learn how a young man of poor health became a strong and respected leader.

**FYI for your information**

Teddy Roosevelt overcame a childhood of sickness to become the twenty-sixth President of the United States. He was police commissioner of New York City before assembling the Rough Riders and fighting in Cuba during the Spanish-American War. He became a national hero during the war and was soon elected governor of New York. Next he was elected Vice President under William McKinley. Roosevelt became President after McKinley was assassinated in September 1901.

# Teddy Roosevelt: The People's President

by Sharon Gayle

## Before Reading

### BUILD BACKGROUND

Explain what the Office of the President is. Point out that a President and a Vice President are elected by the citizens of the United States. Explain that if a President cannot do the job, then the Vice President becomes the President. Brainstorm a list of facts about the President and the presidency. Ask:

- *Who is the current President of the United States? Who is the current Vice President?*
- *Why might a President be unable to fulfill the duties of the presidency?*

### PREVIEW AND SET PURPOSES

Ask students to look at the cover, read the title, name the author, and look at the illustrations. Explain that this is a biography, which tells the true story of a real person's life. Then have students set a purpose for reading, such as to find out why Roosevelt is called the "people's President."

## During Reading

### APPLY COMPREHENSION SKILLS AND STRATEGIES

Students can read this book in smaller, more manageable sections as suggested below. For each section Think Alouds and discussion questions are provided. Use these to review comprehension strategies and skills taught in this unit.

Chapter 1

**STRATEGY**
**MONITOR COMPREHENSION**

**Teacher Think Aloud** I should stop after each section to make sure I understand what I have just read. I can reread to look for the most important information. The first chapter is about how sick Theodore Roosevelt was as a child and how he overcame it. When he was eighteen, he entered Harvard University. I will stop after each chapter and then reread and look for the main ideas to make sure I understand what I have read.

CA CONTENT STANDARD R 3.2.5 Distinguish the main ideas and supporting details in expository text.

**Main Idea and Details** How did Teddy change from a weak child to a strong, healthy eighteen-year-old? (First he lived outdoors in Maine. Then Teddy began to exercise daily.)

Chapter 2

**STRATEGY**
**MONITOR COMPREHENSION**

**Teacher Think Aloud** I don't understand why the Rough Riders yelled "Remember the *Maine*." I'll stop and try to figure it out by rereading pages 19 and 20, looking for the word *Maine*. On page 19, I see that a battleship called the *Maine* blew up, and the Americans blamed the Spanish. On page 20, I see that the Rough Riders yelled "Remember the *Maine*!" as they attacked the Spanish army. This cry reminded them why Spain was their enemy.

**Cause and Effect** What terrible things happened in one day in 1884 that caused Roosevelt to move West? (His wife and mother both died.)

Chapter 3

**STRATEGY**
**MONITOR COMPREHENSION**

**Teacher Think Aloud** I want to stop and make sure I understand what I have read. One way I can do this is by paraphrasing, or putting into my own words, what I read. I can paraphrase the first page of the third chapter like this: Teddy Roosevelt became President when President McKinley was assassinated.

**Main Idea and Details** What details show Teddy Roosevelt's concern for wildlife? Why was this important? (He made sure that many animals and birds were protected. He once released a bear cub that had been tied to a tree. This was important because many animals or birds might have otherwise become extinct.)

## After Reading

**LITERATURE CIRCLES**

Use page 267 in the **Teacher's Resource Book** to review Listening and Speaking guidelines for discussion. Have students discuss the book in small groups, using questions such as these:

- *Who was Teddy Roosevelt? Why was he famous?*
- *How did Roosevelt's experience in the Spanish-American War with the Rough Riders lead to his becoming President?*

### Write About It

What if Teddy Roosevelt were still alive? Have students write an invitation to him asking him to speak to the class about an important event in his life. Review the parts of a formal letter with students, including the date, greeting, body, closing, and signature.

## Connect to Standards

**Presidential Biography**

Have students find out more about Theodore Roosevelt and write their own short biographies. Let students share these biographies in groups.

CA CONTENT STANDARD
**HSS 3.4.6** Describe the lives of American heroes who took risks to secure our freedoms.

Classroom Library

Classroom Library

## Objectives

- Make inferences and analyze
- Summarize
- Make and confirm predictions
- Understand character, plot, and setting

**Genre** Historical Fiction

On Level

## Summary


Ten-year-old Frederika tells about the year Miss Agnes came to her Athabascan village in Alaska to be the town's one and only schoolteacher.


**FYI for your information**

Set in Alaska in 1948, this book gives a child's view of life in a small Alaskan Native American village. The families depend on the rivers and the woods for food—whole families leave town during winter and summer to gather food. The book provides wonderful descriptions of the clothing and other items people make.

# The Year of Miss Agnes

by Kirkpatrick Hill

## Before Reading

**BUILD BACKGROUND**

Explain that in the past, in some parts of the country, a school had just one teacher who taught all subjects to all of the children. Brainstorm a KWL chart about what students know about schoolhouses. Ask students:

- *What do you see in your mind when you think of a one-room schoolhouse?*
- *What might be some of the advantages and disadvantages of going to school in one room with all the kids in town?*

**PREVIEW AND SET PURPOSES**

Have students look at the cover illustration and read the title. Read a page or two aloud to give students a sense of what the book might be about. Then have them set a purpose for reading, such as to find out whether Miss Agnes is a good teacher.

## During Reading

**APPLY COMPREHENSION SKILLS AND STRATEGIES**

Following are suggestions for dividing the reading into manageable sections. For each section, Think Alouds and discussion questions are provided. Use these to review comprehension strategies and skills taught in this unit.

Chapters 1-6

**STRATEGY**
**MAKE INFERENCES AND ANALYZE**

CA CONTENT STANDARD R 3.2.2 Ask questions and support answers by connecting prior knowledge with literal information found in, and inferred from, the text.

**Teacher Think Aloud** I know that I have to use what I read and what I know to understand more than the author tells me. As I read descriptions of the village, the new teacher, and the schoolhouse, I can infer that this town is small and far away from other towns and that the people are poor. I will look for more information about the people and the way they live. I can use this information to make more inferences about what living in this village was like. Making predictions helps me to understand plot development.

CA CONTENT STANDARD R 3.2.4 Recall major points in the text and make and modify predictions about forthcoming information.

**Make and Confirm Predictions** The village gets a new schoolteacher because the last one did not stay. Make a prediction. Do you think Miss Agnes will stay for long? (Readers' predictions will vary. At least the fish smell will not cause Miss Agnes to leave, since she has sinus problems and cannot even smell the fish. )

Chapters 7–11

**STRATEGY**
**SUMMARIZE**

**Teacher Think Aloud** I want to stop and summarize what has happened so far before I read on. Miss Agnes is the new teacher at the village school, and she is teaching the kids all kinds of new things. The kids really like her, and she thinks every child should go to school, even Bokko, who is deaf.

CA CONTENT STANDARD R 3.3.3 Determine what characters are like by what they say or do and by how the author or illustrator portrays them.

**Character, Setting, Plot** What does Miss Agnes do for Bokko? What does this show about her character? (She convinces Bokko and Fred's mother to let Bokko to come to school. Then Miss Agnes teaches the class sign language. This shows that she cares about her students and wants to give Bokko a chance to learn.)

Chapters 12-17

**STRATEGY**
**MAKE INFERENCES AND ANALYZE**

**Teacher Think Aloud** I learn that the kids leave school at times to go and help their families catch and dry fish. I can infer that because of their poverty, finding food is more important for these families than going to school. Making inferences or predictions helps me to see the plot.

**Make Predictions** Miss Agnes plays a record of the King's Choir in England and tells how pretty the flowers are there. Fred thinks Miss Agnes will stay only one year. What do you predict will happen? (Answers will vary. Miss Agnes does plan a trip to England, but returns the next year, surprising the students.)

## After Reading

**LITERATURE CIRCLES**

Use page 267 in the **Teacher's Resource Book** to review Speaking and Listening guidelines for discussion. Have students discuss the book in small groups, using questions such as these:

- *Based on the descriptions in this book, what do you think it was like to be a child growing up in this village in 1948?*
- *Why do you think Miss Agnes leaves the map and the pictures on the wall at the end of the school year?*

## Write About It

Reread pages 21 and 22 aloud, focusing on the descriptions of the mittens and boots Mamma sews. Point out phrases that help readers "see" the mittens, pom-poms, and boots in their minds. Then have students choose an object to describe. Tell them to use descriptive words to tell about the object so that someone who has never seen one can understand what it looks like. Remind students to use complete sentences and to check their writing for end punctuation.

## CA Connect to Standards

**Maps**

Miss Agnes shows her students a map of Alaska and helps them locate places they know. Have students find a map of their state and locate their town. Partners can locate lakes, rivers, mountains, and other physical features of their state. Then ask them to locate Alaska and England to see how far away from home Miss Agnes was.

CA CONTENT STANDARD HSS 3.1.1 Identify geographical features in their local region.

Classroom Library

## Objectives

- Analyze story structure
- Monitor comprehension
- Understand cause and effect

**Genre** Folktale

Beyond Level

## Summary

Elena wants to be a glassblower like her father, but girls can't be glassblowers. Or can they? To prove they can, Elena sets off for Monterrey, where the best glassblowers live. She helps many creatures along the way with the use of her glassblowing pipe. When she gets to Monterrey, she misses her father, so she blows out a large bird-shaped piece of glass and rides it all the way back home.

**FYI for your information**

Glassblowers can make glass bottles, figurines, and other creations by heating glass until it melts. They twirl the melted glass onto the end of a glassblowing pipe and blow into the pipe while the glass is still in liquid form. They set the finished glass into a pile of sand to cool.

# Elena's Serenade

by Campbell Geeslin

## Before Reading

**BUILD BACKGROUND**

Explain that folktales are stories that are passed down from one generation to another. Unrealistic events and objects often play a part in folktales. Brainstorm a list of fantastic happenings in folktales. Ask students:

- *What folktales can you name that have fantastic happenings?*
- *Do all folktales have these elements? Do you think that unrealistic occurrences are a necessary element of folktales?*

**PREVIEW AND SET PURPOSES**

Have students look at the cover, read the title, and scan the illustrations. Discuss with students what the book may be about. Have each student set a purpose for reading, such as to find out what a serenade is.

## During Reading

**APPLY COMPREHENSION SKILLS AND STRATEGIES**

Students may want to read this book in one sitting. Use the Think Alouds and discussion questions to review comprehension strategies and skills taught in this unit.

**STRATEGY**
**SUMMARIZE**

Pages 1–6

**Teacher Think Aloud** I know that it is important to understand how a story is written. So far I am learning about a girl who wants to be a glassblower. Her father says she cannot do it because she is a girl. This sounds like a problem to me. Then Elena leaves for the city of Monterrey, where the best glassblowers in the world live. So I think she will try and solve her problem as the story goes on.

**Cause and Effect** What causes Elena to leave home? Why does she wear boys' clothing? Where does she go? (She wants to be a glassblower, but her father will not let her because she is a girl. So she dresses up like a boy and goes to Monterrey, where she can learn how to blow glass.)

Pages 7–16

## STRATEGY
### MONITOR COMPREHENSION

**Teacher Think Aloud** One way I monitor my comprehension is by visualizing, or picturing, what I am reading. When I read "Burro lies down and I use him as a pillow," I form a picture in my mind of what the characters are doing and how they look. If Elena uses Burro as a pillow, he is probably soft and comfortable to lean on. Visualizing helped me monitor my comprehension in this part of the story.

CA CONTENT STANDARD R 3.2.4 Recall major points in the text and make and modify predictions about forthcoming information.

**Make and Confirm Predictions** After Elena meets the coyote, she tries to teach him to sing. Predict whether you think she will be successful. Why or why not? (She has already found the burro with her song and taught a roadrunner to run so she will probably be successful with the coyote.)

Pages 17–end

## STRATEGY
### SUMMARIZE

**Teacher Think Aloud** At the start of the story, Elena has a problem. She wants to be a glassblower. As the story continues, she tries to solve her problem by going to Monterrey, where the best glassblowers live. In the end she solves her problem by showing her father that she can blow glass. Paying attention to the plot helped me find the problem and solution.

CA CONTENT STANDARD R 3.3.3 Determine what characters are like by what they say or do and by how the author or illustrator portrays them.

**Character, Setting, Plot** Recall the events of the plot, telling what happens at the beginning, middle, and end. Tell where these events take place. (First Elena leaves home because she wants to be a glassblower. Next she meets various animals, whom she helps with songs from her pipe. Then she works for a glassblower in Monterrey and makes glass stars. Finally she flies home, showing her father that she can blow glass.)

## After Reading

**LITERATURE CIRCLES**

Use page 267 in the **Teacher's Resource Book** to review Speaking and Listening guidelines for a discussion. Have students discuss the book in small groups. Ask:

- *Do you think this story is realistic? Why or why not?*
- *Why does Elena go to Monterrey? Do you think she should have gone? What would you have done?*

## Write About It

Have students write a journal entry from the point of view of one of the characters from *Elena's Serenade*. Make sure students write their entries as though they really are the character, using first-person pronouns. Have students reread their writing to see that they have various types of sentences.

## Additional Readings

| | UNIT 1 | |
|---|---|---|
| **By the Authors and Illustrators**<br>For additional information on authors, illustrators, and selection content, go to **www.macmillanmh.com**. | **Danneberg, Julie.** ***First Year Letters.*** **Charlesbridge, 2003.** A teacher's first year is related in a series of humorous letters through short notes written by her students and colleagues.<br>ON LEVEL | **Hoffman, Mary.** ***Starring Grace.*** **Frances Lincoln Children's Books. 2000.** Grace leads her friends on many adventures during their summer vacation, using her imagination to become anything she dreams up.<br>BEYOND |
| **Related to the Theme (spans 3+ grade levels)**<br>Use these and other classroom or library resources to ensure students are reading at least 30 minutes a day outside of class. Enlist the help of your school librarian to teach students how to use library resources, such as card catalogs and electronic search engines, to find other books related to the unit theme. | **Fraser, Mary Ann.** ***I. Q. Goes to the Library.*** **Walker & Co., 2003.** When I.Q., a pet mouse, accompanies his class to the library, he decides that he wants his own library card.<br>APPROACHING | **Boelts, Maribeth.** ***When It's the Last Day of School.*** **Putnam, 2004.** As excited as James is on the last day of school, he is determined to follow all the rules and earn a gold star.<br>APPROACHING |
| | **Bunting, Eve.** ***My Special Day at Third Street School.*** **Boyds Mills Press, 2004.** A children's book author visits a school and everyone has a good time.<br>ON LEVEL | **Danziger, Paula.** ***Get Ready for Second Grade, Amber Brown.*** **Puffin Books, 2002.** Amber Brown is faced with the anxieties that come with going back to school for a new year.<br>ON LEVEL |
| | **Morris, Ann.** ***That's Our Librarian.*** **Millbrook Press, 2003.** Introduces a school librarian and describes what she does during the school day.<br>BEYOND | **Hurwitz, Johanna.** ***Fourth Grade Fuss.*** **HarperCollins, 2004.** Julio and his friends have fun throughout fourth grade, but it's time to get serious for the end-of-year statewide test.<br>BEYOND |

| | | |
|---|---|---|
| **Editors of TIME For Kids. TIME FOR KIDS: *Storms!* Harper, 2005.** From summer thunderstorms to winter blizzards, TIME For Kids takes you into the eye of the storm! ON LEVEL | **Bloom, Becky. *Leo and Lester.* Mondo, 2003.** When Leo the raccoon and Lester the hippo go to town, Leo must keep an eye on Lester's manners. APPROACHING | **Pérez, Amada Irma. *My Diary from Here to There.* Children's Press, 2002.** A girl discovers her strengths and weaknesses as she is about to move from Mexico to Los Angeles. ON LEVEL |

| | | |
|---|---|---|
| **Forward, Toby. *What Did You Do Today?* Clarion Books, 2004.** As a young boy describes the events of his first day at school, his mother's day at work is shown on the opposite pages. APPROACHING | **Rylant, Cynthia. *Poppleton.* The Blue Sky Press, 1997.** Poppleton the pig reads a library book about an adventure and then helps a sick friend get better. APPROACHING | **Numeroff, Laura Nate. *Beatrice Doesn't Want To.* Candlewick Press, 2004.** After much resistance about going to the library, Beatrice finally discovers something she likes. APPROACHING |
| **Salat, Cristina. *Peanut's Emergency.* Charlesbridge, 2002.** When no one picks up Peanut after school, she starts for home, remembering the safety rules she has learned. ON LEVEL | **Pattou, Edith. *Mrs. Spitzer's Garden.* Harcourt, 2001.** Mrs. Spitzer, a teacher, nurtures her garden just as much as she nurtures her students. ON LEVEL | **Hill, Kirkpatrick. *The Year of Miss Agnes.* Aladdin, 2002.** Miss Agnes takes over a one-room schoolhouse on the Alaskan frontier and makes a difference in the lives of the kids. ON LEVEL |
| **Malam, John. *Library.* Peter Bedrick Books, 2000.** Reveals the inner workings of a large public library by examining different departments, the equipment used, and the duties of the librarians. BEYOND | **Seuling, Barbara. *Oh No, It's Robert.* Front Street, 1999.** Robert is in the remedial reading group, but enters the classroom achievement contest to show everyone he can succeed. BEYOND | **Kelly, Katy. *Lucy Rose: Here's the Thing About Me.* Delacorte Press, 2004.** Eight-year-old Lucy Rose has just moved to Washington, D.C., and is struggling to fit in at her new school. BEYOND |

## Library Resources

### Organization of Research Resources

**Explain/Discuss** Tell students that they can find resource books in a library, including dictionaries to look at word meanings, thesauruses to find antonyms and synonyms, atlases to find maps, and encyclopedias to find information about topics. Show an example of each resource, point out its structure and organization, and show how to use it: alphabetical order in the dictionary, thesaurus, and encyclopedia, tables of contents and indexes for the encyclopedia and atlas.

**Apply** Tell students that as they do research, they can use these resources. Have students use the resources to look up the word *public* in a dictionary, find a map of their home state in the atlas, and find an article on libraries in the encyclopedia.

# Selection Honors, Prizes, and Awards

## First Day Jitters

Unit 1, p. 10
by ***Julie Danneberg***
**Storytelling World Award (2001), Nevada Young Readers' Award Nominee (2003)**

**Author: *Julie Danneberg,*** winner of Teacher's Choice Award for Children's Books (2004) for *First Year Letters*; the Colorado Center of the Book Children's Book Award (2000) for *Margaret's Magnificent Colorado Adventure;* Mountains and Plains Booksellers Association Regional Book Award for Children's Chapter Book (2003) for *Women Artists of the West.*

## Amazing Grace

Unit 1, p. 38
by ***Mary Hoffman***

**Author: *Mary Hoffman,*** winner of Children's Africana Book Award; Primary English Award (1995) for Song of the Earth; Waldenbooks Silver Picture Book Award (1991).

## Wolf!

Unit 1, p. 82
by ***Becky Bloom***
**California Young Reader Award Nominee (2002), Nevada Young Readers Award Nominee (2001)**

## My Very Own Room

Unit 1, p. 116
by ***Amada Irma Pérez***
**Tomás Rivera Award (2000), Americas Award for Children's and Young Adult Literature Honorable Mention (2000); Pura Belpre Honor Award (2004)**

# Resources

**Audio Bookshelf**
44 Ocean View Drive
Middletown, RI 02842
800-234-1713
www.audiobookshelf.com

**Discovery Communications**
4540 Preslyn Drive
Raleigh, NC 27616
888-892-3484

**Dorling Kindersley**
375 Hudson Street
New York, NY 10014
Tel: 800-631-8571
Fax: 201-256-0000
http://us.dk.com

**Great Plains National Instructional Television Library**
GPN Educational Media
1407 Fleet Street
Baltimore, MD 21231
800-228-4630
www.shopgpn.com

**Innovative Educators**
P.O. Box 520
Montezuma, GA 31063
888-252-KIDS
Fax: 888-536-8553
www.innovative-educators.com

**The Learning Company**
(Dist. for Broderbund)
1 Athenaeum Street
Cambridge, MA 02142
800-716-8506
www.learningcompanyschool.com

**Library Video Co.**
P.O. Box 580
Wynnewood, PA 19096
800-843-3620
www.libraryvideo.com

**Listening Library**
400 Hahn Road
Westminster, MD 21157
800-243-4504

**Live Oak Media**
P.O. Box 652
Pine Plains, NY 12567
800-788-1121
www.liveoakmedia.com

**Macmillan/McGraw-Hill**
220 East Danieldale Road
DeSoto, TX 75115-9960
Tel: 800-442-9685
Fax: 972-228-1982
www.macmillanmh.com

**MCA Video**
MCA Records/Universal Studios
100 Universal City Plaza
Universal City, CA 91608
818-777-1000

**Microsoft Corp.**
One Microsoft Way
Redmond, WA 98052
800-426-9000
www.microsoft.com

**Mindscape, Inc.**
The Learning Company
88 Rowland Way
Novato, CA 94945
Tel: 415-895-2000
Fax: 415-895-2102
www.mindscape.co.uk

**National Geographic Society**
1145 17th Street N.W.
Washington, DC 20036
800-647-5463
www.nationalgeographic.com

**Recorded Books**
270 Skipjack Road
Prince Frederick, MD 20678
800-636-3399
www.recordedbooks.com

**Sunburst Communications Sunburst Technology**
1550 Executive Drive
Elgin, IL 60123
888-492-8817
www.sunburst.com

**SVE & Churchill Media**
6465 North Avondale Avenue
Chicago, IL 60631
800-253-2788

**Tom Snyder Productions**
100 Talcott Avenue
Watertown, MA 02472
800-342-0236
www.tomsnyder.com

**Weston Woods**
143 Main Street
Norwalk, CT 06851
800-243-5020
www.teacher.scholastic.com/products/westonwoods/

Go to www.macmillanmh.com.
Use the zip code finder to locate other resources in your area.

# CA Web Sites

BERKELEY
**Habitot Children's Museum**
1563 Solano Avenue, #326
Berkeley, CA 94707
Phone: (510) 647-1111
www.habitot.org

CULVER CITY
**Museum of Jurassic Technology**
9341 Venice Boulevard
Culver City, CA 90232
Phone: (310) 836-6131
www.mjt.org

DAVIS
**Explorit Science Center**
3141 Fifth Street
Davis, CA 95617-1288
Phone: (530) 756-0191
www.dcn.davis.ca.us/go/explorit

DEATH VALLEY
**Death Valley National Park**
P.O. Box 579
Death Valley, CA 92328
Phone: (760) 786-3200
www.nps.gov/deva/index.htm

EUREKA
**Redwood Discovery Museum**
501 Third Street
Eureka, CA 95501
Phone: (707) 443-9694
www.discovery-museum.org

FREMONT
**Ardenwood Historic Farm**
34600 Ardenwood Boulevard
Fremont, CA 94555
Phone: (510) 791-4196
www.ebparks.org/parks/ardenwood

FRESNO
**Fresno Chaffee Zoo**
894 West Belmont Avenue
Fresno, CA 93728
Phone: (559) 498-5910
www.fresnochaffeezoo.com/

HEMET
**KidZone Youth Museum**
123 S. Carmalita Street
Hemet, CA 92543
(951) 765-1223
www.kidzone.org

LA HABRA
**Children's Museum at La Habra**
301 South Euclid Street
La Habra, CA 90631
Phone: (562) 905-9793
www.lhcm.org/

LONG BEACH
**Aquarium of the Pacific**
100 Aquarium Way
Long Beach, CA 90802
Phone: (562) 590-3100
www.aquariumofpacific.org/

LOS ANGELES
**El Pueblo de Los Angeles**
622 N. Main Street
Los Angeles, CA 90012
Phone: (213) 628-1274
www.lasangelitas.org

**La Brea Tar Pits**
5801 Wilshire Boulevard
Los Angeles, CA 90036
Phone: (323) 934-7243
www.tarpits.org/

**California African American Museum**
600 State Drive
Los Angeles, CA 90037
Phone: (213) 744-7432
www.caam.ca.gov/

**Natural History Museum of Los Angeles County**
900 Exposition Boulevard
Los Angeles, CA 90007
Phone: (213) 763-3466
www.nhm.org

**Museum of Tolerance**
Simon Wiesenthal Plaza
9786 West Pico Boulevard
Los Angeles, CA 90035
Phone: (310) 553-8403
www.museumoftolerance.com

**J. Paul Getty Museum**
1200 Getty Center Drive
Los Angeles, CA 90049-1679
Phone: (310) 440-7300
www.getty.edu/museum

**Los Angeles Zoo & Botanical Gardens**
5333 Zoo Drive
Los Angeles, CA 90027-1498
Phone: (323) 644-4200
www.lazoo.org/

MARTINEZ
**Martinez Museum**
1005 Escobar Street
Martinez, CA 94553
Phone: (925) 228-8160
www.martinezhistory.org

MONTEREY
**Monterey Bay Aquarium**
886 Cannery Row
Monterey, CA 93940-1085
Phone: (831) 648-4800
www.mbayaq.org

OAKLAND
**Chabot Space & Science Center**
10000 Skyline Boulevard
Oakland, CA 94619
Phone: (510) 336-7300
www.chabotspace.org/

PASADENA
**Kidspace Children's Museum**
480 N. Arroyo Boulevard
Pasadena, CA 91103
Phone: (626) 449-9144
www.kidspacemuseum.org

REDWOOD CITY
**Marine Science Institute**
500 Discovery Parkway
Redwood City, CA 94063-4715
Phone: (650) 364-2760
www.sfbaymsi.org/

SACRAMENTO
**California State Railroad Museum**
111 "I" Street
Sacramento, CA 95814-2265
Phone: (916) 445-6645
www.csrmf.org/

SAN DIEGO
**San Diego Natural History Museum**
P.O. Box 121390
San Diego, CA 92112-1390
Phone: (619) 232-3821
www.sdnhm.org

**San Diego Zoo**
2920 Zoo Drive
San Diego, CA 92101
Phone: (619) 231-1515
www.sandiegozoo.org/

SAN FRANCISCO
**Alcatraz Island**
Fort Mason, Building 201-Alcatraz
San Francisco, CA 94123
Phone: (415) 705-1045
www.nps.gov/alca/index.htm

**California Indian Museum & Cultural Center**
5250 Aero Drive
Santa Rosa, CA 95403
Phone: (707) 579-3004
www.cimcc.org/index.html

**Exploratorium**
3601 Lyon Street
San Francisco, CA 94123
Phone: (415) 397-5673
www.exploratorium.edu/

SAN JOSE
**Children's Discovery Museum of San Jose**
180 Woz Way
San Jose, CA 95110
Phone: (408) 298-5437
www.cdm.org/

SAN LUIS OBISPO
**San Luis Obispo Children's Museum**
1010 Nipomo Street
San Luis Obispo, CA 93401-3870
Phone: (805) 544-5437
www.slokids.org/index1.html

SANTA ANA
**The Bowers Kidseum**
2002 North Main Street
Santa Ana, CA 92706
Phone: (714) 567-3600
www.kidseum.org/link1.htm

SANTA BARBARA
**Santa Barbara Zoological Gardens**
500 Niños Drive
Santa Barbara, CA 93103
Phone: (805) 962-6310
www.santabarbarazoo.org/

SANTA MONICA
**Santa Monica Pier Aquarium**
1600 Ocean Front Walk
Santa Monica, CA 90401
Phone: (310) 393-6149

STOCKTON
**Children's Museum of Stockton**
402 W. Weber Avenue
Stockton, CA 95203
Phone: (209) 547-2770
www.visitstocktongov.com/childrensmuseum

TWENTYNINE PALMS
**Joshua Tree National Park**
74485 National Park Drive
Twentynine Palms, CA 92277
Phone: (760) 367-5500
www.desertusa.com/jtree/jtmain.html

WHITTIER
**Jonathan Bailey Home & Park**
13421 E. Camilla Street
Whittier, CA 90601
Phone: (562) 945-3871
www.whittiermuseum.org/bailey.html

YOSEMITE
**Yosemite National Park**
P.O. Box 577
Yosemite, CA 95389
Phone: (209) 372-0200
www.nps.gov/yose/

# Meeting Grade-Level Expectations

The chart below shows the prerequisite standards (from the previous grade) for key instructional skills and strategies in Unit 1. It also shows the correlated standards for the upcoming grade. You can use the chart to determine individual student skill deficiencies (e.g., weaknesses in prerequisite skills) that need to be taught in small group differentiated lessons (Approaching Level lessons). You can also use the chart to have a clearer sense of how you are preparing students for the next grade level's expectations and to accelerate those students performing above grade level (Beyond Level lessons).

| READING | | |
|---|---|---|
| **GRADE 2** | **GRADE 3** | **GRADE 4** |
| R 2.1.6 Read aloud fluently and accurately and with appropriate intonation and expression. | R 3.1.3 Read aloud narrative and expository text fluently and accurately and with appropriate pacing, intonation, and expression. | R 4.1.1 Read narrative and expository text aloud with grade-appropriate fluency and accuracy and with appropriate pacing, intonation, and expression. |
| | R 3.3.1 Distinguish common forms of literature (e.g., poetry, drama, fiction, nonfiction). | R 4.3.1 Describe the structural differences of various imaginative forms of literature, including fantasies, fables, myths, legends, and fairy tales. |
| R 2.1.3 Decode two-syllable nonsense words and regular multisyllabic words. | R 3.1.2 Decode regular multisyllabic words. | |
| R 2.3.1 Compare and contrast plots, settings, and characters presented by different authors. | R 3.3.3 Determine what characters are like by what they say or do and by how the author or illustrator portrays them. | R 4.3.3 Use knowledge of the situation and setting and of a character's traits and motivations to determine the causes for that character's actions. |
| R 2.2.5 Restate facts and details in the text to clarify and organize ideas. | R 3.2.5 Distinguish the main idea and supporting details in expository text. | R 4.3.2 Identify the main events of the plot, their causes, and the influence of each event on future actions. |

## WRITING/LANGUAGE CONVENTIONS

| GRADE 2 | GRADE 3 | GRADE 4 |
|---|---|---|
| W 2.1.1 Group related ideas and maintain a consistent focus. | W 3.1.1 Create a single paragraph:<br>a. Develop a topic sentence.<br>b. Include simple supporting facts and details. | W 4.1.2 Create multiple-paragraph compositions:<br>a. Provide an introductory paragraph.<br>b. Establish and support a central idea with a topic sentence at or near the beginning of the first paragraph.<br>c. Include supporting paragraphs with simple facts, details, and explanations.<br>d. Conclude with a paragraph that summarizes the points.<br>e. Use correct indention. |
| W 2.1.2 Create readable documents with legible handwriting. | W 3.1.2 Write legibly in cursive or joined italic, allowing margins and correct spacing between letters in a word and words in a sentence. | W 4.1.4 Write fluidly and legibly in cursive or joined italic. |
| W 2.2.1 Write brief narratives based on their experiences:<br>a. Move through a logical sequence of events.<br>b. Describe the setting, characters, objects, and events in detail. | W 3.2.1 Write narratives:<br>a. Provide a context within which an action takes place.<br>b. Include well-chosen details to develop the plot.<br>c. Provide insight into why the selected incident is memorable. | W 4.2.1 Write narratives:<br>a. Relate ideas, observations, or recollections of an event or experience.<br>b. Provide a context to enable the reader to imagine the world of the event or experience.<br>c. Use concrete sensory details.<br>d. Provide insight into why the selected event or experience is memorable. |
| W 2.1.4 Revise original drafts to improve sequence and provide more descriptive detail. | W 3.1.4 Revise drafts to improve the coherence and logical progression of ideas by using an established rubric. | W 4.1.10 Edit and revise selected drafts to improve coherence and progression by adding, deleting, consolidating, and rearranging text. |
| LC 2.1.8 Spell basic short-vowel, long-vowel, *r*- controlled, and consonant-blend patterns correctly. | LC 3.1.8 Spell correctly one-syllable words that have blends, contractions, compounds, orthographic patterns (e.g., qu, consonant doubling, changing the ending of a word from *-y* to *-ies* when forming the plural), and common homophones (e.g., hair-hare). | LC 4.1.7 Spell correctly roots, inflections, suffixes and prefixes, and syllable constructions. |

Standards Alignment

| LISTENING AND SPEAKING | | |
| --- | --- | --- |
| **GRADE 2** | **GRADE 3** | **GRADE 4** |
| LAS 2.1.3 Paraphrase information that has been shared orally by others. | LAS 3.1.1 Retell, paraphrase, and explain what has been said by a speaker. | LAS 4.1.2 Summarize major ideas and supporting evidence presented in spoken messages and formal presentations. |
| | LAS 3.1.2 Connect and relate prior experiences, insights, and ideas to those of a speaker. | LAS 4.1.8 Use details, examples, anecdotes, or experiences to explain or clarify information. |
| LAS 2.1.6 Speak clearly and at an appropriate pace for the type of communication (e.g., informal discussion, report to class). | LAS 3.1.9 Read prose and poetry aloud with fluency, rhythm, and pace, using appropriate intonation and vocal patterns to emphasize important passages of the text being read. | LAS 4.1.9 Use volume, pitch, phrasing, pace, modulation, and gestures appropriately to enhance meaning. |
| LAS 2.2.1 a, b Recount experiences or present stories<br>a. Move through a logical sequence of events.<br>b. Describe story elements (e.g., characters, plot, setting). | LAS 3.2.1 a, b, c Make brief narrative presentations:<br>a. Provide a context for an incident that is the subject of the presentation.<br>b. Provide insight into why the selected incident is memorable.<br>c. Include well-chosen details to develop character, setting, and plot. | LAS 4.2.1 a, b, c Make narrative presentations:<br>a. Relate ideas, observations, or recollections about an event or experience.<br>b. Provide a context that enables the listener to imagine the circumstances of the event or experience.<br>c. Provide insight into why the selected event or experience is memorable. |

# Unit 1



| Week | | Vocabulary | Differentiated Spelling |
|---|---|---|---|
| 1 | First Day Jitters | chuckled<br>nervous<br>nonsense<br>fumbled<br>trudged | APPROACHING clap, step, **sick**, rock, mess, shut, **miss**, jump, pond, bag, fan, fed, yet, hid, top<br><br>ON LEVEL clap, step, **sick**, rock, **luck**, crop, snack, mess, **head**, shut, **miss,** stamp, jump, click, pond<br><br>BEYOND crops, snacks, messy, **head**, shut, stamp, click, pond, bathtub, anthill, clammy, slump, tunnel, gushed, chuckled |
| 2 | Amazing Grace | auditions<br>adventure<br>exploring<br>sparkling<br>fantastic<br>success | APPROACHING date, fine, rose, lake, life, **home**, safe, rice, wise, grade, smile, base, code, use, woke<br><br>ON LEVEL date, fine, rose, lake, life, **home**, safe, rice, globe, plane, wise, smoke, grade, smile, come<br><br>BEYOND fine, rice, globe, plane, wisely, smoke, graded, smiled, come, whale, envelope, crime, shapes, skated, stripes |
| 3 | Earth Smart | donate<br>unaware<br>members<br>contribute | APPROACHING fail, bay, pail, ray, tray, may, sway, gray, **plays**, paint, lady, tail, day, pain, way<br><br>ON LEVEL fail, bay, pail, ray, plain, tray, trail, may, braid, sway, gray, **plays**, paint, snail, **great**<br><br>BEYOND bay, pail, plainly, trail, braid, swaying, painted, snails, **great**, ladies, afraid, unfair, acres, explained, maybe |
| 4 | Wolf | passion<br>bothering<br>admire<br>concentrate<br>ached<br>splendid | APPROACHING gold, bowl, sold, snow, loaf, coal, slow, grows, show, blow, road, cold, boat, low, coat<br><br>ON LEVEL gold, bowl, soak, sold, snow, loaf, roast, coast, scold, coal, slow, grows, **show**, float, blow<br><br>BEYOND bowl, soaked, loaves, roasted, coast, scolded, floating, window, program, shown, growth, folk, throat, swallow, roam |
| 5 | My Very Own Room | separate<br>determination<br>storage<br>exact<br>ruined<br>luckiest | APPROACHING sky, pie, **might**, find, flight, **right**, fry, tight, child, buy, wind, fly, try, sigh, bite<br><br>ON LEVEL mild, sky, pie, **might**, find, fight, **tied**, **right**, fry, tight, child, flight, **bright**, buy, dye<br><br>BEYOND mild, mighty, fight, **right**, fry, tightly, flight, brightness, buy, dye, wind, **children**, satisfy, delight, grind |

**Key** Spelling words in bold appear in the selection.

LOG ON For additional spelling activities, go to **www.macmillanmh.com**.

# Language Transfers:

## *The Interaction Between English and Students' Primary Languages*

**Dr. Jana Echevarria**
*California State University, Long Beach*

**Dr. Donald Bear**
*University of Nevada, Reno*

It is important for teachers to understand why English Learners (ELs) use alternative pronunciations for some English words. Many English sounds do not exist or transfer to other languages, so English Learners may lack the auditory acuity to "hear" these English sounds and have difficulty pronouncing them. These students are not accustomed to positioning their mouth in a way the sound requires. The charts that appear on the following pages show that there is variation among languages, with some languages having more sounds in common and thus greater transfer to English than others.

For example, an English speaker may be able to pronounce the /r/ in the Spanish word *pero* ("but"), but not the /rr/ trill in *perro* ("dog"). The English speaker may also lack the auditory acuity to detect and the ability to replicate the tonal sounds of some Chinese words. Similarly, a Vietnamese speaker may have difficulty pronouncing /th/ in words such as *thin* or *thanks*.

Further, English Learners make grammatical errors due to interference from their native languages. In Spanish, the adjective follows the noun, so often English Learners say "the girl pretty" instead of "the pretty girl." While English changes the verb form with a change of subject (*I walk. She walks.*), some Asian languages keep the verb form constant across subjects. Adding /s/ to the third person may be difficult for some English Learners. Students may know the grammatical rule, but applying it consistently may be difficult, especially in spoken English.

When working with English Learners, you should also be aware of sociocultural factors that affect pronunciation. Students may retain an accent because it marks their social identity. Speakers of other languages may feel at a social distance from members of the dominant English-speaking culture.

English Learners improve their pronunciation in a nonthreatening atmosphere in which participation is encouraged. Opportunities to interact with native English speakers provide easy access to language models and give English Learners practice using English. However, students should not be forced to participate. Pressure to perform—or to perform in a certain way—can inhibit participation. In any classroom, teacher sensitivity to pronunciation differences contributes to a more productive learning environment.

Phonics, word recognition, and spelling are influenced by what students know about the sounds, word structure, and spelling in their primary languages. For example, beginning readers who speak Spanish and are familiar with its spelling will often spell short *o* with an *a*, a letter that in Spanish makes the short *o* sound. Similarly, English Learners who are unaccustomed to English consonant digraphs and blends (e.g., /ch/ and *s*-blends) spell /ch/ as *sh* because /sh/ is the sound they know that is closest to /ch/. Students learn about the way pronunciation influences their reading and spelling, beginning with large contrasts among sounds, then they study the finer discriminations. As vocabulary advances, the meaning of words leads students to the sound contrasts. For example, *shoe* and *chew* may sound alike initially, but meaning indicates otherwise. Students' reading and discussions of what they read advances their word knowledge as well as their knowledge in all language and literacy systems, including phonics, pronunciation, grammar, and vocabulary.

# Phonics Transfers:

## Sound Transfers

This chart indicates areas where a positive transfer of sounds and symbols occurs for English Learners from their native languages into English. This symbol (✔) identifies a positive transfer. "Approximate" indicates that the sound is similar.

| Sound Transfers | Spanish | Cantonese | Vietnamese | Hmong | Korean | Khmer |
|---|---|---|---|---|---|---|
| **Consonants** | | | | | | |
| /b/ as in bat | ✔ | approximate | approximate | approximate | approximate | ✔ |
| /k/ as in cake, kitten, peck | ✔ | ✔ | ✔ | ✔ | ✔ | ✔ |
| /d/ as in dog | ✔ | approximate | approximate | ✔ | approximate | ✔ |
| /f/ as in farm | ✔ | ✔ | ✔ | ✔ | | |
| /g/ as in girl | ✔ | approximate | ✔ | approximate | approximate | |
| /h/ as in ham | ✔ | ✔ | ✔ | ✔ | ✔ | approximate |
| /j/ as in jet, page, ledge | | approximate | approximate | | approximate | |
| /l/ as in lion | ✔ | ✔ | ✔ | ✔ | ✔ | |
| /m/ as in mat | ✔ | ✔ | ✔ | ✔ | ✔ | ✔ |
| /n/ as in night | ✔ | ✔ | ✔ | ✔ | ✔ | ✔ |
| /p/ as in pen | ✔ | ✔ | ✔ | approximate | ✔ | ✔ |
| /kw/ as in queen | ✔ | approximate | ✔ | | ✔ | ✔ |
| /r/ as in rope | approximate | | | | | ✔ |
| /s/ as in sink, city | ✔ | ✔ | ✔ | ✔ | ✔ | approximate |
| /t/ as in ton | ✔ | ✔ | approximate | approximate | ✔ | ✔ |
| /v/ as in vine | ✔ | | ✔ | ✔ | | |
| /w/ as in wind | ✔ | ✔ | | | ✔ | ✔ |
| /ks/ as in six | ✔ | | | | ✔ | ✔ |
| /y/ as in yak | ✔ | ✔ | | ✔ | ✔ | ✔ |
| /z/ as in zebra | | | ✔ | | | |
| **Digraphs** | | | | | | |
| /ch/ as in cheek, patch | ✔ | approximate | | ✔ | ✔ | ✔ |
| /sh/ as in shadow | | | ✔ | ✔ | ✔ | |
| /hw/ as in whistle | | | | | ✔ | ✔ |
| /th/ as in path | approximate | | approximate | | | |
| /TH/ as in that | approximate | | | | | |
| /ng/ as in sting | ✔ | ✔ | ✔ | ✔ | ✔ | approximate |

| Sound Transfers | Spanish | Cantonese | Vietnamese | Hmong | Korean | Khmer |
|---|---|---|---|---|---|---|
| **Short Vowels** | | | | | | |
| /a/ as in cat | approximate | | approximate | ✔ | ✔ | |
| /e/ as in net | ✔ | approximate | approximate | | ✔ | |
| /i/ as in kid | approximate | approximate | | | ✔ | |
| /o/ as in spot | approximate | approximate | approximate | approximate | approximate | ✔ |
| /u/ as in cup | approximate | approximate | ✔ | | ✔ | ✔ |
| **Long Vowels** | | | | | | |
| /ā/ as in lake, nail, bay | ✔ | approximate | approximate | approximate | ✔ | ✔ |
| /ē/ as in bee, meat, cranky | ✔ | approximate | ✔ | ✔ | ✔ | ✔ |
| /ī/ as in kite, tie, light, dry | ✔ | approximate | ✔ | ✔ | ✔ | ✔ |
| /ō/ as in home, road, row | ✔ | approximate | approximate | | ✔ | |
| /ū/ as in dune, fruit, blue | ✔ | approximate | ✔ | ✔ | ✔ | ✔ |
| /yü/ as in mule, cue | ✔ | approximate | | | ✔ | |
| ***r*-Controlled Vowels** | | | | | | |
| /är/ as in far | approximate | approximate | | | | |
| /ôr/ as in corn | approximate | approximate | | | | |
| /ûr/ as in stern, bird, suburb | approximate | approximate | | | | |
| /âr/ as in air, bear | | | | | | |
| /îr/ as in deer, ear | | | | | | |
| **Variant Vowels** | | | | | | |
| /oi/ as in boil, toy | ✔ | approximate | approximate | | ✔ | ✔ |
| /ou/ as in loud, down | ✔ | approximate | ✔ | approximate | ✔ | ✔ |
| /ô/ as in law | approximate | ✔ | ✔ | approximate | approximate | ✔ |
| /ô/ as in laundry | approximate | approximate | ✔ | approximate | approximate | ✔ |
| /ôl/ as in salt, call | approximate | approximate | | | approximate | ✔ |
| /ōō/ as in moon, drew | ✔ | approximate | approximate | ✔ | ✔ | ✔ |
| /ŏŏ/ as in look | | approximate | approximate | | approximate | ✔ |
| /ə/ as in askew | | | approximate | | ✔ | |

Phonics Transfers

# Phonics Transfers:
## Sound-Symbol Match

| Sound-Symbol Match | Spanish | Cantonese | Vietnamese | Hmong | Korean | Khmer |
|---|---|---|---|---|---|---|
| **Consonants** | | | | | | |
| /b/ as in bat | ✔ | | ✔ | | | |
| /k/ as in cake | ✔ | | ✔ | | | |
| /k/ as in kitten | ✔ | | ✔ | ✔ | | |
| /k/ as in peck | | | | | | |
| /d/ as in dog | ✔ | | ✔ | ✔ | | |
| /f/ as in farm | ✔ | | | ✔ | | |
| /g/ as in girl | ✔ | | ✔ | | | |
| /h/ as in ham | | | ✔ | ✔ | | |
| /j/ as in jet, page, ledge | | | | | | |
| /l/ as in lion | ✔ | | ✔ | ✔ | | |
| /m/ as in mat | ✔ | | ✔ | ✔ | | |
| /n/ as in night | ✔ | | ✔ | ✔ | | |
| /p/ as in pen | ✔ | | ✔ | ✔ | | |
| /kw/ as in queen | | | ✔ | | | |
| /r/ as in rope | approximate | | | | | |
| /s/ as in sink, city | ✔ | | ✔ | | | |
| /t/ as in ton | ✔ | | ✔ | ✔ | | |
| /v/ as in vine | ✔ | | ✔ | ✔ | | |
| /w/ as in wind | ✔ | | | | | |
| /ks/ as in six | ✔ | | | | | |
| /y/ as in yak | ✔ | | | ✔ | | |
| /z/ as in zebra | | | | | | |
| **Digraphs** | | | | | | |
| /ch/ as in cheek, patch | ✔ | | | | | |
| /sh/ as in shadow | | | | | | |
| /hw/ as in whistle | | | | | | |
| /th/ as in path | | | ✔ | | | |
| /TH/ as in that | | | | | | |
| /ng/ as in sting | ✔ | | ✔ | | | |
| **Short Vowels** | | | | | | |
| /a/ as in cat | | | ✔ | ✔ | | |
| /e/ as in net | ✔ | | ✔ | | | |
| /i/ as in kid | | | | | | |
| /o/ as in spot | | | ✔ | ✔ | | |
| /u/ as in cup | | | | | | |

| Sound-Symbol Match | Spanish | Cantonese | Vietnamese | Hmong | Korean | Khmer |
|---|---|---|---|---|---|---|
| **Long Vowels** | | | | | | |
| /ā/ as in lake | | | | | | |
| /ā/ as in nail | | | | | | |
| /ā/ as in bay | | | | | | |
| /ē/ as in bee | | | | | | |
| /ē/ as in meat | | | | | | |
| /ē/ as in cranky | | | | | | |
| /ī/ as in kite, tie, light, dry | | | | | | |
| /ō/ as in home, road, row | | | | | | |
| /ū/ as in dune | | | ✔ | ✔ | | |
| /ū/ as in fruit, blue | | | | | | |
| /yü/ as in mule, cue | | | | | | |
| ***r*-Controlled Vowels** | | | | | | |
| /är/ as in far | ✔ | | | | | |
| /ôr/ as in corn | ✔ | | | | | |
| /ûr/ as in stern | ✔ | | | | | |
| /ûr/ as in bird, suburb | | | | | | |
| /âr/ as in air, bear | | | | | | |
| /îr/ as in deer, ear | | | | | | |
| **Variant Vowels** | | | | | | |
| /oi/ as in boil | ✔ | | ✔ | | | |
| /oi/ as in toy | ✔ | | | | | |
| /ou/ as in loud | | | | | | |
| /ou/ as in down | | | | | | |
| /ô/ as in law | | | | | | |
| /ô/ as in laundry | | | | | | |
| /ôl/ as in salt | ✔ | | | | | |
| /ôl/ as in call | | | | | | |
| /o͞o/ as in moon, drew | | | | | | |
| /o͝o/ as in look | | | | | | |
| /ə/ as in askew | | | | | | |

# How to Use the Phonics Transfer Charts

To read and speak fluently in English, English Learners need to master a wide range of phonemic awareness, phonics, and word study skills. The Phonics Transfer Charts are designed to help you anticipate and understand possible student errors in pronouncing or perceiving English sounds.

1. **Highlight Transferable Skills** If the phonics skill transfers from the student's primary language to English, state that during the lesson. In most lessons an English Learner feature will indicate which sounds do and do not transfer in specific languages.

2. **Preteach Non-Transferable Skills** Prior to teaching a phonics lesson, check the chart to determine if the sound and/or spelling transfers from the student's primary language into English. If it does not, preteach the sound and spelling during Small Group time. Focus on articulation, using the backs of the small **Sound-Spelling Cards**, and the minimal contrast activities provided.

3. **Provide Additional Practice and Time** If the skill does NOT transfer from the student's primary language into English, the student will require more time and practice mastering the sound and spellings. Continue to review the phonics skill during Small Group time in upcoming weeks until the student has mastered it. Use the additional resources, such as the extra decodable stories in the **Teacher's Resource Book**, to provide oral and silent reading practice.

# Teaching Supports for Students Transitioning from Spanish to English

The **Sound-Spelling Cards** have been created to assist you in working with English Learners. For example:

1. The dotted border on many of the cards indicates that the sound transfers from Spanish to English. On these cards, the same image is used in both English and Spanish (e.g., *camel/camello*). Therefore, students learning the sound in Spanish can easily transfer that knowledge to English.

2. Students whose primary language is not English will need additional articulation support to pronounce and perceive non-transferable English sounds. Use the articulation photos on the backs of the Sound-Spelling Cards and the student-friendly descriptions of how to form these sounds during phonics lessons.

## Sound-Spelling Cards

Transfer Skill Support

**Description of Sound** The sound of *a* in *apple* is called short *a*. It is a vowel. The vocal cords vibrate when making the short *a* sound. The tongue is behind the lower teeth and the sound is made at the front of the mouth.

**How to Make the Sound** Position your tongue behind your bottom teeth. With your mouth wide open, pull back your lips in a partial smile.

Articulation

**Words for Oral Practice**

**Initial Position** add, ah, an, and, ant, as, ask, at

**Medial Position** bad, bag, cat, dad, gap, jam, last, map, mat, nap, pan, ran, sat, tap, zap

Small Group Word Lists



Articulation Support

# Grammar Transfers:
## Grammatical Form

This chart can be used to address common mistakes that some English Learners make when they transfer grammatical forms from their native languages into English.

| Grammatical Form | Transfer Mistakes in English | Native Language | Cause of Difficulty |
|---|---|---|---|
| **Nouns** | | | |
| **Plural Marker -*s*** | **Forgets plural marker -*s***<br>*I have 3 sister.* | Cantonese, Haitian Creole, Hmong, Korean, Vietnamese, Khmer | Native language does not use a plural marker. |
| **Countable and Uncountable Nouns** | **Confuses countable and uncountable nouns**<br>*the homeworks* or *the informations* | Haitian Creole, Spanish | Countable and uncountable nouns are different in English and native language. |
| **Possessives** | **Uses prepositions to describe possessives**<br>*the book of my brother* as opposed to *my brother's book* | Haitian Creole, Hmong, Spanish, Vietnamese | Possession is often described using a prepositional phrase. |
| | **Avoids using *'s***<br>*dog my father* as opposed to *my father's dog* | Haitian Creole, Vietnamese, Khmer | A noun follows the object in the native language. |
| **Articles** | | | |
| | **Consistently omits articles**<br>*He has book. They want dog not cat.* | Cantonese, Haitian Creole, Hmong, Korean, Vietnamese, Khmer | There is no article in the native language or no difference between *the* and *a*. |
| | **Overuses articles**<br>*The English is difficult. The soccer is popular in the Europe.* | Haitian Creole, Hmong, Spanish | Some languages use articles that are omitted in English. |
| ***a/an*** | **Mistakes *one* for *a/an***<br>*She is one nurse.* | Haitian Creole, Hmong, Vietnamese | The native language either does not use articles or uses articles differently. |
| **Pronouns** | | | |
| **Gender-Specific Pronouns** | **Uses pronouns with the inappropriate gender**<br>*He is my sister.* | Cantonese, Haitian Creole, Hmong, Korean, Spanish, Khmer | The third person pronoun in the native language is gender free, or the personal pronoun is omitted. |
| | **Uses inappropriate gender, particularly with neutral nouns**<br>*The day is sunny. She is beautiful.* | Spanish | Nouns have feminine or masculine gender in the native language, and the gender may be carried over into English. |

| Grammatical Form | Transfer Mistakes in English | Native Language | Cause of Difficulty |
|---|---|---|---|
| **Pronouns** | | | |
| **Object Pronouns** | **Confuses subject and object pronouns**<br>*Her talks to me.* | Cantonese, Hmong, Khmer | The same pronoun form is used for subject and object in the native language. |
| | **Omits object pronouns**<br>*That girl is very rude, so nobody likes.* | Korean, Vietnamese | The native language does not use direct objects. |
| **Pronoun and Number Agreement** | **Uses the wrong number for pronouns**<br>*I saw many red birds. It was pretty.* | Cantonese, Korean | The native language does not require number agreement. |
| **Subject Pronouns** | **Omits subject pronouns**<br>*Mom isn't home. Is at work.* | Korean, Spanish | Subject pronouns may be dropped because in the native language the verb ending gives information about the number and/or gender. |
| **Pronouns in Clauses** | **Omits pronouns in clauses**<br>*If don't do homework, they will not learn.* | Cantonese, Vietnamese | The native language does not need a subject in the subordinate clause. |
| **Pronouns and Nouns** | **Overuses pronouns with nouns**<br>*This school, it very good.* | Hmong, Vietnamese | This is popular in speech in some languages. The speaker mentions a topic, then makes a comment about it. |
| | **Avoids pronouns and repeats nouns**<br>*Carla visits her sister every Sunday, and Carla makes a meal.* | Korean, Vietnamese | In the native language, the speaker repeats nouns and does not use pronouns. |
| **Pronoun *one*** | **Omits the pronoun *one***<br>*I saw two dogs, and I like the small.* | Spanish | Adjectives can stand alone in the native language, but English requires a noun or *one*. |
| **Possessive Forms** | **Confuses possessive forms**<br>*The book is my.* | Cantonese, Hmong, Vietnamese | Cantonese and Hmong speakers tend to omit the final *n* sound, which may create confusion between *my* and *mine*. |

# Grammar Transfers:
## Grammatical Form

| Grammatical Form | Transfer Mistakes in English | Native Language | Cause of Difficulty |
|---|---|---|---|
| **Verbs** | | | |
| **Present Tense** | **Omits *-s* in present tense, third person agreement** *He like pizza.* | Cantonese, Haitian Creole, Hmong, Korean, Vietnamese, Khmer | Subject-verb agreement is not used in the native language. |
| **Irregular Verbs** | **Has problems with irregular subject-verb agreement** *Tom and Sue has a new car.* | Cantonese, Hmong, Korean, Khmer | Verbs' forms do not change to show the number of the subject in the native language. |
| **Inflectional Endings** | **Omits tense markers** *I study English yesterday.* | Cantonese, Haitian Creole, Hmong, Korean, Vietnamese, Khmer | The native language does not use inflectional endings to change verb tense. |
| **Present and Future Tenses** | **Incorrectly uses the present tense for the future tense** *I go next week.* | Cantonese, Korean | The native language may use the present tense to imply the future tense. |
| **Negative Statements** | **Omits helping verbs in negative statements** *Sue no coming to school.* | Cantonese, Korean, Spanish | The native language does not use helping verbs in negative statements. |
| **Present-Perfect Tense** | **Avoids the present-perfect tense** *Marcos live here for three months.* | Haitian Creole, Vietnamese | The native language does not use the present-perfect verb form. |
| **Past-Continuous Tense** | **Uses the past-continuous tense for recurring action in the past** *When I was young, I was talking a lot.* | Korean, Spanish | In the native language, the past-continuous tense is used but in English the expression *used to* or the simple past tense is used. |
| **Main Verb** | **Omits the main verb** *Talk in class not good.* | Cantonese | Cantonese does not require an infinitive marker when using a verb as a noun. Speakers may confuse the infinitive for the main verb. |
| **Main Verbs in Clauses** | **Uses two or more main verbs in one clause without any connectors** *I took a book went studied at the library.* | Hmong | In Hmong, verbs can be used consecutively without conjunctions or punctuation. |
| **Linking Verbs** | **Omits the linking verb** *He hungry.* | Cantonese, Haitian Creole, Hmong, Vietnamese, Khmer | In some languages, *be* is implied in the adjective form. In other languages, the concept is expressed with a verb. |
| **Helping Verb in Passive Voice** | **Omits the helping verb in the passive voice** *The homework done.* | Cantonese, Vietnamese | In Cantonese and Vietnamese, the passive voice does not require a helping verb. |

| Grammatical Form | Transfer Mistakes in English | Native Language | Cause of Difficulty |
|---|---|---|---|
| **Verbs** | | | |
| **Passive Voice** | **Avoids the passive voice**<br>*They speak English here.*<br>*One speaks English here.*<br>*English is spoken here.* | Haitian Creole | The passive voice does not exist in the native language. |
| **Transitive Verbs** | **Confuses transitive and intransitive verbs**<br>*The child broke.*<br>*The child broke the plate.* | Cantonese, Korean, Spanish | Verbs that require a direct object differ between English and the native language. |
| **Phrasal Verbs** | **Confuses related phrasal verbs**<br>*I ate at the apple.*<br>*I ate up the apple.* | Korean, Spanish | Phrasal verbs are not used in the native language, and there is often confusion over their meaning. |
| ***Have* and *be*** | **Uses *have* instead of *be***<br>*I have thirst.*<br>*He has right.* | Spanish | Spanish and English have different uses for *have* and *be.* |
| **Adjectives** | | | |
| **Word Order** | **Places adjectives after nouns**<br>*I saw a car red.* | Haitian Creole, Hmong, Spanish, Vietnamese, Khmer | Nouns often precede adjectives in the native language. |
| | **Consistently places adjectives after nouns**<br>*This is a lesson new.* | Cantonese, Korean | Adjectives always follow nouns in the native language. |
| ***-er* and *-est* Endings** | **Avoids *-er* and *-est* endings**<br>*I am more old than you.* | Hmong, Korean, Spanish, Khmer | The native language shows comparative and superlative forms with separate words. |
| ***-ing* and *-ed* Endings** | **Confuses *-ing* and *-ed* forms**<br>*Math is bored.* | Cantonese, Korean, Spanish, Khmer | Adjectives in the native language do not have active and passive meanings. |
| **Adverbs** | | | |
| **Adjectives and Adverbs** | **Uses an adjective where an adverb is needed**<br>*Talk quiet.* | Haitian Creole, Hmong, Khmer | Adjectives and adverb forms are interchangeable in the native language. |
| **Word Order** | **Places adverbs before verbs**<br>*He quickly ran.*<br>*He ran quickly.* | Cantonese, Korean | Adverbs usually come before verbs in the native language, and this tendency is carried over into English. |
| **Prepositions** | | | |
| | **Omits prepositions**<br>*I like come school.* | Cantonese | Cantonese does not use prepositions the way that English does. |

# How to Use the Grammar Transfer Charts

The grammar of many languages differs widely from English. For example, a student's primary language may use a different word order than English, may not use parts of speech in the same way, or may use different verb tenses. The Grammar Transfer Charts are designed to help you anticipate and understand possible student errors in speaking and writing standard English. With all grammar exercises, the emphasis is on oral communication, both as a speaker and listener.

1. **Highlight Transferable Skills** If the grammar skill transfers from the student's primary language to English, state that during the lesson. In many lessons an English Learner feature will indicate which skills do and do not transfer.

2. **Preteach Non-Transferable Skills** Prior to teaching a grammar lesson, check the chart to determine if the skill transfers from the student's primary language into English. If it does not, preteach the skill during Small Group time. Provide sentence frames and ample structured opportunities to use the skill in spoken English. Students need to talk, talk, and talk some more to master these skills.

3. **Provide Additional Practice and Time** If the skill does NOT transfer from the student's primary language into English, the student will require more time and practice mastering it. Continue to review the skill during Small Group time. Use the additional resources, such as the grammar lessons in the **Intervention Kit** (K–3) or review lessons, in upcoming weeks.

4. **Use Contrastive Analysis** Tell students when a skill does not transfer and include contrastive analysis work to make the student aware of how to correct their speaking and writing for standard English. For example, when a student uses an incorrect grammatical form, write the student sentence on a **WorkBoard**. Then write the correct English form underneath. Explain the difference between the student's primary language and English. Have the student correct several other sentences using this skill, such as sentences in their Writer's Notebooks.

5. **Increase Writing and Speaking Opportunities** Increase the amount of structured writing and speaking opportunities for students needing work on specific grammatical forms. Sentence starters and paragraph frames, such as those found in the lessons, are ideal for both written and oral exercises.

6. **Focus on Meaning** Always focus on the meanings of sentences in all exercises. As they improve and fine-tune their English speaking and writing skills, work with students on basic comprehension of spoken and written English.

To help students move to the next level of language acquisition and master English grammatical forms, recast their responses during classroom discussions or provide additional language for them to use as they respond further. Provide leveled-language sentence frames orally or in writing for students to use as they respond to questions and prompts. Below are samples.

| English Learner Response Chart | |
|---|---|
| **Beginning**<br>(will respond by pointing or saying one word answers) | **Sample Frames** (simple, short sentences)<br>*I see a* ______.<br>*This is a* ______.<br>*I like the* ______. |
| **Early Intermediate**<br>(will respond with phrases or simple sentences) | **Sample Frames** (simple sentences with adjectives and adverbs added, and compound subjects or predicates)<br>*I see a* ______ ______.<br>*The* ______ *animal is* ______.<br>*There are* ______ *and* ______. |
| **Intermediate**<br>(will respond with simple sentences and limited academic language) | **Sample Frames** (harder sentences with simple phrases in consistent patterns; some academic language included)<br>*The animal's prey is* ______ *because* ______.<br>*The main idea is* ______ *because* ______.<br>*He roamed the park so that* ______. |
| **Early Advanced**<br>(will begin to use more sophisticated sentences and some academic language) | **Sample Frames** (complex sentences with increased academic language, beginning phrases and clauses, and multiple-meaning words)<br>*When the violent storm hit,* ______.<br>*As a result of the revolution, the army*______.<br>*Since most endangered animals are* ______, *they* ______. |
| **Advanced**<br>(will have mastered some more complex sentence structures and is increasing the amount of academic language used) | Use the questions and prompts provided in the lessons for the whole group. Provide additional support learning and using academic language. These words are boldfaced throughout the lessons and sentence starters are often provided. |

# Cognates

Cognates are words in two languages that look alike and have the same or similar meaning (e.g., *school/escuela, telephone/teléfono*) and can be helpful resources for English Learners. This list identifies some Spanish cognates for the academic language used during the lessons.

Students must also be aware of false cognates—words that look similar in two languages, but have different meanings, such as *soap* in English and *sopa* (meaning *soup*) in Spanish.

| | |
|---|---|
| **accent** | *acento* |
| **action** | *acción* |
| **action verb** | *verbo de acción* |
| **adjective** | *adjetivo* |
| **adverb** | *adverbio* |
| **alphabetical order** | *orden alfabético* |
| **analogy** | *analogía* |
| **analyze** | *analizar* |
| **antecedent** | *antecedente* |
| **antonym** | *antónimo* |
| **apostrophe** | *apóstrofe* |
| **article** | *artículo* |
| **author** | *autor* |
| **cause** | *causa* |
| **classify** | *clasificar* |
| **combine** | *combinar* |
| **compare** | *comparar* |
| **complex** | *complejo* |
| **comprehension** | *comprehensión* |
| **conclusion** | *conclusión* |
| **confirm** | *confirmar* |
| **conjunction** | *conjunción* |
| **connotation** | *connotación* |
| **consonant** | *consonante* |
| **context** | *contexto* |
| **contrast** | *contrastar* |
| **definition** | *definición* |
| **demonstrative** | *demostrativo* |
| **denotation** | *denotación* |
| **description** | *descripción* |
| **dialogue** | *diálogo* |
| **dictionary** | *diccionario* |
| **direct** | *directo* |
| **effect** | *efecto* |
| **evaluate** | *evaluar* |
| **event** | *evento* |
| **example** | *ejemplo* |
| **exclamation** | *exclamación* |
| **family** | *familia* |
| **fantasy** | *fantasía* |
| **figurative** | *figurativo* |
| **fragment** | *fragmento* |
| **future** | *futuro* |
| **generalization** | *generalización* |
| **generalize** | *generalizar* |
| **glossary** | *glosario* |
| **Greek** | *Griego* |
| **homophone** | *homófono* |

| English | Spanish |
|---|---|
| **idea** | *idea* |
| **identify** | *identificar* |
| **illustration** | *ilustración* |
| **indirect** | *indirecto* |
| **introduction** | *introducción* |
| **irregular** | *irregular* |
| **language** | *lenguaje* |
| **Latin** | *Latín* |
| **myth** | *mito* |
| **negative** | *negativo* |
| **object** | *objeto* |
| **opinion** | *opinión* |
| **order** | *orden* |
| **origin** | *orígen* |
| **paragraph** | *párrafo* |
| **part** | *parte* |
| **perspective** | *perspectiva* |
| **persuasion** | *persuación* |
| **phrase** | *frase* |
| **plural** | *plural* |
| **possessive adjective** | *adjetivo posesivo* |
| **predicate** | *predicado* |
| **prediction** | *predicción* |
| **prefix** | *prefijo* |
| **preposition** | *preposición* |
| **prepositional** | *preposicional* |
| **present** | *presente* |
| **problem** | *problema* |
| **pronunciation** | *pronunciación* |
| **punctuation** | *puntuación* |
| **reality** | *realidad* |
| **relationship** | *relación* |
| **sequence** | *secuencia* |
| **singular** | *singular* |
| **solution** | *solución* |
| **structure** | *estructura* |
| **subject** | *sujeto* |
| **suffix** | *sufijo* |
| **syllable** | *sílaba* |
| **synonym** | *sinónimo* |
| **technique** | *técnica* |
| **text** | *texto* |
| **theme** | *tema* |
| **verb** | *verbo* |
| **visualize** | *visualizar* |
| **vowel** | *vocal* |

# African American Vernacular English (AAVE)

Some of your students will be speakers of African American Vernacular English (AAVE). AAVE is a language system with well-formed rules for sounds, grammar, and meanings. Throughout the year you will help these students learn standard academic English by focusing on those places where AAVE differs from the standard and on those patterns that will have the most immediate impact on the students' reading and writing development.

These students will need help in understanding that what is appropriate in one setting is not appropriate in another, so they can shift easily and competently between varieties in different social contexts. Instruction will be more effective if it identifies nonstandard varieties of English as different, rather than inferior. All students should be taught standard English in a way that respects their home language.

Use the charts that follow to identify AAVE linguistic differences and instructional modifications that can help students as they learn to successfully and fluently speak, read, and write standard English. The modifications focus on the following:

- Providing students with clear enunciation examples during phonics and phonemic awareness lessons targeting difficult sounds. Then additional pronunciation practice is provided during small group phonics lessons.
- Using contrastive analysis during whole group and small group time in which students code switch between AAVE and standard English. The difference in each grammatical structure is highlighted and students are provided ample opportunities to practice standard English in speaking and writing. They are also taught the proper context for each usage.
- Using Discrimination Drills in which two sentences are read aloud or written on the board. One is standard English, the other reflects common AAVE structures. Students must determine which is standard English.
- Using Translation Drills in which students change an AAVE sentence into standard English.

## PHONICS DIFFERENCES

| English/Language Arts Skill | Linguistic Differences and Instructional Modifications |
|---|---|
| Digraph *th* as in *bathroom* | For many speakers of African American Vernacular English, the initial /th/ sound in function words such as *this* and *then* is often produced as a /d/ sound. In some words, such as *thing* and *through*, the /th/ sound is produced as a /t/ sound. At the ends of words and syllables, such as *bathroom* and *death,* the /th/ sound is replaced by the /f/ sound. This will affect students' spelling and speaking. Students will need additional articulation support prior to spelling these words. |
| Final Consonant *r* | Many speakers of African American Vernacular English drop the /r/ sound in words. For example, these students will say *sto'* for store or *do'* for door. Clearly pronounce these words, emphasizing the /r/ sound. Have children repeat several times, exaggerating the sound before spelling these words. |
| *r*-Blends | Many speakers of African American Vernacular English drop the /r/ in words with *r*-blends. For example, these students will say *th'ow* for *throw*. Clearly pronounce these words in the lesson, emphasizing the sounds of the *r*-blend. Have children repeat several times, exaggerating the sound. |
| Final Consonant *l* and Final *l*-Blends | Many speakers of African American Vernacular English drop the /l/ sound in words, particularly in words with *-ool* and *-oal* spelling patterns, such as *cool* and *coal*, and when the letter *l* precedes the consonants *p, t,* or *k* as in *help, belt,* and *milk*. These students will drop the *l* when spelling these words, as well. Provide additional articulation support prior to reading and spelling these words. |
| Final Consonant Blends | Many speakers of African American Vernacular English drop the final letter in a consonant blend (e.g., *mp, nt, nk, lo, lt, lk*). For example, they will say *des'* for *desk*. Clearly pronounce the final sound in these words and have students repeat several times, exaggerating the sound. |
| Plurals | When the letter *-s* is added to a word ending in a consonant blend, such as *test* (*tests*), many speakers of African American Vernacular English will drop the final sounds. Therefore they will say *tes'* or *tesses*. These students will need additional articulation support. |
| Contractions | Many speakers of African American Vernacular English drop the /t/ sound when pronouncing the common words *it's, that's,* and *what's*. These words sound more like *i's, tha's,* and *wha's*. These students will need additional articulation support in order to pronounce and spell these words. |
| Short Vowels *i* and *e* | When the /i/ and /e/ sounds appear before the consonants *m* or *n* in words, such as *pen/pin* and *him/hem,* many speakers of African American Vernacular English won't pronounce or hear the difference. Focus on articulation, such as mouth position for each vowel sound, during the lesson. |
| Inflectional Ending *-ing* | Many speakers of African American Vernacular English will pronounce words with *-ing* as /ang/. For example, they will say *thang* for *thing*. Emphasize the /i/ sound in these words to help students correctly spell and pronounce them. |

## GRAMMAR, USAGE, MECHANICS DIFFERENCES

| English/Language Arts Skill | Linguistic Differences and Instructional Modifications |
|---|---|
| Subject-Verb Agreement (*he is* , *he goes*) | To acquire standard academic English speech and writing, speakers of African American Vernacular English need to learn to use *-s* with a verb and the third person and only there, as in *he is* and *he goes*. Many speakers of AAVE will leave out the *-s* or place it elsewhere, as in *he go* or *we goes*. Write a sentence from students' speech or writing. Then provide contrastive analysis work. Write the standard English form above that sentence. Discuss the key differences. |
| Subject-Verb Agreement (*do/does, have/has, was/were*) | Many speakers of African American Vernacular English have difficulties with subject-verb agreement when the verbs *do/does*, *have/has*, and *was/were* are used. Additional grammar instruction and practice will be needed. Write a sentence from students' speech or writing. Then provide contrastive analysis work. Write the standard English form above that sentence. Discuss the key differences. |
| Past Tense (*-ed*) | Many speakers of African American Vernacular English understand the use of *-ed* to form the past tense, but leave it out or add sounds when pronouncing the word, as in *pick* or *pickted* for *picked*. Students will need additional work during Small Group time with *-ed* in order to know when and where to use it in writing. |
| Past Tense (simple past tense vs. past perfect tense) | Many speakers of African American Vernacular English will add *had* to the simple past tense, saying *We had picked* for *We picked*. The use of had indicates the past perfect tense in standard academic English. Other common nonstandard forms of irregular past-tense verbs include *He seen that* and *He had ran over there*. |
| The Verb "to be" (pronunciation) | In the first person present tense, many speakers of African American Vernacular English will properly use *I am* or *I'm*, but say it more like "uhm." Focus on pronunciation. |
| The Verb "to be" (writing) | To learn standard academic English, many speakers of African American Vernacular English will need to learn not to delete *is* and *are* when speaking and writing. For example, students might say *He my brother* or *She goin' over there*. Additional grammar instruction and practice will be needed. Use Discrimination and Translation Drills. |
| The Verb "to be" (speaking) | Many speakers of African American Vernacular English will use *was* in the singular and plural forms, as in *He was* and *They was*. Additional grammar instruction and practice will be needed. |
| The Verb "to be" | To learn standard academic English, many speakers of African American Vernacular English will need to learn to avoid using nonstandard forms, such as *He always be doing this*, in favor of *am*, *are*, and *is*. Also, additional instruction and practice will be needed to show the proper placement of the adverbs *always*, *never*, and *others*. For example, *He is always doing this* rather than *He always is doing this*. Write a sentence from students' speech or writing. Then provide contrastive analysis work. Write the standard English form above that sentence. Discuss the key differences. |

## GRAMMAR, USAGE, MECHANICS DIFFERENCES

| | |
|---|---|
| Possessives (*'s*) | In standard academic English, *'s* is added to a noun to show possession. For many speakers of African American Vernacular English the *'s* is absent. However, the *'s* is regularly added to *mine,* as in *This is mines*. |
| Possessive (*whose*) | The possessive pronoun *whose* is often not used by many speakers of African American Vernacular English. For example, students will say *I don't know who book this was*. Students will need additional instruction and practice to acquire this skill. |
| *There is/There are* | Many speakers of African American Vernacular English will need help in pronouncing *its* in standard academic English and in properly using the patterns *there is* and *there are*. In AAVE it is common to replace the word *there* with *it*, as in *It's a man at the door* rather than *There's a man at the door*. Use Discrimination and Translation Drills. |
| Plurals (nouns of measure) | Most speakers of African American Vernacular English correctly use plurals, except when it involves "nouns of measure," as in *It cost five dollars* or *She owe me five dollars*. However, the plural /s/ is often absent in writing, and students will need additional instruction and practice during small group time. |
| Negatives | Many speakers of African American Vernacular English will use several negatives in a sentence when only one is required, as in *Nobody never said nothing*. To master standard academic English, speakers of AAVE will need considerable practice to gain control of *any, ever,* and *either* after a negative word. Write a sentence from students' speech or writing. Then provide contrastive analysis work. Write the standard English form above that sentence. Discuss the key differences. In addition, use Discrimination and Translation Drills. |

# California Treasures 2010 Scope and Sequence

| | K | 1 | 2 | 3 | 4 | 5 | 6 | 7 | 8 |
|---|---|---|---|---|---|---|---|---|---|
| **READING PROCESS** | | | | | | | | | |
| **Concepts About Print** | | | | | | | | | |
| Recognize own name | | | | | | | | | |
| Understand directionality (top to bottom; tracking print from left to right; return sweep) | ✔ | | | | | | | | |
| Locate printed word on page | ✔ | | | | | | | | |
| Develop print awareness (concept of letter, word, sentence) | ✔ | | | | | | | | |
| Identify separate sounds in a spoken sentence | ✔ | | | | | | | | |
| Understand that written words are represented in written language by a specific sequence of letters | ✔ | ✔ | | | | | | | |
| Distinguish between letters, words, and sentences | ✔ | ✔ | | | | | | | |
| Identify and distinguish paragraphs | | | ✔ | | | | | | |
| Match print to speech | ✔ | ✔ | | | | | | | |
| Name uppercase and lowercase letters | ✔ | | | | | | | | |
| Understand correct book handling | ✔ | | | | | | | | |
| Identify parts of a book; (front cover, back cover, title page) recognize that parts of a book contain information | ✔ | ✔ | | | | | | | |
| **Phonological Awareness** | | | | | | | | | |
| Understand alliteration | ✔ | ✔ | ✔ | | | | | | |
| Segment sentences into correct number of words | ✔ | | | | | | | | |
| Identify, blend, segment syllables in words | ✔ | ✔ | ✔ | | | | | | |
| Recognize and produce rhyming words | ✔ | ✔ | ✔ | | | | | | |
| Identify, blend, segment onset and rime | ✔ | ✔ | ✔ | | | | | | |
| **Phonics and Decoding** | | | | | | | | | |
| Understand the alphabetic principle | | ✔ | | | | | | | |
| Sound/letter correspondence | ✔ | ✔ | ✔ | ✔ | | | | | |
| Blend sounds into words, including VC, CVC, CVCe, CVVC words | ✔ | ✔ | ✔ | | | | | | |
| Blend common word families | ✔ | ✔ | ✔ | ✔ | | | | | |
| Initial consonant blends | | ✔ | ✔ | ✔ | | | | | |
| Final consonant blends | | ✔ | ✔ | ✔ | | | | | |
| Initial and medial short vowels | ✔ | ✔ | ✔ | ✔ | ✔ | ✔ | ✔ | | |
| Decode one-syllable words in isolation and in context | ✔ | ✔ | ✔ | ✔ | | | | | |
| Decode multisyllabic words in isolation and in context | | ✔ | ✔ | ✔ | ✔ | ✔ | ✔ | | |
| Identify common irregular words, high-frequency words | ✔ | ✔ | ✔ | ✔ | | | | | |
| Identify compound words, contractions | | ✔ | ✔ | ✔ | ✔ | ✔ | ✔ | | |
| Use knowledge of spelling patterns to identify syllables | | | ✔ | ✔ | ✔ | ✔ | ✔ | | |
| Recognize abbreviations, regular and irregular plurals | | | ✔ | ✔ | ✔ | ✔ | ✔ | | |
| Long vowels | | ✔ | ✔ | ✔ | ✔ | ✔ | ✔ | | |
| Variant vowels | | ✔ | ✔ | ✔ | ✔ | ✔ | ✔ | | |
| *r*-Controlled vowels | | ✔ | ✔ | ✔ | ✔ | ✔ | ✔ | | |
| Hard/soft consonants | | | ✔ | ✔ | ✔ | ✔ | ✔ | | |
| Initial consonant digraphs | | ✔ | ✔ | ✔ | ✔ | ✔ | ✔ | | |

| KEY | |
|---|---|
| | ✔ = Assessed Skill |
| | Tinted panels show skills, strategies, and other teaching opportunities. |

| | K | 1 | 2 | 3 | 4 | 5 | 6 | 7 | 8 |
|---|---|---|---|---|---|---|---|---|---|
| Medial and final consonant digraphs | | ✔ | ✔ | ✔ | ✔ | ✔ | ✔ | | |
| Diphthongs | | ✔ | ✔ | ✔ | ✔ | ✔ | ✔ | | |
| Identify and distinguish phonemes (initial, medial, final) | ✔ | ✔ | ✔ | | | | | | |
| Count phonemes | ✔ | ✔ | ✔ | | | | | | |
| Blend phonemes | ✔ | ✔ | ✔ | | | | | | |
| Segment phonemes | ✔ | ✔ | ✔ | | | | | | |
| Manipulate phonemes (addition, deletion, substitution) | ✔ | ✔ | ✔ | ✔ | | | | | |
| Silent letters | | | ✔ | ✔ | ✔ | ✔ | ✔ | | |
| Schwa words | | | | ✔ | ✔ | ✔ | ✔ | | |
| Inflectional endings | | ✔ | ✔ | ✔ | ✔ | ✔ | ✔ | | |
| Triple-consonant clusters | | ✔ | ✔ | ✔ | ✔ | ✔ | ✔ | | |
| Unfamiliar and complex word families | | | | ✔ | ✔ | ✔ | ✔ | | |
| **Structural Analysis/Word Analysis** | | | | | | | | | |
| Common spelling patterns (word families) | | ✔ | ✔ | ✔ | ✔ | ✔ | ✔ | | |
| Common syllable patterns | | | ✔ | ✔ | ✔ | ✔ | ✔ | | |
| Inflectional endings | | ✔ | ✔ | ✔ | ✔ | ✔ | ✔ | | |
| Contractions | | | ✔ | ✔ | ✔ | ✔ | | | |
| Compound words | | ✔ | ✔ | ✔ | ✔ | ✔ | ✔ | | |
| Prefixes and suffixes | | | ✔ | ✔ | ✔ | ✔ | ✔ | | |
| Root or base words | | | ✔ | ✔ | ✔ | ✔ | ✔ | | |
| Comparatives and superlatives | | | ✔ | ✔ | ✔ | ✔ | ✔ | | |
| Greek and Latin roots | | | ✔ | ✔ | ✔ | ✔ | ✔ | ✔ | ✔ |
| **Fluency** | | | | | | | | | |
| Apply letter/sound knowledge to decode phonetically regular words accurately and quickly | ✔ | ✔ | ✔ | ✔ | ✔ | ✔ | ✔ | ✔ | ✔ |
| Recognize high-frequency and familiar words | ✔ | ✔ | ✔ | ✔ | | | | | |
| Read regularly on independent and instructional levels | ✔ | ✔ | ✔ | ✔ | ✔ | ✔ | ✔ | ✔ | ✔ |
| Read orally with fluency from familiar texts (choral, echo, partner, Readers Theater) | ✔ | ✔ | ✔ | ✔ | ✔ | ✔ | ✔ | | |
| Use appropriate pace, expression, intonation, and phrasing | | ✔ | ✔ | ✔ | ✔ | ✔ | ✔ | ✔ | ✔ |
| Read with automaticity (accurately and effortlessly) | ✔ | ✔ | ✔ | ✔ | ✔ | ✔ | ✔ | ✔ | ✔ |
| Use punctuation cues in reading | ✔ | ✔ | ✔ | ✔ | ✔ | ✔ | ✔ | ✔ | ✔ |
| Adjust reading rate to purpose, text difficulty, form and style | ✔ | ✔ | ✔ | ✔ | ✔ | ✔ | ✔ | ✔ | ✔ |
| Repeated readings | ✔ | ✔ | ✔ | ✔ | ✔ | ✔ | ✔ | ✔ | ✔ |
| Timed readings | | ✔ | ✔ | ✔ | ✔ | ✔ | ✔ | ✔ | ✔ |
| **Self-Selected Reading** | | | | | | | | | |
| Use personal criteria to choose own reading: including favorite authors, genres, recommendations from others | | | | | | | | | |
| Read a variety of literature for assigned tasks as well as for enjoyment | | | | | | | | | |
| **Vocabulary Development** | | | | | | | | | |
| Develop oral vocabulary | | | | | | | | | |
| Identify academic language | ✔ | ✔ | ✔ | ✔ | ✔ | ✔ | ✔ | ✔ | ✔ |
| Identify persons, places, things, actions | ✔ | ✔ | ✔ | ✔ | ✔ | ✔ | | | |
| Classify and categorize words | ✔ | ✔ | ✔ | ✔ | ✔ | ✔ | ✔ | | |
| Identify salient features of vocabulary | | ✔ | ✔ | ✔ | ✔ | ✔ | ✔ | ✔ | ✔ |
| Synonyms, antonyms, and opposites | | ✔ | ✔ | ✔ | ✔ | ✔ | ✔ | | |
| Use context clues: word, sentence, paragraph; definition, example, restatement, description | | ✔ | ✔ | ✔ | ✔ | ✔ | ✔ | ✔ | ✔ |

| | K | 1 | 2 | 3 | 4 | 5 | 6 | 7 | 8 |
|---|---|---|---|---|---|---|---|---|---|
| Use word identification strategies | | ✔ | ✔ | ✔ | ✔ | ✔ | ✔ | | |
| Unfamiliar words | | ✔ | ✔ | ✔ | ✔ | ✔ | ✔ | | |
| Multiple-meaning words | | ✔ | ✔ | ✔ | ✔ | ✔ | ✔ | | |
| Use dictionary to locate meanings, pronunciation, and derivatives | | ✔ | ✔ | ✔ | ✔ | ✔ | ✔ | | |
| Compound words | | ✔ | ✔ | ✔ | ✔ | ✔ | ✔ | | |
| Words ending in *-er* and *-est* | | | ✔ | ✔ | ✔ | ✔ | | | |
| Base (root) words and their derivations | | ✔ | ✔ | ✔ | ✔ | ✔ | ✔ | ✔ | |
| Prefixes and suffixes | | ✔ | ✔ | ✔ | ✔ | ✔ | ✔ | | |
| Greek and Latin roots | | | ✔ | ✔ | ✔ | ✔ | ✔ | ✔ | ✔ |
| Denotation and connotation | | | | | ✔ | ✔ | ✔ | ✔ | ✔ |
| Word families | | ✔ | ✔ | ✔ | ✔ | ✔ | ✔ | | |
| Inflectional endings | | ✔ | ✔ | ✔ | ✔ | ✔ | ✔ | | |
| Use a thesaurus | | | ✔ | ✔ | ✔ | ✔ | ✔ | | |
| Use reference sources for word meaning, such as a dictionary | | ✔ | ✔ | ✔ | ✔ | ✔ | | | |
| Homographs | | | | ✔ | ✔ | ✔ | ✔ | | |
| Homophones | | | ✔ | ✔ | ✔ | ✔ | ✔ | | |
| Contractions | | ✔ | ✔ | ✔ | | | | | |
| Figurative language (metaphors, similes) | | | ✔ | ✔ | ✔ | ✔ | ✔ | ✔ | ✔ |
| Idioms | | | ✔ | ✔ | ✔ | ✔ | ✔ | ✔ | ✔ |
| Analogies | | | | | | ✔ | ✔ | ✔ | ✔ |
| Listen to, read, discuss familiar and unfamiliar challenging text | | | | | | | | | |
| Relate new vocabulary to prior knowledge | | | | | | | | | |
| Use vocabulary to express spatial and temporal relationships | | | | | | | | | |
| Identify shades of meaning in related words | | | | ✔ | ✔ | ✔ | ✔ | ✔ | ✔ |
| Word origins | | | | ✔ | ✔ | ✔ | ✔ | ✔ | ✔ |
| Morphology | | | | ✔ | ✔ | ✔ | ✔ | ✔ | ✔ |
| **Comprehension Strategies** | | | | | | | | | |
| Build background | | | | | | | | | |
| Use prior knowledge | | | | | | | | | |
| Preview and predict | ✔ | ✔ | ✔ | ✔ | ✔ | ✔ | ✔ | ✔ | ✔ |
| Set and adjust purpose for reading | | | | | | | | | |
| Evaluate | | | | | ✔ | ✔ | ✔ | ✔ | ✔ |
| Generate questions | ✔ | ✔ | ✔ | ✔ | ✔ | ✔ | ✔ | ✔ | ✔ |
| Inferences, making | ✔ | ✔ | ✔ | ✔ | ✔ | ✔ | ✔ | ✔ | ✔ |
| Monitor comprehension: including reread, adjust reading rate, paraphrase, self-correct, read ahead, seek help | | ✔ | ✔ | ✔ | ✔ | ✔ | ✔ | ✔ | ✔ |
| Retell | | | | | | | | | |
| Summarize | ✔ | ✔ | ✔ | ✔ | ✔ | ✔ | ✔ | ✔ | ✔ |
| Story structure (identifying and analyzing) | ✔ | ✔ | ✔ | ✔ | ✔ | ✔ | ✔ | ✔ | ✔ |
| Text structure (identifying and analyzing) | | ✔ | ✔ | ✔ | ✔ | ✔ | ✔ | ✔ | ✔ |
| Identify text features | ✔ | ✔ | ✔ | ✔ | ✔ | ✔ | ✔ | ✔ | ✔ |
| Visualize | ✔ | ✔ | ✔ | ✔ | ✔ | ✔ | ✔ | ✔ | ✔ |
| **Comprehension Skills** | | | | | | | | | |
| Author's perspective (author's point of view) | | | ✔ | ✔ | ✔ | ✔ | ✔ | ✔ | |
| Author's purpose (inform, entertain, persuade) | | ✔ | ✔ | ✔ | ✔ | ✔ | ✔ | ✔ | |
| Cause and effect | ✔ | ✔ | ✔ | ✔ | ✔ | ✔ | ✔ | ✔ | |
| Compare and contrast (including character, setting, plot, topics) | ✔ | ✔ | ✔ | ✔ | ✔ | ✔ | ✔ | ✔ | ✔ |

| KEY | |
|---|---|
| | ✔ = Assessed Skill |
| | Tinted panels show skills, strategies, and other teaching opportunities. |

CA

Scope and Sequence

| | K | 1 | 2 | 3 | 4 | 5 | 6 | 7 | 8 |
|---|---|---|---|---|---|---|---|---|---|
| Classify and categorize | ✔ | ✔ | ✔ | | | | | | |
| Conclusions, drawing | | ✔ | ✔ | ✔ | ✔ | ✔ | ✔ | | |
| Fact and opinion | | | | | ✔ | ✔ | ✔ | | |
| Fantasy and reality | ✔ | ✔ | ✔ | ✔ | ✔ | ✔ | ✔ | | |
| Generalizations, making | | | | | ✔ | ✔ | ✔ | | |
| Illustrations, using | ✔ | ✔ | ✔ | | | | | | |
| Inferences, making | | ✔ | ✔ | ✔ | ✔ | ✔ | ✔ | | |
| Instructions/directions (written and oral) | | | ✔ | ✔ | ✔ | ✔ | ✔ | ✔ | ✔ |
| Judgments, making | | | | ✔ | ✔ | ✔ | ✔ | | |
| Main idea and relevant supporting details | ✔ | ✔ | ✔ | ✔ | ✔ | ✔ | ✔ | | |
| Implied message | | | | ✔ | | ✔ | ✔ | ✔ | |
| Persuasion/persuasive techniques | | | | | | ✔ | ✔ | ✔ | ✔ |
| Predictions, making/confirming | ✔ | ✔ | ✔ | ✔ | ✔ | ✔ | ✔ | ✔ | ✔ |
| Problem and solution (problem/resolution) | ✔ | ✔ | ✔ | ✔ | ✔ | ✔ | ✔ | | |
| Sequence, arrange events in; chronological order of events | ✔ | ✔ | ✔ | ✔ | ✔ | ✔ | ✔ | | |
| Summarize | ✔ | ✔ | ✔ | ✔ | ✔ | ✔ | ✔ | ✔ | ✔ |
| **LITERARY ANALYSIS AND RESPONSE** | | | | | | | | | |
| **Genre: Fiction** | | | | | | | | | |
| Drama/play | | | | ✔ | ✔ | ✔ | ✔ | ✔ | ✔ |
| Fantasy | | | | ✔ | ✔ | ✔ | ✔ | ✔ | ✔ |
| Historical fiction | | | | ✔ | ✔ | ✔ | ✔ | ✔ | ✔ |
| Humorous fiction | | | | ✔ | ✔ | ✔ | ✔ | ✔ | ✔ |
| Mystery | | | | ✔ | ✔ | ✔ | ✔ | ✔ | ✔ |
| Picture book | | | | | | | | | |
| Realistic fiction | | | | ✔ | ✔ | ✔ | ✔ | ✔ | ✔ |
| Rhyming story | | | | | | | | | |
| Science fiction | | | | | ✔ | ✔ | ✔ | ✔ | ✔ |
| Short story | | | | ✔ | ✔ | ✔ | ✔ | ✔ | ✔ |
| Traditional stories: fairy tale, fable, folktale, tall tale, myth, legend | | | | ✔ | ✔ | ✔ | ✔ | ✔ | ✔ |
| **Genre: Poetry** | | | | | | | | | |
| Forms (refrain, cinquain, free verse, haiku, limerick, lyric, narrative, simple) | | | | ✔ | ✔ | ✔ | ✔ | ✔ | ✔ |
| Tone | | | | | | | ✔ | ✔ | ✔ |
| **Literary Devices and Elements** | | | | | | | | | |
| Alliteration | ✔ | ✔ | ✔ | ✔ | ✔ | ✔ | ✔ | | |
| Character | ✔ | ✔ | ✔ | ✔ | ✔ | ✔ | ✔ | ✔ | ✔ |
| Consonance and assonance | | | | ✔ | ✔ | ✔ | ✔ | | |
| Dialect | | | | | | | | | |
| Descriptive and figurative language (metaphors, similes, personification, hyperbole) | | ✔ | ✔ | ✔ | ✔ | ✔ | ✔ | ✔ | ✔ |
| Foreshadowing; flashback | | | | ✔ | ✔ | ✔ | ✔ | ✔ | ✔ |
| Imagery | | | | ✔ | ✔ | ✔ | ✔ | | |
| Meter | | | | ✔ | ✔ | ✔ | ✔ | | |
| Onomatopoeia | | | | ✔ | ✔ | ✔ | ✔ | | |
| Plot development | ✔ | ✔ | ✔ | ✔ | ✔ | ✔ | ✔ | ✔ | ✔ |
| Repetition | | ✔ | ✔ | ✔ | ✔ | ✔ | ✔ | | |
| Rhyme/rhyme schemes | | ✔ | ✔ | ✔ | ✔ | ✔ | ✔ | | |
| Rhythm | | ✔ | ✔ | ✔ | ✔ | ✔ | ✔ | | |

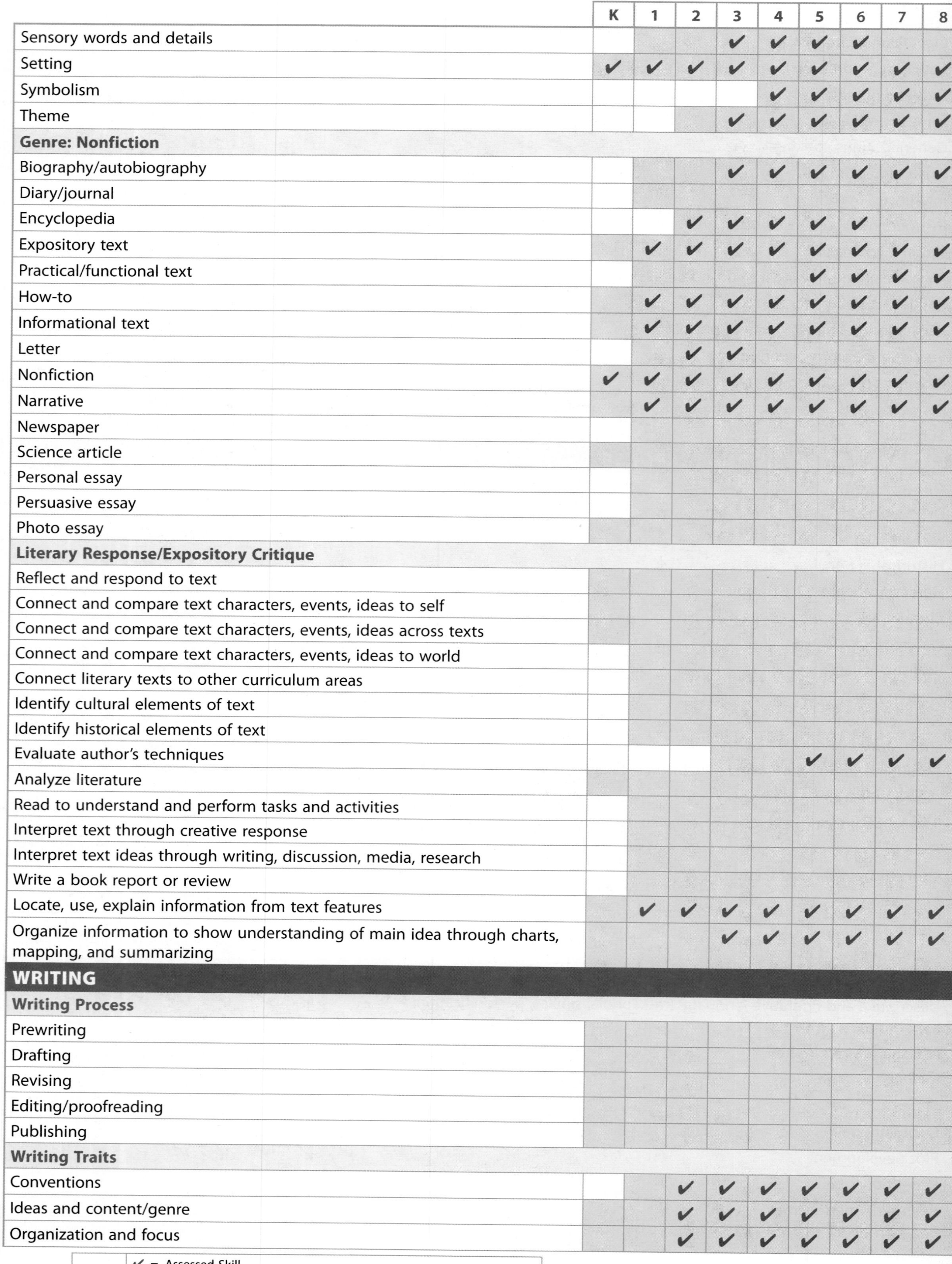

| | K | 1 | 2 | 3 | 4 | 5 | 6 | 7 | 8 |
|---|---|---|---|---|---|---|---|---|---|
| Sensory words and details | | | | ✔ | ✔ | ✔ | ✔ | | |
| Setting | ✔ | ✔ | ✔ | ✔ | ✔ | ✔ | ✔ | ✔ | ✔ |
| Symbolism | | | | | ✔ | ✔ | ✔ | ✔ | ✔ |
| Theme | | | | ✔ | ✔ | ✔ | ✔ | ✔ | ✔ |
| **Genre: Nonfiction** | | | | | | | | | |
| Biography/autobiography | | | | ✔ | ✔ | ✔ | ✔ | ✔ | ✔ |
| Diary/journal | | | | | | | | | |
| Encyclopedia | | | ✔ | ✔ | ✔ | ✔ | ✔ | | |
| Expository text | | ✔ | ✔ | ✔ | ✔ | ✔ | ✔ | ✔ | ✔ |
| Practical/functional text | | | | | | ✔ | ✔ | ✔ | ✔ |
| How-to | | ✔ | ✔ | ✔ | ✔ | ✔ | ✔ | ✔ | ✔ |
| Informational text | | ✔ | ✔ | ✔ | ✔ | ✔ | ✔ | ✔ | ✔ |
| Letter | | | ✔ | ✔ | | | | | |
| Nonfiction | ✔ | ✔ | ✔ | ✔ | ✔ | ✔ | ✔ | ✔ | ✔ |
| Narrative | | ✔ | ✔ | ✔ | ✔ | ✔ | ✔ | ✔ | ✔ |
| Newspaper | | | | | | | | | |
| Science article | | | | | | | | | |
| Personal essay | | | | | | | | | |
| Persuasive essay | | | | | | | | | |
| Photo essay | | | | | | | | | |
| **Literary Response/Expository Critique** | | | | | | | | | |
| Reflect and respond to text | | | | | | | | | |
| Connect and compare text characters, events, ideas to self | | | | | | | | | |
| Connect and compare text characters, events, ideas across texts | | | | | | | | | |
| Connect and compare text characters, events, ideas to world | | | | | | | | | |
| Connect literary texts to other curriculum areas | | | | | | | | | |
| Identify cultural elements of text | | | | | | | | | |
| Identify historical elements of text | | | | | | | | | |
| Evaluate author's techniques | | | | | | ✔ | ✔ | ✔ | ✔ |
| Analyze literature | | | | | | | | | |
| Read to understand and perform tasks and activities | | | | | | | | | |
| Interpret text through creative response | | | | | | | | | |
| Interpret text ideas through writing, discussion, media, research | | | | | | | | | |
| Write a book report or review | | | | | | | | | |
| Locate, use, explain information from text features | | ✔ | ✔ | ✔ | ✔ | ✔ | ✔ | ✔ | ✔ |
| Organize information to show understanding of main idea through charts, mapping, and summarizing | | | | ✔ | ✔ | ✔ | ✔ | ✔ | ✔ |
| **WRITING** | | | | | | | | | |
| **Writing Process** | | | | | | | | | |
| Prewriting | | | | | | | | | |
| Drafting | | | | | | | | | |
| Revising | | | | | | | | | |
| Editing/proofreading | | | | | | | | | |
| Publishing | | | | | | | | | |
| **Writing Traits** | | | | | | | | | |
| Conventions | | | ✔ | ✔ | ✔ | ✔ | ✔ | ✔ | ✔ |
| Ideas and content/genre | | | ✔ | ✔ | ✔ | ✔ | ✔ | ✔ | ✔ |
| Organization and focus | | | ✔ | ✔ | ✔ | ✔ | ✔ | ✔ | ✔ |

| KEY | ✔ = Assessed Skill |
|---|---|
| | Tinted panels show skills, strategies, and other teaching opportunities. |

| | K | 1 | 2 | 3 | 4 | 5 | 6 | 7 | 8 |
|---|---|---|---|---|---|---|---|---|---|
| Sentence structure/fluency | | | ✔ | ✔ | ✔ | ✔ | ✔ | ✔ | ✔ |
| Voice | | | ✔ | ✔ | ✔ | ✔ | ✔ | ✔ | ✔ |
| Word choice | | | ✔ | ✔ | ✔ | ✔ | ✔ | ✔ | ✔ |
| **Writer's Craft** | | | | | | | | | |
| Good topic, topic sentence | | | ✔ | ✔ | ✔ | ✔ | ✔ | ✔ | ✔ |
| Paragraph(s) | | | ✔ | ✔ | ✔ | ✔ | ✔ | ✔ | ✔ |
| Supporting details | | | ✔ | ✔ | ✔ | ✔ | ✔ | ✔ | ✔ |
| Unimportant details | | | | | | | | | |
| Fact and opinion | | | | ✔ | ✔ | ✔ | ✔ | ✔ | ✔ |
| Strong opening, strong conclusion | | | ✔ | ✔ | ✔ | ✔ | ✔ | ✔ | ✔ |
| Beginning, middle, end | | ✔ | ✔ | ✔ | ✔ | ✔ | ✔ | ✔ | ✔ |
| Precise words, vary words | | | ✔ | ✔ | ✔ | ✔ | ✔ | ✔ | ✔ |
| Figurative language | | | | | | | ✔ | | |
| Informal/formal language | | | | | | | | | |
| Mood/tone | | | | | | | | ✔ | ✔ |
| Dialogue | | | | ✔ | ✔ | ✔ | ✔ | ✔ | ✔ |
| Transition words, transitions to multiple paragraphs | | | | ✔ | ✔ | ✔ | ✔ | ✔ | ✔ |
| Select focus and organization | | | ✔ | ✔ | ✔ | ✔ | ✔ | ✔ | ✔ |
| Use reference materials (dictionary, thesaurus, online encyclopedia) | | | ✔ | ✔ | ✔ | ✔ | ✔ | ✔ | ✔ |
| **Writing Applications** | | | | | | | | | |
| Personal and fictional narrative (also biographical and autobiographical) | | ✔ | ✔ | ✔ | ✔ | ✔ | ✔ | ✔ | ✔ |
| Write a variety of expressive forms | | ✔ | ✔ | ✔ | ✔ | ✔ | ✔ | | |
| Write a variety of informational/expository forms | | ✔ | ✔ | ✔ | ✔ | ✔ | ✔ | ✔ | ✔ |
| Write a description | | ✔ | ✔ | ✔ | ✔ | ✔ | ✔ | | |
| Write simple directions | | | | | | | | | |
| Write a variety of communications (including technical documents) | | ✔ | ✔ | ✔ | ✔ | ✔ | ✔ | ✔ | ✔ |
| Write a research report | | | ✔ | ✔ | ✔ | ✔ | ✔ | ✔ | ✔ |
| Write responses to literature | | | | ✔ | ✔ | ✔ | ✔ | ✔ | ✔ |
| Write summaries | | | ✔ | ✔ | ✔ | ✔ | ✔ | ✔ | ✔ |
| Write letters | | | ✔ | ✔ | | | | | |
| **Grammar, Mechanics, and Usage** | | | | | | | | | |
| Sentence concepts: statements, questions, exclamations, commands | | ✔ | ✔ | ✔ | ✔ | ✔ | ✔ | ✔ | |
| Complete and incomplete sentences; sentence fragments, word order | | ✔ | ✔ | ✔ | ✔ | ✔ | ✔ | ✔ | ✔ |
| Compound sentences, compound-complex sentences | | | | | ✔ | ✔ | ✔ | ✔ | ✔ |
| Combining sentences | | ✔ | ✔ | ✔ | ✔ | ✔ | ✔ | ✔ | ✔ |
| Nouns: including common, proper, singular, plural, irregular plurals, possessives | | ✔ | ✔ | ✔ | ✔ | ✔ | ✔ | ✔ | |
| Verbs: including action, helping, linking, irregular | | ✔ | ✔ | ✔ | ✔ | ✔ | ✔ | ✔ | |
| Verb tenses: including past, present, future, perfect, and progressive | | ✔ | ✔ | ✔ | ✔ | ✔ | ✔ | ✔ | ✔ |
| Pronouns: including possessive, subject and object, pronoun-verb agreement, indefinite | | ✔ | ✔ | ✔ | ✔ | ✔ | ✔ | ✔ | |
| Adjectives: including articles, demonstrative, adjectives that compare | | ✔ | ✔ | ✔ | ✔ | ✔ | ✔ | ✔ | |
| Adverbs: including telling how, when, where, comparative, superlative, irregular | | | ✔ | ✔ | ✔ | ✔ | ✔ | ✔ | |
| Subject, predicate; subject-verb agreement | | | ✔ | ✔ | ✔ | ✔ | ✔ | ✔ | ✔ |
| Contractions | | ✔ | ✔ | ✔ | ✔ | ✔ | ✔ | | |
| Conjunctions | | | | | ✔ | ✔ | ✔ | ✔ | ✔ |

| | K | 1 | 2 | 3 | 4 | 5 | 6 | 7 | 8 |
|---|---|---|---|---|---|---|---|---|---|
| Commas | | | ✔ | ✔ | ✔ | ✔ | ✔ | ✔ | ✔ |
| Colons, semi-colons, dashes, hyphens | | | | | | ✔ | ✔ | ✔ | ✔ |
| Quotation marks | | | ✔ | ✔ | ✔ | ✔ | ✔ | ✔ | ✔ |
| Prepositions and prepositional phrases, appositives | | | | | ✔ | ✔ | ✔ | ✔ | ✔ |
| Independent and dependent clauses | | | | | | ✔ | ✔ | ✔ | ✔ |
| Negatives, correcting double negatives | | | | | ✔ | ✔ | ✔ | ✔ | ✔ |
| Use correct capitalization in sentences, proper nouns, titles, abbreviations | | ✔ | ✔ | ✔ | ✔ | ✔ | ✔ | ✔ | ✔ |
| Use correct punctuation | | ✔ | ✔ | ✔ | ✔ | ✔ | ✔ | ✔ | ✔ |
| Antecedents | | | | ✔ | ✔ | ✔ | ✔ | ✔ | ✔ |
| Homophones | | | ✔ | ✔ | ✔ | ✔ | ✔ | | |
| Parallelism | | | | | | | | | ✔ |
| **Spelling** | | | | | | | | | |
| Write irregular high-frequency words | ✔ | ✔ | ✔ | | | | | | |
| ABC order | | | | ✔ | | | | | |
| Write letters | | | | | | | | | |
| Words with short vowels | ✔ | ✔ | ✔ | ✔ | ✔ | ✔ | ✔ | | |
| Words with long vowels | | ✔ | ✔ | ✔ | ✔ | ✔ | ✔ | | |
| Words with digraphs, blends, consonant clusters, double consonants | | ✔ | ✔ | ✔ | ✔ | ✔ | ✔ | | |
| Words with variant and ambiguous vowels | | ✔ | ✔ | ✔ | ✔ | ✔ | ✔ | | |
| Words with diphthongs | | ✔ | ✔ | ✔ | ✔ | ✔ | | | |
| Words with *r*-controlled vowels | | ✔ | ✔ | ✔ | ✔ | ✔ | ✔ | | |
| Schwa words | | | | ✔ | ✔ | ✔ | ✔ | | |
| Words with silent letters | | | ✔ | ✔ | ✔ | ✔ | ✔ | | |
| Words with hard and soft letters | | | ✔ | ✔ | ✔ | ✔ | ✔ | | |
| Inflectional endings: including plural, past tense, drop final *e* and double consonant when adding *-ed* and *-ing* | | ✔ | ✔ | ✔ | ✔ | ✔ | ✔ | | |
| Compound words | | ✔ | ✔ | ✔ | ✔ | ✔ | ✔ | | |
| Homonyms/homophones | | | ✔ | ✔ | ✔ | ✔ | ✔ | | |
| Prefixes and suffixes | | | ✔ | ✔ | ✔ | ✔ | ✔ | | |
| Root and base words (also spell derivatives) | | | | ✔ | ✔ | ✔ | ✔ | ✔ | |
| Syllables: patterns, rules, accented, stressed, closed, open | | | | ✔ | ✔ | ✔ | ✔ | | |
| Words with Greek and Latin roots | | | | | | ✔ | ✔ | ✔ | ✔ |
| Words from mythology | | | | | | | ✔ | | |
| Words with spelling patterns, word families | | ✔ | ✔ | ✔ | ✔ | ✔ | ✔ | | |
| **Penmanship** | | | | | | | | | |
| Write upper and lowercase letters using correct formation and spacing | ✔ | ✔ | ✔ | ✔ | ✔ | | | | |
| Write using left-to-right and top-to-bottom directionality | ✔ | ✔ | | | | | | | |
| Write using appropriate spacing between letters, words, and sentences | | ✔ | ✔ | ✔ | | | | | |
| Write using appropriate margins and indentations | | | | ✔ | ✔ | | | | |
| Write legibly in manuscript | ✔ | ✔ | ✔ | | | | | | |
| Write legibly in cursive | | | | ✔ | ✔ | | | | |
| **Listening** | | | | | | | | | |
| Identify musical elements in language | | | | | | | | | |
| Determine the purpose for listening | | | | | | | | | |
| Understand and follow directions | | | | | | | | | |
| Develop oral language and concepts | | | | | | | | | |
| Listen responsively, attentively, and critically | | | | | | | | | |

| KEY | ✔ = Assessed Skill |
|---|---|
| | Tinted panels show skills, strategies, and other teaching opportunities. |

| | K | 1 | 2 | 3 | 4 | 5 | 6 | 7 | 8 |
|---|---|---|---|---|---|---|---|---|---|
| Listen to distinguish fact from fiction; fact from opinion | | | | | | | | | |
| Listen responsively to oral presentations | | | | | | | | | |
| Ask and answer relevant questions (for clarification to follow-up on ideas) | | | | | | | | | |
| Apply comprehension strategies and skills in listening activities | | | | | | | | | |
| Recall and interpret speakers', verbal and nonverbal messages, purposes, and perspectives | | | | | | | | | |
| **Speaking** | | | | | | | | | |
| Use repetition, rhyme, and rhythm in oral texts | | | | | | | | | |
| Participate in classroom activities and discussions | | | | | | | | | |
| Ask and answer questions | | | | | | | | | |
| Stay on topic when speaking | | | | | | | | | |
| Use language appropriate to situation, purpose, and audience | | | | | | | | | |
| Use nonverbal communications such as eye contact, gestures, and props | | | | | | | | | |
| Use verbal communication in effective ways | | | | | | | | | |
| Retell a story, presentation, or spoken message by summarizing | | | | | | | | | |
| Oral presentations: focus, organizational structure, audience, purpose | | | | | | | | | |
| Give and follow directions | | | | | | | | | |
| Consider audience when speaking or preparing a presentation | | | | | | | | | |
| Speak audibly (volume, pitch, pace, phrasing, modulation) | | | | | | | | | |
| Recite poems, rhymes, songs | | | | | | | | | |
| Use complete, coherent sentences | | | | | | | | | |
| Organize presentations | | | | | | | | | |
| Deliver presentations (narrative, oral summaries, research, persuasive) | | | | | | | | | |
| **INFORMATIONAL AND MEDIA LITERACY** | | | | | | | | | |
| **Informational Text and Text Features** | | | | | | | | | |
| Recognize and identify text and organizational features of nonfiction texts | | ✔ | ✔ | ✔ | ✔ | ✔ | ✔ | ✔ | ✔ |
| Recognize and identify text features of poetry, fiction, drama, popular media, workplace and public documents, consumer materials | | ✔ | ✔ | ✔ | ✔ | ✔ | ✔ | ✔ | ✔ |
| Captions and labels, headings, subheadings, footnotes, endnotes, key words, bold print | | ✔ | ✔ | ✔ | ✔ | ✔ | ✔ | ✔ | ✔ |
| Graphics, including photographs, illustrations, maps, charts, diagrams, graphs, time lines | | ✔ | ✔ | ✔ | ✔ | ✔ | ✔ | ✔ | ✔ |
| **Study Skills** | | | | | | | | | |
| Directions: read, write, give, follow (includes technical directions) | | | ✔ | ✔ | ✔ | ✔ | ✔ | ✔ | ✔ |
| Evaluate directions for sequence and completeness | | | | ✔ | ✔ | ✔ | ✔ | ✔ | ✔ |
| Use library/media center | | ✔ | ✔ | ✔ | ✔ | ✔ | ✔ | ✔ | ✔ |
| Use parts of a book to locate information | ✔ | ✔ | ✔ | ✔ | ✔ | ✔ | ✔ | ✔ | ✔ |
| Interpret information from graphic aids | | ✔ | ✔ | ✔ | ✔ | ✔ | ✔ | ✔ | ✔ |
| Use graphic organizers to organize information and comprehend text | | ✔ | ✔ | ✔ | ✔ | ✔ | ✔ | ✔ | ✔ |
| Use functional, everyday documents | | | | ✔ | ✔ | ✔ | ✔ | ✔ | ✔ |
| Apply study strategies: skimming and scanning, note-taking, outlining, K-W-L | | | ✔ | ✔ | ✔ | ✔ | ✔ | ✔ | ✔ |
| **Research Process** | | | | | | | | | |
| Generate and revise questions for research | | | | ✔ | ✔ | ✔ | ✔ | ✔ | ✔ |
| Narrow focus of research | | | | ✔ | ✔ | ✔ | ✔ | ✔ | ✔ |
| Find and locate information using print and electronic resources | ✔ | | ✔ | ✔ | ✔ | ✔ | ✔ | ✔ | ✔ |
| Record information systematically (note-taking, outlining) | | | | ✔ | ✔ | ✔ | ✔ | ✔ | ✔ |
| Develop a systematic research plan | | | | ✔ | ✔ | ✔ | ✔ | ✔ | ✔ |
| Evaluate reliability, credibility, usefulness of sources and information | | | | | | ✔ | ✔ | ✔ | ✔ |

# Scope and Sequence

| | K | 1 | 2 | 3 | 4 | 5 | 6 | 7 | 8 |
|---|---|---|---|---|---|---|---|---|---|
| Use primary sources to obtain information | | | | | ✔ | ✔ | ✔ | ✔ | ✔ |
| Synthesize, evaluate, and draw conclusions from information | | | | | | | | ✔ | ✔ |
| Cite and list sources of information (record basic bibliographic data) | | | | | ✔ | ✔ | ✔ | ✔ | ✔ |
| Demonstrate basic keyboarding skills | ✔ | ✔ | ✔ | ✔ | ✔ | ✔ | ✔ | ✔ | ✔ |
| **Media Literacy** | | | | | | | | | |
| Summarize the main idea, message or content, supporting details from media message | | | | | | | | ✔ | ✔ |
| Use graphics, illustrations to analyze and interpret information | | | | | | ✔ | ✔ | ✔ | ✔ |
| Identify structural features of popular media and use the features to obtain information: including newspapers, magazines, and digital technology | | | | ✔ | ✔ | ✔ | ✔ | ✔ | ✔ |
| Distinguish between fact and opinion in visuals and print media message | | | | | | ✔ | ✔ | ✔ | ✔ |
| Analyze media source: recognize effects of media in one's mood and emotion | | | | ✔ | ✔ | ✔ | ✔ | ✔ | ✔ |
| Make informed judgments about print and nonprint media | | | | ✔ | ✔ | ✔ | ✔ | ✔ | ✔ |
| Critique persuasive techniques | | | | | | ✔ | ✔ | ✔ | ✔ |
| **Technology** | | | | | | | | | |
| Use computer, Internet, CD-Rom, and other technology resources to access information | | | | ✔ | ✔ | ✔ | ✔ | ✔ | ✔ |
| Use text and organizational features of electronic resources: including search engines, keywords, e-mail, hyperlinks, URLs, Web pages, databases, graphics | | | | | ✔ | ✔ | ✔ | ✔ | ✔ |
| Use digital tools to present and publish in a variety of media formats | | | | | | | | ✔ | ✔ |

| KEY | ✔ = Assessed Skill |
|---|---|
| | Tinted panels show skills, strategies, and other teaching opportunities. |

# Index

# A

# B





**Key** 1 = Unit 1

# C

# Index





**Key** 1 = Unit 1

Key 1 = Unit 1

# F

**Key** 1 = Unit 1

# H



# I





Key 1 = Unit 1

# J



# K



# L

**Key** 1 = Unit 1

# Index



## M



## N

# O



# P





**Key** 1 = Unit 1

# R





**Key** 1 = Unit 1

# S





**Key** 1 = Unit 1

# Index



## T





**Key** 1 = Unit 1

# U



# V





**Key** 1 = Unit 1

Index



# W





**Key** 1 = Unit 1

# Index

# Index





**Key** 1 = Unit 1

## Acknowledgments

*The publisher gratefully acknowledges permission to reprint the following copyrighted material:*

"Amazing Grace" by Mary Hoffman, illustrations by Caroline Binch. Text copyright © 1991 by Mary Hoffman. Illustrations copyright © 1991 by Caroline Binch. Reprinted by permission of Dial Books for Young Readers, a division of Penguin Young Readers Group.

"Author: A True Story" by Helen Lester. Copyright © 1997 by Helen Lester. Reprinted by permission of Houghton Mifflin Books.

"Boom Town" by Sonia Levitin, illustrations by Cat Bowman Smith. Text copyright © 1998 by Sonia Levitin. Illustrations copyright © 1998 by Cat Bowman Smith. Reprinted with permission by Orchard Books a Grolier Company.

"A Castle on Viola Street" by DyAnne DiSalvo. Copyright © 2001 by DyAnne DiSalvo. Reprinted with permission of HarperCollins Children's Books, a division of HarperCollins Publishers.

"The Caterpillar" by Christina Rossetti from BOOK OF POEMS by Tomie dePaola. Text copyright © 1988 by Tomie dePaola. Reprinted with permission.

"A Child's Call to Aid the Zoo" by Jim Davis. Copyright © 2003 by Jim Davis. Reprinted with permission by The Fresno Bee, a division of the The McClatchy Company.

"Dear Juno" by Soyung Pak, illustrations by Susan Kathleen Hartung. Text copyright © 1999 by Soyung Pak. Illustrations copyright © 1999 by Susan Kathleen Hartung. Reprinted with permission of Penguin Putnam Books for Young Readers, Penguin Books Ltd.

"First Day Jitters" by Julie Danneberg, illustrations by Judy Love. Text copyright © 2000 by Julie Danneberg. Illustrations copyright © 2000 by Judy Love. Reprinted with permission of Charlesbridge, Charlesbridge Publishing, Inc. All rights reserved.

"Home-Grown Butterflies" by Deborah Churchman from RANGER RICK®. Copyright © 1998 by National Wildlife Federation. Reprinted with permission of the National Wildlife Federation, May 1998.

"The Jones Family Express" by Javaka Steptoe. Text and illustrations copyright © 2003 by Javaka Steptoe. Reprinted by permission of Lee & Low Books, Inc.

"Listen" is from A RUMPUS OF RHYMES: A BOOK OF NOISY POEMS is by Bobbi Katz and illustrated by Suan Estelle Kwas. Text copyright © 2001 by Bobby Katz. Illustrations copyright © 2001 by Susan Estell Kwas. Printed by permission of Dutton Children's Books, a division of Penguin Putnam Books for Young Readers.

"Monarch Butterfly" by Marilyn Singer from FIREFLIES AT MIDNIGHT by Marilyn Singer. Text copyright © 2003 by Marilyn Singer. Reprinted with permission by Atheneum Books for Young Readers, an imprint of Simon & Schuster Children's Publishing Division.

"My Very Own Room" by Amada Irma Pérez, illustrations by Maya Christina Gonzalez. Text copyright © 2000 by Amada Irma Pérez. Illustrations copyright © 2000 by Maya Christina Gonzalez. Reprinted with permission by Children's Book Press.

"The Storytelling Stone" is from KEEPERS OF THE EARTH: NATIVE AMERICAN STORIES AND ENVIRONMENTAL ACTIVITIES FOR CHILDREN by Joseph Bruchac. Copyright © 1989 by Joseph Bruchac. Reprinted by permission of Fulcrum Press.

"What Do Illustrators Do?" by Eileen Christelow. Copyright © 1999 by Eileen Christelow. Reprinted with permission by Clarion Books, an imprint of Houghton Mifflin Company.

"Wolf!" by Becky Bloom, illustrations by Pascal Biet. Copyright © 1999 by Siphano, Montpellier. Reprinted with permission by Orchard Books, a Grolier Company.

**ILLUSTRATIONS**
**Cover Illustrations:** Leland Klanderman

10–29: Judy Love. 36–37: Lindy Burnett. 38–59: Caroline Binch. 60–63: Robert McGuire. 65: Ken Bowser. 69: Sarah Beise. 80: Jason Abbott. 82–105: Pascal Biet. 116–139: Maya Christina Gonzalez. 146–147: Laura Ovresat. 160–183: Cat Bowman Smith. 240–241: Traci Van Wagoner. 248–269: DyAnne DiSalvo. 276: Kathleen Kemly. 279: Joe Taylor. 290–303: Helen Lester. 304–307: Susan Estelle Kwas. 314–339: Susan Kathleen Hartung. 362–385: Eileen Christelow. 386–389: Chris Boyd. 396–419: Javaka Steptoe. 424–425: Amanda Hall. 426–427: Cathi Mingus.

**PHOTOGRAPHY**
*All Photographs are by Ken Cavanagh, Ken Karp or Dave Mager for Macmillan/McGraw Hill (MMH) except as noted below:*

Inside front and back cover: Dynamic Graphics Group/Creatas/Alamy. v: Spencer Grant/Photo Edit. vi: William Dow/CORBIS. vii: (t) Superstock; (c) Darrell Wong/The Fresno Bee. ix: David Young-Wolff/Photo Edit. 2-3: BananaStock/PunchStock. 3: Michael Newman/PhotoEdit. 4: Michael Newman/PhotoEdit. 5: Maria Azucena Vigil. 6-7: Jeff Cadge/Getty Images. 8: (t) Don Tremain/Getty Images; (tr) Royalty Free/CORBIS. 9: David Young-Wolf/Photo Edit. 28: (tr) Courtesy Charlesbridge Press; (bl) Courtesy Charlesbridge Press. 30: Alan Oddie/Photo Edit. 31: Radius/PunchStock33: Amos Morgan/Photodisc/Punchstock. 34-35: Bill Bachmann/Index Stock Imagery. 58: (tl) Courtesy Mary Hoffman; (tr) Courtesy Caroline Binch. 66-67: Spencer Grant/Photo Edit. 68: (t) Jon Soo Hoo/Los Angeles Dodgers; (b) Major League Baseball/Urban Youth Academy. 69: Free the Children, www.freethechildren.com. 70-73: Bridget Barrett. 74: (tc) Bob Daemmrich/Photo Edit; (tr) Smart Creatives/Corbis. 78-79: Bettmann/CORBIS. 106-107: (bkgd) Tom Brakefield/The Image Works. 107: (tr) Robert E. Barber/Alamy; (c) Tom Brakefield/The Image Works, Inc. 108: (t) Johnansen Krause/National Geographic/Getty Images. 109: Jeff Lepore/Photo Researchers. 111: (r) © Image Source/Corbis. 112-113: CORBIS/PunchStock. 114: (tr) Tom Stewart/CORBIS; (bl) Michael Pole/CORBIS. 115: (cl) C Squared Studios/Getty Images. 138: (tr) Courtesy Children's Book Press; (cl) Courtesy Children's Book Press. 140: (l) Esselte/Phototone/Earthlink Textures; (bl) Marvin Koner/CORBIS. 141: (tl) Farrel Grehan/CORBIS; (bc) Western Pennsylvania Conservancy/Art Resource, NY. 142: (l) Esselte/Phototone/Earthlink Textures; (cr) Angelo Hornak/CORBIS; (c) Wetzel&Company. 143: Catherine Karnow/CORBIS. 145: Amos Morgan/Photodisc/Getty Images, Inc. 148: Nature Picture Library/Alamy. 149: Suzanne L. & Joseph T. Collins/Photo Researchers, Inc. 152-153: Jeff Greenberg/PhotoEdit. 153: Michael Newman/PhotoEdit. 154: Blend Images/Alamy. 155: Cathy Blaivis, Photographer. 156-157: The Art Archive/Culver Pictures. 158: (tr) Charles O'Rear/CORBIS; (cl) Michael Newman/Photo Edit; (bl) David Young-Wolff/Photo Edit. 159: Michael Newman/Photo Edit. 182: (tl) Courtesy Scholastic; (cl) Courtesy Cat Bowman Smith. 184: Bronwyn Kidd/Getty Images. 185: Lynda Richardson/CORBIS. 187: Ariel Skelley/CORBIS. 189: Amos Morgan/Photodisc/Punchstock. 190-191: Christi Carter/Grant Heilman Photography. 192: Millard H. Sharp/Photo Researchers. 193: (tr) Ken Thomas/Photo Researchers; (c) Valerie Giles/Photo Researchers. 194-195: William Dow/CORBIS. 196: (c) Ralph A. Clever/CORBIS; (bl) J.H. Pete Carmichael; (br) J.H. Pete Carmichael. 197: J.H. Pete Carmichael. 198-199: J.H. Pete Carmichael. 199: Whit Bronaugh. 200: (All Photos) Whit Bronaugh. 201: (tl) J.H. Pete Carmichael; (r) Whit Bronaugh. 202: Craig W. Racicot/Game Day Pictures. 203: Craig W. Racicot/Game Day Pictures. 204: (cl) J.H. Pete Carmichael; (cr) Ralph A. Clever/CORBIS; (br) J.H. Pete Carmichael. 204-205: Getty Images. 205: (tl) Craig W. Racicot/Game Day Pictures; (br) Whit Bronaugh. 206: Bill Beatty/Animals Animals/Earth Scenes. 206-207: Craig Tuttle/CORBIS. 207: (tr) Sharon Cummings/Dembinsky Photo Associates; (cl) Raymond Mendez/Animals Animals/Earth Scenes. 208: William Dow/CORBIS. 209: Frank Siteman/Photo Edit Inc. 210-211: Superstock. 212: Tom Bean/Corbis. 213: (tr) Tom Bean/Corbis; (cr) Glow Images/Alamy. 214: The Granger Collection, New York. 215-216: The Bancroft Library/University of California, Berkeley. 217: David Young-Wolff/Getty Images. 218: Yan Butchofsky/Corbis. 222-223: Creatas/PunchStock. 224: Peter Kaplan/Photo Researchers. 225: Heifer International. 226: Robert Cranston/RJ's Images of Nature. 227: Darrell Wong/The Fresno Bee.

446

**Photo Credits** All photographs are by Ken Cavanagh and Ken Karp for MacMillan/McGraw-Hill (MMH) except as noted below:

iii: Row 2 (l) Photography by Monet; (cl) Courtesy of Vicki Gibson. Row 3 (bl) Deborah Attoinese Photography. iv: (bl) Ferguson & Katzman Photography. xii: Michael Newman/PhotoEdit. xiii: Veer. xvi: Michael Newman/PhotoEdit. S1: Creatas/SuperStock. 6A: Brad Perks Lightscapes/Alamy. 6B: (l) David Young-Wolf/Photo Edit; (r) Radius/PunchStock. 6F-G: (bkgd) Brad Perks Lightscapes/Alamy. 6H: Courtesy Mary Hoffman. 33H: Gabe Palmer/CORBIS. 34A: Medioimages/PunchStock. 34F-G: (bkgd) Medioimages/PunchStock. 34H: Courtesy Mary Hoffman. 66A: Rich Reid/National Geographic/AGE Fotostock. 66F-G: (bkgd) Rich Reid/National Geographic/AGE Fotostock. 66H: Courtesy Mary Hoffman.

78A: Susan J. Banta. 78B: (br) Tom Brakefield/The Image Works; (tl) Johnansen Krause/National Geographic/Getty Images; (tr) Robert E. Barber/Alamy. 78F-G: (bkgd) Susan J. Banta. 78H: Courtesy Mary Hoffman. 111H: Jim Cummings/CORBIS. 112A: Photodisc/SuperStock. 112B: (tl) Tom Stewart/CORBIS; (bl) Michael Pole/CORBIS; (bc) C Squared Studios/Getty Images. 112F-G: (bkgd) Photodisc/SuperStock.

112H: Courtesy Mary Hoffman. 146A: Image Source. 151C: Ryan McVay/Getty Images. 151F: Ariel Skelley/CORBIS. 151H: Royalty-Free/CORBIS. 151L: Michael Newman/PhotoEdit.

Teacher's Notes: (tr) Pixtal/PunchStock; (bl) Royalty Free/Corbis.

# Acknowledgments

228: Courtesy Stacey L. Caha. 229: Courtesy of The Fresno Bee. 230: Courtesy Stacey L. Caha. 231: Robert Cranston/RJ's Images of Nature. 232: David Hunter/The Fresno Bee. 233: Courtesy Stacey L. Caha. 234: Courtesy Stacey L. Caha. 235: Courtesy Stacey L. Caha. 236: Courtesy Stacey L. Caha. 237: Robert Cranston/RJ's Images of Nature. 238: Courtesy Gary Soto. 239: Robert Cranston/RJ's Images of Nature. 242: Darrell Wong/The Fresno Bee. 243: Amos Morgan/Photodisc/Getty Images, Inc. 244-245: Paul Burns/Photodisc/Getty Images. 246: Siede Preis/Getty Images. 246-247: Henry Diltz/CORBIS. 247: (tr) David Hiller/Photodisc blue/Getty Images; (c) Dennis MacDonald/Photo Edit. 268: Courtesy DyAnne DiSalvo. 270: (tr) Tim Matsui/Getty Images; (bl) Billy Hustace/Stone/Getty Images. 271: Erik S. Lesser/Getty Images. 272: Erik S. Lesser/Getty Images. 272-273: Mark Peterson/CORBIS. 275: Frank Siteman/PhotoEdit Inc. 278: (All Photos) Steve Ruark/Syracuse Newspapers/The Image Works. 279: Steve Ruark/Syracuse Newspapers/ The Image Works. 282-283: IPNstock. 283: Ulana Switucha/Alamy. 284: ImageSource/PunchStock. 285: Courtesy Kathleen Krull. 286-287: Scott T. Smith/CORBIS. 288: Lulu Delacre. 289: (c) F. Schussler/Photolink/ Getty Images; (cr) Siede Preis/Getty Images. 302: Courtesy Houghton Mifflin. 309: JupiterMedia/Alamy. 310-311: Craig Hammell/CORBIS. 312: (tr) Steve Cole/Masterfile; (cl) Paul Wenham-Clark/Masterfile; (bl) Jeff Greenberg/The Image Works. 313: (inset) Jeff Greenberg/The Image Works; (tr) Photodisc/Picture Quest. 338: (tl) Courtesy Soyung Pak; (cr) Courtesy Susan Kathleen Hartung. 340: (bc) Underwood & Underwood/CORBIS; (br) Leonard de Selva/CORBIS. 341: (tr) J. Richards/Alamy; (c) Leonard de Selva/CORBIS; (bl) Bettmann/CORBIS; (bc) National Archive/Newsmakers/Getty Images; (br) Roberts H. Armstrong/Robertstock/Retrofile. 342:(tr) Rubberball Productions/ Getty Images; (cl) Photodisc/Getty Images; (b) Myrleen Ferguson Gate/Photo Edit. 343: (tr) Stewart Cohen/Stone/Getty Images. 345: Digital Vision/Punchstock. 346-347: David Young-Wolff/Photo Edit. 349: David Young-Wolff/Photo Edit. 354: Colin Young-Wolff/Photo Edit. 357: (c) Lars Lindblad/Shutterstock; (r) Siede Preis/Getty Images. 358-359: JIStock/Masterfile. 360: Bettman/CORBIS. 360-361: (top and bottom) C. Walker/Topham/The Image Works. 361: Bob Rowan/ Progressive Image/CORBIS. 384: Courtesy Eileen Christelow. 388: (cr) CMCD/Getty Images; (br) ELIPSA/CORBIS Sygma. 389: (tr) Digital Vision/Getty Images; (cr) Robbie Jack/CORBIS. 391: Michael Newman/ Photo Edit Inc. 392-393: LWA-Dann Tardif/CORBIS. 394: (tr) Royalty-Free/CORBIS; (bl) Royalty-Free/CORBIS. 395: (tl) The Image Bank/Getty Images; (cl) Royalty-Free/CORBIS; (cr) Bob Krist/CORBIS. 418: Courtesy Javaka Steptoe. 420: SuperStock. 421: Royalty-Free/CORBIS. 423: Pierre Arsenault/Masterfile. 430: (br) Jim Brandenburg/Minden Pictures; (bl) ©Royalty-Free/CORBIS. 432: © Kim Kulish/Corbis. 433: Stockbyte/ PictureQuest. 434: Skip Nall/Getty Images, Inc. 435: Siede Preis/Getty Images, Inc. 436: © Randy Faris/Corbis. 437: Imagebroker/Alamy. 438: © APIX/Alamy. 439: PhotoLink/Getty Images, Inc. 440: ©Royalty-Free/ CORBIS. 442: (t) © David Papazian/Corbis; (b) Digital Art/CORBIS. 444: Margot Granitsas/The Image Works, Inc. 445: C Squared Studios/Getty Images, Inc. IBC: Dynamic Graphics Group/Creatas/Alamy.

# Correlations to the California Standards

- English-Language Arts
- History-Social Science
- Science

# English-Language Arts California Content Standards Grade 3

**Each standard is coded in the following manner**

| R | 3 | 1.1 |
|---|---|---|
| Domain | Grade | Standard |

| KEY | | | |
|---|---|---|---|
| | **TE** = Teacher's Edition | **PR** = Practice Reader | **CCR** = California Content Reader |
| | **OVC** = Oral Vocabulary Cards | **RAA** = Read Aloud Anthology | **DR** = Decodable Reader |
| | **SB** = Student Book | **IK** = Intervention Kit | **TRB** = Teachers' Resource Book |

| DOMAIN: READING | | Macmillan/McGraw-Hill CALIFORNIA TREASURES | |
|---|---|---|---|
| **1.0 Word Analysis, Fluency, and Systematic Vocabulary Development** Students understand the basic features of reading. They select letter patterns and know how to translate them into spoken language by using phonics, syllabication, and word parts. They apply this knowledge to achieve fluent oral and silent reading. | | | |
| **Substrand:** Decoding and Word Recognition | | **Primary Citations** | **Supporting Citations** |
| **R 3.1.1** | Know and use complex word families when reading (e.g., *-ight*) to decode unfamiliar words. | **TE: UNIT 1:** 6N, 43, 63B, 66N, 77AA, 78N, 112N, **UNIT 2:** 156N, 310N, **UNIT 3:** 358N, 392N, **UNIT 4:** 68N | **TE: UNIT 1:** 65U, 65W, 112J, 112M, 145S, **UNIT 3:** 423J, **UNIT 6:** 384J |
| **R 3.1.2** | Decode regular multisyllabic words. | **TE: UNIT 1:** S4, 34O, 6O, 66O, 77AA, 78O, 112O, **UNIT 2:** 156O, 190O, 220O, 244O, 286O, 310O, **UNIT 3:** 346O, 358O, 392O, **UNIT 4:** 38N, 38O, 6O, 68D, 80O, 110O, **UNIT 5:** 142O, 172O, 200N, 200O, 212O, 234O, **UNIT 6:** 310O, 278O, 336O, 384O | **TE: UNIT 1:** 33L, 33U, 33Y, 65J, 65S, 65W, 77R, 77EE, 111L, 111U, 111Y, 145J, 145S, 145W, **UNIT 2:** 189I, 189U, 189Y, 209J, 209S, 209W, 210O, 221R, 221AA, 221EE, 243L, 243U, 243Y, 275J, 275W, 309L, 309U, 309Y, 345J, 345S, 345W, **UNIT 3:** 357R, 357EE, 391L, 391U, 423J, 423S, 423W, **UNIT 4:** 37L, 37U, 37Y, 67J, 67S, 67W, 79R, 79AA, 79EE, 109L, 109U, 131J, 131S, 131W, **UNIT 5:** 171L, 171V, 199J, 199S, 200J, 211R, 211AA, 211EE, 234J, 267J, 267S, 267W, **UNIT 6:** 309L, 309U, 309Y, 310J, 335J, 335S, 335W, 347R, 347AA, 347EE, 411J, 411S, 411W |

| Substrand: Decoding and Word Recognition | | Primary Citations | Supporting Citations |
|---|---|---|---|
| R 3.1.3 | Read aloud narrative and expository text fluently and accurately and with appropriate pacing, intonation, and expression. | **TE: UNIT 1:** S21, 29A, 59A, 73A, 105A, 139A, **UNIT 2:** 156M, 183A, 190M, 190N, 205A, 217A, 222M, 239A, 269A, 303A, 339A, **UNIT 3:** 385A, **UNIT 4:** 6L, 33A, 105A, 110M, 127A, **UNIT 5:** 172M, 193A, 207A, 212M, 229A, 234M, 261A, **UNIT 6:** 278M, 303A, 310L, 329A, 336M, 343A, 348M, 348O, 377A, 384M, 405A | **TE: UNIT 1:** 6J, 6M, 33S, 33V, 33X, 33Z, 33BB, 33CC, 33FF, 33JJ, 34J, 65AA, 65DD, 75II, 77LL, 78J, 65P, 65T, 65X, 65Z, 66J, 66M, 77X, 77FF, 78M, 111R, 111V, 111Z, 111CC, 111FF, 112J, 145T, 145AA, **UNIT 2:** 14HH, 156J, 189Q, 189R, 189S, 189V, 189X, 189Z, 189BB, 189CC, 189FF, 190J, 209O, 209P, 209Q, 209T, 209V, 209X, 209Z, 209AA, 209DD, 210J, 210M, 221W, 221BB, 221DD, 221FF, 221II, 221LL, 225J, 243Q, 243R, 243S, 243V, 243X, 243Z, 243BB, 243CC, 243FF, 244J, 275P, 275T, 275X, 275AA, 275DD, 286J, 286M, 309V, 309Z, 309CC, 309FF, 310J, 310N, 345P, 345T, 345V, 345Z, 345AA, 345DD, 375II, 375LL, 391CC, 391FF, 423AA, 423DD, **UNIT 3:** 346J, 357W, 357X, 357Y, 357BB, 357DD, 357FF, 357HH, 358J, 358M, 391Q, 391V, 391X, 391Z, 392J, 392M, 419A, 423O, 423T, 423X, **UNIT 4:** 6J, 37Q, 37R, 37S, 37V, 37X, 37Z, 37BB, 38J, 67O, 67P, 67Q, 67T, 67V, 67X, 67Z, 68J, 79W, 79X, 79Y, 79BB, 79DD, 79FF, 79HH, 80J, 80M, 109R, 109S, 109V, 109Z, 110J, 131O, 131P, 131Q, 131T, 131V, 131X, 131Z, **UNIT 5:** 142M, 167A, 171R, 171V, 171Z, 172J, 199P, 199T, 199X, 199AA, 199DD, 200J, 200M, 211W, 211BB, 211FF, 234J, 267O, 267P, 267Q, 267T, 267V, 267X, 267Z, 267AA, 267DD, **UNIT 6:** 278J, 309R, 309V, 309Z, 309CC, 309FF, 310J, 335O, 335P, 335Q, 335T, 335V, 335X, 335X, 336J, 347X, 347II, 347LL, 411O, 411P, 411J, 411V, 411X, 411Z |

| Substrand: Vocabulary and Concept Development | | Primary Citations | Supporting Citations |
|---|---|---|---|
| R 3.1.4 | Use knowledge of antonyms, synonyms, homophones, and homographs to determine the meanings of words. | **TE: UNIT 1:** S8, 31B, 126, 63B, 68, **UNIT 2:** 212, 221B, **UNIT 3:** 288, 298, 360, 394, 421B, **UNIT 4:** 80N, 107B, **UNIT 5:** 144, 153, 174, 197B, 202, 211A, 231B, **UNIT 6:** 280, 307A, 307B, 307D, 376 | **TE: UNIT 2:** 65S, 66J, 187B, 189Y, 207B, 209W, 221W, 234, 241B, **UNIT 3:** 210J, 221W, 221CC, 348, 357A, 357B, 357CC, 392J, 409, 425, **UNIT 4:** 35B, 37N, 38J, 40, 47, 55, 65A, 65B, 79B, 80J, 110J, 112, 118, 129A, 129B, 131U, **UNIT 5:** 171k, 172J, 179, 265B, **UNIT 6:** 278J, 290, 294, 309Y, 312, 334A, 334B, 335U, 335W, 409B |
| R 3.1.5 | Demonstrate knowledge of levels of specificity among grade-appropriate words and explain the importance of these relations (e.g., *dog/ mammal/ animal/ living things*). | **TE: UNIT 1:** 109B, **UNIT 2:** 241B, **UNIT 3:** 344B, 421B, **UNIT 4:** 79B, 129B, **UNIT 6:** 409B | **TE: UNIT 6:** 409B |
| R 3.1.6 | Use sentence and word context to find the meaning of unknown words. | **TE: UNIT 1:** S10, 115, **UNIT 2:** 212, 246, **UNIT 3:** 288, 307B, 312, 360, 365, 389B, **UNIT 5:** 174, 202, **UNIT 6:** 307A | **TE: UNIT 1:** 10, 18, 50, **UNIT 2:** 165, 222J, 224, 228, 241A, 243W, 260, **UNIT 3:** 286J, 296, 310J, 320, 345O, 358J, 391Q, 391W, **UNIT 4:** 21, **UNIT 5:** 190, 200J, 211W, 211CC, 246, **UNIT 6:** 312, 334A, 335U |
| R 3.1.7 | Use a dictionary to learn the meaning and other features of unknown words. | **TE: UNIT 1:** S12, 73C, 80, 100, **UNIT 2:** 221B, **UNIT 3:** 360, 394, 400, 421B, **UNIT 6:** 356 | **TE: UNIT 1:** 78J, **UNIT 2:** 156J, 158, 176, 190J, 192, 198, 207A, 210J, **UNIT 3:** 286J, 320, 345W, 346J, 348, 357A, 357EE, 391Y, **UNIT 4:** 6J, 8, 12, 35A, 37W, **UNIT 5:** 171Q, 171Y, 211EE, 234J, 236, 245, 248, 255, 265A, 267U, **UNIT 6:** 384J, 386, 397, 409A |
| R 3.1.8 | Use knowledge of prefixes (e.g., *un-, re-, pre-, bi-, mis-, dis-*) and suffixes (e.g., *-er, -est, -ful*) to determine the meaning of words. | **TE: UNIT 1:** S11, 8, 22, 77B, 102, 109B, 114, 143B, **UNIT 2:** 221B, 261, 273B, **UNIT 3:** 298, 389B, **UNIT 4:** 82, 88, **UNIT 5:** 212N, 214, 231B, 231D, **UNIT 6:** 278N, 287, 307C, 338, 347B, 381B, 384N | **TE: UNIT 1:** 6J, 33Y, 112J, 136, 149, **UNIT 2:** 187B, **UNIT 3:** 346J, 357B, 357C, 357D, 357R, 357AA, 357EE, **UNIT 4:** 14, 35B, 50, 55, 68J, 70, 79A, 79B, 79CC, 80J, 96, **UNIT 5:** 158, 160, **UNIT 6:** 289, 318, 334B, 336J, 347CC, 398, 399, 409B, 409C, 409D |

**2.0 Reading Comprehension** Students read and understand grade-level-appropriate material. They draw upon a variety of comprehension strategies as needed (e.g., generating and responding to essential questions, making predictions, comparing information from several sources). The selections in *Recommended Literature, Kindergarten Through Grade Twelve* illustrate the quality and complexity of the materials to be read by students. In addition to their regular school reading, by grade four, students read one-half million words annually, including a good representation of grade-level-appropriate narrative and expository text (e.g., classic and contemporary literature, magazines, newspapers, online information). In grade three, students make substantial progress toward this goal.

| **Substrand:** Structural Features of Informational Materials | | **Primary Citations** | **Supporting Citations** |
|---|---|---|---|
| R 3.2.1 | Use titles, tables of contents, chapter headings, glossaries, and indexes to locate information in text. | **TE: UNIT 1:** xvi, 30, 45, 106, 140, **UNIT 2:** 217C, 270, **UNIT 3:** 340, 341, 386, **UNIT 5:** 207C, 211D | **TE: UNIT 1:** 107, 142, **UNIT 2:** 185, 271, 272, **UNIT 5:** 244 |
| **Substrand:** Comprehension and Analysis of Grade-Level-Appropriate Text | | **Primary Citations** | **Supporting Citations** |
| R 3.2.2 | Ask questions and support answers by connecting prior knowledge with literal information found in, and inferred from, the text. | **TE: UNIT 1:** 37A, 38, 40, 46, 48, 52, 81A, 82-83, 88, **UNIT 2:** 193A, **UNIT 3:** 321, 372, 395A, 396, 425, **UNIT 4:** 9A, 9B, 63B, 83A, **UNIT 6:** 282, 329B, 351A, 352 | **TE: UNIT 1:** 10, 65M, 65U, 95, 96, T4,T5, **UNIT 2:** 190J, 194, 197, 199, 200, 205, 209M, 209N, 209O, 209U, 209V, 209Y, 209Z, 267, 269, T3, **UNIT 3:** 345T, 399, 400, 405, 406, 407, 410, 415, 416, 423M, 423U, 423Y, T3, T7, **UNIT 4:** 10, 13, 14, 15, 16, 17, 18, 19, 21, 25, 27, 28, 29, 31, 33, 37O, 37P, 37Q, 37W, 37X, 37AA, 37BB, 47, 50, 53, 83A, T2, T5, T6, T7, **UNIT 5:** 181, **UNIT 6:** 284, 285, 288, 289, 291, 292, 293, 297, 298, 300, 309O, 332, 347U, T3, T5<br>**IK: Comprehension:** 28, 29, 30, 31, 32, 33 |
| R 3.2.3 | Demonstrate comprehension by identifying answers in the text. | **TE: UNIT 1:** 29, 38, 59, 83, 98, 105, 139, 146, **UNIT 2:** 218, 276, **UNIT 3:** 303, 339, 358, 385, 419, **UNIT 5:** 208, 215A, 216 | **TE: UNIT 1:** 146, **UNIT 2:** 73, 183, 205, 239, **UNIT 3:** 391AA, 424, **UNIT 4:** 63, 109Y, 127, **UNIT 5:** 211DD, 211HH, |
| R 3.2.4 | Recall major points in the text and make and modify predictions about forthcoming information. | **TE: UNIT 1:** 11, 27, 39, 83, 103, 115A, 116-117, 118, 119, 122, 125, 127, 137, 145N, 145U, 145Y, **UNIT 2:** 183B, 249, 267, **UNIT 3:** 291, 301, 315, 337, 363, 383, 397, 417, **UNIT 4:** 85, **UNIT 5:** 147, 165, 177, 205, 227, **UNIT 6:** 283, 288, 301, 341, 375 | **TE: UNIT 1:** 33II, 65N, 65U, 65GG, 71, 77V, 77CC, 77GG, 77OO, 111P, 111W, 111II, 112J, 145GG, T4, T7, **UNIT 2:** 161, 162, 164, 181, 189P, 189W, 195, 203, 215, 221V, 221CC, 221GG, 227, 237, 243P, 243W, 255, 256, 275N, **UNIT 3:** 189II, 209GG, 221OO, 342II, 375GG, 309P, 309W, 309AA, 309II, 329, 330, 332, 333, 334, 336, 345N, 345GG, 351, 375OO, 391W 391AA, 391II, 392J, 423N, 423GG, **UNIT 4:** 11, 23, 24, 31, 37P, 37W, 37AA, 43, 61, 67N, 67U, 67Y, 73, 79V, 85, 109P, 109W, 109AA, 115, 125, 131N, 131U, 131Y, **UNIT 5:** 171P, 191, 199G, 239, 261, 267GG, **UNIT 6:** 295, 296, 309II, 315, 326, 347OO, 385, 401, 408, |
| R 3.2.5 | Distinguish the main idea and supporting details in expository text. | **TE: UNIT 1:** 69A, 70, 105B, 148, **UNIT 2:** 213A, 214, 239B, **UNIT 3:** 289A, 290, 293, 298, 299, 300, 366, 426, **UNIT 4:** 71A, 71B, **UNIT 5:** 145A, 146-147, 175A, 176, 193B, 261B, **UNIT 6:** 343B | **TE: UNIT 1:** 66J, 77U, 77V, 77CC, 77GG, 108, 141, T2, T3, **UNIT 2:** 216, 221U, 221V, 221CC, 221GG, 232, T4, T5, T7, **UNIT 3:** 309O, 342, 379, **UNIT 4:** 35, 72, 73, 79U, 79V, 79W, 7CC, 79DD, 79GG, 79HH, 122, **UNIT 5:** 148, 149, 152, 153, 157, 163, 164, 171O, 171P, 171AA, 171W, 178, 181, 184, 185, 188, 189, 196, 199M, 199U, 242, 246, 249, 256, 267M, T2, T3, T7, **UNIT 6:** 407<br>**IK: Comprehension:** 88, 89, 90, 91, 92, 93 |
| R 3.2.6 | Extract appropriate and significant information from the text, including problems and solutions. | **TE: UNIT 1:** 90, 102, **UNIT 3:** 349A, 349B, 368, 385B, 412, **UNIT 4:** 71A, 71B, 83A, 84, 127B, **UNIT 5:** 215B, **UNIT 6:** 371 | **TE: UNIT 2:** 267, 269, **UNIT 3:** 346J, 350, 352, 353, 357U, 357V, 357W, 357CC, 357DD, 357GG, 357HH, 370, 371, 373, 378, T4, **UNIT 4:** 68J, 72, 74, 75, 79U, 79V, 79W, 79CC, 79DD, 79GG, 79HH, 80J, 88, 92, 95, 100, 102, 109O, 109W, 109AA, 123, T3, T5, T6, T7, **UNIT 5:** 200J, **UNIT 6:** 320<br>**IK: Comprehension:** 100, 101, 102, 103, 104, 105 |
| R 3.2.7 | Follow simple multiple-step written instructions (e.g., how to assemble a product or play a board game). | **TE: UNIT 3:** 420, **UNIT 5:** 194, 211L, **UNIT 6:** 368, 379 | **TE: UNIT 3:** 426, 427, **UNIT 4:** 6K, 34, 35, 421, **UNIT 5:** 195, **UNIT 6:** 278K |

**3.0 Literary Response and Analysis** **Students read and respond to a wide variety of significant works of children's literature. They distinguish between the structural features of the text and literary terms or elements (e.g., theme, plot, setting, characters). The selections in *Recommended Literature, Kindergarten Through Grade Twelve* illustrate the quality and complexity of the materials to be read by students.**

| **Substrand:** Structural Features of Literature | | Primary Citations | Supporting Citations |
|---|---|---|---|
| R 3.3.1 | Distinguish common forms of literature (e.g., poetry, drama, fiction, nonfiction). | **TE: UNIT 1:** S15, 6L, 10, 34L, 38, 48, 55, 66L, 70, 82, 112L, 116, **UNIT 2:** 156I, 190I, 210L, 214, 222I, 244L, 248, **UNIT 3:** 286I, 290, 310I, 314, 318, 340, 346L, 358L, 362, 386, 392L, 396, 420, **UNIT 4:** 38L, 68L, 80L, 84, 110L, **UNIT 5:** 142L, 146, 172L, 176, 204, 212L, 234L, **UNIT 6:** 278I, 282, 310L, 340, 348L, 352, 384L | **TE: UNIT 1:** 14, 18, 62, 78L, 84, 91, 111Y, 129, **UNIT 2:** 160, 161, 175, 184, 194, 196, 206, 225J, 226, 231, 240, 250, **UNIT 3:** 286J, 294, 367, 413, **UNIT 4:** 10, 30, 34, 37Y, 58, 64, 72, 92, 101, 110J, 114, 119, 128, **UNIT 5:** 151, 156, 162, 186, 200L, 234J, 238, 257, **UNIT 6:** 296, 300, 314, 324, 330, 390, 406 |
| **Substrand:** Narrative Analysis of Grade-Level-Appropriate Text | | **Primary Citations** | **Supporting Citations** |
| R 3.3.2 | Comprehend basic plots of classic fairy tales, myths, folktales, legends, and fables from around the world. | **TE: UNIT 1:** 59B, 60, 94, **UNIT 4:** 6L, 10, 33B, 38L, 42, 38L, 230, **UNIT 5:** 128, 262 **UNIT 6:** 282, 336L, 348L, 354, 387A, 387B, 406 **OVC:** *Ming's Teacher, I Knew I Could!, The Farmers and Their Children, The Legend of Tutokanula, The Sheep and the Pig Who Set Up House, Ama's Choice, The Big Voice, The Magic Paintbrush, The Legend of Roland and Oliver, Heracles and the Golden Apples, The Husband and Wife Who Switched Places, The Animals and the Birds Play Ball, The Coyote and the Turtle, Babe the Blue Ox, The Wolf and the Fox, Feathers in the Wind, Uwabami, Brer Rabbit in the Well, Gordita, Rumpelstiltskin* | **TE: UNIT 4:** 12, 26, 54 **UNIT 6:** 296, 384K, 388, 390, 391, 392, 395, 396, 397, 398, 400, 402, 405, 411M, 411N, 411O, 411U, 411V, 411Y, 411Z, T2, T3, T4, T5 |
| R 3.3.3 | Determine what characters are like by what they say or do and by how the author or illustrator portrays them. | **TE: UNIT 1:** 9A, 10-11, 59B, 96, **UNIT 2:** 254, **UNIT 3:** 313A, 314, 317, 322, 323, 325, 327, 328, 330, 331, 403, 412, **UNIT 4:** 33B, 36, 87, 105, 105B, **UNIT 5:** 217, 219, **UNIT 6:** 387A, 387B | **TE: UNIT 1:** 6J, 13, 15, 16, 17, 19, 20, 22, 23, 24, 25, 26, 330, 33W, 33AA, 42, 45, 48, 56, 91, 92, 94, 99, T5, T7, **UNIT 2:** 169, 171, 173, 176, 179, **UNIT 3:** 345M, 345U, 345Y, 411, T2, T6, **UNIT 4:** 6J, 22, 26, 53, 55, 95, 96, **UNIT 6:** 309D, 368, 372, 373, 411M, 411N, 411O, 411U, 411V, 411Y, 411Z, T6, T7 |
| R 3.3.4 | Determine the underlying theme or author's message in fiction and nonfiction text. | **TE: UNIT 1:** 101, **UNIT 2:** 247A, 248-249, 278, **UNIT 3:** 303B, **UNIT 4:** 41A, 41B, 75B, 89, 105B, **UNIT 5:** 226, 230, 231, **UNIT 6:** 300, 405B | **TE: UNIT 1:** 145M, **UNIT 2:** 244J, 251, 257, 259, 262, 266, **UNIT 4:** 30, 38J, 42, 45, 46, 49, 51, 53, 57, 60, 63, 67M, 67N, 67O, 67T, 67U, 67V, 67Y, 67Z, 74, **UNIT 6:** 336J, 374, 402 |
| R 3.3.5 | Recognize the similarities of sounds in words and rhythmic patterns (e.g., alliteration, onomatopoeia) in a selection | **TE: UNIT 1:** 58, 90, 112L, **UNIT 2:** 258, **UNIT 3:** 304, 305, 306, **UNIT 4:** 106, **UNIT 5:** 168 | **TE: UNIT 1:** 14, 126, **UNIT 2:** 206, 207, 240, 241, **UNIT 4:** 107, 109Y, 128, **UNIT 5:** 169, 171Y |
| R 3.3.6 | Identify the speaker or narrator in a selection. | **TE: UNIT 2:** 252, **UNIT 3:** 295, 398, **UNIT 4:** 37F, 106, **UNIT 5:** 221, **UNIT 6:** 392 | **TE: UNIT 2:** 162, 164, **UNIT 5:** 107 |

| DOMAIN: WRITING | | Macmillan/McGraw-Hill CALIFORNIA TREASURES | |
|---|---|---|---|
| **1.0 Writing Strategies** Students write clear and coherent sentences and paragraphs that develop a central idea. Their writing shows they consider the audience and purpose. Students progress through the stages of the writing process (e.g., prewriting, drafting, revising, editing successive versions). | | | |
| **Substrand:** Organization and Focus | | **Primary Citations** | **Supporting Citations** |
| W 3.1.1 | Create a single paragraph:<br>a. Develop a topic sentence.<br>b. Include simple supporting facts and details. | **TE: UNIT 1:** 34K, 145A, 151B, **UNIT 2:** 275A, 281B, **UNIT 3:** 423A, **UNIT 4:** 67, **UNIT 5:** 199D, | **TE: UNIT 1:** 34K, 65D, 66K, 78K, 112K, **UNIT 2:** 190K, 209D, 210J, 210K, 222K, 244J, 244K, T3, T5, **UNIT 3:** 286K, 345D, 346K, 356, 392K, **UNIT 4:** 6K, 67, 80K, 110K, 131, **UNIT 5:** 172K, 198, 200K, 234K, T7, **UNIT 6:** 310K, 335A, 336K, 347H, 411A, T7,<br>**IK: Grammar and Writing:** 212, 213, 214, 215, 216, 217, |
| **Substrand:** Penmanship | | **Primary Citations** | **Supporting Citations** |
| W 3.1.2 | Write legibly in cursive or joined italic, allowing margins and correct spacing between letters in a word and words in a sentence. | **TE: UNIT 1:** 77H, 151E, **UNIT 3:** 357H, **UNIT 4:** 37H, 67F, 78H, 78N, 109H, 131F, | **TE: UNIT 1:** 33H, 65F, 77N, 111H, 145F, **UNIT 2:** 189H, 209F, 221N, 243H, 275F, **UNIT 3:** 309H, 345F, 357N, 391H, 423F, **UNIT 4:** 137E, **UNIT 5:** 211H, 273E, **UNIT 6:** 347H, |
| **Substrand:** Research | | **Primary Citations** | **Supporting Citations** |
| W 3.1.3 | Understand the structure and organization of various reference materials (e.g., dictionary, thesaurus, atlas, encyclopedia). | **TE: UNIT 1:** xvi, S13, 73C, 151C, **UNIT 2:** xvi, 28IC, **UNIT 3:** xvi, 353C, 353D, **UNIT 4:** 75C, 75D, **UNIT 6:** 411D, 417K | **TE: UNIT 1:** 34K, 145B, **UNIT 2:** 210K, 243D, 244K, **UNIT 3:** 346K, **UNIT 4:** xvi, 38K, 68K, 80K, 110K, **UNIT 5:** xvi, 200K, 273D, **UNIT 6:** xvi, 278K, 336K, 384K, 417K |
| **Substrand:** Evaluation and Revision | | **Primary Citations** | **Supporting Citations** |
| W 3.1.4 | Revise drafts to improve the coherence and logical progression of ideas by using an established rubric. | **TE: UNIT 1:** S23, 33H, 65F, 77N, 111H, 145F, 151D, 151F, **UNIT 2:** 189H, 209F, 221N, 243H, 275F, 281F, **UNIT 3:** 429F, 309H, 345F, 357N, 391H, 423F, **UNIT 4:** 37H, 67F, 78N, 109H, 131F, 137D, 137F, **UNIT 5:** 171H, 199F, 211N, 233H, 267F, 273D, 273F, **UNIT 6:** 309H, 335F, 347N, 383H, 411F | **IK: Grammar and Writing:** 144, 145, 164, 165, 186, 186, 204, 205, 222, 223 |
| **2.0 Writing Applications (Genres and Their Characteristics)** Students write compositions that describe and explain familiar objects, events, and experiences. Student writing demonstrates a command of standard American English and the drafting, research, and organizational strategies outlined in Writing Standard 1.0. Using the writing strategies of grade three outlined in Writing Standard 1.0, students: | | | |
| | | **Primary Citations** | **Supporting Citations** |
| W 3.2.1 | Write narratives:<br>a. Provide a context within which an action takes place.<br>b. Include well-chosen details to develop the plot.<br>c. Provide insight into why the selected incident is memorable. | **TE: UNIT 1:** 77G, 77H, 77I, 77J, 77K, 77L, 77M, 77N, 151A, 151B, 151C, 151D, **UNIT 4:** 78G, 78H, 78I, 78J, 78K, 78L, 78M, 78N, 79, 137A, **UNIT 5:** 211G, 211H, 211I, 211J, 211K, 211L, 211M, 211N | **TE: UNIT 1:** 6K, 34K, 66K, 76, 77, **UNIT 3:** 310K, 358K, 392K, **UNIT 4:** 68K, **UNIT 5:** 234K, T5, **UNIT 6:** T3, T5, **IK: Grammar and Writing:** 170, 171, 172, 173, 174, 175, 176, 177, 182, 183 |
| W 3.2.2 | Write descriptions that use concrete sensory details to present and support unified impressions of people, places, things, or experiences. | **TE: UNIT 1:** 111A, 144, **UNIT 2:** 188, 221G, 281A, **UNIT 3:** 390, 391A, 422, **UNIT 4:** 137C, **UNIT 5:** 227, **UNIT 6:** 375 | **TE: UNIT 1:** 6K, 78K, T5, **UNIT 2:** 131W, 156K, 189F, 190K, 210K, 220, **UNIT 3:** 358K, **UNIT 4:** 38K, 80K, **UNIT 5:** 234K, 260, **UNIT 6:** 278K, 335W, 384K, 403<br>**IK: Grammar and Writing:** 148, 149, 150, 151, 152, 153, 154, 155 |
| W 3.2.3 | Write personal and formal letters, thank-you notes, and invitations:<br>a. Show awareness of the knowledge and interests of the audience and establish a purpose and context.<br>b. Include the date, proper salutation, body, closing, and signature. | **UNIT 3:** 357G, 429A, 429B, 429C, **UNIT 6:** 347G, 347H, 347I, 347J, 347K, 347L, 347M, 347N, 357H, 357I, 357J, 357K, 357L, 357M, 357N | **TE: UNIT 1:** T3, **UNIT 2:** 244K, **UNIT 3:** 286K, T3, **UNIT 3:** 346K, **UNIT 4:** T7, **UNIT 5:** 267D, **UNIT 6:** 328, 404<br>**IK: Grammar and Writing:** 130, 131, 132, 133, 134, 135, 136, 137, 138, 139, 140, 141, 142, 143 |

| DOMAIN: WRITTEN AND ORAL ENGLISH LANGUAGE CONVENTIONS The standards for written and oral English language conventions have been placed between those for writing and for listening and speaking because these conventions are essential to both sets of skills. | | Macmillan/McGraw-Hill CALIFORNIA TREASURES | |
|---|---|---|---|
| **1.0 Written and Oral English Language Conventions** Students write and speak with a command of standard English conventions appropriate to this grade level. | | | |
| **Substrand:** Sentence Structure | | **Primary Citations** | **Supporting Citations** |
| LC 3.1.1 | Understand and be able to use complete and correct declarative, interrogative, imperative, and exclamatory sentences in writing and speaking. | **TE: UNIT 1:** 31F, 143F, 151E, **UNIT 2:** 244N, 273D, **UNIT 3:** 308, 344, 429E | **TE: UNIT 1:** 112K, **UNIT 2:** 207F, **UNIT 3:** 345B, **UNIT 4:** 65F, 67Q |
| **Substrand:** Grammar | | **Primary Citations** | **Supporting Citations** |
| LC 3.1.2 | Identify subjects and verbs that are in agreement and identify and use pronouns, adjectives, compound words, and articles correctly in writing and speaking. | **TE: UNIT 2:** 273F, 281E, **UNIT 3:** 344F, 389F, 421F, **UNIT 5:** 197F, 211E, **UNIT 6:** 307E, 347F | **TE: UNIT 3:** 307E, 307F, 309Y, **UNIT 4:** 129E, 129F, **UNIT 5:** 265E, 265F, **UNIT 6:** 309JJ, 334E, 334F |
| LC 3.1.3 | Identify and use past, present, and future verb tenses properly in writing and speaking. | **TE: UNIT 3:** 63F, 344F, 389D, 389E, **UNIT 4:** 137F, **UNIT 5:** 172N, 211F | **TE: UNIT 2:** 275B, **UNIT 3:** 357E, 357F, **UNIT 4:** 21, 35E, 35F, 65E, 65F, **UNIT 5:** 199HH, **UNIT 6:** 309JJ, 347PP |
| LC 3.1.4 | Identify and use subjects and verbs correctly in speaking and writing simple sentences. | **TE: UNIT 1:** S23, 77E, 109E, **UNIT 2:** 221E, 242, 273F, **UNIT 3:** 307E, 308, **UNIT 4:** 107F, **UNIT 5:** 231E, **UNIT 6:** 197F | **TE: UNIT 2:** 207E, 207F, 241E, 241F |
| **Substrand:** Punctuation | | **Primary Citations** | **Supporting Citations** |
| LC 3.1.5 | Punctuate dates, city and state, and titles of books correctly. | **TE: UNIT 2:** 273F, **UNIT 3:** 307F, 417F, **UNIT 6:** 307F | |
| LC 3.1.6 | Use commas in dates, locations, and addresses and for items in a series. | **TE: UNIT 3:** 307F, 421F, **UNIT 6:** 409F | **TE: UNIT 3:** 357F, **UNIT 6:** 409F |
| **Substrand:** Capitalization | | **Primary Citations** | **Supporting Citations** |
| LC 3.1.7 | Capitalize geographical names, holidays, historical periods, and special events correctly. | **TE: UNIT 3:** 308, **UNIT 6:** 307F | **TE: UNIT 2:** 187E, 187F, **UNIT 3:** 309D, 421E, **UNIT 6:** 309S |
| **Substrand:** Spelling | | **Primary Citations** | **Supporting Citations** |
| LC 3.1.8 | Spell correctly one-syllable words that have blends, contractions, compounds, orthographic patterns (e.g., *qu*, consonant doubling, changing the ending of a word from *-y* to *-ies* when forming the plural), and common homophones (e.g., *hair-hare*). | **TE: UNIT 1:** S7, 31C, 34J, 63C, 77C, 109C, 143D, **UNIT 2:** 221C, 222N, **UNIT 3:** 307D, 344D, 421D, **UNIT 4:** 107C, 110N, **UNIT 5:** 197D, **UNIT 6:** 307C, 381C | **TE: UNIT 1:** 34J, 66J, **UNIT 2:** 187C, 187D, 207B, 207C, 207D, 222J, 241C, 241D, 244J, **UNIT 3:** 358J, 392J, **UNIT 4:** 6J, 35C, 35D, 65C, 68J, 79C, 79D, 79E, 79F, 110J, 129C, 129D, 131J, 131S, 131W, **UNIT 5:** 172J, 265C, 265D, 265E, 265F, **UNIT 6:** 278J, 336J, 334C, 334D, 384J, 409C, 409D |
| LC 3.1.9 | Arrange words in alphabetic order. | **TE: UNIT 1:** 77D, **UNIT 2:** 221D, **UNIT 6:** 347D, 348M | **TE: UNIT 1:** 142, **UNIT 3:** 357D, **UNIT 4:** 79D |

| DOMAIN: LISTENING AND SPEAKING | | Macmillan/McGraw-Hill CALIFORNIA TREASURES | |
|---|---|---|---|
| **1.0 Listening and Speaking Strategies** Students listen critically and respond appropriately to oral communication. They speak in a manner that guides the listener to understand important ideas by using proper phrasing, pitch, and modulation. | | | |
| **Substrand:** Comprehension | | **Primary Citations** | **Supporting Citations** |
| LAS 3.1.1 | Retell, paraphrase, and explain what has been said by a speaker. | **TE: UNIT 1:** 61II, 65II, 65Q, 65X, 77Y, 77BB, 111S, 111KK, 151E, **UNIT 2:** 209II, 243KK, 275Q, 275T, 281E, **UNIT 3:** 300, 345Q, 345II, 391S, 391V, 391Z, 391KK, 423Q, 423X, 429E, **UNIT 4:** 102, **UNIT 5:** 211Y, 226, **UNIT 6:** 417K | **TE: UNIT 2:** 189S, **UNIT 3:** 423T, **UNIT 4:** 137K, 131T, **UNIT 5:** 273K, **UNIT 6:** 417K |
| LAS 3.1.2 | Connect and relate prior experiences, insights, and ideas to those of a speaker. | **TE: UNIT 1:** 33KK, 145II, 151E, **UNIT 2:** 189KK, 275II, 281E, **UNIT 3:** 309KK, 423II, 429E | **TE: UNIT 1:** 33JJ, 65HH, 77PP, 111FF, 145HH, **UNIT 2:** 145HH, 189JJ, 209HH, 221PP, 243JJ, 275HH, **UNIT 3:** 309JJ, 345HH, 357PP, 391JJ, 423HH, **UNIT 4:** 79Y, 79BB, **UNIT 5:** 267HH, 273K, **UNIT 6:** 335Q, 335T, 335X, 347PP |
| LAS 3.1.3 | Respond to questions with appropriate elaboration. | **TE: UNIT 1:** 2/3, 33V, 61II, 65II, 77FF, 111KK, 145II, **UNIT 2:** 209II, 243KK, 275II, **UNIT 3:** 345II, 391S, 391KK, 423II, **UNIT 4:** 2/3, **UNIT 6:** 274/275, 417K | **TE: UNIT 1:** 33E, 33JJ, 65C, 65HH, 77PP, 111E, 111FF, 145C, 145HH, **UNIT 2:** 189E, 189JJ, 209C, 209HH, 221PP, 243E, 243JJ, 275C, **UNIT 3:** 309E, 309JJ, 345C, 345HH, 391E, 391JJ, 423C, 423HH, **UNIT 4:** 37E, 67C, 67X, 79Y, 79FF, 109E, 124, 131C, 137K, **UNIT 5:** 171E, 199C, 233E, 267C, 267HH, 273K, **UNIT 6:** 309E, 335C, 347Y, 347FF, 383C, 383E, 411C, 417K |
| LAS 3.1.4 | Identify the musical elements of literary language (e.g., rhymes, repeated sounds, instances of onomatopoeia). | **TE: UNIT 4:** 68M, 109V, **UNIT 5:** 77E, 171S, 171Z, 171V | **TE: UNIT 1:** 34M, 112M, **UNIT 2:** 207, 209X, 243S, **UNIT 3:** 286M, 309S, 309V, 309Z, **UNIT 4:** 37E, 47, 67C, 67T, 80M, 109E, 128, 131C, 109S, 109Z, **UNIT 5:** 200M, **UNIT 6:** 383F |
| **Substrand:** Organization and Delivery of Oral Communication | | **Primary Citations** | **Supporting Citations** |
| LAS 3.1.5 | Organize ideas chronologically or around major points of information. | **TE: UNIT 1:** 61II, 65II, 145II, **UNIT 2:** XVI, 209II, 275II, **UNIT 3:** 345II, 423II, **UNIT 6:** 417K | **UNIT 4:** 131Q, **UNIT 5:** 273K, **UNIT 6:** 417K |
| LAS 3.1.6 | Provide a beginning, a middle, and an end, including concrete details that develop a central idea. | **TE: UNIT 1:** 33KK, 65T, **UNIT 2:** 189KK, 275Q, 275X, 281K, **UNIT 3:** 309KK, **UNIT 4:** 78L | **TE: UNIT 2:** 189V, 189Z, **UNIT 4:** 131X, 137K |
| LAS 3.1.7 | Use clear and specific vocabulary to communicate ideas and establish the tone. | **TE: UNIT 1:** 33S, 77KK, 77QQ, **UNIT 2:** 221QQ, 281E, **UNIT 3:** 357QQ, 391V, 391Z | **TE: UNIT 2:** 209Q, 209T, **UNIT 3:** 423T, **UNIT 4:** 131T, 137K, **UNIT 5:** 273K |
| LAS 3.1.8 | Clarify and enhance oral presentations through the use of appropriate props (e.g., objects, pictures, charts). | **TE: UNIT 1:** 111KK, **UNIT 2:** 243KK, **UNIT 3:** 391KK, **UNIT 6:** 417K | **TE: UNIT 2:** 243Z, **UNIT 4:** 37S, 37V, 37Z, 137K, **UNIT 5:** 267O, 267X, 273K, **UNIT 6:** 417K |
| LAS 3.1.9 | Read prose and poetry aloud with fluency, rhythm, and pace, using appropriate intonation and vocal patterns to emphasize important passages of the text being read. | **TE: UNIT 1:** 33Z, **UNIT 2:** 156M, 190M, 222M, **UNIT 3:** 346M, **UNIT 4:** 6M, 38M, 68M, **UNIT 5:** 211Y, 211BB, 211FF, 212M | **TE: UNIT 1:** 6M, 34M, 78M, 112M, 145O, 145T, 145X, **UNIT 2:** 209Q, 210M, 243S, 243V, 243Z, **UNIT 3:** 309S, 310M, 357BB, 357FF, 358M, **UNIT 4:** 37S, 110M, **UNIT 5:** 142M, 200M, 234M, **UNIT 6:** 310M, 384M, 411Q, 411T, 411X **IK: Fluency:** G3 |

| Substrand: Analysis and Evaluation of Oral and Media Communications | | Primary Citations | Supporting Citations |
|---|---|---|---|
| LAS 3.1.10 | Compare ideas and points of view expressed in broadcast and print media. | **TE: UNIT 4:** 98, **UNIT 6:** 347J | **TE: UNIT 2:** 231, **UNIT 3:** 282/283 |
| LAS 3.1.11 | Distinguish between the speaker's opinions and verifiable facts. | **TE: UNIT 1:** 77QQ, **UNIT 2:** 221QQ, **UNIT 3:** 357QQ, **UNIT 6:** 417K | **TE: UNIT 3:** 357Y, **UNIT 4:** 60, **UNIT 5:** 267T, **UNIT 5:** 273K, **UNIT 6:** 417K |

**2.0 Speaking Applications (Genres and Their Characteristics)** **Students deliver brief recitations and oral presentations about familiar experiences or interests that are organized around a coherent thesis statement. Student speaking demonstrates a command of standard American English and the organizational and delivery strategies outlined in Listening and Speaking Standard 1.0. Using the speaking strategies of grade three outlined in Listening and Speaking Standard 1.0, students:**

| | | Primary Citations | Supporting Citations |
|---|---|---|---|
| LAS 3.2.1 | Make brief narrative presentations:<br>a. Provide a context for an incident that is the subject of the presentation.<br>b. Provide insight into why the selected incident is memorable.<br>c. Include well-chosen details to develop character, setting, and plot. | **TE: UNIT 1:** 151E, **UNIT 4:** 67D, 94, 137F, 273A, **UNIT 5:** 211J, 273A, 273C | |
| LAS 3.2.2 | Plan and present dramatic interpretations of experiences, stories, poems, or plays with clear diction, pitch, tempo, and tone. | **TE: UNIT 2:** 221Y, 221BB, 221FF, **UNIT 3:** 304, 345Q, 345X, **UNIT 5:** 233F, **UNIT 6:** 336M | **TE: UNIT 1:** 34M, 66M, 112M, 151K, **UNIT 2:** 210M, 344M, **UNIT 3:** 286M, 310M, 392M, **UNIT 6:** 335B |
| LAS 3.2.3 | Make descriptive presentations that use concrete sensory details to set forth and support unified impressions of people, places, things, or experiences. | **TE: UNIT 1:** 151E, **UNIT 2:** 281E, **UNIT 3:** 429K, **UNIT 4:** 78L, 131D, **UNIT 5:** 226 | **TE: UNIT 2:** 221J, **UNIT 3:** 423B, **UNIT 6:** 402 |

# History-Social Science California Content Standards Grade 3

**Each standard is coded in the following manner**

| HSS | 3 | 1.2 |
|---|---|---|
| History/ Social Science | Grade | Standard |

| KEY | TE = Teacher's Edition | PR = Practice Reader | CCR = California Content Reader | SB = Student Book |
|---|---|---|---|---|

| GRADE 3 HISTORY-SOCIAL SCIENCE *Continuity and Change* | | Macmillan/McGraw-Hill CALIFORNIA TREASURES | |
|---|---|---|---|
| **Standard 3.1:** Students describe the physical and human geography and use maps, tables, graphs, photographs, and charts to organize information about people, places, and environments in a spatial context. | | **Primary Citations** | **Supporting Citations** |
| **HSS 3.1.1** | Identify geographical features in their local region (e.g., deserts, mountains, valleys, hills, coastal areas, oceans, lakes). | **CCR:** 96, 97, 98, 99, 100, 101<br>**SB 2:** *A Solution to Pollution:* 72, 73, 74 | **TE: UNIT 1:** 112K, T5, **UNIT 2:** 190K, **UNIT 3:** 419B |
| **HSS 3.1.2** | Trace the ways in which people have used the resources of the local region and modified the physical environment (e.g., a dam constructed upstream changed a river or coastline). | **CCR:** 102, 103, 104, 105, 106, 107 | **TE: UNIT 1:** 112K, **UNIT 2:** 239B |
| **Standard 3.2:** Students describe the American Indian nations in their local region long ago and in the recent past. | | **Primary Citations** | **Supporting Citations** |
| **HSS 3.2.1** | Describe national identities, religious beliefs, customs, and various folklore traditions. | **CCR:** 108, 109, 110, 111, 112, 113<br>**PR:** *The Acjachemen People*<br>**SB 2:** *Tales of the Trickster:* 341, 342, 343 | **TE: UNIT 1:** 59B, 63, **UNIT 4:** 65B, **UNIT 6:** T3 |
| **HSS 3.2.2** | Discuss the ways in which physical geography, including climate, influenced how the local Indian nations adapted to their natural environment (e.g., how they obtained food, clothing, tools). | **CCR:** 114, 115, 116, 117, 118, 119 | |
| **HSS 3.2.3** | Describe the economy and systems of government, particularly those with tribal constitutions, and their relationship to federal and state governments. | **CCR:** 120, 121, 122, 123, 124, 125 | **TE: UNIT 6:** 343B |
| **HSS 3.2.4** | Discuss the interaction of new settlers with the already established Indians of the region. | **CCR:** 126, 127, 128, 129, 130, 131 | **TE: UNIT 2:** 217B |
| **Standard 3.3:** Students draw from historical and community resources to organize the sequence of local historical events and describe how each period of settlement left its mark on the land. | | **Primary Citations** | **Supporting Citations** |
| **HSS 3.3.1** | Research the explorers who visited here, the newcomers who settled here, and the people who continue to come to the region, including their cultural and religious traditions and contributions. | **CCR:** 132, 133, 134, 135, 136, 137<br>**SB 1:** *Coasting to California:* 214, 215, 216, 217 | **TE: UNIT 1:** 6K, **UNIT 2:** 179, **UNIT 3:** 385B |
| **HSS 3.3.2** | Describe the economies established by settlers and their influence on the present-day economy, with emphasis on the importance of private property and entrepreneurship. | **CCR:** 138, 139, 140, 141, 142, 143<br>**SB 1:** *Coasting to California:* 214, 215, 216, 217 | **TE: UNIT 3:** 343, 389 |
| **HSS 3.3.3** | Trace why their community was established, how individuals and families contributed to its founding and development, and how the community has changed over time, drawing on maps, photographs, oral histories, letters, newspapers, and other primary sources. | **CCR:** XVI, 138, 139, 140, 141, 142, 143<br>**SB 1:** *Coasting to California:* 214, 215, 216, 217 | **TE: UNIT 2:** 183B |

| Standard 3.4: Students understand the role of rules and laws in our daily lives and the basic structure of the U.S. government. | | Primary Citations | Supporting Citations |
|---|---|---|---|
| **HSS 3.4.1** | Determine the reasons for rules, laws, and the U.S. Constitution; the role of citizenship in the promotion of rules and laws; and the consequences for people who violate rules and laws. | **CCR:** 144, 145, 146, 147, 148, 149<br>**SB 1:** "How to Be a Good Citizen": 30, 31 | **TE: UNIT 1:** 29B, 30/31<br>**UNIT 6:** 6K |
| **HSS 3.4.2** | Discuss the importance of public virtue and the role of citizens, including how to participate in a classroom, in the community, and in civic life. | **CCR:** 144, 145, 146, 147, 148, 149,<br>**SB 1:** "How to Be a Good Citizen": 30, 31,<br>**SB 2:** *A Solution to Pollution:* 72, 73, 74, 75, *Here's My Dollar:* 227, 228, 229, 230, 231, 232, 233, 234, 235, 236, 237, "Homes for Families": 270, 271, 272, 273 | **PR:** *Jay Beckwith and Julia Morgan: Two Builders*<br>**PR:** *Patching a Playground*<br>**TE: UNIT 1:** 29B, 31, **UNIT 2:** 222K, 236, 273, T7, **UNIT 4:** T7 |
| **HSS 3.4.3** | Know the histories of important local and national landmarks, symbols, and essential documents that create a sense of community among citizens and exemplify cherished ideals (e.g., the U.S. flag, the bald eagle, the Statue of Liberty, the U.S. Constitution, the Declaration of Independence, the U.S. Capitol). | **CCR:** 150, 151, 152, 153, 154, 155 | **TE: UNIT 1:** 143, **UNIT 6:** 75B |
| **HSS 3.4.4** | Understand the three branches of government, with an emphasis on local government. | **CCR:** 156, 157, 158, 159, 160, 161 | **TE: UNIT 4:** 68K |
| **HSS 3.4.5** | Describe the ways in which California, the other states, and sovereign American Indian tribes contribute to the making of our nation and participate in the federal system of government. | **CCR:** 156, 157, 158, 159, 160, 161 | **TE: UNIT 3:** 339B |
| **HSS 3.4.6** | Describe the lives of American heroes who took risks to secure our freedoms (e.g., Anne Hutchinson, Benjamin Franklin, Thomas Jefferson, Abraham Lincoln, Frederick Douglass, Harriet Tubman, Martin Luther King, Jr.). | **CCR:** 162, 163, 164, 165, 166, 167, 168, 169, 170, 171, 172, 173 | **TE: UNIT 1:** 73B, 139B, T3, **UNIT 3:** T7, **UNIT 4:** 38K |

| Standard 3.5: Students demonstrate basic economic reasoning skills and an understanding of the economy of the local region. | | Primary Citations | Supporting Citations |
|---|---|---|---|
| **HSS 3.5.1** | Describe the ways in which local producers have used and are using natural resources, human resources, and capital resources to produce goods and services in the past and the present. | **CCR:** 174, 175, 176, 177, 178, 179 | **TE: UNIT 2:** 202, 272, 269B, **UNIT 5:** T5 |
| **HSS 3.5.2** | Understand that some goods are made locally, some elsewhere in the United States, and some abroad. | **CCR:** 180, 181, 182, 183, 184, 185 | **TE: UNIT 2:** 183B, 205B, **UNIT 6:** 307 |
| **HSS 3.5.3** | Understand that individual economic choices involve trade-offs and the evaluation of benefits and costs. | **CCR:** 180, 181, 182, 183, 184, 185 | **PR:** *Start Your Own Business*<br>**TE: UNIT 2:** 187, 205B |
| **HSS 3.5.4** | Discuss the relationship of students' "work" in school and their personal human capital. | **CCR:** 180, 181, 182, 183, 184, 185 | **TE: UNIT 2:** 205B |

# Science
# California Content Standards
# Grade 3

**Each standard is coded in the following manner**

| PS | 3 | 1.a |
|---|---|---|
| Physical Science | Grade | Standard |

| KEY | TE = Teacher's Edition | PR = Practice Reader | CCR = California Content Reader | SB = Student Book |
|---|---|---|---|---|

| DOMAIN: PHYSICAL SCIENCES | | Macmillan/McGraw-Hill CALIFORNIA TREASURES | |
|---|---|---|---|
| **Standard 3.1:** Energy and matter have multiple forms and can be changed from one form to another. As a basis for understanding this concept: | | **Primary Citations** | **Supporting Citations** |
| **PS 3.1.a** | *Students know* energy comes from the Sun to Earth in the form of light. | **CCR:** 6, 7, 8, 9, 10, 11 | **TE: UNIT 4:** 63B |
| **PS 3.1.b** | *Students know* sources of stored energy take many forms, such as food, fuel, and batteries. | **CCR:** 6, 7, 8, 9, 10, 11 | **TE: UNIT 4:** 63B |
| **PS 3.1.c** | *Students know* machines and living things convert stored energy to motion and heat. | **CCR:** 6, 7, 8, 9, 10, 11 | **TE: UNIT 4:** 63B |
| **PS 3.1.d** | *Students know* energy can be carried from one place to another by waves, such as water waves and sound waves, by electric current, and by moving objects. | **CCR:** 6, 7, 8, 9, 10, 11 | **TE: UNIT 4:** 63B |
| **PS 3.1.e** | *Students know* matter has three forms: solid, liquid, and gas. | **CCR:** 12, 13, 14, 15, 16, 17 | **TE: UNIT 6:** 303B |
| **PS 3.1.f** | *Students know* evaporation and melting are changes that occur when the objects are heated. | **CCR:** 12, 13, 14, 15, 16, 17 | **TE: UNIT 2:** 222K, **UNIT 6:** 303B |
| **PS 3.1.g** | *Students know* that when two or more substances are combined, a new substance may be formed with properties that are different from those of the original materials. | **CCR:** 12, 13, 14, 15, 16, 17 | **TE: UNIT 6:** 303B, 381 |
| **PS 3.1.h** | *Students know* all matter is made of small particles called atoms, too small to see with the naked eye. | **CCR:** 18, 19, 20, 21, 22, 23 | **TE: UNIT 3:** 353B |
| **PS 3.1.i** | *Students know* people once thought that earth, wind, fire, and water were the basic elements that made up all matter. Science experiments show that there are more than 100 different types of atoms, which are presented on the periodic table of the elements. | **CCR:** 18, 19, 20, 21, 22, 23 | **TE: UNIT 3:** 353B |
| **Standard 3.2:** Light has a source and travels in a direction. As a basis for understanding this concept: | | **Primary Citations** | **Supporting Citations** |
| **PS 3.2.a** | *Students know* sunlight can be blocked to create shadows. | **CCR:** 24, 25, 26, 27, 28, 29 | |
| **PS 3.2.b** | *Students know* light is reflected from mirrors and other surfaces. | **CCR:** 30, 31, 32, 33, 34, 35 | |
| **PS 3.2.c** | *Students know* the color of light striking an object affects the way the object is seen. | **CCR:** 30, 31, 32, 33, 34, 35 | |
| **PS 3.2.d** | *Students know* an object is seen when light traveling from the object enters the eye. | **CCR:** 30, 31, 32, 33, 34, 35 | |

| DOMAIN: LIFE SCIENCES | | Macmillan/McGraw-Hill CALIFORNIA TREASURES | |
|---|---|---|---|
| **Standard LS 3.3:** Adaptations in physical structure or behavior may improve an organism's chance for survival. As a basis for understanding this concept: | | **Primary Citations** | **Supporting Citations** |
| **LS 3.3.a** | *Students know* plants and animals have structures that serve different functions in growth, survival, and reproduction. | **CCR:** 36, 37, 38, 39, 40, 41, 42, 43, 44, 45, 46, 47<br>**SB 1:** *The Truth About Wolves:* 106, 107, 108, 109, *Home-Grown Butterflies:* 198, 199, 200, 201<br>**SB 2:** *Penguin Chick:* 146, 147, 148, 149, 150, 151, 152, 153, 154, 155, 156, 157, 158, 159, 160, 161, 162, 163, 164, 165, *Animal Homes:* 190, 191, *Unique Animals:* 240, 241, 242, 243, 244, 245, 246, 247, 248, 249, 250, 251, 252, 253, 254, 255, 256, 257, 258, 259 | **PR:** *The Weddell Seals*<br>**PR:** *Natural Defenses*<br>**TE: UNIT 1:** 6K, 66K, 78K, 109, **UNIT 2:** 190K, T3, T5, **UNIT 4:** 6K, 38K, **UNIT 5:** 197, 234K, 261B |
| **LS 3.3.b** | *Students know* examples of diverse life forms in different environments, such as oceans, deserts, tundra, forests, grasslands, and wetlands. | **CCR:** 48, 49, 50, 51, 52, 53<br>**SB 2:** *Unique Animals:* 240, 241, 242, 243, 244, 245, 246, 247, 248, 249, 250, 251, 252, 253, 254, 255, 256, 257, 258, 259 | **TE: UNIT 5:** 189, 193B, 234K |
| **LS 3.3.c** | *Students know* living things cause changes in the environment in which they live: some of these changes are detrimental to the organism or other organisms, and some are beneficial. | **CCR:** 54, 55, 56, 57, 58, 59 | **PR:** *Purple Loosestrife: The Beautiful Invader*<br>**TE: UNIT 2:** 152/153 |
| **LS 3.3.d** | *Students know* when the environment changes, some plants and animals survive and reproduce; others die or move to new locations. | **CCR:** 60, 61, 62, 63, 64, 65, 66, 67, 68, 69, 70, 71<br>**SB 2:** "Daddy Daycare": 202, 203, *Call of the Wild:* 204, 205, 206, 207, "A Wild Vote": 208 | **TE: UNIT 3:** 303B, **UNIT 5:** 207B |
| **LS 3.3.e** | *Students know* that some kinds of organisms that once lived on Earth have completely disappeared and that some of those resembled others that are alive today. | **CCR:** 72, 73, 74, 75, 76, 77 | **TE: UNIT 1:** 105B |

| DOMAIN: EARTH SCIENCES | | Macmillan/McGraw-Hill CALIFORNIA TREASURES | |
|---|---|---|---|
| **Standard ES 3.4:** Objects in the sky move in regular and predictable patterns. As a basis for understanding this concept: | | **Primary Citations** | **Supporting Citations** |
| **ES 3.4.a** | *Students know* the patterns of stars stay the same, although they appear to move across the sky nightly, and different stars can be seen in different seasons. | **CCR:** 78, 79, 80, 81, 82, 83,<br>**SB 2:** "The Big Dipper": 331, 332 | **PR:** *What's in the Sky?*<br>**TE: UNIT 4:** 110K |
| **ES 3.4.b** | *Students know* the way in which the Moon's appearance changes during the four-week lunar cycle. | **CCR:** 84, 85, 86, 87, 88, 89, 117,<br>**SB 2:** *Out of This World!:* 34, 35 | |
| **ES 3.4.c** | *Students know* telescopes magnify the appearance of some distant objects in the sky, including the Moon and the planets. The number of stars that can be seen through telescopes is dramatically greater than the number that can be seen by the unaided eye. | **CCR:** 78, 79, 80, 81, 82, 83 | **PR:** *What's in the Sky?* |
| **ES 3.4.d** | *Students know* that Earth is one of several planets that orbit the Sun and that the Moon orbits Earth. | **CCR:** 35, 84, 85, 86, 87, 88, 89 | **PR:** *What's in the Sky?* |
| **ES 3.4.e** | *Students know* the position of the Sun in the sky changes during the course of the day and from season to season. | **CCR:** 35, 90, 91, 92, 93, 94, 95<br>**SB 2:** "What Causes Day and Night": 34, 35, 117 | **TE: UNIT 4:** 33B<br>**PR:** *What's in the Sky?* |

Use this page to record lessons that work well or need to be adapted for future reference.

## Lessons that work well

## Lessons that need adjustments

Use this page to record lessons that work well or need to be adapted for future reference.

## Lessons that work well

## Lessons that need adjustments

Teacher Notes

Use this page to record lessons that work well or need to be adapted for future reference.

## Lessons that work well

## Lessons that need adjustments

# Teacher Notes

Use this page to record lessons that work well or need to be adapted for future reference.

## Lessons that work well

Use this page to record lessons that work well or need to be adapted for future reference.

## Lessons that work well

## Lessons that need adjustments

Use this page to record lessons that work well or need to be adapted for future reference.

## Lessons that work well

# Teacher Notes

Use this page to record lessons that work well or need to be adapted for future reference.

## Lessons that work well

## Lessons that need adjustments

Teacher Notes

Use this page to record lessons that work well or need to be adapted for future reference.

## Lessons that work well

# Teacher Notes

Use this page to record lessons that work well or need to be adapted for future reference.

## Lessons that work well

## Lessons that need adjustments